Teaching,

Bearing the Torch

Second Edition

Teaching,
Bearing the Torch

Pamela J. Farris
Northern Illinois University

Boston   Burr Ridge, IL   Dubuque, IA   Madison, WI   New York   San Francisco   St. Louis
Bangkok   Bogotá   Caracas   Lisbon   London   Madrid
Mexico City   Milan   New Delhi   Seoul   Singapore   Sydney   Taipei   Toronto

McGraw-Hill College

A Division of The **McGraw·Hill** *Companies*

TEACHING, BEARING THE TORCH, SECOND EDITION

 This book is printed on recycled, acid-free paper containing 10% postconsumer waste.

1 2 3 4 5 6 7 8 9 0 QPD/QPD 9 3 2 1 0 9 8

ISBN 0–697–37537–4

Editorial director: *Jane E. Vaicunas*
Sponsoring editor: *Beth Kaufman*
Editorial coordinator: *Cara Harvey*
Marketing manager: *Daniel M. Loch*
Project manager: *Brenda K. Lahey-Paisley*
Senior production supervisor: *Sandra Hahn*
Interior design: *Michael Warrell*
Senior photo research coordinator: *Lori Hancock*
Supplement coordinator: *Tammy Juran*
Compositor: *Shepherd, Inc.*
Typeface: *10/12 Palatino*
Printer: Quebecor Printing Book Group/Dubuque, IA

Cover design: *Z Graphics*
Cover images: © *Tony Stone Images, Zigy Kaluzny and* © *Comstock*

Library of Congress Cataloging-in-Publication Data

Farris, Pamela J.
     Teaching, bearing the torch / Pamela J. Farris. —2nd ed.
          p.   cm.
     Includes index.
     ISBN 0–697–37537–4
     1. Teachers—United States.   2. Education—United States–
–Philosophy.   3. Teaching—United States.   4. School management and
organization—United States.   5. Educational sociology—United
States.   6. Classroom management—United States.   7. Educational
change—United States.   I. Title.
LB1775.2.F37   1999
371.1'00973—dc21   98–13921
                                                                    CIP

www.mhhe.com/socscience/education/farris

■ To Kurtis and the children of his generation

Brief
Contents

Detailed Contents

3   *Trends in Education*   49

4   *Philosophical Foundations of Education*   75

7   Legal and Ethical Issues in Education   157

8   Social Issues in Education   201

9 The Administration and Governance of Schools   237

13 *Effective Instructional Strategies*   345

14 *Managing the Classroom Environment*   369

15   *Schools and Their Environment*   *389*

16   *Education in Other Countries*   *409*

Detailed Contents

Preface

> A teacher makes a mark on the world which only a few may see, but from which many will profit. A teacher can change the "course of human events" but may never really know when or to what extent.

These words by Marcella L. Kysilka, a professor of education and former teacher, reflect the importance of teachers. Perhaps no other profession is as rewarding and challenging as teaching. It is also one of the most exciting professions. Each day our students uncover new discoveries as part of their learning, opening new doors to opportunities for them.

We teach our students to be lifelong learners in the belief that "education is the best provision for old age." This is not a recent discovery, for the quote comes from Aristotle, who lived over two thousand years ago.

Teaching, Bearing the Torch is a reflection of contemporary teaching and schooling, which are based on the philosophical and historical underpinnings of education. Both the pleasant and unpleasant aspects of teaching are shared in an attempt to provide those readers considering the teaching profession with a frank, honest view of education and teaching. Anecdotes about teachers and school administrators and their professional encounters are shared so readers can gain insight into how teachers think.

This second edition of *Teaching, Bearing the Torch* focuses on educational change. Not only are current trends outlined, but demographic changes are described and charts and tables updated. Websites have been added to better meet the needs of readers.

New to this edition are *One Teacher's View* and *Talking It Over*. *One Teacher's View* gives an authentic opinion of a topic taken from each chapter. These sections feature real teachers talking about real educational issues. *Talking It Over* permits me to chat with readers about a variety of educational topics, sharing my insights, my successes, and my failures as well in a candid, brief format.

To enhance the contemporary approach of *Teaching, Bearing the Torch,* we offer you a different approach to selecting your course materials. Have you ever visualized a text with only those chapters you cover in your course? A text that is more affordable for students because they pay only for chapters they need? Have you visualized a text that provides expanded coverage where your students need it? Do you prefer a text that includes all of the traditional topics important for students just entering the teaching discipline? Would you like to create your own text to meet your students' needs?

This is the book.

The chapters are organized as they are in traditional texts, but you will notice that instead of numbers, we use icons. This is so you can truly create your text to meet your needs, without following a preset pattern. Choose 10 chapters to concentrate on specific content areas. Choose 17 chapters to expand students' knowledge beyond the basics. Start with philosophy, or start with history. Use one history chapter or two, to give students more information on international education and American education. Include the Student Resource Guide. You decide!

Of course, you can choose not to decide. By using our complete listing of chapters without expanded chapters, you will find all of the traditional topics necessary for your introductory course. Either way, we will provide your students with texts that have the same quality look and feel of all McGraw-Hill coursebooks. Every coursebook will have special features within each chapter to enhance learning, and can be used with other supplements.

Course Supplements

Course supplements are created to add value to your teaching experience and to your students' learning experience. The following supplements will work well with any coursebook you create through *Teaching, Bearing the Torch.*

Instructor's Manual and Test Item File
MicroTest (testing software)
Student Study Guide
Annual Editions
Taking Sides
Audiotape
Guide to Observation & Participation

Special Pedagogical Features

There are several special features in *Teaching, Bearing the Torch.* New to this edition is *A Teacher's View* that opens each chapter by telling the real story of teaching through the voices of different educators. Also new is *Talking It Over.* This feature is an informal forum that presents many current educational issues to students. The many features that made the first edition so engaging are still present in this revision. *Primary Points* direct the reader to the main ideas and concepts presented in the chapter. *Chapter Inquiries* are questions designed to pique the interest of the reader, establishing anticipation for the upcoming textural material. *A Closer Look* boxes concentrate on important issues and on educators giving students an in-depth view of various topics. *Point/Counterpoint* boxes present differing sides to a specific educational issue.

The Student Resource Guide in the back of this book offers a wealth of information, including addresses of state certification offices, professional organizations, and technology sources. In addition, there are suggestions for preparing for and holding parent-teacher conferences, suggestions about the job-search process, lists of resources, and Goals 2000. Terms are explained in a thorough glossary.

Menu-driven products offer you the unique opportunity to match the organization and emphasis of the coursebook to the way you teach your course. You decide which chapters to cover and in what order. It is that simple. Your involvement in this process assures you flexibility and control and it provides your students savings. Your students pay only for the material you wish to cover—a savings of up to one-half the cost of a conventional text. Value to your students and a product which provides what you need for an effective course, all from a reliable publishing source—McGraw-Hill Publishers.

Acknowledgments

A book cannot be written without the support and assistance of many people. I'd like to acknowledge some of them here. Many former students, teachers, and school administrators have offered ideas and support for this textbook. Because of them, it was honed and polished so that those individuals considering teaching as a profession could gain insights into what teaching is all about through reading this book.

Beth Kaufman was a most supportive and encouraging editor for this edition. The project manager was Terry Routley, who paved the way through the myriad of details from copyediting through the final gluing of the cover to the spine of the textbook. Certainly Michelle Oberhoffer deserves a pat on the back for gathering photos literally from far and wide to make the book interesting, relevant, and aesthetically pleasing. Patricia Rieman worked very diligently in obtaining the necessary permissions. Dan Loch prepared the marketing promotion materials, something that all authors greatly appreciate.

Reviewers of *Teaching, Bearing the Torch* 2nd edition

Alan F. Quick
Central Michigan University

Mack Welford
Roanoke College

Elizabeth Ihle
James Madison University

D. Cecil Clark
Brigham Young University

Hal E. Jenkins, II
University of West Alabama

Larry G. Julian
Brewton-Parker College

Nomsa Geleta
Salisburg State University

Michael Kelly
Dominican College of Buffalo

Carlos F. Diaz
Florida Atlantic University

Kay L. Clawson
West Liberty State College

Jerry C. Long
Emporia State University

Susan Blackwell
Marian College

I'd like to thank Patricia Rieman, who assisted with the research and developed the test items.

Writing a book is a time-consuming, grueling effort for any author. My husband, Richard A. Fluck, offered much support on the home front. Kurtis, our son, patiently waited for me to get off the computer to play soccer or read a book with him. To both of them go my love and gratitude.

As for what I have learned through writing this book, that would be another book. As a teacher I learn something new about teaching every day. As a writer/researcher, I find that what other teachers and educators do influences my own work. Ralph Tyler, the great curriculum expert who died in 1994, gave teachers three essential questions to ask ourselves:

What did I learn today?

What does it mean?

How can I use it?

Tyler's words provide a code of ethics and reflection practice for us all. Every day each of us in our teaching learns something new. Good teachers ask what does it mean; great teachers find out how to use it to help their students.

Pamela J. Farris
Presidential Teaching Professor

DON'T FORGET TO EXPLORE OUR COMPANION WEBSITE TO *TEACHING, BEARING THE TORCH:* www.mhhe.com/socscience/education/farris

Peter F. Drucker, *The New Realities*

Within the next decade education will change more than it has changed since the modern school was created by the printed book over 300 years ago.

1

The Teaching Profession

Primary Points

- Teachers and education are very important in our society.

- There are many important issues to consider before deciding on a teaching career.

- The public and parents have many expectations of teachers.

- Teachers are prepared in programs at colleges and universities as well as in alternative certification programs.

- Certification, professional organizations, and unions are all part of the teaching profession.

- The salaries and fringe benefits of teachers have become more competitive with other professions, though they still lag behind.

Chapter Inquiries

- Why is teaching an important profession?

- What demands and expectations are placed on teachers?

- How are teachers prepared?

- How are teachers deemed qualified to teach?

- What are the salary and job prospects for beginning teachers?

The Haunting

Photo Disc/Education

"They arrive at night, unannounced and uninvited, interrupting my sleep. My chest tightens, and I grimace, knowing they will not leave me for days. Their images and their problems come back to me from nineteen years of teaching, as real and as troubling as when I first met these students in my classrooms.

"Joseph was the youngest of seven boys who had lost their father to cancer. The boys and their mother ran the dairy farm with no help, feeding themselves with the crops they grew and the deer they hunted. Joseph and I had a routine; every morning during recess he would come to me so I could rub hand cream into his calloused, cracked eight-year-old hands.

"Gerry was also a farm boy. He had a tough time in first grade because he couldn't learn to read. On the playground children called him 'stupid.' He believed them and repeated first grade. The second year, he sobbed and shook so badly during the first week of school that he had to be taken from the room. The school district tested him and learned he had an IQ of 147 with severe learning disabilities.

"Gerry worked with me in the gifted program for five years. We worked on his strengths: his fascination with machines, his ability to fix anything, and his interest in U.S. history. During an assembly a speaker would never know how this child struggled to learn, because Gerry remembered everything and asked questions that helped the other students conceptualize the message given. In high school now, Gerry does not fit into any easy category, and I worry that the fast-paced system will not meet his special needs.

"Other images come, too; the children who never had the chance to reach their potential, Katie, who maintained an *A* average even though she missed eighty days of fourth grade, was still a high-achieving student when she died of leukemia at age ten. Jennifer died in tenth grade of a gun accident, leaving only her picture in the paper to remind me of the feisty fourth grader I had known.

"Anna haunts me the most. She is in her twenties now, but I remember her as an eight-year-old with long brown braids and blue-speckled frame glasses. The middle child of five, she was not the shining star of her family. When the school nurse informed Anna's mother that Anna was having trouble hearing, her mother sneered, 'She is already ugly enough with those glasses; she will not wear a hearing aid.'

"Anna often acted out in class, and I would ask her to stand in the hall until I could speak with her. One day the principal saw Anna in the hall and asked for an explanation. She replied, 'This is Miss Carney's special time with me. We have a talk every day.' By third grade, she had already learned to manipulate adults to get what she needed.

"Lying awake at 3 A.M., I try to think of my successful students: Laurie, who wants to become the first woman president, and Jeremy, who is married and has just started a car repair business. But my students with the largest needs quickly return. They cry out to me, the child who is teased because he stutters, or the one who gives up trying to learn, saying she doesn't care so her failures won't hurt as much.

"Teachers don't pass students on—we accumulate them. We worry over them, wonder how they're doing, and sometimes cry for them long after they've left our classrooms. It's part of our job."

Source: Pat Carney-Dalton is a teacher from Bucks County, Pennsylvania, and a Teacher-Consultant for the Pennsylvania Writing Project, West Chester University. From Pat Carney-Dalton, "The Haunting" in *Educational Leadership,* 52, 6: 86. Reprinted with permission of the Association for Supervision and Curricular Development. Copyright © 1995 by ASCD. All rights reserved.

Chapter 1 *The Teaching Profession*

Teaching has been described as an honored profession. It is a rewarding and exciting field that holds a tremendous responsibility. No other profession shapes the lives of so many youngsters. As a teacher, you will provide a service for society. No one can become a doctor, lawyer, police officer, secretary, computer technician, or accountant without going to elementary and secondary school first. According to Susan Mandel Glazer (1994, 3),

> As educators, we are continuously discarding the "old" and finding the newest, most innovative, futuristic, avant-garde ideas for teaching children. . . .
>
> The future of our world is in the hands of educators who model behaviors that will guide children to become productive adults. It is, therefore, our responsibility to generate the air of professional confidence and dignity assumed by physicians, lawyers, and chief executive officers of major corporations.
>
> It is incumbent upon all teachers to insist, by our professional behaviors, that we are, in fact, the most important professionals in our world. We are responsible for shaping the thought processes of those who enter those other professions.

This chapter explores teaching as a profession, and subsequent chapters detail the various aspects of teaching.

The Importance of Education and Teachers

Education holds much promise for the youth of today. In writing about education and our society, Sarason (1977, 28) points out that "deeply embedded in the minds of people has been the belief that ours is a society of promise and opportunity, possessing resources—material and human, scientific and technical—which justify belief in an onward and upward conception of progress for individuals and society."

Clearly, it is our educational system that provides a free education for all children that sustains the "onward and upward conception of progress" of which Sarason speaks. Certainly educational leaders, from Rousseau to Thomas Jefferson to Horace Mann to John Dewey to Linda Darling-Hammond, down through the years have held fast to the possibilities education in a democratic society offers. In particular, Sarason (1977, 24) states that John Dewey, an educational philosopher in the early 1900s, shared in this vision: "Dewey both reflected and reinforced the American belief and hope . . . that one could and should expect much from life. . . . This was a 'land of opportunity' in which the only major constraints on the individual were an impoverished imagination, a lack of boldness or initiative, and impersonal bad luck."

What office is there which involves more responsibility, which requires more qualifications, and which ought, therefore, to be more honorable than that of teaching?

—Harriet Martineau

The importance of teachers to this vision of self-enrichment through education cannot be underestimated. As a teacher, you will influence your students. Some teachers make such an impact that their students make career choices based on the teacher's positive example. They become mathematicians, scientists, journalists, musicians, artists, and even teachers because of teachers who spent time with them and displayed interest in nurturing their talents. When teenagers were asked who or what had influenced them to become the kinds of individuals they are, 58 percent, or nearly three out of five, mentioned teachers (Csikszentmihalyi and McCormick 1986).

According to Teeter (1995, 364), our goal as teachers "should be aiming to help children become caring adults, builders of communities, sharers of learning, lovers of the printed word, citizens of the world, and nurturers of nature." Certainly time spent together in a classroom greatly impacts a child's impression of a teacher and his or her own future decisions in life.

Many people credit teachers with influencing them to become who they are. (© James Shaffer)

Burton Blatt (Gooler 1991, 137–38) told this story about his fourth-grade teacher's influence on him:

For whatever reason, Mr. Weiner told the most marvelous stories. One Friday afternoon, he also told me that I had a good mind but that it needed more attention than it was getting from me. What a kind way to advise a child to work more diligently at his numbers and words.

Mr. Weiner also got me thinking about college. . . . Mr. Weiner taught me a little about what college was, about B.S.'s and Ph.D.'s, about classes and giving your mind a good workout just for the fun of it. He also taught me about libraries, real ones, and why the serious student goes to college. And he also taught me why other people go too. That is, Mr. Weiner began to teach me what I needed to know about college. By the end of the fourth grade, I settled on a life's work, deciding at that time to become a scholar.

Blatt not only went on to graduate from college, but he also obtained both master's and doctoral degrees. He began his career as a teacher and, at his untimely death at a relatively young age, was serving as dean of the college of education at Syracuse University.

When considering teaching as a profession you must examine your beliefs about the role of education in our society. The decision to pursue a career in teaching involves weighing a variety of other issues

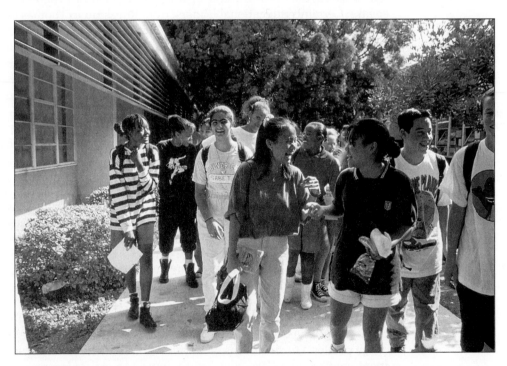

Each student is unique. A teacher must try to find the best way to help each child learn.
(© Mary Kate Denny/PhotoEdit)

as well. Why do you want to become a teacher? Which of your personal characteristics would be positive attributes for teaching? How knowledgeable are you? Do you love a particular subject (e.g., history, math) so much that you can't wait to tell others about it? Are you a patient person? Can you set realistic expectations for yourself? for others? Do you enjoy working with children? Do you find helping others to learn rewarding? Do you have the mental and physical stamina necessary to teach a classroom full of students five days a week?

Take the time now to respond to each of these questions, and then when you come to the end of this text, return to them and see how your answers may have changed.

The following are some key statistics about elementary and secondary teachers in the United States, gathered by the National Center for Education Statistics, U.S. Department of Education:

- Nearly three out of four (73 percent) are women.
- Nearly seven out of eight (87 percent) are white; 7 percent are black; and 4 percent are Hispanic.
- Nearly half (47 percent) have a master's degree or higher.
- Public school teachers earned an average salary of $37,846 in the 1995–96.
- Eighty-five percent of teachers questioned the Schools and Staffing Survey generally felt that their colleagues shared their beliefs and have a similar mission for the school. Likewise, eighty percent of teachers reported their school administrators were supportive and encouraging. And an incredible eighty-seven percent of teachers surveyed reported satisfaction with the intellectual challenges of their positions (Meek 1998).

You can view these and other education statistics at the center's Website:

http://www.ed.gov

Selecting Teaching as a Career

Teachers come from all walks of life and all cultures. Besides wanting to help students learn, the decision to teach, like any occupational decision, requires that you weigh the advantages and disadvantages of teaching.

Certainly one consideration to think about is the public's perception of schools and teaching. For over twenty years, Gallup, a national polling company, in cooperation with Phi Delta Kappa, an educational honorary organization, have conducted an annual poll of the public's attitudes toward the public schools. When asked to give a letter grade—A, B, C, D, or F—to their local public schools, 57 percent of parents who had children in school and 44 percent of individuals who had no children in school gave their local schools a grade of A or B (Elam, Rose, and Gallup 1994). For the first time since 1971, those polled in 1993 indicated that lack of funding was the number-one problem faced by schools (Elam, Rose, and Gallup 1993). However, the 1994 poll indicated that the public viewed the growth of fighting/violence/gangs and poor discipline as the most serious problems facing U.S. schools (Elam, Rose, and Gallup 1994).

Probably one of the most interesting and encouraging findings of the 1993 Gallup/Phi Delta Kappa poll was that 67 percent of those polled would like their children to become teachers—the highest percentage recorded in twenty years. Eighty percent of African Americans expressed the same desire (Elam, Rose, and Gallup 1993). We can speculate as to why this figure is so high. Teachers are viewed as being honest

Parents can offer insights into their children, particularly regarding cultural differences. Here is a letter from a Native American mother to her son's teacher as her son enters school.

"Before you take charge of the classroom that contains my child, please ask yourself why you are going to teach Indian children. What are your expectations? What rewards do you anticipate? . . .

"Write down and examine all the information and opinions you possess about Indians. What are the stereotypes and untested assumptions that you bring with you into the classroom? How many negative attitudes towards Indians will you put before my child? . . .

"Too many teachers, unfortunately, seem to see their role as rescuer. My child does not need to be rescued; he does not consider being Indian a misfortune. He has a culture, probably older than yours; he has meaningful values and a rich and varied experiential background. However strange or incomprehensible it may seem to you, you have no right to do or say anything that implies to him that it is less than satisfactory. . . .

"Like most Indian children his age, he is competent. He can dress himself, prepare a meal for himself, clean up afterwards, care for a younger child. He knows his Reserve, all of which is his home, like the back of his hand.

"He is not accustomed to having to ask permission to do the ordinary things that are part of normal living. He is seldom forbidden to do anything, more usually the consequences of an action are explained to him, and he is allowed to decide for himself whether or not to act. His entire existence since he has been old enough to see and hear has been an experiential learning situation, arranged to develop his skills and confidence in his own capacities. Didactic teaching will be an alien experience for him. . . .

"He has been taught, by precept, that courtesy is an essential part of human conduct and rudeness is any action that makes another person feel stupid or foolish. Do not mistake his patient courtesy for indifference or passivity.

"He doesn't speak standard English, but he is in no way 'linguistically handicapped.' If you will take the time and courtesy to listen and observe carefully, you will see that he and the other Indian children communicate very well, both among themselves and with other Indians. They speak 'functional' English, very effectively augmented by their fluency in the silent language, the subtle, unspoken communication of facial expressions, gestures, body movement, and the use of personal space.

"You will be well advised to remember that our children are skillful interpreters of the silent language. They will know your feelings and attitudes with unerring precision, no matter how carefully you arrange your smile or modulate your voice. They will learn in your classroom, because children learn involuntarily. What they will learn will depend on you.

"Will you help my child to learn to read, or will you teach him that he has a reading problem? Will you help him develop problem solving skills, or will you teach him that school is where you try to guess what answer the teacher wants?

"Will he learn that his sense of his own value and dignity is valid, or will he learn that he must forever be apologetic and "trying harder" because he isn't white? Can you help him acquire the intellectual skills he needs without at the same time imposing your values on top of those he already has?

"Respect my child. He is a person. He has a right to be himself."

Reprinted by permission of the publisher from Ayers, William, *To Teach: The Journey of a Teacher.* (New York: Teachers College Press, © 1994 by Teachers College, Columbia University. All rights reserved.), pp. 39–41.

"Boys and girls, today is my last day of teaching after 36 years at Walnut Hills High. Should we chance to meet along life's highway, I shan't correct your English. However, I may very well give you a good swift kick for no apparent reason." (Copyright © Peter Steiner. Reprinted with permission.)

individuals as compared with attorneys, junk bond arbitrageurs, politicians, and many other professionals. However, teachers typically have not been held in high esteem by society in general. Janet Reno (1994), U.S. Attorney General, points out that teachers should be the ones who are highly paid, not professional athletes, because of what teachers do.

Yet another reason that teaching is viewed in such a positive manner is that unlike other professions, there has been steady employment in recent years for teachers. While many businesses such as ATT, IBM, Proctor and Gamble, Sears, and other major national and international companies have reduced their workforces, local school districts have generally hired new teachers each year. This is due to two factors: an aging teaching population, resulting in many retirements each year, and the mini baby boom, which has increased the number of students. In addition, teaching salaries have increased in recent years.

Expectations of Teachers

Today's teachers have more demands placed on them than ever before. Not only must they be knowledgeable in their content area and like to help students learn, but they also must be familiar with and sensitive to different cultures. The expectations of teachers as posed by the business world, state legislatures, and local communities as well as parents are very high.

Career Satisfaction

Teachers who enjoy their work and can't wait to share their ideas with students tend to be motivated intrinsically rather than extrinsically. That is, rather than receiving large salaries with lots of extra perks such as a company car and frequent flyer miles for vacations to exotic locations, they prefer a smile from a student who catches on to what is taught in a lesson, a thank-you note from a grateful parent at the end of the school year, or a collective moan from a class when they are told they have to wait until tomorrow to finish the learning activity in which they are all excitedly engaged. Teaching can be a fulfilling and gratifying career. Consider Ann Hardesty, who has been a teacher in Wyoming for over twenty-five years, and LouAnne Johnson, who is relatively new to the teaching profession and teaches in an inner-city high school, described in the following "closer looks."

Teacher Preparation

Most teachers receive their professional training from colleges and universities with state-approved programs. Each state regulates teacher certification by establishing criteria that a prospective teacher must meet to be qualified to teach in that state. Typically, such certification specifies the number of course hours in particular areas, such as English, history, and science, as well as in methods coursework. Most states have reciprocal agreements with adjoining states so that upon receiving certification in one state, the teacher is also qualified to teach in a neighboring state. There is much discussion about the development of a national teaching certificate that would enable a teacher to teach in any of the fifty states as well as in Puerto Rico and Washington, D.C.

Preservice Education

Most education programs require that students take a test prior to entering their program. This test is called the Praxis test, which was developed by the Educational Testing Service (ETS) to measure basic skills in reading, writing, and math. Students must score at or above a level specified by the college or university to be admitted to the teacher education program.

Typically, preservice education includes coursework in general studies such as English, literature, history, mathematics, science, and the arts as well as methods coursework. The number of hours of methods coursework varies from state to state, with Texas requiring the least—eighteen hours. Most states specify that each education program have a set number of hours of observation and participation in school settings prior to student teaching.

At the preservice level, you also decide if you want to teach at the early childhood, elementary, middle school or junior high, or secondary level. In the cases of art, music, and physical education, you may be qualified to teach students at all levels as defined by your state's certification guidelines and your college's or university's program. If you decide to teach at the middle school, junior high, or secondary level, you need to select a teaching major, such as biology, English, Spanish, mathematics, history, physics, or some other content area that is taught at these levels. A major is usually forty credit hours of study in a particular discipline. Early childhood and elementary teachers typically have a minor or an area of concentration in a discipline. A minor consists of twenty-four credit hours while an area of concentration usually is eighteen credit hours.

"Who, me, teach? Why? Jobs are no longer plentiful. Funding is not considered a priority most places. Violence has crept into buildings. Days and school years are getting longer. Children are restless.

"Where else, though, can I make a difference? Where else can I be part of exciting changes as education moves from the way I was taught into the age of technology? Where else can I shape the way children are taught and learn? The classrooms of America offer the chance to be on the cutting edge of education.

"Oh, yes, children still must acquire basic skills and knowledge, but not seated in the rows of desks with the teacher acting as a boss. Today's child must be a participant in learning, not a spectator. Today's child's needs of belonging, freedom, and power must be met in an organized way with the teacher serving as a leader, a facilitator.

"What fun it is to plan activities where children learn by discovery! How exciting to hear 'Ah, ha!' when the children learn a new concept through working together and reasoning out a solution! How rewarding to see a reluctant reader turned on to books when given the chance to select books and plenty of time to read without the worry of worksheets to fill out! The place where this happens is in the classroom of a teacher acting as a facilitator, a leader, the classroom of the twenty-first century.

"William Glasser (1992) in *The Quality School* points out that the classroom must be a friendly workplace with courtesy at its center. Rules and standards which all can accept are developed with the students. The teacher is interested in the students and shares his or her interests. The classroom then becomes a workplace in which the workers, the students, can satisfy their needs.

"Students in my fifth grade class have demonstrated that when they learned a skill by discovery, they remembered and applied it in further work. Their need for belonging, power and freedom was met. The work was no longer dull and boring.

"My students have also shown they can take an active role in decision making through setting standards together and using these standards for self-assessment. They had another opportunity to be a participant in their learning. We formed a partnership in assessing work and they didn't sit idly by while I, in isolation, marked papers. They had ownership in their work. They set high standards and goals for themselves.

"Creating a climate in the classroom where students have more opportunity for discovery and self-assessment also enabled my students to become self-directed achievers who set goals and evaluated their progress to those goals. The students became cooperative workers, involved citizens, and perceptive thinkers. This happened because these students had the opportunity to demonstrate their learning in relevant settings. While paper and pencil fill-in-the-bubble tests still had a role, there were other ways for the students to show what they had learned.

"This is what makes education exciting today. It is not easy to plan lessons that allow students to discover new concepts. It takes time to work with students in developing standards for projects. It takes even more time to sit with each child and together evaluate a piece of work. But it is worth it when the child's face takes on a look of understanding and eyes light up with excitement. And it is done one day at a time, not all at once.

"Today's classroom is the place to be if you are willing to face challenges and controversy. It is a place to be if you like trying new ideas for presenting a solid background of learning. It is the place to be if you like working with people and feeling a part of change. It is the place to be if you want to dream and dare to make a difference."

Reprinted by permission of Ann A. Hardesty.

Professional Development Schools

While many preservice education programs are offered on a college or university campus, increasingly these programs are a part of a professional development school in which classroom teachers in public schools serve as instructors as well as teaching supervisors of preservice education majors. In addition, professors of education methods courses go into the field to demonstrate new teaching techniques for preservice and inservice, or current, teachers in school settings.

National Certification

The current movement to raise educational standards was begun in the early 1980s when three major publications came out: *A Nation at Risk, High School,* and *A Place Called School.* Now at the millennium, teachers are being asked to have greater knowledge of both subject matter and teaching practices. Teacher training institutions are increasing their standards for entrance, preparation, and performance.

States, too, are involved in raising standards for teachers as many are reconsidering certification and tenure laws. Some states, such as Ohio, have moved to licensure rather than certification. Every five years, the teacher must take a test to verify that she or he is proficient in her or his subject area and competent in teaching pedagogy. During the five-year period between the teaching exams, the teacher is expected to participate in inservice training and enroll in postgraduate education courses.

The National Council for Accreditation of Teacher Education (NCATE) is an accrediting agency that reviews teacher education programs. Some states, such as Florida, insist that all teacher education programs within its boundaries must meet the academic standards set by NCATE. Other states, such as Wisconsin, do not require teacher education programs to meet NCATE's criteria. Roughly 500 of the 1,200 teacher education programs nationally are accredited by NCATE.

In working with national professional organizations such as the International Reading Association, National Council of Teachers of English, National Council of Teachers of Mathematics, National Council on Social Studies, National Council of Science Teachers, and other subject matter organizations, NCATE is developing New Professional Teacher (NPT) standards. Each professional group has suggested minimum requirements for teachers in their respective fields.

In 1987, the National Board for Professional Teaching Standards (NBPTS) was established to professionalize teaching and raise standards. By the year 2000, thirty different certifications are expected to be issued by NBPTS. The first certification was in the area of "Early Adolescence/Generalist," and this certification was initially granted to eighty-one middle school and junior high teachers in 1995. The NBPTS has the support of the U.S. Department of Education and is endorsed by both Secretary of Education Richard Riley and President Bill Clinton.

In order to obtain NBPTS certification, teachers must have taught at least three years and be certified by their state. A year-long review process then takes place during which the teachers are visited in their classroom as their teaching performance is thoroughly examined. Teaching portfolio evaluations and knowledge-based examinations are also crucial elements of the evaluation process for certification.

Getting NBPTS certification requires a substantial amount of time and effort by teachers. However, meeting the certification demands of the NBPTS has its advantages. In applying for a teaching position, having the certification from the NBPTS enables you to be recognized as a teaching professional who has met high and rigorous requirements. In addition, increasingly states, such as Iowa, New Mexico, and

"I chose to become a teacher because I didn't like what I read in the newspapers—students graduating from our high schools and colleges who can't read or write, kids taking drugs and killing themselves," I continued. "And the newspapers tell me you kids can't read, you hate books, you can't use your own language, and you don't care. Well, I care. And I think you do, too, or you wouldn't be here." I glanced around the room at those ancient eyes in adolescent faces. I saw the fear, the anger, the pain—the truth that the purple mohawks and gang colors were designed to camouflage.

"And please don't waste my time trying to convince me that you're bad," I said. "Bad kids don't go to school. Bad kids are in jail, in juvi hall, in reform schools, on the streets. They aren't sitting in high school."

They weren't sure whether to buy it or not; I could see it in their expressions. Still, they were sitting down and they were not talking. I was on a roll.

"I will make each one of you this guarantee. You come to class every day and do the work I give you here, and you do your homework. And if you *try*, I guarantee you will pass this course. There is nobody in this room who is stupid. You are all valuable human beings, which reminds me—I have only one rule in this classroom and that rule is not negotiable: Respect yourself and everyone else in this room. If you can't respect yourself, you can't respect other people. And if you don't have any self-respect, you have a problem. We're going to fix that problem because every person has the right to his or her personal dignity."

"That's bullshit!" one boy muttered. "That chickenshit rule don't tell us nothing." He raised his voice. "You're supposed to give us a list of rules and shit to follow. 'Respect yourself' don't tell me nothing."

"It tells you everything," I said. "What is your name?"

"Roderick J. Horne."

"All right, Roderick," I said. "Let me give you an example. Do you think it is respectful for you to get up and walk around the room while I am talking?"

"No," he replied.

"Do you think it is respectful for me to yell at you?"

"No," he said, quickly.

"Well, then, do you think it's respectful to say 'shit' in school?"

"No," he snapped, sighing at my stupidity.

"Then you tell me an example of something you could do in class and get in trouble for, that doesn't break my single rule," I said. He offered several suggestions, but his classmates loudly disqualified each example. Roderick refused to give up and the others grew restless. Stacy Wilson, a pretty black girl with about four hundred tiny braids on her head, reached out and smacked Rod on the arm, hard.

"You acting like a stupid nigger, Roderick," she said jovially. "Shut your face." The class broke up.

"That reminds me of my only other rule," I said loudly.

"I knew it," said a voice from the corner. "No teachers have only one rule. They get off on rules."

I ignored the taunt. Although I had not intended to create any other rules, I felt compelled to add one more.

"My second rule isn't really a separate rule," I explained. "It is a result of breaking the first rule. I want you all to understand that there is one thing I will flunk you for on the spot." That was an outright lie; teachers don't have the power to flunk students based on a single incident. But the students didn't know that and I didn't either, at the time.

"I will not tolerate any racial, ethnic, or sexual slurs in this classroom. It is not fair to erase someone's face. In this room, everyone is entitled to equal dignity as a human being."

"Black kids can call each other niggers," Stacy protested.

"Not in this classroom they can't," I insisted.

Stacy shrugged her shoulders. "It don't matter what you say anyway," she said. "Miss Sheppard already done flunked most of us anyway before she left."

(continued)

Without stopping to consider whether I was bound to follow the previous teacher's grading system, I found myself creating yet another rule for this class. Since I had little hope of getting my hands on Miss Sheppard's student files, I decided to use the lack of information to my advantage.

"From this moment," I heard myself say, "each one of you starts with a clean record. I have not opened your previous teacher's files. This is your one break for the year. If you want to pass, all you have to do is try from now on. At this point, everyone has an A. It's up to you to keep it."

"She's lyin'," one student whispered, without conviction.

"Shut up," another kid countered. "I never had an A before. Leave her be before she changes her mind."

The prospect of having A's apparently stunned them, so I decided to knock them out before they had a chance to recover. I waded into the middle of the room, smiling at their upturned faces.

"And, at this point, I like every single person in this room. You can make me dislike you if you want to, but you'll have to try very hard and it won't be worth the effort."

"Hah!" Stacy said, tossing her head. Her braids had little beads on them that clicked musically when she moved. I remembered how much I used to love stomping around the house with bells laced to my shoestrings. "What about Roderick?"

I walked over to Roderick's desk and put my arm on his shoulder. He looked uncomfortable, but secretly pleased. "Yes, I like Roderick very much. I can tell he has a good brain. I hope he uses it."

"You won't like me when you see my grades," Roderick challenged me.

"Oh, yes, I will," I assured him. "I will be sad if you get poor grades, but I will still like you—the person—just as much."

"We'll see," he said, with a weary sigh.

"I believe we will," I said, imitating his huge sigh and his woeful expression until he gave in to a half-smile.

Encouraged by their honesty, I decided to give the kids a real opportunity to express themselves. I wanted to know what had happened in that classroom, why their other teachers quit, but I didn't want the students to exaggerate and brag about how horrible they had been. Moving to the chalkboard, I picked up a piece of chalk and faced the class. "I'm sure you're familiar with the technique of brainstorming?"

A chorus of groans and hisses affirmed my assumption, but I didn't let them slow me down. I drew a vertical line down the middle of the board and wrote Effective Teacher in the center of one side.

"Tell me what you think makes an effective teacher," I said.

"Takes charge!"

"Kicks ass!"

"Interesting!"

"Young!"

"Fair!"

"Controls the class!"

"Smart!"

"Discipline!"

"Shows who's the boss!"

"No homework!"

"No pop quizzes!"

"Likes kids."

"Doesn't wear the same clothes every day!"

After a few minutes, it was quite obvious that the class was begging for discipline and they expected me to provide it. As soon as they started lagging on their responses, I moved to the other side of the board.

"Now tell me what makes an effective student," I said. They were hot. I couldn't write fast enough. They mimicked the voices of their parents and teachers.

"Comes to class on time."

"No cuts."

"Does homework."

"Studies for tests."

"No talking during class."

"No writing notes."

"No throwing paper."

"No smoking in the bathroom."

"No cheating."

They worked hard to outdo each other and we filled the board in just a few minutes. I placed the chalk on the holder and dusted off my hands.

(continued)

Oklahoma, are waiving their own state licensure requirements for those individuals who possess NBPTS certification and who wish to teach in their state. Other states, such as Ohio and Massachusetts, accept the NBPTS certification in lieu of recertification requirements for teachers already teaching in their states.

Alternative Certification

Several states offer alternative certification programs that are not necessarily tied to a college or university. These programs are viewed by some educators as a drastic move toward certifying individuals in areas where there are shortages of teachers, for instance minority teachers and in the areas of math and science.

Many of these alternative certification programs require an individual to have a bachelor's degree, to serve in an internship program under the close supervision of a classroom teacher, and to receive instruction at a regional training center (Farris and Smith 1993). Other alternative certification programs encourage individuals who have taken some college courses in the past to complete a bachelor's degree in education through a modified teacher education program that enables them to work either part-time or full-time while acquiring certification.

Alternative certification programs are one way to recruit members of minorities to the teaching profession. For instance, 52 percent of the individuals in the alternative certification program in Texas are members of minorities as compared with only 12 percent of the actual teaching population. In addition, more men (30 percent as compared with 23 percent in the teaching population) are enrolled in Texas's alternative certification program (Farris and Smith 1993; Texas Education Agency 1992).

The Teaching Profession

While each state regulates the certification requirements of teachers, there are various professional organizations on a national level that teachers can join. (A list of professional education organizations is in the back of this text.) Some organizations deal with the teacher's specific content area, such as the American Alliance for Health, Physical Education, Recreation, and Dance (AAHPERD), the Council for Exceptional Children (CEC), the International Reading Association (IRA), the National Council of Teachers of Mathematics (NCTM), or the National Council for the Social Studies (NCSS).

Other organizations are more general in nature. For instance, the Association for Supervision and Curriculum Development (ASCD) focuses on curriculum from early childhood through high school, while the National Middle Schools Association (NMSA) focuses on issues dealing with teaching sixth through eighth graders.

"I'D LIKE TO OVERWHELM THEM WITH INSTRUCTIONAL EXCELLENCE, BUT I'M NOT ABOVE WINNING THROUGH INTIMIDATION."

(© Martha F. Campbell)

The **American Federation of Teachers (AFT)** and the **National Education Association (NEA)** are two predominate teachers' unions in the United States. They generally have local affiliations to represent teachers in labor negotiations at the local school district level. The NEA is the largest union, with over two million members. The group was originally founded in 1857 as the National Teacher's Association. For nearly 140 years, the NEA has advocated teaching as a profession. It offers its members publications and reports regarding trends and research in educational methods as well as programs and activities.

The AFT began in 1916 with John Dewey, the noted education philosopher, as its first member. The AFT has nearly half as many members as the NEA and is closely affiliated with the AFL-CIO (American Federation of Labor-Congress of Industrial Organizations). Like the NEA, the AFT offers its members publications and reports in addition to professional workshops. In the 1990s, the AFT has focused its attention on teacher leadership.

The AFT receives a substantial amount of public attention because it funds a weekly column written by its president, Al Shanker, in the *New York Times.* This forum often raises questions regarding current educational issues.

During the 1960s and early 1970s, the AFT and NEA competed heavily for members. Whenever the majority of teachers in a school district belong to either the AFT or the NEA, it is that labor union that represents the teachers within that school district during bargaining for salary and fringe benefits.

At this time, both the AFT and the NEA are working on the improvement of schools and teacher empowerment. In recent years, the two organizations have become more similar in their philosophies, and there is even the possibility that in the future the two will merge.

The NEA has developed a Teacher Education Initiative (TEI) designed to improve the preparation of new teachers in teacher education programs. For example, Texas A & M University has raised the admission standards for students in teacher education. In addition, students who enter the program receive counseling throughout the program regarding their performance and fitness for teaching. The University of Memphis has restructured its teacher education program so that its graduates are now better prepared to work with students from diverse backgrounds. The University of Memphis is offering field experiences in urban, suburban, and rural school settings. The University of Southern Maine is developing new standards for its education majors, including requiring a portfolio presentation. Upon graduation, teacher education majors have a one-year internship in a professional development school (Seidel and Williams 1997).

Websites for the AFT and the NEA are available. These contain a variety of information and statistics about teaching.

American Federation of Teachers
http://www.aft.org
National Education Association
http://www.nea.org

The Professionalization of Teaching

In the past two decades, teaching has come to be viewed more as a profession than it was historically. This is in part due to the efforts of educational leaders as well as the AFT and NEA.)

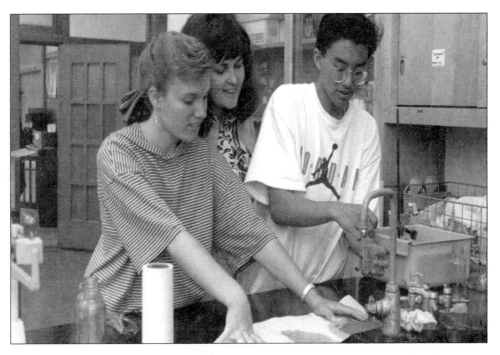

Minoring or majoring in fields which have a known teacher shortage can greatly enhance your opportunity to land a teaching position. For instance there is a shortage of science teachers, especially female science teachers. (© Elizabeth Crews/The Image Works)

Teacher Salaries

Teaching salaries vary from school district to school district within a state as well as among the states. Teachers with master's degrees in education are paid more on the average than those with a bachelor's degree only. However, in some areas, it is often more difficult for a beginning teacher with a master's degree to get a teaching position than one with a bachelor's degree because the school district has to pay a larger salary.

Each school district has a salary schedule. Typically, a teacher goes up the salary schedule with each subsequent year of teaching experience. Whenever a teacher obtains additional professional training, such as a master's or educational specialist degree, his or her salary is also increased. Table 1 shows a salary comparison in one midwestern school district. Some school districts will even pay a portion of tuition for graduate study for their teachers to encourage their professional development.

In 1995–96, the average public school teacher in the United States was paid $37,643. Only twenty-four years before, in 1971, the average salary was $9,705 (U.S. Department of Education 1997). Thus, in recent years teaching salaries have become more competitive with those of other professions, though they still lag behind. For

Table 1 1998–99 Table of Salaries for District 26 (Cary, Illinois)

No. of Years	Degree	Degree +10	Degree +20	Degree +32	Masters	Masters +10	Masters +20	Masters +30	Masters +45
0	22,913	23,738	24,592	25,478	26,395	27,345	28,330	29,349	29,849
1	23,738	24,592	25,478	26,395	27,345	28,330	29,349	30,406	30,906
2	24,592	25,478	26,395	27,345	28,330	29,349	30,406	31,501	32,001
3	25,478	26,395	27,345	28,330	29,349	30,406	31,501	32,635	33,135
4	26,395	27,345	28,330	29,349	30,406	31,501	32,635	33,810	34,310
5	27,345	28,330	29,349	30,406	31,501	32,635	33,810	35,027	35,527
6	28,330	29,349	30,406	31,501	32,635	33,810	35,027	36,288	36,788
7	29,349	30,406	31,501	32,635	33,810	35,027	36,288	37,594	38,094
8	30,406	31,501	32,635	33,810	35,027	36,288	37,594	38,947	39,447
9	31,501	32,635	33,810	35,027	36,288	37,594	38,947	40,349	40,849
10	32,635	33,810	35,027	36,288	37,594	38,947	40,349	41,802	42,302
11	33,810	35,027	36,288	37,594	38,947	40,349	41,802	43,307	43,807
12	35,027	36,288	37,594	38,947	40,349	41,802	43,307	44,866	45,366
13	36,288	37,594	38,947	40,349	41,802	43,307	44,866	46,481	46,981
14		38,947	40,349	41,802	43,307	44,866	46,481	48,154	48,654
15			41,802	43,307	44,866	46,481	48,154	49,888	50,388
16			43,307	44,866	46,481	48,154	49,888	51,684	52,184
17				46,481	48,154	49,888	51,684	53,545	54,045
18				48,154	49,888	51,684	53,545	55,472	55,972

Longevity increases ½ percent per year for each year of experience beyond the end of each column. After the 1995–96 school year, column Degree +32 is closed to any new movement. For the 1998–99 contract years, up to and including column Masters +30, the product of the factor .034825 and year 18, Degree +32, shall be added to the schedule at year 19 only. Effective with the 1996–97 school year the column Masters +45 has been added with a $500 per year cap.

Six percent (6%) of the salary stated will be a tax sheltered contribution made to the Illinois Teachers' Retirement System. In addition, the Board of Education will pay 2.0408 percent annual contribution of the salary stated to the Teachers' Retirement System on each teacher's behalf.

Reprinted by permission of Cary Elementary Schools, Cary Illinois.

Copyright © Cary School District, Cary, Illinois.

instance, Karen Jones, a teacher in South Carolina, recently remarked that she has seen her salary quadruple in the sixteen years she has been teaching (Jones 1994). Table 2 gives the average beginning teacher salary by state in 1995–96. The range was a low of $18,225 in North Dakota to a high of $34,800 in Alaska. The average teaching salary in the U.S. in 1995–96 was $37,643 with $26,800 in Louisiana being the lowest salary per teacher and $50,938 in Connecticut being the highest average salary.

Table 2
Beginning Minimum and Average Teacher Salaries, by State 1995–96

State	1995–96		
	Beginning salary	Average salary	Beginning salary as a percent of average salary
United States	$24,507	$37,643	65.1
Alabama	24,824	31,323	79.3
Alaska	[3]34,800	47,349	73,5
Arizona	[3]24,042	32,843	73.2
Arkansas	[3]21,189	[2]29,845	71.0
California	[3]25,762	[3]42,161	61.1
Colorado	21,472	36,364	59.0
Connecticut	28,840	50,938	56.6
Delaware	24,300	40,533	60.0
District of Columbia	25,937	42,424	61.1
Florida	23,508	33,330	70.5
Georgia	24,693	[5]34,130	72.3
Hawaii	25,436	37,044	68.7
Idaho	19,667	30,894	63.7
Illinois	[6]26,753	[6]40,513	66.0
Indiana	[2]24,216	[2]37,677	64.3
Iowa	21,338	32,376	65.9
Kansas	[7]21,607	[7]32,531	66.4
Kentucky	[3]22,457	33,079	67.9
Louisiana	19,406[3]	26,800	72.4
Maine	20,725	32,869	63.1
Maryland	[6]26,846	41,229	65.1
Massachusetts	[3]25,815	43,025	60.0
Michigan	[3]25,635	[3]47,430	54.0
Minnesota	23,998	36,847	65.1
Mississippi	20,150	27,692	72.8
Missouri	21,996	32,369	68.0
Montana	[3]19,992	29,364	68.1
Nebraska	21,299	31,496	67.6
Nevada	25,576	[8]39,535	64.7
New Hampshire	[3]23,510	35,792	65.7
New Jersey	[3]31,435	48,920	64.3
New Mexico	22,634	29,118	77.7
New York	28,749	48,115	59.8

Table 2
Continued

State	1995–96		
	Beginning salary	Average salary	Beginning salary as a percent of average salary
North Carolina	[3,9]20,620	[2]30,411	67.8
North Dakota	18,225	26,966	67.6
Ohio	[2]20,355	[2]38,075	53.5
Oklahoma	24,187	[7]29,177	82.9
Oregon	[8]24,592	[8]39,311	62.6
Pennsylvania	29,514	46,087	64.0
Rhode Island	24,754	41,829	59.2
South Carolina	21,791	[2]31,397	69.4
South Dakota	19,609	26,369	74.4
Tennessee	21,537	[2]33,126	65.0
Texas	22,642	[10]31,633	71.6
Utah	20,544	30,390	67.6
Vermont	[3]24,445	[3]36,263	67.4
Virginia	[3]25,500	34,687	73.5
Washington	[2]24,590	[2]38,001	64.7
West Virginia	22,011	32,155	68.5
Wisconsin	24,560	[3]37,586	65.3
Wyoming	[3]21,900	31,571	69.4

[1]Based on the Consumer Price Index prepared by the Bureau of Labor Statistics, U.S. Department of Labor. Price index does not account for different rates of change in the cost of living among states.
[2]Preliminary or state estimate.
[3]Estimated by the American Federation of Teachers. See NOTE.
[4]Excludes state-paid health insurance.
[5]Reflects the redefinition of classroom teacher.
[6]Preliminary or state estimate. Includes pay for extra duties.
[7]Estimated to exclude fringe benefits.
[8]Includes 6 percent pension pick-up in Oregon and 9.5 percent in Nebraska.
[9]Median salary.
[10]Including incentive pay or career ladder stipends and revision of classroom teacher definition.
NOTE:Data in this table reflect results of surveys conducted by the American Federation of Teachers. Because of differing survey and estimation methods, these data are not entirely comparable with figures appearing in other tables.
Source: American Federation of Teachers, Washington, D.C., *Surveys and Analysis of Salary Trends,* 1997, p. 13, and U.S. Department of Education, *Statistics of State School Systems,* 1997, p. 86.

One indication of a state's support of its schools is the amount of expenditure per pupil. Table 3 indicates that an average of $5,988 was spent per U.S. student in 1994–95. New Jersey spent an average of $9,774, the highest for all states while Mississippi spent only $4,080 per student during the same period.

Private School Salaries

Teachers in private schools earn less money on the average than their public school counterparts. This is because private schools largely rely on tuition for primary funding, although most private schools also receive federal and state monies through grants and other programs.

Table 3

Expenditures per Pupil in Average Daily Attendance in Public Elementary and Secondary Schools by State 1994–95

State or other area	1994–95	State or other area	1994–95
United States	**$5,988**	Nevada	5,160
Alabama	4,405	New Hampshire	5,859
Alaska	8,963	New Jersey	9,774
Arizona	4,778	New Mexico	4,586
Arkansas	4,459	New York	9,623
California	4,992	North Carolina	5,077
Colorado	5,443	North Dakota	4,775
Connecticut	8,817	Ohio	6,162
Delaware	7,030	Oklahoma	4,845
District of Columbia	9,335	Oregon	6,436
Florida	5,718	Pennsylvania	7,109
Georgia	5,193	Rhode Island	7,469
Hawaii	6,078	South Carolina	4,797
Idaho	4,210	South Dakota	4,775
Illinois	6,136	Tennessee	4,388
Indiana	5,826	Texas	5,222
Iowa	5,483	Utah	3,656
Kansas	5,817	Vermont	6,750
Kentucky	5,217	Virginia	5,327
Louisiana	4,761	Washington	5,906
Maine	6,428	West Virginia	6,107
Maryland	7,245	Wisconsin	6,930
Massachusetts	7,287	Wyoming	6,160
Michigan	6,994	Outlying areas	
Minnesota	6,000	American Samoa	2,046
Mississippi	4,080	Guam	4,969
Missouri	5,383	Northern Marianas	5,227
Montana	5,692	Puerto Rico	2,742
Nebraska	5,935	Virgin Islands	6,003

[1]Based on the Consumer Price Index, prepared by the Bureau of Labor Statistics, U.S. Department of Labor, adjusted to a school-year basis. These data do not reflect differences in inflation rates from state to state.
[2]Estimated by the National Center for Education Statistics.
—Data not available or not applicable.
NOTE:—Beginning in 1980–81, state administration expenditures are excluded. Beginning in 1988–89, extensive changes were made in the data collection procedures. Some data have been revised from previously published figures.
Source: U.S. Department of Education, National Center for Education Statistics, *Statistics of State School Systems*, 1997, 171.

Merit Pay and Differential Pay

In recent years, many school districts have examined different ways of rewarding outstanding teachers. During the 1980s, some districts adopted merit pay programs that rewarded excellent teachers with an additional salary stipend for their efforts. Teachers who receive merit pay must go through a rigorous evaluation of their instructional practices, including classroom observations by other teachers and administrators. Typically, teachers' unions resist merit pay, stating that it causes morale problems among the teaching staff. Largely because of the lack of support by teachers' unions, merit pay has been adopted by a relatively small number of school districts.

In addition to merit pay, differentiated pay also exists within some school districts. Differentiated pay means a higher salary is provided to teachers in fields in which there is a severe shortage of trained teachers, such as speech and hearing, physics, and Japanese. Some school districts pay higher salaries to recruit minority teachers. This salary differential reflects the private sector, where a business may try to lure one employee away from another company by offering a higher salary. Whenever a severe shortage in an instructional area exists, a school district may elect to provide a differentiated salary to attract qualified teachers to that district. When the shortage no longer exists, the differentiated salary is eliminated by the school district as a salary offer to new teachers. Thus, differentiated pay is based on the supply and demand of teachers within fields of specialization.

Fringe Benefits

School districts provide fringe benefits to their employees that usually include retirement benefits, health and dental insurance, and a reduced fee for group life insurance.

Almost all school districts make available certain services for their staff for no fee, such as direct deposit of paychecks to local banks and/or credit unions. In addition, some districts allow teachers to choose a nine-month or twelve-month paycheck schedule. However, most districts pay their teachers every two weeks for a total of twenty-six paychecks.

Most districts and unions have an agreement that allows union dues to be withheld from those teachers' paychecks who are union members. In this way, the dues are prorated over the year rather than paid in one lump sum at the beginning of the school year.

Nearly all school districts make available to their teachers individual retirement annuity accounts (called a 403B account). Each pay period a teacher may contribute up to 20 percent of his or her salary or a maximum of $9,500 a year, whichever is less, to a retirement account supervised by a company usually approved by the state. The monies set aside by a teacher each year in a 403B retirement account are not subject to income tax, either federal or state, until the funds are withdrawn at age 59½ or older.

Employment Opportunities in the Teaching Profession

Rumors of a major teacher shortage surfaced in the mid-1980s but were somewhat premature. However, by the year 2000, many teachers who entered the teaching profession in the 1960s and early 1970s will retire, leaving positions open for new teachers. According to Marshall (1995, 53), "Tight budgets discourage teacher hiring, but early retirement incentives have increased the number of openings available to new graduates." In addition, the mini baby boom has caused an increased need for teachers at the elementary level. This boomlet has also impacted secondary schools. Lastly, the new focus on early childhood education and the increased number of working mothers and single working parents have opened up new opportunities for preschool teachers.

Teacher shortages can occur for various reasons. School districts in areas of high population growth may need to hire several new teachers because of increased numbers of students. New areas of specialization have resulted in a shortage of teachers in fields such as computer science and behavior disorders. Likewise, a surplus of teachers can result whenever the number of students declines or the number of qualified teachers exceeds the number of teaching positions.

Table 4 shows the results of a 1997 ASCUS study of teacher supply and demand in the United States.

Table 4   Teacher Supply and Demand by Field and Region

Region codes: 1–Northwest, 2–West, 3–Rocky Mountain, 4–Great Plains/Midwest, 5–South Central, 6–Southeast, 7–Great Lakes, 8–Middle Atlantic, 9–Northeast, 10–Alaska and 11–Hawaii.

Demand codes: 5.00–4.21 = Considerable shortage; 4.20–3.41 = Some Shortage; 3.40–2.61 = Balanced; 2.60–1.81 = Some Surplus; 1.80–1.00 = Considerable Surplus

Teaching Field	Region											National 1997
	1	2	3	4	5	6	7	8	9	10	11	
Agriculture	2.60	2.78	3.50	3.08	3.00	3.20	3.80	3.50	—	—	3.00	3.17
Art/Visual	2.36	2.70	2.25	2.70	2.63	2.56	2.64	1.97	2.60	—	2.00	2.53
Audiology	3.83	3.71	4.50	4.24	4.00	4.54	4.08	3.67	4.50	—	3.00	4.06
Bilingual Education	4.55	4.75	4.76	4.67	4.00	3.50	4.59	4.00	4.50	—	4.00	4.34
Business Education	2.73	2.81	2.67	2.93	2.30	2.84	2.91	2.15	2.00	—	3.00	2.69
Computer Science/Education	3.56	3.64	3.25	3.74	3.57	3.83	3.77	3.63	4.00	—	3.00	3.70
Counselor Education	3.06	3.17	3.00	4.10	3.23	3.03	3.53	2.81	2.63	4.00	4.00	3.25
Dance Education	2.50	2.78	2.00	2.50	2.43	2.20	2.67	2.00	—	—	3.00	2.45
Driver Education	2.67	2.75	—	2.73	2.31	2.33	3.17	2.80	—	—	3.00	2.59
Elementary–Pre-K	2.07	3.48	2.57	2.58	2.69	2.70	2.50	2.10	2.75	4.00	2.00	2.56
Elementary–Kindergarten	2.33	3.87	2.82	2.44	2.69	2.63	2.31	1.90	2.13	3.50	3.00	2.50
Elementary–Primary	2.26	4.03	2.75	2.25	2.91	2.52	2.10	1.97	2.08	3.50	2.00	2.44
Elementary–Intermediate	2.32	3.66	2.67	2.40	3.03	2.70	2.32	2.00	2.18	3.00	2.00	2.54
English/Language Arts	2.50	2.87	2.43	3.00	2.95	2.83	2.56	2.07	2.00	3.00	3.00	2.64
English as a Second Lang. (ESL)	3.86	4.46	3.33	3.93	4.14	3.88	4.04	3.68	4.00	—	4.00	4.01
Gifted/Talented Education	2.67	3.70	3.00	3.55	3.50	3.29	3.33	3.33	—	—	3.00	3.36
Health Education	2.56	2.71	2.80	2.16	2.12	2.44	2.05	2.41	3.00	—	3.00	2.31
Home Economics	2.80	3.00	3.00	3.19	2.92	3.08	3.21	3.50	2.00	—	4.00	3.09
Journalism	2.38	2.89	2.68	3.00	2.82	2.79	2.33	2.59	2.50	4.00	—	3.00
Language–Classics	3.00	3.09	2.00	3.27	3.36	3.70	3.06	2.18	3.50	—	3.00	3.14
Language–French	2.78	2.76	2.83	3.25	3.22	3.62	3.04	2.76	2.69	4.00	3.00	3.08
Language–German	2.71	3.00	2.60	3.15	3.00	3.56	3.08	2.79	2.67	3.00	3.00	3.07
Language–Japanese	3.43	3.00	—	3.36	5.00	3.77	3.73	4.00	4.00	—	4.00	3.54
Language–Spanish	3.43	3.93	3.70	3.98	3.66	4.03	3.88	3.21	2.93	4.00	3.00	3.72
Library Science	2.57	3.33	3.67	3.82	3.27	3.45	4.08	3.78	—	—	4.00	3.52
Mathematics	3.71	4.03	4.00	3.81	4.02	4.09	3.71	3.50	3.39	4.00	5.00	3.81
Music–Instrumental	3.00	3.07	3.60	3.55	3.03	3.03	3.04	2.66	2.70	5.00	3.00	3.11
Music–Vocal	2.85	2.92	3.33	3.42	2.94	2.97	2.97	2.72	2.50	—	3.00	3.02
Physical Education	2.29	2.36	2.25	2.03	2.05	2.28	1.95	2.04	2.00	—	1.00	2.11
Psychologist (School)	3.89	3.88	3.75	3.76	2.92	3.24	3.75	3.55	3.50	4.00	4.00	3.58
Reading	3.13	3.50	3.17	3.27	3.20	3.27	3.17	2.95	3.09	—	3.00	3.19
Science–Biology	3.43	3.96	3.54	3.59	3.71	3.82	3.46	3.51	3.45	3.00	4.00	3.62
Science–Chemistry	3.79	4.30	3.67	4.14	4.02	4.14	4.14	3.87	3.63	4.00	4.00	4.04
Science–Earth/Physical	3.25	3.96	3.38	3.70	3.89	3.83	3.62	3.63	3.53	4.00	4.00	3.70
Science–General	3.39	4.04	3.27	3.58	3.76	3.93	3.56	3.48	3.38	3.00	4.00	3.64
Science–Physics	3.72	4.08	3.80	4.19	3.94	4.16	4.41	3.97	3.71	3.00	4.00	4.09
Social Sciences/Studies	1.39	1.92	2.31	2.14	2.25	2.24	1.94	1.89	2.05	2.00	2.00	2.05
Social Worker (School)	2.38	3.33	2.00	3.39	2.50	3.04	3.27	3.29	4.33	—	3.00	3.13
Special Ed.–Behavioral Disorders	4.27	4.77	4.17	4.31	4.00	4.40	4.56	4.09	3.79	4.00	5.00	4.29

Table 4 Continued

Region codes: 1–Northwest, 2–West, 3–Rocky Mountain, 4–Great Plains/Midwest, 5–South Central, 6–Southeast, 7–Great Lakes, 8–Middle Atlantic, 9–Northeast, 10–Alaska and 11–Hawaii.

Demand codes: 5.00–4.21 = Considerable shortage; 4.20–3.41 = Some Shortage; 3.40–2.61 = Balanced; 2.60–1.81 = Some Surplus; 1.80–1.00 = Considerable Surplus

Teaching Field	Region											National 1997
	1	2	3	4	5	6	7	8	9	10	11	
Special Ed.–Hearing Impaired	4.11	4.56	5.00	4.18	3.77	4.75	4.00	4.00	4.50	4.00	5.00	4.21
Special Ed.–Learning Disability	4.28	4.58	3.75	4.10	4.30	4.39	4.25	3.79	3.92	4.00	5.00	4.21
Special Ed.–Mentally Hand.	4.21	4.59	4.00	4.14	4.15	4.33	4.27	3.95	3.88	4.00	5.00	4.20
Special Ed.–Multiple Hand.	4.33	4.65	5.00	4.10	4.13	4.58	4.37	3.88	4.00	4.00	5.00	4.25
Special Ed.–Physically Impaired	4.33	4.36	5.00	4.00	4.25	4.59	4.07	4.06	4.33	4.00	5.00	4.23
Special Ed.–Visually Impaired	3.71	4.11	5.00	3.38	4.44	4.64	3.50	4.20	5.00	4.00	5.00	
Speech/Drama/Theatre	2.60	3.00	3.00	2.76	2.82	2.62	2.25	2.54	2.50	3.00	3.00	2.63
Speech Pathology	4.10	4.50	5.00	4.57	3.88	4.78	4.52	3.93	—	5.00	5.00	4.34
Technology Education	4.00	3.71	4.43	4.39	4.11	4.00	4.26	3.56	3.67	4.00	5.00	4.02
COMPOSITE	**3.10**	**3.64**	**3.20**	**3.23**	**3.30**	**3.30**	**3.08**	**2.95**	**3.01**	**3.83**	**3.52**	**3.19**
Number of Participants	26	34	14	87	49	107	96	89	33	2	1	538*

*Questionnaires returned without indication of region were computed in the national averages only. Total of regional participants does not equal national total.

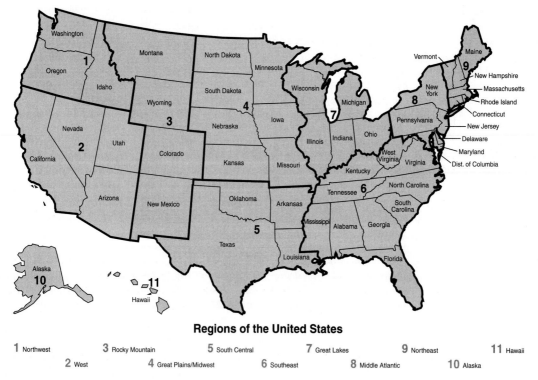

Regions of the United States

1 Northwest 3 Rocky Mountain 5 South Central 7 Great Lakes 9 Northeast 11 Hawaii
2 West 4 Great Plains/Midwest 6 Southeast 8 Middle Atlantic 10 Alaska

Chapter 1 *The Teaching Profession*

Finding a Teaching Position

After you have successfully completed a teacher education program, including student teaching in a public school setting, you will begin your search for a teaching position in either a public or private school. Before you can apply for a teaching position, you need to prepare yourself for the job search by developing a résumé and a teaching portfolio. You also need a list of teaching openings.

Organize yourself by using a file folder for each school district with a checklist to track the materials you send: cover letter describing your interest in the school district and the teaching position, transcript of grades, teaching certificate, résumé, application, and location of college or university placement office that will send copies of your letters of recommendation directly to the school district. Whenever the school district notifies you that your materials have been received, place that information in the file.

To find a teaching position, you must locate schools with openings for teachers trained in your area of specialization. Every college and university has a placement office that receives lists of teaching positions in the geographical area, both public and private. Most colleges and universities sponsor a career day so school districts can send representatives to recruit talented teachers. If you attend a college or university with a large teacher education program, recruiters from school districts not only throughout your state but from large cities in other states as well may attend your career day.

You may also write or call school districts directly in the geographical area in which you want to teach and request a teaching application. Request a list of teaching position openings at that time, but keep in mind that openings may change frequently in the spring and summer months.

Each year there are numerous openings for private school teachers, primarily in religious schools. Although teachers in private schools are required to meet the same certification requirements as their public school counterparts, be aware that when a teacher decides to move from a private school to a public school, very often the public school district will hire the teacher at the same starting salary as a first-year teacher and not give credit for the years taught in a private school. This may be a consideration as you search for your first teaching position.

Most teaching candidates send out several applications to school districts before they land a teaching position. Generally speaking, you probably should send out applications to all school districts within a thirty-mile radius of where you currently live if you are planning to stay in your same geographical area.

Transcript and Teaching Certificate

Long before you graduate, you need to work on your transcript. Plan to take courses that will enhance your marketability as a teacher. If you love physical education and like math but you know your area has a big surplus of physical education teachers and a shortage of math teachers, then major in math and minor in physical education. This will increase your chances of getting a teaching position. As an elementary education major, you might want to enhance your marketability by minoring in science, math, or Spanish or by taking twelve to fifteen extra credit hours in special education or reading.

Certainly the higher your grade point average (GPA) the more likely that you will get an interview. Students with marginal GPAs find it more difficult to find teaching positions than those with solid B and above averages.

When you apply to a particular school district, find out if the district prefers an original copy of your college or university transcript or if they are willing to accept a copy from you. Some districts will interview only those candidates who have original transcripts on file. If the district only accepts or prefers an original copy, have your college or university registrar's office send it directly to the school district.

Almost all school districts will accept a photocopy of your teaching certificate for interview purposes. However, if you are hired, the teaching certificate will need to be filed with either the school district or in the county education office.

Résumé

Your résumé should accompany the application you send to the school district. It will introduce you to the building principal, who generally will interview you, as well as other personnel, such as the personnel director, if the district has one, and the search committee, if the school uses building teachers as part of the hiring process. Your résumé, like the application, should be prepared carefully, with no typing or spelling errors. All information should be dated and listed from current to past. Print your résumé on a laser printer on good-quality paper. Photocopies should be clear and clean with no smudges. Figure 1 is an example of a résumé.

On your résumé, clearly state all the previous jobs you have held, especially those in which you worked with children or adolescents. Beginning teachers who have trouble with classroom management and discipline tend to be those who have had little experience working with children, so principals want to know how familiar you are with helping children.

Typically, between three and five references are listed. More than five makes the candidate seem suspicious. Why would anyone need six or more references unless they have a weakness or are insecure? Usually, your references are those who have written the letters of recommendation in your placement file at your college or university. Ask each person you want to serve as a reference to write a letter of recommendation for your placement file.

You may elect to read all the letters in your placement file or you may decide to trust the individuals you asked to write the letters and not review them. If you decide to have a closed placement file, that is, one where you cannot read any of the materials, you must sign a waiver stating that you have elected not to see your file. Many personnel directors and principals prefer candidates with closed files because it indicates that candidates believe they have nothing to hide.

Teaching Portfolio

"A teacher's portfolio enables us to do exactly what we ask our students to do: self-assess, self-evaluate, and self-regulate" (Van Wagener & Hibbard 1998, 29). The portfolio should not be a collection of your best efforts as a teacher but rather a demonstration of how you are growing and improving as an educator.

Your **teaching portfolio** should begin with your first methods class. Keep copies of professional articles you've read and any summaries you've written. In addition, keep all lesson plans you develop and, with both their own permission and their parents', copy a few samples of students' work that resulted from lessons you taught. Include original ideas you've developed.

Figure 1
Example
résumé of a
beginning
teacher

Catherine J. Hanratty
137 Cardinal Lane
Rochester, MN 55206
(H) (507) 238–4411
(Answering Machine)
or
(W) (507) 238–9325
e-mail: chanratty@StCloud.edu

Professional Goal

    I want to become a mathematics teacher at a high school. In addition, I would like to coach swimming, diving, and or tennis.

Education

B.S. Ed. Degree	1998 St. Cloud State University	
	Major: Mathematics Education	
	Minor: History	
Associate Degree	1996 Sauk Valley Community College	
	Major: Business	

Certification

7–12	Mathematics
7–12	United States History

Experience

Student teaching, Litchfield High School, Litchfield, MN,
    Spring, 1998 (Algebra I and II, Geometry, and U.S. History)

Activities

Kappa Kappa Kappa Sorority
Swim team, St. Cloud State University

Professional Organization

National Council of Teachers of Mathematics

Work Experience

McDonald's, St. Cloud, MN 1995–98
    — Assistant Manager
Office Max, Rochester, MN, Summers 1993 and 1994
Tennis and swimming instructor, Rochester Park District, Summers 1991, 1992

Awards

Dean's List, St. Cloud State University, 1996–98
Swimming scholarship, St. Cloud State University, 1996–98

References

Dr. Joe Smith	Mr. Tom Henson	Mrs. Dorothy Jones
Mathematics Department	Teacher	Principal
St. Cloud State University	Litchfield High School	Litchfield High School
St. Cloud, MN 55307	Litchfield, MN 55319	Litchfield, MN 55319
(507) 631–2365	(507) 437–2934	(507) 437–2934

Probably the biggest concern a teacher education major has is about whether there will be a teaching position available. This has been true for several years, even decades. I had the same concern as a teacher education major in the mid-1970s. Perhaps the best advice I received came from a liberal arts professor who told me there is always a job for good students. In short, for those students who worked hard in methods courses and in clinical experiences in the schools, there would be jobs available. That advice is still true today, provided that flexibility in location is maintained. Southerners have a saying that you have to be willing to move away from "mama and nem"—mother and them. The ability and willingness to relocate adds greatly to the potential for employment in all professions, but particularly so in education.

Consider this fact: there are more students in our public schools now than at any other time in the history of our nation. During the next ten years, high school enrollment will swell 13 percent, resulting in the building of six thousand more high schools. And, unlike the baby boom influx which was followed by a decline in student enrollment, by the year 2007 student enrollment is expected to plateau. New York alone has an increase of over twenty thousand students a year, mostly due to immigration. The states expected to grow over 20 percent in high school enrollment are Arizona, California, Massachusetts, Nevada, and North Carolina. Other states to see a substantial increase in student enrollment are Colorado, Georgia, New Mexico, Texas, and Wyoming (Gannett News Service 1997). Already elementary and middle schools are feeling the crunch of increased numbers of students. Thus, the reduction in force of teachers that took place in some districts in the 1970s and 1980s won't occur this time around. In addition, a sizable proportion of teachers at all levels and in all subject areas are approaching retirement. Some states have reported that as many as 40 percent of current teachers will be eligible to retire by the year 2000.

In the fall of 1998, many school administrators found themselves scrambling to hire teachers for the opening of the school year. Couple this with the knowledge that, due to budget cuts in colleges and universities, during the past few years most teacher education programs have reduced their number of teacher education majors. So, with greater competition by school districts to hire teachers, things look *very promising* for teacher education majors.

The placement office at your university will list teaching positions that are available. Also comb the World Wide Web at the Internet to locate homepages of school districts, as some list openings. Check with your state's department of education as well as the classified ad section of your local newspaper.

There are some ways to enhance your opportunities and avoid interview mistakes. While obtaining an additional area of endorsement or minor is expensive with today's high college tuition rates, such effort can lead to your having a list of teaching positions from which to choose, something that was rare a few years ago. Fifteen hours in Spanish plus a couple of classes in instructional technology and computers can make you very marketable. A 24 credit hour minor in one of the sciences or math also enhances your position.

So, let's say you've taken extra coursework: now what? Plan to attack the job market. Use the information at the back of this book to formulate a strategy for landing the teaching position you want. Have a friend ask you the questions listed that a school administrator is most apt to query new applicants. Some teacher education programs set up mock interviews for students with local principals serving as the interviewers.

Give some thought to the actual interview, months before it is to take place. If you're an "A" student and happen to be into body piercing, the latter fact may mean you'll wind up the last choice of hiring officials. It might be wiser to postpone your piercing plans.

(continued)

(concluded)

My students often ask me how to dress for an interview. I suggest that women interviewing for an early childhood, lower elementary position wear a dress or skirt and blouse. Men should wear a white or light blue shirt, tie, and slacks. Bright, but not gaudy, colors are acceptable. Those seeking upper elementary through high school positions might want to dress up a notch, with women wearing either a nice dress or suit and men wearing a sport coat or a sweater, if the weather is cool. Hair should be neat and close to the mainstream in style. Your shoes should be comfortable dress shoes, flats or modest heels for women and loafers or other dark leather shoes for men. And don't forget to polish them. You are giving yourself a poor image if you don't.

Men, if you're not comfortable tying a tie, get a clip-on tie that's decent looking. Women, avoid wearing a pantsuit to an interview. Pants are quite acceptable (and practical) attire for teaching, but a dress and hose are the accepted dress mode for interviews. Both men and women need to remember to unbutton the bottom button of a blazer when seated. Getting a proper wardrobe to wear to interviews is expensive but necessary. One of my students told me she didn't own a dress or a skirt and her budget was very tight. I suggested that she visit one of the local discount stores. Karen did, locating a dress on sale for $17. She landed a special-education position near her future husband's job.

One of my colleagues said to me, "People don't realize that image is everything." He's right. First impressions can be lasting ones. One principal told me that after an interview with a teaching prospect, she arranges to have an errand to do at another building or in town. She explained, "I like to walk the candidates to the parking lot so I can check out their cars. If a car contains empty pop cans, stale french fries, trash, and the like, that candidate gets a lower rating. If a car, no matter how ancient and minus one or two wheel covers with only imagination holding it together, is reasonably clean outside and inside with no candy wrappers and fast food containers left on the floor, then I up that candidate a notch. Teachers who are comfortable living in squalor tend to have messy classrooms. Our community won't accept that."

Remember to make getting a job a priority. One of my students interviewed in a black cocktail dress and insisted that the principal call her by her nickname, "Gogi." You've probably already figured out that she's in another profession. Another student was bent on getting a job in the suburb she grew up it. Despite being an excellent student with superb recommendations from her classroom supervisors, Cheryl was unable to get a job in her community. She gave up a career in teaching and returned to college where she graduated with a degree in nursing and a job at her local hospital.

So, the bottom line is develop a plan for getting a teaching position and follow that plan. And after you land that job, show up to prepare your classroom wearing the proper attire, a T-shirt and cutoffs, and carrying a bucket of cleaning supplies and an armload of books and classroom displays. And on the first day of school, dress comfortably and appropriately—a notch above your colleagues. Congratulations! You're a teacher now!

Include handouts from professional conferences or meetings you attend in your portfolio. Their presence indicates that you take teaching seriously, and, you will be perceived as a dedicated professional educator willing to give extra effort and open to new ideas and teaching strategies.

Take photos of student projects and activities, bulletin boards, and projects you create or field trips you help supervise. Make captions with notecards to describe briefly how each photo relates to your teaching career. Brief statements on current educational practices such as the inclusion of technology or phonics in your teaching style as well as a reflection regarding your position on classroom management are appropriate pieces for a portfolio.

If you work in other settings with children—day camp counselor, swimming instructor, soccer official—take photos of the children with whom you work. Even better, have someone else take a photo of you working with the children. Be certain to find out if parental permission is needed for photos of students and get it if it is required.

Arrange the lesson plans, articles, summaries, photos, and any other appropriate materials into an album. Prior to going to a job interview, scrutinize your portfolio to make it as clear and succinct as possible. According to one report, "Many administrators have reported that although they value the portfolios, time constraints preclude the reviews of lengthy documents" (McLaughlin and Vogt 1996, 98). Thus, for example, videos may take too much time for administrators to review. During the interview, show the principal and any teachers you may meet with what you have already accomplished. You'll find that school administrators and teachers are very interested in what you have accomplished. The portfolio allows you to provide "unique, interesting, and coherent supportive documentation" of your professional competence (Simmons 1995, 59).

■ Summary

Teachers are professionals. Those who enter any profession must first pass through classrooms in which teachers guide them and facilitate their learning. Students are influenced by the teachers they encounter in school.

Teachers come from all walks of life and all cultures. Their common bond is that they want to help students learn.

Before deciding to become a teacher, you must weigh the advantages and disadvantages of the profession. A recent poll indicates that two out of three parents would like their children to become teachers, a most encouraging view of the teaching field as a vocation.

Most teachers are prepared through teacher education programs at colleges and universities that must meet certain certification requirements in their respective states. Such preparation includes a core of general education and methods coursework and field experiences in actual classroom settings.

There are numerous professional organizations teachers can join in their areas of specialization. In addition, there are two national teachers' unions, the American Federation of Teachers and the National Education Association, to which any teacher may belong.

To locate and land a teaching position, you must prepare yourself to be a professional. This includes the courses you select in your teacher education program and the development of a résumé and teaching portfolio. You need to obtain and complete applications for the teaching positions in which you are interested. The earlier you begin planning for your career, the more successful you will be in obtaining a teaching position.

■ Reflections

Obtain four or five sheets of paper. At the top of each, list a career that appeals to you, either strongly or slightly. For each career, list on the left side of the paper all the positive aspects it has to offer. On the right side, list all of the negative aspects of that career.

Compare all of the careers you have selected. How does teaching stack up against the other careers? If one or more have more positive aspects than teaching, can you really justify becoming a teacher? Be realistic and try not to let your emotions take over.

■ Discussion Questions

1. Should every teacher in a school district be required to join the local branch of a teachers' union?
2. Compare the advantages and disadvantages of having an open versus a closed placement file.
3. Why should a beginning teacher join a professional organization in his or her teaching specialty?
4. If you had a friend who enjoys a particular teaching specialty but you were aware there was a surplus of teachers in that area, what advice would you give your friend?

■ For Further Reading

Ayers, A. 1993. *To teach: The journey of a teacher.* New York: Teachers College Press.

Hurst, B., C. Wilson, and G. Cramer. 1998. Professional teaching portfolios. *Phi Delta Kappan,* 79(8):578–582.

Johnson, L. A. 1992. *My posse don't do homework.* New York: St. Martin's Press.

O'Connor, S. 1997. *Will my name be shouted out?* New York: Touchstone.

Rotberg, I. C., M. H. Futrell, and J. M. Lieberman. 1998. National Board Certification: Increasing participation and assessing impacts. *Phi Delta Kappan,* 79 (6):462–467.

Sornson, R., and J. Scott (eds.) 1997. *Teaching and joy.* Alexandria, VA: ASCD.

Teeter, A.M. 1995. Learning about teaching. *Phi Delta Kappan* 76 (5):360–64.

VanWagener, L. and K. M. Hibbard. 1998. Building teaching portfolios. *Educational Leadership* 55 (5): 26–29.

■ Surfing the 'Net

Educational Organizations

Association for Childhood Education (ACEI)
http://www.udel.edu/bateman/acei

Association for Supervision and Curriculum Development (ASCD)
http://www.ascd.org

Council for Exceptional Children (CEC)
http://www.cec.sped.org

International Reading Association (IRA)
http://www.reading.org

Music Teachers National Association (MTNA)
http://www.mtna.com

National Association of Elementary School Principals (NAESP)
http://www.naesp.org

National Association for the Education of the Young Child
http://www.naeyc.org/naeyc

National Association for Sport and Physical Education (NASPE)
http://www.aahperd.org/naspe/naspe.html

National Association of Secondary School Principals (NASSP)
http://www.nassp.org

National Catholic Educational Association (NCEA)
http://www.ncea.org

National Council for the Social Studies (NCSS)
http://www.ncss.org

National Council of Teachers of English (NCTE)
http://www.ncte.org

National Council of Teachers of Mathematics (NCTM)
http://www.nctm.org

National Education Association (NEA)
http://www.nea.org

National Science Teachers Association (NSTA)
http://www.nsta.org

National Vocational Agricultural Teachers' Association (NVATA)
http://www.nvata.ffa.org

Lesson Plans and Educational Resources

Educational Resources Information Center (ERIC)
http://www.eric.syr.edu

A huge bank of lesson plans plus a wide variety of other information is available from this Website, called Ask ERIC, which is supported by a grant from the U.S. Department of Education.

Search Engines and General Websites

AltaVista
www.altavista.digital.com
   The AltaVista search engine enables you to locate information on the Web very quickly by using keywords in over twenty-five languages. If you receive too much information, you can limit the search.

America Online
www.aol.com
   America Online is the number one commercial on-line service, with over twelve million users. Called AOL, this service provides E-mail and news as well as access to the Internet.

AT&T WorldNet
www.att.net

AT&T's WorldNet is a very reliable Internet service provider.

Deja News
www.dejanews.com

The Deja News service was the first to help people search out discussion groups on the Internet. It is very easy to use

Earthlink Network
www.earthlink.com
Earthlink offers content and information services.

Lycos
www.lycos.com
Lycos can use keywords to search the entire Internet or just a portion, say the top 10 percent of sites. Lycos has an advantage in that it can search for image and sound files as well.

Magellan
www.mckinley.com
Magellan, by the McKinley company, offers thousands of Website reviews. Important to teachers is the "green light" feature which locates only those sites that don't contain any offensive material.

Metacrawler
www.metacrawler.com
Metacrawler relays your request to a number of search sites and brings the results back rapidly, making it very helpful for teachers or students doing research.

Microsoft Internet Explorer
www.microsoft.com/ie
Using Internet Explorer 4.0 is an easy way to navigate the Web. Go to the Microsoft Website and you can download the Internet Explorer free.

Microsoft Network
www.msn.com

Besides Internet access, there are a variety of news and services available, including Microsoft National Broadcasting Corporation (MSNBC), a news source.

Netscape Communicator
home.netscape.com/communicator
This is an all-in-one Internet tool for surfing the Internet, sending E-mail, and having students create a Web page for your school. This includes Netscape's Navigator. There is a fee for downloading this program from the Netscape Website.

Switchboard
www.switchboard.com
This site is good for teachers who want to find E-mail listings or business addresses. It even contains all of the telephone numbers of people and businesses in the United States.

WhoWere
www.whowhere.com
Lists of telephone numbers and addresses of U.S. businesses along with their Web pages can be found here.

Yahoo
www.yahoo.com
This site is the best known for promoting successful online searches. News and free E-mail are a part of this site. Yahoo is great for finding specific information, leading teachers and students alike to rely on it. Some countries, such as France and Germany, and cities, such as Boston and Chicago, have special sites with Yahoo so that students can find even more detailed and current information about local historical and cultural locations and events.

2

The Purpose of Schools

Primary Points

- Historically, schools have had the responsibility of passing on a society's culture to the younger generation.

- The role of a school is influenced by the community in which it exists.

- School is an institution of society.

- There are three sociological perspectives on the purpose of schooling: functionalist, economic-class conflict, and status-group conflict.

- School has three primary functions in meeting the needs of its students: academic, psychological, and physical.

Chapter Inquiries

- What is the difference between education and school?

- How do the three sociological perspectives differ?

- What are the four developmental stages according to Piaget, and how do they differ?

- How do private schools and homeschooling change the socialization process of schooling?

Janet Century/PhotoEdit

Photo Disc/Education

As a new teacher, Jill Frye was adamant that her students were going to succeed. After spending weeks preparing her classroom and developing lessons that would motivate her students, Jill finally met her new charges. Standing outside in the fog were twenty-eight sixth-graders dressed in their best Nikes and Reeboks, oversized T-shirts, baggy shorts, and well-worn baseball caps with colorful bookbags slung over their shoulders. Jill smiled and welcomed them into their classroom.

By the end of the week Jill was exhausted. "Six kids don't know their multiplication tables, two have difficulty even adding, and one doesn't know the capitol of the U.S. is Washington, D.C. And writing! Whoa! It's going to be a long year."

But Jill hung in there. When I saw her at a conference in March, she said, "I'm SO proud of my kids! They've worked so hard. Next month when we take the state tests for math, reading, and writing, they're going to surprise some people. Hey, they believe they are good and are willing to work to prove it. They're terrific!"

American education has a big lesson to learn. . . . What we need is not a certain system, nor a lot of new methods and equipment, but direction, a conscious purpose towards which the schools shall strive . . . that of educating for democracy.

Evelyn Dewey
New Schools for Old

Education takes place in many settings, including school. We each serve as teachers in different capacities: a parent teaches a child how to tie a shoe; a grocery clerk teaches a customer that a laundry detergent on sale may not be the best buy; a friend demonstrates to another friend how to cast a fishing line; or a child shares a street rhyme with another child. And just as we all are teachers to others at one time or another each day, so do we all engage in our own education: we watch a television news story about a war in another part of the world; we observe a mechanic testing the front-end alignment on our car; we listen to our doctor explain a new medical treatment for an illness; we talk to a stranger on the bus and discover new information about a profession; or we rent a video and learn about other lifestyles.

While education can take place anywhere, anytime, and anyplace, the school has a much more limited definition. A school is a social institution in which teaching and learning are formalized. As a teacher, you must be certified by the state in which you teach to instruct the subjects in your area of specialization. The state also establishes curricular guidelines and course requirements for schools. In addition, many states also have assessment measures such as math, reading, and writing tests. Students must attend school on a regular basis, typically arriving in the morning and leaving midafternoon. Classrooms are organized with desks or tables and chairs, chalkboards, computers, and a teacher's desk.

Schools are an American institution. Historically, schools were established in the United States before the Revolutionary War. Today, the structure of schooling in the United States is viewed as one of the world's best. In particular, no one is denied access to a public education, a rarity among the leading civilized nations of the world.

"A student's connection to a school begins with the feeling that he or she is part of it. . . . A neighborhood's connection to the school in its midst can bind children to education and lend cohesion to the community" (Maeroff 1998, 427).

This chapter examines the purpose of schools. Historical, cultural, and societal perspectives are considered as well as the goals of education in general.

The Bear Creek Township school, Brooklyn, Iowa, circa 1893. (Courtesy of the State Historical Society of Iowa)

The Historical Perspective

You may think that schools were established to teach children the three Rs of "readin', 'ritin', and 'rithmetic." Actually, the fear of God helped establish our public schools. In 1642, the Massachusetts General Court passed a law that required parents and guardians to be responsible for their children's ability to read and understand the principles of religion as well as commonwealth laws. In 1647, the Deluder Satan act was passed in Massachusetts colony to establish public schools that would "fight that Old Deluder Satan." Puritan leaders believed that Satan tricked ignorant, uneducated people into sinning. Education was perceived as an avenue to salvation, not the way to a better standard of living as it is considered today.

The idea of "readin', 'ritin', and 'rithmetic" was actually to teach children the basic skills they would need as adults. For over a century, these three subjects dominated school curricula in the United States. Then, other subjects began to receive more attention—geography, geometry, history, and Latin. Over time, the arts, physical education, and science gained importance.

Some communities have a long history of education. Boston, for example, was the cradle of American education. The city has a lengthy record of educational firsts: from Massachusetts' early laws on compulsory education, to its dame and grammar schools, to the development of formalized teacher education through normal schools, to the proactivism for a free public education for all by Horace Mann, to the development of the first public high school, to the desegregation of its schools in the 1960s. While they do not have the long historical record of the Boston community, many suburban communities and small towns take great pride in having high-quality schools that produce outstanding students.

Other cities and towns, however, may not have such a sustained commitment to education. A small rural town or suburban community may have very little obligation to its school system. The citizens may believe that the school's purpose is to provide vocational training so that upon graduation students can work as tool makers,

The value placed on education is reflected in the financial and moral support a community provides. (© James Shaffer)

mechanics, farm laborers, or secretaries. In those situations an academic curriculum is not viewed important by the community and is not sustained fiscally by its citizens. In addition, there may be little moral support of the teaching staff in such a community.

The Cultural Perspective

Schools provide a means of acculturation for a society. You may not realize the degree of acculturation that took place during your elementary and secondary school years. Values, beliefs, and mores are transmitted to students not only by teachers and school administrators but by other students and school staff members, such as secretaries and custodians. The **curriculum** of a school reflects the values, beliefs, and mores of the local community, as do the textbooks selected for adoption and the tradebooks purchased for the school library.

Citizens who are elected to the school board as the policy makers of the school district typically reflect the tenor of the community as well. Thus, when school board members hire the school district's superintendent to be the instructional leader of the district and employ building principals, they generally try to find individuals who share the same **values** as the local community. They also attempt to employ teachers and staff who reflect the philosophy and ethics of the community.

If, for instance, a community is quite liberal in its thinking, the curriculum as well as the school administrators, teachers, and staff are likely to have liberal views. There may be a generous curfew time imposed by the community itself. Incidents of vandalism or drug abuse by students may be tolerated with a "kids will be kids" attitude. The high school principal may approve a heavy metal or rap band for the homecoming dance, if that is what the students want. A room in which students can smoke might be available for junior high/middle school students as well as those in high school. The high school curriculum may look like a smorgasbord of classes, with choices ranging from African American studies to art of the Plains Indians to daiquiri techniques to food preparation for singles to women's studies to zoology.

Unlike a liberal community, a conservative, middle-class community might have strict curfews. Students caught vandalizing property might find themselves and their parents held responsible for their actions. The homecoming dance might have a local disc jockey spinning CDs of mainstream rock-and-roll favorites. The school district would make no provision for students to smoke on the premises but would allow students access to computer labs before and after school. The high school curriculum would be highly academically oriented, with courses in calculus, chemistry, botany, advanced composition, physics, advanced classes in Spanish, and English literature.

The issues involved in passing on to children and young adults a community's values, beliefs, and mores can be very controversial. For example, sex education is a highly debatable issue that can divide a community into those who believe that the topic should be dealt with by families in the privacy of their homes and those who believe that schools should provide sex education so that every child is informed about safe sex. Many would say the only "safe sex" is abstinence.

Certainly in the United States the emphasis on sports is a controversial issue regarding the academic requirements of players. Some schools permit students with grade point averages (GPA) of 2.0, or even less, to participate in extracurricular sports. Since 1995, the National Collegiate Athletic Association (NCAA) requires that athletes entering college have a GPA of 2.5 and an ACT score of seventeen or a GPA of 2.0 and an ACT score of twenty-two to receive an athletic scholarship.

Beside sex education and sports, a major controversial issue for a school is censorship. For instance, *The Great Gilly Hopkins* (1978), a Newbery Award–winning book about a young foster child who uses a lot of profanity, and *Catcher in the Rye* (1951), an award-winning book about adolescent lovers, are banned from reading lists in many school districts because of their controversial content.

Less argumentative issues today include the offering of home economics classes for boys and car maintenance classes for girls. At the elementary school level, controversy may surround discussions and activities involving ecological issues, such as recycling.

Sociology of Education

Our society, like every society, has its own customs and practices, its own rules and regulations, its own values and mores, and its own institutions. School is an institution of society in which children are educated. Thus, our society expects our schools to transmit the primary elements of our society to our children. This includes the art, music, and literature of our society, so students study the works of Americans Georgia O'Keefe and Norman Rockwell, Irving Berlin and Duke Ellington, and Toni Morrison and John Steinbeck. Through school, students learn about law and order, customs and practices, and values and ethics.

School programs are greatly impacted by the values of the community, for it is the community that determines whose interests the school will serve as well as the functions of the school. Educational sociologists believe that three different perspectives exist. These are the functionalist, the economic-class conflict, and the status-group conflict perspectives, as described on the following pages.

The Functionalist Perspective

According to sociologists, functionalists believe that members of society share common goals, many of which create social institutions such as families, government, religion, and, of course, schools. Each institution has a unique responsibility to perform as part of the overall obligation to preserve and protect the society.

Functionalists believe that schools provide an equal opportunity for all students and that it is up to each student to take advantage of what the school has to offer. Through education, then, students can develop their skills to the fullest and obtain well-paying jobs. The underlying assumption is that by taking advantage of what schools have to offer and then getting a good job, individuals will become taxpaying citizens who support others in the society. Functionalists point out that such individuals as President Bill Clinton and his wife, Hillary Rodham Clinton, are both products of public school systems—he in Arkansas and she in Illinois.

A criticism of this view is that not all students are capable of taking advantage of the opportunities that schools provide. Some are forced to find jobs to help support the family. Others lack the initiative to take advantage of the opportunities available to them. Also, in recent years, many individuals who *did* take advantage of what their schools had to offer and went on to obtain good positions with established companies found themselves out of jobs as their employers tried to become more efficient through the use of technology, lower labor costs in Third World countries, and other means. Opponents of the functionalist view stress that we do not live in a static society and thus there are no guarantees of job security.

Another criticism of the functionalist view is that social groups do not necessarily take care of their obligations, thereby transferring them to another social group. For instance, when parents refuse to talk about sex with their children, it may fall to either the church or the school to provide sex education. Thus, while the functionalists point out the need for school as an institution to fulfill a society's needs, in many cases other institutions, such as the family and church, fail to fulfill their obligations to children and society.

The Economic-Class Conflict Perspective

Supporters of the economic-class conflict perspective believe that society is divided into various groups based on economic status. Rather than working together in harmony, these groups work in opposition. Thus, the capitalists, who own businesses and industry, are opposed by the working class, which provides the labor needed to make the products and provides the services offered by the businesses and industries.

The roots of the economic-class conflict perspective can be traced back to Karl Marx and Fredrick Engels and their writings, which promoted communism. Marx advocated in his work *The Communist Manifesto* (1963) that the working class was suppressed by capitalists, who readily took advantage of them, and that capitalists have an economic edge over the working class, without which the capitalists would have nothing. Marx argued that tension between the two groups would always exist; therefore, he advocated a socialistic, classless society in which every person would earn the same amount of money and receive the same benefits.

Marx's theory was embraced by the Bolsheviks in early twentieth-century Russia, who dethroned the Czar and renamed the country the Union of Soviet Socialist Republics (USSR). After World War II, the USSR took control of several eastern European countries (Albania, Bulgaria, Czechoslovakia, East Germany, Hungary, Poland, Rumania, and Yugoslavia, among others), forcing socialism on their citizens. After

World War II, the people of mainland China, under the leadership of Mao Tse-tung, overthrew the government and established communism in that country.

Under Marx's theory, elementary students were taught a rigid curriculum. At the secondary level, only highly talented students were permitted to take academic coursework. Most high school students received vocational training to become mechanics, factory workers, or agricultural workers. There was government censorship of reading materials and films for students at all levels.

In 1991, the communist government of the USSR fell. The individual states became independent countries and sought democracy and capitalism for their people. The combination of the lack of support from the USSR and the toppling of aging leaders caused the governments of Eastern European countries to fall, thereby ending the period of communism's stranglehold in Eastern Europe.

Sweden has had a socialist government for nearly three decades. Under a monarch rule, the Swedish Parliament, with its members elected by the citizens of the country, was until the 1990s controlled by members of the Socialist Party. While under the party's control, Parliament enacted sweeping socialist reforms including a shorter work week, wage scales for workers, universal health insurance for all, family leave policy enabling the mother to stay at home with a newborn infant until the child reached the age of six months, and child care for preschoolers. To pay for such liberal reforms, taxes were greatly increased. However, in a recent election voters concerned with the extremely high tax rate swept the Socialist Party out of control of Parliament.

The Swedes under socialism view education in a much different light than do people in communist countries. When a toddler reaches age two, a parent takes the child to a clinic to receive inoculations. After the child is given a physical examination by a doctor, a librarian meets with the parent to discuss ways to encourage language development and provides a list of books and activities for the child. Children enter school at age seven, not age five as in the United States. Students have wide choices of subjects in which to enroll. Censorship is very limited in Swedish schools.

There are two primary views of the economic-class conflict perspective: the class conflict view and the class reproduction view. Advocates of the class conflict view consider the changes in schools to be a result of economically disadvantaged groups voicing their concerns over the inadequacy of existing school programs. Examples are the passage of **Title IX,** of the Education Amendments of 1972, which resulted in female students being offered the opportunity to participate in the same number of sports in secondary school and college as their male counterparts, and **Title I,** a federally funded program designed to help low-ability students from economically disadvantaged schools in reading and math. Title I was part of the Elementary and Secondary Education Act (ESEA), which will be discussed elsewhere.

On the other hand, the class reproduction view asserts that capitalists are forcing schools to provide programs that will benefit them. For instance, business leaders complain that the schools are inadequately training future workers. Such leaders insist that schools must stress cooperative learning, basic skills such as math, reading, and writing, and the use of new interactive technology.

Critics of the economic-class conflict perspective contend that Americans are socially mobile and not necessarily tied to an economic class. For instance, Sam Walton, son of an itinerant salesman, became a billionaire through the formation of his WalMart and Sam's Club discount stores, and Oprah Winfrey, daughter of economically disadvantaged parents, is a self-made multimillionaire entertainer and media producer.

*Spoken Languages Present
in One Suburban School District*

Below is a list of 64 first languages other than English of students in Elgin School District Unit 46, a large suburban school district of 28,000 students located just outside of Chicago. While there are large numbers of Spanish and Laotian speaking students, there are many languages, such as Gaelic and Sioux, in which there are five students or fewer represented.

Afrikaans (Taal)	Gujarati	Portuguese
Albanian	Haitian Creole	Punjabi
Amharic	Hebrew	Romanian
Arabic	Hindi	Russian
Armenian	Hindustani	Serbian/Croatian
Assyrian	Hmong	Sindhi
Bengali	Hungarian	Sioux
Bisayan	Iroquoian	Slovak
Bulgarian	Italian	Slovenian
Burmese	Jamaican	Spanish
Chinese—Cantonese	Japanese	Swedish
Chinese—Mandarin	Kannada	Taiwanese
Czech	Khmer/Cambodian	Tamil
Danish	Korean	Telugu
Dutch	Lao	Thai
Farsi (Iranian)	Lithuanian	Tibetan
Finnish	Malayalam	Turkish
French	Marathi	Ukrainian
Gaelic	Norwegian	Urdu
German	Pilipino (Tagalog)	Vietnamese
Greek	Polish	Yugoslavian

Source: P. J. Farris. 1997. *Language Arts: Process, Product, and Assessment,* 2nd ed. Boston: McGraw-Hill Higher Education. Used by permission.

The Status-Group Conflict Perspective

The status-group conflict perspective asserts that modifications in schools occur as a result of conflicts among competing groups. Leaders of social, governmental, religious, or other groups and organizations achieve status, largely due to their influential power. These leaders then seek to meet the needs of constituents within their group, resulting in friction with other groups.

Proponents of the status-group conflict perspective believe that school programs reflect influences of social groups to promote their own interests and/or causes. Examples are the call for more minority teachers to serve as role models for minority students; the emphasis on hiring more women and minority school administrators; the push by Hispanic and Asian groups to teach students in their native languages rather than in English; the support for Reserve Officers' Training Corps (ROTC) units in secondary schools by members of the armed services; and the push by members of the insurance industry for driver's education in the schools.

The Functions of School

As you went through elementary and secondary school, you and your siblings as well as friends had different needs. In the United States, school is the institution designed to fulfill a variety of students' needs, including academic, psychological, and physical needs.

Academic Needs

The fundamental academic needs of students include the acquisition of knowledge and information, as well as learning strategies, and the development of citizenship skills and ethics. Traditionally, local beliefs and mores have been passed on to students by the local schools. As beliefs and mores change, so does what is presented to students in the classroom.

The three Rs—reading, writing, and arithmetic—are emphasized in our schools today just as they were the primary focus of American schools three hundred years ago. The development of skills in these three areas enables individuals to obtain good jobs and to function effectively outside of the workplace in managing money and meeting daily needs.

Students can use the Internet to communicate with students in another state or country.
(© David Young Wolff/PhotoEdit)

Unlike education of three centuries ago, however, other aspects of the curriculum have become increasingly important. Social studies and the study of its social sciences—economics, geography, history, political science, psychology, and sociology—have become important because as citizens we are increasingly members of a global village. For example, the effect of weather on the corn crop in Brazil can affect the price of corn flakes in the United States, while a mild winter in Europe can decrease the demand for heating oil, reducing the cost of oil for Americans. Knowledge of political alignments among Middle Eastern countries is advantageous in understanding the conflicts written about almost daily in our newspapers. Certainly we cannot watch Oprah Winfrey's, Larry King's, or Rosie O'Donnell's television talk shows without some basic knowledge of psychology and sociology.

Like social studies, science has become increasingly important in our everyday lives. In the daily newspaper, individuals read medical research summaries that were first published in the *New England Journal of Medicine* or the *Journal of the American Medical Association.* Information regarding proper nutrition, the effects of secondary smoke on children and adults, new developments in cancer treatment or heart disease, new drugs for the treatment of arthritis, and many other findings are of interest to us all. New discoveries in other areas catch our scientific interest as we try to ensure safety for ourselves and loved ones: new tire designs for driving on rain-soaked highways, airbags in vehicles, bike helmets, and coffee makers that shut themselves off automatically. We're also concerned about how buildings and highways can be built to withstand major earthquake damage and how to protect the environment and wildlife.

Critical thinking skills, which are essential for problem solving, are a part of science education as well as other academic areas. Morality education has been much discussed in recent years. There is much debate over to what degree values clarification and character education should be taught in schools and whose values should be presented.

In our fast-paced society, technological breakthroughs seem to occur daily. Because of technological advances, computers are relatively inexpensive, and one out of every three homes in the United States now has a computer. As a result of advances in computer technology and semiconductor chips, the information superhighway is readily accessible to nearly every home in America via fiber optic phone lines. Messages can be faxed to or from a handheld computer whether you are in an office, at school, or on a mountaintop. **CD-ROM** programs enable students to write

("LUANN reprinted by permission of United Feature Syndication, Inc.")

research reports and include film footage as part of their projects. Such technological advancements impact what is learned by students and how they learn it.

"Beepers," personal pagers, and cellular phones have been banned from many schools because drug pushers and gangs were using them within schools. However, some students still carry portable phones in their cars.

Perhaps most important, school gives students the tools they need to continue their learning long after they have graduated from high school or college. By reading, watching videos, interacting with computer programs, and interacting with other individuals their own age and other ages, students develop their own learning strategies, which they take with them after graduation.

Psychological Needs

The second purpose of school is to meet the psychological needs of students. These include the need for self-esteem, safety, security, and a sense of belonging and the desire to achieve. Remember how you felt when a teacher praised you with or selected you to perform a special task?

Children generally enter kindergarten with high self-esteem. Unfortunately, the high self-esteem of a five-year-old seems to diminish with age, and as a teacher, you must try to counter this. Other kindergartners enter school with low self-esteem, which is often a reflection of their parents' poor self-esteem. You must try to help these children develop a positive self-image, a difficult task indeed. At all grade levels, you must try to develop and maintain a high level of self-esteem in your students if they are to take risks as learners.

Besides self-esteem, safety and security are important factors in a child's psychological makeup. In those urban areas where drive-by shootings are a daily fact of life, many children find that school and home are the safety zones on which they can depend. Children who are abused at home may feel that school offers their only solace and protection. For all children, school must be a positive environment where they feel secure not only bodily but mentally as well.

School typically provides students with a sense of belonging. Remember the good feelings of being part of a team or group effort? Children don't want to be rejected, and acceptance in the classroom is very important to psychological well-being, especially self-esteem. Group activities in which all share the work and the rewards provide children with a sense of being needed and valued. Extracurricular activities such as soccer, basketball, math club, or a school newspaper can help build a student's self-concept and image as he or she becomes part of a community of students.

Lastly, students want to achieve and to perform well. In your teaching you need to provide ample opportunities that challenge students to stretch their abilities. Certainly when a child produces a quality product or tries his or her best, you should duly note the effort put forth. Try to arrange situations in the classroom so that a child who has met with a series of academic or psychological setbacks will have a chance to succeed. The more success a student encounters, the more motivated the student will be in the classroom.

For students to develop their skills, they need to set individual learning goals under your guidance. If you take the time to meet with each student individually in an environment of trust, a positive rapport develops. It is important that you create a supportive learning climate in the classroom.

Acknowledging what a student has accomplished and how much effort he or she has put into learning builds confidence. As a teacher, you will need to observe your students in the classroom, plan successful but challenging activities, assess their

Medical Clinics in High Schools

Over three hundred medical clinics are currently operating in schools throughout the nation, with more opening each year. Most are located in schools that serve low-income students whose parents have no health insurance. By locating these clinics in schools, where students spend much of their time, the belief is that students will be more apt to seek medical attention.

Opponents to school clinics believe that schools have enough problems without serving the health needs, both physical and mental, of students. Funds for these clinics come from a combination of local, state, and federal sources, with many funded through private foundations. Christian fundamentalists fear that school clinics will offer advice on birth control and abortion; however, that has not proved to be the majority of referrals. Twenty-nine percent of all referrals are for acute illnesses and injuries, with 18 percent mental health counseling and 15 percent physical examinations. Only 10 percent of referrals have involved reproductive services (Hill 1994).

Denver has had school-based medical clinics since 1988. The formation of the clinics was fought by Denver's Catholic population, which believed that birth-control counseling would be their primary focus. In practice, the clinics deal with a variety of health problems, primarily ear infections and bronchitis. One out of ten referrals pertains to teenage pregnancy. But the pregnant girls do stand out. According to Connie Boyle (Hill 1994, 24), who works in a school-based clinic, "I'd say that 40 to 60 percent [of those girls] *want* to get pregnant. Some of them come in every three to six weeks to be tested. That's the discouraging thing."

Changes in the nation's health care plan will likely mean changes in access to medical attention by students. The Clinton administration supports school-based health clinics, including giving students free condoms. It is likely that school-based clinics will increase as medical care costs, the spread of tuberculosis and sexually transmitted diseases, and increased substance abuse among students receive media attention.

progress, and require that they take some responsibility for their own learning. To do this, you must have strong interpersonal skills, be proficient in teaching the subject matter, be an attentive observer, and be able to manage record keeping for all of the students.

Physical Needs

Physical needs of students have been a greater topic of interest largely since the John F. Kennedy administration in the early 1960s, when it was found that the majority of elementary and secondary children were physically unfit. However, at that time the emphasis was on competitive physical fitness—the number of situps or pushups you could do or how fast you could run the one-hundred-yard dash, for example. By the 1980s, the emphasis changed to lifelong physical activities such as archery, basketball, golf, jogging, racquetball, soccer, swimming, tennis, and volleyball. The emphasis on cooperative sports, and even individual sports, lessened the previous emphasis on competitive team sports in physical education classes.

Nationally, there is a greater concern than ever before on physical wellness and health. Thousands of health and fitness clubs have been established. Many companies now provide fitness facilities for their workers, and others offer increased benefits for employees who exercise regularly, who are not overweight, and who don't smoke.

Drug use is strongly discouraged in our society, and this is communicated to students as early as kindergarten in most school districts, with some programs reaching out to preschoolers. The prevention of drug and alcohol abuse among elementary and secondary students is seen by many as a way to eventually eliminate it in our society.

Child Development and Schooling

Teacher preparation programs require that you take courses in child and adolescent psychology. School curricula take into account the psychological development of students at each of the various grade levels. The majority of schools in the United States to some extent base their curricula on the cognitive development of children, largely as a result of the research findings of Jean Piaget. A Swiss biologist, Piaget studied his own three children and discovered that all three went through the same stages of development at roughly the same age periods.

Piaget believed that each child developed not only from within but also through interacting with the surrounding outer environment. His developmental stages are as follows:

Sensorimotor: From birth to about two years old

Preoperational: From two to seven years old

Concrete operations: From seven to eleven years old

Formal operations: From eleven years old and up

According to Piaget, children view the world differently than do adults. Youngsters in the sensorimotor stage experiment with their hands and feet as well as their eyes. For example, when thirteen-month-old Kurtis was playing peek-a-boo, he believed that he couldn't be seen whenever a blanket was placed over his head or that whenever his mother left him at day care she completely "disappeared" until she picked him up later that same day. By the time Kurtis moved into the preoperational stage, he was aware that people and things existed even though they were out of his line of vision.

During the preoperational stage, Kurtis's vocabulary expanded more than any other time in his life. During this period he also spent a lot of time classifying things. He made pictures of race cars for a race car book and strong men for a protector of the universe book. Kurtis spent numerous hours placing baseball, basketball, and football cards in various categories he made up—Jets, Astros, and Supersonics in his "space" category; Cowboys, Broncos, Spurs, 49ers, and Rangers in his "cowboy" category; and Bears, Dolphins, Marlins, Seahawks, Lions, Timberwolves, Hornets, and Bulls in his "animals" category.

As Kurtis passed into the concrete operations stage, he still manipulated things, just as he had done during the previous two stages, but now he concentrated on the size, number, and weight of objects. Abstract thinking and cause-and-effect relationships, two aspects of critical thinking that he would use in the formal operations stage, were still too difficult.

Using Piaget's findings, many teachers tend to meet each individual student's needs so that children learn when they are ready. In addition, school curricula today, particularly at the preschool and elementary levels, include the use of many hands-on manipulatives, especially for math and science.

Joe Camel has been a popular, almost cult figure among elementary and secondary students. His picture could be found in magazines and on billboards scattered across America as he smokes Camel-brand cigarettes. He joins the ranks of such successful advertising campaigns as the Marlboro man, a ruggedly handsome, very macho cowboy who is never without his Marlboro cigarettes. The success of these two advertising themes led to a ban on cigarette ads.

What do cigarette ads have to do with schools and students? Educators and politicians are well aware that children are impressionable. As a result, most states have laws that protect students, which range from requiring motorists to reduce their speed while driving through a school zone to prohibiting taverns and gun shops from locating near schools. In recent years, several states have restricted the distance that certain types of billboards, including those advertising alcohol, can be located from schools.

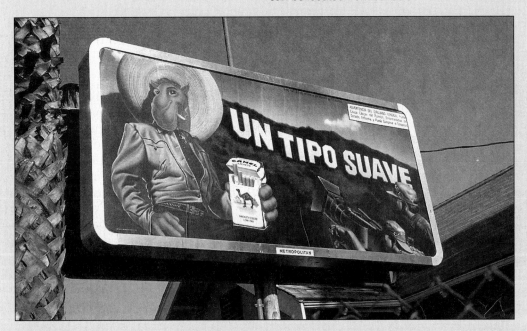

Alcohol and tobacco ads are designed to be appealing to young adults. Unfortunately many children and teenagers are swayed by this appeal. (© Tom Prettyman/PhotoEdit)

The Role of Curriculum

School provides an efficient means of formally educating the young. While children learn from members of their immediate families—mother, father, sisters, and brothers— and their extended families—grandmothers, grandfathers, aunts, uncles, and cousins— school as an institution provides a more uniform, balanced, and shared curriculum.

Public schools hire teachers who have received **certification** by their states to teach specific subject areas. For instance, if you want to teach high school mathematics, you typically must have a major in mathematics, usually forty credit hours of study from a college or university, and in addition complete a teacher education methods program, during which you observe and participate in high school mathematics classes as well as student teach. You must receive a bachelor of science or a bachelor of science in education degree to become certified as a high school mathematics teacher. Failure to complete any of these requirements would deny you a teaching certificate. State departments of education closely monitor schools to make certain that only qualified teachers teach specific subject areas. For example, as a high school mathematics teacher, you would not be permitted to teach a fourth-grade elementary class.

Each school has a curriculum, a program that indicates what material teachers will cover. Each teacher is expected to follow the curriculum and facilitate the learning process for students. The curriculum of a school is important. What children learn in school today must be useful to them in their later lives—lives that will be spent mostly in the twenty-first century.

When parents become very sensitive about what is in the local school curriculum or believe that the school provides an inadequate education for their child, however, they may opt to enroll their child in a private school or to teach their child at home.

Private Schooling

Private schooling enables parents to select the school they believe can best provide socialization and education for their child. Typically parents pay a tuition fee for their child to attend private school. Most private schools are affiliated with a religious group. Four of the largest religious groups that support K–12 schools are Baptist, Catholic, Lutheran, and Quaker. There are more private K–8 schools than there are private schools for grades 9–12, so many students who attend private grade school go on to attend a public high school. Thus, in some communities, there is an increase in enrollment in secondary public schools as compared with the number of students entering the high school(s) from the elementary and middle schools in the district.

Private schools sponsored by religious groups transmit the values, beliefs, and mores of that particular religious group. By working with children when they are young and formable, religious leaders believe that their beliefs are more apt to be instilled in them for a lifetime.

There are several private schools that are not affiliated with any religious group. These include prep schools, which are predominate in the eastern part of the United States and are modeled after the British prep schools. They are residential schools largely for children of affluent families who seek to have their children enter Ivy League colleges. Typically wealthy families have a tradition of sending generation after generation to a specific prep school so that children follow in the footsteps of their ancestors.

Military prep schools are particularly prevalent throughout the South. Many of these schools have a long tradition dating from before the Civil War. Indeed, five out of six military colleges were located in the South at the time of the Civil War, thereby providing the Confederacy with a better-trained group of officers than the Union. Most military prep schools are not coeducational, however higher education schools such as the Citadel and Virginia Military Institute (VMI) have somewhat reluctantly let female students enroll.

*Should There Be Minimum Requirements
for Parents Who Teach Their Children at Home?*

Point: A parent who homeschools his or her children must be licensed.

The parent who serves as teacher must take an exam or have a bachelor's degree before children can be educated at home. These requirements would ensure that the parent would have a specified level of education before attempting to teach his or her own children.

If a parent is unqualified to serve as his or her children's teacher, then society gets a poorly educated individual. Society is also forced in many cases to support that poorly educated child through social services. It is not fair to the child or society for this to happen.

Counterpoint: If a parent elects to homeschool his or her children, there should not be any licensing requirements by the state to do so.

The state doesn't have any requirements parents must meet in order to have children in the first place, so why should there be requirements parents have to meet in order to homeschool? No one knows a child better than his or her parents. If the parents decide to teach their children at home, then they can provide what their children need. There is no need for the state to interfere by requiring a specified level of training before parents can teach their children.

A criticism of private schools is that students are sheltered from society as a whole. In the South, parents avoid poorly funded, integrated schools by sending their children to private schools. Another criticism is that private high schools recruit outstanding athletes from outside of their immediate area and place them on scholarships so that they avoid paying tuition to attend. Thus, many private high schools are able to make their teams far more competitive than their public high school counterparts.

Homeschooling

It is possible for parents to educate their children entirely at home, a practice known as homeschooling. This usually means that one parent must remain at home with the children and create lessons, often using commercially developed textbooks, for each child. While parents may have the intellectual ability to teach their own children, they may lack the skills and resources. Many homeschooled children enter either a private or a public school when they are of upper elementary or junior high/middle school age because the subject matter they need becomes increasingly difficult for their parents to teach them. Typically, homeschooled children are quite proficient in the same areas as their parents' interests. For instance, a parent who is very interested in math may stress its importance over another subject area, say social studies. Homeschooled students generally lack social interaction. Sometimes this results in extreme behavior swings during adolescence.

Some parents and their children believe that homeschooling is best for gifted children. For instance, Gabriel Willow, a gifted teenager who lives in rural Maine, is self-motivated. He owns over a dozen books on fish alone. According to Gabriel, his efforts to learn more aren't restricted in homeschooling as they would be in a regular school: "If I'm reading a book, I'm learning. The book is my teacher. If I'm out by the pond, I'm learning, so the pond is my teacher" (Kantrowitz and Rosenburg 1994, 58).

An only child, Jaime was a growing nine-year-old boy in my fourth-grade class. At home, his diet consisted of cold cereal and bologna sandwiches. His dad was a single parent who worked the second shift in a local factory welding semi trailers. As I was going through the lunch line one day, I noticed Jaime requesting an additional portion of pizza for his school lunch which the cooks denied. When I asked the cooks about it, one of them said, "That kid is always hungry." That settled it. Without his knowing who furnished it, there was an extra lunch for Jaime every day for the rest of the year. I felt good knowing that Jaime wasn't going hungry, even though my meager beginning teacher's salary was barely enough for me to pay my bills and repay my college loans.

As a teacher, I knew that Jaime couldn't learn with hunger foremost in his mind. For him, the purpose of school was not only to learn the three Rs of reading, writing, and arithmetic, but also to serve as a social function. Since Jaime was an only child, he was also starved for interaction with other children his age. Jaime was an average student, but he and others like him will stay with me as long as I live, just as every teacher has students they can't forget.

■ Summary

Historically, schools have had different purposes. School is an institution of society, however, and as such its basic purpose is to transmit culture from one generation to another, including the values and mores and the rules and regulations of society. Thus, the role of a school is influenced by the community in which it exists.

There are three sociological perspectives on the purpose of schooling: functionalist, economic-class conflict, and status-group conflict. School has three primary functions in meeting the needs of its students: academic, psychological, and physical.

The psychological development of children has been classified by Piaget as sensorimotor, preoperational, concrete operations, and formal operations. With the exception of sensorimotor, children go through the stages during their school career.

In recent years there has been a resurgence in private schooling; however, there has been even more rapid growth in homeschooling. Both have given educators in public schools cause for concern.

■ Reflections

Consider the community in which you attended secondary school. Which of the three sociological perspectives (functionalist, economic-class conflict, and status-group conflict) was prevalent in your community? Were there instances in which one of the other two perspectives became evident over a particular issue?

Which sociological perspective do you believe should influence our schools? Why? How would the sociological perspective you selected improve the schools?

■ Discussion Questions

1. Because there are tremendous stresses placed on students, should more emphasis be placed on the psychological needs of students than the physical needs of students? Explain your answer.

2. Give an example of a status group that is trying to influence what is taught in the schools.

3. Interview a classroom teacher and find out what percent of time during a day is actually devoted to academic instruction of students.

4. Since the purpose of school is to transmit culture from one generation to another, should there be a national curriculum for schools?

5. Go to two different communities and drive around. Interview a teacher from each community and determine what is emphasized for students to learn.

■ For Further Reading

Cartwright, M., and M. D'Orso. 1993. *For the children: Lessons from a visionary principal.* New York: Doubleday.

Hill, D. 1994. The doctor is in. *Teacher Magazine* (February):18–25.

Kantrowitz, B., and D. Rosenburg. 1994. In a class of their own. *Newsweek,* 10 January, 58.

Kohn, A. 1998. Only for *My* kid: How privileged parents undermine school reform. *Phi Delta Kappan,* 79(8):568–577.

■ Surfing the 'Net

American Association of Colleges for Teacher Education
http://www.aacte.org
Association for Supervision and Curriculum Development
http://www.ascd.org

Association of Teacher Educators
http://www.siu.edu/departments/coe/ate

3

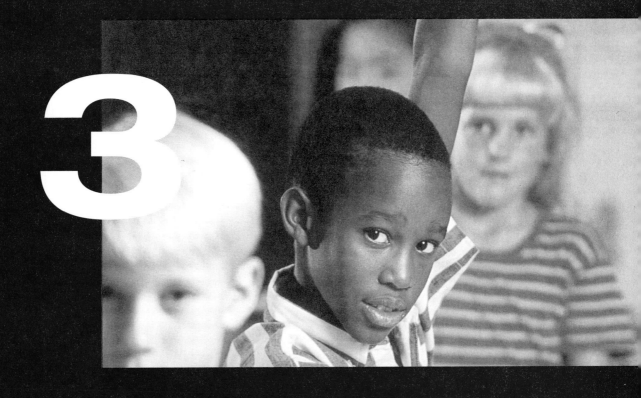

Trends in Education

Primary Points

- Under Goals 2000, national standards for students will be established and assessed.

- Many believe that a longer school day and year will increase student learning.

- Each year, more and more students are homeschooled.

- The need for positive role models has resulted in greater interest in single-sex high schools.

- Technological advancements will enable students to work on projects with students from schools in other states or countries.

Chapter Inquiries

- Why are national standards for teachers and students controversial?

- How would a longer school day or year increase learning?

- What is the primary reason that parents give for homeschooling their children?

- Why are single-sex high schools considered discriminatory?

- Why is there a need for women and minority school administrators?

An honor student, T. J. Lux was the top tennis player in his home state of Indiana. His 6'8" build helped him lead his Merrillville High School basketball team to the state finals. After receiving a full-ride scholarship to play basketball at Northern Illinois University, T. J. enrolled in math education.

Computers, movies, music weight lifting, and just kicking back at times are some of T. J.'s favorite pastimes. But when he talks about teaching kids in the twenty-first century, T. J.'s adrenalin flows.

"I love math. There's a right and a wrong answer. And I like to be around kids. Teaching is the right choice for me. I'll be able to do what I love plus I'll probably get to coach tennis and basketball after school. Who knows, maybe I can coach my team to the state finals in the next millennium."

Photo Disc/Families and Lifestyles

The future of education requires that teachers be involved not only in their classroom instruction but also in the leadership within their schools, their school districts, and their communities. Teachers will be required to work together with colleagues, parents, and community leaders to improve schooling for students.

Education is a debt due from the present to the future generations.

George Peabody
Ely, *I Quote*

Education requires energetic, committed, and dedicated teachers who aren't afraid to take a stand that is in the best interest of helping their students learn. According to Ayers (1993, 138), "Education is bold, adventurous, creative, vivid, illuminating—in other words education is for self-activating explorers of life, for those who would challenge fate, for doers and activists, for citizens."

Before you enter the teaching profession, you need to be aware of the trends and issues that will affect education in the future. Several trends will impact education well into the twenty-first century. These include national standards for teachers and students, the length of the school day and year, homeschooling, inclusion, gender equity and single-sex high schools, the need for more women and minority school administrators, and technological advances.

A Call to Action

In 1997, President Bill Clinton issued his *Call to Action for American Education in the 21st Century.* Comprised of ten goals, the idea is to address educational problems related to increasing international competitiveness in regards to the economy. The ten goals are:

- Set rigorous national standards, with national tests in fourth-grade reading and eighth-grade math to make sure our children master the basics;
- Make sure there is a talented and dedicated teacher in every classroom;
- Help every student read independently and well by the end of third grade;
- Expand Head Start, and challenge parents to get involved early on in their children's learning;

- Expand choice and accountability in public education;
- Make sure our schools are safe, disciplined, and drug free, and instill basic American values;
- Modernize school buildings and help support school construction;
- Open the doors of college to all who work hard and make the grade, and make the thirteenth and fourteenth years of education as universal as high school;
- Help adults improve their education and skills by transforming the tangle of federal training programs into a simple skill grant; and
- Connect every classroom and library to the Internet by the year 2000, and help all students become technologically literate (Community Update, 1997, p. 4).

The U.S. Department of Education set up a Website for President Clinton's Call to Action. The site can be accessed at http://www.ed.gov/updates/PresEDPlan/. Additional information can be obtained by calling 1 (800) USA-LEARN.

Education Reform

Linda Darling-Hammond (1997), a professor at Columbia University's Teachers College, authored the provocative book *The Right to Learn,* in which she says the way to improve schools is for teachers to teach for understanding and to encourage authentic assessment. She believes the reason the performance of American students cannot compare with the performance of foreign students is not because we fail to give them enough work but rather that our teaching is less thoughtful. Darling-Hammond argues that teachers encounter bureaucratic processes that prohibit them from focusing on education outcomes.

Darling-Hammond stresses the need for providing more in-depth learning opportunities for students, including placing an emphasis on Howard Gardner's theory of multiple intelligences (see Chapter 12, The School Curriculum). Teachers, in Darling-Hammond's view, must build a close relationship with each student. She points out that in today's comprehensive high schools, top-heavy with administrative staff, only one-third of adult time is actually spent teaching. Teachers have only 6.2 minutes a week to spend with each child.

Teachers are the primary engine for educational reform, according to Darling-Hammond. It is up to teacher preparation programs and school districts to restructure schools so that schools are less bureaucratic and more friendly to their clientele, the students.

National Standards for Teachers and Students

In the 1980s, a call was made for national standards for both teachers and students. Meeting the educational needs of students was not included in the U.S. Constitution as a responsibility of the federal government; rather, it is the right of the individual states. Since 1787, however, when the Constitution was approved, our society has become a very mobile one. Many teachers leave the states in which they originally received their certification and move to other states. Likewise, thousands of students move from one state to another before they complete their schooling. Thus, many educators and politicians argue that national standards for both teachers and students will improve the overall quality of education nationally. With the passage of Goals 2000 by Congress in 1994, each state is required to have minimum standards for students but not for teachers.

Point /Counterpoint

Should There Be National Standards for Teachers?

Point: National standards will increase the quality of the nation's teachers.

National standards for teachers will help to improve the quality of schooling our students receive. When individual states such as Arkansas implemented teacher certification testing in the 1980s, several inservice teachers were found to be unqualified to teach in their subject areas.

National standards for teachers will allow those states with teachers of lesser ability to send these teachers to remediation programs so their teaching will improve.

National standards will also make the United States more respected internationally. They demonstrate that this country takes the education of its children seriously.

Counterpoint: National standards for teachers will result in several states reducing their present standards while other states will have to raise theirs.

National standards for teachers will cause many teacher preparation programs to change dramatically. These programs will need to implement more rigorous standards for their education majors. In addition, national standards will cause many current teachers to leave the profession if they cannot meet the necessary requirements. If a teacher has taught effectively for several years, it is unfair to require that individual to meet new certification standards.

Our states differ greatly. How can teachers in Mississippi or Rhode Island be expected to meet the same criteria as those in Montana or Pennsylvania? Should teachers in Hawaii or Delaware possess the same knowledge as those in Michigan or Maine? State rather than national certification standards are far more appropriate.

National Standards for Teachers

In 1987, the National Board for Professional Teaching Standards (NBPTS) was established with the assistance of the Carnegie Corporation. A nonprofit organization, the NBPTS issues teaching certificates to those experienced teachers who meet the board's standards for content knowledge and effective teaching methodology. The certification standards are far more rigorous than those of the various states, as teachers are assessed through interviews, portfolio reviews, and video clips of their actual teaching. Certification is available in over twenty different teaching fields.

A case study of teachers in the National Board Certification was undertaken. The findings indicated that "the process of participating in National Board Certification provides a potentially powerful learning experience" (Rothberg, Futrell and Lieberman 1998, 465). However only a very small number of teachers nationally have taken the National Board examination. Thus, the impact of National Board Certification on the quality of education nationwide cannot, at this point, be accurately assessed.

The idea of a national teaching examination and certification appeals to those individuals who have moved from one state to another and discovered that they had to take additional coursework to be qualified to teach in their new state of residence. Critics argue, however, that a national teaching examination and certification program

The development of national standards impacts upon the curriculum in every classroom in the country. (Don Valenti/Tony Stone)

will dilute the standards that some states have already established for their teachers, standards that are more rigorous than those proposed nationally. Others argue that a large number of teachers in their particular state would not be qualified to teach under the proposed national standards.

National Standards for Students

The same arguments for and against national standards for teachers are used for such standards for students. Some educators and legislative leaders argue that by adopting national standards, our country will be more in line with other leading nations that already have national standards in place, namely France, Germany, and Japan. As a result of national standards for students, academic standards will be raised. Since each state is different, national standards for students would inevitably result in some states lowering their standards for their students while others would have students who fall short of meeting the necessary criteria. Thus, many view national standards for students as elitist.

Another issue regarding national standards is that the student population varies dramatically from one state to another. For instance, Alabama and Mississippi have very high percentages of African American students in their school populations, California and Texas have high percentages of Hispanic students, Montana and South Dakota have large numbers of Native Americans, while Idaho and Utah have predominately white student populations. Many educators argue against national standards because they believe that each individual state best knows what the expectations should be for its students.

Goals 2000: Educate America Act

Goals 2000 came out of a meeting of the nation's governors that then President George Bush called in September 1989 in Charlottesville, Virginia. President Bush was concerned about the lack of skills high school graduates possessed as well as the need for incorporating technology in the curriculum and making schools safe havens for students, free of drugs and violence. The meeting was chaired by then Arkansas governor Bill Clinton. Out of this meeting came the Goals 2000 movement.

In 1994, Congress passed the Goals 2000: Educate America Act, one of the most significant pieces of education legislation ever approved at the federal level. Specifically, **Goals 2000** addresses several educational issues, including the following:

- the quality and availability to all students of curricula, instructional materials, and technologies, including distance learning;
- the capability of teachers to provide high-quality instruction to meet the diverse learning needs of all students in the content area;
- the extent to which teachers, principals, and administrators have ready and continuing access to professional development, including the best knowledge about teaching, learning, and school improvement;
- the extent to which curriculum, instructional practices, and assessments are aligned with voluntary national content standards;
- the extent to which school facilities provide a safe and secure environment for learning and instruction and provide the requisite libraries, laboratories, and other resources necessary to provide students an opportunity to learn; and
- the extent to which schools use policies, curricula, and instructional practices that ensure nondiscrimination on the basis of gender (Lewis 1994, 661).

Supporters of Goals 2000 say the act creates a framework for setting up national standards for students that are both clear and high. Students will be required to be competent in challenging subject matter and will face straightforward penalties for not attaining the set standards.

Each state may choose to establish its own standards and assessment of students rather than using the national standards. Federal funding will be provided to states for the initial establishment of standards and the means to evaluate students to determine whether those standards have been met.

The Length of the School Day and Year

Our current school year is based on an agrarian calendar. Students begin school in autumn and are out for the summer by the second week in June—in time to help plant the spring crops, according to the original intent of school officials. Most school districts have a 180-day to 200-day school year calendar. Teachers usually are required to work five to twenty additional days during the school year, during which time they engage in professional development sessions to improve their teaching.

In recent years, there has been a call by some politicians for a longer school year. A 210-day school year is the most often suggested proposal. By having students attend school more days, many people, including some educators, believe that students will learn more. Certainly **time on task** (the amount of time actually engaged in learning) studies support such an idea.

In 1991, the National Education Commission on Time and Learning examined the quality and adequacy of the time students in the United States spent learning. The commission identified ten schools with extended learning programs of 210 school days or longer. The schools, located in different states, each had unique attributes. Several of these schools are described in the following paragraphs.

Many school districts are changing to a year-round calendar, with school closed during July only. (© Myrleen Ferguson/PhotoEdit)

The Murfreesboro city schools in Tennessee have run an extended day program on a year-round basis since 1986. According to John Hodge Jones (1994a, 21), superintendent of the district's eight elementary schools and chair of the National Education Commission on Time and Learning, "While teachers have a personal vested interest in traditional time schedules, most acknowledge that changes are needed." The program in Murfreesboro enables students to be at school from 6 A.M. to 6 P.M., with the academic program beginning at 8 a.m. and concluding at 3 P.M. The remainder of the time students are engaged in child-care activities. The schools focus on "academic learning experiences, skill-building, exploration, experimentation, and problem-solving" (Anderson 1994, 10). A major local company, Nissan, strongly supports the extended day program, which many of its employees use (Jones 1994b).

The James A. Foshay Middle School in Los Angeles, California, has a year-round schedule in which students attend 180 days a year, the normal span of days for a school year. However, the school has four different schedules, each beginning and ending at a different time of the year with one quarter of the school's enrollment. On any given weekday, three-fourths of the students enrolled are in attendance at the school. Two-week intersessions allow students who need extra assistance to receive up to sixty hours of additional instruction. Saturday classes are held in a cooperative effort with the University of Southern California (USC) for sixty talented students. Their parents must also attend the Saturday classes. If these academically talented students complete the Saturday program and score at least one thousand on the Scholastic Aptitude Test, they are given full tuition waivers to USC (National Education Commission on Time and Learning 1994).

Over 1,905 public schools, including 1,627 elementary schools, in thirty-two states have adopted year-round calendars (Knox 1994). The Emerson Elementary School in Albuquerque, New Mexico, has a twelve-week-on, fifteen-day-off, multi-track schedule with the school district shutting down completely for three weeks each July. The school district has eight hundred students, 75 percent members of minorities and 90 percent who qualify for free lunches (Anderson 1994). It is argued that having these students in school most of the school year enables them to learn more since they do not have a three-month summer break away from learning. Also, for older students, being in school prevents them from being on the streets and getting into trouble.

The Crane school district in Yuma, Arizona, has a forty-five-day-on, fifteen-day-off schedule in which students and teachers attend school in four forty-five-day periods separated by fifteen-day vacations or intersessions. Student achievement was found to be equal to or slightly above that of students on the typical school calendar (Knox 1994).

In addition to a longer calendar school year, several school districts have reexamined the length of the school day for students attending their schools. Such action has resulted in lengthening the school day, usually by fifteen to thirty minutes. An increase of just fifteen minutes a day adds up to an hour and fifteen minutes of additional learning time per week for students, a significant amount indeed.

A longer school year has been resisted by some teachers who believe that both they themselves and their students need one long break rather than shorter, more frequent breaks. In addition, many teachers use the long summer break to further their professional development by enrolling in college or university classes or workshops to enhance their teaching knowledge and skills. Family vacations and court-ordered visitation of children with the noncustodial parent are other societal reasons for closing schools during the summer months.

School Choice

According to its proponents, school choice results in greater competition between schools and improves the quality of education. This theory hasn't been validated by research. The basic premise is that good schools will attract students and lousy ones will go out of business.

Tuition tax credits permit parents or caretakers to get an income tax reduction for a portion of the tuition they pay for their child's private schooling. Minnesota was the first state to adopt tuition tax credits. The idea has been proposed in Congress which in 1997 passed a law involving tuition tax credits for college students.

School choice is also provided by vouchers. This idea has been around for over thirty years. Parents or caretakers are given a voucher worth a flat amount for the costs of their child's education. They can then enroll their child in any school, public or private. A strong argument can be made against tuition tax credits and vouchers, since they both suggest a loss of public confidence in public education. Those parents who can afford to transport their children to better schools would likely do so leaving poor students for the public schools to educate.

Diane Ravitch, a noted education scholar and former under-secretary of the United States Department of Education, has a new book entitled *New Schools for the New Century*, coauthored with Joseph P. Viteritti (1997). This book points to charter schools and vouchers as being ways to improve education. Valerie E. Lee of the University of Michigan points out that Catholic schools offer an effective model of schooling that is different from the public schools. According to Lee, a convert to the idea of promoting Catholic schools over public schools, data points out that "impoverished minority children were significantly likelier to graduate, and to go on to college, if they attended Roman Catholic rather than comparative public schools" (Traub 1997, 13). Conservatives argue that Catholic schools are successful because they are not tied to bureaucratic control. For instance, if a student is unruly, the student is expelled from school, and special-education programs are the exception rather than the rule in Catholic schools.

Forming charter schools is yet another way to promote school choice. The state board of education or the local school board issues the charter to a group of community members, parents, or teachers along with the amount of money it costs to educate the students in the regular educational system. Any extra funding must be gained through donations or grants. Currently there are over 200 charter schools throughout the United States, mostly elementary schools. While charter schools have been widely discussed, particularly by the business sector, the idea has not caught on, largely because businesses have failed to contribute funding for them. Those charter schools that have succeeded have done so largely due to the efforts of the teachers and school administrators along with substantial parental involvement and support.

Homeschooling

The number of students being homeschooled has increased dramatically in the last decade. Estimates of the number of families that homeschool their children range from 200,000 to over one million (Knowles, Marlow, and Muchmore 1992). Homeschooling is popular in particular with members of the conservative right wing as well as with some liberal parents. Generally speaking, parents who believe in homeschooling feel that the local public schools and private schools cannot devote as much individual attention to their children's education as they, themselves, can.

In homeschooling, siblings help each other with their studies. (© Andy Sacks/Tony Stone)

In most instances, mothers who are not employed in the workplace serve as the teaching parent. These mothers may have high school or college degrees but most are not certified teachers. In some cases the father serves as the teacher, while in other instances the parents divide the teaching duties between themselves.

Typically, homeschooled children come from two-parent families with the father working outside of the home rather than from single-parent families. Most homeschooled children have never been enrolled in a public school, but they do enter secondary school when the content of the subject areas becomes more difficult.

The strength of the homeschooling movement became evident when members of Congress were pressured to rewrite a portion of education legislation. The Goals 2000 legislation was changed to drop the requirement that only certified teachers be allowed to teach in schools because many parents who homeschooled their children thought that they, too, would be required to be certified to teach. In fact, the original legislation excluded them.

A Closer Look   *Disney's Model School*

The late Walt Disney once was quoted as saying, "I'd love to be part of building a school of tomorrow." The Walt Disney company built a new public school for grades K–12 in Celebration, a housing development at Walt Disney World, near Orlando, Florida. Promoting brochures hailed it as being a "unique public/private collaboration" and "a model for education" for the twenty-first century. The school was located in the midst of a new housing development owned by the Disney company (Stecklow 1997).

Opened in the fall of 1996, Celebration School enrolled 170 students with 19 full-time teachers. By the end of the school year, the building principal and six teachers had quit. Despite having received thousands of inquiries from teachers about positions, the low pay ($23,000 for new teachers with no teaching experience)

discouraged most from applying. Even the school nurse left, citing the low pay of $9,116 a year.

Over twenty students were removed from the school by their parents. Parents complained that their children regressed in both academics and in discipline. However test results indicated that students from Celebration School outperformed others in the Osceola County School District in standardized reading tests for fourth, sixth, seventh, and eighth graders and in mathematics for sixth, seventh, and eighth graders. Dr. Lois Hetland, a Harvard University researcher, points out that the current students come from affluent, white families who tend to score well on such tests while many of the new students for the 1997–98 school year come from less affluent and more and more ethnically diverse communities.

Inclusion

Inclusion means placing students who are emotionally, mentally, or physically disabled in regular classrooms. Often, regular classroom teachers have had limited special training in working with these students. For instance, many states require that teachers take a course on inclusion. In addition, teachers with large classes find it difficult to work individually with present students without adding students with special needs. According to Albert Shanker (1994, E23), president of the American Federation of Teachers, "The movement in American education that is taking hold the fastest and is likely to have the profoundest—and most destructive—effect is not what you might think. It's the rush towards full inclusion of disabled children in regular classrooms."

Those in support of full inclusion for all students with emotional, mental, and physical disabilities point out the similarities between inclusion and the separate but equal education provided to African Americans prior to desegregation. They believe that through inclusion, students with emotional, mental, and physical disabilities and their regular classroom counterparts are better socialized as a result.

Gender Equity and Single-Sex High Schools

In the 1980s and 1990s, there has been a greater emphasis on gender equity issues. In addition, some educators have pointed out the need for role models for minority students. The result has been interest in creating separate all-boy and all-girl public

Chapter 3   *Trends in Education*

A High School in a Shopping Mall

Five school districts in Minnesota, all located near Bloomington, a suburb of the Twin Cities, have collaborated on an innovative secondary school in the Mall of America. Located just down from Sunglass Hut International and between Knott's Camp Snoopy and Bloomingdale's department store on the first level of the world's largest shopping mall is the Metropolitan Learning Alliance's Leila Anderson's Learning Center.

The school enrolled two hundred high school students for the 1994–95 school year and eventually wants to expand to include a kindergarten through third-grade elementary school for children of mall workers. The school itself has no extra frills. There are no windows in the white, soundproof classrooms (Winerip 1994).

Currently, only junior and senior students are enrolled at the Learning Center. Each class has a business partner. For instance, the environmental issues class has guest speakers from Browning-Ferris Industries, a company that collects and recycles one thousand tons of garbage from the mall each month. Students in the marketplace class work with the Camp Snoopy Amusement Park, which offers plays and musical performances as well as rides.

Internships are offered to students who work on an individual basis. For instance, one female student elected to do an internship in restaurant operations at Tony Roma's, an Italian restaurant in the mall. Tom Gotreau, manager of the restaurant, made certain that she saw all facets of the restaurant business, from busing dishes to hostessing to working in the kitchen. Another student interned at the Gap Kids, an apparel store for children. Marcy Richeson, the store manager, helped her intern learn about the product and its quality as well as how to sell it. In addition, the intern learned about the need to beat the sales performance of the previous year (Association Press 1994).

Some of the complaints about the school include claims that the mall setting is distracting to students and hinders their learning. In addition, there is concern by educators that such a tempting shopping and entertainment setting might have a negative effect on student attendance. When a reporter for the *New York Times* asked the teachers at the high school about attendance, they replied that it was good. However, the reporter noted that one-third of the class was absent on the day he was present (Winerip 1994).

The Mall of America is not the only mall with a school. In 1993, the Oglethorp Mall in Savannah, Georgia, opened a high school for sixty students who had done poorly in more traditional classes. The project was so successful that a second school opened in Savannah Mall. The Park City Mall has Lancaster County Academy, which is a collaboration of seven school districts in Pennsylvania. In Toronto, a similar school is located in the Dufferin Mall.

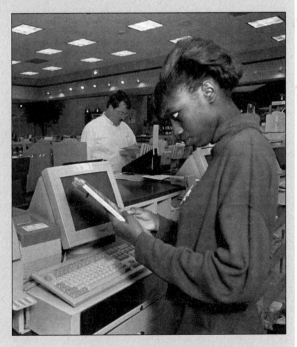

A student at the Metropolitan Learning Alliance Center works at the mall to develop knowledge and skills. (Courtesy of Mall of America)

A Mother's Day of Homeschooling

The following appeared as an article in *The Wall Street Journal* on May 6, 1994. The author is Isabel Lyman, who lives with her family in Amherst, Massachusetts.

"It is 10 A.M. Wid, my eight-year-old, and I have just reviewed the primary colors in Spanish. *Amarillo,* I note, is the one that he has trouble pronouncing. After *español,* we prepare microscope slides with gum-media. Sticky fun! After we ooh and aah over the magnified specimens, I dash out to our little red barn and feed the hens. Sometimes Wid helps me collect the eggs. Before morning expires, Wid will have taken a spelling test, done multiplication and division worksheets, and listened to a cassette recording of "The Hobbit." Daniel, my ten-year-old, is working on his studies as well.

"Welcome to my home school—my private, little rebellion against the enemies of educational excellence and the forces of feminism who say a woman's place is in the paying workplace.

"Patricia M. Lines, a researcher with the U.S. Department of Education, currently estimates the home-schooled population at around 300,000 school-age children. The Home School Legal Defense Association believes the number to be as high as 500,000. The statistics are indicative of a new trend: American women who are bypassing the mommy track to teach their children at home.

"Make no mistake. I'm no retro June Cleaver armed with a stack of designer textbooks to match my pearls. I'm a modern-day, Hispanic-American version of Laura Ingalls Wilder with a personal computer, mini-van and advanced college degree. Part schoolmarm, part activist, part pioneer, part entrepreneur, part entertainer, and part dedicated wife.

"My husband, sons, and I reside on five acres in a college town. We supplement my husband Wid's $25,000-a-year paycheck as a math instructor and private high school director by heating with wood, growing a vegetable garden, raising meat, tutoring public-school children and writing articles. Our lifestyle guarantees us

a vanishing commodity: strong family bonds. Bonds, I hope, that result in young adults who will laud the likes of patriot Nathan Hale, not grunger Kurt Cobain.

"Part of the thrill I derive from home schooling on a shoestring, and sans a teaching certificate, is the superior academic and cultural gains that result when I give my boys one-on-one attention. For instance, when Daniel had the assignment of composing a story from a set of sophisticated vocabulary words, he didn't balk. He wrote these opening sentences:

" 'There was once a man named Jim who went daft, clambered up a hawser, dropped through a bulkhead, and was gravely hurt. He was very nonchalant about the incident and was tantalized to do it again.'

"Dan is also mastering algebra, knows tiny Andorra is near sunny Portugal, plays an aggressive game of ice hockey, has been interviewed by the local media, has shared his bedroom with an inner-city child, has conversed with the last president of Costa Rica, was the runner-up in a spelling bee of about twenty local home-schooled children, and has scored high—ninety-ninth percentile—on his Stanford Achievement Tests.

"Those test scores are fairly typical of home-taught children. Brian Ray, president of the National Home Education Research Institute in Oregon, says that in every study done to date, home schoolers have scored equal to or better than conventionally schooled children. Mr. Ray's analysis of 509 home schoolers who took standardized tests in spring 1992 revealed that they averaged at or above the eighty-second percentile in every category, including social studies and science.

"Yet home educators, for all their hardfought academic and legal victories, are often harshly criticized by the 'pros.' Thomas Shannon of the National School Boards Association gave the Associated Press his two cents' worth on parents who have the gall to be their children's teacher: 'We are very concerned that many parents who think they are qualified to teach their

(continued)

youngsters simply are not. Society ultimately has to pay for any mistakes, not to mention the loss of a child who might otherwise have made a maximum contribution.'

"Well, Mr. Shannon, tell that to the mother of Charlotte Cates, who has empowered her daughter with real skills instead of hollow rhetoric. Former neighbor Charlotte was home schooled through high school. She is now a junior at Mount Holyoke College.

"Colorful anecdotes aside, members of academia are effectively making the case that home-schooled students have not retreated into the cultural catacombs. Homeschool Associates of Maine recently released the findings of Prof. J. Gary Knowles.

"Mr. Knowles, of the University of Michigan, studied fifty-three adults to see the longterm effects of being educated at home. He summarized his findings as follows: 'I have found no evidence that these adults were even moderately disadvantaged. . . . Two thirds of them were married, the norm for adults their age, and none were unemployed or on any form of welfare assistance. More than three quarters felt that being taught at home had actually helped them to interact with people from different levels of society.'

"The contemporary home-schooling movement is a splendid success story because of the sacrifice of societal icons—career advancement and leisure time—on the part of many concerned mothers. They consider the education of their children of utmost importance: a fitting lesson two days before Mother's Day."

high schools. Certainly there are numerous private single-sex high schools in the United States and Canada, as well as in other countries.

The idea of separate-sex high schools is far from new. The first all-female public high school in the United States was the Philadelphia Girls High School, which was founded in 1848 in Philadelphia and continues to operate. During the countercultural upheaval of the 1960s, the Philadelphia Girls High School suffered as the number of girls interested in attending a single-sex school declined greatly. There were discussions about closing the school. However, in the 1980s and 1990s, the downtown school has thrived and now has far more applicants than it can accept, with a current enrollment of four hundred girls (Willis 1994). According to Chris Sagen-Peacock, principal of the Philadelphia Girls High School, between 95 percent and 98 percent of its graduates go on to higher education. The school emphasizes math and science. In coeducational high schools these subjects are taken mostly by boys.

In Detroit, the idea for an all-boy public high school in an inner-city area was developed in the late 1980s. The idea was to have a high school with only male students that would have a preponderance of male African American teachers to serve as role models. Despite the positive achievement and social results demonstrated by the high school, a lawsuit was filed against the school stating that it was discriminatory in nature because only boys were allowed to attend. The judge agreed and the all-boy high school program was discontinued.

Gender equity issues will continue to surface in education. Two-thirds of illiterate adults in the entire world are women (Glazer 1994). The majority of the teachers in higher education are males, whereas in early childhood and elementary education the majority are females.

Mainstreaming Isn't Always Solution for Disabled Students

"Jimmy Peters, six, is described vaguely as 'communicatively handicapped.' He speaks only in disconnected words. According to teachers, when he's frustrated, he lashes out. In his kindergarten class in Huntington Beach, California, teachers say, he threw chairs, toppled desks, repeatedly bit and kicked other children and teachers, and disrupted class by throwing temper tantrums.

"The Ocean View School District wanted to transfer Jimmy to a special education class. His father said no and denies his son is violent. The district sued to remove the boy. A county judge temporarily barred Jimmy from class, but a federal judge ruled that Jimmy is not an immediate danger to himself and others and ordered him readmitted.

"Jimmy's teacher went on medical leave, saying she couldn't take the stress any longer, and twelve of the thirty-one children in Jimmy's class were removed by their parents because of the boy's return. 'We're not against inclusion,' said Karen Croft, one of the parents. 'But if a child is going to be included in a class, he has to behave.'

Mainstreaming

"The Jimmy problem is a byproduct of humane reform: the mainstreaming of hundreds of thousands of disabled youngsters into ordinary public school classrooms. The downside of the movement is that schools have lost most of their ability to maintain order. The state of Virginia is currently battling the U.S. Department of Education to preserve school boards' authority to expel disabled students for behavior unrelated to their disability, such as bringing guns, knives, or drugs into schools.

"In 1988, the U.S. Supreme Court ruled that public schools may not expel or remove disruptive, emotionally disturbed children from their classroom for more than ten days, even to protect others from physical assault, unless they get permission of the parents or a judge. Writing for the majority, Justice William Brennan said

that when school officials remove a disturbed child, they have the burden of proving the child is dangerous.

"This has had the effect of turning placement decisions—whether a child goes to a regular class or a special ed class—over to lawyers and judges. And the high hurdle of having to prove dangerousness to self or others, the same hurdle that keeps some of the wilder deinstitutionalized mental patients on our streets, means that the schools usually lose such suits in court.

"More astonishingly, the right of all schoolchildren to a chaos-free classroom is not taken into account. If proving dangerousness to a judge is the only way to remove a disturbed child, then presumably the child could run around class shrieking every day, toppling desks, and shredding schoolbooks in a non-dangerous manner without running afoul of the Brennan rule.

" 'At what point do we raise the question, Can the rest of the class function?' asks Robert Berne, dean of the Wagner School of Public Service at New York University. 'If mainstreaming is slightly better for the disturbed child, but much worse for everyone else, we have to deal with that.'

Dumped into Classes

"The problem is becoming worse as the call for 'full inclusion' grows. In the 1980s, many school districts started mainstreaming children with mild disabilities, often without special help. Since then, children with severe mental, physical, and behavioral problems have been placed into regular classes. The argument is now made that the 'exclusion' of any youngster, no matter how seriously impaired, is simply unjust.

"There's a more cynical explanation for the sudden mainstreaming of very serious cases: Since special education students are heavily funded, school districts can save millions by 'dumping' these students into regular classes without providing the support of expensive aides and special teachers.

(continued)

"Albert Shanker, president of the American Federation of Teachers, says a lot of dumping is going on. The AFT believes that many teachers are either afraid or skeptical of the inclusion policies. An AFT poll of West Virginia teachers shows that 78 percent of respondents think disabled students won't benefit from the inclusion policy; 87 percent said other students won't benefit either.

"The Toledo AFT points out that some severely disturbed children are already in regular public schools, though still segregated in special classes. Among them are students in diapers, others fed through tubes, suffering from obsessive-compulsive disorders, or extremely violent and destructive. One nine-year-old, whose mother had sued for him to be mainstreamed, had broken the jaw of one staff member and three ribs of another. A high school student urinated on the floor, banged her head against the wall, and tore off her clothes and shred them when she did not get her own way.

"The call for 'full inclusion' should surely lead to some discussion about when exclusion is justified, what the financial and social costs of the program will be, and what kind of learning will go on in classes where severe disturbance is allowed to set the tone. This movement has rolled along without enough input from the public. If it goes much further, it may turn out to be yet another advertisement for school choice programs."

The Need for More Female and Minority School Administrators

The overwhelming majority of school administrators at the elementary and secondary levels are white males. This is a result of low pay for teachers in the 1950s and 1960s when men were often the sole income provider for their families and therefore sought administrative positions to bolster their incomes instead of the lower paying classroom teaching positions. However, in recent years, particularly in larger urban school districts, more minority school administrators have been hired as principals and superintendents.

Like the small number of minority male principals, there is a relatively small percentage of female school administrators. This is due largely to societal expectations that a man can better serve as a manager and a disciplinarian than a woman. Indeed, in the 1940s through 1970s, many men who had been coaches within a school district and who possessed the proper administrative certification were promoted to principalships. The idea was that a coach knew how to work with people, could set goals, and could discipline those individuals who might get out of line. As a result, there were several ex-basketball and ex-football coaches sitting in principals' offices who may or may not have known much about teaching and curriculum.

The school reform movement of the 1980s resulted in a change in the role of the building principal. No longer were the sole requirements that the individual be a good manager and disciplinarian. Half of the principal's time would now be devoted to instructional leadership for the teachers in the school. As a result, the opportunity for more women to become principals arose, since women have traditionally spent more time in classroom settings teaching and working on curriculum development. What was once a higher salaried position dominated by white males has become more accessible to women.

Teach for America

How did someone who grew up in Dallas, Texas, and graduated from Princeton University, an institution without a teacher education program, have an impact on teaching? As a senior at Princeton, Wendy Kopp decided she wanted to make a difference in the lives of others. She believed that many of her friends and acquaintances felt the dame way. So Wendy founded Teach for America with the idea that outstanding recent college graduates might want to give something back to society by enrolling in a teacher corps to fill teaching positions in urban and rural schools.

When the program began in 1989, Wendy naively thought some foundation would give her large sums of money to push the Teach for America program along. It didn't happen overnight, but Wendy pressed onward. Now the program has financial support. Of over 2,500 applicants the first year, 500 were selected to participate. Since 1989, three thousand teachers have been placed in schools from the South Bronx to Los Angeles and in impoverished areas in the deep South, for a total of fifteen school districts across the United States (Morrison 1997).

Applicants for Teach for America undergo a rigorous review process prior to being accepted. Individual interviews with staff members from Teach for America as well as involvement in small-group discussions contribute to the process. In addition, each applicant must teach a short five-minute lesson to other applicants. Teach for America has basic standards that applicants must meet prior to consideration for the teaching corps, including eight teaching performance requirements and eight competencies.

After being selected by staff members, the candidates then engage in an internship program over the summer. Upon successful completion of the internship, candidates are then placed in one of fifteen school districts in urban inner cities or in poor rural areas where they teach for a minimum of two years.

Overall, Teach for America has met with success and continues to be a welcome source of teachers in areas where many teachers choose not to teach. One drawback to Teach for America is that after two years, many of its teachers move on to other careers. This problem is found in the teaching profession in general, however. Fifty percent of beginning teachers leave the teaching profession within seven years, and more than two-thirds of that percentage leave within their first four years (Hewitt 1993).

In the accompanying A Closer Look, written by Alice Waddell, a former middle school and high school teacher who is now principal of Natural Bridge Elementary School, the need for women administrators is pointed out as well as some of the difficulties they may have in attaining such positions. Dr. Waddell lives in Lexington, Virginia, with her husband and son.

Technology

Technological advancements are occurring on an almost daily basis. Faster and faster new computers can be linked to computer networks within a school and/or directly to online services and the **Internet,** which allow students access to information bulletin boards. E-mail allows students to send messages to each other as well as graphics, photos, and even art and music projects. Teachers and students alike will be involved in gleaning knowledge from the information superhighway.

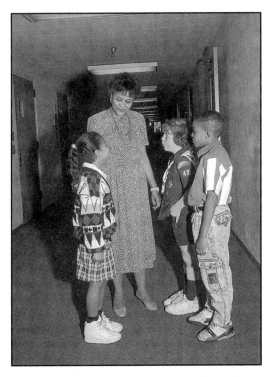

Schools need more females and members of minorities in administrative roles. (© Mary Kate Denny/PhotoEdit)

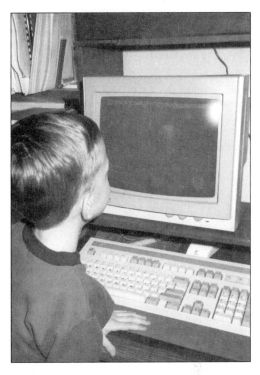

Many children now have access to home computers complete with CD-ROM and Internet hookups. (Courtesy of Pamela J. Farris)

Pett Peeves

by Joel Pett

As you read Alice Waddell's account of the issues women face in their careers, think about your future in the schools. Do you expect your own experience to be different? Do you agree with Ms. Waddell's views?

"We are living in a period of constant change. Today public school administrators are seeking ways of restructuring schools to make them more effective and are examining the leadership that will be required to make schools successful. As we look at the leadership that is necessary to manage schools of the late twentieth and twenty-first centuries, we are examining not only the traditional, male-dominated, transactional leader but also the transformational leader who has the leadership qualities that have been traditionally considered to be female leadership qualities—participatory leadership, shared decision making, and the use of group processes.

"Many people still expect school administrators to be men, particularly at the central office, middle school, and secondary school levels. Women who choose to enter an administrative career and are successful in obtaining a position are defying the expectations. Women who seek and obtain administrative positions are the exception, not the rule.

Career Path

"Let's face it. Women and men tend to follow different career paths in the field of education. Men are usually more assertive and pursue administrative positions more vigorously and do so earlier in their careers. Job advertisements for administrative positions usually work to the advantage of male applicants because they usually require minimal teaching experience and emphasize administrative experience. Teaching experience is often devalued, and this is generally where the women's experience lies. Male administrators spend an average of five years teaching prior to obtaining an administrative position, whereas women spend an average of fifteen

years in teaching (Pigford and Tonnsen 1993, 13–15). As you can see, the cards are stacked against women applicants even before the official screening process begins.

"All of this makes it very difficult for a woman to 'get her foot' in the door. Women have to find ways to challenge the 'good ole boys' network, which has been working successfully for males for centuries. Men tend to have a natural means for gathering and exchanging information whether it be in the locker room, on the golf course, or in men's organizations. Men have realized the need to band together and the need to promote each other. Women must learn from their examples.

Networking

"Women who aspire to be school administrators need to work together to gain the power and support needed to have an impact on the present social and political system (Smith et al. 1982, 84). They must gain access to information and resources, and they need a support system to do this for them. Women need to talk to each other and, in so doing, they need to share their common concerns, problems, experiences, and ideas. They must provide each other with understanding, support, and assistance. Thus, the professional network has become a necessity. This network is usually a group that serves as an official representative or advocate for women in the profession or for those who are seeking to become a member of the profession. Women must seek to combat the 'good ole boys' network by constructing these formal associations that network publicly (Schmuck 1986, 98). Although women do not usually grow up feeling the need to connect, they must realize that this connection is necessary in the professional world. For females networking is not only a replacement strategy for the 'good ole boys' network but also an opportunity to form a bond with other females in an effort to promote each

(continued)

(continued)

other's personal and professional development (Schmuck 1986, 98). Women need to use networking to the maximum extent to further the administrative success of women.

The Importance of Mentors

"Finding a suitable mentor, male or female, is another significant endeavor for a female aspirant to school administration. A mentor has 'walked the walk.' Mentors can provide support by being someone an aspirant can shadow; they can also open doors of opportunity. People who are already in administrative positions are more aware of job openings and are more cognizant of the workings of the administrative and political systems. They can often put the aspirant in contact with the 'right' people.

"Mentors tend to take a special interest in the individuals they have chosen to mentor. The aspirant's personal and professional success are often taken quite personally by the mentor. They see the aspirant's success as a responsibility that cannot be taken lightly.

"If a woman can find a female mentor, she may find more personal assistance. A female mentor may adapt 'feminine' qualities to an acceptable managerial style. She may provide more personal support and provide more understanding of how to balance a personal and professional life. Hopefully, she would understand the problems women face as a group and help women to organize to gain status and strength (Smith et al. 1982, 29).

"Since the benefits of using a mentor are significant, women must know how to find such a mentor. A woman could begin the process by observing administrators and thinking about what they do. It would be beneficial to spend some time 'shadowing' an administrator and asking questions. It is absolutely necessary that a woman make her aspirations known to the appropriate people. She must investigate opportunities for training, as well as for jobs. Women must apply for administrative positions. They do not have the opportunity to obtain these positions if they do not seek them actively (Smith et al. 1982, 32). Having a mentor can guide an individual through the entire process—the training,

the job hunt, the interview, and the on-the-job problems and successes. Both males and females should seek the assistance and companionship that can be gained from mentor-mentee relationships.

Internships

"Yet another means of preparing one's self for the position of a school administrator is to participate in an internship. Many of the universities provide or require internships as part of their preparatory programs. Internships provide opportunities to break the barriers with potential male colleagues. They give men an opportunity to see how women lead in an atmosphere that is nonthreatening to the male ego. Since most of the administrative positions are held by males, internships still leave the male in the position of control. At the same time it allows women the chance to show men and other women their leadership styles and gives them the opportunity to gain the respect of the male administrators in the system. Internships can often lead to job opportunities in this manner. When men can feel that they had a part in the training of women, then these women appear to be less threatening to them (Adkinson 1980–81, 117). Internships can open doors and should not be ruled out as possibilities on the road to advancement.

Internal Barriers

"Women's career paths confront many barriers. Often 'women's biggest enemies are . . . themselves' (Woo 1985, 286). Since women have not been conditioned to be ambitious and determined, they may find it tougher to fight the old values. They may become tired of fighting the system and simply give up. Even though women are not more aware, have better self-images and higher career expectations, these gains may have created psychological and emotional turmoil (Woo 1985, 286).

"Our whole socialization process is a hinderance to women. Gloria Steinem once said that 'the first problem for all of us, men and women, is not to learn, but to unlearn' (Pigford and Tonnsen 1993, 8). Thoughts that people have about themselves are influenced by the experiences they have had throughout their lives and by what they have been taught. The socialization process

(continued)

(continued)

that begins in childhood has tremendous influence on how women and men see themselves and how they view their capabilities.

"The socialization process in the schools also encourages the development of internal barriers. School experiences tend to reinforce behaviors considered to be 'gender appropriate.' For example, 80 percent of the teachers are female, while approximately 80 percent of the principals are male. This sends a clear message as to the accepted roles of men and women in the schools (Pigford and Tonnsen 1993, 9–10).

"A major internal barrier for some women is their definition of leadership. The term 'woman leader' is often viewed as a contradiction of terms. Women often feel that they can be a woman or a leader, but not both. Women are faced with a real dilemma. If they choose to be administrators, they may have to be tough and aggressive, which is often difficult for women who feel that this is contrary to the 'identity' of women. Their self-concepts may pay the price in this struggle (Pigford and Tonnsen 1993, 11).

"The absence of female role models creates still another internal barrier for women. In 1990, only 5 percent of the superintendents, 12 percent of the secondary principals, and 34 percent of the elementary principals were women. This might lead women to assume that only extremely talented and skilled women become administrators, and many will choose not to aspire (Pigford and Tonnsen 1993, 12).

"Fear of being rejected is a major barrier for some women—fear, not only of rejection from males but also from females who have been socialized to accept men as their leaders. Women face the jealousies of their female subordinates or peers and face the views that they are threats to the males.

"The personal cost of success is a stumbling block for some women. One cannot 'have it all.' Something somewhere is going to be sacrificed. Women may find it difficult to face the increased visibility and public scrutiny, the hostility from males, the resentment from females, the work overload, and the increased responsibility. Being an administrator does have an impact on one's personal life. Work may have to become a top priority. For males, this is not as difficult. Most male administrators have wives to depend on for psychological and emotional support. Women are less likely to have such a support system. Ninety-two percent of male principals are married; 59 percent of the females are married (Woo 1985, 13–14).

"The internal barriers are areas over which the individual has some control. Women must take charge of their lives and make decisions that lead to where they want to be. This is possible if women choose to settle for nothing less. The first challenge is to make the choice.

External Barriers

"C. S. Shakeshaft cautions women against blaming internal barriers for their situations in the field of school administration. Internal barriers can be overcome by individuals, whereas external barriers require institutional and social change (Pigford and Tonnsen 1993, 14).

"External barriers control the employment status and opportunities of males and females. The formal screening system determines who gets in the system and who gets promoted. It sets the requirements for credentials such as degrees, certification, and experience. Since women make up 50 percent of the enrollment in school administration programs, the lack of proper credentials is no longer a valid excuse for the lack of women administrators. When school boards set the requirements for experience for particular positions, women often are screened out as viable candidates (Pigford and Tonnsen 1993, 13–15).

"This informal screening system sets a definite barrier for some women. Women may find it easy to meet the formal requirements, but few survive the informal screening process. It is difficult for women to 'fit in' with those in power. Women continue to have difficulty being accepted by the 'good ole boys.' Women miss out on the locker room discussions and thus miss out on a great deal of sharing of information about job openings and the wheeling and dealing that go on for these positions (Pigford and Tonnsen 1993, 15).

(continued)

Chapter 3 *Trends in Education*

The Legacy of Discrimination and Exclusion

"Even though the research studies substantiate that women perform as well as, or better than, men as school administrators, the barriers still exist (Pigford and Tonnsen 1993, 15). The most significant external barrier is sex discrimination (Bonuso and Shakeshaft 1983, 14). Shakeshaft stated that "the primary reason that women are not hired or promoted in administrative positions is due solely to the fact that they are female" (Pigford and Tonnsen 1993, 16). Some people try to convince women that sex discrimination is 'history' because of the forces of the 1980s, such as affirmative action, the feminist movement, and the raised consciousness of educators. Others might say this is wishful thinking.

"Another area that tends to be ignored by those in power is sexual harassment. Sexual harassment is real and it still exists. Women must realize that sexual harassment of any type is not acceptable and they must stand up for their rights. Women often endure verbal abuse from male colleagues on a regular basis—dirty jokes, demeaning remarks, and unfair criticism of their schools, their teachers, and their programs. Often it appears that no one in power cares or has any desire to do anything about these inappropriate behaviors. The perpetrators appear to go 'untouched.' For a female administrator to address this problem legally, she would need to be aware of the possible sacrifice of her career.

The lawyers make it clear that fighting the discrimination and harassment often destroys women's careers.

"It is very difficult to face these circumstances on a daily basis. Women must learn to deal with such circumstances. Women must be willing to confront them, ignore them, or be devoured by them. Sexual harassment is often viewed as being 'just the way things are'—accept it or leave. Sexual harassment in the workplace is far from being a thing of the past. Women need to stand up for their rights and help rid the workplace of inappropriate behavior. Women must take off their 'blinders.'

Conclusion

"Women should consider school administration as a viable aspiration in their career paths. They must be aware of the hurdles, confront them as needed, continue the race, and settle for nothing less than victory—a position in school administration. Women of the new century must take the lead. As long as women continue to accept discrimination, ignore harassment, and step aside when the going gets rough, women will perpetuate the problem. School administrators can wear skirts, and because women have excellent leadership skills, they should be considered to be on equal status with male applicants for administrative positions. Women can see success—they must face the challenge, make the choice, and begin to add a new chapter to the legacy."

Courtesy Alice M. Waddell.

Computer Technology, Multimedia, and CD-ROM

Already students in some secondary schools have their own E-mail addresses and routinely get notes from students in other states or in other countries. Mosaic, a navigation program available free to Internet users, allows students and teachers to "tap into audio and video clips as well as text without having to know where the items are stored in some remote database" (Deutschman and Tetzeli 1994, 98).

Newly developed software enables students in classrooms in different schools and even in different states to work on a project together. Such software is referred to as *groupware* (Deutschman and Tetzeli 1994). Recently, a fourth-grade class in a South Dakota elementary school decided to use technology to study economic concepts. They linked up with students in Alaska, North Carolina, Texas, and other states to do an economic survey. For instance, they discovered that a Big Mac sandwich costs the least in South Dakota and the most in Alaska.

Teachers can program computers so students can choose among a variety of activities to meet a learning objective. Students can touch a picture or words on the screen to find out more information about a particular subject. For instance, in studying the Civil War, fourth-graders can point to pictures of such generals as Stonewall Jackson, Robert E. Lee, Ulysses S. Grant, and others and text appears that provides additional details and information about that person or photos of the Civil War battle sites, along with information about the geography and locale.

Software programs also permit computers with **CD-ROMs** and speakers to produce audio while displaying a picture on the screen. For example, books written and read by their authors will become part of the everyday classroom or a wonderful free-time activity for students. Unlike the early CD-ROM disks, which were called *shovelware* because they were nothing more than printed material or simple software put on CD-ROM disks, new "CD-ROMs blend video, text, graphics, sound, photos, and animation so cleverly that they deliver an experience wholly different from what books or ordinary software can provide" (Sprout 1994, 141). For example, a high school can buy the CD-ROM multimedia program *JFK Assassination: A Visual Investigation* for less than $50. It includes actual footage of the assassination as well as the complete text of the Warren Commission Report and the book *Crossfire: The Plot That Killed Kennedy*. *World Beat* is another CD-ROM program that can be purchased inexpensively. *World Beat* gives samples of the different popular musical styles from throughout the world (Sprout 1994).

New computer screens are larger so students can see more than one program running at once, such as a word processing program and a graphics program at the same time.

Virtual Reality

Virtual reality, now popular with secondary students as a leisure-time activity, is on its way into the classroom. Instead of virtual reality machines that simulate driving in the Daytona 500 stock car race, flying a powerful jet fighter, or playing basketball with Michael Jordan, students will examine what it was like to be a soldier in World War II or discover in an archaeological dig the skeleton of a dinosaur from the Jurassic period.

Interactive software is now being developed not just for high school students but for preschoolers and middle school students as well. DaVinci Time and Space, a California-based software company that leads in this area, has a goal that such an interactive television channel will "create a virtual reality for kids to play and learn in, not just a bunch of computer games transferred to TV" (Losee 1994, 136).

Telecommunications

Many companies, including those that produce both hardware and software, have joined alliances to combine telephone and computer systems in *computer telephony*. Through fiber optics phone lines, teachers will be able to talk to each other and trade lesson plans on their computer screens at the same time. Or, students thousands of miles from each other can work on a musical arrangement over the phone and see the score on their separate computer screens.

School districts or regional offices will use servers that allow area schools to become linked with other schools. These servers will enable conference calls by students in which they and a teacher in another school can see each other while they sit at their computer screens.

A Closer Look — *Evaluating an Educational Website*

With increasing use of the World Wide Web (www), many teachers need to decide which sites are of most value to meet their needs as well as those of their students. Since literally anyone, competent or not, can establish a Website, caution needs to be taken. Web Review is a Web-based resource from Columbia University's Teachers College that provides reviews of educational Web materials. It can be accessed at:

http://webreview.ilt.columbia.edu/web.html

The following checklist was created by Bernard Robin (1997, 6), who teaches instructional technology at the University of Houston.

Checklist for Education Websites

Layout and Design
- Is the site well organized and easy to navigate
- Do all of the hypertext links work?
- Are the graphics informative and not too flashy or overpowering?
- Is additional documentation about the site, or help in using it, available?

Authenticity
- Are the developers of the site identified? Is contact information available for the designer or the development team?
- For a Website developed by an organization, can the potential user tell if it is a university, a government institution, or a commercial business?

- For a Website developed by a commercial institution, is there advertising that overpower or influences the content of the site?
- Does the site contain references with bibliographic information or links to other sources?

Content
- Are the objectives of the site stated clearly and objectively?
- Is the content appropriate for the intended audience?
- How comprehensive is the content? Does it provide a well-rounded view of the topic, or are there "missing pieces"?
- Can the potential user distinguish between fact and opinion in the information that is present?
- If there are media objects on the page, such as audio or video clips, will the content be strongly affected if the site is viewed as text-only?
- Can the site be used to support a constructivist learning style?
- Can the information found on the site be used to supplement other sources of information, such as books, magazines, and videotapes?

Another resource in this area is the Educator's Guide to the Web (1997) by Bernard Robin, Elissa Keeler, and Robert Miller.

Students will be able to collect data on field trips and use laptop computers and cellular telephones to relay the data back to a computer in their classroom or to students in another school in another part of the world.

Funding Technology in the Schools

Obtaining the latest technology is difficult for many school districts, which simply cannot afford them. Affluent school districts, on the other hand, speed along on the information superhighway with all the gadgets and software their teachers and students can use. Indeed, many teacher education programs lack the hardware and software needed to train future teachers for what they will be expected to use as part of the curricula in their own classrooms. Technological advancements are predicted to widen the gap between students in affluent schools and those in poor schools and student achievement.

■ Summary

The future of education begins today. Many current issues must be dealt with by teachers, school administrators, and concerned citizens. The Goals 2000 legislation requires that these individuals examine what students need to know and to what degree. The outcome will affect students well into the twenty-first century.

As national standards are developed and assessed, many states and their respective school districts are giving consideration to the length of the school day and year. By increasing either or both, student learning on the average increases.

Certainly homeschooling has become increasingly popular. Many parents assert that their homeschooled children outperform students in public and private schools on achievement tests. So strong is their voice that the wording of Goals 2000 was changed in Congress so that parents would not have to be certified to teach their children at home.

Like homeschooling, inclusion is another controversial issue. Supporters of inclusion believe that students with physical, mental, or emotional disabilities have the right to be educated in a regular classroom, regardless of the lack of preparation and training the classroom teacher has had in this area and the amount of disruption of learning that occurs for other students in the classroom.

Gender equity in high schools has been talked about for many years. Research has long pointed out that more boys than girls take advanced math and science coursework. Now urban school districts are looking at ways to encourage girls to take math and science as well as to provide positive minority role models for both sexes.

Technological advancements will continue to develop and impact both teaching and learning. The problem will become how can schools afford to purchase the new equipment.

■ Reflections

Think back to when you were in elementary school. Who were the best students in math or science? Were they the same ones in your junior high math and science classes? If you took geometry or calculus in high school, what percent of the class was boys compared with the percentage of girls? Did the teachers do anything to favor one sex of students over the other? Which sex seemed to be called on most? Was it those students who raised their hands?

How would you teach math or science so that girls are encouraged to take additional coursework? Would you have to change your own beliefs or demeanor?

■ Discussion Questions

1. Discuss the pros and cons of Goals 2000.
2. Should parents of homeschooled children be certified teachers?
3. Should there be full inclusion of students with emotional, mental, or physical disabilities within the regular classroom?
4. How can there be equal opportunities for all students in using new technology?

■ For Further Reading

Anderson, J. 1994. Alternative approaches to organizing the school day and year: A national commission examines new structures for improving student learning. *The School Administrator* 3 (51):8–15.

Haberman, M. 1994. Visions of equal educational opportunity: The top 10 fantasies of school reformers. *Phi Delta Kappan* 75 (9):689–92.

Walling, D. R. 1997. *Hot buttons: Unraveling 10 controversial issues in education.* Bloomington, IN: Phi Delta Kappa.

Yaffe, E. 1994. Not just cupcakes anymore: A study of community involvement. *Phi Delta Kappan* 75 (9):697–704.

■ Surfing the 'Net

Elementary and Secondary Schools

Web66.coled.umn.edu/schools.html

This website has links to over six thousand elementary and secondary schools throughout the world.

Alphabet Superhighway
www.ash.udel.edu

The Alphabet Superhighway project, initially funded with a grant from the U.S. Department of Education, offers a variety of sections that are useful to teachers, students, and parents. For example, Kelly McGovern, a doctoral student at the University of Delaware, has a project on the Alphabet Superhighway that describes ways of developing curriculum at the high school level.

For teachers:

- Ask Aristotle: a place to make comments and ask questions about teaching.
- Smart Searcher: a resource for searching the Alphabet Superhighway and the entire World Wide Web.

- Teachers' Lounge: information on using the Alphabet Superhighway and listings of helpful Websites and other teacher resources.

For students:

- Challenge Chaser: an opportunity for students to play word games and enter writing contests.
- Cyberzine: a magazine developed by kids for kids.
- Exhibit Hall: projects by students, organized by category.
- Library: an assortment of references to books, videos, and reference works. In addition, there is a search function and links to numerous Websites.
- Traveling Tutor: tutoring and minilessons on a wide variety of subjects.

For parents:

- Parents' Place: information for parents on using the Alphabet Superhighway, including listings of useful Websites.

4

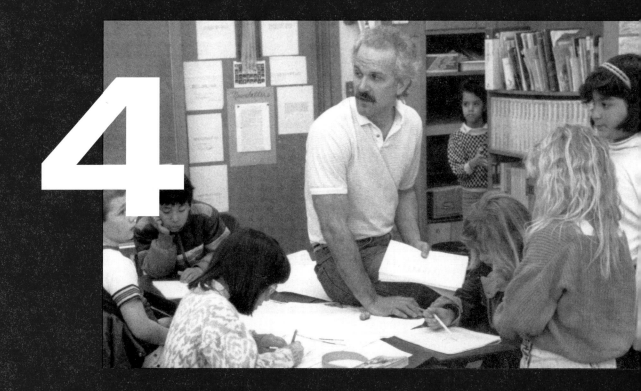

Philosophical Foundations of Education

Primary Points

- The different philosophical stances of education are idealism, realism, existentialism, and pragmatism.

- The different theories of education are experimentalism, progressivism, social reconstructionism, perennialism, and essentialism.

- In education, there exist authoritarian and nonauthoritarian views.

- In recent years, teachers have gained increased power in making educational decisions.

- In recent years, students have more choices in their learning as to how to accomplish it, what resource to use, and the type of final product to be developed.

Chapter Inquiries

- How are the various philosophical stances different?

- Which are the most prominent philosophical stances in education today?

- Why is a philosophical stance needed by teachers?

- What is teacher empowerment?

- Why should students be empowered?

"Until my master's degree work, I really didn't know what my philosophy of education was or even that I had one," Nancy Leifheit, a fifth-grade teacher, said. "Then it all began to fit. I realized I could make choices of what to teach in order to meet the district's goals. I could teach what I knew worked, what I enjoyed teaching, just as long as my students were able to meet the goals."

Nancy discovered that she is a pragmatic teacher, not unlike many others. In her view, "If it works and is effective, then do it. If it doesn't, then try something else."

Teachers learn to be pragmatists or they don't survive. Underneath their veneer of practicality, they are dreamers. Truck drivers and longshoremen might not need a philosophical guiding light from their union leaders, but teachers do. Teachers yearn for commitment, for caring, and for conscience.

**—Susan Ohanian
(Ryan & Cooper 1998)**

In the film *Dead Poets Society*, Robin Williams portrays a teacher at a private all-boys school who embodies the spirit of his educational philosophy. He critically examines, probes, and challenges the pedagogical conformity of teaching put forth by the leaders of the private school where he is employed. The character depicted by Williams stretched his students through his instructional methods rather than demanding simple recall from them. Because his philosophical stance differed from that of the school's leaders, he was dismissed as a teacher.

Developing a philosophy or ideology about teaching requires that we "think most speculatively, reflectively, and systematically about the universe and the human relationship to that universe" (Gutek 1988, 2). Often, a beginning teacher has little time to reflect on and grapple with what is the nature of teaching and what is essential in life itself. Developing a teaching philosophy takes time and much thought before it is truly shaped and established. And every teacher is influenced to some extent by other teachers, both as a student and as a colleague.

A philosophical stance gives a teacher direction in instructional decision making and in interactions with students. For instance, without a philosophy of education, it would be difficult to answer these questions: What should and should not be taught? What does and does not belong in a curriculum? Should students have input into how and what they learn?

One philosopher of education, Van Cleve Morris (1961, 383), wrote: "The most remarkable thing about philosophy is its agonizing unsettledness. What is noteworthy about the questions that philosophy raises is that they never seem to get answered." As teachers, we must continuously examine our own beliefs about teaching, either confirming or rejecting them.

This chapter presents an overview of some of the major philosophical stances in terms of education. These include idealism, realism, existentialism, and pragmatism. In addition, theories of education are examined, including experimentalism, progressivism, social reconstructionism, perennialism, and essentialism. Predominant features of each of these viewpoints are highlighted.

Philosophical Stances

There are four primary philosophical stances that have influenced American education. These are idealism, realism, existentialism, and pragmatism. Each is outlined here.

PEANUTS

"PEANUTS reprinted by permission of United Feature Syndicate, Inc."

Idealism

Many philosophers maintain that **idealism** is the most significant philosophy inasmuch as a great deal of the history of thought can be traced to its origins. Most of the world's religions are based upon idealism. According to Hamm (1974, 211), "Idealism is the forge on which was hammered out the ironwork of every major philosophical position in Western thought today. . . . The idealist would have us look inside to the quality of our lives—the intangibles, the whispers."

Idealism can be described as "idea-ism." Plato opened his Academy, the core of intellectual thought in Greece for over nine hundred years, in 397 B.C. Plato and his followers believed that material things were of little consequence. Some idealists believed that materialistic longings were evil: "The everyday world of things and objects is merely a fleeting, shadowy copy of the true idea which the soul carries within itself from heaven. . . . The highest element of man—reason—is rooted in a spiritual soul" (Hamm 1974, 212).

Several significant philosophers were idealists: Plato, René Descartes, Immanuel Kant, Baruch Spinoza, Gottfried Wilhelm von Leibniz, Georg Wilhelm Fredrich Hegel, and Arthur Schopenhauer. Hegel believed that education was a rigorous process, without which freedom could not be obtained. Kant, another idealist, encouraged democratic tendencies by pointing out that humankind has limitless possibilities for creative growth, both in one's intellectual and personal life (Mayer 1960). They tended to be conservative in their religious and social views. Friedrich Froebel, the father of kindergarten, followed the idealistic philosophy, but unlike other idealists he was very liberal in his thinking.

In today's classrooms, idealism still exerts an influence. Students are encouraged by teachers to stretch themselves through higher-level thinking to become truth seekers. The school curriculum should present the cultural heritage and wisdom so that students can become knowledgeable about it, participate in sharing it, and elaborate and extend it through their own contributions. As Hamm (1974, 250) points out, for the idealist teacher, "Each pupil makes a difference, he counts for something. The teacher will devote considerable time and energy to the one who goes astray."

The truly idealistic teacher should have no discipline problems because he or she knows the content well, likes to teach, and knows the students. If a student's conduct does become a problem, the teacher handles it without taking the child to the principal's office. Usually the teacher would discuss the problem with the child, perhaps even asking the pupil, "What would happen if everyone acted this way?"

The idealistic philosophy views the school as representing the community, with teachers serving as models in the classroom, in the community, and at all times. Sports are important because they provide an opportunity to demonstrate school

Advances in technology have been welcomed by realists as more work can be accomplished in less time. Here a child designs a bicycle in a few minutes, something that would have taken hours without computer-assisted design.
(© Chad Slattery/Tony Stone)

spirit, good conduct, high moral standards, and fair play. (However, failure to have winning seasons can cost a coach a job.)

Realism

Realism, like idealism, is one of the oldest philosophical stances in the world. Realists believe that objects exist regardless of how we perceive them. Realism focuses on the scientific method and personal experience. The crux of realism is science—empirical, objective, and experimental—with its precise measurements. In short, realists take a straightforward, commonsense approach to discovering the truth. Rules and regulations are essential if a society is to survive.

Among the most noted realists are Aristotle, John Amos Comenius, Johann Heinrich Pestalozzi, Johann Friedrich Herbart, Maria Montessori, Thomas Hobbes, Sir Francis Bacon, and John Locke. Thomas Jefferson embraced realism, as can be seen in his words in the Declaration of Independence: "We hold these truths to be self-evident, that all men are created equal, that they are endowed by their Creator with certain unalienable Rights, that among these are Life, Liberty, and the pursuit of Happiness." Like Jefferson, Horace Mann believed in realism. Mann wrote in his tenth annual report in 1846 that education was an absolute right of every human being and it was the duty of every government to see that education is provided for all (Cremin 1957).

Realism still influences education in many ways. The emphasis by most state legislatures on accountability in the schools is an outgrowth of realism. This has led to state-mandated testing programs at specific grade levels. In the classroom, the study of authors of realistic literature and their works still continues—Harriet Beecher Stowe's *Uncle Tom's Cabin* (1965), Charles Dickens's *Oliver Twist* (1840), John Steinbeck's *The Grapes of Wrath* (1978), Ernest Hemingway's *For Whom the Bell Tolls* (1940), and Katherine Paterson's *The Great Gilly Hopkins* (1978). Precision is encouraged in math and science. At the high school level, the various disciplines such as art, biology, chemistry, geography, history, and mathematics, to name a few, are considered to consist of "clusters of related concepts and of generalizations that interpret and explain interactions between the objects which these concepts represent. Each discipline as a conceptual system has a structure. Structure refers to a framework of related conceptual meanings and their generalizations that explain physical, natural, social, and human realities. For instance, biology consists of a number of necessary concepts that are appropriate to the study of plants and animals" (Gutek 1988, 47). Certainly the influx of technology in teaching—televisions and video cassette recorders, word processors, laser discs, and hypermedia—reflects the realist philosophical view.

Existential teachers allow students to have a great deal of freedom in the classroom. (© David Young-Wolff/PhotoEdit)

Existentialism

Existentialism is the most difficult philosophical stance to define for several reasons. First, existentialism focuses on the individual; second, there exists no agreement as to what constitutes an existential thinker; third, not only philosophers but poets, playrights, and novelists have equally influenced existential thought; fourth, it is not a logical theory but one that can be "felt" as an attitude or mood; fifth, ordinary words such as awareness, anxiety, and choice take on new meanings in existentialism; and finally, the primary focus of existentialism is its revolt against the traditional philosophical stance (Hamm 1974).

In existentialism there are no set tenets or no set systematic thought. Carl Michalson distinguished existentialism from other philosophies as being "a way of life which involves one's total self in an attitude of complete seriousness about himself" (Hamm 1974, 79). If a person makes an existential choice, it can be said that, as an individual:

1. I make the choice. Even no choice is a choice.
2. I must consider the alternatives.
3. I must be aware of what the alternatives can do or lead to because I am responsible for the choice I make.
4. I must make the choice as if it is for all humankind.

Three noted existential philosophers were Søren Kierkegaard, a Danish founder of existential thought, Jean-Paul Sartre, and Friedrich Nietzsche. Kierkegaard advocated "themes of passionate choice, absolute freedom, and total responsibility"

(Gutek 1988, 114). Kierkegaard wrote in the first volume of his *Journals and Papers* in 1843 that life must be understood backward but must be lived forward (Bartlett and Kaplan 1992).

Existentialism occasionally turns up in education. The theory focuses on value questions, so it is not by coincidence that the open school and the whole language approach movement had glimpses of existentialism in them. However, once an idea, such as an open concept classroom or "empowering" students by letting them choose what they will learn and how they will learn it, has been adopted and formalized by organizing and specifying it, then the idea is no longer an existential thought. In existentialism it is impossible to classify or categorize others or things. Green (1967, 8) wrote in *Existential Encounters for Teachers* that "no external categorization, naming, or definition can touch that crucial awareness; each man relates himself to the world around from a perspective that is within."

Morris (1970, 311) writes that concerning education and schooling, existentialists are interested in "developing the affective side of man, his capacity to love, to appreciate, to respond emotionally to the world about him." Existentialists are not concerned with elementary education; rather, it is at the secondary level that they believe education should begin focusing. At this point, the humanities (art, music, and drama) instead of the sciences should be emphasized (Morris 1961).

The existential teacher is a free spirit who has no limitations in terms of dress and personal lifestyle. This teacher does as he or she chooses, in short, daring to be different at all times.

In today's classrooms, students are exposed to existentialism in many of the works they read; for instance, Henry David Thoreau's Walden in *A Week on the Concord and Merrimack Rivers* (1968) or his poetry. Thoreau (Torrey 1968, 314) wrote, "Let me forever go in search of myself; never for a moment think I have found myself; be as a stranger to myself, never a familiar seeking acquaintance still."

A more contemporary existentialist is the character of Robert Kincaid, a photographer who views himself as the "last cowboy," in the Waller novel *The Bridges of Madison County* (1992). The main character, Kincaid, does not care what the members of a small, midwestern, rural community think about him, his dress, the length of his hair, his job as a freelance photographer, or even his affair with a local farmer's wife.

Pragmatism

The pragmatic philosophic theory ventures forth with questions about truth. It also deals with both process and product. According to Gutek (1988), **pragmatism** evolved as a philosophical expression of the westward movement in America, caused in part by the encounters of pioneers with their new environment. When western expansion slowed, it was followed by scientific and technological advances, a new frontier of sorts. Charles Peirce, an American mathematician, scientist, and philosopher, was a promoter of pragmatism in the late 1800s and early 1900s. The philosopher William James based much of his work on Peirce's. John Dewey was a pragmatist who later began the experimental and progressive education movements. The social reconstructionist theory had its roots in pragmatism, as did the progressive education movement.

Pragmatism still pervades the classroom setting as the most popular philosophy of education in the United States today. The scientific method is still widely used in not only science courses but in other classes as well. The use of books such as Gary Paulsen's *Hatchet* (1987) or Lois Duncan's *Who Killed My Daughter* (1992) at the middle school level to teach reading as well as geography and sociology through an integrated approach stems from the pragmatic philosophy. Teaching students survey techniques and about the use of equipment to measure the perimeter of a new neighborhood playground for children or a new parking lot for students also would fit this philosophy of education.

Figure 1 summarizes the basic philosophies of education and their classroom applications.

Theories of Education

The various philosophies led to the development of theories of education. These theories include experimentalism, progressivism, social reconstructionism, perennialism, and essentialism, which are discussed in the following sections.

Experimentalism

From pragmatic theory came the educational theories of experimentalism and progressivism. Through John Dewey's emphasis on the testing of ideas through experimentation came the term **experimentalism.** Later, in the late 1910s, a group of educators, many of whom were experimentalists, developed the *progressive education* theory. Practitioner of progressivism resent authoritarian figures and promote firsthand experiences rather than reading books as a means of gaining knowledge and information. Curricula emphasizes experience and child-centered activities, in which the process of learning is stressed over any final product. For instance, in a social studies class a child may draw a map of a community by using graph paper and a map scale of two inches equaling one city block. Going through the process of scaling down the community to fit on an 8 1/2-by-11-inch sheet of paper helps develop the student's mapping and mathematics conceptualization. This process leads to a more important learning development for the child than the final product of a beautiful community map.

George Herbert Meade, a pragmatist who followed William James, was a close friend and colleague of John Dewey, the most widely known pragmatist. They were neighbors in Ann Arbor, Michigan, and both left the University of Michigan to go to the University of Chicago. Meade (1964) developed nine primary points about education.

1. Science courses need to play an important role in the school.
2. Compartmentalization of curricular offerings is not desirable because the relationship of things to each other helps children to more readily assimilate the information and concepts presented.
3. Play has an essential role in teaching and learning, as it requires both competition and cooperation.
4. The subject matter taught should relate to students' problems and experiences, thus making it relevant to them.
5. Education is a dialogue, that is, a conversation between child and teacher, between child and child.
6. The classroom teacher is the most significant factor in instruction. The teacher's personality and relationship with the students plays an important role in the children's learning.
7. Broad fields of learning should be emphasized over narrow boundaries of learning

Figure 1
Philosophies of
education and
their classroom
applications

Idealism

The teacher	Knows the content area that he or she teaches very well. Enjoys teaching and serving as a model for students. Believes each student has value and can make a valuable contribution to society.
Teaching strategies	Encourage students to challenge themselves as learners. Encourage students to "seek the truth."
The student	Is in school to seek the truth.
The curriculum	Is based on cultural heritage and wisdom.
Classroom management	Few discipline problems as teacher's love of subject matter is transferred to students. Any problems with student behavior are handled by the teacher who discusses them with the students involved.

Realism

The teacher	Relies on test scores to place students. Readily adopts new technology.
Teaching strategies	Emphasize realistic novels such as *The Color Purple*; *The Great Gilly Hopkins*. Stress precision and accuracy in math, science, social studies, and writing.
The student	Is expected to focus on accuracy.
The curriculum	Emphasizes accountability. Stresses concept acquisition.
Classroom management	Classroom rules and resultant punishments are established at the beginning of the school year and posted in the classroom. Violators are punished according to the criteria established.

Existentialism

The teacher	Emphasizes individual choice.
Teaching strategies	Stress individual freedom; empowerment of students to make choices about what and how they will learn.
The student	Is an individual who gains meaning from within.
The curriculum	Stresses the arts and literature. Has little emphasis on math and science.
Classroom management	Emphasis on freedom to do as student pleases in the classroom.

Pragmatism

The teacher	Applies democratic methods. Classroom is a community of learners.
Teaching strategies	Encourage problem solving. Apply democratic procedures.
The student	Learns by engaging in activities first-hand.
The curriculum	Emphasizes concrete experiences. Emphasizes the three Rs in elementary school.
Classroom management	Classroom rules are established by the class in a democratic fashion.

John Dewey

John Dewey was born in 1859 in Burlington, Vermont. His family was quite active in the local society and politics, largely of a democratic nature, which probably influenced his later work. Dewey attended public schools as a child. He did his undergraduate work at the University of Vermont and taught in schools in Pennsylvania and rural Vermont. Dewey envisioned himself as a philosopher, and he studied at Johns Hopkins University, a university built on the German scientific model rather than the idealist theories he held at the time. Dewey studied the work of pragmatist philosopher William James at Johns Hopkins University.

Dewey believed that education and philosophy were inseparable; that they were one and the same since both sought to experiment with ideas to improve the human condition. He also wrote in the field of child psychology.

As a trained philosopher, Dewey taught at the University of Michigan. He left that position in 1894 to work at the University of Chicago, where he chaired the Department of Philosophy, Psychology, and Education, three disciplines in which Dewey was well read and a contributor of writings.

At the University of Chicago, Dewey founded the laboratory school and worked closely with Francis Parker, whom Dewey considered to be the founder of the progressive education movement and who was principal of the laboratory school. George Herbert Meade, who had followed Dewey from the University of Michigan to the University of Chicago, was yet another colleague who shared common beliefs with Dewey. Both Meade and Dewey believed that for a democracy to work, its citizens had to be educated to understand and share in the duties and responsibilities of maintaining it. They also believed that morality had to be applied to daily living in terms of personal, political, social, and educational behavior (Crunden 1984). Deeply concerned about the effects of industrialism on society and democratic

John Dewey was the most influential educator during the 1900s. (Bettmann)

ideals, Dewey wrote that schools had to assume a larger social function (Dewey 1899).

Meade's notions that preschoolers needed play and that it was a natural way to learn were congenial to Dewey's ideas. It was Meade who persuaded Dewey to have education students experiment in classrooms of children. Dewey, a proponent of experimentalism, readily adopted Meade's ideas.

Dewey emphasized child-centered education, that is, learning by doing. He wrote, "It is a cardinal precept of the newer school of education that the beginning of instruction shall be made with the experience learners already have; that this experience and the capacities that have been developed during its course provide the starting point for all further learning" (Ratner 1939, 674–75).

(continued)

Believing that the world is everchanging, Dewey suggested, as did other pragmatists, that an answer to an educational problem depends on the situation in which it is viewed. As Dewey (Ratner 1939, 414) asserted, "Since we live in a moving world and change with our interactions in it, every act produces a new perspective that demands a new exercise of preference."

The curriculum of his laboratory school was far more practical than others of its day. Children between the ages of four and fourteen were engaged in activities that involved play, construction, nature study, and self-expression (Gutek 1988). Dewey (1916) argued that children must be taught how to use their knowledge as responsible, productive citizens. He felt that the classroom was to be a community of learners, producing good citizens rather than educated individuals.

Leaving the University of Chicago in 1914, Dewey went to Columbia University's Teachers College in New York City. There he continued to lecture and write on his educational theories. He died in 1952.

While many teachers are quite familiar with Dewey's work in education, his energies did not stop there. Dewey was considered to be a radical by some of his contemporaries as he strongly advocated welfare programs to assist the poor. Very much the social activist and lib-eral thinker, while at the University of Chicago Dewey worked closely with Jane Addams and her Hull House project. He also helped to found the National Association for the Advancement of Colored People (NAACP). A compatriot of Susan B. Anthony, he was one of the most prominent men to march for the right for women to vote. Dewey also was the first member of the American Federation of Teachers. He was a laureate of Kappa Delta Pi, an educational honorary.

Dewey's contributions to American education are significant, perhaps more than any other individual except Horace Mann. Mayer (1960, 363) writes: "Undoubtedly, Dewey has often been misinterpreted. He has been cited as the champion of vocationalism, of extreme permissiveness in the classroom, and as the enemy of the classics. His aim was, in reality, to make education more dynamic and democratic so that a truly liberal society would triumph. Pragmatism is a philosophy of experimentalism; the curriculum is to be plastic; it is to be cooperatively planned; it is to emphasize the interests and ideals of the children."

A prolific writer, Dewey produced over one thousand articles and books. He traveled and lectured not only in the United States but also in Europe and Asia. Dewey's work was very influential in the late 1800s to the middle 1900s. Even today, his work is still read and followed.

8. "The whole is more concrete than the part." Subject matter should be presented so that students can look for interrelationships, connections, and patterns.

9. The research method cannot only be used in science courses, but it can be effective in other classes as well.

According to Gordon (1998, 393), "authentic learning is a laudable goal that should be promoted and pursued vigorously. Students not only *should* see their work in school related to the real world but *must* see it that way, if they are to be able to apply their learning in real-life contexts." Teaching real world experiences is a "sophisticated process that demands refined skills and a tolerance for ambiguity and complexity. While only some teachers and students have an innate capacity for such undertakings, almost all teachers and students can develop such capacity."

Progressivism

Progressivism began as a rebellion against the formalism of traditional education, which these philosophers believed restricted the child from learning. Created in America during the late 1910s, a period of social reform, progressivism was based on the belief that all people are benevolent and that by using human intellect in combination

Progressivism encouraged hands-on activities for students. (© Jean-Claude Lejeune)

with the scientific method, the world would be improved. Followers looked to Jean-Jacques Rousseau, author of *Emile*, who believed in natural education without coercion, and Rousseau's devotee, Johann Heinrich Pestalozzi, who believed that education should engage the entire child—body, emotions, and intellect.

Some early progressive educators followed John Dewey's pragmatism, which considered schooling to be a way to reform society and its institutions. However, other progressive educators were not persuaded by Dewey and his experimentalist view of progressivism.

William Heard Kilpatrick, a follower of Dewey, proved to be a great interpreter of Dewey's work. In addition, Kilpatrick advanced his own beliefs. In his own high school classroom and at Columbia University's Teachers College, Kilpatrick advanced the ideals of cooperative learning, intrinsic rewards rather than the extrinsic rewards of report cards, and liberal classroom discipline. For instance, students were encouraged to work together in small groups on reports and projects and to celebrate each other's triumphs and achievements. Each student was urged to consider each project from the standpoint of how well he or she had done to complete it, including the amount of effort put into it, rather than seeking a letter grade of A or B. Classroom rules were minimal. Students were permitted to roam about and talk with one another regarding their work.

Kilpatrick synthesized Dewey's experimentalism with progressivism and developed the "project method" of teaching. Described as the "purposeful act," Kilpatrick advocated that students be permitted to select, plan, direct, and carry out their work to completion in projects. He suggested four different types of projects:

1. the *creative project*, in which the students designed and implemented a theoretical plan such as writing and acting out a play;

2. the *enjoyment project*, in which aesthetic experiences would be cultivated;

3. the *problem project*, in which an intellectual problem such as universal health care or gender discrimination would be resolved;

4. the *specific learning project*, which would involve the acquisition of knowledge or a skill such as learning to swim or play golf (Gutek 1988).

Kilpatrick was considered a talented lecturer who captivated his audience. His lectures drew large numbers of students to his classes and readers to his writings. Dewey's lectures, on the other hand, were considered to be glimpses into his own thoughts; he would often stare out the window, seemingly ignoring the class completely as he appeared to be talking to himself. At the end of the class period, Dewey would turn to the class and thank the students before leaving the room.

The progressive teacher is sensitive to the child's needs and interests and more concerned with these factors than with academic subject matter. The progressive classroom gives students freedom to make choices and to explore on their own. Teachers must be adroit in following the leads of the students. In a high school math class, for instance, a student may want to calculate how much faster his pickup truck is traveling than the speedometer indicates if he puts oversized rather than standard sized tires on it.

Social Reconstructionism

While some progressive educators believed the child's individuality should be respected, other progressive educators viewed things quite differently. They felt that progressive education should create a new society, using Dewey's example of creating new experiences. Hence, they are referred to as social reconstructionists.

Social reconstructionism, a liberal philosophy, had its roots in progressivism. Two of the premises of social reconstructionism are that culture is always changing and that human beings are capable of resculpting culture so that human growth and development are promoted (Brameld 1956). Its proponents believe that if schools reflect the predominant social values, then the worst part of the problems and ills of society are transmitted to children. The end result is the destruction of society itself. The solution, according to the social reconstructionists, is to have students study their own culture, finding the major causes of problems (e.g., poverty or war) and resolving them. George Counts, in *Dare the School Build a New Social Order?* (1932), put forth the idea that technology advancements occurred at a rate beyond what society and culture were prepared to adjust to and accept.

Social reconstructionists view education from a global standpoint. They suggest that without a global interpretation, the world itself will be destroyed.

Social reconstructionist teachers utilize problem solving and divergent thinking in their classes. Remedies for solutions to social problems such as ecological damage to the environment or health care for the elderly are probed. Developing within their students a sense of caring for others and a need to plan for the future are emphasized. Above all, democratic procedures are encouraged and stressed.

Perennialism

An educational theory that bases much of its principles on the philosophy of realism is **perennialism.** This is a traditional and conservative view, and its followers consider school to be an institution designed solely to develop students' intellects. Perennialists generally follow the beliefs of Aristotle.

There are general principles of perennialism, put forth by Robert Maynard Hutchins, president of the University of Chicago. Hutchins believes that human nature is rational and constant; that is, that humans can be predicted to do things in certain ways. Therefore, education should be universal. In addition, Hutchins (1968) believes that knowledge occupies unchanging, absolute, and universal truths. A good education is based on searching for the truth, which can be found in the great works of civilization.

Perennialists view the "humanities as works that provide insights into the good, true, and beautiful" (Gutek 1988, 272). Insights in art, history, literature, mathematics, and science can be passed from one generation to the next. And it is through the study of the classics of Western culture, which have endured the passage of time, that truth can be found.

The perennial view of philosophy resulted in a program known as the Great Books. Created by Hutchins and Mortimer Adler, a professor at the University of Chicago, the Great Books consist of works considered to be classics, that is, timeless pieces to be valued throughout the history of humankind. "The great books, read and discussed with an eye out for the basic truths and the equally based errors or mistakes to be found in them, should be a part of everyone's general, liberal, and humanistic education" (Adler 1988). Great Books for elementary children include Verna Aardema's *Who's In Rabbit's House?* (1977), Lloyd Alexander's *The Book of Three*

(1964), Pearl S. Buck's *The Big Wave* (1948), Astrid Lindgren's *Pippi Longstocking* (1950), Wilson Rawls' *Where the Red Fern Grows* (1961) and *Summer of the Monkeys* (1976), and Mildred Taylor's *Roll of Thunder, Hear My Cry* (1976). Sophocles's *Oedipus the King* (1978), Rachel Carson's *Silent Spring* (1962), Robert Penn Warren's *All the King's Men* (1982), Mark Twain's (Samuel Clemens') *Huckleberry Finn* (1985), Daniel Defoe's *Robinson Crusoe* (1966), and George Eliot's *Silas Marner* (1861) are among the books suggested for high school age students (Adler 1984).

Precision is important in perennialism. Cowan and Puck (1984, 96) write that "the romance and excitement evoked by learning to deal with the universe in *quantitative* terms, rather than by means of qualitative verbal description should be frequently emphasized. One of the great intellectual accomplishments of a civilized person is the ability to compare two quantities to a precision of four or five significant figures. It sets such a person apart from every other living organism."

This statement holds true for language, which is viewed as an "instrument for shaping, ordering, evaluating, and appreciating our thoughts and feelings. Language can organize them, clarify them, connect one with another, disjoin and reconnect them. Language does all this well or badly, depending on one's command of it" (Van Doren 1984, 61).

The perennialist teacher must be a reader and a writer and encourage students to improve both of these skills. The goals of learning are the acquisition of organized knowledge, the development of intellectual skills, and an enlarged understanding of ideas and values. Three primary approaches to learning are stressed: didactic teaching of concepts, for instance, the operations and uses of mathematics; coaching of skills; and seminars in which various topics are discussed in depth through the Socratic method (Adler 1984).

Essentialism

Essentialism is a very traditional and conservative view of education that is in direct opposition to progressive education. It tends to exhibit some of the elements of idealism and realism. For instance, essentialists consider the primary focus of education to be to teach elementary children to read, write, and perform math computations and then to build on those skills at the secondary school level and emphasize higher thinking skills. A strong liberal arts education is encouraged. Essentialists oppose new educational fads that fail to emphasize the academic function of schools. In addition, proponents of this view believe the classroom teacher should be well trained in his or her discipline.

Calvin and Hobbes   by Bill Watterson

CALVIN AND HOBBES copyright 1989 Watterson./Dist. by UNIVERSAL PRESS SYNDICATE. Reprinted with permission. All rights reserved.

The essentialist movement seems to come and go in twenty-year cycles—it was quite popular in the 1930s, 1950s, 1970s, and 1990s. In the 1930s, William Chandler Bagley, a professor of education at Columbia University's Teachers College, stated that American elementary and secondary students did not meet the same standards as their foreign counterparts and that increasingly large numbers of high school students were illiterate. Bagley (1938) pointed out that American students performed poorly in math and science. He also lashed out at social promotions for students, which had become widespread (Gutek 1988). Regardless of how well the student performed academically, social promotion allowed him or her to move on to the next grade level along with peers.

In the 1950s, the essentialism movement was led by three individuals, Max Rafferty, the state school superintendent of California and author of *Suffer Little Children* (1962), Admiral Hyman Rickover, noted for his work on developing the first atomic submarine, and Arthur Bestor, a history professor at the University of Illinois. Bestor's books, *Educational Wastelands* (1953) and *The Restoration of Learning* (1956), made a major impact in the United States. He helped to form the Council for Basic Education. Bestor (1956, 7) believed that students should be trained "in history, science, mathematics, literature, language, art, and other disciplines" in order to acquire "usable knowledge, cultural understanding, and intellectual power."

The essentialist movement resurfaced in the 1970s as the **back-to-basics** movement. As a result, many states, particularly in the South and Midwest, mandated competency testing of students at specific grade levels as determined by each state. Initially, most of the states that required competency limited the testing to reading and math. In more recent years, writing, science, and social studies have been added.

A Nation at Risk (National Commission on Excellence in Education 1983), one of many documents that came out during the education reform movement, supported many essentialist ideas, in particular more rigorous academic standards. As a result, high schools and colleges increased their liberal arts course requirements for graduation.

The current essentialist movement remains quite vigorous. The push toward national standards for teachers and students is strongly supported by essentialists. They argue that the United States is lagging behind other industrialized nations because of a lack of standards in the schools.

Figure 2 summarizes the theories of education and their classroom applications.

Philosophical Terms

The word **philosophy** is made up of two words, "love" (*philo*) and "wisdom" (*sophos*), or the "love of wisdom." Thus, it is easy to understand why philosophers have devoted much of their study and writings to education.

Because philosophy is a field of study, it is complete with its own vocabulary. In discussing various educational philosophies, four terms are commonly used: metaphysics, epistemology, axiology, and logic.

Metaphysics is the study of the nature of reality, or what is real. In short, philosophers try to draw back the curtain of the nonessentials of life to examine what remains.

Philosophers view metaphysics or reality in a variety of ways. An idealist sees reality in nonmaterial, spiritual terms. However, a realist considers reality as being an objective order, completely independent of humankind. A perennialist views reality as being constant and unchanging, and the meaning of life is considered in the context of the collective wisdom of humankind. An existentialist considers reality in

Figure 2
Theories of
education and
their classroom
applications

Experimentalism

The teacher	Encourages students to test ideas. Develops rapport with students. Encourages play for both cooperation and competition.
Teaching strategies	Use hands-on activities. Emphasis on problem solving. Integrated instruction.
The student	Is encouraged to question ideas.
The curriculum	Stresses science. Emphasizes interrelatedness.
Classroom management	Dialogue is encouraged between student and teacher regarding student behavior.

Progressivism

The teacher	Assists rather than guides learning. Emphasizes intrinsic rather than extrinsic rewards. Is more sensitive to student needs than academic subject matter. Follows lead of students as to what should be taught.
Teaching strategies	Incorporate projects planned, developed, and carried out by students. Aesthetics of learning are stressed. Cooperative learning.
The student	Is self-directed in learning.
The curriculum	Stresses skills attainment. Emphasizes the arts and the aesthetics of learning.
Classroom management	Liberal classroom discipline with students given lots of freedom.

Social Reconstructionism

The teacher	Is a liberal thinker. Challenges the established rules of the school district.
Teaching strategies	Encourage students to address and attempt to solve social problems. Stress experimentation and problem solving.
The student	Needs to study his or her own culture. Is encouraged to be a divergent thinker.
The curriculum	Is heavily multicultural. Emphasizes social issues.
Classroom management	Liberal classroom discipline.

Figure 2
(continued)

Perennialism

The teacher	Emphasizes searching for the truth and rationalization. Stresses the good, true, and beautiful. Is an avid reader and writer.
Teaching strategies	Stress the great works of literature, mathematics, art, music, etc. Didactic learning of concepts. Coaching of skills. Small group discussion using Socratic method.
The student	Is encouraged to organize, clarify, and connect thoughts to make accurate quantitative comparisons.
The curriculum	Focuses on the classics in literature. Emphasis on concept acquisition in math, science, and social studies.
Classroom management	Students are expected to behave in a rational behavior.

Essentialism

The teacher	Teaches students basic skills and knowledge. Strives to develop students' higher thinking skills. Each subject is taught separately. No social promotions to higher grade level. Competency testing.
Teaching strategies	Incorporate paper and pencil activities. Emphasize reading the classics and skill and drill work in math and other subject areas.
The student	Is encouraged to set high personal goals.
The curriculum	Stresses reading, writing, mathematics, science, and social sciences.
Classroom management	Time on task is emphasized. Students are expected to follow directions and behave appropriately.

Chapter 4 *Philosophical Foundations of Education*

Scientific and technological breakthroughs enable today's students to develop their logical thinking skills. (© Tony Freeman/PhotoEdit)

terms of its relationship to oneself. A pragmatist perceives reality as the result of human experiences, both in the physical and social environments. A progressivist considers reality in terms of being sensitive to the needs of others. On the other hand, an experimentalist sees reality in terms of firsthand experiences that call for the individual to engage in research. To a social reconstructionist, reality means discovering what is wrong in life and attempting to rectify it. An essentialist views reality as being constant and orderly.

Thus, the school curriculum, as developed by teachers, school administrators, and other educators, and influenced by textbook authors, is an attempt to describe some of the aspects of reality—geography, history, math, religion, etc.—to students.

Epistemology is the theory of knowing and of knowledge. It deals with the nature of learning itself. As such, it is significant for teachers because it is closely affiliated with teaching methods and how students learn.

Like metaphysics, the different philosophical stances view epistemology in different ways. Idealists regard knowing, or the cognitive process, as the recollection of ideas that are latently present in the mind. Therefore, an idealist teacher might rely on the Socratic method of asking leading questions to get students to bring forth latent ideas to consciousness. On the other hand, realists believe that knowledge begins in the sensations we get from objects in the environment, such as viewing a beautiful work of art or reading a poignant piece of prose. By making abstractions based on sensory information, concepts are developed that correspond with the objects. This is referred to as the sensory-abstraction formula (Gutek 1988). A realist teacher might use classroom demonstrations and modeling as primary teaching methods. A perennialist views knowledge as something to be handed down from generation to generation with each generation contributing to the knowledge base. A perennialist teacher would emphasize the reading of the "classics" of literature—those written by Dante, William Shakespeare, Sir Walter Raleigh, and Emily Dickinson as well as modern classics by Emily Wharton and Sinclair Lewis and the more recent classics by Toni Morrison and Alice Walker. An existentialist believes that

Should Teachers In a School Share a Common Educational Philosophy?

Point: Faculty members in a school should all have the same philosophy of education.

If all teachers in a school share the same philosophy, a student understands teacher expectations and teaching approaches because they are shared by the entire staff. As a result, a student is more at ease in the learning environment.

When teachers share a common educational philosophy, they are more willing to share and discuss ideas with their colleagues. This enhances learning.

Parents and the community also gain a greater sense of what is taught and how teachers work. This reduces outside pressures on both teachers and students.

Counterpoint: Faculty members in a school should represent a variety of philosophies of education.

Students differ greatly and should be exposed to teachers with different philosophies. For instance, a school with only perennialists would focus on precision and measurement, thereby emphasizing mathematics and the sciences. A student who might be more artistic in nature would encounter problems in such a school setting. A school filled with idealists would stress the classics in literature, art, and music, thereby limiting a student who is more mathematically or scientifically oriented.

By being exposed to teachers with different philosophical beliefs, students are better able to develop their own philosophical stances. Only one philosophical stance in a school would tend to bias students toward that stance and against other philosophies.

Diverse philosophical stances better help students adjust to the real world. In actuality, the population of a typical neighborhood or community represents different philosophies.

each individual is free to make his or her own meaning. A teacher who follows the existentialist philosophy would focus on individual or group activities that students themselves select as being relevant for them.

The pragmatist considers knowledge as being created by acting and interacting with the environment through a series of problem-solving incidents. A teacher with a pragmatic view would have students engage in a series of problem-solving events until the teaching objective or goal is achieved. A progressivist believes that knowledge is gained by using our intellect in learning how to learn and becoming lifelong learners. The progressivist teacher would challenge students to use their intellect and, in particular, apply the scientific method to problems. An experimentalist believes that knowledge comes from firsthand experiences and discoveries. An experimentalist teacher would engage students with hands-on activities. A social reconstructionist considers knowledge to be constantly changing since society is everchanging. A social reconstructionist teacher would expect students to consider knowledge in terms of how it can be used for the betterment of humankind.

An essentialist teacher values knowledge, particularly within his or her own subject area. Such a teacher would encourage students to develop their knowledge in the academics and use their higher-level thinking skills.

Axiology is concerned with value, and as such it is divided into two areas, **ethics** and **aesthetics.** Ethics deals with moral values and appropriate conduct; aesthetics considers values in beauty and art. Educators have always addressed the need for students to engage in proper conduct and ethics. Indeed, in colonial schools in the 1600s and 1700s, a primary focus was for children to learn right from wrong, good from bad. Generally speaking, aesthetics has received limited attention in American education. Aesthetics is the development and cultivation of taste and appreciation for that which is beautiful. Discussions of the artistic merit of a best-selling novel, play, film, or piece of art are a part of the aesthetic realm.

In terms of axiology, an idealist as well as a realist contends that the *objective* value theory is of most importance. That is, that the good, true, and beautiful are rooted in the universe and are valid anywhere and any time. A perennialist and an essentialist believe that values are essentially changeless and are determined by a culture. An existentialist believes that values are determined by the individual. A pragmatist asserts that the *subjective* value theory is the primary concern. That is, that values are personal or group choices that change with the situation, place, and time and thus are not universally valid. A progressivist, like the experimentalist and social reconstructionist, considers values to be individually determined as we interact with our culture.

Logic addresses the rules of correct and valid thinking and considers the rules of inference that we use to frame propositions and arguments. *Deductive logic* is reasoning that moves from general statements to particular instances and applications. The most frequently used method is that of syllogism. Two statements are made followed by a concluding statement, which is deduced from the first two statements. For instance, the teacher might say:

1. All men are mortal.
2. Tom is a man.
3. (Conclusion) Therefore, Tom is mortal.

Deductive logic is most frequently associated with idealism and realism.

Inductive logic is reasoning that moves from particular instances and applications to generalizations, the reverse order of deductive logic. For instance, particulars are given and then a general proposition is derived. A teacher may decide to use inductive reasoning to teach students the need for exercising. After giving students the general proposition that exercise is needed to prevent obesity, he or she may divide them into pairs, giving each pair two guinea pigs of equal size. The students must weigh their guinea pigs at the beginning of the project and once a week thereafter. Each day, the students feed the two animals the same amount of food and water, but they exercise only one of the guinea pigs. The students conclude that the heaviest guinea pig is the one that didn't exercise.

Perennialists and essentialists believe logic develops as reasoning, which can be acquired as a result of reading the classics. On the other hand, existentialists believe that logic comes from within oneself. Pragmatists, progressivists, experimentalists, and social reconstructionists rely upon inductive logic.

When you think about teaching, the terms *metaphysics, epistemology, axiology,* and *logic* may seem foreign and far removed from the classroom environment. However, in instructional practices, each of these terms is incorporated into daily

Discovering one's philosophy of education is not something that occurs overnight. In fact, many first year teachers may not identify with any one philosophical stance. Their primary thoughts are of staying ahead of the students.

Most teacher education programs emphasize the progressive education focus which recognizes the developmental needs of children and adolescents and the need for relevance to be a part of the learning process. However, this philosophical view is being faulted by some individuals outside of the field of education as many students fail to meet basic academic standards. And yet the theory is still sound.

I struggled for some time in my attempt to identify my own philosophical view. In many ways I felt that I was a realist in that I wanted a right answer. Then in other ways I was idealistic, like most young teachers just entering the profession. But it was the diversity of my student clientele that finally caused me to distinguish my true philosophy. Trying to meet the needs of mentally challenged students as well as gifted students and not overlook the "average" students and trying to help my students respect the various cultures respresented in our class all led me to be a pragmatist.

classroom activities. Teachers introduce students to what is real by looking through a microscope at a tiny organism or a fleck of precious metal in the study of the biological and physical sciences. Studying the social sciences brings awareness of economic, political, and sociological realities. Appreciating a piece of artwork on a laser disc from the Metropolitan Museum of Art brings to the forefront aesthetics and its concern for beauty. Even a high school football coach relies on logic to create and explain to his team successful plays against an opponent.

■ Summary

Philosophies of education vary greatly and to a large degree impact teaching methodologies. Which philosophy a teacher adopts influences his or her thinking and actions.

Philosophies such as idealism and realism have been around for centuries. Most of the religions of the world have their roots in idealism, or "idea-ism." Realism, on the other hand, deals with the individual's own experiences and the scientific method. Precise measurement is the crux of realism.

Perennialism is an educational theory based on realism. The behavior of human beings can be predicted. As such, education should be universal, with an emphasis on the classics. As with the philosophy of realism, precision is important to perennialists.

Unlike idealism, realism, and perennialism, existentialism is difficult to define in that it focuses on the individual and is not considered to be a "logical" philosophy but instead an attitude or mood.

While existentialism has realitively few educational followers, pragmatism has been a popular educational philosophy. Many educators believe that philosophy can be used to solve the problems of the world. Pragmatism recognizes the importance of both the process and the product of human actions.

From pragmatism comes progressivism, which is divided into two educational theories, experimentalism and social reconstructionism. The experimentalism movement was led by John Dewey and his friend George Herbert Meade. They believed that ideas should be tested and tried. The social reconstruction movement was led by William Heard Kilpatrick, a follower of Dewey who also advanced his own philosophical theories. Kilpatrick asserted the "project method" in which students selected what they would learn, designed a plan for learning, and worked together in small groups to accomplish such learning.

Essentialism continues to gain support as community leaders as well as educators adopt this educational theory. Essentialists advocate strong academic standards. The widespread base of support for essentialism is evident in the movement for national standards for students and teachers.

■ Reflections

Your philosophy of education determines how you teach and interact with students. Consider which philosophy of education you most closely follow. Give examples of your beliefs and actions that suggest you follow that philosophy. Give examples of beliefs and actions of your former teachers, and speculate as to their respective philosophies of education.

■ Discussion Questions

1. Should a preservice teacher develop a philosophy of education prior to engaging in the senior student teaching process?

2. Teachers rarely openly discuss their philosophies of education, yet they do have such beliefs. In what ways can you determine a teacher's philosophy of education?

3. Should the teachers in a school have the same philosophy of education as their principal? Why or why not?

4. Should a school district adopt a philosophy of education? What would be the pros and the cons of such an action?

5. The essentialist movement is often associated with conservative people, while progressivism is considered to be followed by liberals. Why? What are the strengths of each of these educational theories?

■ For Further Reading

Bestor, A. 1953. *Educational wastelands: Retreat from learning in our public schools.* Urbana, IL: University of Illinois Press.

Counts, G.S. 1932. *Dare the school build a new social order?* New York: John Day.

Dewey, J. 1916. *Democracy and education: An introduction to the philosophy of education.* New York: Macmillan.

Dewey, J. 1899. *School and society.* Chicago: University of Chicago Press.

Gordon, R. 1998. Balancing real-world problems with real-world results. *Phi Delta Kappan* 79 (5): 390–393.

Gutek, G.L. 1988. *Philosophical and ideological perspectives on education.* Needham Heights, MA: Allyn & Bacon.

Meehan, P. 1998. Beyond a chocolate crunch bar: A teacher examines her philosophy of teaching reading. The Reading Teacher 51 (4): 314–328.

Wagner, T. 1993. Rethinking the purpose of school. *Educational Leadership 51*(1): 24–29.

5

International Influences on the Foundations of Education

Primary Points

- The beginnings of education were in ancient civilizations.

- European educational leaders influenced educational practices in the New World.

- The role of the teacher changed during the seventeenth and eighteenth centuries from disciplinarian to nurturer and role model.

- The need for instructional activities to fit the needs of the child rather than fitting the child to the activities evolved over a period of several hundred years.

Chapter Inquiries

- What curricular changes evolved over time? Why?

- In what ways did the ancient Greek philosophers influence how we teach today?

- How have early childhood instructional practices changed?

- How did integrated instruction evolve?

- Why were the senses considered to be so important in learning?

"We talk about multicultural education when in reality, education IS multicultural!" Joe Risbak said. "If we hadn't borrowed so many of our ideas from other cultures, then we wouldn't be where we are today. Much of our math comes from Arabic countries and Greece. The idea of respecting the student has roots in Germany and Austria. Even hands-on learning that Dewey promoted came from Prussia. For me, it is interesting to trace back an educational theory to its roots. Then I understand it better."

David Frazier

"No formal structure, certainly no "system" of public schools, was ever envisioned by the early settlers in the English colonies. The family was the only binding social institution in a land of uncertainty and struggle."

—S. Alexander Rippa,
**Education in a Free Society:
An American History**

The historical roots of education go back to the ancient civilizations. As civilization developed throughout the world, there were numerous advances in educational thought.

Long ago, only males were educated since it was considered a waste of time and resources to teach females, who would only get married, have children, and be responsible for household duties. Thus, for thousands of years, men were far better educated than their female counterparts. This is still true in many Third World nations today.

This chapter reviews the historical foundations of education, from its ancient Middle Eastern roots to the time when schools were first established in the New World.

Ancient Civilizations

Four primary geographical areas of ancient civilizations have been discovered and carefully examined by archaeologists. These include the Middle East (Mesopotamia and Egypt), the Indus Valley (now Pakistan), the Huang He Valley of China, and Central America. Each began as fertile farming areas. These ancient societies all built cities, developed forms of writing, domesticated animals, and learned to make pottery and use metals. They each created somewhat complex social structures that included class systems and different types of work.

Middle Eastern Civilizations

Mesopotamia was an area between the Tigris and Euphrates rivers, now part of Iraq. About 10,000 B.C., small towns and villages began to develop in this area, largely because the climate and vegetation made farming profitable. Once farmers could produce a surplus of food, society changed. Everyone no longer needed to farm because food was available for purchase, so other occupations arose and settlements were created. Farming also advanced science and mathematics. The movements of the moon, sun, and planets were studied to calculate the different seasons and create the first calendars. Measurements became important for the division of land or seeds and grains. Barter was the primary method of commerce, and monetary systems were not created until much later. Measurement also led to the need for record keeping.

The founder of Islam, Muhammad was born in the year A.D. 570 as measured by the Christian calendar in Mecca to a poor family. His father died before Muhammad's birth, and by age six when his mother died, Muhammad was an orphan. Abu Talib, Muhammad's uncle and protector, took him in. Muhammad was reflective and quiet.

As a young man, Muhammad, like many of his tribesmen, became a trader and traveled about the Middle East, including making numerous trips to Syria. Later he managed the assets of a wealthy widow, Khadija. Impressed by his honesty and skills in managing her riches, Khadija proposed marriage which Muhammad accepted.

Frequently, Muhammad would spend time in a cave outside of Mecca meditating and praying for guidance. During one such retreat, he had a vision of the archangel Gabriel, who declared Muhammad to be a prophet of God. Muhammad found this to be unsettling, but other revelations followed. Muhammad began to preach in public and recited verses that came to him during the revelations, which became the Koran.

According to Muhammad, there is but one God who had sent out other prophets to nations. When the prophets had failed, God had destroyed their nations. Muhammad was to be the last prophet, and the one possessing the most importance.

Muhammad's teachings included social reform as he advocated improving the living conditions of orphan, slaves, and women. Tribal loyalties were to replace friendships as dictated by the Islamic faith. Furious with the suggestion of such reforms, rich merchants struck out against Muhammad and his followers.

Upon the death of his wife and uncle, Muhammad was approached by rival tribesmen in Yathrib (now Medina) to negotiate a peaceful settlement to their differences. Upon the conclusion of the negotiations, Muhammad and his followers moved to Medina just as his enemies in Mecca plotted to kill him. His flight from Mecca to Medina is called the Hegira, which means emigration in Arabic, and marks the beginning of the Islamic calendar.

By A.D. 630, Muhammad was the most powerful man in the Middle East. He ordered idols destroyed and gave Jews and Christians religious automony because the revelations of these religions had anticipated his own coming. Muhammad dismissed claims of superiority due to class, color, or race.

After his death in 632, Muhammad's followers embellished the story of his life, patterning it upon mythology and other religions. For instance, Muhammad's ascension to heaven from Jerusalem may have been modeled on the ascension of Jesus Christ.

After his first wife's death, Muhammad took nine wives. All of his sons died as infants and only one daughter, Fatima, survived.

In the 1890s, archaeologists discovered that in about 5000 B.C., the Sumerians, a non-Semitic society, established Sumer in Mesopotamia. Unlike the Semites who were descendants of Noah's son Shem which included Arabs, Assyrians, Caroanites, and Hebrews, who were mostly pastoral and seafaring peoples, the Sumerians were a highly developed society with a bent toward business. They were highly successful buying and selling goods, and they developed record-keeping methods, including the first system of writing. In 2500 B.C., their writing system changed from picture-signs or symbols to that of a combination of alphabet letters as symbols for words. The Sumerian writing method, called cuneiform writing, was very complicated. The Sumerians wrote on clay tables to record commerce transactions and to preserve their history. They introduced their writing to students by beginning with the simplest concepts

Avicenna was a follower of Islam. Born to a government official, Avicenna studied medicine and philosophy. Avicenna became recognized as one of the greatest Islamic philosophers. He denied prevailing Islamic views of the period of personal immortality, God's interest in individual people, and the creation of the world. Avicenna's work in medicine was recognized throughout the Middle East and Europe. His book, *The Canon of Medicine,* was a systematic classification and summary of medical and pharmaceutical knowledge up to and including Avicenna's time (980–1037). Avicenna believed that the study of philosophy would enrich the study of religion.

Like Avicenna, Averroës (1126–98) was an Islamic philosopher and physician. He lived in Spain and Morrocco. His father, a judge in Cordoba, Spain, taught him law. Averroës believed that metaphysical truths can be expressed in two ways: through philosophy, such as that represented by the views of Aristotle, and through religion, such as the truths being presented in ways the common individual can understand. Averroës believed that teachers were responsible for seeking truth and transmitting it to their students, a widespread belief that is still held today.

Like Avicenna, Averroës translated Aristotle's works into Arabic. Had it not been for the two of them, most of Aristotle's philosophical writings would have been lost.

Averroës maintained that the world had no creation, no beginning. He believed that God was the "prime mover" who was the self-moved force that stimulates all motion, who transforms potential into the actual. Because of his beliefs, Averroës was exiled. However, just prior to his death, Averroës was pardoned and restored to power.

Mathematics, medicine, and science were greatly advanced by Arabic scholarship. European and American education were influenced by their early efforts (Lewis 1993).

and then adding increasingly more complex concepts. This teaching strategy is still used today (Armstrong, Henson, and Savage 1993).

The Sumerians were conquered by neighboring Semitics, however, the Sumerian civilization was carried on by their successors, which included the Akkadians, Babylonians, Assyrians, and Chaldeans. In particular, the Babylonians contributed to education by making advancements in astronomy and mathematics.

A few hundred miles away along the Nile River, the ancient Egyptian civilization also began in about 5000 B.C. The Nile River area had a mild climate that fostered an agrarian culture. The Egyptian rulers, called pharoahs, were deeply concerned about religion, in particular what would happen to them after they died. Hence, they built huge pyramids beginning around 2700 B.C. to house the possessions they would need in the afterlife. Education became important as men were trained as engineers to build the pyramids and in methods of preserving the human bodies of the rulers. Priests were the teachers of the ruling family. The Egyptians are noted for developing Egyptian hieroglyphics, a term meaning sacred carvings. Hieroglyphics were pictures carved in stone that represented both sounds and objects.

Another ancient people in the Middle East were the Hebrews. Deeply religious, the Hebrews were often scorned and threatened by other societies. The Hebrews impressed upon the young males the need for an education and were quick to scold or even severely punish those students who failed to work hard in their studies (Armstrong, Henson, and Savage 1993).

Name K'ung Ch'iu at birth (about 551 B.C.) and later given the name that became known to millions worldwide, Confucius was born into the noble K'ung clan of China. Confucius lived during the second half of the Chou dynasty (about 1027–256 B.C.). His father died when Confucius was only three years old, causing the family to live in poverty. However, Confucius was well educated. Married at nineteen, he had a son and two daughters.

Early in his life, Confucius performed menial work for the chief of the district in which he lived. After Confucius's mother died, he went into mourning. Afterwards, Confucius decided to become a teacher.

Traveling throughout the province of Lu, now present-day Shandong Province, Confucius's notoriety as a teacher spread and he gained disciples of his work. Noted for his teaching ability and character, he was also recognized for his respect for Chinese ideals and customs. During this period in Chinese history, feudalism was on the decline and disorder and vice were widespread. Confucius bemoaned the state of social conditions and tried to convince people to return longstanding Chinese principles.

Adults and children were taught to respect one another as deemed by family order. The eldest male family member, usually the grandfather, was the most revered, followed by the eldest female family member, then the father with the mother next, the eldest son, the second son, etc., with the eldest daughter, second daughter, etc., until the last daughter, who received the least amount of respect in the family. Reverence for one's elders, even if they were deceased, was important in Confucius's beliefs.

At age fifty, Confucius was named magistrate of Chung-tu. The next year, he became minister of crime of the state of Lu. In these positions, Confucius introduced numerous reforms and dispensed justice fairly, as his disciples followed his teachings. Crime was drastically reduced in Lu, so much so that a stronger but corrupt neighboring sate eventually managed to force Confucius out of office. During his forced retirement, Confucius wrote commentaries on the Chinese classics.

Confucius never wrote down the principles of his philosophy. Rather, these were handed down by his disciples. The *Lün Yu* (Analects) is a book of Confucius's works compiled by some of his disciples and is considered to be the most accurate source of knowledge about his life and teachings. Confucius's own teachings and those of his primary disciples can be found in the *Shih Shu* (Four Books) of Confucian literature. These Four Books were used as textbooks for later generations of Chinese.

The teachings of Confucius focused on the practical and ethical aspects of life instead of on religion. In essence, he was the restorer of ancient Chinese morality. According to Confucius, proper outward acts are based on five virtues: kindness, uprightness, decorum, wisdom, and faithfulness. These five virtues constitute the whole of human duty.

Confucius is best known for his reverance for parents, both living and dead, and the concept that government was paternalistic. Confucius stressed that all individuals should be good citizens of the state, respectful and obedient. The ruler is to be benevolent and honorable. It is the ruler's responsibility to cultivate moral perfection. As such, the ruler becomes a good example for the people.

Despite living during the feudal period, Confucius advocated that in education, no class distinction exists. Everyone should have an opportunity. Thus, the extensive testing system of Chinese students is supported in Confucius's beliefs.

Confucianism, the major system of thought in China, developed from the teachings of Confucius and his followers. It focuses on the principles of good conduct, practical wisdom, and proper social relationships. Confucianism has greatly influenced Chinese society

(continued)

including setting patterns for living and social expectations as well as impacting political theories and structure.

Confucianism spread to Korea and Japan and is known throughout the world. Its principles are contained in the *Wi Ching* (Five Classics) and the *Shih Shu* (Four Books).

While Confucius is honored as a great scholar, he has never been worshiped as a god. Temples were built in honor of Confucius's teachings, not as places of religious worship.

The gist of Confucian ethics is *jen*, which has been translated to mean "love," "goodness," "humanity," and "human-heartedness." *Jen* is considered to be a supreme virtue representing the human qualities at their finest. In relations between one person and another, *jen* is apparent in *chüng*, or faithfulness to oneself and others, and *shu* or altruism, best expressed in the Confucian golden rule, "Do not do to others what you do not want done to yourself."

Additional Confucian virtues include righteousness, propriety, integrity, and filial piety. Possessing these virtues along with *jen* qualifies the individual as a *chun-tzu* (perfect gentleman).

Confucius died in 479 B.C. Today his birthday continues to be celebrated with festivities at the various temples erected in China to honor his teachings.

Led by Alexander the Great in 332 B.C., the Greeks conquered much of the Middle East. The extent to which Middle Eastern philosophy influenced the Greeks is unknown. However, it is known that Arabic numerals and computation and certain Egyptian art forms were adopted.

Asian Civilizations

In Asia, the valley of the Indus River was the birthplace of the Indian civilization around the year 4000 B.C. Located in what is now Pakistan, the early Indians developed the art of writing in addition to engineering feats such as complex irrigation and drainage systems.

Another ancient civilization was China, which began in 3000 B.C. as a settlement along the Huang He (Yellow River) Valley in what is now northern China. The first documented formal schooling began around 2000 B.C. These schools were created during the Shang dynasty and were for boys. In particular, leaders were needed for their highly organized armies.

Also by 2000 B.C., the Chinese began their form of writing. It was a complicated system of picture writing using forms called ideograms, pictograms, and phonograms. Animal bones were inscribed with writings for record keeping.

It was during the Chou dynasty (1122–221 B.C.) that ancient Chinese civilization reached its height. During this dynasty, the Chinese empire was united, iron was introduced, and a middle class developed. In addition, Confucius (551–479 B.C.) developed the code of ethics that dominated Chinese thought and culture for the following twenty-five centuries.

Ancient Greece and Rome

Two major civilizations were ancient Greece and Rome. Paths forged by these two civilizations still are influential in today's world.

Hagar the Horrible

Chris Brown

Ancient Greece

Ancient Greece was settled by nomadic herdsmen between 1900 B.C. and 1650 B.C. Because of the mountainous geography of Greece, early settlements tended to be in valleys where food could be grown. Little is known about the earliest Greek settlements and the lifestyle of the people.

Ancient Greece gave us philosophy and advanced mathematics including geometry, which had its roots in Babylon. The sciences, art, and Western literature were also further developed by the Greeks.

In ancient Greece, education was first looked upon as a means of contributing to the development of good citizens. The role of education in economic, political, and social change was also important.

Greece was made up of several city-states that were quite competitive. Athens and Sparta were the two most prominent city-states. In the fifth century B.C., Athens became the first democracy in the world. Individual freedom was important. Freedom was possible because the citizens believed in obedience to the laws. Self-control and moderation were emphasized. Unlike Athens, Sparta was a military state whose citizens believed that only the strongest and fittest should survive. Children born with handicaps were killed. Loyalty to the city-state was stressed. Freedom was not possible. The focus of education was to train loyal, obedient men for a military lifestyle.

Each city-state, or *polis*, had its own form of citizenship education. For each city-state, it was critical that acculturation, the immersion and participation in the city-state's total culture, take place (Cordasco 1976).

Education was considered to be of lesser importance than acculturation and was largely accessible only to boys whose families had the money to pay the tuition to the private schools. No public schools existed. A liberal education was regarded as being essential if a man was to perform his civic duties. Women, slaves, and noncitizens of the city-state were largely uneducated, so the majority of the population received little, if any, formal education.

In Athens, women had no economic or legal rights. Only women born to affluence received an education, and then only from tutors who came to their homes. In Sparta, women fared somewhat better. They received a limited education which included athletic training. Spartan leaders felt this would contribute to the women rearing healthy boys suitable for becoming soldiers and engaging in warfare.

Greek mythology provided heroes such as Achilles and Ulysses. Homer's epic poems, the *Iliad* and the *Odyssey*, provided role models and also helped to define the

Greek culture. As students read the *Iliad* and learned of the brave deeds of Greek warriors against the Trojans of Troy, they were exposed to heroes and encouraged to model their own behavior after that of the valiant warriors. Loyalty to their city-state was emphasized.

According to Beck (1986), Homer's epic poetry served three educational purposes: (1) it preserved the Greek culture by transmitting it from the adults to their children; (2) it cultivated Greek cultural identity based on historical and mythical origins; and (3) it was used to shape the character of the young.

The Sophists

By the middle of the fifth century B.C., the landed aristocracy was being replaced by the commercial classes of citizenry. This socioeconomic change helped support the rise of the Sophists, a group of wandering, itinerant teachers. They taught the children of the commercial classes rhetoric and oratory techniques. The ability to speak well in public and sway an assembly of people was held in high esteem. Sophists claimed they could teach any person any skill or subject. (Gutek 1991). Members of the commercial classes were impressed with such claims, however unrealistic, and hired Sophists to educate their children. This resulted in an increased percentage of the populace being educated.

Communication skills were stressed in order that students would become successful legislators and jurists. Grammar, logic, and rhetoric were the primary subjects. These subjects emerged as the liberal arts.

Some Sophists were excellent teachers, but others relied on gimmicks. The most successful Sophist was Protagoras (485–415 B.C.), who developed his own approach to teaching. First, Protagoras would model his outstanding speaking style for his students. Next he would take his students to hear outstanding orators. At that point, Protagoras would have his students critique the orators's presentations. Protagoras emphasized that his students study rhetoric, grammar, and logic in order to speak effectively. Students would deliver their own speeches, first in a small group with Protagoras critiquing them, and later in public. Protagoras's teaching methods are similar to teacher education programs in today's colleges and universities. Appropriate teaching behavior is modeled for preservice teacher education majors who also take classes in liberal arts and other professional areas. After learning various teaching strategies, the preservice teacher education majors go into the field and teach students in schools under the guidance of classroom teachers and university supervisors.

Both Socrates and Plato criticized the Sophists as being opportunists who stressed appearance and technique while ignoring truth and honesty. However, the Sophists did not believe in elitism, the education of only the best students. The Sophists were early democratic teachers who taught any student regardless of social class so long as the student paid for his education.

Ancient Greek Philosophers

Three noted Greek philosophers and teachers who influenced educational thought were Socrates, Plato, and Aristotle. These men greatly influenced education in ancient Greece, and their work has heavily influenced education in the United States and Canada.

Socrates

Plato

Socrates's and Plato's work still influence education over 2,000 years later. (Stock Montage)

Socrates

Not interested in fame or money, Socrates (*ca.* 470–399 B.C.) spent his days wandering around Athens as he sought the universal principals of truth, beauty, and goodness. Socrates would talk to anyone who would listen to him. His conversational style was unique: he asked questions, criticized answers, and poked holes in imperfect arguments. This became known as the Socratic method. The major topics of discussion examined by Socrates and his students included life, truth, and justice.

The idea of academic freedom has been tied to Socrates, because he believed that teachers needed the freedom to think and question as part of their teaching. Socrates put forth the idea of knowing oneself, for he believed that if a person really knew himself or herself, then that individual could learn what was actually good instead of what may only be beautiful on the surface. Socrates stressed the need for individuals to construct, criticize, and reconstruct their basic concepts. Reflection and self-criticism was essential if individuals were to undergo self-examination.

Honesty was important to Socrates, and he devoted much of his life to exposing fraud. As a result, he made some enemies. His support of critical thinking was considered to be a threat to the status quo of society, thereby making even more enemies for Socrates.

In Socrates's view, an individual should be ethical, striving for moral excellence. A person should live wisely, use good judgment, and act in a rational manner. Education should develop morally excellent people. It was far more important, in Socrates's opinion, to produce morally commendable people than the technicians who were the result of the Sophists's teaching.

Socrates was sentenced to death by three self-serving rulers whom he opposed because he thought they were corrupt.

Plato, Founder of the University

The most famous student of Socrates was Plato (*ca.* 427–348 B.C.). As a follower of Socrates, Plato was forced to hide after Socrates's death.

The most celebrated teacher of his time, Plato is best known for authoring *The Republic,* in which he outlined an educational institution designed to prepare citizens for social roles for which they were best suited. According to Plato, this would create an ideal society. The Republic required that only knowledgeable people rule. The purpose of the Republic itself was to cultivate truth and virtue in its citizens. Residents of the Republic would be divided into three classes: the intellectual rulers (called the philosopher-kings); the auxiliaries and military defenders; and the workers, who produced goods and provided services. An individual's intellectual capacity would determine his or her class rank.

Women and men should have the same privileges and responsibilities, according to Plato. Women would receive an education, just as men, that would be appropriate for their intellectual level and class assignment. Although Plato's Republic was never implemented, his book is noted as a literary classic.

Plato contended that reality consisted of an unchanging world of perfect ideas that were universal concepts. These universal concepts included truth, goodness, justice, and beauty. The appearance of these concepts, such as the beauty of a red rose when we look at it and see it, are but imperfect representations of the universal and eternal concepts that reside in an absolute idea, the Form of Beauty.

According to Plato, **reminiscence** was a process by which individuals recall the truths or ideas present in latent forms in their minds. Reminiscence suggests that before birth, the human soul has lived in a spiritual world of ideas, the reservoir of all truth and knowledge. These ideas are repressed a birth and brought forth again only through learning, when these perfect ideas are recollected. True knowledge is permanent and unchanging.

The curriculum advocated by Plato was based on an hierarchical rather than an egalitarian society. He was convinced that ignorant, prejudiced parents would pass along their inabilities and beliefs to their children. Plato proposed taking children away from their parents and placing them in the care of qualified, trained child-care workers in state-run facilities. The environment would develop good habits in the children and eliminate inappropriate ones.

At age six, students would be placed in schools that taught music, reading, writing, literature, arithmetic, choral singing, dancing, and gymnastics. The classics would be studied as well. As children progressed through school, astronomy and geometry would be added. Between the ages of eighteen and twenty, the emphasis would be on physical and military training. At age twenty, those deemed future philosopher-kings would begin ten years of additional education in mathematics, geometry, astronomy, music, and science. At age thirty, those less intellectually capable would become civil servants while the others studied metaphysics and eventually began leading military and political affairs. At age fifty, the philosopher-kings would become the elder statesmen for the Republic.

In 387 B.C., Plato opened the Academy in Athens, the forerunner of today's colleges and universities. The curriculum included philosophy, law, mathematics, and science. The Academy remained open until A.D. 529, closing only at the order of Justian, emperor of the roman Empire.

Chapter 5   *International Influences on the Foundations of Education*

Plato believed that the individual should be happy and content. He taught his students how to think for themselves, something Plato believed was important for a democracy to survive and grow.

Aristotle, Student of Plato

The third noted Greek philosopher and teacher was Aristotle (382–322 B.C.), a student of Plato. Aristotle studied at Plato's Academy for twenty years, leaving after Plato's death. Aristotle was the tutor of Alexander the Great.

Aristotle's work, *Politics*, examines education in relation to society and government. In it, he contends that the good of a community rests on its members' rationality. If education, which cultivates and nurtures rationality, is neglected or poor, then the community suffers.

Through the study of the liberal arts, individuals broadened their horizons, consciousness, and choices. On the other hand, technical or vocational training resulted in reduced intellectual development. This argument, over the value of studying liberal arts versus vocational education, still lingers today.

Aristotle's work in the natural and social sciences continues to influence modern-day thinking. In particular, Aristotle believed that we learn through our senses. At his school, the Peripatetic (which means to walk about), Aristotle had his students observe nature as they studied the habits of insects and dissected animals. He was adament that students be taught categories, now referred to as concepts.

Another important educational contribution of Aristotle was his definition and classification of the various subject matter. He defined these as physics, metaphysics, psychology, rhetoric, poetics, and logic.

Compulsory schooling was advocated by Aristotle. Infant schooling, what is today referred to as nursery school, would consist of play, physical activity, and the oral sharing of stories. By age seven, male students would be taught basic numeracy, reading, writing, and proper moral behavior. Beginning at age fifteen, the young men would study geometry, mathematics, astronomy, grammar, literature, poetry, rhetoric, ethics, and politics. At age twenty-one, students would be taught physics, biology, psychology, logic, and metaphysics.

Unlike Plato, Aristotle advocated that women be subservient to men and believed they were of low intellectual ability. Women were to be trained to cook, clean, and perform other household duties in addition to learning about child-rearing.

When he was accused by some Athenian leaders of impiety, Aristotle fled. He died the following year.

Teachers who follow the Aristotelian educational ideas focus on a body of knowledge, referred to as a subject-matter discipline such as history or geometry. Teaching is viewed as being scientific rather than an art. Thus, teachers need to be experts in the subject matter in order to teach and motivate their students.

Ancient Rome

With the rise of the Roman Empire, the Greek city-states fell to Roman rule. Greek slaves were brought back to Rome, where many served as teachers. The Romans were noted for their laws and system of government.

Unlike Greek schools, the Romans believed in harsh discipline of their students. This was perhaps an outgrowth of their interest in war and conquering new lands. Students were taught not only how to read but to write. In addition, oratory skills were emphasized and students were expected to develop their public speaking abilities. This required that students be able to organize information in a logical manner.

Only a small portion of the Roman population was educated. Schooling was expensive and limited to those families who could afford to pay the tuition. Only girls from wealthy families received an education, and then only in their homes. Boys attended a *ludus,* a primary school, before going on to their secondary schooling where they learned Latin and Greek. Educated Greek slaves, called *pedagogues,* ushered the boys to and from school each day. *Pedagogy,* meaning the art of instruction, comes from the word *pedagogues.*

The focus of education in the Roman Empire was to produce effective politicians, competent government administrators, and skilled military leaders, unlike the focus of the Greeks, who sought to produce philosophers. The Romans desired to produce students who were good orators, essential for those who were to become politicians, civil servants, or teachers.

Cicero

A Roman writer, statesman, and orator, Cicero (106–43 B.C.), also called Tully by the English, was known as Rome's best orator. He had a distinguished political career as a Roman Senator as well as being known for his works as a writer. Cicero wrote *On the Republic, On the Orator, On Old Age,* and *On Friendship,* the latter two being recognized for their tone of cultivated geniality. His wide vocabulary is credit with enriching the languages of Europe, in which his works were widely translated.

Cicero promoted the idea of educating students to win debates. In order to do so, students would have to receive a broad, liberal education. Greek and Latin, the language of the Roman Empire, should both be taught to secondary students. In addition, there would be the study of poetry, grammar, literature, and history. Higher studies would encompass astronomy, geography, natural science, psychology, ethics, medicine, and military science. History and geography would be taught to give students a perspective of the background of the Roman Empire. Speeches of famous orators were to be examined.

Orators, according to Cicero, needed precision in using words, selecting them carefully for the impact they would carry with an audience. Arguments had to be persuasive and well structured. Having a background in psychology would help orators in swaying and motivating their audiences.

Cicero had been aligned with Pompey, the archrival of Julius Caesar. When Caesar defeated Pompey, Cicero accepted Caesar as a political friend. This enabled Cicero to live quietly, reading and writing philosophy. After Caesar's assassination, Cicero returned to politics and supported Caesar's adopted son, Octavian (later called Augustus). Upon becoming emperor, Augustus engaged in a power struggle with Marc Antony. Later, Augustus and Antony patched up their differences, leaving Cicero the odd man out. Cicero was murdered on December 7, 43 B.C.

Quintilian

A Roman rhetorician, Marcus Fabius Quintilian (*ca.* A.D. 35 to *ca.* A.D. 95) was born in Spain and educated in Rome. Appointed by the emperor to be the first chair of Latin rhetoric, he is best known as a teacher and writer. Since the emperor held tremendous power, Quintilian's work influenced education in the vast expanse of the Roman Empire.

Quintilian authored twelve books, called *Institutio Oratoria,* which outlined three aspects of education: (1) the education preparatory to studying rhetoric, (2) rhetorical and educational theory, and (3) the practice of public speaking. Education was to consist of four stages. During the first stage, from infancy to age seven, the children would learn developmentally. Children should be surrounded by articulate nurses, pedagogues, and friends—all of whom were to be selected by the child's parents. Quintilian believed that character was formed in the early years and changed little in later life.

At age seven, students would begin the second stage of development in which they would learn from their senses, much as Aristotle had advocated. The primary teacher was to possess both high moral character and teaching competence. In learning to read and write, students would begin by tracing letters with their index fingers. Time would be set aside each day for students to play and engage in recreational games. Quintilian believed this would refresh students so that they would learn more upon their return to their studies.

The third stage of education, from age fourteen to seventeen, would emphasize the liberal arts. The study of both the Greek and roman cultures was encouraged as well as music, geometry, astronomy, and gymnastics. From seventeen to twenty-one, students would be in the fourth, and final, stage of education. This stage emphasized rhetoric and included drama, poetry, law, philosophy, public speaking, and debate (Smail 1966).

Quintilian's work had a huge impact upon humanist education theories during the Renaissance. It was he who took educational theories and put them into practice. Quintilian stressed that teachers needed to know their students and to accommodate for individual differences and abilities. Students' mistakes were to be corrected by the teacher by using patience, tact, and consideration. According to Quintilian, the teacher's role was to make the subject interesting to students.

Table 1 summarizes the contributions made by ancient educational leaders.

The Middle Ages

The Middle Ages were the years from the middle of the fifth century A.D. through the middle of the fifteenth century. This was a period of great religious influence, when primarily those who were wealthy, royal, royal family members, or affiliated with the Christian Church, primarily the Roman Catholic Church, received an education. The primary locations for schooling were monasteries and cathedrals, forerunners of today's parochial elementary and secondary schools.

The early part of the Middle Ages is referred to as the Dark Ages (A.D. 400–1100), when there was great political and religious oppression of the masses. The Roman Catholic Church held great power during this period. Some historians believe there was little advancement of knowledge during this time. Charlemagne (A.D. 742–814) was a ruler who highly valued education. He insisted that an educator be found who could improve the quality of education in his country. The educator who was named to be Charlemagne's advisor was Alcuin (A.D. 734–804), a teacher in England. Alcuin changed the curriculum of schools, which at that time was almost entirely religious teachings.

Table 1 Ancient Educational Leaders

Culture or Leader	Primary Contributions	Teacher's Role	Curriculum	Impact on Today's Schools
Sumerians (*ca.* 5000–2500 B.C.) (middle Eastern people)	Introduced writing by first presenting simplest concepts then increasingly more difficult concepts.	Make learning simple and easy for students.	Math, reading, and writing	Emphasis on training students to keep records, especially for business. High school accounting and computer instruction.
Confucius (*ca.* 551–479 B.C.) (Chinese)	Children and adults should respect one another and conduct themselves according to the five virtues: kindness, uprightness, decorum, wisdom, and faithfulness.	Provide all students with an opportunity to learn.	Ethics and character education.	Character and values education
The Sophists (*ca.* 400's–300's B.C.) (Greek)	Teach students to speak well and be persuasive.	Teachers should develop effective teaching methods.	Rhetoric, logic, public speaking and grammar	Speech and drama; teaching methods are refined and new ones adopted.
Socrates (*ca.* 470–399 B.C.) (Greek)	The Socratic method.	Teachers should ask questions, criticize answers, and find fault in weak arguments.	Ethics	Reflection and self-criticism by students.
Plato (*ca.* 427–348 B.C.) (Greek)	Men and women should be considered equals. Students should be taught the roles they will be expected to fill as citizens of a society.	Students should be taught how to think for themselves.	Reading, writing literature, arithmetic, dancing, singing, and gymnastics	His academy was the predecessor of today's colleges and universities.
Aristotle (384–322 B.C.) (Roman)	We learn through our senses. School should be compulsory.	Teachers should view teaching as a science, not an art.	Nature and the social sciences	Subjeact matter areas (e.g., history, physics, or geometry).
Cicero (106–43 B.C.) (Roman)	Students should be taught psychology and argumentation in order to sway others.	Teachers should train students in public speaking.	Liberal arts (Greek, Latin, math, ethics, history, and astronomy).	Speech
Quintilian (*ca.* A.D. 35–*ca.* 95) (Roman)	Children learn developmentally. He stressed the importance of parents' role in educating the young child.	Teachers should be highly competent and of high moral character. Teachers should use tact, patience, and consideration in helping students learn.	Study of nature and use of one's senses for learning.	Humanism in education, inclusion
Muhammad (A.D. 570–632) (Syrian)	Advocate of classless society.	Teach those who are not of the privileged classes.	Values education.	Conflict resolution and mediation of student disagreements.
Avicenna (A.D. 980–1037 (Egyptian)	Stressed the importance of studying philosophy to understand religion and wrote *The Canon of Medicine,* a systematic summary of medicine.	Teach a variety of philosophies to students.	Biology, religion, and philosophy gained importance in the curriculum.	Classification system scientists use today.
Averroës (A.D. 1126–1198) (Spanish/ Monoccan)	Present truths so that the common individual can understand.	Teachers are responsible for seeking truth and transmitting it to their students.	Math and science.	Hands-on science and math.

During the eleventh century, a group of intellectuals called the Scholastics began asserting the need to develop rational thinking in order to build a logical argument for their own religious commitment. These Christians helped to found universities during the Middle Ages. One of the better-known Scholastics was St. Thomas Aquinas (1225–74), an Italian, who believed that men should not only be well educated in religion but in other intellectual areas as well. At a time when reading the works of Greek and Roman authors was scorned because they were believed to be pagans and godless, Aquinas felt that these works deserved study.

Education During the Middle Ages (500–1400)

The Middle Ages, often referred to as the medieval period in Europe, began with the fall of the Roman Empire. Education fell into disarray. The Roman Catholic Church gained political power and took over much of the educational duties with parish and monastic schools. Major universities existed in large cities such as Bologna, London (Cambridge and Oxford), Paris, and Salerno, with the primary curriculum being theology. The framework of medieval universities served as the model for today's universities. Faculty in medieval universities taught and preserved knowledge. Today's college faculty teach and are expected to contribute to scholarly knowledge through research and the publishing of the results.

Merchants and craft guilds provided vocational training. Feudalism arose, as lords controlled local farmlands that surrounded their manors. The largest group of people were serfs who worked the land as farmers for the feudal lords.

Only a small portion of the population received formal education, mainly the wealthy and those who planned to enter religious life as priests or monks. Women who planned to become nuns were taught in convents which had libraries. In general, however, women during the Middle Ages were poorly educated, with their roles viewed as housekeepers and child-rearers. For women in the noble classes, education consisted of music appreciation and training, reading and writing, sewing, manners, and supervision of the manor's workers, namely servants and ladies-in-waiting.

St. Thomas Aquinas

An Italian philosopher and theologian, St. Thomas Aquinas (1225–1274) was educated by Benedictine monks. Heavyset and sometimes difficult to get along with, his classmates nicknamed him "Dumb Ox." After earning his doctorate in theology, Aquinas taught at the University of Paris.

Scholasticism, a method of inquiry, scholarship, and teaching, had been developed by educators during the Middle Ages. Clerics who taught were known as Scholastics. They put forth the writings of the leaders of the Roman Catholic Church and those of the scriptures. Aquinas became the best known of the Scholastics.

A prolific writer, Aquinas is credited with producing eighty works. His most significant was *Summa Theologica*. Prior to being influenced by Aquinas, Western thought was dominated by the philosophy of St. Augustine, who taught that in the search for truth people must depend upon sense experience. Because of the availability in the thirteenth century of the translations of Aristotle's writings, the Averroists asserted that philosophy was independent of revelation. This belief threatened the integrity and supremacy of the Roman Catholic doctrine. Aquinas was able to reconcile the Augustinian emphasis upon the human spiritual principle with the Averroist claim of autonomy for knowledge derived from the senses. According to Aquinas, the truths of faith as presented in the scriptures and those of the sense experience, as Aristotle introduced, are compatible and complementary.

Aquinas believed that human beings possess both a physical body and a spiritual soul. While humans live temporarily on earth, the ultimate goal is to reside in eternity with God. Aquinas agreed with Aristotle that human knowledge begins in sensation and is completed in conceptualization. It is the action of the intellect that elevates through to higher levels.

In *de Magistro*, which translates into *Concerning the Teacher*, Aquinas asserted that teachers must combine faith, love, and learning in their instruction. Teachers should conduct research and teach, and both should be done well. As experts in their subjects, teachers were to be knowledgable and serve as models of learning.

Deductive reasoning, called syllogism, was used by educators to create organized bodies of knowledge. Basic principles and their implications were emphasized.

Lifelong learning was acknowledged by Aquinas. While he believed in formal education, family, friends, and the environment also provided learning opportunities.

After Aquinas's death he was canonized by the Roman Catholic Church.

Erasmus

Born in Rotterdam in the Netherlands, Desiderius Erasmus (1465–1536) became a priest but found that religious life disagreed with him. He received papal dispensation so he could live and dress as a secular scholar. As such, Erasmus moved from city to city as a tutor and lecturer. He sought out ancient manuscripts and wrote, often poking fun at exalted scholars with his satirical writings. He claimed that grammar teachers confused students and ignored the practicality of the subject. Philosophers, he believed, ignored realities and lived in the abstract.

In *De Ratione Studii* (On the Method of Study), which came out in 1511, and *De Pueris Satim ac Liberaliter Instituendis* (On Teaching Children Firmly but Kindly), which followed in 1529, Erasmus argued that elementary Latin and basic principles of character and behavior should be taught at home prior to children enrolling in formal schooling at age seven. Like Quintilian, Erasmus stressed the importance of early childhood as a major stage in human development to be guided by children's parents. Latin was to be taught first in conversation, later as grammar. This approach is still used today.

The meaning of literature was considered by Erasmus to be more important than having students imitate the writer's style. Through a six-step instructional approach, Erasmus described how literature should be taught: (1) present the author's biography; (2) identify the piece of literature by its type; (3) discuss the basic plot of the piece; (4) analyze the author's style; (5) consider the moral implications; and finally, (6) explore the work's broader philosophical issues and implications. Teachers were encouraged to have discussions with students about literature. Through activities and games, students were taught the meaning of literature.

Erasmus advocated physical education as a subject. He opposed severe discipline of students by teachers. Rather, he urged that teachers arouse the interest of students in the various subjects.

The Renaissance

The Renaissance began in the fourteenth century and lasted through the sixteenth century and led to the demise of the Middle Ages. Beginning in Italy, the Renaissance was a rebellion by the common people against the upper class and the rulers of the Church. It was a time when art, literature, and music were valued. Most important, individualism as opposed to the oppressiveness of the upper classes was emphasized.

The Reformation

The Roman Catholic Church dominated the common people during the fifteenth through the seventeenth centuries. The religious laws set forth had to be followed by the masses of people. The pope held more power than any other leader of the period and indeed was feared by most leaders.

In 1517, Martin Luther began the Protestant Reformation when he nailed his ninety-five theses to the door of the Roman Catholic Church at Wittenburg, Germany. Prior to this time, the Roman Catholic Church advocated that people did not need to learn to read or write, since the Church would pass on the true meaning of the Bible. Luther and his followers asserted that the commoners should receive formal schooling so that they could read and make their own interpretations of the Bible. This began the movement for universal elementary education, something that John Amos Comenius promoted about a hundred years later.

The feudal system which had fostered two primary classes of people, the peasantry and nobility, succumbed during the Protestant Reformation. With the rise of the new middle class, some people enjoyed financial success through business and commercial means. European nations and cultures changed; the population of Europe as a whole became better educated.

Many reformers followed Martin Luther's belief that children should be taught to read the Bible in their own language. The invention of the moveable type printing press by Guttenberg in the fifteenth century made the Bible a book nearly every family could afford to own. While the Roman Catholic religion held that Masses and liturgies as well as the Bible should be presented in Latin, reformers were busy translating it into the vernacular languages (German, English, French, Swedish, etc.) of the various nations. Children began to be taught to read in their own language with the text being the Bible.

Reformers established vernacular schools in which instruction was delivered in children's own language rather than Latin. Because of the popularity such instruction gained, Catholic schools began to teach in the vernacular while maintaining religious instruction in Latin.

Catechisms, started by Protestant educators, were textbooks which had religious questions about the Protestant Church followed by answers. Students memorized the catechisms. Other types of catechism textbooks included geography and history. Catechisms were also adopted by the Catholic Church.

Because of the emphasis upon educating the children of the common people, including increased attendance and greater supervision of schools by the state, literacy rose greatly during this period. In 1500, it was estimated that only 12 percent of the people in England were literate (10 percent men, 2 percent women). By 1600, the proportion of literate adults was 37 percent (28 percent men, 9 percent women) and by 1700, 72 percent (40 percent men, 32 percent women) (Maynes 1985).

European Leaders

There were several European leaders who greatly influenced educational practices. Among these were John Amos Comenius, John Locke, Johann Pestalozzi, Jean Rousseau, Johann Friedrich Herbart, Friedrich Froebel, and Maria Montessori.

Descended from the peasantry, Martin Luther was born in 1483 in Eisleben, Prussia (now Germany), to a copper miner and his wife. After receiving a good education, including bachelor's and master's degrees, Luther was to study law. Instead, he unexpectedly entered the monastery. Luther later explained his change of career as being due to having several sudden brushes with death.

Luther was assigned to the University of Wittenburg, one of many German universities that had monks as the teaching staff. Luther taught moral philosophy.

In his readings of the New Testament, Luther believed that Christians are saved by God's grace, which they accept in faith. This ran counter to the teachings of the Roman Catholic Church, and turned Luther against the Catholic Church.

On October 31, 1517, Luther published his Ninety-Five Theses. In this work, Luther condemned the actions of the Catholic Church which was having individuals pay money to build St. Peter's Basilica in Rome in turn for being forgiven of sins and being given indulgences. Legend has it that Luther nailed his theses to the door of the church at Wittenberg, but historians doubt that this event took place. This is considered the beginning of the Protestant Reformation and the Lutheran Church.

Luther was excommunicated by the Catholic Church in 1521, but he continued to write and lecture. Luther's insistence that rulers should rule independent of the Catholic Church won him the support of several princes. In 1525, he married Katharina von Bora, a former nun, who supported his work.

The teachings of Luther greatly influenced education. Luther viewed the church, state, family, and school as being essential reform vehicles. The family was key to the character building of children and their behavior. Luther encouraged families to read and discuss the Bible together. He advocated that parents should insist that their children have vocational training to ensure that they would become productive citizens.

In his "Letter to the Mayors and Aldermen of All Cities of Germany in Behalf of Christian Schools," Luther emphasized that schooling held benefits in three important areas: economic, political, and spiritual. He supported school inspections by state officians in order that children would be well trained, literate, and productive citizens.

Influenced by the writings of St. Paul, Luther's views toward gender roles were traditional. The husband was the dominant figure in the house with the wife meeting his needs and demands. The home was to be maintained by the wife, who also had all child-rearing responsibilities. Luther was more open-minded about the educational needs of women, for he believed that if women were educated they would then help their husbands in the education of their children.

In order to promote his education views, Luther sought the assistance of Philip Melanchthon (1497–1560). During this period, schools were controlled by the Roman Catholic Church. Luther and Melanchthon wanted the state to control and supervise the schools as well as to license teachers. In 1559, Melanchthon wrote the "School Code of Wutemberg," which was used by other German states as a model for education. Primary schools were created in villages to teach religion, reading, writing, arithmetic, and music to children of the common people. Secondary schools, called *gymnasiens* in German, after the gymnasiums of Denmark were limited to adolescent males who were taught Greek and Latin.

The Protestant Reformation led by Luther reaffirmed the classical model of schooling. Primary schools were to educate children of the common people; secondary schools were to educate young men to prepare them for university study (Harran 1985). Thus, the dual track school system was established.

John Amos Comenius lived during the seventeenth century in what is now Czechoslovakia. He believed that education should be available to all and argued for compulsory education until children had completed six years of formal, organized schooling.

John Locke

At about the same time that Comenius was making his contributions to education, John Locke (1632–1704), an English philosopher, stressed the need for teaching to the senses. Because Locke believed that each child was born as a *tabula rasa*, or blank slate, he felt children needed firsthand experiences in which they could use their senses to acquire knowledge.

Although Locke targeted his educational views for children of England's upper class, many of his ideas have remained. He was the first to emphasize the need to teach personal hygiene as well as physical education. Locke asserted that it was impossible to develop a good mind without being in good health.

Locke also emphasized the need for teaching "useful information." Thus, he stressed the teaching of the basic skills of reading, writing, and mathematics.

Jean Jacques Rousseau

Another European education leader was Jean Jacques Rousseau (1712–78), who was born in Geneva, Switzerland. His mother died giving birth, and because his father could not care for him, Rousseau was apprenticed at a young age to an engraver who was cruel to him. When he was sixteen, he ran away.

Unlike Comenius, Rousseau was not a teacher, but he did develop his own educational philosophy. Rousseau lived during the period in which the divine powers of the French monarchy were challenged by the populace. The movement toward a natural, clean lifestyle as opposed to corrupt practices of political leaders had begun prior to Rousseau's birth, paving the way for many of Rousseau's ideas to be adopted.

Rousseau's first major success came when he entered a writing contest and his entry, *Discourse of 1750*, won first prize. In response to the essay contest question as to whether the arts and sciences had contributed to the purity of manners, Rousseau pointed out that man had missed the goal completely and that the current civilization had created an artificial and insincere culture.

Rousseau put forth his ideal that a child was born with capabilities and knowledge. He was adamant that a child was born with inherently good tendencies at a time when the predominant belief was the Calvinistic one that a child was born in sin and was thereby evil.

Rousseau believed that the very young should be given freedom in a nurturing setting. According to Rousseau, there are three types of learning: (1) the education of nature, or the gradual maturation of our organs and the sharpening of our faculties (the physical and mental maturation process); (2) the education of things, or from the physical world, as a child learns that in autumn, leaves are dry and brittle and can be piled high to make a soft bed (sense experience); and (3) the education of men, or one's connection with others, both in cooperation and conflict (social experience).

Emile (1911), a story about a young boy isolated from the outside world with contact only with his tutor, was Rousseau's best-known work. His basic premise was that "to develop good men and through them a better society, education must consider the child. And to teach the child, you must understand him" (Rippa 1992, 48).

John Amos Comenius

An early influence on the philosophy and principles of education was a seventeenth-century Moravian bishop, teacher, and educational theorist, John Amos Comenius (1592–1670). Born a hundred years after Christopher Columbus's first voyage to the New World, Comenius grew up in a religious community called the Unity of Brethren. The Brethren were often subject to persecution and denied access to schooling. Thus, the Brethren believed that education should be provided by the family (Capkova 1970).

Comenius's parents and two of his sisters died of the plague when Comenius was twelve, so he went to live with a guardian until he was sixteen. Comenius "suffered at the hands of an improvident guardian and of incompetent teachers," causing him in future years to "feel intense pity for all those children who were exposed to the care of teachers ignorant of their art" (Sadler 1970, 9). When he was sixteen, friends sent Comenius to a grammar school, where he performed well in his studies. Later, members of the Brethren sent him to universities in Germany to study for the ministry.

Much of Comenius's adult life was spent in hiding because of his religious beliefs or in exile because of the Thirty Years' War. It was during this period in which Comenius did much of his writing. Two of his better-known works are *The Great Didactic*, which means the great art of teaching, and *Orbus Sensualium Pictus*, which was the first illustrated textbook for student instructional purposes (Pedram 1963).

Comenius believed that society could be reformed through education. In his view, the lack of social and political harmony in the world was the result of a lack of understanding. Thus, Comenius promoted universal education for everyone in the world, regardless of sex, nationality, status, or ability, and he envisioned a Collegium Lucim (college of light) for adults (UNESCO 1957).

A knowledge of the order of nature (animals, plants, etc.) was in Comenius's opinion the key to the proper understanding of learning and the development of methods of instruction. By following the example of nature, such as the development of a seed into a grown

(continued)

Rousseau pointed out that the best approach to learning was to encourage a child such as Emile to discover on his own what needs to be learned for living. For instance, Emile learned to read through the letters and notes that he received. Thus, experiences are an essential part of the learning process. Rousseau also made clear that a child cannot learn until he or she is ready to learn.

Prior to Rousseau, children were expected to dress and act like miniature adults, to be seen and not heard. Rousseau's work was important because it gave respect to childhood itself as an important stage of life at a period of time when only adulthood was viewed as consequential and worth considering.

Rousseau was considered a genius but was emotionally unstable. He was viewed as being strange or even crazy, and even accused his best friends of trying to plot against him (Thut 1957). He died in 1778; eleven years before the French Revolution, which resulted in the fall of the monarchy. However, his writing and political ideology played an important part in the overthrow of the monarchy (Rippa 1992).

Johann Heinrich Pestalozzi

Like Rousseau, Johann Heinrich Pestalozzi (1746–1827) was born in Switzerland. When he was five, his father died and left his mother to care for him and his older plant, there would be appropriate timing for instruction. Thus, a pattern of development of the child, readiness, and decisions as to the suitability of materials would be evident to the teacher (Pedram 1963).

In *The Great Didactic*, Comenius (Lascarides 1990, 5) outlined his educational theory as he patterned it after nature:

Following in the footsteps of nature we find that the process of education will, to paraphrase Comenius, be easy

- if it begins early
- if the mind be duly prepared to receive it
- if it proceed from general to the particular
- and from what is easy to what is more difficult
- if the pupil be not overburdened by too many subjects
- if progress be slow in every case
- if the intellect be forced to nothing to which its natural bent does not incline it, in accordance with its age and with the right method
- if everything be taught through the medium of the senses
- if the use of everything taught be continually kept in view

These educational principles of Comenius are as accurate and applicable today as they were over three hundred years ago, when he first developed them.

Comenius emphasized the need for hands-on experiences and believed that firsthand experiences were lasting. He wrote in *The Great Didactic*, "If I have once tasted sugar, seen a camel, heard a nightingale, or been to Rome, the incidents will remain" (Lascarides 1990, 5). He asserted that if firsthand experiences cannot be provided, secondary or vicarious experiences through the use of pictures need to accompany lessons. Thus, Comenius is responsible for laying the foundation for the use of today's audiovisual instructional aids such as overhead transparencies and interactive video disks.

Comenius was offered the presidency of Harvard College (now Harvard University) but declined the offer at his wife's insistence. She did not speak English and thought that it would be difficult to learn the customs and language of the New World.

brother and younger sister. A female servant, Babeli, promised Pestalozzi's father on his deathbed that she would stay with the family, which she did for over forty years (Pinloche 1901).

As a child, Pestalozzi had a vivid imagination and was known to be helpful to others. When an earthquake hit Zurich, the teachers and students ran out of the school building. It was Johann who volunteered to go back into the school and retrieve their personal belongings.

After trying several careers including the ministry, law, farming, and managing an orphanage, Pestalozzi became a teacher. He later opened his own school in an old castle at Yverdon. His teaching methods became well known throughout Europe, and educators came from Prussia, Denmark, Holland, Germany, and France to observe his methods firsthand.

Pestalozzi believed that teachers should emphasize the natural stages of development of children. Thus, a student's developmental level was considered in curriculum development. He also stressed the need for children to express the impressions they gained through the use of their senses. For instance, a child would observe an object or event and then express his or her impressions or thoughts in words (De Guimps 1896).

Pestalozzi believed that what children already knew formed a foundation on which new concepts could be built, moving from the concrete to the abstract. For example, children can be taught to count by using seeds and then moving to adding groups of seeds and progressing to higher-level problems.

Pestalozzi also stressed the need for teaching the known first and then expanding to the unknown. These practices continue today, for instance, in how we teach social studies. We begin with the family, then expand to the neighborhood and community before moving to the nation and then to other nations.

Pestalozzi was an advocate of teaching writing along with reading, and his methods are still practiced in today's elementary classrooms. His practices were adopted in the normal schools in the United States in the 1800s.

Perhaps no educator had such conviction that education could regenerate and save society as did Pestalozzi. According to Rippa (1992, 49), a noted education historian, "In the history of education, few men possessed greater faith in the school as a social instrument for uplifting people from misery and degradation."

Johann Friedrich Herbart

Johann Friedrich Herbart (1776–1841) was a German philosopher who believed that moral education should be the main role of formal schooling. Herbart asserted that children should learn that when they do something positive toward others, the results are positive. Likewise, when they do something negative, they are held accountable for such negative behavior. Thus, Herbart stressed concern for the social welfare of others. By developing children's thinking and knowledge, Herbart felt that they would naturally develop a moral conscience and behave in an ethical way.

In addition to moral education, Herbart emphasized the need for an organized, coordinated, and integrated curriculum. Teachers needed to be well prepared with clear and organized lessons that fit together in an orderly manner. Today's lesson and unit plans that teachers prepare have their roots in Herbart's theory.

Herbart also stressed an integrated curriculum. History was impacted greatly by geography, so he believed they should be studied together. For instance, large cities were primarily built along waterways for agricultural and transportation reasons. In addition, Herbart believed literature should be taught simultaneously with history and geography since literature reflects the culture of a society.

Friedrich Froebel

Another prominent German educator was Friedrich Froebel (1782–1852). When he was nine months old, Froebel's mother died. Perhaps because of this, Froebel had a great respect for the importance of early childhood and the young child.

Having worked in several other professions—forestry, pharmacy, and a museum—before becoming an educator, Froebel used the knowledge gained from these experiences and related them to what young children need. Through nature, children could learn a great deal according to Froebel.

Froebel was influenced by Pestalozzi and elaborated on his ideas. Froebel, like Pestalozzi, stressed the need for a supportive, secure learning environment for children.

Froebel believed the teacher should be a role model for children, both morally and culturally. Thus, the teacher was someone to be admired and emulated by students. Previous to this, the teacher was viewed solely as a disciplinarian. This was a significant historical change in the role played by teachers in the education of students.

Today's kindergartens are much more academically oriented than what Froebel first proposed. (© Paul Conklin/PhotoEdit)

In 1837, Froebel opened his **kindergarten,** or child's garden, to nurture children's socialization and mental and physical development. Rather than rigid lessons taught to children sitting on benches at tables, activities and games were used to teach the lessons. Children were encouraged to play in sandboxes, make clay animals and people, and examine plants. This was the first school to emphasize hands-on learning for the very young child.

Maria Montessori

Like Froebel, Maria Montessori (1870–1952) was greatly interested in the young child. Montessori first broke with tradition by becoming the first female medical doctor in Italy. Because of her medical work, she came in contact with children who were considered to be mentally retarded. At that time, people believed these children were unable to learn. Montessori believed differently and developed activities for these children. The positive results led her to open her own school, *Casa dei Bambini*, for disadvantaged and orphaned children from the slums of Rome.

Montessori discovered that young children were capable of concentrating on an activity that they enjoyed for fairly long periods of time. Because of this, she felt they could learn if the activities both interested them and were playlike in nature.

The curriculum in Montessori's school also stressed the need for structure and practicality. Reading, writing, and arithmetic were taught through things that interested children. Hands-on materials were used for science and math. Books were small enough that children could easily hold them in the palms of their hands. Students were also taught how to set the table, wash dishes, and dress themselves neatly. In addition, proper manners were emphasized. Improper behavior was not accepted from children.

Talking It Over

The linkages between our educational programs and those of other nations may seem remote upon first glance. Certainly the European, and particular, Prussian, influence can be readily seen in most classrooms. By understanding the different historical viewpoints regarding education, we can make better decisions for meeting the new demands education will be confronted with in the next millennium. The "been there, done that" response can either be avoided or adopted depending on the situation that arises.

Some people find the history of educational leaders and practices interesting, and others think it's boring. Still, if you understand the linkages between the past and the present, you'll have a better grasp of teaching methodologies and philosophies.

Montessori's methods are still used in schools today. There are thousands of Montessori schools throughout the world in which young preschoolers and kindergartners are taught in a relevant, playlike but structured atmosphere.

Jean Piaget

Yet another Swiss-born educational leader was Jean Piaget (1896–1980). Piaget was trained as a biologist and then studied psychology at the University of Paris under Alfred Binet, who had developed the first intelligence test (IQ test). Piaget was interested in the responses of children to the test items. In particular, he discovered that children of the same age level tended to have similar answers. This led Piaget to develop his theory of cognitive development.

According to Piaget, children between birth and age two, are in the *sensorimotor stage* of development. During this stage they explore their environment through their senses: eyes, hands, ears, noses, and mouths. It is during this stage that rapid development occurs; they learn to sit up, crawl, walk, and talk.

From ages two to seven, children are in the *preoperational stage,* during which they learn to organize their thoughts and language as well as acquire new concepts. During this stage children acquire more new words in their vocabulary than at any other stage.

The third stage is *concrete operations* and is roughly between the ages of seven and eleven. Children become more precise in their use of language and they acquire higher-level concepts. They become proficient in mathematical functions such as addition, subtraction, multiplication, and division. They can see relationships such as cause and effect and sequencing.

The final stage is *formal operations,* from about eleven and on through adulthood. This stage involves abstract thinking.

Because of Piaget's work, teachers give greater consideration to the abilities of students and to the need to provide appropriate activities to meet their skills and mental development as they are ready.

Table 2 presents a summary of the contributions made by European educational leaders.

Table 2 European Educational Leaders

Leader	Primary Contributions	Teacher's Role	Curriculum	Impact on Today's Schools
St. Thomas Aquinas (1225–1274) (French)	.Students should study a variety of subjects, not solely religion.	To teach students to be lifelong learners.	Use of the senses to learn.	Teachers are to model learning as researchers themselves.
Erasmus (1465–1536) (Dutch)	Parents are the child's first teachers.	To motivate students gain their interest.	Stressed understanding of literature; physical education; foreign languages.	Physical education; critical thinking skills stressed.
Luther (1483–1546) (German)	Students should learn to read and write in their own language.	Should be proficient and stress character building and literacy.	Reading, writing, math, and religion should be taught in elementary schools. Secondary schools don't prepare young men for college.	Literacy programs; vocational education; school inspections by state officials.
Comenius (1592–1670) (Czech)	Children learn developmentally, and teachers should teach to this fact.	Teach from the general to the particular. Firsthand experiences are the best way for children to learn.	Reading, writing, math, history, religion, Latin.	Schools organized by childhood development. Use of multimedia and computers to teach.
Locke 1632–1704) (English)	Children need hands-on experiences.	To teach children "useful information."	Reading, writing, Latin, arithmetic, and civics education.	Hands-on math and science; physical education and health.
Rousseau (1712–1778) (Swiss/French)	Children need a nurturing learning environment. Children cannot learn until they are ready to learn.	Need to encourage students. Discipline should not be administered harshly.	Nature, surrounding environment.	Students are given choices in their learnings.
Pestalozzi (1746–1827) (Swiss)	Consider children's developmental level in curriculum development.	Need to emphasize the natural stages of students' development. Teach from concrete to abstract.	Social studies, integrate writing with reading.	Balanced reading and writing instruction.
Herbart (1776–1841) (German)	Moral education should be primary role of schooling.	To teach ethics and values.	Organized and integrated curriculum.	Lesson and unit plans; values education.
Froebel (1782–1852) (German)	Children learn from hands-on experiences. Early childhood education should be stressed.	The teacher is a role model who creates a secure, nurturing learning environment.	Nature, social skills.	Hands-on activities.
Montessori (1870–1952) (Italian)	Children learn if they are kept interested.	Need to set up a structure of classroom activities.	Integrated curriculum with social applications.	Hands-on math and science.
Piaget (1896–1980) (Swiss)	Children learn developmentally.	Match learning activities to the child's abilities.	Reading, writing, math, and science.	Ability-appropriate activities.

■ Summary

The foundations of education began in ancient civilizations with the advent of writing. Greek philosophers such as Socrates, Plato, and Aristotle helped to formalize education and develop early educational practices.

During the Middle Ages, there were minimal cultural, educational, and scientific advancements. However, during the seventeenth century, Comenius and Locke greatly influenced educational theory. Comenius, probably more than any other person up to that time, caused more changes in how children were taught. He believed that the teacher had to be knowledgeable and that children should be treated with respect. Comenius emphasized the need for a structured curriculum and having students learn by doing. During this same period, Locke stressed the need for activities that allowed students to use their senses to learn and the need for personal hygiene and physical education.

Pestalozzi emphasized the need for a compassionate learning environment. Froebel, Pestalozzi's student, believed that the teacher should not only provide a supportive learning environment but also serve as a moral and social example for students.

In the early and mid-1900s, Maria Montessori, a medical doctor, observed that children were more likely to learn if they were interested in the subject and if it was enjoyable. Thus, she incorporated playlike activities into a structured, practical curriculum.

During the twentieth century, Jean Piaget, a biologist and psychologist, made great contributions to educational thought with his stages of cognitive development. As a result teachers began teaching children on an individual basis as they were ready to acquire new concepts.

■ Reflections

Select any four educational leaders discussed in this chapter. Describe how each of their theories influenced how you were taught. For instance, were you taught hands-on math or science? through an integrated curriculum?

■ Discussion Questions

1. How are Herbart's views on the need for schools to emphasize moral education reflected in today's society?
2. Divide into groups of three or four students. As a group, select the individual who has made the biggest difference in education. Be prepared to defend your selection.
3. How did the Renaissance contribute to educational theory?
4. Why weren't more early educational leaders women, particularly when many leaders were women (Queen Elizabeth I, Queen Victoria, Catherine the Great)?

■ For Further Reading

De Guimps, R. 1896. *Pestalozzi: His life and work.* New York: D. Appleton and Company.

Rippa, S. A. 1992. *Education in a free society: An American history.* 7th ed. White Plains, NY: Longman.

Rousseau, J. J. 1911. *Emile.* Translated B. Foxley. New York: Dutton.

UNESCO. 1957. *John Amos Comenius on education.* With introduction by J. Piaget. New York: Teachers College Press.

6

Historical Foundations of American Education

Primary Points

- Schools were initially created to ensure that children would learn to read the Bible.

- The agrarian lifestyle influenced education, including the school calendar and school size.

- The common school movement, led by Horace Mann, recognized the need for women to serve as teachers and professionalized teaching.

- As the population of the United States grew and increased skills were needed by industry, high schools were created.

- As the United States changed from an agrarian society to an industrial one, the goals of education changed.

Chapter Inquiries

- What were the educational priorities of the colonists?

- How did the colonial schools differ regionally? Why?

- Why was the common school significant in American education?

- How did western expansion impact educational practices?

- What curricular changes evolved over time? Why?

- How were diverse populations educated?

- In what ways did higher education develop in the United States?

Courtesy of the State Historical Society of Iowa

Corbis/Bettmann

Margaret Fogelsong Ingram was born in a small Missouri town around 1885. Upon her graduation from high school, she began her teaching career in a one-room rural school at a salary of $7 a week with a one-term contract. During the summers she attended teachers' institutes and later enrolled in the State Normal School at Kirksville, where she obtained a life teaching certificate. At that point, she left Missouri and her salary of $40 a month to take a teaching/principal position in a Montana high school at a salary of $80 per month. The following year, the school board decided to hire a man to serve as teaching/principal and to move her to a second-/third-grade combination class at a reduced salary of $75 per month. Miss Fogelsong accepted; however, the high school students revolted and refused to cooperate with the new male principal. The school board offered her the old position that she had previously held, and Miss Fogelsong angrily rejected their offer (Labaree 1989).

At that time, to teach at the high school level, an individual needed to have some college education. Fogelsong wanted to teach high school students, so each summer she enrolled in courses at the University of Chicago. While holding a number of different teaching positions in Missouri, Montana, and Kentucky during the ten years following her initial teaching position, Fogelsong had earned an average salary of $430 a year. She wrote in her journal:

> What rankled within my soul was the discrimination against me because of sex, upon the very threshold of my career. Too many good men left the profession. Too many weak superintendents leaned heavily upon their strong teachers, usually women, while they drew the lion's share of the pay, took the credit, and bossed, merely because they were men. Meantime, localities engaged in the expensive pastime of wrangling, the petty larceny of Nepotism, and the exacting of missionary devotion from their women teachers (Ingram 1954, 289).

Fogelsong pursued a career in journalism while she still taught. Upon graduating from the University of Chicago, she was determined to find a teaching position that paid a minimum of $100 a month. Not immediately finding such a position, she worked as a sales representative for a textbook publisher. Later she received her master's degree from the University of Chicago. She eventually enrolled in Columbia Teachers College and obtained a Ph.D. and later married. She had taught in several states: Missouri, Montana, Iowa, Kentucky, Texas, and New York (Labaree 1989).

The ladder was there, "from the gutter to the university," and for those stalwart enough to ascend it, the schools were a boon and a path out of poverty.

—Diane Ravitch

Throughout the history of the United States, education has been influenced by myriad outside forces. Initially, schools were founded because children needed to learn how to read the Bible. Societal expectations during the 1600s through the early 1900s resulted in families sending boys to school while girls typically received minimal educational experiences. This pattern continued well into the early part of the twentieth century, when it was considered by many families to be a waste of money to send a girl to college. Even today, religion, societal expectations, economic factors, and political factors greatly influence our schools.

This chapter presents an overview of the history of schooling in the United States from colonial times to the present. It examines the influence of Europe on this country's educational system as well as innovations from American educators, including study of the classics, women as teachers, the common school movement, and progressive education.

Colonial Schools

During the colonial period, three geographic areas formed three very different forms of **schooling.** In the New England colonies of the Massachusetts Bay Colony, Connecticut, New Hampshire, and Vermont, schools were dominated by religion. Of these, Massachusetts set the tone for much of how formal education was established. In the Middle Atlantic colonies of New York, Delaware, New Jersey, Rhode Island, and Pennsylvania, a common language and religion did not exist as it did in the New England colonies. Thus, cultural and religious diversity was prevalent. Finally, the southern colonies of Maryland, Virginia (which included the current state of West Virginia), North and South Carolina, and Georgia had a much smaller population than did the New England and Middle Atlantic colonies and that population was scattered over a large area of land. The wide distances between houses led to itinerant teachers who traveled by horseback from plantation to plantation, staying a few weeks at a time to educate the children of the plantation owner. Private libraries were popular among the wealthy plantation owners, who paid private tutors to instruct their children to read the classics, learn French, play a musical instrument, and calculate mathematics.

New England Colonies

In Massachusetts in 1642, a law was passed that required parents to educate their children. In 1647, the infamous Old Deluder Satan Act strengthened the 1642 law. These legal actions were strongly supported by the Puritans, who believed it was critical that everyone be able to read the Bible and interpret its meaning. The Old Deluder Satan Act suggested that Satan would not want children to learn how to read because he would "keepe men from the knowledge of y Scriptures" (Shurtleff 1853). The act required that a school be established and maintained in communities of fifty or more families. In communities of over one hundred families, a grammar school was required to prepare youth to attend the university, which was Harvard.

With these two Massachusetts laws, education became a civil responsibility of the state. This was the first colony to establish public education, and it served as a model for the other colonies. While it might appear that these two laws were democratic acts, this was not the case at all. Indeed, Puritan leaders such as John Winthrop staunchly opposed all democratic ideals. The true impetus for the laws' passage was to enable the Puritans as a group to maintain and preserve their way of life, thus the legislation provided continuity in terms of social conformity and commitment to religion.

The influence of religion, along with the "three Rs" of reading, writing, and arithmetic, constituted the "four Rs" of early education in the United States. While boys were typically educated in formal schools, girls were generally taught by homemakers in what were known as **dame schools.** These women charged a small fee to teach young girls basic skills in reading, writing, and arithmetic in addition to household skills of cleaning, cooking, and sewing. Some boys also attended dame schools, later leaving for more advanced educational training at another school. For the majority of girls, however, the dame schools were the extent of their formal education. Girls were not encouraged to seek higher education after learning to read, write, and do simple math. It was believed that their purpose in life was to make their husbands comfortable and teach their children proper manners. All matters of business, with the exception of basic household purchases, were left to the husbands to conduct.

The town schools of New England were locally controlled, largely by prominent community leaders, including religious leaders. The teachers were male and often incompetent "n'er do wells" and social misfits who taught from the front of the classroom to students seated in rows on benches. Duncecaps and hickory switches were commonly used as punishment. Teacher incompetency was commonplace during this period. Teaching was a low-paying profession, and there were few competent teachers available because formal training of teachers was lacking. It was not unusual for schools to dismiss a teacher for lack of instructional ability at the end of a school year only to replace that individual with another teacher equally incompetent.

Children as young as five attended the town schools for about eight years, or until the family needed their services. Frequently weather intervened in students' attendance—a warm, sunny spring day might mean large absenteeism because children helped plow fields and plant crops. Likewise, on a cool, crisp autumn day children were needed to butcher hogs and cattle for the winter's larder. In winter, even a moderate snowfall with drifting might prevent children from attending school.

The curriculum consisted of the three Rs plus religious catechism. Rote memorization and recitation was stressed, and music consisted of singing religious hymns of the day, such as "Praise God From Whom All Blessings Flow," "A Mighty Fortress Is Our God," and "Let All the World in Every Corner Sing." Young children used **hornbooks,** which are small, handheld books shaped like a Ping-Pong paddle with a single sheet of parchment protected by a covering of clear material made from flattened horns of cattle, hence the name *hornbook.* The single page of the hornbook typically contained the letters of the alphabet, syllables of words, words, a sentence or two, or often the Lord's Prayer. Children often used their hornbooks to bat objects at each other, thus few have survived as artifacts.

Reading was integrated with the teaching of religion. Students read and memorized biblical verses and passages, such as the Twenty-third Psalm and the Ten Commandments, and older children read from *The New England Primer,* a collection of religious writings and other moralistic readings. The *Primer,* first introduced in 1690, remained a popular and widely used basic textbook for over one hundred years. Arithmetic in the town school was referred to as "cipherin'," in effect merely counting, adding, and substracting numbers.

The **Latin grammar school** was a secondary, precollege school for sons of upperclass families. By this age, daughters were usually deemed by their fathers as being ready for marriage, homemaking, and childbearing. Only on rare occasions did girls attend grammar school.

Teachers, who were usually men, taught Greek and Latin classics. Mathematics, history, and science received little attention. The boys entered school at about eight years of age and stayed until they were sixteen. Advanced students read the works of Cicero, Caesar, Vergil, Horace, Socrates, and Homer. Students then went on to a college, such as Harvard, which required command of the Latin and Greek languages and also stressed grammar, logic, rhetoric, geometry, and the natural sciences as well as the study of the Bible.

In colonial times, particularly in New England, it was quite common for children of poor families to be apprenticed to tradespeople for periods of two to ten years. The family of the apprenticed child would typically receive a small sum of money in

Examples of hornbooks. (Courtesy of the State Historical Society of Iowa).

exchange for the child's labor, while the child not only learned the trade but was taught reading and writing, and some arithmetic, in addition to being provided room and board. Both boys and girls served such apprenticeships. Girls often were servants in households, while boys worked for printers, blacksmiths, shoe cobblers, and tailors.

Middle Atlantic Colonies

Compared with the New England and southern colonies, the Middle Atlantic colonies were more diverse in their populations. A number of religious groups came to the New World and settled in the Middle Atlantic colonies: Baptists, Catholics, Huguenots, Mennonites, and Quakers, among others. The people of the Middle Atlantic colonies spoke a variety of languages, in particular Dutch, German, and Swedish, and held different religious beliefs and values. For example, New York had been founded by the Dutch as New Amsterdam. The Dutch people set up parochial schools to teach reading, writing, and religion. These schools were under the control of the Dutch Reformed Church. Later, New Amsterdam was renamed New York when the English took over control as a colony of England. At that point, the Church of England began operating charity schools in New York as part of its missionary society.

Schools in the Middle Atlantic colonies were largely denominational and not supported by public funds. The instructor was paid by families to educate their children. Typically, parents were concerned that their children not only learn to read, write, and acquire proficiency in basic computational skills but also to receive proper religious training.

New York City grew rapidly into a major trade center. Workers who could speak other languages, such as French and Spanish, and skilled tradespeople with geographical and nautical knowledge were in demand. To meet this demand, **academies** devoted to teaching specific skills or trades were created. Unlike apprentices, students of these schools came from middle-class families who had the funds to pay tuition fees. The idea of the academy spread to nearby colonies.

Benjamin Franklin published his *Proposals Relating to the Education of Youth in Pensilvania [sic]* in 1749. Using John Milton, John Locke, and others as references, Franklin proposed that an academy would be secular in both tone and content. He stressed the need for "vocational training and practical preparation for a life of usefulness in society, government, occupation, and professional service." Franklin envisioned "a pleasant and attractive school life for the students in his hope that the school would have a garden, orchard, meadow, and fields and be well stocked with books, maps, globes, scientific apparatus, and machines. Attention to physical education was also recommended" (Butts and Cremin 1953, 78). Drawing and mathematics were also stressed in the curriculum. Franklin opened the Philadelphia Academy in 1751.

Like New York, the Pennsylvania colony had a variety of different nationalities and religious sects. These included people of English, Welsh, Dutch, French, and German descent who flooded into eastern Pennsylvania to settle. One prominent religion in the area was the Society of Friends, founded by William Penn and commonly called the Quakers. Penn believed, as did his followers, that violence, including war for whatever reason, was intolerable. Thus, corporal punishment was disavowed in their school. The Society of Friends provided schools that were open to all children, male and female, whites, African Americans, and Native Americans. They believed that children deserved respect. The Quaker schools taught vocational skills such as handicrafts, agriculture, and, for the girls, domestic science, in addition to reading, writing, arithmetic, and religion.

Many of the principles set forth in the Middle Atlantic colonies' schools are still prevalent today. Vocational education is a major part of high school curricula. Certainly mathematics and physical education have retained their importance. The Quakers' beliefs that students are to be respected and that corporal punishment should not be allowed in schools are written into most school districts' policy handbooks.

Southern Colonies

Because of the distance between plantations in the South, children from affluent families were educated by private tutors, often local ministers or itinerant scholars who rode a circuit of plantations, or they were sent away to private schools. Teaching was not an acceptable profession for upper-class women because of the need to travel from plantation to plantation. However, it was suited to young men who did not have any family obligations and who later planned to enter a profession such as law or the ministry (Rury 1989). Many of the plantation owners were from the English upper class and were members of the Anglican Church.

Southern plantations harvested one prominent crop each year, such as cotton or tobacco. Mechanization was virtually nonexistent in the 1600s and 1700s. Manual labor was supplied by slaves, purchased from slave traders who brought them from Africa or from other slave owners. New generations of African Americans raised on the plantations became the slaves of their owner. African American slaves were taught skills needed for maintaining the agrarian life, that is, how to plant, cultivate, and weed; how to harvest cotton, tobacco, or rice; and how to do housework and cook. Slaves were prohibited from learning to read and write. Poor whites who owned and tilled the less productive marginal land of either the back country or the hills and mountains were, like the slaves, uneducated. Because wealthy landowners controlled education in the southern colonies, large public school systems were not formed until after the Civil War (Ornstein and Levine 1989).

*Slavery and the Lack of Education
of African Americans*

Slaves greatly outnumbered the owners and their families. Thus, authoritarian means were used to keep slaves under the control of their white owners. We are quite familiar with Harriet Beecher Stowe's portrayal of the evil and cruel slavemaster Simon Legree in her monumental book, *Uncle Tom's Cabin* (1972).

Slaves were forbidden to learn how to read and write. Consider what Sarah Wilson, a former slave, said:

I's larned to read de Bible, an' my chillun larned to read and write, but our white folks didn't believe in niggers larnin' anything. Dey thought hit would make de niggers harder to keep slaves, an' to make dem work. All de slaves dat I knowed couldn't read nor write (Mellon 1988, 197).

Anyone who taught a slave to read and write was also punished. William McWhorter, another former slave, said this during an interview in the 1930s:

Lordy, mist'ess, ain't nobody never told you it was agin' de law to larn a nigger to read and write, in slavery time? White folks would chop your thumbs off for dat quicker dan dey would for 'most anything else. Dat's jus' a sayin', "Chop your thumbs off." Why mist'ess, a nigger widout no thumbs wouldn't be able to wuk much, and his owner couldn't sell him for nigh as much as he could git for a slave wid good hands. Dey jus' beat 'em up bad when dey cotched 'em studyin', readin', and writin', but folks did tell 'bout some of de owners dat cut off one finger evvy time dey cotch a slave tryin' to get some larnin' (Mellon 1988, 197).

Learning simple arithmetic was also prohibited. Slaves were not allowed to count change because they could be a potential threat economically. Thus, if a slave borrowed a dollar bill, he or she would have to pay it back as a dollar bill, not as four quarters, ten dimes, two fifty-cent pieces, or any combination that would total a dollar.

The Common School

During the late 1700s and the 1800s as the frontier expanded, interest in education was nationwide. The U.S. Constitution itself does not mention education; however, Article X states: "The powers not delegated to the United States by the Constitution, nor prohibited by it to the States, are reserved to the State respectively, or to the people." Thus, education is the legal responsibility of the states.

Congress enacted the Land Ordinance of 1785, commonly referred to as the Northwest Ordinance, which incorporated the Northwest Territory. The ordinance divided the lands into townships consisting of thirty-six sections, each one mile in a six-mile-by-six-mile square block. The section numbered sixteen, the center of each township, was designated as the site of the school for the community. As the states of Ohio, Indiana, Illinois, and Michigan joined the original thirteen, the Land Ordinance of 1785 determined the educational opportunities on the frontier.

With the War of 1812, citizens were concerned about maintaining their nation. New states were being added in the South, including Kentucky, Tennessee, Louisiana, and Alabama. Indeed, Tennessee, a frontier state, produced a president, Andrew Jackson. Pioneers settling in frontier states lacked strong ties to the social conventions of New England and parts of the Middle Atlantic and southern states. As Rippa (1992, 75) wrote, "Streaming in from the old seaboard states, the frontier

Horace Mann was a persuasive orator and an astute politician. To gain support for public schools, Mann would tell differing factions what they wanted to hear—even though he sometimes contradicted himself. Lack of news media benefited Mann's strategy. (Courtesy of Northern Illinois University)

settlers became imbued with a rugged independence and a new liberalism in politics that flourished in the backwoods climate. Unopposed by religious- and private-school traditions, the idea of public education also took root and slowly grew." This interest in education climaxed with the common school movement, which sought to provide free public schooling for all children.

The common school movement was led by Horace Mann, a lawyer who served as a member of the Massachusetts legislature. Mann was appointed the first secretary of education of Massachusetts in 1837. Mann's twelve *Annual Reports* shared his philosophy of education as well as gave an indication of the state of schools in Massachusetts. In the *First Report*, Mann's salient points included the basic requirements for an education, such as adequately built and maintained school buildings, qualified teachers, responsible members of school committees, and robust support by citizens for public education.

Mann knew he needed the support of several groups throughout Massachusetts if the common school movement was to succeed. Working fifteen-hour days, writing his own reports, and answering correspondence without any clerical assistance (Rippa 1992), Mann doggedly fought for the cause of public education. He was a master at political strategy. For example, Mann skillfully persuaded the wealthy class that it was their social and moral responsibility to assist in the education of all children; indeed it would ensure the protection of the upper class.

Mann traveled abroad in 1843 to study the schools of Europe. He praised the Prussian schools, which followed Pestalozzian principles of respect for and understanding of the child. Like Johann Pestalozzi (discussed later in this chapter), Mann believed that women were better suited than men to teach young children. This

Chapter 6   *Historical Foundations of American Education*

Point /Counterpoint — *Should Public Funds Be Used to Educate Children?*

Point: There is a great need for a common school supported by public funds.

A common school provides for the education of all children, no matter what a family's socioeconomic level. Thus, all of society will be an educated society, making for better-trained workers and increasing productivity.

A free education for all is a basic human right and provides equal educational opportunity. Children whose families lack the funds for a private education are still able to develop their talents and contribute to the societal good.

An educated populace is essential for the survival of a democracy. A well-informed citizenry is needed if the principles of democracy are to be maintained and upheld.

Counterpoint: One family should not have to pay for the education of another family's children.

It is unfair to have wealthy families pay for the education of children from impoverished families. Parents are responsible for providing food and clothing for their children. When parents also provide education for their children, they can choose how their children are to be educated and for what length of time. To have wealthy families pay for the education of children from poor families is to penalize the affluent members of society and reward those who are not prosperous.

---

caused an outcry among those who believed men were the only fit teachers of children. The shortage of male workers for mercantile positions and as industrial workers aided Mann's position and helped influence business leaders of the period that women could play a role in education. Naturally, Mann supported education for both boys and girls, again a controversial stance in that day.

Mann's *Annual Reports* were read throughout the United States as well as in Europe and in South America. His educational philosophy spread to other states and territories. Mann's influence led to the passage in 1852 of the first compulsory education law, which required all children of elementary school age to attend school. This occurred at a time when the affluent owners of the mills of Lowell, Massachusetts, hired mostly illiterate young women to work in sweatshop conditions. Many of the young workers died from injuries caused by dangerous machines or because their lungs became filled with lint. While some mill owners hired young children as workers, Horace Mann's efforts began to sway the populace that child labor was not in the best interest of children. Without Horace Mann's insistence that women made good teachers, the teaching profession would have remained dominated by males for a much longer period of time. No one person did more to contribute to the success of the common school movement and the education of women than did Horace Mann.

While Mann was leading the common school movement in Massachusetts, Henry Barnard worked toward the same goal in Connecticut and Rhode Island. Unlike Mann, who had a difficult and impoverished childhood, Barnard was born of wealth and educated in private schools. He was a lawyer who graduated from Yale, and like Mann, he traveled to Europe to study the Pestalozzian methods of teaching.

Horace Mann was one of the most influential leaders in the history of American education. He worked tirelessly to push for the establishment of common schools, an effort recognized as a milestone in American education.

Mann was born on May 4, 1796, on a farm in New England, not far from Franklin, Massachusetts. His parents had little money to spare for a formal education for their son; however, they did instill in him a desire for the acquisition of knowledge, an aspiration he maintained throughout his life. Mann graduated from Brown University in 1819, the top student in the class. Still with little financial means, Mann tutored students at Brown University before enrolling in law school at Litchfield, Connecticut. He returned to his home state of Massachusetts, where he passed the bar exam in 1823.

Mann's first wife died shortly after they were married. After her death, he went to Boston and entered politics. He was elected to the state senate of Massachusetts in 1833 and in his role as a state senator, Mann was highly instrumental in the creation and passage of a law that formulated the Massachusetts Board of Education. In 1837, Mann resigned from his senate position to become the first secretary of the Massachusetts Board of Education. It was in this position that he would carve out new pathways for education that would make his name synonymous with the common school movement.

As secretary of the Massachusetts Board of Education, Mann wielded profound influence on the common school movement, which resulted in free public schooling for the masses. His philosophical stance, though seemingly conservative by present-day standards, was revolutionary for his time. Mann's philosophical point of view was grounded in four ideas: (1) education should be universal, regardless of economic status; (2) education should be free; (3) education should be dependent on carefully trained teachers; and (4) education should train both men *and* women.

During Mann's tenure on the Massachusetts Board of Education, he had a great and lasting influence on American education through his intense dedication in his personal beliefs about education, the publication of his twelve *Annual Reports* of the status of education, and his founding and editing of the *Common School Journal*. These efforts changed the direction of American education. His publications helped sway public opinion in favor of the common school movement.

Mann is also credited with supporting the education of females at a time when society valued only the schooling of males. Mann argued that women could be successful teachers, a rebellious cry unheard of in his day. He went even further in staunchly supporting that women teach children in their early school years because he believed that women were more caring and insightful with younger children than were their male counterparts.

A vigorous advocate of professionally trained teachers, Mann established the first public normal school at Lexington, Massachusetts, in 1839. Students enrolled in the normal school engaged in a curriculum that focused on educational theory. They also worked with children in practice schools under close supervision.

Strongly influenced by the European schools, particularly those in Prussia (which later became Germany), Mann incorporated Pestalozzian methods. He persistently demanded that a more humane approach be used in schools and that the use of corporal punishment be minimized. Mann was one of the first American educators to encourage teachers to build rapport with students based on mutual respect and admiration. This was in a time when the common motto in most schools was, "Spare the rod and spoil the child."

Mann put forth a nonsectarian approach to education. He saw the need to keep church and state separated, with the school system being effectively and efficiently run by the state. Schools were to be accessible to all. Mann believed that religious instruction was

(continued)

(concluded)

most appropriately taught in a church setting and should not detract from academic endeavors in school.

Prior to Mann, there was little support for school libraries. Mann made the public aware that good school libraries are vital to education.

Mann also created one of the first mental health institutes in the United States. He believed that the mentally ill deserved kind treatment. Working with his contemporary, Dorothea Dix, individuals confined to mental health institutes were provided with clean surroundings, good food, and ample care.

Under Mann's direction, Massachusetts led the nation in the common school movement. His goal was to provide a free public education for every child. According to Mann, the foundation for a free society was a universal system of public education. Today, Mann's ideas still prevail: professional training of teachers; women and men equally accepted as teachers; free public education for all, regardless of financial abilities; and the separation of church and state. His untiring efforts changed the direction of American education dramatically. Mann died on August 2, 1859, but his educational innovations and contributions live on in today's society.

Barnard was impressed with Pestalozzi's emphasis on the individual. Three elements of the individual were most important to learning in Pestalozzi's view: the head, heart, and hand. Pestalozzi stressed the need for children to become aware of their environment, and he would often take children on strolls through the countryside. He used clay models to demonstrate geography, making it as realistic as possible. Barnard incorporated these ideas and expanded on them.

Also like Mann, Barnard became the first secretary of education for his state, Connecticut. Both men strongly supported the education of women. Meeting with great resistence to his common school ideals, Barnard was removed from office. He went to Rhode Island as the first commissioner of education for that state, where he continued his writings on the common school movement.

During this period of the early 1800s, Emma Willard, Mary Lyon, and Julia and Elias Mark opened seminaries for girls. These schools provided an education for girls that was of equal quality to that already provided for boys. It was not until well into the 1900s, however, that women were allowed equal access to higher education.

While the common school movement spread, it met with great resistence in the South (Butts and Cremin 1953). The southern social structure differed greatly from that found in New England and the Middle Atlantic states. The long distance between plantations, the southern aristocratic class, and the question of slavery all contributed to constraining the common school movement. Progress was made in the Midwest, however, by Caleb Mills, who wrote in support of public education from his post at Wabash College. Mills was said to have "expanded the basis of education in Indiana" (Mayer 1960, 348). Likewise, California was responsive to the common school movement largely because of the efforts of John Swett, who worked to support legislation in support of public schools (Rippa 1992).

Common School Curriculum

The common school curriculum still emphasized the three Rs of reading, writing, and arithmetic. Religion was still a part of the curriculum in stories emphasizing Victorian values of reverence, honesty, and industry. Other subjects included geography, history, and music.

The schools of the common school era had two major books. One was Noah Webster's *Grammatical Institute of the English Language*, the first part of which was published as the *American Spelling Book* and immediately was referred to as the *Blue Back Speller*

(Farris 1993). Webster was deeply interested in creating an American culture. He worked to develop the first American dictionary, appropriately entitled the *American Dictionary*, which continues to be updated and published today.

The majority of children in the mid- to late 1800s learned to read from William Holmes McGuffey's readers. In 1835, prior to the publication of his readers, McGuffey gave a speech entitled "Lecture on the Relative Duties of Parents and Teachers." According to McGuffey (1835, 135), "It is knowledge and morality, the offspring of knowledge that alone can give general prosperity to society." McGuffey gathered stories and poetry that illustrated the values of honesty, perserverance, kindness, courage, gratitude, reverence, industriousness, and patriotism and put them into a series of graded readers, creating one of the first basal reading series (Farris 1980, 1993). An example is lesson XXXIX of the *First McGuffey Eclectic Reader* (McGuffey 1879, 51–52), which follows:

> *See my dear, old grandma in her easy-chair! How gray her hair is! She wears glasses when she reads.*
> *She is always kind, and takes such good care of me that I like to do what she tells me.*
> *When she says, "Robert, will you get me a drink?" I run as fast as I can to get it for her. Then she says, "Thank you, my boy."*
> *Would you not love a dear, good grandma, who is so kind? And would you not do all you could to please her?*

McGuffey included work from writers of his day, for example, Henry Ward Beecher, as well as writers from the past, including Shakespeare.

Ironically, McGuffey did not include educational practices of his day in his readers. He largely ignored the Prussian educational system and Horace Mann's efforts to improve education through the common school movement (Commager 1962). While the moral values of the McGuffey readers reflect those of the Victorian age, it was the middle-class children of America who were his primary audience. Mosier (1947, 123) wrote, "The great achievement of the McGuffey readers is the complete integration of Christian and middle-class ideals." Because of this integration, the McGuffey readers are considered to be "the great textbook of American middle-class structure" (Mosier 1947, 123).

Over 122 million copies of the McGuffey readers were sold prior to 1920. Often the books passed from one child in the family to the next, generation after generation (Farris 1980). Because of their popularity and moralistic content, McGuffey readers have been acknowledged as a major influence on the character of civilization of the nineteenth and early twentieth centuries (Minnich 1936; Walker 1976).

European Influences

Like the unique system of government in the United States, the system of education differed from that of Europe due to the adoption of public rather than private education. However, four Europeans greatly influenced education in the United States in the 1800s. In Germany in 1837, the same year that Horace Mann became secretary of education of Massachusetts, Friedrich Froebel introduced the concept of **kindergarten,** a children's garden.

In 1855, Mrs. Carl Schurz, a former student of Froebel, opened a private kindergarten for German-speaking students in Watertown, Wisconsin. Five years later, Elizabeth Palmer Peabody, a sister-in-law of Horace Mann, opened a private kindergarten in Boston for English-speaking children. By 1873, kindergarten was incorporated as part of the public school system in St. Louis, Missouri, due in part to the influence of its large German population.

A Closer Look — *Rules of Conduct for Rural Teachers*

Taken from a Boone County school in the 1920s:

1. Teachers must have legal qualifications.
2. They must keep the classroom neat and clean; sweep the floor at least once a day; clean blackboards each day; scrub the floor and toilets at least once a month.
3. Ring school bell, promptly at 9.
4. Raise the flag before the start of school.
5. Start the fire early enough to have the school warm by 9 a.m.
6. Keep the school in session until 4 p.m.
7. Prepare and present a Christmas program for the community.
8. Observe Arbor Day to beautify the school grounds.
9. Women teachers may not dress in bright colors.
10. Dresses must be of an appropriate length.
11. Bobbed hair is forbidden. If hair is cut short, a switch must be worn in the classroom.
12. Married teachers will not be hired.
13. Good conduct must be kept in the school, to warrant a renewal of a contract.
14. Teachers who engage in unseemingly conduct will be dismissed.
15. Any teacher who smokes, uses liquor in any form, frequents pool or public halls, will give good reason to suspect his worth.
16. The length of the school term is stated in the contract (either eight or nine months).
17. Palatable water must be available in the building each day.
18. The teacher's instruction must prepare the eighth grade students to pass the county exam, which will qualify them for high school graduation.

Source: Local history department of Rockford, IL, Public Library, Boone County Historical Society Museum

Today, Froebel's ideas are a part of the American educational system. Kindergartens are fixtures in public school systems. The developmental curriculum of elementary and secondary schools also reflects Froebel's theory of teaching as the child develops.

Like Froebel, Johann Pestalozzi's theories were readily adopted in the United States. Studied and praised by both Mann and Barnard, Pestalozzi's methods of treating the child with respect, love, patience, and understanding greatly differed from the often harsh and cruel punishment doled out to children in the United States in the 1700s and early 1800s (Johnson et al. 1991).

Johann Friedrich Herbart, like Pestalozzi and Froebel, was also interested in how children were treated by teachers. Herbart believed that a child's interest in a subject greatly influenced the amount of learning that took place.

In 1908, Maria Montessori opened a school for impoverished children in Rome. She believed that children enjoy order and structure as well as work. Montessori schools are still popular in both Europe and the United States, primarily as private preschools. The curriculum of the schools is based on practical, sensory, and formal skills. Materials are small and childlike, designed so that young children can easily manipulate them with their hands. Motor coordination, reading, writing, and basic math are stressed. The focus is child-centered rather than group-centered so that children are encouraged to expand on their own individual interests.

The Secondary School

While academies and Latin grammar schools met the needs of the sons of middle- and upper-class families, respectively, there still existed a need for additionally trained workers. The nation was changing from a predominantly rural, agrarian populace to an industrial society. Cities grew into large urban populations, and workers with specialized training were needed. Massachusetts, once again, led the way in fulfilling the needs of the country with an American invention: the **high school.** In 1821, the first public high school opened its doors to boys in Boston. The curriculum was simple: English (reading and writing), mathematics, history, and science. Other courses of study were later added: philosophy, chemistry, logic, and trigonometry, among others.

The high school class of 1891, possibly in Elkader, Iowa. The original is a stereograph view, cut in half and bordered with a pink ribbon. (Courtesy of the State Historical Society of Iowa)

Nearly one hundred years later, in 1910, the first **junior high school** (grades seven, eight, and nine) opened to compensate for the differences between elementary and high school students. By the 1960s, **middle schools** were introduced as another way of meeting the educational and developmental needs of preadolescents—sixth, seventh, and eighth graders. Unlike the junior high schools, which followed a more secondary orientation, middle schools are often considered to be an extension of the elementary school.

Goals of Public Education

As we have discussed, early colonial schools were established for religious purposes. In order for children to understand the Bible, they had to learn to read. As the country grew, schools provided unity in that a common language, English, was shared. Common values of honesty, courage, industriousness, and above all patriotism were shared in schoolrooms across the country. Providing knowledge and training for future farmers, mill workers, and industrial workers were also important.

By the late 1800s, the common school movement had had a significant impact on our nation. Subsequently, three different groups developed goals for education in the United States: the Committee of Ten, the Seven Cardinal Principles of Education, and the Eight-Year Study.

At the end of World War II, federal legislation provided funding for training and furthering the education of returning soldiers and sailors. In the late 1950s, during the cold war, federal legislation once again provided funding, this time to enhance the math and science skills of elementary and secondary students. By the early 1980s, there was considerable public concern about the quality of public education. In 1994, Congress passed Goals 2000, which was designed to make schools more accountable and set higher academic standards for elementary and secondary students.

The New England states provided several educational leaders, including Francis W. Parker. Born on October 9, 1837, in a small village in New Hampshire, Parker was greatly influenced by his mother, Millie Rand Parker. She was an exceptional teacher, which undoubtedly accounted in part for his learning to read at the very young age of three as well as his strong desire to be educated. When Parker was six, his father died. With little to provide for the family, Parker's mother boarded Parker and his younger sister with a relative until they were old enough to "earn their keep." This Parker did when he was eight years old as a farm hand, "bound-out" to a local farmer until he was twenty-one (Campbell 1967).

While he served as a farm hand, Parker received only eight weeks of formal schooling each year. Later, he considered the farm to be where he received his "true" education. He believed that the years on the farm were one of the best preparations for his teaching career. Parker later reminisced that a farm served as the basis for elementary learning because it is one place where a child can be made responsible for something important as well as acquire good work habits. In addition, the child is surrounded by a simple, peaceful environment. At age thirteen, Parker broke his farming apprenticeship and enrolled in a local academy; however, insufficient finances prevented him from finishing his last term.

At sixteen, Parker was engaged to teach in a country school. In 1859, he became both teacher and principal of a school in Carrolton, Illinois. The school included primary grades through high school, which was commonplace in most rural communities. With the beginning of the Civil War, Parker joined the Union Army and earned the rank of colonel, a title by which he was often later called. Wounded in action in 1864, he was on a furlough when he married another schoolteacher, Phenie E. Hall. The next year, Ann, their only child, was born (Campbell 1967).

After the war ended, Parker resumed teaching, this time in Dayton, Ohio. It was during this period that Parker became disenchanted with the harsh discipline and rigid traditional teaching methods prevalent for the day. Parker's ideal was to free children from the constraints, regulations, and almost military-like regimentation that existed in classrooms. He loathed rote learning and advocated that learning must be meaningful to the child to be understood. Concrete, hands-on experiences were to be the primary form of instruction for children.

Parker believed there were no bad children, just children who were victims of bad homes, bad habits, and bad conditions. Thus, he treated children with compassion, kindness, understanding, and, above all, respect. He emphasized the need for adults to believe in children and demonstrate faith and confidence in them. Through security and encouragement, children would think of themselves as successful and never as failures. Through a strong belief in human potential, Parker felt that every child had the ability to develop a skill and the right to be successful in life. Parker wrote, "Nothing that is good is too good for the child, no thought too deep, no toil too great, no work too arduous" (Parker 1894, 451).

The death of his wife in 1870 led Parker to reexamine his ideals and beliefs about teaching. He traveled to Europe and studied at the University of Berlin. There Parker discovered that he was a kindred spirit of the likes of Froebel, Herbart, and Pestalozzi, all of whom held a similar philosophy regarding children and their education.

Upon his return to the United States in 1875, Parker returned to New England, where he had grown up. He became the superintendent of schools in Quincy, Massachusetts. There Parker put into practice what was to become known as the Quincy System of education. The Quincy System gained worldwide recognition as an experimental curriculum and replaced the rote learning and textbooks of the day. The "whole word method" was used for reading rather than the alphabet spelling system, which introduced letter-sound correspondences such as *ab, ac,* and *ad,* followed by parts of words,

(continued)

(concluded)

such as *tab*, before the entire word *table* (Lapp and Flood 1992). Rather than emphasizing the rules of grammar, students were encouraged to construct their own sentences, write letters, and create their own short compositions, which were intended to be "real" and "meaningful" to the child. Arithmetic, too, was modified and no longer taught in a concrete fashion. Rather than rely on textbooks for instruction in the sciences and geography, field trips became the primary vehicle for instruction. Parker advocated that students learn to read, write, and think without differentiating between subjects, quite similar to the whole language approach of today.

Like Horace Mann before him, Parker had a profound effect on the training of teachers. His teachers were encouraged to share ideas and visit one another's classrooms. Parker himself served as a model and gave weekly demonstration lessons for teachers. He also tried to promote the development of creative and critical thinking in teachers. He would probe and push them with such questions as, How shall we educate? Is education necessary? What new notions about education have come to you this week? and the even more revealing, Are you a growing teacher?

Parker's teachers were given total freedom to develop their own educational system within their classrooms as long as the system was grounded in simple, but solid, scientific educational principles. The Quincy System offered unity in schools without uniformity; teachers taught to their own preferences. The curriculum was a reflection of the individuality brought forth by each of the teachers. Thus, in actuality, there was no "system" to the Quincy System. Critics argued that fundamentals were ignored. Parker, himself, denied that a Quincy System really existed; rather he believed it was a system of continuous change.

Parker served for a short time as supervisor of schools in Boston before he returned to the Midwest as principal of the Cook County Normal School in Chicago, Illinois, in 1883. This was considered by Parker to be a superb educational opportunity; not only would he work with children but he would also train teachers. Under Parker's leadership, the Cook County Normal School became a model for training teachers in the United States. He expanded the length of the time required for professional study from forty weeks to two complete years. Those enrolled in the program devoted a large amount of time to observation and practice teaching as part of the school's curriculum (Campbell 1967).

After serving sixteen years at the Cook County Normal School, Parker moved to the Chicago Institute, which then merged with the University of Chicago to create the University of Chicago School of Education. It was there that Parker worked with, and greatly influenced, John Dewey. It was Dewey who called Parker the father of progressive education.

The Committee of Ten

The Committee of Ten, including five college presidents and no women, was created by the National Education Association in 1892 to examine the function of the high school. At that time, only a small number of youth actually attended high school. The Committee of Ten was chaired by Charles W. Eliot, president of Harvard University, an influential leader in higher education and a man greatly interested in both elementary and secondary education. The Committee of Ten recommended the following:

1. A high school should consist of grades seven through twelve.
2. Courses should be arranged sequentially, with one a prerequisite for another.
3. A unit of study, called a Carnegie unit, should be awarded for each course that met daily for the entire school year.
4. Students should not be given many choices of courses as electives; the curriculum would be largely intact (National Education Association 1893).

The goals of high school were largely to meet the entrance requirements of college.

Perhaps no other person influenced educational policy in the twentieth century as did Ralph W. Tyler. Born in Chicago in 1902, the son of a minister, he attended rural schools in Nebraska.

Tyler disliked school, which he thought was for "sissies." Like many high school boys in Nebraska at that time, he trapped animals to sell for their fur. When he first trapped a skunk, he was curious about why it made such an awful smell. He extracted the juice from the glands of the skunk and as he was returning home, spied a bucket of paint destined for the school's radiators. Tyler poured the skunk juice into the bucket of paint. Later during the fall, the heat was turned on and the school was filled with the skunk odor. Tyler was held accountable for his actions, but he protested that he didn't think he was learning anything in school. However, his father and the principal convinced him to stay in school. He attended school part-time and worked full time at a local creamery (Hiatt 1994).

Tyler graduated from Doane College in Crete, Nebraska, in 1921. The same year he married Flora Olivia Volz, and the young couple moved to Pierre, South Dakota, where Tyler took a position as a high school science teacher. During the summers he was director of the community swimming pool. He planned to use the money to attend medical school but instead changed his mind and stayed in education.

Tyler attended the University of Nebraska, where he received a Master of Arts degree in 1923. His thesis dealt with the development and standardization of high school science tests for the state of Nebraska. Tyler then began working on his doctorate at the University of Chicago and later, in 1927, he took a position as associate professor at the University of North Carolina (Ohles 1978). He moved to Ohio State University in 1931.

In 1932, Tyler became director of evaluation for the Eight-Year Study, one of the landmark studies in American education. The Eight-Year Study involved

Ralph W. Tyler worked diligently during the twentieth century to better schools in the United States and throughout the world. His contributions include the development of educational objectives and authentic assessment of students. (Courtesy of Phi Delta Kappa)

thirty secondary schools, both public and private, and over three hundred colleges. The secondary schools each designed and offered their own college preparatory curricula. The study included 1,475 pairs of college students, each pair consisting of one student from one of the experimental secondary schools and another student from a nonexperimental secondary school but who was of the same age, gender, and race and who had a similar home and community background. In addition, each pair had similar aptitude and achievement test scores. The result of the study found that the students

(continued)

(concluded)

from the experimental schools earned a slightly higher grade point average in college and were more precise, systematic, and objective in their thinking. Because the results of the Eight-Year Study were published during the height of World War II, the importance of the study was overshadowed by the war (Rippa 1992).

In 1938, Tyler became head of the Department of Education at the University of Chicago, where he later became dean of the Division of Social Sciences. In 1953, he created the Center for Advanced Study in the Behavior Sciences at Stanford University in California and became the director, a position he held for fourteen years.

Tyler served as an education consultant to five U.S. presidents. For fifteen years, Tyler chaired the National Commission on Resources for Youth. He was among the first U.S. educators to visit schools in the former Soviet republics and China.

Tyler had a long and distinguished career in education. While in his eighties, he still continued to write and speak as well as teach three college courses a week. The courses were not on a single university campus but were in fact in three separate states: New York, Illinois, and California. He commuted each week to all three campuses. When asked how at his age he kept up, he replied, "Oh, I'm lucky. I can sleep on planes" (Farris 1986).

According to Rubin (1994, 784), "Few public figures blend extraordinary capacities and vision to fashion a career that can truly be called awesome in its breadth and significance. Ralph Tyler was this sort of rarity." Rubin went on to describe the roots of Tyler's genius: "As with others marked by greatness, much of his talent resulted not from inherent gifts alone but from a portfolio of meticulously honed skills. Similarly, the exceptional length of his productivity stemmed neither from good fortune nor from special blessings, but rather from a systematically choreographed program to preserve his abilities and combat the ravages of time."

Tyler believed that education needs differed for individuals: "The notion that the goals of education should be the same for everyone is wrong. Education is a matter of trying to help the individual move forward from his present position, regardless of where that might be" (Lackey and Rowls 1989, 35–36). He also believed that "the purpose of life is learning. When one ceases to learn, one ceases to live life to the fullest. The biological basis of man has changed little since the cave days. However, each generation creates new ideas and elaborates on those ideas which have previously existed" (Hiatt 1994, 787).

Tyler felt that teaching students was a complex process that itself required constant learning: "Students should move in a step-by-step fashion which carries them forward at all times. This means that none of the steps should be so easy as to be boring, while at the same time they must not be so difficult that the student will fall flat on his face" (Lackey and Rowls 1989, 81).

Perhaps one of the greatest aspects of Tyler's genius was his foresight. In the 1960s, he asserted that evaluation and curriculum should follow different objectives than those currently in use. In the 1970s, he advanced the idea that the curriculum should be a good fit between what is taught and what is tested. These ideas were finally adopted in the 1990s, when authentic assessment practices such as the use of student-generated portfolios and teacher anecdotal records became commonplace (Rubin 1994).

Tyler was acutely aware of the need to maintain community ties with the schools: "One of the greatest tasks facing education today is that of strengthening the relationship among the schools, the home and other community groups. Strong bonds among these community resources and groups are one of the most effective means I know of to promote excellence in education" (Lackey and Rowls 1989, 52).

Tyler's pragmatic view was carried out in his own learning. Every night, before going to sleep, Tyler would ask himself what he learned that day, what it meant, and how could he use it.

On February 18, 1994, a month short of his ninety-second birthday, Ralph Tyler died. He had devoted nearly seventy years to the betterment of educational practices.

The Seven Cardinal Principles of Education

In 1918, the Commission on Reorganization of Secondary Education, a committee created again by the National Education Association, developed a report entitled *Cardinal Principles of Secondary Education*, typically referred to as the Seven Cardinal Principles of Education. These principles provided high school teachers with guidance about what to teach students. The seven principles were as follows:

1. health;
2. command of fundamental processes;
3. worthy home membership;
4. vocation;
5. civic education;
6. worthy use of leisure;
7. ethical character.

In essence, the Seven Cardinal Principles of Education shifted the direction of the high school from a college preparatory school to that of a **comprehensive school.** In the opening remarks, the committee wrote: "Secondary education should be determined by the needs of the society to be served, the character of the individuals to be educated, and the knowledge of educational theory and practice available. These factors are by no means static" (Commission on the Reorganization of Secondary Education 1918, 1).

The Eight-Year Study

Over twenty years after the Seven Cardinal Principles of Education were published, the Progressive Education Association produced the Eight-Year Study. From 1933 until 1940, students in thirty high schools were studied to determine how well they performed in college. The Eight-Year Study resulted in the following goals of education:

1. physical and mental health;
2. self-assurance;
3. assurance of growth toward adult status;
4. a clear philosophy of life;
5. wide range of personal interests;
6. aesthetic appreciations;
7. intelligent self-direction;
8. progress toward maturity in social relations with age-mates and adults.

G.I. Bill

In 1944, near the end of World War II, Congress passed the Servicemen's Readjustment Act. This act, commonly referred to as the G.I. Bill, provided federal monies to veterans to continue their education by subsidizing their tuition, books, and living expenses. As a result, enrollment in colleges and universities across the nation doubled and numerous trade and technical schools were established.

National Defense Education Act (NDEA) of 1957

The 1950s began the cold war era in which the United States and its allies cautiously viewed communist nations as rivals. At the end of World War II, the former Soviet Union had greatly increased its influence in Europe with the communist regimes in such countries as Albania, Czechoslovakia, East Germany, Hungary, Poland, and Yugoslavia.

The 1950s was also the advent of the space age, and the United States and the former Soviet Union both sought to be the first in space. In 1957, the Soviet Union won the first round of the space race with the successful launch of *Sputnik,* a space satellite. There was an outcry in Congress and across the nation deploring not only our nation's space program but blaming schools for producing students with low math and science scores. Congress rapidly passed the National Defense Education Act (NDEA) of 1958, which funded curricula improvements in math, science, and foreign languages. Audiovisual equipment such as film and overhead transparency projectors were purchased by schools with NDEA funds. Thousands of teachers received inservice training in math, science, and foreign languages at colleges and universities throughout the country.

A Nation at Risk

In 1983, *A Nation at Risk* (National Commission on Excellence in Education) was published. At the time, the American economy was struggling while the German and Japanese economies were flourishing. *A Nation at Risk* heavily criticized American schooling, again pointing out student deficiencies in math and science as well as a general lack of teacher competence. As a result, several states instituted legislation that mandated stricter high school graduation requirements, particularly in math, science, and English. In addition, several states, particularly those in the South, instituted teacher competency exams. Colleges and universities also increased their entrance requirements for math, science, and English. In addition, many added a requirement of two years of a foreign language.

Goals 2000

In 1994, Congress passed **Goals 2000.** This bill encourages states to work together to develop curriculum for students. In addition, each state is to assess and establish requirements for the different curricula and grade levels. Goals 2000 is viewed by many as a step toward national standards for both students and teachers.

Education of Diverse Populations

Initially, schools and academies in America focused on educating white males. Eventually, largely due to the work of Horace Mann and his supporters, white females were also educated beyond rudimentary reading, writing, and arithmetic skills. When large numbers of immigrants arrived, schools were used to teach a common language, English, to the overwhelming numbers of Western European immigrants (mainly Swedes, Germans, and Dutch). Schools also ensured a sense of unity for the young nation. Later, the schools served to assimilate the Irish, Russian, Polish, Sicilian, Finnish, and other peoples who immigrated to this country.

Madeline Hunter

At the age of twelve, Madeline Hunter made up her mind to become a psychologist. She attended the University of California at Los Angeles (UCLA) and majored in psychology. After graduation she continued her work in psychology at Children's Hospital in Los Angeles. Hunter did not like this position because it often involved preparing a child and his or her parents for the child's death, which was very depressing. After leaving the hospital Hunter worked at Juvenile Hall, where she said, "At least what those kids had was curable" (Goldberg 1990). She left this position because interventions in that setting were "too little, too late."

Madeline Hunter decided she would rather work at the preventive rather than the remedial end of things. She decided to become a school psychologist. While working in Inglewood, California Hunter found teachers to be dedicated and intelligent; however, she found that they didn't know much about the cause-and-effect relationships between teaching and learning. Hunter felt that teachers didn't ask enough questions and were unaware of names like Thorndike and Guthrie, American educator who stressed the psychological aspects of learning.

Hunter began working with teachers by translating psychological theory into language a teacher could understand Hunter's mission was to take psychological theory, much of which has been around for a hundred years, and translate it for classroom teachers. Hunter worked in the Inglewood and Los Angeles city school districts for thirteen years. She then became a professor at UCLA and principal of the UCLA Lab School.

Hunter spent twenty years at the Lab School and while there, she began to implement her ideas. Madeline read many research studies and translated them into practice. Hunter admired the work of Benjamin Bloom but added that he did not write for a teacher audience. Hunter stated that the researchers "often didn't know what the teacher was facing in the class room. They're researchers. The research is impeccably done by brilliant people, but it needs

Madeline Hunter stressed the need for teachers to structure lessons and include assessment as a component. (*Los Angeles Times Photographic Archive,* Department of Special Collections, University Research Library, UCLA)

translation before it can affect the classroom" (Goldberg 1990).

Hunter is probably best known for her seven step model. This model was developed from watching effective teachers teach. Hunter's model can increase the probability of learning. It tells the teacher what to consider before teaching and while teaching; it does not tell the teacher what to do. Using this model, the teacher is a decision maker who must know when and under what conditions to use the generalizations of the model (Batesky 1987).

(continued)

(concluded)

Prior to planning a lesson, the teacher must make three key decisions:

1. What content am I going to teach?
2. What behavior do I want from the learner?
3. What behavior will I as the teacher exhibit?

The seven steps of the lesson are as follows:

1. *Anticipatory set*—gets the student's attention focused on the lesson. The instructor is developing a state of readiness for instruction. Having a worthwhile anticipatory set will increase motivation, increase retention, and help in making efficient use of class time.

2. *Objective/why*—enables students to know what they will learn and why it is relevant or important to them. Without an objective, the students, teacher, and lesson have no sense of direction.

3. *Input*—provides the key information necessary to achieve the objective. Information is presented by the teacher in a simple to complex sequential manner.

4. *Modeling*—shows the students what is expected of them. The sequence of events in which modeling occurs, not simply the modeling itself, facilitates learning.

5. *Checking for student understanding*—checks comprehension as the teacher asks students questions in a variety of ways, including signaled answers, choraled response, or individual responses, to determine if the student truly understands the material. This step prevents teachers from proceeding when students do not understand.

6. *Guided practice*—allows monitored practice while the teacher is present. The student attempts the new skill while the teacher gives specific feedback about what is being done correctly, what needs to be improved, and how to improve performance.

7. *Independent practice*—occurs when the teacher is not present or monitoring student progress. New learning should be performed without major errors, discomfort, or confusion. Homework, a written test, or out-of-school activities are examples of independent practice (Batesky 1987).

In Hunter's design, all seven steps do not have to be completed in one day. This design allows for flexibility and recycling. Hunter stressed that this model is not a checklist; therefore, an observer should not expect to see all seven steps occur in one lesson.

Districts interested in this model must understand that it takes more than two hours of lecture with two handouts for follow-up. Hunter said the training should take at least two years of dedicated work. Districts must send staff members to valid workshops time and time again, provide continual support in the home district, and send the trainees back for research updates as often as possible. (Goldberg 1990).

Hunter was quoted as saying, "I hope I live to see public recognition of the incredible complexity of teaching." Most people believe that "teaching is just telling kids what to do and maintaining discipline" (Goldberg 1990), but Hunter compared teaching to surgery, "where you think fast on your feet and do the best you can with the information you have. You must be very skilled, very knowledgeable, and exquisitely well trained, because neither a teacher nor a surgeon can say, 'Everybody sit still until I figure out what in the heck we're gonna do next'" (Goldberg 1990).

When asked what she wanted to be remembered for most, Hunter replied, "If I could have my wish, I would hope my work would help move teaching from a craft to a profession based on research translated into artistic practice, where the professional is a decision maker and where the professional never stops learning" (Goldberg 1990).

Albert Shanker, Voice of the AFT

For over twenty-two years, the American Federation of Teachers (AFT) was led by Albert Shanker. Referred to as the father of collective bargaining for teachers, Shanker was a powerful leader and strong voice for public education. Noted for his quick decision making and bold stances on educational issues, Shanker built the AFT into a powerful labor union. But it was more than that, for it reflected Shanker himself as it became known as an organizational think tank and crusader for public education.

A graduate of the University of Illinois in 1949, Shanker then enrolled in Columbia University to study philosophy. In 1952, he became a substitute teacher in East Harlem, New York, a position he described as being a "lousy job." Later he moved to a regular classroom position where he taught mathematics at a Manhattan junior high school.

In 1960, Shanker took part in a one-day strike that resulted in the first collective bargaining agreement for teachers in the United States. By 1964, he was elected president of the United Federation of Teachers in New York City. During the next decade, Shanker would march with Dr. Martin Luther King in Selma, Alabama, to promote equal rights for blacks, be arrested in New York City for having a labor strike in favor of smaller class sizes, and spend fifteen days in jail during the Ocean Hill-Brownsville strike.

Neither a liberal nor a conservative, Shanker defined his political stance as being "common sense." Liberal reforms, he believed, were "faddish" and too radical to work. Likewise, he dismissed the vouchers and privatization of public schools plans offered by conservatives (Bradley and Ponessa 1997).

In the early 1980s, some teachers were taken aback when Shanker agreed with the negative reports, often scathing, on the quality of schooling in the United States. Using a weekly column in the Sunday edition of *The New York Times* paid for by the AFT as his pulpit, Shanker lashed out each week, attacking the way schools were run

Perhaps the foremost advocate of public education in the 20th century, Al Shanker kept the major issues of schooling in view of education's critics. He never backed down in his support for standards for teachers and the need for professionalism in the field. (Reprinted with permission of the American Federation of Teachers, AFL-CIO)

and the quality of teachers in the profession itself. The AFT, he stressed had a greater purpose than just improving the salaries of teachers through collective bargaining. The goal of the AFT, in Shanker's view, was to find avenues to improve the nation's schools.

(continued)

Shanker advocated minimum competency testing of teachers, saying that incompetent teachers had no place in the classroom. His support for national certification of teachers led to the development of the National Board for Professional Teaching Standards.

Teachers, in Shanker's view, needed empowerment as that they would have a voice in the decision making. As part of the national reform movement, building principals were required to develop instructional leadership skills. In addition, school districts across the nation began implementing site-based management in which the building principal and a team of teachers worked together to make decisions. Such programs failed to result in improved student achievement scores, causing Shanker to reevaluate his position. He concluded that there was little incentive for students to study hard.

In the 1990s, Shanker again shifted his position. In the 1960s he had stated that the public's opinion of him didn't matter to him, but in reality it did. Having been depicted in a 1973 Woody Allen movie as a madman who ultimately blew up the world with a nuclear bomb, Shanker moved toward more positions the general public found acceptable, such as higher standards for teachers and students. He promoted a national curriculum for all students.

Shanker shared conservative views that public schools should socialize young people into America's democracy. Multicultural education, in Shanker's view, needed to be viewed carefully. Taking too liberal a stance would result in divisive and destructive education that would not produce a democratic citizenry. Shanker even supported certain kinds of academic tracking and strongly opposed full inclusion programs.

In 1995, Shanker led the AFT's "Lessons for Life" campaign. "Lessons for Life" stresses high standards of conduct and academic achievement for students. This effort was perceived by Shanker as being achievable only if teacher unions, local elected officials, and communities worked together.

Upon Shanker's death in 1997, President Bill Clinton referred to him as one of the greatest educators of the twentieth century. According to Clinton, Shanker "believed that all children could learn—with high standards, high-quality teaching, and high accountability. He literally lived a lift that was nothing less than a crusade, with intense passion and power" (Bradley and Ponessa 1997, 30).

Native Americans

Tribal traditions served to educate Native American children so that boys became hunters, fishermen, or, for a few tribes, farmers, while girls learned to cook, sew clothing, and build the family shelter. The skills and knowledge passed from generation to generation, along with the religious and cultural beliefs of the tribe.

Native Americans were not formally educated in the colonial or later the common schools but rather primarily through the efforts of missionaries and religious groups, often in defiance of tribal leaders. In the Northeast, missionaries from the Church of England worked with Native Americans, while French Catholic missionaries were commonplace in the Mississsippi Valley region. In the Southwest, under Spanish rule at that time, Franciscan priests instituted missions to help protect the Native Americans from ruthless Spanish landowners who tried to use them as slaves.

Today, many Native American children are educated in schools based on reservations. Additional federal aid is provided to meet the needs of these students.

Hispanics

Hispanics were in Mexico before the Pilgrims landed on Plymouth Rock. By the 1700s, Hispanics had settled northward in what are now California, Arizona, New Mexico, Texas, and Colorado.

Wilma P. Mankiller is the first female to be elected deputy chief of the Cherokee Nation. In 1987, she became the first female elected by her tribe as principal chief. Since then, Mankiller has used her influence and devoted her energies toward helping the Cherokee people achieve both economic independence and renewed pride in their culture.

Born in 1945 into rural poverty in Stilwell, Oklahoma, Mankiller realized the need to develop strong self-esteem early in a child's life through community involvement and education. Today, Mankiller travels throughout the country encouraging community involvement within Native American tribes. According to Mankiller, "To me, the only people who are going to solve our problems are ourselves—people like you and me. We have got to personally take charge and solve our problems" (Boyko and Colen 1996, 143).

Just as every teacher should be, Mankiller is very concerned about stereotypes. She writes, "Sometimes I sit down with a diverse group of people in Oklahoma to work on some problem that we all have in common; it is almost like sitting down with people who have some kind of veil over their face or something. We all look at each other through this veil that causes us to see each other through these stereotypes. . . . we need to lift back the veil and deal with each other on a more human level in order to continue to progress" (Boyko and Colen 1996 144–5).

Mankiller believes that tolerance should prevail as she writes

"the minority population in this country is dramatically increasing, and that is a fact. If we continue to have this increase in minority population, we need to find ways of dealing with each other and working with each other in much better ways, because it affects everybody."

(Boyko and Colen 1996, 145)

In the mid-1800s, pioneers from the United States moved westward into what are now the states of Texas, New Mexico, Utah, and California. Spurred on by the defeat of Santa Anna and Mexico in 1847 and the 1849 California gold rush, settlers pushed into these territories to discover a population of Hispanic descent. These people had been educated in parochial schools through the efforts of the Roman Catholic Church. Like the Native Americans, Hispanic leaders often protested such education. It was not until nearly one hundred years later, in the mid-1900s, that **bilingual education** became a component of public education.

Today, the term *Hispanic* is often used to refer to any individual who speaks Spanish as a first language or who is of Spanish decent. However, it should be pointed out that not all Spanish-speaking people prefer to be called Hispanics. Natives of Puerto Rico may prefer to be called Puerto Ricans, while those from Latin America may favor the terms Latinos and Latinas. While Spanish may be the common language, there are many different distinct dialects that are indicative of the various regions from which individuals and their parents and grandparents came.

Currently, the education of Hispanics is somewhat controversial. Some Hispanic leaders believe that their cultural heritage and language are being lost in the U.S. educational system. These individuals promote the teaching of Spanish as Hispanic children's primary language. Other educational leaders believe that English is the language of the United States and failure to teach English as the primary language will result in Hispanics being relegated to serving as second-class citizens.

In the mid-1900s, segregated schools were commonplace in the south. Prior to World War II, there were several segregated schools in northern cities. (Courtesy of the Mississippi Department of Archives)

Thurgood Marshall was a young civil rights attorney when he represented Olive Brown in *Brown v. Board of Education of Topeka* before the U.S. Supreme Court. (© Bettmann)

African Americans

During the Civil War, with the passage of the Thirteenth Amendment to the U.S. Constitution, which abolished slavery, came a change in the education of African Americans. In some of the northern states, free African Americans had been educated in public schools prior to 1861. In the South, such education was prohibited, and individuals caught teaching slaves to read and write were severely punished or banned from the community. Southerners largely believed that if slaves were educated they would demand the same rights as whites, particularly the right to live freely.

At the close of the Civil War, Congress created the Freedmen's Bureau to assist slaves in making the transition to "freed men." This act allowed for the establishment of schools throughout the South. The curriculum was similar to those of the New England

Chapter 6 *Historical Foundations of American Education*

James Banks: Leading the Mainstream into Multiculturalism

James Banks is known throughout America's higher educational institutions as a challenging voice of reason, demanding equality and integrity throughout elementary, secondary, and college curricula. Director of the Center for Multicultural Education at the University of Washington, Banks focuses on his desire to "transform the mainstream" (Brandt 1994) to enable all students to be able to perform better both within their neighborhoods and in the outside, larger world community.

Banks refers to three basic approaches to multicultural education. The first approach, contributions, occurs when school systems set aside certain days to honor the contributions of members of marginalized groups. The additive approach is used when books by nonwhites are added to existing curricula. The final approach is the transformative approach, in which students are encouraged to consider facts from a variety of viewpoints and in which instructional materials, teaching techniques, and student learning are all changed (Banks 1994).

Another means by which, according to Banks, teachers can reach more students is by using equity pedagogy. When educators use equity pedagogy, they use teaching strategies that will reach students of all races and cultures in their classrooms. For example, teachers should take note of how successful students work together in groups and encourage the less successful, isolated students to do the same.

One misconception Banks battles is the idea that multiculturalism implies cultural relativism, or the idea that we must accept and respect all other cultures re-gardless of the values of the culture. The difference is, says Banks, that we as multiculturalists must "make a strong, unequivocal commitment to democracy, to basic American values of justice and equality" (Brandt 1994, 4).

According to Banks, there are five dimensions of multicultural education to support teachers' efforts to respond to student diversity. Educators should use these five steps as guidelines when examining their own curricula and strategies. Content integration, the first dimension, examines the above-mentioned concepts of the contributive and additive approaches. The second dimension, knowledge construction, addresses how much educators aid students in understanding how perspectives influence conclusions, as well as whether students learn to form their own knowledge. Prejudice reduction deals with attempting to help students to develop positive attitudes about groups outside their own mainstream. As mentioned earlier, equity pedagogy, the fourth dimension, involves educators finding ways to modify their teaching strategies to better reach all students. The final dimension, empowering school culture and social structure, determines how large a role a school's culture and organization play in ensuring educational equality and cultural empowerment.

As a strong advocate of activism, James Banks points out that one of the most important goals of multicultural education is to aid students in the acquisition of "the knowledge and commitment needed to think, decide, and take personal, social, and civic action" (Banks 1994, 12).

common schools: reading, writing, arithmetic, geography, and music. Predominant textbooks were the *Blue Back Speller* of Noah Webster and the McGuffey readers.

The teachers were typically natives of northern states who held the cultural values of the North rather than of the South. These teachers believed that the white race was superior to that of African Americans. Although northerners largely did not believe in slave ownership and supported education of African Americans, they did not welcome them into the public schools and workplace.

Schools remained largely segregated in the South until 1954, when the **Brown v. Board of Education of Topeka,** 347 U.S. 483, case was heard by the U.S. Supreme Court. Thurgood Marshall, a young civil rights lawyer, successfully argued that separate educational opportunities were not equal. The result was integration of public schools, a process that slowly took place over the next decade. Desegregation led to "white flight" as many white families left inner city areas for the suburbs.

Private Education

Private schools were present in colonial America and are still prevalent today. Early colleges such as William and Mary, Harvard, Princeton, Yale, and King's College (Columbia) were all established as private schools.

Both Protestant and Roman Catholic Churches established private, parochial schools. Today, the Missouri Synod Lutheran Church operates about 1,700 elementary and secondary schools throughout the United States (Johnson et al. 1991). The Roman Catholic parochial school system grew in the 1800s because of the large immigrant population. Today, the Roman Catholic Church operates the largest private school system in the United States.

The Development of Colleges and Universities

College students today are often unaware of the long and rich history of the schools they attend. For the most part, colleges and universities in the eastern part of the United States have very old roots and traditions, with some over two hundred years of age. There are several colleges and universities in the Midwest and South over one hundred years old.

The first college in the new colonies was Harvard University, founded in 1636 in Cambridge, Massachusetts. Its primary focus was to educate the sons of prominent citizens and to produce ministers. William and Mary was established in 1693 by a royal charter. Thus, William and Mary had close ties with the English university structure of Oxford and Cambridge.

In addition, the early colleges of colonial America were supported by religious groups. William and Mary was founded as a Church of England school; Harvard, founded in 1636, was established to prepare men for leadership in the Puritan Church. In 1701, a gift of books to churchmen in Bradford, CN, let to Yale University being established as an alternative to Harvard. Yale was later moved to New Haven, CN. Princeton, founded in 1746, was affiliated with the Presbyterian Church, while Rhode Island College (today known as Brown University) was created in 1764 by the Baptist Church. In fact, all of the colleges founded prior to 1776 were church-related, the exception being King's College (now known as Columbia University). King's College was chartered in 1754 as primarily nondenominational, largely due to a dispute between members of the Anglican and Presbyterian churches (Rippa 1992).

Churches established colleges for three reasons: first, to train ministers to convey the group's religious beliefs to colonists, thereby ensuring that the church would grow; second, to train scholars who would in turn educate children, primarily boys; and third, to educate the sons of wealthy and prominent citizens, who would likely become politicians who would look favorably on the religious views of that particular church.

Early instructors in these schools were generally ministers; later, colleges sought to hire their own graduates, who were thought to be the best trained to carry on the intellectual beliefs and ideas of the colleges. This continues to be the tradition even today in colleges such as Harvard, Princeton, and Yale.

The tradition of educating politicians also continues today. Harvard has educated such politicians as Vice President Albert Gore and Yale two of the most recent presidents of the United States, George Bush and Bill Clinton.

Normal Schools

Early teachers generally received little or no training, either formal or informal, in the instruction of students until the establishment of the **normal school.** Horace Mann and others in Massachusetts staunchly believed that teachers needed formal training. In 1823, the first private normal school opened in Massachusetts.

The normal school was created for a variety of reasons besides the need for more proficient and skilled teachers. For instance, better-trained teachers meant that teaching would be viewed as a profession, thereby raising the social status of teachers and, likewise, their salaries. At the time that the normal school was established, teachers were earning a mere $2 a week for their efforts. For this, teachers not only taught school but served as the building's janitor.

Female Seminaries

As a result of the common school movement, women were encouraged to be teachers, particularly at the elementary level. Because colleges educated only male students, female seminaries were established by feminist leaders to provide educational equity for women.

Emma Willard opened a female seminary in Troy, New York, in 1821. Willard knew that women from poor families were largely educated at home, so those reared in families with no one who could read or write were likely to be illiterate. Willard argued that female seminaries would strengthen the minds of young women and enhance their moral philosophy and well-being. Later in the nineteenth century, Mary Lyon initiated a female seminary in Mount Holyoke, as did Julia and Elias Mark in Barhamville, South Carolina.

Another of these schools was the Hartford Female Seminary, founded by Catherine Beecher in 1828. The curriculum educated women as well as trained them in pedagogy so that upon completion of their studies, the women would be capable teachers. Like her sister, Harriet Beecher Stowe, the author of *Uncle Tom's Cabin,* Catherine Beecher was interested both in education and social reform.

Catherine Beecher was familiar with the western frontier because she had family members in Ohio. This sparked her interest in training teachers for the small, one-room schoolhouses spread across the rural countryside of the western frontier. Several women, natives of eastern states such as Connecticut, Massachusetts, and Rhode Island, were trained as teachers at the Hartford Female Seminary and then traveled west to frontier states and territories. Their job was to move among families in the school district, who provided room and board for a month. The primitive conditions caused much hardship. Poor sanitary conditions and lack of medical care led to the spread of disease among students, and sometimes death. The harsh winters made it dangerous to venture out. Indeed, because of the long distances that students were forced to travel to rural, one-room schools, it was necessary during snowstorms for both teacher and pupils to spend the night in the school. In the extreme northern

Jane Addams and Ellen Gates Starr, a good friend and former classmate from the Rockford (Illinois) Female Seminary, now Rockford College, opened Hull House in the fall of 1889. Addams was influenced by the social movement in England and was concerned that schools emphasized only the three Rs. She saw that the slums of the large cities fostered poverty, vice, disease, and crime. Hull House served the families of impoverished immigrants in Chicago—largely German, Greek, Italian, Russian, and Sicilian families—with an enriched curriculum that Addams believed added "human significance"

to an individual's life. At its peak, over forty thousand people went to Hull House each week.

Supported through donations, Hull House became internationally known. It stressed fulfilling the social needs of people and thus contained a day nursery, a dispensary for medicine, a playground and gymnasium for physical activity, and a boardinghouse for young women. Classes were taught at Hull House, including basic cooking and sewing skills.

Addams continued her liberal social philosophy by teaming with Felix Adler. She won the Nobel Peace Prize for her efforts.

states of the Dakotas, Minnesota, and Montana, stories tell of blizzards that resulted in children freezing to death as they attempted to go home at the end of a school day.

Coeducational Colleges

Changes in society resulted in changes in educational institutions. As the westward movement continued in the 1800s, women were required to share greater roles with men. While still considered second-class citizens and denied the right to own property and to vote, women began to emerge from the home into the workplace. This was partly due to the Industrial Revolution, which required more workers than the male population could provide. Another reason was the frontier life and its accompanying hardships. Women widowed by wars and disease were left to fend for themselves and their children. Some took over their husbands' businesses, and others gained employment in local establishments as clerks or seamstresses.

With men working in industry or seeking their fortunes as frontiersmen, teaching, which had been predominantly a male profession, opened up to increasing numbers of women. Women crowded into the newly formed normal schools to be trained in the teaching vocation.

The often unconventional societal life on the frontier helped to bring about the first coeducational colleges. In 1837, Oberlin College in Ohio admitted four women, the first college to be coeducational. Later, in 1853, Antioch College opened its doors to women. By 1858, the State University of Iowa became the first coeducational state college.

Land-Grant Colleges

State universities were established through an act of Congress. Generous land donations for these universities, known as **land-grant colleges,** were made as a result of the Land-Grant Act of 1862, also known as the Morrill Act after its sponsor, Senator

Booker T. Washington was born to a slave mother and a white father in 1856, prior to the Civil War. In 1881, Washington initiated the first African American normal school in the United States, Tuskegee Institute in Tuskegee, Alabama. The school had only a handful of students. The nearby white community strongly opposed Washington's work. He believed that African Americans needed to "live" down rather than "talk" down the race question (Butts and Cremin 1953). Washington believed that rather than reading the classics, African American students should become productive societal members by training themselves in practical skills.

With his belief in learning by doing, Washington directed his students in the construction of the building of the school itself. The students learned practical knowledge of mathematics and basic construction skills. Students grew produce and sold it to members of the white community.

It was at Tuskegee Institute that George Washington Carver, a faculty member, experimented with peanuts. He found that they were a valuable food source that actually restored nutrients to the soil rather than taking them away, as did "king cotton." Peanuts replaced or supplemented cotton as an income crop on many Southern farms and plantations.

Justin S. Morrill of Vermont. The Morrill Act provided a federal allocation of thirty thousand acres of land for each senator and representative to Congress from a state, provided that for each thirty thousand acres a college be created that would teach both agriculture and mechanical arts. Hence, many of the schools were referred to as "A and M" schools. The Big Ten, Pac-Ten, and Big Eight schools, with the exception of the few private schools in these conferences, are largely universities initiated as a result of the Morrill Act of 1862.

In 1890, a second Morrill Act was passed that gave state colleges matching federal dollars. This act encouraged state legislatures to also match funds for public higher education institutions.

African American Colleges

Among the distingushed African Americans of the 1700s and 1800s was Benjamin Banneker, who not only surveyed Washington, D.C., but in 1770 also manufactured the first clock built in the colonies. His talents were recognized by Thomas Jefferson, who invited him to visit Monticello in 1803. Jefferson's reputation as a statesman and inventor was widely known at the time. Therefore, when Jefferson invited Banneker into his home, it served to recognize that African American people were capable of important achievements.

Another important African American was Fredrick Douglas, who had been born a slave in 1817. A fluent speaker and prolific writer, Douglas spurred on the abolitionist movement.

Despite the efforts of these and other individuals, only a small number of colleges opened their doors to African Americans. Oberlin, which had been the first to admit women, Bowdoin, Franklin, and Harvard were among the few that did. The first African American colleges were Lincoln University, which opened in 1854 in Pennsylvania,

Talking It Over

Our country's history of education is both a rich and a troubled one. Early schools had strong religious ties. Indeed, the Old Deluder Satan Act was passed solely so children could learn to read the Bible. Today, public schooling is still influenced to some degree by the religious beliefs of the community, particularly when character or sex education are discussed.

We've been fortunate as a nation to have had strong educational leaders who devote their entire lives to promoting their beliefs. It's difficult to imagine today's teachers and educational leaders being as dedicated.

Some people, myself included, argue that we lack the educational leaders who possess the fervor for teaching and educating children. We need individuals such as yourself to become actively involved in teaching and teaching organizations. Then go out and spread the good news about what terrific things are happening in your classroom, your school. If enough teachers do this, then the new educational leaders will emerge for us to follow. You could very well be the leader we've been searching for.

and Wilberforce University, which was founded in 1856 in Ohio. Booker T. Washington's Tuskegee Institute was founded in 1880. Because of its success and that of its founder, it became known for its broad curriculum for African Americans, which primarily emphasized vocational and practical education.

Mary McLeod Bethune, an African American woman born in 1875, was the only one of seventeen children born of slave parents not to have been born a slave. Bethune spent her entire life improving education for African American girls. She moved from South Carolina to Florida, where she created the Daytona Normal and Industrial School for Negro Girls. The school later was renamed Bethune-Cookman College, with Bethune serving as its president until 1942. Bethune served in many other capacities, including as President Franklin D. Roosevelt's special advisor on minority affairs and as a consultant in the drafting of the charter of the United Nations.

■ Summary

Education in the United States was initially influenced by religious groups. The Old Deluder Satan Act was passed in the Massachusetts Bay Colony in 1642 to ensure that children would be taught to read so they could understand and interpret the Bible. Later, a compulsory schooling law was likewise passed.

Schools initially taught boys only, and girls were educated either at home or in dame schools. Boys were encouraged to pursue an advanced education, while girls were taught basic reading, writing, and arithmetic along with cooking, sewing, and housekeeping duties.

Early colleges and universities were also established by religious groups to meet their own needs. By having their own higher education systems, they could perpetuate their own beliefs and influence future politicans educated by their institutions.

Until Horace Mann became a predominant educational figure in the early 1800s, schools were a hodgepodge of private and public institutions. Mann led the common school movement, which advocated a free and equal education for all. Since Mann believed that women would be excellent teachers, he thus opened a new vocation for them. This occurred at roughly the same time that women began demanding more educational and social rights.

The need for better-trained workers resulted in an American creation, the high school. As the demand for educated employees increased, the curriculum was examined more closely. Both the Seven Cardinal Principles of Education and the Eight-Year Study considered what was to be taught in high school.

Unlike the high school, colleges and universities were largely based on English models. It was not until 1837 that an American college permitted both men and women to be educated together. The westward movement resulted in Congress enacting the Morrill Act, which established land-grant colleges.

Like women, African Americans were largely denied access to education. Unlike women, however, in the southern states African Americans were not taught to read and write for fear that they would stage an uprising and demand their freedom. After the Civil War, free schools were set up in the South to educate African Americans. These schools were usually staffed by teachers from northern states. It was not until 1954, when the U.S. Supreme Court ruled that separate schools were not equal in terms of educational opportunities, that all public schools were integrated.

In the 1900s, changing societal demands greatly influenced schooling. High schools were formed, followed by junior high schools. World War II brought about the G.I. Bill, which enabled numerous veterans to obtain degrees from technical schools and colleges. The 1950s brought the cold war. With the 1957 launch of *Sputnik,* critics of the schools demanded more emphasis on math, science, and foreign languages. The result was the NDEA of 1958, which provided federal funds for such programs. In 1983, with *A Nation at Risk,* and again in 1994, with Goals 2000, public concerns about lack of student and teacher standards were raised.

■ Reflections

In the eighteenth and nineteenth centuries, young men and women had to give up any idea of family obligations if they wanted to teach. Many school boards discouraged even meeting someone of the opposite sex for an ice cream soda after daylight had passed. Most teachers had contracts that prohibited marriage by women unless they gave up their teaching positions. Men who married found it difficult to support a wife and children on a teacher's salary.

Today's teachers have fewer restrictions, however, the low salaries make it difficult for some teachers to purchase a new car, nice clothes, and a home. Do you see yourself as an individual who could have made such major sacrifices as a teacher in the 1800s? In what ways have you already sacrificed to become a teacher? Are you willing to spend money from your teaching salary to further your education by obtaining a master's degree in education?

■ Discussion Questions

1. Compare and contrast schooling in colonial America with that of the Middle Atlantic states and the South.

2. In what ways were the southern plantation owners, who limited the education of slaves, like modern-day produce farmers, who employ migrant farm workers?

3. If you had already decided to become a teacher when you were in high school, what courses were you encouraged to take then?

4. When considering today's high schools, what suggestions would you make to strengthen the curriculum? What about elementary schools? middle schools?

■ For Further Reading

Goldberg, M. 1998. Bringing the voices of the people to the people. *Phi Delta Kappan, 79*(8), 613–615.

Mellon, J. 1988. *Bullwhip days: The slaves remember.* New York: Avon.

Spring, J. 1986. *The American school, 1642–1985.* White Plains, NY: Longman.

Warren, D., ed. 1989. *American teachers: Histories of a profession at work.* New York: Macmillan.

7

Legal and Ethical Issues in Education

Primary Points

- The U.S. Constitution requires separation of church and state, which has proven to be the basis of many court decisions regarding schools and their funding.

- The teaching of creationism and evolution continues to be controversial.

- Teachers are protected by a teaching contract.

- Tenure is given to teachers after they have successfully taught in a school district for a set period of time, usually three years.

- Teachers and students have the right to due process.

Chapter Inquiries

- Can a teacher require students to read the Bible or recite the Pledge of Allegiance to the Flag of the United States of America?

- Under what conditions can a teacher be dismissed from a teaching position?

- Do students have the same right to freedom of speech in school as do adults in public?

- Can a student's locker be searched for drugs?

© James Shaffer

"My students show no remorse, no guilt. In previous years, if I just hinted at an apology, the students would catch on. This year's students don't, or even worse, won't take the hint. They won't yield that they made a mistake or were in the wrong." The speaker is Jennifer Schroeder, a fifth year teacher. "They lack respect for their peers. And these kids are just *second graders!* What will they be like in high school?

"If a pencil or a quarter is found on the classroom floor, most of my students will pick it up and keep it instead of looking for its rightful owner. Their idea of ethics is 'finders keepers, losers weepers.' Even if they hurt someone's feelings by something they said, they are reluctant to say they are sorry. Forget etiquette. I almost think that these students are beyond that."

Legal Issues

Increasingly the courts have become involved in school issues. Prior to 1960, there was little litigation against school districts. Today, every school district has its own legal counsel, and large school districts sometimes employ three or four legal firms, each with special legal expertise. As teachers, we need to be aware of laws and court decisions regarding schooling.

Many of the legal decisions involve the separation of church and state, freedom of speech by teachers and students, and the rights of individuals, including both teachers and students. As such, the rulings are based largely on the Constitution.

Along with legal issues, schools encounter ethical issues. Teachers deal with ethics every day, and how teachers are perceived by their students is important.

Jurisdiction Rights

Laws may be local, state, or federal. School districts must abide by all three. Local ordinances are typically those that involve health or safety regulations that are not covered by state laws. Local ordinances or laws that may affect school districts include a curfew for individuals under the age of eighteen. For example, evening school activities such as plays or sporting events must be finished by 10:30 P.M. if the curfew was set for 11:00 P.M. Some other examples of local ordinances that affect school districts include parade permits for homecoming activities, speed limits and parking restrictions in the area near a school, and local building codes for public buildings.

We have failed to teach an ethic of concern and to model a culture of responsibility. We have created a culture characterized by dysfunctional families, mass schooling that demands only minimal effort, and media idols subliminally teaching disrespect for authority and wisdom. It is as if there were a conspiracy of parents and educators to deliberately ruin our children.

Richard H. Hersh
The Culture of Neglect

In many states, school districts have the right to negotiate agreements with the local municipality. The local police department may be given the authority to arrest drivers who speed on school parking lots or individuals found trespassing on school grounds. Such agreements may also result in the joint funding of elementary school crossing guards and police officers within elementary and secondary schools. Local ordinances and laws are enforced at the local level.

Since schools are the responsibility of each respective state and not the federal government, each state has a large section of its state statutes, or laws, designated especially to school code. State laws that affect school districts include such areas as certification and tenure laws, state fire and building safety codes, and motor vehicle laws for public vehicles. Several states have laws that prohibit smoking in public buildings, including schools and arenas. Most states have environmental laws that school districts must follow.

There are also state laws to protect children in schools. In a number of states, laws prohibit the sale of firearms and liquor close to school property. Many states have stiffer penalties than usual for individuals found guilty of selling drugs on or near school grounds.

Members of a school district's school board are state officials with local jurisdiction even though they are elected locally. They are responsible for overseeing that state laws, rules, and regulations are followed by the school district personnel.

Unlike local and state laws, federal laws must be adhered to by all schools that receive any federal funds. Federal laws include prohibiting discrimination against students because of race, disability, sex, or religion; the right to due process for students; and the prohibiting of mandatory school prayer.

The Judicial System

The court system in the United States consists of state and federal courts. Each state's judicial system is outlined in its constitution. The levels of courts differ by states. Generally, legal concerns pertaining to a state's constitution or laws are assigned to the state court system and are initially assigned to the lowest level of the court. Any appeals are heard at the next level, which may be a district court, and then by the state appellate court. The final level of appeal at the state level for all states is the state supreme court. Depending on the nature of the case, at that point an appeal may be made to the federal court system. In the case of any appeal, the higher-level court does not have to hear the case and may refuse to review it.

Legal concerns relating to violation of the U.S. Constitution or federal laws are filed with the federal judicial body. The lowest level is the U.S. District Court, and the U.S. Circuit Court is the next level of judicial authority. The U.S. Supreme Court is the highest court in the nation. Cases reviewed and heard at that level are generally significant ones, and we read and hear about them in the media.

The United States is divided into twelve judicial districts, each with a U.S. District Court. Only litigation from within the specific area may be heard by that area's U.S. District Court. At the U.S. District Court level, trials are held. These would include cases such as the violation of interstate commerce laws and U.S. customs laws, for instance.

The next level is the U.S. Circuit Court, each of which hears cases from three U.S. District Courts. Cases from the four U.S. Circuit Courts may be appealed to the U.S. Supreme Court. However, for a case to be heard at the highest level, the U.S. Supreme Court, a minimum of four of the nine U.S. Supreme Court judges must agree to such a hearing. Should fewer than four agree to such a hearing, the decision by the U.S. Circuit Court stands.

Since the decisions handed down by U.S. Circuit Courts have jurisdiction only for their respective geographic areas, there may be rulings in one U.S. Circuit Court that conflict with rulings by another. However, a ruling handed down by one U.S. Circuit Court may set a precedence for rulings in federal courts in other parts of the United States.

Religion and the Public Schools

The U.S. Constitution calls for separation of church and state. However, there have been many religious issues over the years that have involved court decisions. These include the provision of tax monies to purchase textbooks for parochial schools, school prayer, school attendance as related to religious beliefs, and the teaching of creationism.

Separation of Church and State

The First Amendment to the U.S. Constitution states that "Congress shall make no law respecting an establishment of religion, or prohibiting the free exercise thereof." One of the major U.S. Supreme Court decisions regarding the right to private, parochial schools was *Pierce v. Society of Sisters*, 268 U.S. 510 (1925). An Oregon law was set to go into effect in September 1926 that would require all healthy children between the ages of eight and sixteen to attend public schools until they had completed the eighth grade. Obviously the law would have seriously damaged private schools, the majority of which were parochial schools with religious affiliations, and forced most to close. The U.S. Supreme Court ruled that the state may regulate all schools and may require all children to attend school, but children have the right to attend adequate private schools.

Many states now have laws that regulate private schools. These may include the regulation of curriculum, certification of teachers, and the number of days of required attendance. Other laws also impact private schools, such as meeting health department standards and fire codes.

Use of State Monies for Private Schools

Several states provide tax money to purchase textbooks for all students, both in public and private schools. This is to prevent private schools from offering an inferior education by using old, outdated textbooks. This practice has been ruled constitutional as has the practice of providing transportation for nonpublic school students. The U.S. Supreme Court has ruled that if such financial aid assists the child, then it is appropriate. If the monies assist the nonpublic school or institution, it is not permissible. This is known as the child benefit theory and came about as a result of a 1947 U.S. Supreme Court case, *Everson v. Board of Education, Irving Township*, 330 U.S. 1, in which the court held that the state (New Jersey) could provide transportation for students to attend nonpublic schools. In a later case, *Wolman v. Walter*, 433 U.S. 229 (1972), the U.S. Supreme Court ruled that state support may be provided to private schools for the loan or purchase of secular (nonreligious) textbooks and standardized tests; for speech, hearing, and psychological services at the private school; and to fund remedial services for private school students at a site other than the private school. However, state funds cannot be used for purchase or loan of instructional materials such as audiovisual equipment or globes or to pay for field trips for private school students.

In 1971, the use of direct aid from the state to support nonpublic schools was challenged in the U.S. Supreme Court in *Lemon v. Kurtzman*. Over twenty states had considered state legislation to provide direct aid in one way or another to nonpublic schools. In 1968, Pennsylvania passed a law to provide funding for services not related to religion, or, in other words, secular services. In *Lemon v. Kurtzman*, the Supreme Court ruled against the Pennsylvania law, pointing out that three questions had to be answered to determine whether the First Amendment had been violated. These three questions became known as the *Lemon test* and are as follows:

1. Does the act have a secular purpose?
2. Does the primary effect of the act either advance or inhibit religion?
3. Does the act excessively entangle government and religion?

If excessive entanglement between government and religion was a possibility, then increased state supervision would be needed. However, the Supreme court ruled that state aid supporting only secular education (nonreligious education) was permissible and in accord with the First Amendment (Zirkel and Gluckman 1991).

Support of parochial schools through state funding continues to be an issue in many states. Tuition tax credits and vouchers are related issues and are discussed further in Chapter 3, "Trends in Education."

The Bible and School Prayer

As recently as the 1950s, many public schools required that students read the Bible and say prayers. Even today students daily recite the Pledge of Allegiance to the Flag of the United States of America, which includes the statement "one nation, under God." In a 1962 decision, the U.S. Supreme Court ruled that students could not be required to recite a nondenominational prayer, stating that reading the Bible and saying prayers in school were violations of the First Amendment (*Engle v. Vitale*, 370 U.S. 421). In 1963, the U.S. Supreme Court ruled in another case, Abington School District v. Schempp, 374 U.S. 203, upholding the earlier decision that students could not be required to read the Bible or recite the Lord's Prayer. However, the court ruled that students may be required to read the Bible as part of civics, history, or literature studies of Western civilization, just as they would be required to read the Koran or the writings of Confucius to study Asian or Middle Eastern cultures.

This controversy continues today. In a 1994 Colorado lawsuit, there was a twist. A group of five parents sued the Woodland Park school district, which is in a suburb of Colorado Springs, because their children were required to learn about ancient Greek and Roman religions but not those found in the Bible. This case,

These Amish children from Indiana are checking their lunch boxes as they walk to school. (Courtesy of Jack Westhead)

Skipworth v. Board of Education, 874 P. 2d 487 (Colo. Ct. App. 1994), was heard before the Colorado Appellate Court, which dismissed the plaintiffs' arguments, thereby siding with the school district.

The federal courts have ruled that a student cannot be required to stand and recite the Pledge of Allegiance to the Flag of the United States of America if the student's religious beliefs conflict with saying the pledge (*West Virginia State Board of Education v. Barnette,* 319 U.S. 624 [1943]). Other court decisions based on this case have ruled that even if a student's personal beliefs conflict with reciting the pledge, then that student must be excused from reciting the pledge (Zirkel and Gluckman 1990).

School Attendance and Religious Beliefs

Whether or not students must attend school even if it violates their religious beliefs has been challenged in the courts. The Old Order Amish has been a Christian religious sect in the United States for over three centuries. Probably they are best known as an agrarian community that shuns the use of modern equipment, such as telephones, gasoline engines, and electricity, and uses horse-drawn farming machinery. Many Amish reside in Lancaster County in Pennsylvania, near Napanee and Worthington in Indiana, and in other small farming communities throughout the Midwest.

Members of the Old Order Amish in Wisconsin were sued because they failed to comply with a state compulsory education law. According to Amish religious teaching, children are to attend school through the eighth grade but no further. They believe that going to school after eighth grade impedes their children's preparation for adult life, which is taught by their parents, as well as their religious preparation. After the eighth grade, Amish children are expected to engage in farming and housework. The U.S. Supreme Court ruled in *Wisconsin v. Yoder*, 406 U.S. 205 (1972), in favor of the Amish inasmuch as the Amish way of life and religious belief and practice are inseparable from their daily work.

Teaching Creationism and Evolution

Perhaps the most notorious case involving religion and education was *Scopes v. State of Tennessee*, 154 Tenn. 105, 289 S.W. 363 (1925). There had been substantial national debate over whether teaching evolution or creationism in public schools was most appropriate. John Scopes was a young high school science teacher who taught the theory of evolution even though the Tennessee state constitution stated that only creationism be taught. The two sides were represented by arguably the most well-known and talented lawyers of the day, William Jennings Bryan, a leading figure in the populist movement, and Clarence Darrow, a nationally prominent attorney who represented Scopes. Hundreds of reporters flocked to Tennessee for the trial, which became so famous that a Hollywood studio made a movie of it.

When the appeals reached the U.S. Supreme Court, the Court held that evolution could be taught in schools, striking down the Tennessee law. Later, in 1982, the Louisiana Legislature passed a law that was referred to as the Balanced Treatment Act, which stated that whenever evolution would be taught, so would creationism. However, if a school chose only to teach creationism, it would not be required to teach evolution. In 1987, in *Edwards v. Aguillard*, 197 S. Ct. 2573, the U.S. Supreme Court ruled against the Balanced Treatment Act. Despite this Supreme Court ruling, creationists still protest to boards of education throughout the United States. In California, the state board of education now recognizes evolution as a theory and not as a fact (Mydans 1989).

Special School Districts for Religious Sects

In 1994, the U.S. Supreme Court heard a case that involved an insular Satmar Hasidic Jewish community, an ultraorthodox Jewish sect (*Kiryas Joel Village School District v. Grumet*, U.S. 93-517). The children from the community spoke only Yiddish, and their parents would not send them to public schools with non-Hasidic children. The state legislature of New York passed a law that created a school district solely for the Hasidic Jewish students. The law was challenged by the New York State School Board Association, which contended that the special school district unconstitutionally favored a religious sect. The association argued that special school districts for religious groups could lead to "religious apartheid in America as different sects press for separate public schools" (Savage 1994, 1). In 1994, the U.S. Supreme Court agreed with the New York State School Board Association when it ruled that it was unconstitutional for a state to create a school district for a religious group. In writing for the majority opinion, Justice David Souter wrote, "Because this unusual act is tantamount to an allocation of political power on a religious criterion . . . we hold that it violates the prohibition against establishment" of religion found in the First Amendment (Press 1994, 58).

Rights of Students with Disabilities

The "Individuals with Disabilities Education Act Amendments of 1997" passed by Congress addresses student discipline, individual education plans (IEPs), and attorney's fees for students with disabilities. An IEP is a plan that denotes the goals and the educational plan for a student with disabilities to meet those goals. Benchmarks for progress must be measurable, and general progress reports must be given out on a regular basis. The new law requires that students with disabilities must be assessed in terms of the general curriculum as well as be administered standardized tests. Every IEP team must consider how technology and special services can be used to meet the child's needs. Representatives of the school district, at least one of the child's regular classroom teachers, the special education teacher or coordinator, and the parents or guardians must approve the IEP.

States are required to pay for the mediation process should the parents object to the IEP. Previously, school districts could be required to pay a parent's attorney fees if the parent objected to the IEP or wanted a legal representative during the IEP process. Under the new law, attorney fees may be denied if the parent's attorney fails to state the "nature of the problem and the relief sought" by the parent on behalf of the child within a specified framework of time (Underwood 1997, 25).

Since the passage of the original bill in 1975, educators have voiced concerns that the "rules for disciplining those with disabilities have resulted in barriers to effective discipline. In addition, parents and educators alike have complained that the statute had grown unnecessarily prescriptive in some areas, too vague in others" (Underwood 1997, 24).

Under the new law, any disciplinary action exceeding ten days (including suspension) that changes the student's placement requires that the student be returned to the original placement awaiting the outcome of an IEP meeting and the resolution of any dispute over the placement decision. However, if a student with disabilities brings a weapon such as a gun to school or possesses or uses drugs on school grounds, school authorities may place the student in an interim alternative placement for up to forty-five days. If a student with disabilities violates rules other than those for weapons and drugs, she or he may be disciplined in the same way as any other student in the school.

Court decisions have ruled that students with disabilities can be suspended from school provided that misconduct was not caused by the disability. The courts have also ruled that students who are not identified as having disabilities can evade disciplinary action by proving that they should have been identified as being disabled at the time the misconduct took place (Underwood 1997).

Legal Issues for Teachers

As teachers, we encounter numerous legal issues. The teaching certificate itself is a legal document issued by the state in which you reside. The certificate verifies that you have successfully completed a state-approved teacher education program and are qualified to teach in a specified instructional area. Should you commit a felony, such as child abuse, the state has the right to rescind the teaching certificate.

Even before a teacher can accept a position, many states require that school districts conduct a police background check on all teaching and school administration candidates as well as school administrators and other staff members such as secretaries and classroom aides. Some school districts even require checks on volunteers who may work with students.

Teachers need to be aware of many legal issues. From the teaching contract and tenure to legal issues that relate to students and their rights, it is important that every teacher, including the beginning teacher, be familiar with these issues.

The Teaching Contract

Many southern states have laws against collective bargaining. In these states the school districts establish salaries and expectations of teachers. However, in most school districts, a **contract** is negotiated between the school district and the teachers' union in that district. A teacher generally does not have to be a member of the teachers' union to benefit from those negotiations. The contract is long and extensive, and it specifies not only salary but numerous aspects of teaching and administrative responsibilities (figure 1). The contract specifies the amount and degree of dental and medical insurance coverage provided by the school district for teachers and their families. In addition, the length of both the school year and the school day, including arrival and departure times for teachers; the number of sick days granted (usually ten to twenty per year, which can be accumulated over the years); the number of personal days granted (usually two per year, which may or may not be accumulated); areas of instruction; and extra duties, such as lunchroom or recess supervision, are all written out in the contract. Any compensation for extra work is also included, for example, coaching tennis or directing a class play.

Some contracts specify the maximum number of students to be taught at a time by a teacher. For example, San Diego's public schools require twenty-five students or fewer in grades K–2.

A contract also specifies the grievance procedure for teachers. That is, if a teacher believes he or she is being treated unfairly, a grievance may be filed against the school district. For example, if a teacher is assigned to teach thirty-seven students and the contract states that there will be no more than thirty-five students in a class, that teacher could file a grievance against the school district. If, however, a teacher objects to being transferred to another school for the next school year, the teacher cannot file a grievance because the school board makes all teaching assignments and is within its legal rights to do so.

After negotiators for the school district, acting on behalf of the school board, and the teachers' union agree to the terms of a contract during contract negotiations, the school board and the members of the teachers' union must vote their approval. The terms of the contract between the school district and the teachers' union are for a specified period of time—usually one or two years.

Each teacher signs an individual contract with the school district on an annual basis. For new teachers, this is renewed until tenure is granted or denied.

Changes in Teacher Certification and Licensing

During the past decade, states have reviewed their teacher certification and licensing. Some states have moved to make tenure more difficult to acquire by increasing the number of years required to teach before tenure is granted or by raising their standards. Other states, such as Ohio have adopted licensing practices which require that teachers be tested on current teaching practices every few years, typically five. Usually, most states require that teachers pay a fee to renew their certification or license. For most states, this is done annually with the fee being nominal, five dollars or less.

Even with increased standards for certification and licensing, over 12 percent of newly hired teachers have had no training at all and another 15 percent fail to fully meet the standards set by their respective states. This is particularly evident at the secondary level, where 56 percent of high school students taking physical science are taught by out-of-the-field teachers as are 27 percent of those taking mathematics, especially higher-level mathematics courses, and 21 percent of students taking

Figure 1
The elements
typically
contained in a
teaching
contract.

Middleton-Cross Plains Area School District

[REVISED]

1997–1998 TEACHER CONTRACT

PRELIMINARY TEACHER ASSIGNMENT:

Name:

School:

Grade/Subject:

Additional Assignment(s):

The Middleton-Cross Plains Area School District Board of Education (hereinafter the "Board") does hereby contract with _____ (hereinafter the "teacher"), a professionally trained educator legally qualified in the State of Wisconsin as follows:

TERM: This _____ contract covers a term of _____ months, (_____ days) commencing on or about _____, and terminating on or about _____, in accordance with the school calendar.

COMPENSATION: The teacher is to be paid for his/her services by the school district at an annual wage of _____ for the aforesaid term payable in 24 equal installments. This salary is based on (Range) _____, (Step) _____ of the current salary schedule.

EMPLOYMENT: The teacher is employed subject to such rules and regulations as may have been or may be hereinafter adopted by the Board of Education and subject to the supervision and control of the school administrator. This agreement is also made and shall remain subject to the provisions of Sections 118.21 and 118.22 and other applicable provisions of the Wisconsin Statutes. This agreement is further subject to all valid provisions of the collective bargaining agreement applicable to the Board and teacher.

STATE RETIREMENT, SICK LEAVE, AND HEALTH LAWS APPLICABLE: The provisions of the Statutes relative to teachers' sick leave, deductions for and payments to the teachers' retirement fund, and to physical examinations, constitute a part of this contract.

TERMINATION: The disqualification of the teacher to continue teaching for any legal cause whatsoever shall automatically terminate this contract. This contract may be modified or terminated at any time during the term hereof by the mutual written agreement of the parties hereto.

EXECUTION OF CONTRACT: This contract is not valid unless executed by the teacher and filed in the Office of Human Resources within fourteen (14) days of receipt of this contract.

BOARD OF EDUCATION

President: _____   Clerk: _____

Date: _____

I, the undersigned teacher, represent to the Board that I am not now under a contract of employment with another school district for any period covered by this contract. I hereby accept employment under the terms as set forth in this contract.

Teacher: _____   Address: _____

Date: _____

Courtesy Middleton-Cross Plains Area School District, Middleton, Wisconsin

English. The proportions are greater in high schools in impoverished communities (Education Commission of the States 1996).

Twelve states (California, Georgia, Hawaii, Indiana, Iowa, Kentucky, Minnesota, Nevada, North Dakota, Oregon, West Virginia, and Wyoming) have created "autonomous" teacher professional standards boards that have the authority to make decisions about their state's teacher policies. Thirty-four states have advisory professional standards boards that present recommendations, usually to the state superintendent of instruction.

The state boards serve a variety of purposes. They set standards and requirements for obtaining and maintaining teaching certification or licenses. The boards set standards for teacher examinations as well as create policies or make recommendations to improve teacher education, induction, and professional development. To some extent, the boards develop plans to attract and retain qualified, competent teachers in their respective states.

In addition, the state boards issue, renew, suspend, and revoke teaching certification or licenses. If a teacher's certification or license is to be suspended, the state board ensures that due process is provided for the teacher.

Peer Review of Teachers

In the wake of numerous states proposing an end to tenure laws, in 1997 the National Education Association voted to approve peer review so that teachers can assist colleagues to improve—or help them get dismissed if necessary. The concept of peer review came about during the early 1980s with the education reform movement. Some states, such as Georgia, adopted peer review in addition to administrative review as part of the tenure process for new teachers. In 1986, the idea of peer review for tenured teachers who were experiencing difficulty in the classroom was proposed by the NEA, but its members failed to endorse it. While the concept was accepted by NEA members in 1997, there was no date indicated as to when peer review would go into effect (Gannett News Service 1997).

The concept of peer review at the elementary and secondary levels is not unlike peer review at the college level as part of the tenure/promotion process. Decisions by personnel committees to deny tenure and/or promotion to a colleague have generally been upheld by the judicial system. Peer review at the elementary and secondary levels will most certainly bring lawsuits as teachers will be expected to recommend whether their colleagues are fit to continue as teachers or should be fired. Building morale will be affected. On the other hand, if there s a teacher who is not performing adequately, then the teaching load is increased for the other teachers. The algebra teacher who fails to teach basic algebraic concepts then forces the calculus teacher to review material, slowing down the learning process for all students, not just those who had the poor teacher.

On the surface, peer review looks promising as the teaching profession moves in effect to police itself much as the American Medical Association and the American Bar Association do. On a local level, however, even when a teacher has a noted reputation for being awful, there will be much energy spent and tension created when peers attempt first to work to remediate the teacher, and then, if necessary, to remove the teacher. Few teachers will be willing to make the sacrifice to serve in such a capacity. Those who do will be the truly dedicated teachers.

National Board for Professional Teaching Standards

In 1987, the National Board for Professional Teaching Standards (NBPTS) was established to recognize outstanding teachers. The NBPTS has developed high and rigorous standards for what proficient teachers should know and be able to do, and it has a national voluntary system to assess and certify teachers who meet these standards. Certification by the NBPTS complements, but does not replace, state licensing. Each state still sets its own entry-level requirements for teachers.

Over sixteen states have adopted measures to support teachers who pursue national board certification. Some of the actions include:

- Providing salary increases or one-year bonuses;
- Accepting board certification for licensing renewal requirements and/or awarding the highest rank in the state licensure system;
- Paying for, supplementing, or reimbursing the teacher's fee for the assessment and certification process;
- Awarding special status, such as "master teacher," which carries greater responsibility and salary bonuses;
- Accepting board certification or participation in the process as professional development credits;
- Granting a license to board-certified teachers from out of state;
- Providing release time to teachers to prepare for the intensive assessment process; and
- Modifying the state's teacher licensing categories to be compatible with national board certification categories (Education Commission of the States 1996).

The movement toward standards for teachers has been led by the NBPTS, the Interstate new Teacher Assessment and Support Consortium, and the National Council for Accreditation of Teacher Education (NCATE). The majority of colleges and universities with teacher education programs belong to NCATE. Every few years, NCATE, usually accompanied by a respective state teacher education review team, critiques teacher education programs of its member institutions.

Tenure

In most states, after successfully teaching in a school district for a probationary period of time specified by state law, usually two or three years, a teacher receives **tenure.** Tenure provides security for public school teachers. A teacher is granted tenure as a *teacher* in the school district. Thus, a junior high physical education teacher is a tenured teacher and not a tenured physical education teacher at the junior high level. If that teacher is certified to teach physical education in grades K–12, then that individual may teach physical education at either the elementary or high school level in that school district provided the school administration and school board approve such an assignment change. The teacher would not have to gain tenure again at another school in that school district.

After being granted tenure, a teacher cannot be dismissed unless there is substantial misconduct; for example, being found grossly incompetent as a teacher, guilty of a felony such as child molestation, negligent in overseeing the safety of students, or lying about teaching credentials. For instance, an elementary teacher who hit a student in the face with his fist was dismissed as was a social studies teacher and football coach who lured female students into his office and had sex with them. It is important to note that a teacher cannot be dismissed for any rights that are protected under the U.S. Constitution. For example, a teacher who runs for a political office or who is active in a political cause could not be dismissed.

Until you gain tenure, your teaching will be closely monitored by the building principal, and, in states such as Georgia, by a teacher who will serve as your mentor. In most states, a first- through third-year teacher may not be rehired without any explanation from the school district. In many states, if the school administration and school board decide not to rehire a first- through third-year teacher by a date specified by the state, a due process hearing is not necessary. In some states, the dismissal must be in writing.

When you are hired as a teacher, it is for the entire school year, which means a school district cannot decide to dismiss you during the middle of your first year. Most school administrators recognize that the first year of teaching is very difficult and is very much a learning experience for the new teacher. However, in cases of gross incompetence or negligence, a school district may decide that it is in the best interests of the students involved to terminate a teacher. In such instances, the teacher may request a formal hearing.

While the school district cannot dismiss you without cause during a school year, neither can you break a contract. If as a first-year teacher you decide after three weeks in the classroom that teaching is not the profession you thought it would be, or if you receive another offer at higher pay from another school district two days into the school year, you cannot break your contract with the school district. You are obligated to complete the school year. By breaking a contract, you can be sued by the school district for *breach of contract.* Courts have ruled that a teacher who breaks a contract must pay the school district the costs of finding a replacement. In some instances, school districts willingly agree to break the contract. For example, a teacher's spouse may be transferred to another state or some unusual circumstances may occur during the year—such as a terminally ill child or parent needing the teacher's full attention. School administrators and school boards are concerned people who take into account life's circumstances. If it is close to the end of a semester, the teacher whose spouse has been transferred two states away may be encouraged to continue to teach until the end of the semester before being released without penalty from the contract. The teacher with a terminally ill child or parent would most likely be encouraged to take a leave of absence and return to the classroom at a later time.

The basic premise of tenure is to protect teachers so that a school district will have a competent, ongoing teaching staff. Before tenure laws were enacted, a variety of questionable activities took place in many school districts. In one bizarre instance, teachers who failed to buy their cars from the president of the school board's car dealership were not rehired. Other instances include the dismissal of teachers for religious reasons, for opposing political views of the school board, and even to make an opening available to hire a relative of a school board member. Tenure laws protect tenured and, to some degree, nontenured teachers from actions such as these.

Tenure laws specifically outline how teachers are to be treated and have been upheld by the courts. State boards of education, in addition to state statutes, clearly indicate the procedures for review of the teaching practices of both probationary and tenured teachers. Such state laws explicitly state how tenure is acquired as well as the procedures for dismissing tenured teachers. As mentioned, only in rare instances are tenured teachers dismissed. In fact, many educators argue that tenure laws protect incompetent rather than competent teachers. According to a principal in a large suburban school district, the cost of dismissing an incompetent teacher is about $400,000 (Carmony 1994). This is due to the legal fees and the long duration of the process. The dismissal process of an incompetent teacher may drag on for several years in the courts. Obviously, few districts have the funds to pay for such costs, even though most have legal insurance that covers their legal costs. Regardless, the legal process is quite expensive and few school boards elect to pursue the dismissal of a teacher, no matter how inept and unprofessional that individual might be in the classroom. Unfortunately for the other teachers in a school district, an incompetent colleague reflects poorly on them as well.

Discrimination

School districts must follow state and federal laws regarding equal employment opportunities for all personnel. This includes employment, promotion, dismissal, and demotion of faculty and staff. Typically, lawsuits regarding discrimination by a school district fall into one of the following categories: age, gender, disability, race, and/or religion.

Age cannot be a factor when hiring a teacher. However, some school districts prefer to hire experienced teachers over new college graduates, who tend to be young. This practice is not against the law. Newly certified teachers have found that substituting in such districts can be one way to become noticed, particularly if they go beyond the basics of substituting and demonstrate initiative, such as carefully following all lesson plans and requests made by the classroom teacher, volunteering for lunchroom or recess duty, and grading all student assignments made during the day.

At the other end of the age spectrum, under federal law, school districts cannot force a teacher or staff member to retire. This has not always been the case. Until 1994, mandatory retirement at age seventy could be enforced by any school district or business. When this law was changed, it meant that teachers could continue teaching in the classroom beyond age seventy. Since older teachers generally have several years of teaching experience and command large salaries, often twice as much as

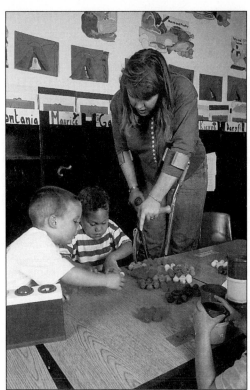

A school district is prohibited from discriminating against a teacher with a disbility. (Michael Newman/PhotoEdit)

a beginning teacher, school districts with limited financial resources create retirement packages that are beneficial to both the teacher and the school district. For instance, a school district may create a plan that pays teachers who agree to retire in two years a 10 percent higher salary for their final two years of teaching. While the school district must pay the higher salary during those last two years, it benefits three years later when a teacher with a lower salary is hired. The retiring teacher is also rewarded for contributions made over a long teaching career. In addition, retirement benefits increase because of the salary increase. A drawback to the school district can be the loss of valuable experience when the retiring teacher is replaced by a younger, less-experienced teacher.

Gender is another category in which school districts cannot discriminate. Title IX of the Education Amendments was enacted in 1972. Probably best known for establishing sports opportunities for girls and women equal to those for boys and men in public schools and colleges, Title IX strongly states that no individual can be excluded from participating in sports or be discriminated against in educational and employment opportunities. For example, female teachers cannot be paid lower salaries than male teachers. This extends to the pay scale for extracurricular activities. The courts have ruled that female coaches must be paid the same rate as male coaches in the same sport.

If a teacher has a disability, he or she cannot be discriminated against. The school district may make provisions to assist the teacher; for example, a teacher with a degenerating eye disease may be given a classroom aide to assist with evaluating student papers and typing exams. A school district cannot discriminate against an applicant with a disability. However, that does not mean that a disabled applicant receives priority over a nondisabled individual. For instance, an Arkansas school district had an opening for a librarian. One of the applicants was a legally blind but otherwise qualified librarian. The school district hired another qualified candidate. The visually impaired librarian filed a lawsuit against the school district. The U.S. District Court in Arkansas ruled that the school district had a rational basis for employing the candidate whom they had hired and had not discriminated against the visually impaired candidate.

Health conditions cannot be used to punish teachers. In 1974, the U.S. Supreme Court ruled in *Cleveland Board of Education v. LaFleur,* 414 U.S. 632 (1974) that school boards cannot dictate when a pregnant teacher takes a maternity leave or returns to teaching full-time (Zirkel 1978). The teacher does have the responsibility of notifying the school district early in a pregnancy so that provisions can be made to hire a substitute teacher. Some districts have the substitute teacher overlap a day or two with the classroom teacher to ensure a smooth instructional transition for students.

The federal courts have ruled that teachers who carry the HIV virus cannot be dismissed. In addition, under federal law it is prohibited for any agency that receives federal funds to discriminate against anyone who has AIDS (Holmes 1990).

A school district cannot discriminate against teachers because of race or religious beliefs. Indeed, minority teachers are in great demand and are actively sought by most school districts, particularly those in urban and suburban areas.

Teachers cannot practice their religious beliefs in the classroom. For example, an Oregon school district employed a teacher who was a Sikh, a Hindu religious sect, who insisted on wearing a turban in the classroom. His principal informed him that he could not wear the turban in the classroom. He sued the school district and lost.

Due Process

Laws that protect individual rights include **due process,** which ensures that the individual is treated fairly. States have statutes regarding the rights of teachers. A tenured teacher dismissed for gross negligence of duty, for example, has a right to a hearing. The school district must set up that hearing within a specified period of time as well as meet the procedures outlined within the state statutes. For instance, there must be substantial written and dated documentation that the teacher did not perform the assigned duties—such as leaving students unsupervised on more than one occasion or having students engage in a dangerous activity, such as building explosive devises in a chemistry class.

Basically, due process requires that tenured teachers be provided with detailed, written comments on the charges over a period of time, not within a couple of weeks. The teacher must be allowed to have a formal hearing based on the charges and be given sufficient time to prepare for it. The teacher may have a lawyer or union representative. During the hearing, the teacher may submit written and oral statements as well as ask questions of any witnesses. The hearing is held before an impartial body, usually the school board. All written transcripts of the hearing must be provided to the teacher upon request. Should the teacher lose the case, he or she may appeal the case in court, usually within the state judicial system.

Thus, a teacher cannot be immediately dismissed without due process. Consider a teacher who has been with a school district for several years and is arrested for the felony charges of child molestation and engaging in child pornography. The school district could not immediately dismiss the teacher. The school district can remove the teacher from the classroom setting by suspending the teacher with pay. Until the

Schools must provide a safe environment for students. Here students are separated from the street by a chain-link fence. (Courtesy of Pamela J. Farris)

This playground has no fence, so a teacher or other school employee must watch carefully to prevent a child from going out into the street. (Courtesy of Pamela J. Farris)

teacher is found guilty of the felony, the school district, regardless of the amount of evidence the police and prosecutors have against the teacher, cannot take dismissal action. If, in this case, the teacher is found guilty of child molestation and engaging in child pornography, the school district then dismisses the teacher and notifies the state board of education to retract that individual's teaching certificate because of the felony charge. However, the school district still has to provide for due process for the teacher and hold a formal dismissal hearing.

Liability

A legal term you need to become familiar with is **tort liability.** Torts are civil, rather than criminal, wrongs. Under tort law, a person who has endured damages as a result of another individual's improper behavior or conduct may sue for damages. For instance, if a person bought a used car but was not told that it had been submerged in water during a flood, even though the salesperson knew this, the owner may sue for damages under tort law.

Tort liability is important for teachers and school administrators in that if a child is accidentally injured at school due to negligence, the child's parents or guardians may sue the school on the child's behalf. As a result of tort liability, boards of education have policy manuals for teachers and school administrators as well as for students. In addition, safety measures are taken to ensure that students are not injured. Most school districts no longer have dangerous playground equipment such as merry-go-rounds, slides, and wooden seat swings. If a teacher must leave the classroom for any reason, another adult employee of the school must be present to supervise the students. Written permission must be obtained from a student's parents or guardian before a student can leave the school grounds to go on a field trip. These and other precautions have reduced the number of instances of student injury and the liability of local boards of education.

It is important to note that tort law is based on the degree of reasonableness of the case. If a student is playing kickball and falls over the base, breaking an arm in the process, the teacher and school cannot be sued. Likewise, if a child under a teacher's supervision accidently cuts a finger on a desk or metal locker, the teacher is not liable. However, if the teacher brings in a dangerous chemical for a science experiment and a student drinks it to show off for the other students, the teacher may be sued.

Negligence is ruled by the courts to be a result of a lack of reasonable care to protect students from harm, for example, leaving students unsupervised. Also, if the teacher's actions resulted in the student's injury, negligence can be found. For instance, if a physical education teacher tells students to run the length of the gym floor as fast as they can but there is insufficient room for them and they run into the wall, negligence is evident.

School districts make every attempt to eliminate potentially dangerous situations. In addition, they seek parental permission for unusual educational events. School districts typically require written parental permission for students to take part in special events such as field trips to museums. While permission is intended to protect the school or teachers from any tort liability, it offers little or no protection against lawsuits.

Not every state allows for tort liability. Some hold that school districts and their employees are exempt; however, most states do follow tort law for schools.

School districts carry liability insurance to protect teachers, school administrators, and members of the board of education against damages awarded in lawsuits. In addition, teachers' organizations such as the AFT and NEA and school administrative organizations such as AASA also provide liability insurance for their members. Because in our society the courts are filled with lawsuits, it is vitally important that as teachers we be extra cautious in our interactions with students. Written rules and regulations, oral directions for safety, and advance, thoughtful planning are all important to protect student welfare.

Freedom of Expression

As a teacher, you must follow the policies set forth by the board of education in your school district and outlined in your contract. This includes following the curriculum guidelines as well as other codes of behavior. For instance, you are responsible for evaluating and returning students' work within a reasonable time period so students know how they are performing in class.

A school district may require you to dress and groom yourself in a manner deemed appropriate for teachers in that community. Such a dress code must be adopted by the school board and disseminated to the faculty. For instance, Max Miller, a teacher in Illinois, grew a beard and sideburns. When he refused to shave the extra facial hair, his contract was not renewed. The judges ruled in favor of the school district in stating that the teacher's dress should not unduly affect students and that choice of dress or grooming is "subordinate to the public interest" (*Miller v. School District No. 167 of Cook County, Illinois*, 495 F. 2d

Teachers' dress has become more relaxed in some districts, particularly in liberal communities. (Mary Kate Denny/PhotoEdit)

Point /Counterpoint

*Can School Officials Set Standards of Conduct
for Student Speech, or Do Students Have
Complete Freedom of Speech?*

Over the years, freedom of speech has become an increasingly sensitive issue in schools. This Point/Counterpoint examines Bethel School District No. 403 v. Fraser, 478 U.S. 675 (1986) by examining the opinions of the justices of the U.S. Supreme Court.

In this box, Counterpoint directly follows Point.

Point: School officials have the right to set standards of conduct, including speech, for students.

Chief Justice Burger delivered the opinion of the U.S. Supreme Court. He wrote:

"Matthew N. Fraser, a student at Bethel High School in Pierce County, Washington, delivered a speech nominating a fellow student for student elective office. Approximately six hundred high school students, many of whom were fourteen-year-olds, attended the assembly. Students were required to attend the assembly or to report to the study hall. The assembly was part of a school-sponsored educational program in self-government. Students who elected not to attend the assembly were required to report to study hall. During the entire speech, Fraser referred to his candidate in terms of an elaborate, graphic, and explicit sexual metaphor.

"Two of Fraser's teachers, with whom he discussed the contents of his speech in advance, informed him that the speech was 'inappropriate and that he probably should not deliver it,' App 30, and that his delivery of the speech might have 'severe consequences.' Id., at 61.

"During Fraser's delivery of the speech, a school counselor observed the reaction of students to the speech. Some students hooted and yelled; some by gestures graphically simulated the sexual activities pointedly alluded to in respondent's speech. Other students appeared to be bewildered and embarrassed by the speech. One teacher reported that on the day following the speech, she found it necessary to forgo a portion of the scheduled class lesson in order to discuss the speech with the class. Id., at 41–44. . . ."

Burger went on to state:

"The process of educating our youth for citizenship in public schools is not confined to books, the curriculum, and the civics class; schools must teach by example the shared values of a civilized social order. Consciously or otherwise, teachers—and indeed the older students—demonstrate the appropriate form of civil discourse and political expression by their conduct and deportment in and out of class. Inescapably, like parents, they are role models. The schools, as instruments of the state, may determine that the essential lessons of civil, mature conduct cannot be conveyed in a school that tolerates lewd, indecent, or offensive speech and conduct such as that indulged in by this confused boy.

"The pervasive sexual innuendo in Fraser's speech was plainly offensive to both teachers and students—indeed to any mature person. By glorifying male sexuality, and in its verbal content, the speech was acutely insulting to teenage girl students. See App 77–81. The speech could well be seriously damaging to its less mature audience, many of whom were only fourteen years old. . . ."

Burger further stated:

"The role and purpose of the American public school system were well described by two historians, who state: '[P]ublic education must prepare pupils for citizenship in the Republic. . . . It must inculcate the habits and manners of civility as values in themselves conducive to happiness and as indispensable to the practice of self-government in the community and the nation.' C. Beard & M. Beard, New Basic History of the United States 228 (1968). In Ambach v Norwick, 441 US 68, 76-77, 60 L Ed 2d 49, 99 S Ct 1589 (1979), we echoed the essence of

(continued)

Chapter 7   *Legal and Ethical Issues in Education*

(continued)

this statement of the objectives of public education as the 'inculcat[ion of] fundamental values necessary to the maintenance of a democratic political system.'

"[2] These fundamental values of 'habits and manners of civility' essential to a democratic society must, of course, include tolerance of divergent political and religious views, even when the views expressed may count consideration of the sensibilities of others, and, in the case of a school, the sensibilities of fellow students. The undoubted freedom to advocate unpopular and controversial views in schools and classrooms must be balanced against the society's countervailing interest in teaching students the boundaries of socially appropriate behavior. Even the most heated political discourse in a democratic society requires consideration for the personal sensibilities of the other participants and audiences."

Justice Brennan offered a concurring opinion. He wrote:

"Respondent gave the following speech at a high school assembly in support of a candidate for student government office:

'I know a man who is firm—he's firm in his pants, he's firm in his shirt, his character is firm—but most . . . of all, his belief in you, the students of Bethel, is firm.

'Jeff Kuhlman is a man who takes his point and pounds it in. If necessary, he'll take an issue and nail it to the wall. He doesn't attack things in spurts—he drives hard, pushing and pushing until finally—he succeeds.

'Jeff is a man who will go to the very end—even the climax, for each and every one of you.

'So vote for Jeff for A. S. B. vice-president—he'll never come between you and the best our high school can be.' App 47.

"The Court, referring to these remarks as 'obscene,' 'vulgar,' 'lewd,' and 'offensively lewd,' concludes that school officials properly punished respondent for uttering the speech. Having read the full text of respondent's remarks, I find it difficult to believe that it is the same speech the Court describes. To my mind, the most that can be said about respondent's speech—and all that need be said—is that in light of the discretion school officials have to teach high school students how to conduct civil and effective public discourse, and to prevent disruption of school educational activities, it was not unconstitutional for school officials to conclude, under the circumstances of this case, that respondent's remarks exceeded permissible limits."

Counterpoint: Students should have the right of freedom of speech under the U.S. Constitution.

Justice Marshall was one of two justices who voted in the minority in *Bethel School District No. 403 v. Fraser.* Here is an excerpt from Marshall's dissenting opinion:

"I agree with the principles that Justice Brennan sets out in his opinion concurring in the judgment. I dissent from the Court's decision, however, because in my view the School District failed to demonstrate that respondent's remarks were indeed disruptive. The District Court and Court of Appeals conscientiously applied Tinker v Des Moines Independent Community School District, 393 US 503, 21 L Ed 2d 731, 89 S Ct 733, 49 Ohio Ops 2d 222 (1969), and concluded that the School District had not demonstrated any disruption of the educational process. I recognize that the school administration must be given wide latitude to determine what

forms of conduct are inconsistent with the school's educational mission; nevertheless, where speech is involved, we may not unquestioningly accept a teacher's or administrator's assertion that certain pure speech interfered with education. Here the School District, despite a clear opportunity to do so, failed to bring in evidence sufficient to convince either of the two lower courts that education at Bethel School was disrupted by respondent's speech. I therefore see no reason to disturb the Court of Appeals' judgment."

Justice Stevens wrote in his dissenting opinion:

" 'Frankly, my dear, I don't give a damn.'

"When I was a high school student, the use of those words in a public forum shocked the Nation. Today Clark Gable's four-letter expletive is less offensive than it was then. Nevertheless, I assume that high school

(continued)

65 [7th Cir. 1974]). Female teachers have been dismissed for wearing miniskirts, while male teachers have lost their teaching positions for wearing earrings or growing ponytails. Religious apparel, such as a Christian cross on a lapel pin or necklace, can also be prohibited by a school district. The courts have upheld school districts in such judicial decisions.

You must also consider the language you use in the classroom. If you allow profanity or obscene jokes in the classroom, even by students who have your permission, you can be dismissed.

Child Abuse

If teachers, school administrators, and/or members of the board of education ignore complaints about a teacher sexually harassing or even abusing students, they and the school district can be held liable. Any such complaints by a student about another teacher or school employee, even about a school crossing guard or cafeteria worker, should be immediately directed to the building principal.

In almost every state, teachers are legally responsible for reporting cases of child abuse. Failure to do so may result in a teacher's arrest. Because of the prevalence of child abuse, most school districts have specific procedures as part of their board of education policy that outline how to deal with suspected cases of child abuse of any type, physical, mental, or sexual.

Technology and Its Legal Ramifications for Schools

By the year 2000, the U.S. Department of Education wants every classroom hooked up to the Internet. With computer access available for all students from their own classrooms, certain legal problems arise. There is no censorship on the Internet. While in the past the worst problem with information access was when elementary and middle school students sneaked peeks of nude statues in encyclopedias or unclothed natives in the *National Geographic,* teachers and school administrators now have to guard against students viewing the pure porn that can be found on the World Wide Web as students cruise the information superhighway.

Following is a statement that teachers in Rochelle School District in Rochelle, Illinois, must sign as part of their contract to teach in the school district. Students (or their parents) must also sign this statement.

Instruction

Exhibit—Authorization for Internet Access

• Each teacher must sign this Authorization as a condition for using the District's Internet connection. Each student and his or her parent(s)/guardian(s) must sign the Authorization before being granted unsupervised access. School Board members and administrators are treated like teachers for purposes of this Authorization. Please read this document carefully before signing.

All use of the Internet shall be consistent with the District's goal of promoting educational excellence by facilitating resource sharing, innovation, and communication. This Authorization does not attempt to state all required or proscribed behavior by users. However, some specific examples are provided. **The failure of any user to follow the terms of the Authorization for Internet Access will result in the loss of privileges, disciplinary action, and/or appropriate legal action.** *The signature(s) at the end of this document is legally binding and indicates the party who signed has read the terms and conditions carefully and understands their significance.*

Terms and Conditions

1. *Acceptable Use—Access to the District's Internet must be for the purpose of education or research, and be consistent with the educational objectives of the District.*

2. *Privileges—the use of the District's Internet is a privilege, not a right, and inappropriate use will result in a cancellation of those privileges. The system administrator will make all decisions regarding whether or not a user has violated this Authorization and may deny, revoke, or suspend access at any time; his or her decision is final.*

3. *Unacceptable Use—You are responsible for your actions and activities involving the network. Some examples of unacceptable users are:*
    a. *Using the network for any illegal activity, including violation of copyright or other contracts, or transmitting any material in violation of any U.S. or State regulation;*
    b. *Unauthorized downloading of software, regardless of whether it is copyrighted or devirused;*
    c. *Downloading copyrighted material for other than personal use;*
    d. *Using the network for private financial or commercial gain;*
    e. *Wastefully using resources, such as file space;*
    f. *Gaining unauthorized access to resources or entities;*
    g. *Invading the privacy of individuals;*
    h. *Using another user's account or password;*
    i. *Posting material authored or created by another without his/her consent;*
    j. *Posting anonymous messages;*
    k. *Using the network for commercial or private advertising.*
    l. *Accessing, submitting, posting, publishing, or displaying any defamatory, inaccurate, abusive, obscene, profane, sexually oriented, threatening, racially offensive, harassing, or illegal material; and*
    m. *Using the network while access privileges are suspended or revoked.*

4. *Network Etiquette—You are expected to abide by the generally accepted rules of network etiquette. These include, but are not limited to, the following:*
    a. *Be polite. Do not become abusive in your messages to others.*
    b. *Use appropriate language. Do not swear, or use vulgarities or any other inappropriate language.*
    c. *Do not reveal the personal addresses or telephone numbers of students or colleagues.*
    d. *Recognize that electronic mail (E-mail) is not private. People who operate the system have access to all mail. Messages relating to or in support of illegal activities may be reported to the authorities.*
    e. *Do not use the network in any way that would disrupt its use by other users.*
    f. *Consider all communications and information accessible via the network to be private property.*

5. *No Warranties—The District makes no warranties of any kind, whether expressed or implied, for the service it is providing. The District will not be responsible for any damages you suffer. This includes loss of data resulting from delays, non-deliveries, missed-deliveries, or service interruptions caused by its negligence or your errors or omissions. Use of any information obtained via the Internet is at your own risk. The District specifically denies any responsibility for the accuracy or quality of information obtained through its services.*

6. *Indemnification—The user agrees to indemnify the School District for any losses, costs, or damages, including reasonable attorney fees, incurred by the District relating to, or arising out of, any breach of this Authorization.*

7. *Security—Network security is a high priority. If you can identify a security problem on the Internet, you must notify the system administrator or Building Principal. Do not demonstrate the problem to other users. Keep your account and password confidential. Do not use another individual's account without written permission from that individual. Attempts to log-on to the Internet as a system administrator will result in cancellation of user privileges. Any user identified as a security risk may be denied access to the network.*

8. *Vandalism—Vandalism will result in cancellation of privileges and other disciplinary action. Vandalism is defined as any malicious attempt to harm or destroy data of another user, the Internet, or any other network. This includes, but is not limited to, the uploading or creation of computer viruses.*

9. *Telephone Charges—The District assumes no responsibility for any unauthorized charges or fees, including telephone charges, long-distance charges, per-minute surcharges, and/or equipment or line costs.*

Students, parent(s)/guardian(s), and teachers need only sign this Authorization for Internet Access once while enrolled or employed by the School District.

Copyright Laws

In 1976, Congress passed new copyright laws far more stringent than those previously on record. Authors and artists use these copyright laws to protect their property, including articles, poetry, stories, books, artwork, photos, musical scores and lyrics, films, computer software, and videotapes. No one can make a photocopy of a book or copy a videotape without written permission.

To assist educators, a committee comprised of authors, librarians, and publishers, along with educators, reviewed the copyright laws and developed what is known as **fair use.** Fair use enables teachers to make copies of materials for use with students in their classrooms under certain limited conditions. Here are the guidelines set forth for fair use of copyrighted materials by the Association of American Publishers (1991).

Copying of prose is limited to no more than 1,000 words.

A poem may be copied if it is less than 250 words, and an excerpt of no more than 250 words may be copied from a longer poem.

Distribution of copies from the same author more than once a semester or copying from the same work or anthology more than three times during the semester is prohibited.

Books that are no longer in print may be photocopied.

Teachers may make one photocopy per student for class distribution.

Students cannot be charged more for the copies than the actual photocopying expenses.

Teachers may not photocopy anthologies or compilations of articles, etc., as a substitute for purchasing the same or similar materials.

Workbooks, standardized tests, and other consumable materials may not be photocopied.

Single copies of printed materials may be made for personal study, lesson planning, or research.

Most magazine and newspaper articles may be photocopied freely unless they are particularly designed for student use.

Each teacher must decide what to photocopy for student or his/her own use. A higher authority such as a principal cannot direct the teacher to decide.

There are three types of material that can be copied without permission: written material published before 1978 that does not have a copyright; books published over seventy-five years ago; and any U.S. government publications.

If a teacher or school district wants to use certain copyrighted material for a curriculum project, they may contact the publisher and request written permission to use the material. Usually the publisher wants to know how the material will be used and for what purpose. Often the publisher asks that the school district pay a royalty fee, which goes to the publisher and the author of the material. For instance, using a song by Alan Jackson or Whitney Houston in a middle school play in which admission will be charged requires permission from their record companies.

In some instances, the state may negotiate to use certain materials. California, Illinois, and other states, for example, negotiated with Steven Spielberg to permit every high school to have copies of his film *Schindler's List*, an award-winning film that depicts the efforts of German businessman Oskar Schindler to save Jews from Nazi concentration camps during World War II, to show to their students as part of curriculum units on the Holocaust.

As teachers, we need to be aware that showing a Walt Disney video such as *Snow White and the Seven Dwarfs* or *White Fang* or a video about underwater life rented from a local video store to our classes may be illegal. Walt Disney reserves such rights solely for home viewing, whereas other studios permit use in schools. Such restrictions are usually clearly identified on the case of the video.

Likewise, teachers are avid users of video cassette recorders. A teacher may videotape a television program or sports event to show to a class, but there are several restrictions. The program may be shown to the class only once in the ten-day period following the original airing of the program on television. The videotape may be re-shown to the class one more time after that ten-day period, and the videotape must be destroyed within forty-five days after the program was originally televised.

Teachers are notorious for sharing ideas and materials. This has often included software, videotapes, and compact disks. Copying software, videotapes, or compact disks is a federal offense and is subject to the same restrictions as written copyrighted materials.

Lifestyles

School districts cannot dismiss teachers for living with someone of the opposite sex. Nor can they dismiss a teacher who routinely gets drunk every weekend. As long as they are competent in the classroom and successfully perform their teaching duties, teachers cannot be terminated. However, if a teacher solicits a student for sexual favors, the teacher can be dismissed. Likewise, if a teacher who enjoys drinking offers a student liquor, the teacher is contributing to the delinquency of a minor and could be dismissed.

There are a few states that have laws to protect teachers who are homosexuals. In 1977, the U.S. Supreme Court refused to hear a case from Washington in which a teacher was dismissed for his homosexuality (*Gaylord v. Tacoma School District No. 18*, 434 U.S. 879 [1977]). Some states, however, have laws stating that homosexual teachers can be dismissed for being gay.

Legal Issues for Students

Ever since the 1954 Supreme Court decision in *Brown v. Board of Education of Topeka*, 347 U.S. 483, the courts have played a major role in education. That 1954 decision struck down the separate-but-equal educational policy that had been upheld for years in the southern states. However, once a ruling is made by the U.S. Supreme Court, it may take years to actually see changes take place as a result. While African American students have been permitted to attend public schools along with white students for over fifty years, there still are questions of equal opportunities in education since public schools do not receive equal funding.

A Closer Look   *Residence Requirements*

Residence requirements necessitate that students who attend a school reside within the boundaries of the school district. In recent years, Hispanic students who live in Mexico have given Texas schools the addresses of relatives who legally reside within the school district as their own. However, the students cross the border at the end of each day and return to their real homes in Mexico, where the schools have lower academic standards and fewer resources. Thus, the taxpayers of several Texas school districts are paying for the education of children from Mexico. Today, many foreign students are brought from Asia and other parts of the world by adult relatives, usually parents or uncles, to the United States to obtain a quality education. Some are left on their own in rented apartments or to live with other relatives or even strangers.

Similarly, state borders are often crossed by students who have relatives living within the school district of their neighboring state. In some cases, students lie about their true addresses to get into a school because of better academic or extracurricular programs. For example, several years ago, Illinois was a leading state in assisting students with mental and physical disabilities. Many parents from the bordering states of Iowa, Kentucky, and Indiana used relatives' addresses who lived within Illinois school districts to register their children in school.

Legal issues for students include the right to education, conduct, the role of teachers in supervision, school dress codes, due process, discipline and corporal punishment, search and seizure, and right to privacy. According to Zirkel (1998, p. 410), there is "increasing education litigation concerning hostile atmosphere based on protected civil rights. At the leading edge of such case law are court decisions based on student-to-student sexual harassment. Following not far behind are hostile environment suits based on disability, religion, and national origin," or cultural background. As a teacher, you need to be aware of the civil rights of your students.

Right to Education

Since the first compulsory education law in Massachusetts in 1647, American children have had the opportunity for free public schooling. In addition, the courts have ruled that education cannot be denied to students with disabilities.

In 1982, the U.S. Supreme Court heard a case from the state of Texas regarding the right of children whose parents were not U.S. citizens to attend public school. Under Texas law, children of illegal aliens were denied access to public education. These children, most of whom were Hispanics from Mexico, were not permitted to attend school. The U.S. Supreme Court in a five-to-four decision ruled that the Texas law was unconstitutional. As long as the children lived within the boundaries of the school district, they were entitled to a free public education. The majority opinion wrote that not allowing these children to obtain an education would result in a subclass of illiterates that would add to the problems of unemployment, high welfare costs, and crime.

In 1994, California voters passed Proposition 147, which limits funding for education, health care, and welfare for illegal aliens and their children. Other states are considering similar legislation.

Student Conduct

One of the major areas of litigation during the past four decades involves student conduct. A student has the right to a free public education; however, it is a privilege that may be taken away if the student violates the rules and regulations of the school. Boards of education adopt policies that are in effect rules and regulations regarding student conduct. This is to ensure the safety and education of all students.

Board of education policies include guidelines for suspensions and expulsions from school. A suspension from school may result from a student's misconduct. The suspension may be for a short period of time, usually one to three days, and may be given to the student either orally or in writing, with the latter the preferred notification. Expulsion is for a very serious misconduct charge and can be for the remainder of the semester or school year. Before a student can be expelled, the student must be given a hearing in which he or she or a representative can question all witnesses. This is an example of due process for students.

There have been several legal challenges in the courts by students over a variety of school issues: corporal punishment, dress codes, the rights of homosexual students, freedom of expression, and rights of privacy. Many of these cases are examined in the following sections.

In Loco Parentis

Schools function under the *in loco parentis* principle, meaning that they serve in place of a parent. Thus, the school has nearly complete authority over students during the school hours. Court decisions in the past few decades have varied regarding the amount of control schools have over students. Generally, courts uphold the rules and regulations established for students set forth by school boards. However, during the 1960s and 1970s, a liberal U.S. Supreme Court often ruled that the rules and regulations of schools regarding student behavior violated the constitutional rights of students. One of the most famous cases was *Tinker v. Des Moines Independent Community School District*, 393 U.S. 503 (1969), which took place during the height of the Vietnam War. High school students wore black armbands to protest the war, and this behavior violated school rules. The U.S. Supreme Court ruled against the school district in citing that wearing armbands was a demonstration of free speech. The Court was careful to point out that students did not have the right to engage in disruptive action or group demonstrations.

Another decision involving the rights of students to free speech was a 1986 decision by the U.S. Supreme Court. In *Bethel School District No. 403 v. Fraser*, 478 U.S. 675 (1986), Matthew Fraser, a high school senior, gave a nomination speech before over six hundred students in the school assembly for one of his friends who was a candidate for vice president of student government (see Point/Counterpoint). Fraser had written the speech in advance and shared it with two of his teachers. Both teachers warned Fraser that his speech was inappropriate because it included several sexual innuendos that compared the candidate to a sexual organ. Fraser ignored their warnings and gave the speech, which was met with hooting, snickers, and obscene, suggestive gestures from the audience. Fraser was promptly suspended from school for two days. He filed suit against the school district, alleging that his First Amendment rights had been violated. The U.S. District Court of the Western District of Washington agreed with Fraser and awarded him damages, as did the U.S. Court of Appeals for the Ninth District. However, when the school district appealed to the U.S. Supreme Court, the court ruled in favor of the school district, stating that the school is responsible for determining conduct and cannot permit indecent or offensive speech by students. Whether Fraser's lewd speech was a help or a hindrance to his candidate is uncertain, since the court records do not include how the school election turned out.

A third case regarding the First Amendment was the *Hazelwood School District v. Kuhlmeier*, 86-836 S. Ct. (1988). According to school policy, the student newspaper was to be reviewed by the high school principal before going to press. The principal approved all but two articles that were to appear in an issue. The principal objected to a story in the newspaper that dealt with three pregnant students, including explicit details of each student's sex life, and a second article that focused on divorce and its effects on student lives. While the articles did not include names of students, most were known to the student body. The two articles were deleted and the issue was published. Three of the journalism students who had written the articles sued the school district, claiming their First Amendment rights had been violated. The U.S. Supreme Court ruled in favor of the school district, citing that writing the newspaper was part of a journalism class and a supervised learning experience (Robbins 1990).

A fourth federal court case involved two brothers, Jeffrey and Jonathan Pyle, both students in the South Hadley, Massachusetts, school district. Jeffrey, a senior, wore a T-shirt with the message, "See Dick Drink. See Dick Drive. See Dick Die. Don't Be a Dick." His brother, Jonathan, a sophomore, wore a T-shirt with the even more explicit message, "Coed Naked Band; Do It to the Rhythm." The boys were both banned from wearing the T-shirts to school by school administrators for two reasons: (1) the T-shirts were suggestive and somewhat vulgar, thereby interfering with the school's educational mission, and (2) the sexually charged messages were demeaning to female students. Jeffrey and Jonathan's father, a political science professor at Mount Holyoke College who specialized in constitutional law, sued the school district on his sons' behalf, claiming that the school district violated his sons' First Amendment rights. The federal judge cited the three U.S. Supreme Court decisions discussed previously: *Tinker v. Des Moines Independent Community School District, Bethel School District No. 403 v. Fraser,* and *Hazelwood School District v. Kuhlmeier.* The judge pointed out that the *Tinker* decision involved wearing armbands as a political message, whereas the *Fraser* decision involved the sexual terms used by Fraser in his speech in front of the school assembly. The judge ruled that the Pyle brothers' T-shirts were more like the *Fraser* case and ruled in favor of the school district.

Other federal court cases involving student dress codes have resulted in the courts upholding school districts' right to prohibit students from attending a prom wearing clothes of the opposite sex, from wearing earrings that are a gang symbol, and from wearing T-shirts with caricatures of school administrators in a drunken stupor. Some decisions have ruled in favor of students, but, generally speaking, any clothing that is sexually suggestive, gang-related, or drug-related can be prohibited by a school district (Zirkel 1994). Thus, a student's First Amendment right to freedom of speech remains somewhat unclear.

Due Process

The Fourteenth Amendment guarantees the right to due process, or the right of equal protection. As we saw earlier, teachers have the right to due process. Students, as well, have a right to due process. That is, if a student violates school policy, say by bringing a gun to school and pointing it at another student, the student may be expelled for the remainder of the semester or school year. However, the student has a right to a hearing prior to the expulsion.

Middle school and high school students are usually sensitive to changes in student dress codes. Many teenagers spend much of their allowances or the money they earn on apparel to create an image of themselves for their peers. However, several school districts have banned a variety of clothing for safety reasons and personal hygiene. Boston public schools have banned hats, including baseball caps, because some students used them to hide small handguns and knives. Backpacks or bookbags have also been found to hide contraband and have thus been banned in many high schools. Students may use see-through, mesh bags instead. The Atlanta public schools have a drug-free policy that prohibits students from wearing T-shirts that support the use of drugs and alcohol. Baltimore schools have banned gold chains, bracelets, and large earrings. In Detroit, some schools have placed leggings on the taboo list for clothing. Some high schools have banned any clothing with the name of a sports team, professional or college, since it was discovered that gangs used these logos as their gang insignia. Many California middle schools and high schools have banned baggy jeans, which are sometimes worn pulled down so that the wearer's underwear is easily seen (Howard and Rogers 1994).

Many schools, including elementary through secondary schools, believe that student apparel is a significant problem. Students have been shot and killed for a leather jacket or one bearing the insignia of a sports team. Other problems include students wearing gang-related colors. In many public schools, students are required to wear a school uniform. This is typically a white shirt or blouse, navy or black pants or skirt, and black shoes. Schools that have adopted this policy believe that it causes students to focus more on learning and less on their wardrobes.

School Discipline and Corporal Punishment

Students who misbehave interfere with the learning of others. Teachers and school administrators have the responsibility and authority to enforce a school district's student conduct codes.

Corporal punishment as a disciplinary action dates back to the earliest American schools, when teachers used hickory sticks to swat the behind or legs of a student who misbehaved. Some states have enacted laws that forbid corporal punishment; however, it is permissible in many states. In those states each school board must make specific policies regarding corporal punishment. If a teacher violates the local school board's policy regarding corporal punishment, for instance giving a student ten swats when three is the maximum permitted under school district policy, the teacher may be dismissed. The student may sue the teacher if excessive force was used or if school board policy is violated.

Corporal punishment includes paddling a student. However, some school officials have used battery-charged cattle prods to give students an electrical shock, shoved students into lockers or walls, or kicked them. While paddling under certain circumstances is permissible, all of these other forms of corporal punishment are not. Research indicates that over a million students receive corporal punishment such as paddling each year (Gursky 1992).

Search and Seizure

Searches of student lockers and students themselves may be conducted if there is "reasonable" suspicion that the student has contraband or has engaged in a crime. In contrast, a person's home may not be searched by police without a search warrant, which indicates there is "probable" cause. Thus, school officials may search students with a lower degree of suspicion to protect the safety of other students. School administrators may have specially trained dogs sniff lockers and even students' cars but not students themselves.

Students may not be strip-searched, which is unconstitutional. However, schools may have students walk through metal detectors, a common practice in large urban and suburban high schools.

Right to Privacy

In 1974, the Family Educational Rights and Privacy Act, more commonly referred to as the Buckley Amendment, was passed by Congress. The act allows parents to have access to their child's academic records. Information about special education or criminal records as well as academic records cannot be given out to anyone without the parents' permission.

As teachers, this law means that student records must be kept confidential. However, you still may write notes for your own records and portfolios. Grade books are also the property of teachers and may not be revealed to parents.

In 1993, a suburban middle school student in the Midwest challenged her school's policy of publishing a list of honor roll students in the local newspaper. The student was on the honor roll but felt that by publishing her name in the paper, the school was invading her privacy. The school opted to make the publication of names of honor roll students optional.

Legal Issues Websites

Bilingual Education

National Clearing house for Bilingual Education. This site has information on U.S. and state legislation, court decisions, and bilingual education.

http://www.ncbe.gwu.edu/

Homeless Children

U.S. Congress on the Internet. Within this website is the reference to the Stewart B. McKinney Homeless Assistance Act which states that "each State educational agency shall ensure that each child of a homeless individual and each homeless youth has equal access to a free, appropriate public education."

http://www.ed.gov/legislation/ESEA/sec323.html

U.S. Supreme Court Rulings

Cornell University's Law School. This site contains both recent and archived U.S. Supreme Court decisions.

http://supct.law.cornell.edu/supct/

U.S. Congress on the Internet

The Thomas site within the U.S. Congress on the Internet site contains the Illegal Immigration Reform and Immigrant Responsibility Act of 1996.

http://thomas.loc.gov/

Should Student Names Not Be Given Out for any Reason, Including Publication In Local Newspapers?

Point: It is an invasion of students' privacy to give their names to local newspapers.

Students should have the right to keep their names out of the press. When student names, along with their parents' names, are printed in newspapers, their home addresses can be discovered by looking up their names in telephone books. In one instance, several families in a suburban Chicago neighborhood were terrorized by an individual who claimed he had kidnapped their children on their way to school. The terrorist had gotten the names of the children by reading about school activities in the local newspaper.

Counterpoint: Such extrinsic rewards as an article or photo in the newspaper boosts self-esteem and self-concept in students, so it is appropriate to give out student names to the media.

When students do outstanding work, such as help clean up a local playground, receive an award for a state music or speech contest or a scholarship from the local Rotary or Lions Club, or perform well in basketball, baseball, golf, swimming, tennis, track, or volleyball, they deserve to have their names in the newspaper. This shares good news with the local community, and while it helps to maintain a positive image for the school, it also promotes the talent and effort put forth by the students.

Certainly parents, grandparents, and other relatives are pleased to read about the positive exploits of a student. In effect, it also rewards the support and encouragement that families provide as well.

Ethics

As teachers, we need to keep in mind ethics—a major concern of parents and citizens in every school district. In 1994, a major scandal rocked the U.S. Naval Academy when it was found that several students were involved in a cheating scheme in which stolen copies of tests were sold to fellow students. The scandal received national attention for several weeks. Polls of high school honor students indicate that cheating is not only accepted but commonplace for many of them. This news is discouraging to both educators and parents. Maintaining a high ethical standard is important for all of us as we interact with children and adolescents.

History of Ethics and Education

Ethics education is not new to schools. Scholars taught ethics to their students in ancient civilization. In 1647, just over two decades after the landing at Plymouth Rock, the Old Deluder Satan Act was passed, requiring the establishment of schools to foster morality in children (ASCD Panel on Moral Education 1988). In Asia, Europe, and the United States, educators were historically concerned about ethics.

Confucianism

During the Chou dynasty (*ca.* 1027–256 B.C.) in China, Confucius (*ca.* 551–479 B.C.) was born. Considered the greatest teacher in China, today his teachings on ethics and morals are known throughout Asia and the world.

Confucius lived during a time of intense turmoil in China as the feudal system was breaking down. During the ensuing chaos, corruption, disobedience, and iniquities occurred. Confucius and his followers deplored such behavior and sought to have people return to the ancient values of reverence for elders and social standards for family and government.

Confucius was a scholar and sage. He stressed that ethics were essential to mankind. In Confucianism, the primary theme is that of *jen,* which means "love" and "goodness," the supreme virtue of human beings at their best. In interactions with others, *jen* is manifested in faithfulness to oneself and others, or *chung.* Altruism, known as *shu,* is consideration of others. *Shu* is the basis for the Confucian golden rule, "Do not do to others what you do not want done to yourself." This is similar to that of the golden rule of Christianity, "Do unto others as you would have them do unto you."

Confucious led the Chinese in returning to their cultural roots of respecting their elders. (© Shumsky/The Image Works, Inc.)

Jen is the foremost virtue in Confucianism. There are four other Confucian virtues. These include righteousness, propriety, integrity, and filial piety. Possession of all five of these virtues makes a person a *chun-tzu* (perfect gentleman).

After Confucius died, two opposing schools of Confucianism evolved. Mencius, like Confucius, stressed the innate goodness of human beings. In Mencius's view, human goodness can become corrupted through an individual's own destructive effort or through contact with evil surroundings. The challenge is maintaining or restoring human goodness.

Unlike Mencius and Confucius, Hsun-tzu considered human beings to be born with an evil nature. Through moral education, individuals followed the rules of propriety. Character was molded by the observance of rites and the practice of music, which provided discipline. Such a code heavily influenced one's character by directing emotions in a positive manner and by providing inner harmony. It was Hsun-tzu who promoted ritualism in Confucianism.

In the Sung dynasty (960–1279), Confucianism was blended with elements from Buddism and Taoism. Scholars who were knowledgeable in the latter two philosophies were interested in the theories of the universe and origin of human nature. Basically, these scholars were teachers of ethics.

This blending of philosophies was known as Neo-Confucianism. As with Confucianism, two major schools of thought emerged. Chu Hsi, an eminent scholar, second only to Confucius and Mencius in distinction in China, organized scholarly opinion into a cohesive system. According to the system Chu Hsi established, all objects in nature are composed of two inherent forces: *li,* an immaterial universal principle or law; and *ch'i* the substance of which all material things are made. *Li* may change and dissolve, but *li,* the underlying law of the myriad thing, remains constant and indestructible.

Chu Hsi identified *li* in human beings as human nature, which is basically the same for everyone. The phenomenon of specific differences can be a trait due to the varying portions and densities of the *ch'i* found among individuals. Purity can be achieved by extending one's knowledge of the *li* in each individual object. When, after lengthy effort, one has explored and understood the universal *li* or natural law inherent in all animate and inanimate objects, one becomes a sage.

Unlike the *li* (law) school proposed by Chu Hsi, the *hsin* (mind) school of Neo-Confucianism emphasizes the unity of knowledge and practice. This school of thought was developed by Wang Yang-ming, whose major premise was that "apart from the mind, neither law nor object" exists. Nothing exists without the mind, for it embodies all the laws of nature. The *hsin* school emphasized intense thought and calmness meditation as a means of developing intuitive knowledge.

By the end of the nineteenth century, the Chinese were encountering the outside world. The emphasis changed to value old customs. Neo-Confucianism gave way to Confucianism. The collapse of the monarch and takeover of the government by communists in 1949, as well as the changing family structure on which Confucianism was rooted, resulted in the decline of Confucianism as a philosophy in China. However, during the Vietnam conflict, many American and Canadian military personnel became familiar with Confucianism. This resulted in its adoption by some North Americans during the 1960s and 1970s.

European Educators' Contributions to Ethics Education

In the 1800s, two German educational leaders concerned about ethics were Friedrich Froebel, the founder of the kindergarten, and Johann Herbart, a philosopher. Froebel believed that the teacher should be a model for students to emulate. Thus, according to Froebel's views, it is imperative that teachers have high moral standards and be of good character. Froebel's views have prevailed, especially at the early childhood level with teachers of preschoolers and primary grade students.

It was Herbart who developed the first model of moral education. He believed that human beings will choose virtue over evil and that it was essential to present ethical ideas to children. Herbart wanted students to be sympathetic to others, maintain good social relationships, and develop religious beliefs. In Herbart's model of moral education, five major areas form the foundation of the development of moral character:

1. *Inner freedom*, which refers to the actions an individual takes based on his or her own personal beliefs and convictions.
2. *Perfection*, which refers to the harmony and integration of behavior.
3. *Benevolence*, which refers to an individual being concerned with the social welfare of other people.
4. *Justice*, which refers to the individual reconciling his or her own personal conduct with that of the group.
5. *Retribution*, which refers to what reward or punishment should accompany appropriate or inappropriate action.

Herbart believed that knowledge and the development of cognitive (thinking) abilities were essential if schools were to produce a person of high moral standards and good, sound character.

U.S. Educators' Contributions to Ethics Education

Early schools were founded in the mid-1600s on the basis of educating children so that they might follow religious doctrine. Through the 1800s, reading materials in such textbooks as the McGuffey readers included biblical verses and prayers in a didactic form of moral and ethical education.

By the late 1800s, character education was introduced into the public school curriculum and continued to be popular until the period of the Great Depression, which began in 1929 (Yulish 1980). Character education required that students be taught lessons that often failed to relate to real-life behavior.

In the early 1900s, John Dewey (1909, 1916), the foremost philosopher of American education during the twentieth century, believed that "one day the United States would become a utopian society, strongly committed to the ideals of human compassion and brotherhood among people of different races and creeds" (Rippa 1992, 173). Dewey felt that social reform had to begin with children and their social development. Ideally, in Dewey's view, the United States would become a nation of "humanism, compassion, and equality."

It was Dewey, a pragmatist, who introduced reflective thinking as a way to resolve moral dilemmas in life rather than having students work through character education problems. Dewey believed that in a democratic society, individuals needed to make decisions based on reasoning and thought. It was from Dewey's early work in this area that values clarification later evolved and became part of the curriculum in the 1960s and 1970s (Raths, Harmin, and Simon 1978).

From the 1950s through the 1980s, Lawrence Kohlberg (1958, 1969, 1986), a professor at Harvard University, advanced a view of moral development based on moral reasoning. Kohlberg believes that moral development advances in stages, similar to the cognitive stages put forth by Jean Piaget. For instance, a five-year-old volunteers to help his mother get ready for a party. As the child is carrying a stack of plates into the dining room, one falls off and breaks. A typical four- or five-year-old will say he should be punished, even though the child was trying to be helpful. A seven- or eight-year-old child will usually say that the plate broke accidentally and he should not be punished.

Kohlberg based his research findings on the reactions of children to eleven moral dilemmas he devised similar to the one described previously. Kohlberg's most popular dilemma is that of Heinz, whose wife is extremely ill:

In Europe a woman was near death from a special kind of cancer. There was one drug that the doctors thought might save her. It was a form of radium that a druggist in the same town had recently discovered. The drug was expensive to make, but the druggist was charging ten times what the drug cost him to make. He paid $200 for the radium and charged $2,000 for a small dose of the drug. The sick woman's husband, Heinz, went to everybody he knew to borrow the money, but he could only get together $1,000 which is half of what it cost. He told the druggist that his wife was dying and asked him to sell it cheaper or let him pay later. But the druggist said, "No, I discovered the drug, and I am going to make money from it." So Heinz got desperate and broke into the man's store to steal the drug for his wife (Kohlberg 1969, 379).

The child is then asked if Heinz did the right thing and why or why not.
Kohlberg's three levels of moral development each have two stages.

Level 1. *Preconventional reasoning (the lowest level). The child demonstrates no internalization of moral values.*

Stage 1. *Punishment and obedience orientation. At this stage, moral thinking is based on punishment. For instance, children believe they should obey their parents because their parents tell them to obey.*

Stage 2. *Individualism and purpose. At this stage, moral thinking is based on rewards and self-interest. Children obey when they want to obey and when it is in their best interest to obey. What is right is what feels good and what is rewarding.*

Level 2. *Conventional reasoning. At this level, children's internalization is intermediate. The child abides by certain standards that are internal, but they are the standards of others (external), such as parents or teachers, or laws of society.*

Stage 3. *Interpersonal norms. At this stage, children make moral judgments based on trust, caring, and loyalty to others. Thus, parents view their child as a "good boy (or girl)."*

Stage 4. *Social system morality. At this stage, moral judgments are based on understanding the social order, law, justice, and duty. For instance, a child may say that it's always wrong to steal because there are laws against stealing.*

Level 3. *Postconventional reasoning (the highest level in Kohlberg's development levels). At this level, morality is completely internalized.*

Stage 5. *Community rights versus individual rights. At this stage, the individual understands that values and laws are relative and that standards may vary from one person to another.*

Stage 6. *Universal ethical principles. At this stage, the individual has developed a moral standard based on universal human rights. When the person is faced with a conflict between law and conscience, the person follows conscience, even though the decision might involve danger or risk.*

Kohlberg's theory of moral development has been greatly criticized because his research is based on how people think rather than how they behave in actual life. For instance, people may say it is wrong to cheat on paying their taxes but they cheat anyway.

Carol Gilligan (1982), also of Harvard University, believes that ethics and morality should be viewed from a care perspective rather than from a justice perspective such as Kohlberg does. According to Gilligan, the care perspective views people from their connectedness with others and focuses on interpersonal communication, relationships with others, and concern for others.

Gilligan argues that there are three levels of moral development:

Level I. *Preconventional morality. At this level the individual demonstrates a concern for self and survival.*

Level II. *Conventional morality. At this level the person shows a concern for being responsible and caring for others.*

Level III. *Postconventional morality. At this level the person shows a concern for self and others as interdependent.*

In her research, Gilligan has found that girls have the ability to sensitively pick up different rhythms in relationships based on listening and watching what happens between people (Brown and Gilligan 1990; Gilligan 1990; Gilligan, Brown, and Rogers 1990). Other researchers have found support for Gilligan's claim that females' and males' moral reasoning often centers around different concerns and issues (Galotti, Kozberg, and Farmer 1990; Hanson and Mullis 1985; Yussen 1977).

Research on ethics and moral reasoning continues to be of interest to educators. The findings will influence teaching at the elementary and secondary levels.

Ethics in Today's Schools

Ethics in our schools has become a greater concern during the past few years as evidenced by more and more articles published in newspapers, magazines, and professional journals. According to Richard Hersh (1994, 12), president of Hobart and William Smith Colleges, the lack of ethics begins "at home, where social and economic factors . . . result in less family time. Young people have been allowed to or must take part-time jobs rather than spending time in school, on homework, or with their families. More children and adolescents are being reared in a vacuum, with television as their only supervisor, and there is little expectation that they learn personal responsibility. Immersed in themselves, they're left to their peers."

A Bill of Rights and Responsibilities for Learning

Standards of Conduct, Standards for Achievement

The traditional mission of our public schools has been to prepare our nation's young people for equal and responsible citizenship and productive adulthood. Today, we reaffirm that mission by remembering that democratic citizenship and productive adulthood begin with standards of conduct and standards for achievement in our schools. Other education reforms *may* work; high standards of conduct and achievement *do* work—and nothing else can work without them.

Recognizing that rights carry responsibilities, we declare that:

1. All students and school staff have a right to schools that are safe, orderly and drug free.

2. All students and school staff have a right to learn and work in school districts and schools that have clear discipline codes with fair and consistently enforced consequences for misbehavior.

3. All students and school staff have a right to learn and work in school districts that have alternative educational placements for violent or chronically disruptive students.

4. All students and school staff have a right to be treated with courtesy and respect.

5. All students and school staff have a right to learn and work in school districts, schools and classrooms that have clearly stated and rigorous academic standards.

6. All students and school staff have a right to learn and work in well-equipped schools that have the instructional materials needed to carry out a rigorous academic program.

7. All students and school staff have a right to learn and work in schools where teachers know their subject matter and how to teach it.

8. All students and school staff have a right to learn and work in school districts, schools and classrooms where high grades stand for high achievement and promotion is earned.

9. All students and school staff have a right to learn and work in school districts and schools where getting a high school diploma means having the knowledge and skills essential for college or a good job.

10. All students and school staff have a right to be supported by parents, the community, public officials and business in their efforts to uphold high standards of conduct and achievement.

American Federation of Teachers

James Comer, the Maurice Falk Professor of Child Psychiatry at the Yale University Child Study Center, says that "to be successful, one needs a threshold level of cognitive ability. But many other things are just as important: creativity, personal discipline, the ability to relate to other people. I call this 'effective intelligence'" (O'Neil 1997, 10). In Comer's view, our society has had a breakdown in the sense of community. The community provides social and emotional support for children and is necessary for children to attain high academic levels. If we can restore a sense of community, children today can attain what was possible for previous generations.

As teachers, we must create ethical classroom and school environments where our students can develop a sense of personal responsibility for their actions and behavior.

Ray Mims

Teachers as Role Models

When we walk into our school buildings and classrooms, we serve as role models to our students. This is a significant responsibility. How we dress, talk, and interact with others and our actions all are seen and weighed by our students. For instance, Al Canon, a high school teacher, believes that what he does greatly influences his students. When Al goes out to a pizza parlor in his community, he never orders a beer because one of his students might see him. "Sure a beer would taste good with a pepperoni pizza," he says, "but what am I saying to my students? I can drink alcoholic beverages when my students aren't around to see me do it."

Other teachers express a variety of other concerns about being a role model. Shawn Green, an elementary teacher, tries very hard to be fair to all students. Shawn consciously notes which students she has called on as well as those she has given positive comments to so that every child will be involved and every child complimented every day. She believes that students look up to teachers. Thus, she tries to be a good listener, giving each student their due time, and to be supportive of all of her students.

Political climates exist in schools as well as every other workplace. Betty Taglieri, who has taught in several schools in two different states, has often served on curriculum and textbook adoption committees. Regardless of the school district, Betty finds that there is always a teacher who tries to force his or her preference on other teachers on the committee. Usually, the teacher tries to coax less-experienced teachers into siding with him or her without a valid curricular reason.

Harmin (1988) gives five recommendations for teachers regarding ethics and moral education. While he doesn't believe that a teacher should promote one personal value over another one, he does advocate that teachers take a stand for ethics and morality.

Recommendations for Teaching Moral Education in Our Schools

In 1988, the Association for Supervision and Curriculum Development Panel on Moral Education (1988, 7–8) made the following recommendations regarding moral education:

1. "We urge all those involved in American education—from school board members to district and building administrators to individual teachers—to renew their commitment to promoting moral education in the schools. Indeed, we urge that moral education be made a powerful unifying and energizing force in the curriculum.

2. "We recommend that educators form partnerships with parents, the mass media, the business community, the courts, and civic, racial, ethnic, and religious groups to create a social and cultural context that supports the school's efforts to develop morally mature citizens.

3. "We recommend that schools define and teach a morality of justice, altruism, diligence, and respect for human dignity. These are universal moral values that coincide with traditional religious teachings but stand on their own as authentic secular values. As part of a genuine respect for pluralism, schools should also teach students about the different ultimate sources for morality, including religion.

4. "We urge schools and school systems to make sure their moral education efforts extend beyond the cognitive domain to include the affective and the behavioral. Moral education must go beyond simply knowing what is good; it must also involve prizing what is good and doing what is good.

5. "We recommend that moral education include, especially for younger children, socialization into appropriate patterns of conduct and, especially for older students, education for the critical thinking and decision making that are part of adult moral maturity. The latter may include examination of the complex issues that stir ethical debate in society at large.

6. "We recommend that educators continually examine the institutional features of school life to ensure that climate and instructional practices contribute to the same moral growth.

7. "We urge further research on what works in moral education, drawing on research findings from other fields and presenting those findings to the profession forcefully and clearly.

8. "We recommend that educators regularly assess the moral climate of schools and the conduct of students and communicate the results of these assessments to their communities. Many schools take steps now, including notations about conduct on pupils' report cards, notes of praise or criticism to parents, and recognition for individuals or groups whose conduct is praiseworthy. We acknowledge, however, that there is still much work to be done in the articulation of moral principles and the development of methods to assess their place in the school.

9. "We recommend that schools establish and convey clear expectations for teachers and administrators regarding their roles as moral educators. Furthermore, we recommend that their performance as moral educators be included as a regular and important part of their evaluation.

10. "We recommend that teacher educators, both preservice and inservice, give major attention to moral education to ensure that teachers have the necessary knowledge, attitudes, and skills to fulfill their moral education responsibilities."

1. *Teachers should speak up for morality and ethics.* For example, a teacher could say that everyone will get an opportunity to voice their opinion in a group or class discussion, or that everyone needs to learn to work cooperatively, with each person making a contribution to the group's work.

Ethics is a sensitive issue in the classroom. What is acceptable in one culture can be tabu in another. Teachers must wrestle with the problem of whose ethics and values should be taught. (© James Shaffer)

2. *Teachers should state personal positions.* Teachers frequently avoid making statements on issues. However, there are often instances when we as teachers should share our views. For instance, stating that you believe in equal pay for equal work or that government officials should be held accountable if they break the law are personal opinions. Students can be asked if they agree or disagree.

3. *Teachers should explain classroom and school rules.* Rather than just establishing rules or requiring students to follow them, we need to explain why they are important; for instance, the danger of walking between buses or failing to respect another student's property.

4. *Teachers should speak forthrightly.* We need to speak up honestly about our own values while not diminishing those of other individuals who hold different views. If we fail to speak up, we fail to respect our own values and beliefs. In addition, students must see that freedom of speech is part of our democracy.

5. *Teachers need to increase moral experiences for students.* We as teachers need to demonstrate moral and ethical experiences for students. We need to be tolerant of others, listen carefully, keep an open mind, and forgive ourselves for our own imperfections.

   According to Harmin (1988, 30): "Young people today . . . need us to speak up for the value wisdom of the past, to inspire them to do good and be good, to call them up short when they slip into bad habits, to voice indignation when we see violations of what is right, and to be living examples of what we know is good. They need guidance and support."

Preamble

"The educator, believing in the worth and dignity of each human being, recognizes the supreme importance of the pursuit of truth, devotion to excellence, and the nurture of democratic principles. Essential to these goals is the protection of freedom to learn and to teach and the guarantee of equal educational opportunity for all. The educator accepts the responsibility to adhere to the highest ethical standards.

"The educator recognizes the magnitude of the responsibility inherent in the teaching process. The desire for the respect and confidence of one's colleagues, of students, of parents, and of the members of the community provides the incentive to attain and maintain the highest possible degree of ethical conduct. The *Code of Ethics of the Education Profession* indicates the aspiration of all educators and provides standards by which to judge conduct.

"The remedies specified by the NEA and/or its affiliates for the violation of any provision of this Code shall be exclusive and no such provision shall be enforceable in any form other than one specifically designated by the NEA or its affiliates.

PRINCIPLE I
Commitment to the Student

"The educator strives to help each student realize his or her potential as a worthy and effective member of society. The educator therefore works to stimulate the spirit of inquiry, the acquisition of knowledge and understanding, and the thoughtful formulation of worthy goals.

"In fulfillment of the obligation to the student, the educator—

1. Shall not unreasonably restrain the student from independent action in the pursuit of learning.

2. Shall not unreasonably deny the student access to varying points of view.

3. Shall not deliberately suppress or distort subject matter relevant to the student's progress.

4. Shall make reasonable effort to protect the student from conditions harmful to learning or to health and safety.

5. Shall not intentionally expose the student to embarrassment or disparagement.

6. Shall not on the basis of race, color, creed, sex, national origin, marital status, political or religious beliefs, family, social or cultural background, or sexual orientation, unfairly—

    a. Exclude any student from participation in any program.

    b. Deny benefits to any student.

    c. Grant any advantage to any student.

7. Shall not use professional relationships with students for private advantage.

8. Shall not disclose information about students obtained in the course of professional service unless disclosure serves a compelling professional purpose or is required by law.

PRINCIPLE II
Commitment to the Profession

"The education profession is vested by the public with a trust and responsibility requiring the highest ideals of professional service.

"In the belief that the quality of the services of the education profession directly influences the nation and its citizens, the educator shall exert every effort to raise professional standards, to promote a climate that encourages the exercise of professional judgment, to achieve conditions that attract persons worthy of the trust to careers in education, and to assist in preventing the practice of the profession by unqualified persons.

(continued))

"In fulfillment of the obligation to the profession, the educator—

1. Shall not in an application for a professional position deliberately make a false statement or fail to disclose a material fact related to competency and qualifications.

2. Shall not misrepresent his/her professional qualifications.

3. Shall not assist any entry into the profession of a person known to be unqualified in respect to character, education, or other relevant attribute.

4. Shall not knowingly make a false statement concerning the qualifications of a candidate for a professional position.

5. Shall not assist a noneducator in the unauthorized practice of teaching.

6. Shall not disclose information about colleagues obtained in the course of professional service unless disclosure serves a compelling professional purpose or is required by law.

7. Shall not knowingly make false or malicious statements about a colleague.

8. Shall not accept any gratuity, gift, or favor that might impair or appear to influence professional decisions or action."

We as teachers, then, must not only serve as role models for our students but help guide them as they make ethical and moral decisions.

According to Dianne Berreth and Sheldon Berman (1997), educators and teachers can help children develop social skills as well as moral values through "modeling, direct instruction, experience, and continual practice" (p. 25). The foundation on which moral behavior is built is empathy and self-discipline. Berreth and Berman believe that empathy enables "the child to appreciate the perspectives and feelings of another, to sense violations of justice and care, and to better distinguish right from wrong" (p. 24). On the other hand, self-discipline is essential, for it "provides the ability to take action and delay or even forego gratification in order to remain committed to a set of values or goals" (p. 24). Empathy and self-discipline work together as a foundation for moral behavior.

Teachers need to nurture empathy and self-discipline so that students will:

- Learn basic decision-making and perspective-taking skills;
- Delay gratification and persist through obstacles;
- Develop a consistent set of positive values they can translate into action;
- Learn how to act responsibly; and
- Have opportunities to successfully test skills (Berreth and Berman 1997, 24).

Implementation of such a program entails reducing the size of schools to create a community atmosphere in which every teacher knows every student and students know each other. Teachers and volunteers are essential as well as caring adults who model the appropriate behavior. Perhaps the most critical element is parental involvement so that appropriate behavior is reinforced outside of the school setting.

Evaluating and Assessing Students

Ethics are involved in evaluating and assessing students. Diane Harshburger, a parent, complained that students whose parents served on the school board or were volunteers in her children's elementary school received preferential treatment in terms of grades. In some school districts, teachers feel they must give children of school board members higher grades. This is not only unfair to the other students but gives the impression that it is "who you are or who you know" rather than hard work and effort that is important in the evaluation process.

Parents and students as well as teachers can cite instances in which grades seemed not to be based on the student's academic work but on other reasons. Bob Wells, a high school junior, remarked that his grade for his U.S. history class was always a full letter grade higher during the cross country and track seasons than during the other grading periods. He said as long as he was willing to participate in these sports, he could pass the course since his history teacher was also the cross country and track coach.

In another high school, the daughter of a prominent citizen finished second in class rank. Her parents complained to the superintendent and principal that the valedictorian award should go to the student who maintained the highest grade average over the senior year, which she had done, rather than throughout high school.

Students observe their teachers for ethical examples. Failure to assess and evaluate fairly can cause a teacher to lose esteem in students' eyes.

Confiding in Administrators

Like teachers, school administrators need to hold to a high ethical standard. Most superintendents and principals fit this mold. They are able to keep a confidence, they seek to treat students fairly, they do not give preferential treatment to students from prominent families within the community, and they treat teachers and staff with respect and equitably.

"What kind of human being do we want to emerge from our efforts at moral education? What are the characteristics of the morally mature person?

"A moment's reflection tells us that moral maturity is more than just knowing what is right. The world is full of people who know what is right but set moral considerations aside when they find it expedient to do so. To be moral means to *value* morality, to take moral obligations seriously. It means to be able to judge what is right but also to care deeply about doing it—and to possess the will, competence, and habits needed to translate moral judgment and feeling into effective moral action.

"We submit that the morally mature person has six major characteristics, which are derived from universal moral and democratic principles. These characteristics offer schools and communities a context for discourse about school programs and moral behavior.

"The morally mature person habitually:

1. *Respects human dignity,* which includes
   - showing regard for the worth and rights of all persons,
   - avoiding deception and dishonesty,
   - promoting human equality,
   - respecting freedom of conscience,
   - working with people of different views, and
   - refraining from prejudiced actions.
2. *Cares about the welfare of others,* which includes
   - recognizing interdependence among people,
   - caring for one's country,
   - seeking social justice,
   - taking pleasure in helping others, and
   - working to help others reach moral maturity.
3. *Integrates individual interests and social responsibilities,* which includes
   - becoming involved in community life,

- doing a fair share of community work,
- displaying self-regarding and other-regarding moral virtues—self-control, diligence, fairness, kindness, honesty, civility—in everyday life,
- fulfilling commitments, and
- developing self-esteem through relationships with others.
4. *Demonstrates integrity,* which includes
   - practicing diligence,
   - taking stands for moral principles,
   - displaying moral courage,
   - knowing when to compromise and when to confront, and
   - accepting responsibility for one's choices.
5. *Reflects on moral choices,* which includes
   - recognizing the moral issues involved in a situation,
   - applying moral principles (such as the golden rule) when making moral judgments,
   - thinking about the consequences of decisions, and
   - seeking to be informed about important moral issues in society and the world.
6. *Seeks peaceful resolution of conflict,* which includes
   - striving for the fair resolution of personal and social conflicts,
   - avoiding physical and verbal aggression,
   - listening carefully to others,
   - encouraging others to communicate, and
   - working for peace.

"In general, then, the morally mature person understands moral principles and accepts responsibility for applying them."

Our society is rampant with lawsuits, and teachers are not exempt from becoming involved in a lawsuit involving a student. A disgruntled parent or guardian's last words prior to exiting the school building may be "my attorney will be contacting you."

Teachers may not always have a clear understanding of their basic responsibilities involving students. Certain standards of care apply when a lawsuit involves negligent acts. Consider these actual incidents cited by Philip Corkill, a superintendent in Arizona, and Robert Hendricks, a former superintendent and current faculty member at the University of Arizona.

A third-grade student was abducted from a classroom and raped in a nearby empty field during the time when her teacher stepped out of the classroom 'for just a few minutes' to return a personal phone call (Corkill and Hendricks 1997, 6).

A high school student was involved in a minor traffic accident while driving his teacher's personal car during school hours to the local 'lube pit.' The *teacher requested his student aide do him this favor and had released him from class (Corkill and Hendricks 1997, 6).*

A male coach discovered $20 missing from his office desk during a third-period physical education class. He retained the students and confronted them with the charge of theft before searching each student's pockets and backpack. He then ordered the students to remove their clothing and conducted an unsuccessful strip search. Later he expressed surprise when a lawsuit was brought against him and the school by a group of parents (Corkill and Hendricks 1997, 9).

For the new teacher, it is always best to be on the cautious side of maintaining your responsibilities. Unfortunately a principal or fellow teacher who possesses a cavalier attitude toward following the rules can result in misleading a new teacher and result in a legal issue arising.

Teachers, staff members, and students should be able to confide in their school administrators. If the principal cannot be trusted or fails to back teachers in difficult situations with students or parents, the entire school suffers.

Likewise, each teacher must determine in whom he or she can confide as a colleague. No one wants a confidence broken in the faculty lounge and spread throughout the school district and out into the community.

Confronting Issues

Ethics requires that we as teachers take certain stands. Establishing standards that challenge our students, making a point to stay current in our field of study, and dealing with social issues in an appropriate manner are but a few positions that teachers must take. If a teacher says that a test will be given on Wednesday and the class complains that they aren't ready to take it, the teacher must take a stand at that moment. Are the students ready? If the test is delayed, will they perform better and will the curriculum content to be covered during the year still be covered? If a teacher is challenged by a student regarding course content, the teacher must make a stand. If a student asks a question and the teacher doesn't know the answer, it is far better for the teacher to be frank and say, "I don't know the answer to that. Let's see if we can find it," than to say, "Go look it up yourself."

Teaching about controversial issues is an ethical dilemma. In what context is it appropriate for a teacher to express his or her opinion about sensitive issues? Ramon Parks, a teacher in a small suburban high school, asked this question when his students wanted to know his opinion in a discussion about a nurse who failed to summon help for a terminally ill patient during a crisis period and the patient died. Parks wanted his students to debate the issues. Was the nurse's action morally justifiable? Was her act legally justifiable? But high school students have difficulty establishing and formulating positions and developing arguments. According to Parks, "Kids tend to be very poor debaters. Their notion of debating is to say things louder and louder, rather than searching for some evidence. . . . Kids usually see things right away as either right or wrong, or [look for] instant answers and tend not to go much farther than that" (Lyons 1990, 167).

One experimental ethics curriculum for gifted high school students involved students from Australia, Canada, Cyprus, Israel, Jordan, and the United States. Students wrote papers on such questions as the right of parents to prohibit immunization of their children, even if it might put the community in danger. At the end of the study, students indicated the interaction with students throughout the world "opened their eyes to different perspectives and taught them a lesson in tolerance (Sappir 1998, 80).

If high school students look for what is clearly right or wrong, then elementary and middle school students certainly delineate issues even more precisely as being absolutely right or absolutely wrong.

■ Summary

As our society has become more litigant, so have school districts been drawn into more lawsuits. Teachers must be aware of relevant laws and court decisions to understand their own liability in the classroom.

Court decisions regarding the separation of church and state have become important with the increasing number of private, church-related schools. Students' rights as well as teachers' rights need to be fully understood before an individual takes a teaching position.

Like laws and court findings, ethics plays an important role in a teacher's life. We need to be aware that our actions and words make a substantial impression on students.

Froebel and Herbart were the earliest educational leaders to recognize the need for ethics and moral education. They believed that teachers must demonstrate ethical and moral behavior. As such, they believed that teachers must be good examples both inside and outside the classroom.

Following on Froebel's and Herbart's ideas, Dewey stressed the need for developing children's sense of reason. He believed that without reflecting on one's actions and those of others, that there would be a lack of morality, something that democracy demands.

In more recent years, Kohlberg's theory of moral development has become prominent. In addition, Gilligan's theory that female and male children develop different moral viewpoints has been supported by a number of researchers.

Ethics plays an important role in a teacher's life. We need to be aware that our actions and words make a substantial impression on students. We must also be aware that we help to mold our students and greatly influence them. Failure to take a position on an issue as a teacher can also influence students.

■ Reflections

When you were in high school, was there a teacher who represented highly ethical behavior: honesty, loyalty, the ability to keep a confidence, fairness, and trustworthiness? What did that teacher do that made you remember him or her in this way? Outline three characteristics of that teacher that you want to emulate in your own teaching style. Outline three other characteristics that you plan on including as part of your own teaching style that you believe exemplify strong ethics.

■ Discussion Questions

1. Why should there be a separation of church and state where schools are involved?

2. If you signed a teaching contract with a school district and then received another offer from a school district in another state with higher pay, would you break the original contract? Why or why not?

3. Someone once joked that everyone's middle name is "sue," short for lawsuit. Give three suggestions for preventing a lawsuit against you and your colleagues as teachers.

4. Should the curriculum be a safe curriculum, thereby limiting all potentially dangerous or politically incorrect subjects (e.g., a fourth-grade teacher would not obtain live crayfish for a unit on pond studies but would use plastic crayfish instead; a high school chemistry teacher would teach chemistry through videotapes and lectures rather than with hands-on laboratory experiments)?

5. If a teacher is arrested for cheating on his or her income taxes, should the school district dismiss the teacher on ethical grounds?

■ For Further Reading

Fege, A. F. 1998. Parental rights: Yes! Parental rights legislation: No! *Educational Leadership* 55(3):76–79.

Gallagher, J. J. 1995. Education of gifted students: A civil rights issue? *Phi Delta Kappan* 76 (5):408–10.

Gursky, D. 1992. Spare the child? *Teacher Magazine* (7):17–19.

Nash, R. J. 1997. *Real world ethics: Frameworks for educators and human services professionals.* New York: Teachers College Press.

Robbins, J. 1990. *Public schools as public forums.* Bloomington, IN: Phi Delta Kappa.

Sappir, S. 1998. Global ethics in a high school curriculum. *Educational Leadership* 55(6):80–82.

Underwood, J. K. 1997. Four implications of IDEA's reauthorization. *The School Administrator* 54 (10):24–27.

Zirkel, P. A. 1995. A doomed prayer for relief. *Phi Delta Kappan* 76 (6):496–97.

Zirkel, P. A. 1994. Student dress goads. *Phi Delta Kappan* 75 (7):570–71.

8

Social Issues in Education

Primary Points

- Children encounter numerous social problems.

- Disadvantaged children often have problems learning.

- The family unit as we know it continues to change.

- There are an increased number of abused children in the United States.

- The population of the United States is quite diverse.

- Violence in the schools is on the rise.

Chapter Inquiries

- What are the primary social issues children face?

- Who are children "at risk"?

- What are the problems faced by children in different types of family units?

- How are children abused and to what extent?

- What problems are caused by the diversity of our population?

- How does violence in the schools impact students?

Jill Simpson has taught a variety of grade levels. "They talk about kids being streetwise. Teaching makes you streetwise. Like Tommy. In my second-grade class he drew a picture of naked women—all with big breasts. His parents were getting a divorce and his mom had moved in with another man. Drugs were a problem. Goodness knows what he saw at home."

"When I taught eighth graders, I'm not certain whether they learned as much from me or I from them. They're adults, they're kids, they're sophisticated, they're awkward, they're cool, they're frightened, they're hot stuff, they're at the end of their rope. And you can't help but love them, pity them, laugh with them."

© Nita Winter/The
Image Works, Inc.

Students face a variety of social problems both inside and outside of school. Dishonesty is not just prevalent among some Wall Street arbitrage experts and shady politicians but in the classroom as well. A recent poll of top high school students in the United States, all of whom had at least a B or higher grade average, revealed that 40 percent had cheated on a test or quiz. A substantial number, 67 percent, admitted to copying someone else's homework and turning it in as their own work. Among the reasons given for cheating was that students had fewer than seven hours a week to study (Feldman 1993). Extracurricular activities and jobs also place time demands on secondary students.

Cheating in the classroom is but one of the social issues that pervade students' lives at all grade levels. Violence on our streets and in rural areas is increasing at a rapid rate. When the television is turned on, violence often enters into children's own homes. In addition, some children are victims of verbal and/or physical abuse by a parent or parents.

Schools cannot be effective when they work in isolation from the familial, cultural, and community context.

**Linda J. Stevens
and Marianne Price**

*Meeting the Challenge
of Educating Children at Risk*

Other social issues include teenage pregnancy, with an estimated one million births a year (Males 1993). Some junior high students have two roles, that of young adolescent student and parent. Indeed, some female high school students have two or three children. These students are able to attend school only because another family member serves as caretaker for the children. Some high schools now provide day care for children of students. Some states require young teenage mothers to attend high school or graduate equivalency programs to qualify to receive welfare benefits.

There is an increased prevalence of sexually transmitted diseases among students. While many believe that HIV or AIDS is transmitted only among drug users through the use of dirty needles or homosexuals and their sexual partners, statistics show this is not the case. And while AIDS was once considered a big-city problem, the spread of AIDS is growing fastest in rural, not urban, communities. Television ads now promote sexual abstinence and the use of condoms, an unheard of practice just a decade ago.

The quality of child care and health care is also of concern. The most rapidly growing group of workers are mothers of children under the age of six. Nationally, political leaders continue to discuss how every citizen can receive adequate health care, including preventative medicine such as free inoculations for preschoolers.

Increasingly, both parents are involved in taking their children to and from day care. (© James Shaffer)

The problems for children from low socioeconomic backgrounds are severe. Sixty-three percent of children of unmarried mothers live in poverty. Of that group, 33 percent are likely to repeat a grade and 17 percent are expelled or suspended from school. Thirty-nine percent of children of unmarried mothers live in families that have been on welfare for over ten years (Whitman and Friedman 1992).

It is not just impoverished children who face the severity of social problems. According to Urie Bronfenbrenner, a leading expert on family life at Cornell University, "After those at the bottom of society, the second most threatened group are those at the top, those who are supposed to be the leaders of the world—the college graduates who are having children at the start of their careers" (Magnet 1992, 46). Parents who work in demanding occupations or put in more than forty hours a week and then take work home place themselves, and their children, under tremendous stress. "Quality time" for these parents may mean a two-minute phone call before their children's bedtime instead of being home reading a bedtime story. Children tend to acquire the values and beliefs of those adults who spend the most time with them, which may be a nanny or babysitter.

This chapter considers the many social issues that affect students and educators.

Demographic Changes in the School Population

The changing demographics of the U.S. population and the pressures of societal problems greatly impact our nation's schools. Beginning in 1972, the number of students enrolled in public elementary and secondary schools in the United States declined as the generation of baby boomers passed school age. However, in 1985, the enrollment trend was reversed due to a baby boomlet. Between 1985 and 1991, public elementary education enrollment increased by an astonishing 12 percent, while secondary enrollment actually declined by 7 percent (U.S. Department of Education 1994a), due in part to the lower student numbers that followed the original baby boom and increasing dropout rates. Figure 1 illustrates the increase in enrollment over the past decades, as well as information on pupil-teacher ratios and school expenditures.

While the elementary population soared in the late 1980s and early 1990s, the number of three- to five-year-olds enrolled in preschools jumped substantially as well. Between 1970 and 1991, the percentage of three- to five-year-olds enrolled in preprimary education increased a whopping 49 percent. By 1991, 38 percent of these children attended full-day programs, a number up from 32 percent in 1980 (U.S. Department of Education 1994a).

Table 1 gives a breakdown of the school population by age and race. Student populations are becoming increasingly more diverse. In 1986, only three states, Hawaii, Mississippi, and New Mexico, had larger minority than white student populations. By 1990, California and Texas, both states with large Hispanic populations, had joined that group. By the year 2000, Florida is expected to join those ranks (U.S. Department of Education 1997).

In 1997, the Civil Rights Project at Harvard University issued a report entitled "Deepening Segregation in American Schools." Its findings state that during the 1994–95 school year, 67 percent of African American students were in schools with less than half white enrollment. Nearly 35 percent of Latino students attend intensely segregated schools, that is, schools having at least 90 percent minority enrollment. In addition, African American and Latino students are more apt than white students to attend schools in areas where poverty is concentrated. The Northeast region of the United States is the most segregated portion of the nation (Civil Rights Project 1997).

The majority of teachers are white, and it is argued by some that minority students are not understood by teachers from another culture. Others argue that minority students are not exposed to teachers as mentors if there are no or few teachers who share a common cultural background.

Some states have encountered tremendous growth in their overall student populations during the past decade (figure 2). In particular, Arizona, California, Florida, Oregon, Nevada, and Washington each had an increase in their elementary and secondary school-age children of over 10 percent (U.S. Department of Education 1994a). This has resulted in a strain on the fiscal and material resources of school districts. California, for example, has had the largest influx of immigrants, in particular Hispanics and Asians, of any U.S. state. If a new school opened every day for the next 365 days, schools in California would still suffer from overcrowding; the average class size in Los Angeles is now approaching forty students.

Student Population of Private Schools and Homeschooling

Since 1981, there has been little change in the percentage of elementary and secondary students enrolled in privately funded schools, many of which have a religious affiliation. The range of students in private schools is between 11 percent and 12 percent of the total elementary and secondary student population. These figures include students who are disabled and have been placed in private educational settings because their local school districts do not have the appropriate educational services to meet their specific needs (U.S. Department of Education 1994a).

Figure 1
Enrollment,
number of
teachers, pupil/
teacher ratios,
and
expenditures in
public schools:
1960–61 to
1995–96
SOURCE: U.S.

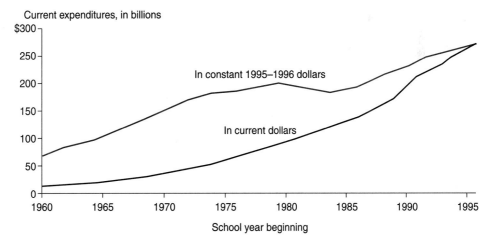

Department of Education, National Center for Education Statistics, *Statistics of State School Systems; Statistics of Public Elementary and Secondary School Systems; Revenues and Expenditures for Public Elementary and Secondary Education;* and Common Core of Data surveys.

Table 1 Percent of the population 3 to 34 years old enrolled in school,[1] by race/ethnicity, sex, and age: October 1975 to October 1996

Year and age	Total				Male				Female			
	All races	White, non-Hispanic	Black, non-Hispanic	Hispanic origin	All races	White, non-Hispanic	Black, non-Hispanic	Hispanic origin	All races	White, non-Hispanic	Black, non-Hispanic	Hispanic origin
1	2	3	4	5	6	7	8	9	10	11	12	13
1975												
Total, 3 to 34 years	53.7	53.0	57.7	54.8	56.1	55.2	60.4	58.1	51.5	50.8	55.3	51.7
3 and 4 years	31.5	31.0	34.4	27.3	30.9	31.1	31.4	26.7	32.1	30.9	37.5	27.9
5 and 6 years	94.7	95.1	94.4	92.1	94.4	94.8	94.8	89.7	95.1	95.4	94.0	94.4
7 to 9 years	99.3	99.4	99.3	99.6	99.2	99.2	99.4	99.6	99.5	99.6	99.2	99.5
10 to 13 years	99.3	99.3	99.1	99.2	98.9	99.0	98.9	98.8	99.6	99.6	99.3	99.7
14 and 15 years	98.2	98.5	97.4	95.6	98.4	98.6	97.6	97.4	98.0	98.4	97.2	93.8
16 and 17 years	89.0	89.5	86.8	86.2	90.7	91.2	88.1	88.3	87.2	87.8	85.5	84.0
18 and 19 years	46.9	46.8	46.9	44.0	49.9	49.4	49.6	51.9	44.2	44.2	44.6	37.1
20 and 21 years	31.2	32.1	26.7	27.5	35.3	36.7	28.4	31.3	27.1	27.8	25.3	24.3
22 to 24 years	16.2	16.4	13.9	14.1	20.0	20.8	14.5	15.9	12.6	12.2	13.4	12.5
25 to 29 years	10.1	10.1	9.4	8.3	13.1	13.2	11.6	11.9	7.2	7.2	7.6	5.3
30 to 34 years	6.6	6.6	7.1	5.5	7.7	7.5	8.7	7.2	5.6	5.8	5.9	4.1
1980												
Total, 3 to 34 years	49.7	48.8	54.0	49.8	50.9	50.0	56.2	49.9	48.5	47.7	52.1	49.8
3 and 4 years	36.7	37.4	38.2	28.5	37.8	39.2	36.4	30.1	35.5	35.5	40.0	26.6
5 and 6 years	95.7	95.9	95.5	94.5	95.0	95.4	94.1	94.0	96.4	96.5	97.0	94.9
7 to 9 years	99.1	99.1	99.4	98.4	99.0	99.0	99.5	97.7	99.2	99.2	99.3	99.0
10 to 13 years	99.4	99.4	99.4	99.7	99.4	99.4	99.4	99.4	99.4	99.3	99.3	99.9
14 and 15 years	98.2	98.7	97.9	94.3	98.7	98.9	98.4	96.7	97.7	98.5	97.3	92.1
16 and 17 years	89.0	89.2	90.7	81.8	89.1	89.4	90.7	81.5	88.8	89.0	90.6	82.2
18 and 19 years	46.4	47.0	45.8	37.8	47.0	48.5	42.9	36.9	45.8	45.7	48.3	38.8
20 and 21 years	31.0	33.0	23.3	19.5	32.6	34.8	22.8	21.4	29.5	31.3	23.7	17.6
22 to 24 years	16.3	16.8	13.6	11.7	17.8	18.7	13.4	10.7	14.9	15.0	13.7	12.6
25 to 29 years	9.3	9.4	8.8	6.9	9.8	9.8	10.6	6.8	8.8	9.1	7.5	6.9
30 to 34 years	6.4	6.4	6.9	5.1	5.9	5.6	7.2	6.2	7.0	7.2	6.6	4.1
1985												
Total, 3 to 34 years	48.3	47.8	50.8	47.7	49.2	48.7	52.6	47.5	47.4	46.9	49.2	47.9
3 and 4 years	38.9	40.3	42.8	27.0	36.7	39.1	34.6	26.4	41.2	41.6	50.3	27.7
5 and 6 years	96.1	96.6	95.7	94.5	95.3	95.6	94.5	95.3	97.0	97.6	97.1	93.7
7 to 9 years	99.1	99.4	98.6	98.4	99.0	99.3	98.4	98.9	99.2	99.4	98.9	98.0
10 to 13 years	99.3	99.3	99.5	99.4	99.2	99.2	99.1	99.1	99.4	99.3	99.9	99.7
14 and 15 years	98.1	98.3	98.1	96.1	98.3	98.4	98.5	96.2	97.9	98.1	97.6	96.0
16 and 17 years	91.7	92.5	91.8	84.5	92.4	92.9	92.0	88.9	90.9	92.2	91.6	80.0
18 and 19 years	51.6	53.7	43.5	41.8	52.2	53.4	49.4	38.6	51.0	54.0	37.8	44.7
20 and 21 years	35.3	37.2	27.7	24.0	36.5	38.8	29.9	20.3	34.1	35.7	25.8	27.4
22 to 24 years	16.9	17.5	13.8	11.6	18.8	19.8	13.5	12.6	15.1	15.4	14.0	10.4
25 to 29 years	9.2	9.6	7.4	6.6	9.4	9.7	5.8	8.2	9.1	9.4	8.7	4.9
30 to 34 years	6.1	6.2	5.2	5.7	5.4	5.6	3.9	4.0	6.8	6.9	6.2	7.5
1990												
Total, 3 to 34 years	50.2	49.8	52.2	47.2	50.9	50.4	54.3	46.8	49.5	49.2	50.3	47.7
3 and 4 years	44.4	47.2	41.8	30.7	43.9	47.9	38.1	28.0	44.9	46.6	45.5	33.6
5 and 6 years	96.5	96.7	96.5	94.9	96.5	96.8	96.2	95.8	96.4	96.7	96.9	93.9
7 to 9 years	99.7	99.7	99.8	99.5	99.7	99.7	99.9	99.5	99.6	99.7	99.8	99.4
10 to 13 years	99.6	99.7	99.9	99.1	99.6	99.6	99.9	99.0	99.7	99.7	99.8	99.1

14 and 15 years	99.0	99.0	99.4	99.0	99.1	99.2	99.7	99.1	98.9	98.9	99.1	98.8
16 and 17 years	92.5	93.5	91.7	85.4	92.6	93.4	93.0	85.5	92.4	93.7	90.5	85.3
18 and 19 years	57.2	59.1	55.0	44.0	58.2	59.7	60.4	40.7	56.3	58.5	49.8	47.2
20 and 21 years	39.7	43.1	28.3	27.2	40.3	44.2	31.0	21.7	39.2	42.0	25.8	33.1
22 to 24 years	21.0	21.9	19.7	9.9	22.3	23.7	19.3	11.2	19.9	20.3	20.0	8.4
25 to 29 years	9.7	10.4	6.1	6.3	9.2	10.0	4.7	4.6	10.2	10.7	7.3	8.1
30 to 34 years	5.8	6.2	4.5	3.6	4.8	5.0	2.3	4.0	6.9	7.4	6.3	3.1
1996												
Total, 3 to 34 years	54.1	54.0	56.3	50.3	54.4	54.2	57.8	49.2	53.8	53.8	54.9	51.4
3 and 4 years[2]	48.3	50.3	49.9	38.1	46.9	48.0	47.7	39.5	49.8	52.9	52.1	36.8
5 and 6 years	94.0	96.1	90.5	89.5	93.8	95.5	89.8	91.0	94.3	96.7	91.2	87.8
7 to 9 years	97.2	97.3	97.4	96.6	97.2	97.2	98.0	95.4	97.3	97.3	96.7	97.9
10 to 13 years	98.1	98.3	97.3	97.6	98.0	98.1	97.1	97.9	98.2	98.6	97.6	97.4
14 and 15 years	98.0	98.2	99.0	96.6	98.5	98.8	98.1	98.0	97.5	97.7	100.0	95.0
16 and 17 years	92.8	93.6	92.1	88.7	93.2	93.5	93.5	90.4	92.4	93.7	90.6	86.9
18 and 19 years	61.5	65.5	53.2	47.0	60.8	63.7	55.4	46.8	62.2	67.3	51.1	47.2
20 and 21 years	44.4	48.9	37.5	25.3	43.9	48.7	39.7	19.5	44.8	49.0	35.8	31.1
22 to 24 years	24.8	25.9	21.2	17.6	25.2	27.3	19.2	16.2	24.5	24.5	22.9	19.3
25 to 29 years	11.9	11.8	13.7	8.6	11.4	11.4	12.4	6.8	12.5	12.1	14.7	10.5
30 to 34 years	6.1	5.8	7.0	5.0	4.9	4.3	5.5	4.3	7.3	7.3	8.3	5.7

[1]Includes enrollment in any type of graded public, parochial, or other private schools. Includes nursery schools, kindergartens, elementary schools, high schools, colleges, universities, and professional schools. Attendance may be on either a full-time or part-time basis and during the day or night. Enrollments in "special" schools, such as trade schools, business colleges, or correspondence schools, are not included.
[2]Preprimary enrollment collected using new procedures. May not be comparable to figures for earlier years.
NOTE—Data are based upon sample surveys of the civilian noninstitutional population.
SOURCE: U.S. Department of Education, National Center for Educational Statistics

Figure 2 Percentage change in public elementary secondary enrollment, by state: Fall 1990 to fall 1997
SOURCE: U.S. Department of Education, National Center for Education Statistics, Common Core of Data surveys.

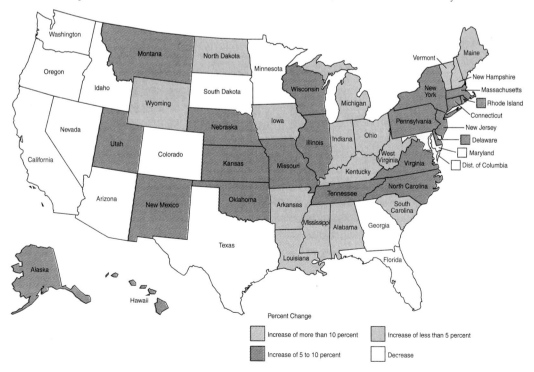

Percent Change

- Increase of more than 10 percent
- Increase of 5 to 10 percent
- Increase of less than 5 percent
- Decrease

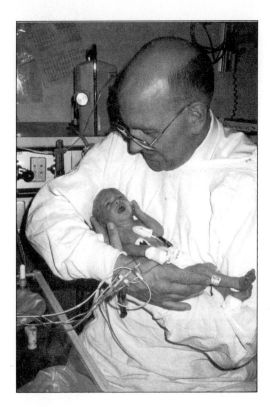

This infant will be treated in a neonatal center for a few weeks until he has developed sufficiently to be sent home with his parents. (Courtesy of Pamela J. Farris)

Increasingly, more and more students are being educated at home. There are a multitude of reasons for this. Some families have given up on public schools because they believe they fail to teach proper values and morals to children. Other families feel that public schools are too dangerous and fear for the physical safety of their children. Yet another justification by some parents is that too much emphasis is placed on meeting the educational needs of lower-achieving students, thereby lowering standards for their children and restricting their learning potential.

It is estimated that out of 49 million children in grades K–12, 350,000 are homeschooled, with the majority from religious fundamentalist families (Kantrowitz and Rosenberg 1994). Increasingly, gifted students are also removed from public schools and homeschooled in an attempt by their parents to foster their children's talents.

At-Risk Students

Infants who weigh less than three and one-half pounds at birth generally require medical intervention to keep them alive. Because of this, they are more apt to face learning problems (Stevens and Price 1992). Prenatal health care greatly reduces the number of premature infants and has improved the infant mortality rate, now at 9.8 per 1,000 live births in the United States, surprisingly higher than nineteen other industrialized nations in the world despite our leading advances in medical research. And healthier babies have increased success in school as well. Unfortunately, over 25 percent of all mothers who give birth every day receive no prenatal care, resulting in low birth weights and children with a higher incidence of learning disabilities (Richman 1992).

Other prenatal factors are important to note. Between 30 percent and 40 percent of mothers who consume large amounts of alcohol during their pregnancies give birth to babies with fetal alcohol syndrome (Burgess and Streissguth 1992). Fetal alcohol syndrome is a birth defect that can result in physical abnormalities, such as retarded physical growth or facial malformation, as well as learning disabilities, such as attention deficit disorder (ADD), or hyperactivity.

Alcoholism has been found to run in families. Thus, middle school and high school students of alcoholic parents face additional problems. A significant relationship has been found between alcoholism of biological parents and alcohol abuse by teenage boys. In addition, sons of alcoholic fathers are four times more likely to become alcoholics than other males, while daughters of alcoholic mothers are three times more likely to be alcoholic. Teenage children of alcoholic fathers are more likely than other adolescents to use marijuana and cocaine (Children of Alcoholics Foundation 1992).

Children of mothers who smoke, either during or after pregnancy, or who are exposed to secondary smoke may have learning problems. In addition, many develop respiratory disorders such as frequent cases of bronchitis or asthma, which typically result in frequent absences from school.

Table 2

Consumption standards of today's poorest households

Percent of households with	All Households in 1971	Poor Households* in 1994
Washing machine	71.3	71.1
Clothes dryer	44.5	50.2
Dishwasher	18.8	19.6
Refrigerator	83.3	97.9
Freezer	32.2	28.6
Stove	87.0	97.7
Microwave	<1.0	60.0
Color television	43.3	92.5
VCR	0	59.7
Personal computer	0	7.4
Telephone	93.0	76.7
Air conditioner	31.8	49.6
One or more cars	79.5	71.8

*At or below the poverty line, as defined by the U.S. Census Bureau. Many of today's **poorest** households have more than the **average** household of two decades ago. By today's consumption standards, the majority of Americans were "poor" just a few years ago.
Michael Cox and Richard Alm, "By Our Own Bootstraps: Economic Opportunity and the Dynamics of Income Distribution," Federal Reserve Bank of Dallas 1995 Annual Report.

Babies of mothers who used crack cocaine during pregnancy are likely to develop language acquisition problems and have difficulty controlling their own behavior (Griffith 1992).

The number of single women between the ages of fifteen and thirty-four having babies continues to increase among both whites and African American females. Between the years 1960 and 1964, 9 percent of single white females and 42 percent of single African American females had babies; by the years 1985–89, those figures increased to 22 percent and 70 percent, respectively. This is a drastic change since 1950, when African American women between the ages of twenty and twenty-four were more likely to get married than white women (Ingrassia 1993), a statistic that is somewhat skewed due to the large number of deaths of white servicemen during World War II. Twenty-five percent of U.S. babies born in 1993 were to unmarried mothers who ran their households alone (Blankenhorn 1995). The importance of these statistics to our discussion is that children raised by single mothers typically have fewer educational opportunities and often live in poverty.

The number of disadvantaged, **at-risk students** who come from impoverished homes is increasing at an alarming rate. According to the figures of the U.S. Bureau of the Census, the national poverty rate of all Americans has increased by 7 percent, growing by almost 10 percent for children since 1970 (Children's Defense Fund 1991). "Black children are nearly three times as likely to be poor as whites. . . . In 1993, 46 percent of black children were living in poverty, compared with 17 percent of white children" (What's news 1995). Table 2 shows the percent of persons living in poverty by state.

While it is typically believed that poverty is primarily limited to urban areas and members of minority populations, that is not the true picture. In the United States, out of one hundred impoverished children, twenty-eight live in suburban areas,

Figure 3 Percent of persons in poverty by state.

Source: U.S. Department of Commerce. Bureau of the Census

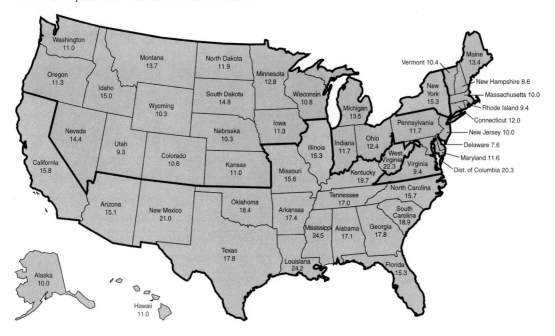

twenty-seven in rural areas, and forty-five in cities. Their cultural heritage is primarily European American (forty-one), and thirty-five are African American, twenty-one are Latin Americans, and the remaining three are either Asian Americans, Pacific Islanders, Native Americans, or Alaskan natives. Shockingly, the fastest growing group among the poor in our country is children under the age of six (Children's Defense Fund 1991). About 40 percent of those living in poverty are children under the age of eighteen, despite the fact that they represent only 26 percent of the total population (U.S. Department of Commerce Bureau of Census 1993).

Some states have a far greater percentage of impoverished children than do others (figure 3). Overall, nearly 47 percent of African American and 40 percent of Hispanic children under the age of eighteen are impoverished. Thus, those states with large African American or Hispanic populations tend to have very high poverty rates. Forty percent of the poor live in the South, while slightly less that 22 percent of the poor live in midwestern states (U.S. Department of Commerce Bureau of the Census 1993).

The social problems faced by teachers in classrooms across the country on a daily basis and continued attacks on public education by business leaders, politicians, and media have led some educators to strike out. One is Timothy Shannon (1993, 87–88), a professor at Pennsylvania State University, who writes: "Educators are not the cause of any decline or rise of poverty in the United States. Government officials, chief executive officers (CEOs), and media pundits use a curious logic to link the two. . . . It is not school policy and practices, but rather American governmental and corporate mismanagement and poor policy that have caused economic decline and growing poverty."

At-risk students come from prosperous as well as impoverished families. Latch-key children in affluent suburbs with working parents and children in single-parent homes as a result of divorce are often left to fend for themselves much of the day.

AMERICA'S NEW TWO-PARENT FAMILY

(Reprinted with special permission of North America Syndicate.)

Lacking self-discipline, it is easy for these children, like other at-risk children, to be absent from school. Indeed, the relationship between poor attendance and dropout rates is so strong that poor attendance is a predictive factor, as early as fifth grade, that a student will drop out of school later (Barrington and Hendricks 1989; Bucci and Reitzammer 1992).

The need for quality child care is recognized nationally, particularly as more and more major business firms develop child-care programs within the workplace. According to one study, "The lasting benefits of preschool experiences are seen in the reduced number of retentions, special education placements, delinquents, and drop-outs" (Slavin, Karweit, and Wasik 1993, 11). Unfortunately, teachers in preschool programs receive low wages, often living at or slightly above the poverty line.

It is important not only morally but also socially and economically for children to succeed in school. It costs the school district about $4,000 per child when a child fails kindergarten or first grade or is required to go through an extra-year program to get a better educational start (Slavin, Karweit, and Wasik 1993). The cost of educating a full-time special education student is $17,500, or roughly seven times the amount spent on regular students (Gough 1992). Obviously, it is better to try to prevent these educational problems from occurring in the first place.

The U.S. government spends almost as much to finance the national debt ($184 billion) as it does on education in kindergarten through grade 12 ($199 billion). At the same time, corporations spend an average of $750,000 on the salary of their chief executive officer (Pollin 1992). One in seven American children is now supported by some kind of social funding, with about two thousand of these children joining the rolls every day (Rase 1992). While federal spending to assist children is significant, it doesn't compare with the monies spent on the elderly. In 1990, the federal government spent $68.6 billion on programs for children but nearly six times as much, $354.5 billion, on programs for the elderly (Richman 1992).

In 1995, only 36 percent of preschool children eligible for Head Start were served (Polakow 1997). In a 1995 study of the quality of U.S. child-care centers, most centers were rated poor to mediocre. Only 8 percent of infant care rooms were rated "good," while 40 percent were rated as meeting less than minimal requirements (Helburn 1995).

Child-care costs continue to rise. The costs for high-quality infant care in the Midwest can run $800 a month or more. In Washtenaw County, Michigan, full-time, high-quality child care runs $10,000 a year, a sum that is 40 percent higher than the costs of undergraduate tuition at the University of Michigan (Polakow 1997).

The pressure of welfare expenses on state and federal budgets has resulted in new programs. For instance, Wisconsin announced in 1993 that a time limit would go into effect so that no one would be on welfare for over three consecutive years. As part of the program, the welfare recipient must complete high school or obtain a general education diploma (GED) or a training program. Because the state was paying higher welfare benefits than neighboring states, there was an influx of welfare recipients from such cities as Chicago and the result was an overburdening of its social welfare system. Thus, Wisconsin designed the program in part as a defensive measure. Massachusetts has adopted a similar law.

The Family Unit

The family unit has changed dramatically during the past two decades. Substantial shifts took place in the composition of families during the twenty-year period between 1970 and 1990. For instance, in 1970, 50 percent of families with children included both parents compared with 37 percent in 1990 (U.S. Department of Education 1994a). Obviously, the number of children living in single-parent homes is on the increase, as are children born out of wedlock. Consider, for instance, that an African American child has only one chance in five of growing up with two parents (Ingrassia 1993).

Over eleven million preschoolers are placed each weekday in some form of child care as their parents work (Richman 1992). The growing role of fathers as primary caretakers has changed in recent years. In 1988, 15 percent of preschoolers were cared for by their fathers while their mothers worked. By 1991, that figure had increased to 20 percent (More dads at home, too 1994).

Approximately 1.6 children, or 8 percent of the elementary and middle school students between the ages of five and fourteen in the United States, come home to empty houses or apartments each day and take care of themselves during the summer and other school vacation periods. While this seems to be a large number, many school administrators believe it is conservative. Eli Baker, an elementary principal in Sumter, South Carolina, says that 45 percent of his students go home to empty houses. However, the percentages differ greatly by school and by region. According to Christina Olson, principal of Mountain View Elementary in Boise, Idaho, only 10 percent of her students go home to an empty house. Suburban students are twice as likely to be latchkey children as are rural students. Also, latchkey children are found across all socioeconomic groups (1.6 million kids home alone 1994).

The increase in the number of working parents has made it difficult for them to be involved in their children's school activities. For instance, many women who used to serve as room mothers now work weekdays at jobs to earn money for the family. One in four employed parents reports that it is a problem for them to take time off from work to attend a school activity, care for a sick child, or even attend a parent-teacher conference (A look at parental involvement in schools 1993).

There is little doubt, however, that parents care how their children do in school and that they are willing to help their children do better. A survey conducted by the National Parent Teachers Association (PTA) and *Newsweek* found that parents devote an average of 6.3 hours per week to their child's formal education and an average of 7.6 hours per week to their child's informal education (i.e., teaching new ideas or concepts and skills, such as that the San Francisco 49ers football team is named after the California gold rush in 1849, or their family's address and phone number). This same survey found that three out of four parents help their children with homework at least once a week (A look at parental involvement in schools 1993).

Two-Parent Families

While the media and many politicians point out that the family unit is breaking down, in actuality the statistics point in a different direction. Seven out of ten children under the age of eighteen live with *both* biological parents. The rate is highest for white children (77 percent) and Hispanic children (65 percent). The rate for African American children is 36 percent (U.S. Census Bureau 1993).

Traditionally, most schools assumed that children lived with two biological parents, one, usually the father, working full-time outside of the home, and the other, usually the mother, working inside the home. This traditional family profile is accurate in only one out of every three families with school-age children (Kirst 1993). Forty-six percent of all children live in homes where both parents or the only parent living in the home works (Hodgkinson 1992).

A survey of two-parent families found that fathers and mothers were equally involved in their children's learning. Both parents engaged in helping their children with their homework, reading and talking to them, and taking them to the public library (A look at parent involvement in schools 1993).

Single-Parent Families

Every day the parents of nearly 2,750 children in the United States separate or are legally divorced. Currently, 22 percent of children under the age of eighteen live in single-parent homes. It is predicted that if divorce rates begin to rise again and single-parent pregnancies continue to increase, over 50 percent of all white children and 75 percent of all African American children will spend a part of their childhood in a single-parent household (Richman 1992).

The majority of couples that divorce each year, 57 percent, have children under the age of eighteen. Thus, over one million children each year must cope with their parents' divorce (Magnet 1992). Divorce has an unsettling effect on the emotions of children. Those between the ages of five and eight typically experience feelings of rejection and abandonment, particularly by the parent who doesn't have custody, whereas children between the ages of nine and twelve are typically angry with both parents (Adler 1990).

Divorce has the greatest impact on children over twelve years of age. Sixty-eight percent of teenagers from divorced families engaged in illegal or even self-destructive activities—alcohol abuse, drug use, theft, or traffic violations—in the months following a divorce. Even a year later, their stress rates continued to rise (Adler 1990). A longitudinal study of 130 children of divorce by Wallerstein and Blakeslee (1989) indicated that no scale can measure the intensity of the wounds of children of divorce. The researchers found that, after a divorce, many boys began having learning and behavior problems in school, despite the fact that most of the boys in the study were above average in intelligence. By adolescence, the boys began to drift, falling behind in their schoolwork and seemingly lacking direction in their lives. Girls did better, but their success was sometimes fragile.

Typically, 35 percent of single-parent families headed by women fall under the poverty rate (U.S. Department of Commerce Bureau of the Census 1993). And it is estimated that 75 percent of children from single-parent families will be impoverished during some period before they reach the age of eighteen as compared with

Children and Divorce

The incidence of divorce is very high in our society. Thus there exists the likelihood that you will have students in your classroom whose parents are undergoing divorce. As teachers, we need to be alert to the warning signs of stress in students as a result of divorce, for example:

- lack of interest in friends;
- lack of interest in enjoyable activities;
- problems working or playing with other students in class;
- lack of interest in school, even subjects in which he or she excels;
- irregular sleep habits, either too little or too much;
- excessive conflicts with siblings and parents;
- unusually negative and even rebellious behavior;
- health problems, including headaches, stomach-aches, and an unusually high number of colds.

Often parents undergoing family problems such as divorce turn to teachers for advice. Here are some suggestions that as a teacher you can offer:

- Don't fight with your spouse in front of the child.
- Don't blame the divorce on the child or the spouse.
- Don't put the child in the middle by having the child convey messages to your spouse.
- Don't expect the child to act in an adult role. The child shouldn't be expected to give emotional support or deal with financial or legal problems. Call on family, friends, and professionals instead.
- Don't make the child feel guilty for loving both parents.
- Do reassure the child that you love him or her. Hugs and pats on the back are appropriate.
- Do convince the child that the divorce wasn't his or her fault.
- Do help the child in releasing his or her feelings of fear or anger.
- Since children have greater emotional problems if they lose contact with one parent, do keep in touch on a regular basis. Even a weekly postcard in the mail helps the child maintain an important family link.

20 percent of children from two-parent families (Magnet 1992). This is because many fathers fail to provide child support even though this is their legal obligation. Also, women tend to work in jobs that do not pay as well as those held by men.

Single parents of preschoolers need child care for their youngsters. Unfortunately, quality child care is very expensive, often between $15 and $25 per day per child in a good child-care center. This greatly diminishes a parent's paycheck. In addition, it is important to note that "attendance at a high-quality preschool program has long-term benefits for children, but it is equally clear that preschool experience is not enough to prevent early school failure" (Slavin, Karweit, and Wasik 1993, 16).

Children from single-parent families are 100 percent more likely to have emotional and behavioral problems than children from two-parent families. They are 50 per-cent more likely to have learning disabilities. As adolescents, children from single-parent families are more apt to be treated for severe mental illness; over 80 percent of all adolescents admitted to hospitals for psychiatric care are from single-parent fam-ilies (Magnet 1992). Reasons for these problems include the fact that children blame themselves for their parents' divorce, thus creating a guilt complex. In addition, chil-dren from single-parent families are more apt to have lower self-esteem than their

In 1997, economist Susan Mayer of the University of Chicago published a book that shocked many liberal thinkers. In *What Money Can't Buy,* Mayer, who describes herself as a liberal, asks the question: how important is money in helping families to help their children escape poverty? Health and living conditions have improved for children living in poverty. For instance, in 1970, a survey showed that 26 percent of children hadn't visited a doctor in a year. By 1989, that percentage had dropped to 14. In 1973, a survey showed that 71 percent of children in poverty lived in homes that didn't have air conditioning but by 1991, the percentage had dropped to 45. During this same period, however, crime and out-of-wedlock births both increased.

Mayer states that employers value certain characteristics that parents can pass along to their children without monetary obligations: diligence, honesty, reliability, and basic academic skills. However, welfare alone cannot guarantee that these characteristics will be passed along to the children.

Currently the trend is toward welfare reform. However, in Mayer's view, previous welfare programs merely supported the existence of a permanent condition of poverty. The results of her study suggest that even a country as wealthy as the United States may be unable to end poverty.

peers. Children in two-parent families have the advantage of the emotional and, sometimes, financial support of two parents. The stress of being breadwinner, homemaker, and parent overwhelms many single parents.

Extended Families

Among elementary students and even older preschoolers are children who refer to their "first" family and "second" family. These children attempt to distinguish stepparents, stepbrothers, stepsisters, and step-grandparents as well as half brothers and half sisters. Indeed, it is not unusual to have students who are stepbrothers or stepsisters in the same classroom.

Children from extended families often have difficulty developing their own identity. For some, a gray area exists regarding who is and who isn't a blood relative in their families. Children whose parents have been married numerous times tend to isolate themselves as a form of self-protection and in an attempt to insulate themselves emotionally.

For many minority children, particularly from African American, Asian, or Hispanic families, the extended family provides an important role. Oftentimes the grandparents or aunts and uncles live with the child's family. Older relatives may provide child care, thereby enabling a child's parent(s) to work outside of the home.

Foster Children

Three percent of children in the United States live with no biological parent at all. Many of these children are foster children who have been placed by state social welfare agencies in homes to receive care. The state then pays the foster parents a fee. In

A Closer Look

Overcoming the Odds

Many individuals have overcome social problems and become successful. Many individuals come from dysfunctional families. Here is one such story.

As a young teenager, Judy fell in love with who she thought was the man of her dreams. She dropped out of school and married without her parents' consent. Judy and her husband had four children in rapid succession.

But Judy's husband badly abused her. She was determined to turn her life around. With her arm in a sling, both eyes blackened, and much of her body black and blue from bruises, Judy went to the Adult Resource and Training Center in Manhattan, Kansas. Depressed and

unable to concentrate on studying, she spent the first few days talking with the center's secretary. As her depression diminished, her concentration level increased. After scoring high on the initial achievement tests given by the center, Judy's self-esteem increased. She received her GED and then called her parents to let them know of her success.

Judy divorced her husband, and she and her four children moved in with her parents. Judy entered Kansas State University and graduated with a bachelor's degree. She now is a working single parent who is trying to make a good family life for her children (Farris 1992; Kansas Department of Education 1991).

1990, there were a record 407,000 children placed in foster homes throughout the United States, with most of the placements due to the parents' inability to provide basic clothing, food, and shelter for the child or to neglect. The cost of foster home placement is a burden on each of the states. Michigan, for example, estimates that it costs $14,000 a year to keep a child in a foster home (Richman 1992).

Unfortunately, foster children are often moved from one foster family to another for a variety of reasons: the family may be unable to properly care for the child, the family may move due to a transfer within the workplace, or the child or the family may have difficulty adjusting. In addition, foster children are often separated from their siblings, especially if there are a large number of children in the family. These aspects and others can lead to a tremendous amount of stress for the foster child, typically resulting in some kind of misbehavior.

Many foster children are unadoptable children with special needs. For instance, foster children who are members of a minority group, who are physically and mentally disabled, or who have AIDs are less likely to be adopted. Also, it is more difficult for social agencies to place these children in foster homes because the need exceeds qualified foster home settings available. Sadly, the number of families willing to take in foster children has declined greatly in the past few years (Richman 1992).

Homeless Children

There are around three million homeless people in the United States. A fast-growing segment of the homeless population is families with children. Phi Delta Kappa, an educational honorary, reports that estimates of the number of homeless children on any given night range from 68,000 to half a million (Children at risk: A photo essay 1992). The plight of homeless children is heartwrenching. Ill-fed, inadequately clothed, and usually lacking access to medical and health care, these children face a daily struggle to survive. Homeless children are often moved from shelter to shelter, since most agencies allow the homeless to stay for only four to six weeks.

An undetermined number of homeless children fail to attend school because they lack clothes and school supplies, as well as adequate diet and medical attention. Some carry communicable diseases such as tuberculosis, a concern for both local health officials and school officials. Homeless children are often denied access to schools for a variety of reasons—residency requirements within the school district boundaries, lack of transportation, lost school records, and inability to determine legal guardianship. School districts are within their legal parameters to deny admission to students for these reasons. Only recently have states acknowledged and taken action regarding the education of homeless children. In 1987, only two state boards of education reported the number of homeless children in their states, and only New York reported state and local initiatives to deal with the problem (First and Cooper 1992).

In 1987, Congress passed the Stewart B. McKinney Homeless Assistance Act. Under this legislation, barriers to educating homeless children were addressed in seven provisions.

1. Each state educational agency shall assure that each child of a homeless person and homeless youth shall have access to a free appropriate public education, which would be provided to the children of a resident of that state.

2. Each state that has a residency requirement for school attendance purposes shall review and revise such laws to assure that such children are provided a free and appropriate public education.

3. Each state shall establish an Office of Coordinator of Education of Homeless Children and Youth to gather data on homeless children in the state and develop a plan providing for their education.

4. The plan developed shall contain provisions designed to authorize the state education agency, the local education agency, the parent or guardian of the homeless child to place that child in the proper school setting.

5. The local educational agency of a homeless child will either continue the child's enrollment in the school district for the remainder of the school year or enroll the child in the school district where he or she is presently living, whichever is in the best educational interests of the child.

6. Each homeless child will be provided with service comparable to those provided to other students in the school.

7. The educational records of each homeless child will be maintained so that those records can be accessible in a timely fashion.

After the passage of the McKinney Act, several states took action regarding homeless children. For instance, in 1988, the New York Board of Regents established regulations that allow the parents of homeless children the right to decide where their children will attend school. The state of Washington set up a computer system designed to keep track of students' health and birth certificates. Thus, homeless children are required to produce these records only once per school year (First and Cooper 1992) rather than every time they attempt to enroll in another school.

Whether homeless children are enrolled in schools depends on many factors. Certainly the motivation of the parent(s) or guardians plays an important role, but so does the proximity of the school to where the child is presently located and the degree of acceptance of homeless children into the schools by the local and school community.

Websites Pertaining to Homeless Children

Legal Issues

Homeless Children

U.S. Congress on the Internet. Within this website is the reference to the Stewart B. McKinney Homeless Assistance Act which states that "each State educational agency shall ensure that each child of a homeless individual and each homeless youth has equal access to a free, appropriate public education."

http://www.ed.gov/legislation/ESEA/sec323.html

Children of Immigrants

U.S. Congress on the Internet. The Thomas site within the U.S. Congress on the Internet site contains the Illegal Immigration Reform and Immigrant Responsibility Act of 1996.

http://thomas.loc.gov/

Homeless Shelters

Homes for the Homeless

The Institute for Children and Poverty sponsors this website. The focus of the site is American Family Inns, an innovative shelter program that includes child care, job training, educational, and medical services for over five hundred families at a time.

http://www.opendoor.com/hfh/

Children of Illegal Aliens

Illegal immigration is a societal problem that the schools cannot ignore. Every day, thousands of aliens illegally cross the borders into the United States. California alone gains an estimated 300,000 new illegal aliens each year. Other states, particularly Arizona, Florida, New Mexico, and Texas, have substantial numbers of illegal aliens. The overwhelming majority of these illegal aliens and their children speak English as a second language.

In 1982, the U.S. Supreme Court addressed the question of whether children of illegal aliens could be denied entrance into the public schools. The Texas State Legislature had passed legislation that would have withheld funding from school districts if those funds were used to educate students who were not legal residents of the United States. Furthermore, the law authorized Texas school districts to deny children of illegal aliens access to schools. In *Plyer v. Doe*, 457 U.S. 202 (1982), the U.S. Supreme Court ruled that the children of illegal aliens were entitled to access to public education based on the rights given in the Equal Protection Clause of the Fourteenth Amendment to the U.S. Constitution. The Supreme Court also ruled that all children, regardless of their nationality, are subject to laws of the state. Because Texas had established its education system as being free and compulsory, all children, even those of illegal aliens, had the right to a public education.

In some school districts, particularly at the high school level, students attend classes illegally. New Trier High School, a secondary school in an affluent suburb northwest of Chicago, has a national and international reputation for its outstanding academic program and produces a high percentage of National Merit Scholars annually. Because of this reputation, illegal attendance is a major problem that requires that the hallways be patrolled daily in search of student violators. For example, it is not unusual for a parent or aunt or uncle of an Asian student to bring the child to the United States and rent an apartment in Chicago. The older relative then returns to Asia while the student commutes to New Trier High School each day by train and bus.

Abused Children

Nearly two million cases of child abuse are reported to the authorities each year (Sawyer 1989). Child abuse can take one of four forms: physical abuse, physical neglect, sexual abuse, and emotional maltreatment. Physical abuse is nonaccidental injury to a child, such as slapping, shaking, hitting, kicking, burning, pushing, or smothering. Physical neglect occurs when the caretaker/parent does not provide sufficient food, clothing, shelter, or supervision. Sexual abuse is the sexual exploitation, molestation, or prostitution of a child. Emotional maltreatment, perhaps the most difficult to prove, is the constant belittlement or rejection of a child, resulting in the child living in a nonpositive emotional environment (Bear, Schenk, and Buckner 1993; Colorado Department of Education 1988).

Research indicates that parents who were abused as children are six times as likely to abuse their own children (Kantrowitz 1988). Child abuse appears to be on the increase. Each year the number of reported cases climbs. According to Richman (1992, 35) "Every day more than three children die of injuries inflicted by abusive parents. Nearly ninety kids a day are taken from their parents' custody and added to the overburdened foster care system."

Research by the Child Welfare League found that abused or neglected children are sixty-seven times more likely to be arrested between the ages of nine and twelve than those children who aren't abused or neglected. Children who are considered most at risk to become juvenile offenders are those who have a parent who is incarcerated, who has serious mental health problems, or who abuses drugs and/or alcohol. Another factor is inadequate housing. Children who get into trouble at a young age at school are also more likely candidates for becoming juvenile offenders. The study involved 75,000 children in California, 1,026 of whom had been targeted by child welfare workers as being victims of child abuse or neglect (Whitmire 1997). The study concluded that there is a very strong tie between having a parent in prison and committing a crime. The current U.S. prison population is 1.5 million. It is estimated that 1.6 million children have one or both parents who are currently prison inmates.

The Child Welfare League believes that increased federal funding of early childhood programs such as Head Start is needed, as are improved health care for children and more after-school and recreational programs. Such programs can help to stop the "volatile and predictive situation," according to Michael Pettit, deputy director of the Child Welfare League.

By law, teachers and school administrators must notify authorities whenever they suspect child abuse. As such, teachers and school administrators may find themselves serving as child advocates in difficult family situations.

Diversity Issues

The population in the United States is becoming ever more diverse. There is a greater awareness of the needs and rights of persons who are physically and mentally disabled, the percentage of minority groups is increasing, advocates of women's rights are becoming more vocal about women's issues, and sexual orientations are discussed more openly than in the past. These issues are encountered by children as well as adults and influence all of our lives.

Marian Wright Edelman is the founder and president of the Children's Defense Fund, an organization whose mission is to enlighten Americans about the needs of children. The Children's Defense Fund is a strong advocate of children's and women's rights. The 1997 positive changes in the U.S. budget to support funding of children's health care were actively lobbied for by Edelman and other members of her organization.

As a child, Edelman's father, a minister, taught her that a young black girl was capable of becoming anything she wanted to be, "that race and gender are shadows, and that character, self-discipline, determination, attitude, and service are the substance of life" (Edelman 1992).

In the mid-1960s, Edelman became the first black woman admitted to the Mississippi Bar. Her first job as an attorney was the directorship of the National Association for the Advancement of Colored People (NAACP) in Jackson, Mississippi.

Born in 1939 in Bennettsville, South Carolina, Edelman has devoted her entire life to being an advocate for disadvantaged Americans. She was awarded a Mac-Arthur Prize Fellowship for her talents.

Edelman continues her crusade to help neglected children. She writes,

Nowhere is the paralysis of public or private conscience more evident than in the neglect and abandonment of millions of our shrinking pool of children, whose futures more than any other factor will determine our nation's ability to compete and lead in the new era.

Yet every eight seconds of every school day an American child drops out. These are all of our children, not just poor and minority children. Every twenty-six seconds an American child will run away from home. Every thirteen seconds an American child will be abused or neglected. Every sixty-four seconds an American teenager will have a baby. Every seven minutes one of our children is arrested for a drug offense. Every thirty minutes an American child is arrested for drunken driving. Every fifty-three minutes in our rich land an American child dies from the effects of poverty.

It is disgraceful that we permit children to be the poorest Americans (Edelman 1992, 4).

Physically and Mentally Disabled Population

The number of individuals who are physically and mentally disabled in the general population continues to grow, as it does in schools (table 3). Inclusion of these students into regular classroom settings is increasing. For instance, in 1976–77, 3,692,000 students were served in federally supported special-education programs. By 1989–90, that number had grown to 4,641,000, with 31 percent of those in regular classroom settings as part of inclusion programs (U.S. Department of Education 1994a).

There is an evergrowing awareness of the problems of the physically disabled population, as can be seen by the accessibility of parking spaces, by wheelchairs provided in grocery and retail stores, and by the presence of railings in stalls in public rest rooms.

Point /Counterpoint

Should Schools Focus on Education Only or Become Involved in Social Problems as Well?

Point: Schools are responsible for educating students and should not become involved in societal issues.

The primary focus of schools is to educate students so they will become contributing citizens of society. Diverting funding from this purpose to social issues in the schools is not a proper use of taxpayer monies.

The tremendous focus on multicultural education greatly overshadows the contributions of the majority population. Students are often told that minority leaders or groups made positive contributions, whereas those made by white leaders or groups were in some way bad or harmful.

Societal issues have invaded schools in other ways. Some junior high and high schools now provide day care for the young children of their students. These secondary students are but children themselves. Having day care available encourages teenage pregnancy. Peer pressure is placed on other students of both sexes to be promiscuous. Indeed, one pregnant student bragged that she "lost her water" in a social studies class.

Likewise, handing out free condoms at school encourages promiscuity among an age group that is not sexually responsible. AIDS is rapidly spreading among teenagers, and handing out condoms is not the solution.

Schools have become overly tolerant of students who engage in disruptive behavior. Students who bring dangerous weapons to school should be expelled for the remainder of the school year. Instead, the culprit students generally receive a short suspension of a few days or a week.

Counterpoint: Schools have no choice but to become involved in social issues.

Public schools must become involved in societal issues. Indeed, schools offer the last hope for our society. If they aren't involved, society's problems may become even more severe.

Many elementary schools now offer before- and after-school care for students for a small fee. This trend came about because parents and educators became concerned about the safety of elementary students who were latchkey children. These students left home after their parents went to work and likewise arrived home before their parents.

Social problems are brought into the school and the classroom. They don't stop at the edge of the school grounds. Consider the first grader who burst into tears in class because her father took her mirror—he needed it to separate cocaine. Or consider the fifteen-year-old teenagers in an inner-city high school who devote their free time in math class to calculating the costs of their own funerals because they don't expect to live long enough to graduate from high school.

If schools don't intercede, societal problems will worsen.

Multiculturalism

There exists a vast amount of diversity in our nation as represented by cultural, racial, and ethnic groups. According to the 1990 census figures, 31.8 million people in the United States communicate in 329 different foreign languages. Spanish is the most common foreign language. It is spoken by over 17 million people, of whom 54 percent do not speak English at home (Vsdansky 1993).

Table 3 Percentage Distribution of Disabled Persons Three to Twenty-One Years Old Receiving Education Services for the Disabled, by Age Group and Educational Environment: 1992–93

Type of disability	All environments	Regular class	Resource room	Separate class	Public separate school facility	Private separate school facility	Public residential facility	Private residential facility	Homebound/ hospital environment
1	2	3	4	5	6	7	8	9	10
All persons, 3 to 21 years old	100.0	40.5	29.9	24.1	2.7	1.4	0.6	0.2	0.6
3 to 5 years old	100.0	47.5	12.2	30.6	4.8	2.9	0.3	0.1	1.6
6 to 21 years old	100.0	39.8	31.7	23.5	2.4	1.2	0.6	0.3	0.5
Mental retardation	100.0	7.1	26.8	56.8	6.8	1.1	0.6	0.3	0.5
Speech or language impairments	100.0	81.7	10.7	6.0	0.2	1.1	0.1	(^{1})	0.1
Visual impairments	100.0	45.4	21.0	18.0	3.9	1.7	8.6	0.8	0.5
Serious emotional disturbance	100.0	19.6	26.7	35.2	8.5	5.3	1.8	1.7	1.3
Orthopedic impairments	100.0	35.1	20.0	34.1	5.2	1.5	0.4	0.2	3.5
Other health impairments	100.0	40.0	7	4	20.6	1.7	0.8	3	9.1
Specific learning disabilities	100.0	34.8	43.9	20.1	0.4	0.3	0.1	(^{1})	0.2
Deaf-blindness	100.0	12.5	9.9	31.5	15.6	5.7	22.1	1.6	1.0
Multiple disabilities	100.0	7.5	19.0	44.6	17.9	5.8	2.2	1.3	1.8
Hearing impairments	100.0	29.5	19.7	28.1	5.6	2.7	13.2	0.9	0.4

^{1}Less than 0.05 percent.
NOTE: This table reflects a compilation of data reported by the states as of October 1, 1994. There are some reporting variations, e.g., estimated or incomplete data and nonstandard definitions, from state to state. Data include Puerto Rico. Data for 3- to 5-year-old children are no longer collected by type of disability. Because of rounding, details may not add to totals.
SOURCE: U.S. Department of Education, Office of Special Education and Rehabilitative Services, *Seventeenth Annual Report to Congress on the Implementation of The Individuals with Disabilities Education Act, 1995.* (This table was prepared April 1996.)

The minority population of the United States by 2000 is expected to be 35.4 million individuals of African American descent, 31.3 million Hispanics, 8.7 million Asian Americans, and 1.6 million Native Americans (Vsdansky 1993). If present trends continue, by the year 2000, one out of every three schoolchildren will be nonwhite (Banks and Banks 1989). Many school districts have modified their curriculum to present more multicultural coverage. According to the Twenty-Sixth Annual Phi Delta Kappa/Gallup Poll (Elam, Rose, and Gallup 1994, 52), "The long-running debate over multiculturalism in the schools has heated up in recent years as some groups protest a tendency to abandon the melting-pot metaphor in favor of 'tossed salad' and as the number and size of racial and ethnic minority groups increases." Seventy-five percent of those polled stated they preferred that both one common tradition and diverse traditions of different populations be promoted in the schools.

The high school dropout rate is a concern to educators. However, the dropout rate is decreasing for whites, African Americans, and all other ethnic groups with the exception of Hispanic students. In 1991, high school dropout rates by race were 8.9 percent for whites, 13.6 percent for African Americans, and 35.3 percent for Hispanics (U.S. Department of Education 1994b). Thus, it was nearly four times higher for Hispanics than whites and almost three times higher for Hispanics than African Americans. However, it should be noted that half of all Hispanic dropouts are immigrants. In addition, Hispanic immigrants between the ages of sixteen and eighteen who never enroll in a U.S. high school and who failed to complete high school in their native country are counted as dropouts even though they never even enrolled, or "dropped in," to U.S. schools (Huelskamp 1993).

Political leaders debate the problems and issues concerning multiculturalism. Children today are exposed to a greater variety of cultural activities in their daily lives. Even the types of foods served in school cafeterias today represent a variety of cultures (e.g., spaghetti, Italian; tacos, Hispanic; egg rolls, Asian), a menu that continues to expand culturally. Schools now celebrate holidays of a variety of cultures, including Kwanza, Swahili for "first fruits," a seven-day celebration at the end of December that emphasizes family, community development, and self-esteem.

Differences in cultural behavior are now acknowledged by both the public and private sectors. The Japanese rely heavily on a teamwork concept in the workplace. U.S. schools now realize the value of teamwork, and cooperative and collaborative learning are commonly encouraged in the classroom. Analysis of and appreciation for different cultures is encouraged at all levels. For example, high school students studying economics may examine Japanese business practices. The Japanese seek to contract their business with acquaintances they trust. These business deals are often done in very private situations, unlike transacting business in formal business settings with individuals from Western European cultures such as the United States.

In the family unit, Hispanic families are typically child-centered, and young children are given the most attention. Asian American families tend to emphasize the need for children to perform well in school as part of the family's honor.

Gender Bias and Sexual Harassment

A national study found that as children grow up, both boys and girls lose some self-esteem in a variety of different areas. However, the loss is most dramatic and has the most long-lasting impact for girls. For example, girls were found to be more apt than boys to lower their career aspirations (American Association of University Women 1993).

Gender issues are prevalent in today's society. There have been gradual strides toward gender equity since the passing of Title IX, the Women's Educational Equity Act of 1974. Title IX prohibited discrimination against women in programs that received federal assistance. The result was the addition/expansion of sports programs, in particular at the secondary and college levels.

Like in the workplace, sexual harassment of females in school settings has received much attention, both in the media and in the courts. In a survey of 1,600 male and female students, four out of five indicated that they had experienced some form of sexual harassment during their school years. Most of the harassment occurs in the school hallways. Girls are more likely to have their clothes pulled in a sexual way or to be grabbed or pinched than are boys. However, boys are often targets of sexual harassment in rest rooms and locker rooms. The worst harassment reported by those in this study was to be referred to as being gay or lesbian (85 percent of the boys; 87 percent of the girls) (American Association of University Women 1993).

In Minnesota, a mother complained to the school that her sixth-grade daughter was being sexually harassed on the school bus. When the school district failed to respond to her complaints, she sued the school district.

In a case in Illinois, the parents of a fourth-grader complained that she was sexually harassed on the school grounds by other students prior to school and during the lunch period. The school took action by discussing the problem with the students involved and telling them such behavior was unacceptable and would be punished.

Children have a natural tendency to tease one another. However, when is it teasing and when is it sexual harassment? This is a difficult question for educators. Some schools have said the line is crossed when the students use derogatory comments or refer to body parts. However, is it sexual harassment if a girl who doesn't like math is teased about missing a geometry problem? Or is it sexual harassment if a boy is kidded by his peers for winning a baking contest?

Physical harassment has also become prevalent. Bra-snapping is a fad among junior high and upper elementary students. When one parent was notified that her son was being suspended from school for one day for grabbing a female classmate's bra and releasing it, she was astonished. She told the principal that her son was "just being a boy" and that there was nothing wrong with such behavior.

The severity of the problem is greatly disturbing. A survey of urban school districts found that 15 percent reported that a student had been raped on the school grounds (Henry 1994).

Educators continue to define the limits of what is and what is not sexual harassment.

When asked about being sexually harassed, a sixteen-year-old white female said, "It made me feel that a woman isn't worth much, and it shouldn't be that way" (American Association of University Women 1993, 18). Few schools have equity issues as part of their curricula. Few teachers feel comfortable in addressing such issues in their classes.

Sexual Orientation

Gay and lesbian sexual orientations in adults are being more openly presented. Children's books are being published that discuss "daddy's friend" and even show two men sleeping together. The book *My Two Mommies* points out that mother's female companion is accepted by the child as a second mother. President Clinton brought the issue to the headlines when he advocated a greater role for the gay and lesbian population in the military through his "don't ask, don't tell" policy for members of the armed services.

Some high schools now counsel high school students who think they are gay or lesbian. In recent years, lawsuits have been filed by gay and lesbian high school couples who wanted to attend their high school prom but were banned by school rules and regulations.

In 1993, Massachusetts became the first state to pass a law to protect homosexual students in schools. This law penalizes students who harass or physically harm homosexual students on school property.

Gangs are present in urban, suburban, and even rural schools in many parts of the U.S. and Canada. (© Timothy Ross/The Image Works, Inc.)

Substance Abuse

Besides the media, the relatively easy access many children have to illegal drugs and alcohol is yet another reason cited for increased violence. Every day over five hundred children between the ages of ten and fourteen experiment with drugs for the first time, while over one thousand start drinking alcohol. By the time children reach middle school, over half abuse drugs and alcohol, participate in unprotected sex, or live in poverty (Richman 1992). Many of us believe it is only students of low ability who engage in substance abuse, but among 1,957 high school juniors and seniors with outstanding academic records surveyed, 11 percent admitted to having driven a car after drinking and 40 percent to having ridden in a car even though they knew the driver had been drinking (Feldman 1993).

Substance abuse rates among teenagers in the United States are higher than for any other industrialized nation in the world (Lemming 1992). This is in part because of the relative ease with which teenagers can acquire alcohol. Children are now beginning to use alcohol at very early ages; the average age for males is twelve years, five months and only slightly higher for females (Horton 1992). However, casual use of marijuana by teenagers between the ages of twelve and seventeen has decreased from 23 percent in 1979 to 13 percent in 1991, though it is still a large percentage (U.S. Census Bureau 1993). According to one researcher, "The prime determinant of drinking or drug use is how many hours the child is left alone during the week" (Magnet 1992, 46).

Violence in the Society

Violence in our society is commonplace. The evening news is filled with reports of murders and drive-by shootings, and many children and adolescents are exposed to violence on a daily basis. A 1994 U.S. Justice Department report indicated that juveniles between the ages of twelve and seventeen are five times more likely to be victims of assault, rape, and robbery than are adults thirty-five years old and older (Whitmire 1994). Cindy Rodriguez, a fourteen-year-old resident of a gang-infested area of south Los Angeles was shot by a gang member a few years ago. Paralyzed as a result of the shooting, Cindy states that "we hear gunshots every day. . . . Sometimes I get scared. I'm in the shower and I hear it and I get all scared. But you have to live with the reality" (Rosenberg et al. 1993, 43).

The U.S. Justice Department reports that each year nearly a million youths between the ages of twelve and nineteen are raped, robbed, or assaulted, often by their peers. In addition, 2,200 murder victims, an average of six per day, during 1991 were under the age of eighteen. In 1991, children between the ages of ten and seventeen accounted for 17 percent of all violent crime arrests (Rosenberg et al. 1993). "Youthful violence . . . is not new. But some recent crimes seem to disregard even the barest of human boundaries" (Ingrassia et al. 1993). In 1991, 5,356 people under the age of nineteen were killed by guns, or roughly fifteen youngsters a day. During the same year, the National Association of Children's Hospitals and Related Institutions reported that children wounded by gunfire had hospital bills alone that averaged $14,434, almost the same amount of tuition for a year at a private college (Connell 1993).

Crimes are committed by girls and boys alike. In 1987, in Massachusetts, 15 percent of the crimes that girls were convicted of were classified as violent offenses. By 1991, that number had zoomed to 38 percent, or roughly four out of every ten violent crimes (Leslie et al. 1993).

Some individuals blame the media, particularly television, for the increase in violence. Since the typical fourteen-year-old watches three hours of television each day but does only one hour of homework, the influence of television on our youth is reason for worry (Richman 1992). Attorney General Janet Reno has urged senators to pass legislation to control television violence, particularly programs that dramatize bloodshed, if the television industry does not do so itself (Reno urges crackdown on TV violence "soon" 1993). MTV's popular "Beavis and Butt-head," an animated television series, changed its direction when a five-year-old copied Butt-head's habit of lighting fires. The five-year-old's actions resulted in a fire that killed his two-year-old sister (Senator no fan, of "Buffcoat and Beaver" [sic] 1993). As a result, the show stopped portraying the main character as a pyromaniac.

Society's mistrust of how the media portrays violence has even led some movie producers to reexamine their films. For instance, the film *The Program*, the story of a player who makes a college football team, was reedited when a scene that depicted players testing their bravery by lying end-to-end in the middle of a busy highway resulted in several copycat incidents among junior high and high school students. The students were tragically injured or killed. *The Program* is produced by Touchstone Pictures, a division of the Walt Disney Company, a name long synonymous with family values.

In 1992, the Minnesota legislature appropriated four times as much money for crime prevention programs as it did new money for incarceration of criminals. Almost $1.5 million was appropriated for education-related programs, including funds to provide for home visits by early childhood/preschool teachers. In addition, $3 per student was allocated to allow school districts to develop violence prevention programs and additional monies for cities, counties, and school districts to establish community councils for violence prevention. However, all of the programs that involve school districts are voluntary and are not required by the state (Pipho 1992).

In addition to violence, increasingly schools are dealing with student depression and suicide prevention. Teenage suicides continue to increase in the United States, although Japan has the highest suicide rate among adolescents. These teens are often top academic students or star athletes. The problem is so widespread that most school districts have suicide prevention programs.

Violence in the Schools

In 1997, an FBI report indicated that violent crime in our society has been steadily decreasing since 1991 (CNN Plus 1997). However, "because of the carryover effect of the violence in the society at large, . . . school violence has been on the rise. Many schools that once were safe havens from the violence that has plagued homes and communities are now themselves experiencing significantly more violent episodes" (Shen 1997, 18).

Increasingly we hear reports of students carrying guns and knives as weapons to protect themselves at school. "Every two days, guns kill the equivalent of a class of twenty-five youngsters and injure sixty more" (Sautter 1995 K2). In 1993–94, there were 20.3 percent of secondary teachers who viewed student possession of weapons as a serious or moderately serious problem as compared with 3.4 percent of elementary teachers.

A national study of adults, both with and without children in school, found that the biggest problems in school after lack of proper financial support for schools were drug abuse (16 percent), lack of discipline (15 percent), and fighting/violence/gangs (13 percent) (Elam, Rose, and Gallup 1993). By 1994, the same poll found fighting/violence/gangs rated the number-one problem by 18 percent of those polled, nearly a 50 percent increase for that category. Also in 1994, lack of discipline was rated the biggest problem by 18 percent of respondents with drug abuse rated first by 11 percent (Elam, Rose, and Gallup 1994). Studies of school violence support these perceptions. A 1993 study by the Harvard School of Public Health indicated that 59 percent of students in grades 6–12 said that they had access to a handgun if they wanted one (Rosenberg et al. 1993). Another study of top male students, those with a B average or higher, found 20 percent who indicated that they either owned or had access to a handgun (Feldman 1993).

A recent national study entitled *Metropolitan Life Survey of the American Teacher* (Metropolitan Life 1993) found that more than one in ten teachers and almost one in four students have been subjects of violence in or near their public schools. Thirteen percent of the students surveyed said they had carried weapons to school. The primary reasons given for carrying weapons were to impress their friends and to make themselves feel important.

In Rockford, Illinois, a middle-class midwestern community, an elementary student brought a loaded gun to school to give to a friend who he thought needed it for protection. In a meeting to discuss the problem with educators and concerned parents, an assistant superintendent from the school district said, "This has sent a shock wave throughout the community. That shock wave cannot be responded to in words" (Justin 1993).

In Boston, emergency medical technicians talking to a group of fifth-grade students were shocked to learn that nearly 75 percent of the children knew someone who had been stabbed or shot (Rosenberg et al. 1993). For some children, violence is almost a daily occurrence. In 1992, there were thirty-three homicides, including both students and teachers, in schools. In 1993, the number dropped to seven (Associated Press 1993).

Gangs are now in suburban as well as urban schools (Feldman 1993) and are now spreading into rural schools. Many schools now ban not only guns and knives but technological devices such as pagers and cellular phones, both used by drug pushers

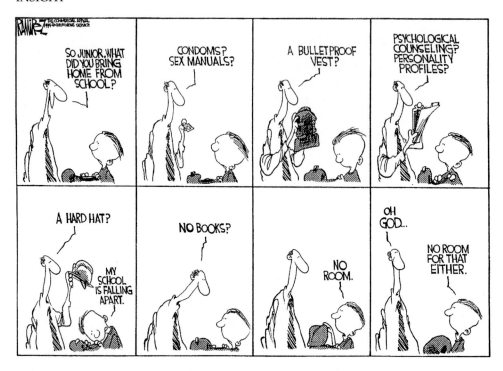

(Mike Ramirez. Copyright © 1994 Copley News Service. Reprinted by permission.)

and gang members as communication devices to avoid being caught by the police as well as to hide their covert actions. Attorney General Janet Reno states that violence among youths is "the greatest single crime problem in America today" (Rosenberg et al. 1993). Reno advocates spending more money on public education to stress academics so students have the skills needed to get good-paying jobs and have an alternative to life on the streets.

During a typical one-month period in the United States, the following occurs:

- 282,000 students and 5,200 teachers are attacked physically, with 4 percent of the students and an incredible 19 percent of the teachers requiring medical attention;
- 112,000 students and 6,000 teachers are robbed;
- 2.4 million students and 128,000 teachers have property stolen from them while at school;
- one out of every ten schools is broken into, a rate, incidentally, that is higher than that of businesses;
- 7 percent of high school students stay at home at least one day each month out of fear for their own safety;
- 24 percent of students avoid three or more places in high school because of fear of being victimized (Kenny and Watson 1993).

A national study conducted by the National School Board Association of seven hundred school districts found that 78 percent of the districts reported student assaults and fights as the most frequent kind of violence, with 93 percent of urban districts, 81 percent of suburban districts, and 69 percent of rural districts reporting

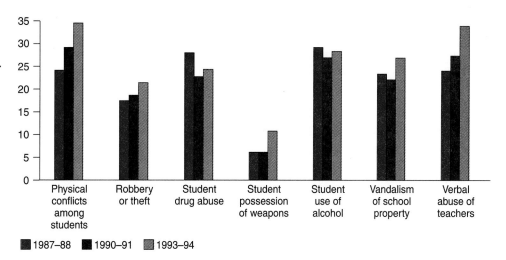

Figure 4
School problems over the past decade. Percentage of teachers who see each problem as serious or moderately serious in their schools

1987–88 ■ 1990–91 ■ 1993–94

—National Center for Education Statistics, U.S. Department of Education

such behavior. Weapons were reported to be a problem in 91 percent of urban districts, 61 percent of suburban districts, and 45 percent of rural districts (Henry 1994). Figure 4 shows the changing levels of teacher concern about student behavioral problems during the last decade.

In an effort to combat such violence, school districts suspend guilty students. In addition, closed circuit televisions are present in school hallways and classrooms and video cameras are used on school buses. Some schools use metal detectors to screen students for weapons as they enter the school building each day.

Because of a problem with drive-by shootings, a Tucson, Arizona, school built a fence eight feet high around the school grounds to keep perpetrators off the campus. In San Diego, California, all lockers were removed from the high schools. Perhaps one of the most innovative efforts was done by the Broward County, Florida, school system, which hired a former gang member from a New York City gang to work with teachers, parents, and students. The program seeks to prevent students from joining gangs (Henry 1994).

Some scholars doubt that schools and society itself can do much to deter crime: "Perhaps its causes are locked so deeply into the human personality, the intimate processes of family life, and the subtlest aspects of the popular culture that coping is the best that we can hope to do" (Wilson 1992, A40). According to research by the American Psychological Association (1993), the strongest developmental predictor of a child's involvement in violence is a history of previous violence, including being abused as a child.

Walter Annenberg, an American philanthropist known as one of the most generous donors of the twentieth century, contributed $500 million in 1993 to improve the nation's elementary and secondary schools. Annenberg blames parents for much of the problem. He believes that they are not concerned about their children. Other perpetrators in Annenberg's view are music with violent messages, questionable movies, and television shows—all of which undermine "the morality of youth today." In explaining his substantial gift to the country's schools, Annenberg states, "When I see grade-schoolers with knives and guns in their lockers, I don't need the roof to fall in to tell me what to do. We can't just wait around for this. We have to get to it immediately" (Nicklin 1994, A29).

"A profound clash of values is being played out in our public schools. Specific battles revolve around religion, creationism, sex education, values education, vouchers, school-linked health clinics, and educational reform. The broader battle focuses on the role of the public school in assuring a balanced, open curriculum that provides for a free exchange of ideas. At issue is how a school district can maintain intellectual freedom while simultaneously guaranteeing the parent's and community's right to be heard.

"Public schools have generally operated under the premise that tolerating various community viewpoints has value. But the tolerance level is being strained. On one side, Robert Simonds, president of Citizens for Excellence in Education, writes that 'we can take back our public schools from the hands of atheistic humanistic manipulators.' On the other, Americans United for Separation of Church and State write that 'anti-separationist leaders are on the scene rallying the troops and whipping up pro-voucher frenzy. . . . Forcing citizens to support sectarian education is imposing a religious tax.'

"Local control of education, a privilege with substantive political resonance, is easily exploited by those who would suppress materials or ideas that they find objectionable. At the same time, many parents accuse the school establishment of intolerance for not teaching religious doctrine nor allowing prayer in the classroom. These differences in perspective reflect not only the growing vocalism of the Far Right and Fundamentalists, but also a backlash against an educational reform movement that to some personifies an attack on traditional values.

"In fairness, terms such as *Far Right* and *Fundamentalist* do not adequately reflect the depth of the cultural wars being waged over our schools. Labels are too easily applied to characterize any citizen who may have some beef with the public schools, and they may limit our ability to understand the dynamics of public school opposition and to seek a valid community consensus.

To be sure, a powerful and effective movement is building that would like to subsume for itself community decision making in education, but the picture of community decision making is far more complex than that.

"Many who seek change in the public schools are not unbalanced trouble-makers, but sincere people who are concerned that school materials or programs will corrupt their children. They feel that their values are not incorporated in the current definition of the 'common' school. There are times when the interests of the school may be incompatible with the values of some parents. Problems arise, however, when parents seek to deny the entire school community the use of certain materials, programs, or educational opportunities because they believe they will corrupt *all* children. Finding the fine line between a parent's right to be involved in his or her child's education versus the exploitation of that right by a few parents with special interests requires adept leadership.

"Public speech that is intimidating, untruthful, or intolerant by any special interest group, either from the Right or Left, should be followed by more and better speech from those of us who believe in open community forums. Parents and community members concerned about attacks on the free exchange of ideas must be prepared to act on their convictions.

"Public speech that is intimidating, untruthful, or intolerant by any special interest group, either from the Right or Left, should be followed by more and better speech from those of us who believe in open community forums. Parents and community members concerned about attacks on the free exchange of ideas must be prepared to act on their convictions.

"Special interest groups take advantage of their audiences in a number of ways. One is through the doublespeak of anti-public school theology, which often confuses rational debate. Parental involvement comes to mean control; equal time, to mean inclusion of religious

(continued)

instruction in the curriculum; secular humanism, to mean anything except the views of the special interest group; back to basics, to mean imposing Christian values on everyone else; and values education, to mean the teaching of one religious doctrine to the exclusion of teaching about all religions.

"Another advantage special interest groups press is the threat of an organized campaign. Even the threat of such a campaign may have a chilling effect on the decisions made by boards of education. Boards wishing to avoid conflict may subtly restrict academic freedom by approving materials that are noncontroversial or by bypassing existing material selection and complaint policies in an effort to placate parents who wish to ban certain material from the library or classroom.

"Special interest groups present many school battles as a test of religious faith. While the religious faith of no one should be questioned, the error of these groups is often not one of religion, but of policy. God has taken no position on school-linked health clinics, or psychological tests, or condom distribution. Although religious values cannot be excluded from every public issue, not every public issue involves religious values. Each school district has an obligation to teach those values that are held in common—honesty, citizenship, patriotism, cooperation, tolerance, democracy.

"These controversies challenge those of us who believe that tolerance should be institutionalized by school policy. We can come out looking as though we support the status quo because we oppose opening the school curriculum to conservative ideology, even though in some cases it may present its own intolerances of race, class, and religion. A case in point is the Far Right's fear of federal government control of public education but its strong support of an amendment to the current HIV/AIDS reauthorization bill that would ban federal monies to fund condom distribution—in effect removing the decision to distribute condoms from more than 14,700 school units. The support by conservative organizations for local community decisions breaks down when communities may differ with far right positions. Such anomalies tax the tolerance levels of public officials in their roles of mediating various cultural conflicts.

"The debate over tolerance, however, conceals a much more devious issue—who controls the institutions of culture and value transmission. Our commitment to tolerance in developing public school policy and programs is desirable in developing a common school agenda responsive to changing public attitudes, mores, and needs. We must, however, be prepared to limit our tolerance when it could lead to the creation of intolerant policy. It is not persuasive to argue that a single group should be able to 'take back the public schools' because we believe in tolerance.

"If we believe that the progress of an educated citizenry depends on the freest possible expression of diverse points of view, then we must feel that we have come to a sort of halting place in American history. We, the American people, with a revolutionary tradition of independence and toleration, find ourselves enmeshed in battles of doctrine and uncompromising demands. Will toleration emerge as a critical national value in the midst of an increasingly diverse and intolerant population? The results of this debate will have an impact on how we, the people, live with one another. When we hear people speak of respecting others' viewpoints, we will know that the principle of toleration continues to establish what is common among us and is not simply being manipulated by those groups wishing to impose their own views on our schools."

Others also believe there is hope. According to Curio and First (1993, 50),

> School employees working in their schools and school districts to prevent violence are connected, knowingly or unknowingly, to concurrent efforts on the local, state, and federal levels. There are

indicators every day of groups and coalitions forming on all levels to defuse and prevent the growing violence that impacts schools. . . . In all, there is definitely an affirmative push from many corners to support local school administrators in their efforts to proactively defuse and prevent violence.

During the 1997–98 school year, three incidents of violence in schools made the front pages of national newspapers as students and teachers in Arkansas, Kentucky, and Pennsylvania were shot and killed by middle school and high school students. Certainly preventing violence among children and youths will be a primary concern of yours as an educator. How to control violence in the face of its prevalence throughout society is an ongoing problem.

School/Family/Community Partnerships

During the 1990s, many schools strove to foster greater community involvement in school affairs. Schools in affluent communities, particularly elementary schools, have been more successful than schools in poor communities and middle/junior high schools or high schools. Two-parent families tend to be more willing to be involved in local schools than are single-parent families, probably due in part to the time constraints single parents encounter. Research on school/family/community has found that nearly all families care about their children. Parents and guardians want children to succeed and are willing to be a partner in their children's education. Likewise, nearly all teachers and school administrators want to build a positive relationship with families. Students themselves at all levels—elementary, middle/junior high, and high school—want their families to be more involved with their schooling (Epstein 1995).

Everyone involved needs to receive some training in communication skills if school/family/community partnerships are to succeed. As John Markgraf, an elementary principal, said, public relations is more important today for teachers and school administrators than ever before. He believes that to do their job right, building principals must use the majority of their school day or public relations (Markgraf 1997).

Teachers can keep parents informed via weekly letters home to parents notifying them of upcoming events such as tests, field trips, or special activities. The same information can be put on the teacher's voicemail or posted on E-mail. Many school districts now have homework phone lines which students can call after school to get assistance in completing their assignments. Reaching out to the community beyond students' families might include inviting the local newspaper to school events or even submitting photos of special projects. Teachers who maintain contact with the current community trends and incorporate those into the curriculum help build close linkages between their school and the community. For instance, when an increased community interest in area historical buildings surfaced, Kim McKenna and Barbara Schwantes, third-grade teachers, immediately capitalized on it. Though neither lived in the community, they modified their curriculum to encourage their students to become actively involved. The students mapped out the city in a collage and took a walking field trip to identify the year each major building was built. In addition, the city had once had a car manufacturing plant which produced a vehicle known as the Palmer car. When local historians found the only remaining Palmer car, Kim and Barbara's students participated in the fund drive to purchase the car. As a result of their efforts, each student's name was recorded in a book in the town's historical museum.

Teachers can't help but become involved with social problems, as many students come from difficult home settings. Even teachers in wealthy school districts have to deal with child abuse, drug problems, and children whose parents are divorcing or divorced. You'll encounter situations that are pathetic, some unbelievable.

Early in my first year of teaching, I was asked to accompany a special-education teacher, one of whose students had stolen ten dollars from another of her students. The two girls, Brenda and Iris, were about thirteen. The first house we visited was that of Iris. The small, three-room house had a metal roof and a dirt floor. A dog with a litter of pups and their feces was in the kitchen. The stench in the home was indescribable. While the special-education teacher talked to Iris and Iris's mother, it was impossible for me not to notice Iris's mother's boyfriend. His eyes never left Iris for a moment, so obvious was his lust. I shuddered to think what Iris would go through after we left.

The next visit was to a rural setting; we met the student and her mother at their mailbox at the end of their driveway. Brenda had taken the money from Iris, and the special-education teacher was trying to right the situation. During the discussion, Brenda's older brother kept interrupting. He claimed he had purchased rifle shells that afternoon. When his mother asked him where he got the money, he replied, "From your purse." His mother didn't seem to be upset in the least that he had lifted a few dollars without her permission.

After the boy left, the special-education teacher continued her conversation with Brenda. Soon Brenda's brother came out of the house and pointed a rifle at our little group. The special-education teacher never let the rifle deter her in the least. Finally, after what seemed like hours to me, the conversation ended and we got into the car. I was in shock, dismayed at what I had seen.

Since then, I've seen worse things that have happened to kids, but the impressions gained that day probably impacted upon me and my teaching more than I'd like to admit. I try to go beyond the extra mile for my students, knowing full well that my classroom may be the only haven in their dark world.

In *Breaking Ranks: Changing an American Institution* (National Association of Secondary Principals 1996), a recent report on high school reform, anonymity and apathy are cited as being the foremost reasons for problems in large high schools. "Students feel anonymous when they have no adult to turn to who knows them well and cares about their welfare. Students become apathetic when they must take required courses that have nothing to do with their goals and interests" (McPartland, Jordan, Legters, and Balfanz 1997, 14).

Once noted for violence in its hallways and a high dropout rate, Patterson High School in Baltimore, Maryland, has turned the situation around by personalizing relationships and focusing the curriculum. The high school adopted the Talent Development Model, under which the school reorganized into smaller, self-contained units for its two thousand students. Students find teachers to be supportive and approachable. Those students who have poor attendance or discipline problems attend the Twilight School, an alternative school with evening school hours within the same facility.

Volunteers

In 1997, a summit on volunteerism chaired by former Armed Services Chief of Staff Colin Powell was held in Philadelphia (Associated Press 27 April 1997). The summit was originally envisioned by George Romney, former governor of Michigan. Called the Presidents' Summit for America's Future, former presidents George Bush, Jimmy Carter, and Gerald Ford joined President Bill Clinton as summit leaders. A stated summit goal is that by the year 2000, volunteers will improve the lives of at least 2 million of America's 15 million poor children. Organizers of the summit hope that "each child will have a stable relationship with at least one adult, a safe place to go after school, adequate health care, and marketable skills."

The summit urged businesses to release workers on a regular basis to assist students in learning to read. Over two hundred businesses and volunteer organizations endorsed the summit.

In conjunction with the summit, President Bill Clinton unveiled a $2.75 billion program over a five-year period to pay for twenty-five thousand reading specialists and tutor coordinators. Over three million students in twenty thousand schools would participate in the reading program. The goal is to have a million American adults to volunteer to help teach children to read. Volunteers are urged to call (800) USA-LEARN to join in the effort which will enhance the literacy level of the next generation.

Studies show that children who cannot read well by the end of the third grade are more apt to become dropouts or be underachievers throughout the rest of their school career. According to the 1994 National Assessment of Educational Progress, 40 percent of fourth-graders scored below the basic level of reading skill (Lacey 1997).

■ Summary

Teachers must be aware of the social issues that impact today's children. The number of impoverished children, from the preschool level through high school, is increasing. Disadvantaged and at-risk students often face learning problems in school and social problems outside of it.

One of the greatest societal changes over the years has been the composition of the family. The basic family unit has changed dramatically from that depicted on television shows that showed the traditional two-parent family—"The Donna Reed Show," "Leave It to Beaver," and "Bill Cosby." Many students come from single-parent homes. In addition, the population of the United States as a whole is changing as percentages of minorities increase.

Ever-growing problems for children are those of substance abuse and violence. Physical attacks on teenagers at school are at an all-time high. Murders of teenagers continue to swell in numbers.

These and other problems are the social issues children encounter, often on a daily basis. As a teacher, you must understand such issues and pressures to help students cope with them.

■ Reflections

Certainly schools face more outside pressures due to societal problems now than ever before in history. Impoverished children, single-parent families, an increasing minority population, gender issues, substance abuse, and violence are potent problems facing today's teachers. Yet, these problems are not new ones. Select one of these issues and think about a classmate in elementary, middle, or high school who encountered this problem. Give the student a fictitious name and write about that individual and how he or she functioned inside and outside of the school setting. Then project what you could have done as a teacher to help that student with the knowledge you now possess.

■ Discussion Questions

1. What factors determine if a student is labeled as "at risk"?
2. How does poverty affect a child's learning?
3. What changes do you see in the diversity of the population?
4. Recall and relate to the class any acts of violence you saw as a student in middle school or high school.
5. Should students who engage in violent acts at school, such as threatening a teacher with bodily harm, be permanently suspended from that school?

■ For Further Reading

Adler, A. J. 1990. *Divorce recovery: Healing the hurt through self help and professional support.* New York: PIA Press.

American Association of University Women. 1993. *Hostile hallways: The AAUW Survey on sexual harassment in America's schools.* Washington, D.C.: American Association of University Women.

Ayers, W. 1997. I walk with delinquents. *Educational Leadership* 55 (2):48–51.

Bancroft, S. 1997. Becoming heroes: Teachers can help abused children. *Educational Leadership* 55 (2): 69–71.

Blankenhorn, D. 1995. *Fatherless America: Confronting our most urgent problem.* New York: Institute for American Values.

Bucci, J. A., and A. F. Reitzammer. 1992. Teachers make the critical difference in dropout prevention. *The Educational Forum* 57 (1): 63–70.

Curio, J. L., and P. F. First. 1993. *Violence in the schools: How to proactively prevent and defuse it.* Newbery Park, CA: Corwin Press.

Klonsky, S. 1995. To learn in peace: What schools are trying now. *City Schools* 1 (1): 18–25.

Sautter, R. C. 1995. Standing up to violence. *Phi Delta Kappan* 76 (5): K1–K12.

Stevens, L. J., and M. Price. 1992. Meeting the challenge of educating children at risk. *Phi Delta Kappan* 74 (1): 18–23.

Surfing the 'Net

Social Issues Websites

Attention Deficit Disorder, Eating Disorders, and Substance Abuse. Assistance with students who have attention deficit disorder, eating disorders, or substance abuse or who are dealing with grief is available from the PsychWeb at Georgia Southern University.

http://www.gason.edu/psychweb/psychweb.htm

Bilingual Students. The Southwest Educational Development Laboratory (SEDL) has an online newsletter, *SEDLetter,* that contains online articles pertaining to minority languages. The newsletter focuses on issues important to educators who teach immigrant children.

http://www.sedl.org/culture/welcome.html

Child Abuse Victims. The National Child Rights Alliance focuses on the problems of the victims of child abuse.

http://linux.hartford.edu/jerry/ncra.html

Children's Rights. The Children's Defense Fund "exists to provide a strong and effective voice for all the children of America, who cannot vote, lobby, or speak for themselves." (Edelman 1992, p. 4)

http://www.childrensdefense.org/

Gangs. The University of Pacific offers two online courses on gangs: "Online Guide to Gang Signs and Graffiti," and "Gangs: Prevention, Remediation, and Parent Conferencing."

http://www.courses.edu/gang_resources.html

9

The Administration and Governance of Schools

Primary Points

- The board of education oversees the administration of schools within a school district.

- School districts are defined geographical areas that are administered by a central administrative structure.

- The chief executive officer of a school district is the superintendent of schools.

- Various administrative assistants and building principals assist the superintendent in administering the schools and following policies.

- Teachers today have increased input into the governance of schools.

- State statutes and federal laws impact on school districts.

- Outside groups may impact on a school district's policies and procedures.

Chapter Inquiries

- Who actually controls the neighborhood school?

- How does a citizen get to serve on a local board of education?

- What are the responsibilities of a local board of education?

- What are the responsibilities of the superintendent of schools in a school district?

- What are the primary responsibilities of principals?

- What power lies with the state board of education?

- How do the state and federal courts impact school governance?

David Frazier Photo CD

Dr. Richard Fluck, a school superintendent for twenty-eight years, sees the administration of schools continuing to change. "In the past, school administrators were expected to be visible in the community. For a few years, the trend was away from that. School superintendents and even principals were invisible outside of the school day. Now the public expects them to attend concerts and ball games. Public relations is a big part of the school administrator's day.

"Community leaders want the people in charge of their schools to be familiar with the local culture and to support community activities. That's why many superintendents and principals are active in local service clubs such as Rotary or Lions Clubs."

Besides the increased public relations role, the management of schools has changed. "Since I first became a superintendent, the amount of paperwork has drastically increased. Frankly, it's ludicrous to have to fill out ten pages of information to get a $1,000 grant. The bureaucracy in the state and federal departments of education deny funding that should go to school districts. The more paperwork, the more bureaucrats are needed in the state capitol and Washington to sift through the reports.

"Teachers want an increased voice in school management. And many have excellent ideas. Unfortunately, some superintendents committee their teachers to death so they have no energy left with which to teach. Superintendents and principals need to judge what are realistic and accomplishable goals and work with their teachers to meet them. Trying to accomplish too much results in very little getting done other than creating animosity amongst your staff."

The administration of the school depends to a large extent upon local practices.

Frederick Mayer
A History of Educational Thought

In all states except Hawaii, which has one unified school district, schools are organized by specific territorial boundaries. In most states these are referred to as school districts, although in Indiana they are called school corporations.

State statutes specify how schools are to be governed in their respective states. Since schools are governed locally, the community and its citizens have great influence in the education of students. Thus, many educational decisions are influenced by politics at the local, state, and even federal level. This chapter describes how schools are administered and governed.

Local School Governance

Schools are administered from a central administrative structure that is overseen by a board of education. The chief administrative official is the superintendent of schools, who heads an administrative team. Teachers work with administrators to a lesser extent in the administration of schools. The following describes how school districts are administered and the role of the board of education.

School Districts

A **school district** is a governmental unit created under state statutes. It administers the school system within a defined territory, typically a local community. School districts have fundamentally the same purpose—to educate students who live within their boundaries. However, because school districts are governed locally, they vary tremendously. Each school district has its own **board of education,** which governs the school district, whose members are citizens from the community. Thus, a school board tends to reflect the values and concerns of the local community.

From a historic standpoint, today's school districts have evolved from the small, one-room schoolhouses of the eighteenth and nineteenth centuries. In 1930, there were over one hundred thirty thousand school districts in the United States. Today there are fewer than fifteen thousand. As horse-drawn school buses became motorized, one- and two-room schools began consolidating into larger schools. In the late 1950's, large school districts were thought to be more efficient and offer students a superior education. Thus, the number of small districts continued to diminish. The largest district is that of New York City, with nearly a million students; however, there exist thousands of small districts throughout the country with enrollments of less than one thousand students. A study in the mid-1980s found that school districts with slightly fewer than five thousand students had higher student achievement scores, were more cost effective, and had a lower dropout rate than those districts with enrollments of over five thousand students (North Carolina State Department of Public Instruction 1986).

The chief executive officer of a school district is the **superintendent of schools.** In large districts, this individual may have assistants with titles of assistant, associate, coordinator, director, or manager who have special administrative assignments in the school district.

The schools within a school district usually serve a neighborhood area. In some cases, schools have special curricula such as math and science or the arts. These schools are called **magnet schools** because they attract students from throughout the school district.

Boards of Education

The local board of education, more commonly referred to as the school board, is a governmental unit that was established by state law. The primary duty of the school board is to develop local policies for the governance and operation of a defined district's schools. The policies and practices of the local board of education must comply with state statutes to obtain state monies; likewise, federal guidelines must be met for receiving federal funds. The second primary duty of most school boards is to hire the superintendent.

Typically the board of education has distinct responsibilities. For instance, it is responsible for employing teachers, administrators, and staff and overseeing their services as well. It is accountable for the curriculum and programs of study for the students, in particular textbook adoption.

The board of education establishes attendance areas, the boundaries for each school within the district, thereby assigning students to the various schools within the district depending on where they live. Students who live within a school district must attend a school within that same district, unless they either have special educational needs that cannot be met by the district school or pay tuition to attend a private school or a public school in another school district. Students may be bused to another school within the district as part of a desegregation program.

The board of education is also responsible for the general welfare of students during the school day and for those students engaged in after-school activities sponsored by the school district. In addition, the board of education must see that the school facilities are maintained to meet federal and state safety codes as well as purchase building sites and oversee the construction of school buildings. A major responsibility is to obtain revenue to fund the building fund and the general revenue fund of the school district. Purchasing of materials and supplies, both maintenance and scholastic, is yet another responsibility.

Members of the board of education are typically citizens who live within the school district and who are elected to a set term of office. If a vacancy occurs, the remaining members may appoint a person to serve out the elected member's term of office. In some instances new members may be appointed by the original appointing authority, such as the mayor of a large city. The election of individuals to the board of education rather than appointment is designed to make the board members more accountable to the electorate.

Many states require that the board of education be comprised of individuals who are elected from areas within the school district itself as well as members elected at large, from the entire school district. For instance in a small district, four members may be from four distinct areas within the district, elected by the voters of their respective areas, and the remaining three members elected by all voters living in the school district. This ensures that representation is from throughout the school district and not just the most heavily populated area.

In small school districts, the members of the board of education may know the majority of their constituents through their encounters in the community, for example through business, church, or neighborhood associations. In large districts, the members tend to be business and religious leaders of the community.

Usually a local board of education has an average of seven members but may range from as few as three in small rural school districts to as many as nineteen for a large city school board. The number allowed to serve on the board of education is usually an odd number to avoid tie votes on issues.

In large urban cities such as Chicago, Los Angeles, and New York City, board of education members are political appointees. This provides stability and prevents the school board from being controlled by individuals who may not have the best interests of the schools and their students as their primary concern. Possible appointees are reviewed prior to their appointment by government officials, usually from the mayor's office. The term of office is usually four years. Appointment of board members ensures diverse representation. Competent appointees are sought to reflect the African American, Asian, Hispanic, and/or Native American student populations served by the school district.

In a recent national random survey of 5,271 school board members, the typical prototype of a board of education member was a white, married male between the ages of forty-one and fifty, a parent of one or more children in school, a homeowner, and someone who holds an advanced educational degree. By far, most board members are white (93.9 percent) with 3.2 percent African American, 1.5 percent Hispanic, and less than 1 percent either Native American or Asian. Males dominate school boards by 65.2 percent to 34.8 percent over females (Michener, Underwood, and Fortune 1993).

A board of education member holds tremendous responsibility. While the superintendent oversees the daily operation of the schools, the school board is ultimately the body responsible for the education of all students within the school district. The school board deals with the tax levy on local citizens' property. It determines when to hold a referendum to increase taxes as well as how much to increase the property tax levy for schools. If a referendum is passed by the voters, the property taxes local citizens must pay are increased. It is these taxes that provide the general funding as well as the building funds for the school district.

During 1991–92, education expenditures increased by 5.8 percent (Michener, Underwood, and Fortune 1993), largely due to salary and health care costs. Unfortunately, education funds from the states and the federal government decreased, in part due to the recession, during the same period. This resulted in fewer purchases of classroom and maintenance supplies, as well as textbooks. Fewer teachers and teacher aides were hired as replacements for those individuals who retired or left the district for other reasons. Library holdings were reduced in many schools. Some districts were forced to eliminate athletics completely, while others obtained partial funding for athletic programs from business and/or other community support.

School Administrators

The number of school administrators in a district and their responsibilities vary dramatically. Large school districts typically have a central office staff in addition to the principals and assistant principals of the school buildings. In small districts, school administrators may have dual roles as superintendent/principal or principal/teacher. Figure 1 shows the administrative hierarchy from the citizens of the state down to the students in the schools.

Superintendent of Schools

Every school district has a superintendent, who is the chief administrative officer of the school district. In very small districts, the superintendent may also serve as a building principal. In large districts, the superintendent may have several assistant superintendents and even associate superintendents to facilitate the administration of the school district.

The superintendent of schools is responsible for providing data and making recommendations to the board of education about any and all aspects of the operation of the school district. This includes budget, buildings, curriculum, personnel, and policies. The superintendent is responsible for both short-range and long-range planning and for making recommendations to the board of education regarding these areas. As part of this responsibility, the superintendent must oversee record keeping within the school district, including academic and fiscal reports mandated by the state.

While the board of education serves as a policy-making board, the superintendent assists and sometimes guides the board in creating policies for the district. For instance, a new state law that specifies no smoking in public buildings may require a school district to revise its smoking policy if smoking is presently permitted on school premises.

In every school district, the superintendent encounters community members or groups with special interests. Rural, suburban, and urban school districts are in some ways similar and in some ways unique. All have to deal with curricular and fiscal issues as well as social issues that impact the district. In rural districts, there is often pressure to keep small schools open and avoid consolidation with other districts to keep community spirit and pride alive. In suburban school districts, there is pressure for increased achievement scores and to provide after-school care for elementary-level students. Urban district superintendents are under pressure to hire minority teachers as models for their large minority populations as well as to provide vocational education. Opportunities for in-school child care for infants and toddlers of secondary students are also being stressed in many parts of the country.

Figure 1
Typical organizational structure of a state school system

Citizens of the State

State Constitution

State Legislature

Governor

State Courts

Attorney General

State Board of Education

State Regulary Commissions (i.e. State Fire Marshall)

State Superintendent of Schools

State Department of Education

Local School Districts (School Boards)

Local School District Superintendents

Local School Principals

Teachers

Students

Assistant Superintendents

Large school districts generally have assistant superintendents; extremely large school districts have associate superintendents. Typically, an assistant or associate superintendent is given one primary area of control under the supervision of the superintendent. For instance, a school district with five assistant superintendents may have one in charge of business affairs, a second in charge of curriculum, a third in charge of facilities and transportation, a fourth in charge of personnel, and a fifth in charge of special services.

An assistant superintendent in charge of business affairs is responsible for fiscal record keeping. This individual must oversee the district payroll as well as payments for purchases made by the district. If school district money is invested, this individual ensures that investments are made within the options provided by state statutes as well as ensures a competitive interest yield with as little risk as possible to

Superintendent or Board Member:
Can the Two Be One?

"Some school superintendents think and act as though they were a member of the board of education. Some board of education members think and act as though they were the superintendent. The difference in most school systems is that the members of the board of education are elected or appointed to set policy while the superintendent is employed by the board to implement that policy. At times individuals in each role, whether it be superintendent or board member, confuse their responsibilities and act as though they were in the other position—superintendents attempting to set policy and board members trying to run the school system on a day-to-day basis. This confusion of roles usually leads to disastrous consequences.

"However, what happens when one person serves in both capacities—superintendent *and* member of the board of education? Of course, this cannot legally occur within one school system because the superintendent cannot be one of his or her own employers. But what happens when an individual is a superintendent in one school system and is a member of the board of education in another school system? Does this unusual combination of roles lead to confusion and educational schizophrenia or does it improve both school systems and make the individual a better superintendent and board member because of the background brought to each position? The answer is a resounding *yes* to all of the above. It only depends at what time and on which day the question is posed.

"How, one may ask, do I know the answer to that question? Because I have had the wonderful experience of serving simultaneously as a superintendent *and* a member of a board of education. I happen to live in one city and work in another city which makes this dual role possible. However, there is one additional twist to the story. The community in which I reside is near the border of one midwestern state and I work in a community on the other side of the border of an adjacent state. Not only are the policies, procedures, rules and regulations of one school system different from the other, the two school systems operate under different state laws and

state boards of education. That situation accounts for the earlier statement concerning educational schizophrenia. There are times that I have to consciously think about which state I happen to be in at the moment and which school system is currently under discussion.

"Nevertheless, despite my occasional disorientation, the experience has been as exciting as one can imagine! Not only does one have the opportunity to make a difference in the education of children in one school system, but one can help to influence the quality of education provided to the children in another school system.

"I was in my fourth year as a superintendent when the opportunity to fill a vacancy on a board of education presented itself. The board position became vacant due to the illness of a board member and I was asked to fill the remainder of the term. I had some hesitation in accepting the appointment to the board since the responsibilities of being a superintendent or a member of a board of education can each be quite demanding and time consuming. I approached my employing board of education and asked if there was any concern if I became a member of a different board. After some discussion, my employing board was of the opinion that the experience would probably make me a better superintendent since I would also gain the perspective of being a board member. With that vote of confidence, I accepted the appointment to the board of education and, as of this writing, continue to serve nearly five years later.

"A number of benefits have accrued for each school system because of my dual role. There have been numerous instances in which I have had the opportunity to take an idea, practice, policy or program from one school system and transplant it in the other school system. At this point in my experience, I have found that one of the most important attributes that I have been able to transfer from one system to the other is a positive change in attitude.

(continued)

(continued)

"The attitude of boards, administrators, teachers and other employees is critical in the success of a school system. Poor attitudes contribute to mistrust, suspicion and even open hostility between the groups that must work together to provide an effective education for the students.

"When I became superintendent in my employing school district eight years ago, the union and the board were embroiled in a contract dispute over a misunderstanding as to what had actually been agreed to during collective bargaining. It took approximately eighteen months, federal mediation, the filing and counter-filing of unfair labor practice charges, numerous trips to the educational labor relations board, and a binding arbitration decree to resolve a twenty-four-month contract. As we concluded that contract it was time to begin negotiations on the ensuing contract. The next two-year contract took over thirteen months to resolve. This type of relationship between the board and the teachers' union could not go on. All of our energies were being consumed by negotiations and, in my opinion, the students suffered because of the deteriorating relationship between the board of education and the union.

"What was the answer to this dilemma? Both the board and the union would have to be amenable to breaking down that wall of distrust. That change finally occurred when the union and the board were willing to take a risk, a large risk, and trust each other by participating in unprecedented informal discussions that would precede formal contract negotiations for the upcoming school year. The risk was taken and if the process did not work, the consequences could have been disastrous!

"Fortunately, the process was successful and a three-year contract was settled in one formal negotiation session that lasted only one hour and twenty minutes. History had been made and it was a true turning point in the relationship between the board and the union. Never before had a contract in the district been settled without many months of formal negotiations. Following the conclusion of negotiations, the union invited the board to a local restaurant where board members and union officers toasted each other. What an unbe-

lievable scene! I never thought that those two groups, having been at extreme odds only a few months earlier, would ever congratulate and compliment each other.

"The three years since that momentous event has seen a vast improvement in the attitude of faculty members, administrators and members of the board. Voluntary participation in staff development activities has increased dramatically, concerns of the union and the board have been resolved informally rather than resorting to formal grievance procedures, teachers and administrators have focused on the improvement of instruction and the students have benefited from this positive change in attitude.

"However, there was an unanswered question. Was this process an aberration or was it truly a long-term change in the relationship between the board and the union? The answer came this last year when this process was utilized a second time. With even more contractual items to discuss than during the previous contract negotiations, a three-year contract was again agreed upon in only one formal negotiating session of less than four hours. It appears that there has been a true change in the previous adversarial relationship that had existed between the board and the union.

"Now for the 'other' school system, the system in which I have been a board member for nearly five years. Once again we find a school system that had been engaged in an extremely adversarial relationship. Besides normal contract disputes and grievances, the district experienced an exceptionally bitter strike by the teachers' union two years ago. The embers from that strike had continued to smolder since that time.

"Nevertheless, both before and after the strike, I had been attempting to plant the seeds of cooperation and trust in other members of the board, the union leadership, administrators and faculty members in the school system. The germination of those efforts has finally been seen in the past six months due to events that had been set in motion due to a serious financial crisis facing the school system.

"One of the cost-cutting measures that was implemented mid-year was an administrators' contractual buy-out/retirement package that would take effect on

(continued)

January 1 of that school year. The desired result of that measure was to entice various administrators to retire or to leave the system, eliminate their positions and reduce the cost of administration. An unexpected consequence of that offer was that the superintendent accepted the buy-out and we were faced with a search for a new superintendent at mid-year. The board appointed an interim superintendent for the remainder of the school year and the search for a new superintendent began.

"One of the fortunate events that occurred before we were aware of our financial crisis was that I was elected president of the board. Consequently, I could speak for the board at various meetings and functions with the added authority of being the board president. By speaking of the positive change the board desired in the school system, we were able to enlist the financial support of local industries in funding the services of a nationally recognized educational consulting firm to conduct a nation-wide search for a new superintendent.

"During the initial stages of the search, I made a suggestion to the other members of the board that could have easily been construed as being irrational and absurd. The suggestion was that we include a representative from industry and a representative from the teachers' union to participate in the interviews of the five finalists for the superintendency. That was a radical recommendation, especially since industry had regularly criticized the quality of education we offered in the system and the union and board were still experiencing the repercussions of the strike. I pointed out that these representatives would not have a vote in the selection of the superintendent (since that is the legal responsibility of the board), but rather that those individuals would have input into the process. The rationale for the representative from industry was that they were funding the search, industry was the largest taxpayer in the school system and that industry had a vested interest in the quality of students we prepared to work in their facilities. The rationale for participation by the union was that we had to make an initiative in developing a sense of trust with the teacher's union. If the union had a voice in the choice of the superintendent, they would have a stake in ensuring that the new superintendent would be successful.

"Fortunately, the board concurred with that suggestion. As the process unfolded, industry became very supportive of the superintendent selection process (and the candidate chosen for the position), the union has been convinced that the board is sincere in its attempt to build bridges to organized labor, and the community in general (which also had input into the selection of the superintendent) has seen a radical change in the way we conduct business in that school system. The board, members of industry, the teachers' union, administrators, faculty members and the community are all excited about the prospects for the future of our schools.

"As of this writing, this change is in its infancy but it holds promise of further fruition and significant improvement in this school system, not only in academics but also in human relationships. All this in a rather short time-frame of six months because the board was willing to take a risk to develop trust between various segments of their publics.

"There have been numerous other changes in the two systems due to the exchanging of exemplary programs and practices. While these changes have not been as singularly significant as the change in attitudes described herein, their cumulative effect should have a major impact on both school systems over time.

"It should be quite apparent that being a superintendent in one school system and a board member in another system can be quite gratifying personally while assisting in the improvement of conditions in both school systems. While it has been difficult at times to juggle schedules and responsibilities between the two school systems, the positive results have been worth the time and energy expended in the effort. I've been told I must be a masochist in attempting to make positive change in two school systems simultaneously. However, rather than being masochist, I would rather look upon my acceptance of this mantle of responsibility as taking the proverbial 'busman's holiday.' I enjoy working for the betterment of education and enjoy seeing major changes in what's good for kids, wherever they may live!"

Reprinted by permission of Dr. James Rajchel.

the school district's money. If the school district sells bonds for building a new school, this person must work with bankers, rating agencies such as Moody's and Standard and Poor's, and bond houses to get the lowest interest yield possible for the district.

The assistant superintendent in charge of curriculum oversees student instruction and principal and teacher training to ensure that these individuals keep current with new methodologies and theories. This superintendent works with faculty to organize the curriculum as well as updates and revises it as necessary. He or she may suggest inservice workshops for teachers or work with area universities to offer graduate courses in specific curriculum areas. All instructional materials, including textbooks, library materials, and computer software, fall under this superintendent's responsibility. Typically, the assistant superintendent in charge of curriculum chairs at least one or two textbook adoption committees each year in addition to serving on all other curriculum committees (e.g., art, foreign languages, language arts, math, music, physical education, science, and social studies).

The assistant superintendent in charge of facilities and transportation is responsible for keeping the schools well maintained and safe. For instance, this individual must check on the necessity of replacing a building's roof, resurfacing the driveways and parking lots, maintaining school buses, and ordering enough fluorescent lightbulbs and chalk for the classrooms. This person works with the architect on any remodeling or new building projects.

The assistant superintendent in charge of personnel conducts interviews with and makes recommendations to the superintendent for hiring candidates for administrative, teaching, and staff positions, with the exception of the superintendent and the assistant superintendents. Other responsibilities include maintaining personnel records, negotiating personnel contracts, and supervising and enforcing personnel policies and procedures. Personnel policies are developed by this individual and recommended to the superintendent.

The assistant superintendent in charge of special services is responsible for such programs as gifted education, special education, and health services, in addition to psychological and social work services. In addition, this person works closely with the assistant superintendent in charge of curriculum to ensure regular classroom teachers are aware of the educational needs of students with special needs in their classes.

Assistant superintendents as well as other central office administrators and, in small districts, building principals report directly to the superintendent, who in turn reports to the board of education.

Principals

The building **principal** is the school administrator students and their parents encounter most frequently. The principal is responsible for the operation of the local school. In small schools, the principal may also teach, either part-time or full time. In large schools, the principal may have one or two assistant or vice principals to assist with the various duties. Large middle schools, junior highs, and high schools may have department heads or team leaders in addition to a dean of students and a guidance director.

The principal's role differs by grade level of students (i.e., elementary, middle school, junior high, or high school), as well as by school size and by region. Specifically, the principal must execute the various aspects of the school's operations and instructional program. This includes carrying out the district's curricula, adhering to

John Markgraf, an elementary principal in a suburban school district, is a hard-working school administrator who wants the best for his students and his staff. He arrives early and stays late. He works hard to improve his school's curriculum by keeping abreast of current trends and findings as well as assisting his teachers in adopting new teaching strategies.

John's job includes supervising the curriculum and discipline, evaluating the teaching staff, and overseeing building maintenance. He completes reports for his district as well as those mandated by the state and federal governments. When his district decided to replace his school building with a new one, he worked to pass the referendum to increase the property tax levy. When the first referendum failed, he worked to pass the second one. John put in many extra hours through the process of designing, building, and moving into the new building.

Employing building personnel is an important part of John's administrative duties. When he hires a new teacher, John doesn't sleep well for a week afterwards because he questions whether he made the right choice from all the candidates he considered and the input from the teachers on the selection committee.

Meeting students' needs is the most important job an educator can do, according to John. He tries to get to know his students and set a community atmosphere in the elementary school. For instance, each spring the school has an international studies month. Each teacher selects a country for his or her class to study, and the entire curriculum is devoted to that particular country. One year the countries included Canada, China, Great Britain, Egypt, Italy, Japan, India, Mexico, the Netherlands, Germany, Norway, Spain, Portugal, Poland, and Greece. Parental volunteers contributed to the project. Students studied the culture, economics, history, and political system of their respective country. As a culminating activity, each class shared what it learned about its country with two other classes. Thus, kindergarteners taught second-graders about the traditions of the Netherlands and sixth-graders taught fifth-graders about Greece and Greek customs and history, including the Greek alphabet.

John finds his work to be both exciting and stimulating. His enthusiasm is carried over into his staff and students' work.

personnel policies, evaluating teachers and staff, supervising building maintenance, overseeing school discipline, and working with parent-teacher organizations. As you can see, a principal must be a good manager and organizer.

While each principal has a unique style, ideally principals tend to be very child-oriented, supportive, and humanistic, and they are likely to be viewed as nurturers of both students and faculty. As one teacher noted, her principal motivated the faculty "through her actions. If we are going to have a long day, we are sure *she* is going to have a long day" (Sagor 1992, 14). In addition, they interact well with others as well as being good managers. Some principals, while interested in their students, may be very businesslike and assertive. You may recall how your own principals differed in personality and in professional style.

In recent years, largely due to the school reform movement of the 1980s, principals have served less as authoritarian figures and more as instructional leaders of their schools. A principal must be familiar with curricula, teaching methodology, and evaluation and assessment, as well as know how to create positive learning environments.

The building principal must not only interact with the school's staff and parents of students, but with the students themselves. (© David Frazier)

Teachers now have greater input into the decision-making process as a result of increased shared governance of the school. This has made the role of the principal change in that he or she must have strong interpersonal and communication skills.

Teachers

Teachers are involved to a lesser extent in the administration of a school district. Their major responsibilities are following the district's adopted curricula, maintaining discipline, keeping daily attendance records, assessing and evaluating student performance, and discussing student progress with a child's parents.

Local School Authority

Many factors influence the governance of a local school district. The school is governed by the principal and the teachers and overseen by the superintendent of schools and the board of education. As we have discussed, the board of education is accountable to the state and federal governments as well as the local electorate.

Local boards of education evolved largely because it was thought that citizens within a community could best determine the type of education students needed to become productive citizens within that community. This practice dominated schools in the nineteenth century, when the United States was largely an agrarian culture. Large cities employed a superintendent of schools to handle administrative matters, while in small rural towns, the school board carried out administrative functions, including hiring personnel. Teaching principals were quite commonplace during this period.

In the mid-1800s, Colonel Francis Parker of the Quincy School permitted his teachers a great deal of freedom. While each morning he demonstrated a teaching method or improvisation, he did not require his teachers to adopt all of his ideas; they were encouraged to be creative in their teaching. The resultant Quincy System included a group of teachers with no two teaching styles exactly alike. The Quincy System was most unique and progressive. Most other schools had an authoritarian principal who rigorously enforced the district's curriculum and discipline policies.

By the early 1900s, the influx of people to the cities from rural America led to larger central administrative staffs for the schools. Small school districts often consolidated to form larger, more efficient districts with improved curricula. Members of the board of education were now a mix from at large as well as from distinct areas within the school district. They were also no longer required to run as a member of a political party as had been the case previously, when political parties each ran a slate of candidates for the school board. Under the old system, newly employed teachers were predominately from the political party that dominated the school board. By not requiring school board candidates to reveal their political ties, partisan politics was thereby removed from the operation of the schools.

In the 1950s and 1960s, another wave of school district consolidations occurred as a result of a report by James S. Conant (1959) of Harvard University. The Conant report indicated that high schools had to be large in order to provide a comprehensive and diverse curriculum. Conant's recommendations were quite explicit as to academic offerings, ability grouping of students, tracking of students, counseling, and vocational training. Many boards of education followed Conant's recommendations and as a result enormous high schools were built during the 1960s and 1970s. Conant's suggestions regarding ability grouping and tracking of students were later found to be discriminatory by the courts.

During the 1980s, the trend among school districts was to decentralize power. The education reform movement led by Ernest Boyer (1983), John Goodlad (1984), and Theodore Sizer (1985) was greatly responsible for this effort. Decisions that had largely been made at the central office headquarters were now made by administrators and teachers at the local school level. Some urban school districts such as Chicago even established local school councils for each school. These councils gave input on such things as the school's curriculum, discipline policies, and even the amount of money given to each teacher to purchase classroom supplies. The idea was to get more parents and community members involved in the school in their neighborhood.

Research indicates that teachers often teach as they themselves were taught. As Goodlad (1984, 238) writes, "Teachers are oriented to teaching particular things—the particular things that they were taught in school. Relating these particular things to some larger purpose is not something they think about very much or have been prepared to do." School reform in the 1980s resulted in several changes: teachers and administrators were encouraged to become continuous students of the new techniques and approaches, new management styles, and new governance strategies at the school level. This has resulted in more openness to change by educators at all levels.

Teacher Empowerment

The school reform movement of the 1980s also led to **teacher empowerment,** meaning that teachers had increased influence and choices over what and how they taught in the classroom. While teachers had been encouraged to serve on curriculum committees for many decades, the school reform movement gave their individual voices more consideration than in the past. Teachers were given more freedom to experiment within the confines of the curriculum.

Also as a result of the school reform movement, teachers now serve on building personnel committees along with the building principal, who generally chairs the committee when interviewing prospective teaching candidates. This gives teachers an influence in choosing their teaching colleagues.

Teacher empowerment has also led to greater and stronger ties to the community as teachers seek recognition for their students and school. Likewise, teacher empowerment has resulted in greater respect for teachers within the community.

Site-Based Management

Site-based management is a process that education has adopted from business. Rather than decisions about a school's operation being handed down from a central administration, known as top-down decision making, more and more decisions are now made at the school democratically. The principal meets with members of the teaching staff and serves as a facilitator rather than the sole decision maker for the building. This is referred to as bottom-up decision making. This democratic process allows input from the various faculty, a discussion of the issue, and, finally, a vote on the issue itself.

In site-based management, the principal usually chairs the management team, which consists of all of the teachers in a small school or six or seven teachers from a large school. Teachers may be either elected or serve as representatives from the various grade levels (in elementary schools) or departments (in secondary schools). A structured procedure is established for submitting issues to the committee, which may include curriculum planning within the building, discipline, or coordination of field trips and school assemblies.

According to Aronstein, Marlow, and Desilets (1990, 63), who themselves are involved as a principal and teachers in a site-based management style at their middle school, site-based management "may seem inefficient and cumbersome at first, but the faculty is in the driver's seat—it has the ability to control acceleration and the mechanism to brake. When its members feel more comfortable with their roles and responsibilities, the road to self-governance should become a lot smoother."

Site-based management has resulted in less tension and greater respect between administration and teachers. For instance, the faculty at Central-Hower High School in Akron, Ohio, a school that changed to site-based management, developed a "new understanding of and appreciation for the principal's role in the successful operation of the school" (Strauber, Stanley, and Wagenknecht 1990, 65).

Odden and Wohlstetter (1995, 32–33) found that for site-based management to work, the following resources had to be controlled at the school level:

- professional development and training opportunities to strengthen teaching, management, and problem-solving skills of teachers;
- adequate information to make informed decisions about student performance, parent and community satisfaction, and school resources;
- a reward system to recognize improved performance and to acknowledge the increased effort site-based management requires of participants.

Three large cities have adopted a variation of site-based management. In the 1970s, Detroit and New York City adopted regional boards of education, which operated on a smaller scale much like their large boards of education. However, after several years of political upheaval, Detroit later dropped its regional councils. In 1989, Chicago adopted a plan to improve the quality of education and increase achievement scores. This plan was approved as part of the Chicago School Reform Act, which was supported by the mayor. Each school has a local school council that serves as a miniature school board. Like the regular board of education, members are typically elected to serve specified terms. The local council is involved with budget oversight and curriculum for the school. The primary idea behind the local councils is to provide more involvement with and concern for students at the neighborhood level. Like Detroit and New York City, Chicago has encountered much political strife among dissident community groups.

Central Administration

School districts have a central administrative office from which the superintendent and any assistant or associate superintendents work. The central administration conducts the record keeping for the district, manages district finances, coordinates the curricula, oversees and employs personnel, and maintains the district's buildings. Figures 2 and 3 show typical administrative structures of large and small school districts.

Because of fiscal necessity and the need for unified negotiations, the central administration will always maintain power. Newly mandated laws and court decisions (Frymier 1984) regarding the education of students with disabilities, minorities, and illegal aliens, for example, necessitate the need for central administration.

State Authority

Each state is responsible for educating the students within its boundaries. Following the limits outlined in the U.S. Constitution and their respective state constitutions, state legislatures serve as education's primary policy makers. State boards of education, chief state school officials, and local boards of education all receive their powers from their state constitutions and legislation passed by the state legislatures.

State Board of Education

Each state has a **state board of education,** which serves both regulatory and advisory functions. In most states, the state board of education has the right to deny an individual teaching certification. In some states, teaching certification is denied to or revoked from individuals who have committed a felony. Other states have a separate certification board chaired by the state's chief school officer that deals with certification matters as well as approves programs of higher education to meet state certification.

Regardless of the board structure, little communication exists between states and the criminal justice systems to verify whether an individual seeking certification has been convicted of a serious crime in another state. For example, until recent years, it was possible for an individual convicted of child molestation and who had served a sentence for this crime to be employed as a teacher in another state. In December 1993, Congress passed the so-called Oprah Law, named for one of its supporters, Oprah Winfrey. The Oprah Law was designed to help states monitor the activity of child molesters and, in particular, to prevent them from gaining employment at preschools and day-care centers.

Figure 2 Lubbock Independent School District organizational chart (Reprinted by permission of the Lubbock Independent School District, Lubbock, Texas.)

Figure 3 Winterset Community School District organizational chart
(Reprinted by permission of the Winterset Community School District, Winterset, Iowa)

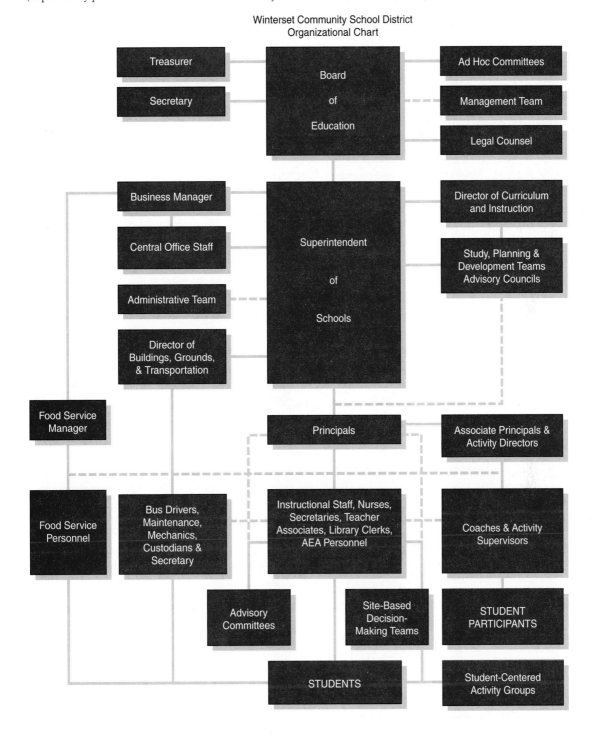

When a school district hires teachers or other employees, the school board and the district's administrators are responsible for selecting qualified individuals. Administrators want good teachers for their students. This is an extremely difficult and important task. Administrators carefully interview candidates and review transcripts and recommendations before they employ teachers. However, sometimes even a thorough review such as this is not enough.

While many states carefully monitor who receives teacher certification, states have failed to exchange background information regarding individuals with other states. In one case, a new teacher was hired by an Oregon school district to teach students who were mentally disabled. The new teacher had excellent written recommendations as well as a master's degree in education. Early during the fall semester of his second year in the school district, the teacher shot his principal and buried him in a nearby woods. He was distraught at having been caught stealing from lockers at a health club to which he belonged. His principal had met with the other teachers and was trying to help the teacher with his situation.

When the principal requested that the teacher meet with him after school, the teacher began plotting the principal's murder. He went to a wooded area and dug a shallow grave. A few days later, the teacher met with the principal in his office. After the meeting, the teacher asked the principal for a ride home, at which point the teacher invited the principal into his house under the pretense of showing him a book. When the principal walked into the garage to enter the house, the teacher locked him in. Then the teacher went into the house, grabbed a butcher knife, and returned to the garage and stabbed the principal to death. He then drove the body to the grave and buried it.

The next day, the teacher went to school and taught his classes. Several days later, he confessed to the slaying. He led police to the shallow grave. While the police were at the gravesite, the teacher attempted to steal the police car. He was shot by police and later died.

What the school administrators in Oregon did not know was that the teacher had a record of shoplifting in Illinois and had lost his teaching position as a result. He had also been accused of child molestation, but the charges had been dropped. When asked by those in Oregon if he had a criminal record, the teacher had said no. His criminal record was never uncovered until the principal's death. As a result of this case, states now share information regarding teachers' criminal backgrounds. Certainly this incident is highly out of the ordinary, but it does point out the heavy burden placed on school administrators and the local school board in employing personnel.

The state school boards also set standards for approving and accrediting schools in their respective states. Evaluation and assessment of data gathered from local school districts and reported at the state level are important roles of the state school boards.

State school boards serve an advisory function in that they weigh educational strengths and the needs of the state. They make recommendations to their governors and state legislatures regarding the educational needs of students within the state.

State Chief School Official

The chief school official for a state is commonly referred to as the state superintendent of public instruction or state commissioner of public instruction. This individual is generally a professional educator who serves as the overseer of the state department of education as well as chair of the state board of education and, if the state has a separate certification board, the state certification board for teachers and administrators.

In nearly two-thirds of the states, this individual is appointed by the state board of education. However, in a few states the office is filled by appointment by the governor, while in the remaining states, a statewide election is held for the position.

The duties and responsibilities as well as powers of the chief school official vary greatly among the states. Those who are appointed by the governor generally are expected to meet the political agenda for schooling set forth by that governor. On the other hand, those who are elected to office generally serve independently of the governor. In most cases, the chief school official advises the governor and the state legislature as to the needs and strengths of schools within the state.

State Department of Education

The **state department of education** is a primary state agency. Operating under the control of the state board of education, it is administered by the chief school official of the state. The main function is to collect and disseminate data regarding schools within the state. In addition, the department is responsible for accrediting schools at the elementary and secondary levels and teacher education programs at the higher education level; certifying teachers and administrators at the elementary and secondary levels; apportioning monies to school districts; regulating school transportation and safety; monitoring state and federal compliance with laws and regulations; conducting educational research; evaluating programs; issuing reports, including those on curriculum and evaluation; and improving education programs to meet the needs of impoverished, bilingual, and/or special needs students.

During the past two decades the state departments of education have considered a plethora of issues: asbestos removal from school buildings; accountability; state-mandated competency testing; mainstreaming and inclusion of special needs students; reduced fiscal resources for funding education; school funding reform; student rights; financial aid to educate an increasing minority population; increased student population for whom English is a second language; and collective bargaining for teachers and supportive staffs.

Because the state department of education deals in depth with a wide variety of issues, it is a large agency located in the capitol city of a state. Often branch offices with specific functions are located in two or three large cities throughout the state.

State Legislature

The state legislature serves as the education policy maker of the state. Advised by the state department of education and the chief school official, it can pass laws and mandates for local school districts. Among the responsibilities of the state legislature are the creation, operation, management, and maintenance of public school systems within the states.

State legislatures approve laws regarding compulsory attendance by students, certification and tenure rights of teachers, programs for research, taxation and distribution for schools, and building standards for schools. In recent years, many of the state legislatures have considered issues related to accountability, teacher competency, sex education, and the adoption of a state lottery for partial funding of education in the state. State legislatures have also passed tighter laws for screening new teachers to determine if they have committed a felony or sex-related crime.

Special-interest groups as well as individual citizens influence legislatures. However, large numbers of individuals and lobbying groups tend to be most persuasive in getting legislative members to listen to their opinions and beliefs. And even after legislation is passed, most governors have the right to veto bills.

State Courts

According to each respective state's constitution, the state courts may rule on education issues that affect schools in their states. A ruling by a state court is not binding in another state, however, often a state court ruling may set a precedent for other states.

A ruling by a state court may be appealed to and overturned by a federal district court or the U.S. Supreme Court. State courts have held that state legislatures as well as other governmental units (counties, municipalities, or school districts) can levy taxes to provide an education for students within the state.

Federal Authority

While we have considered local and state authority, federal authority plays an important role in school administration as well. Although education is not mentioned in the U.S. Constitution, the federal government provides significant fiscal resources to local schools. In addition, federal laws passed by Congress affect all public schools in all states. For instance, a school cannot deny admission to children who live within its legal boundaries.

Federal Education Agencies

The primary federal agency responsible for education is the **U.S. Department of Education,** which was initially created by President Andrew Johnson immediately following the Civil War in 1867. Over the years, the agency was shifted from one federal department to another, including at one time the Department of the Interior, and later the Federal Security Agency, and then the Department of Health, Education, and Welfare. Finally in 1979, President Jimmy Carter signed legislation that created the U.S. Department of Education. The new law included the appointment of a secretary of education with cabinet-level status. This meant that education received a higher level of recognition at the federal level than ever before.

The U.S. Department of Education compiles the education statistics for all of the states. In addition, it issues reports and funds research studies to improve the quality of education. Federal programs such as Head Start and Chapter I, among others, are operated out of the U.S. Department of Education.

U.S. Secretary of Education

The **U.S. Secretary of Education** may be a professional educator or a politician who is appointed by the president of the United States and confirmed by the U.S. Senate. The secretary of education takes part in cabinet meetings and engages in promoting programs to improve the quality of education throughout the United States, thereby making education highly visible across the country.

Federal Courts and the U.S. Supreme Court

The federal courts and the U.S. Supreme Court are often called upon to rule on appeals from lower courts that pertain to schools and students. Cases in recent years

Title IX has resulted in the addition of new school sports opportunities for women, including volleyball. (© James Shaffer)

have included the right of African American students and students with disabilities to equal educational opportunities, the illegality of sexual harassment of a student by fellow students, the right of children who are illegal aliens to receive a free education, and prayer in schools.

U.S. Congress

The U.S. Congress has passed several laws and bills to enhance student learning. For instance, the year after the successful launch of *Sputnik* in 1957, Congress passed the National Defense Education Act to help fund the college education of individuals who wanted to become teachers. The National Science Foundation, created by Congress in 1950, stressed the need for basic research in the sciences. In 1954, the Cooperative Research Program passed by Congress allowed universities and state education agencies to work with the public schools in the teaching of science in the elementary and secondary levels.

More recently, the passage of Title IX of the Educational Amendment Act by Congress in 1972 ensured that female students would have the same opportunities to participate in sports as their male counterparts. Schools that receive federal funds and that deny female students access to school-sponsored athletic programs are breaking the law. Goals 2000 will impact all states and public schools with its increased emphasis on literacy and technology as well as its nonviolence measure.

Point /Counterpoint

Should Schools Be Centrally Governed by the Federal Government?

Point: Schools should be centrally governed by the federal government.

If all schools were governed by the federal government, an equal amount of money would be spent for every child. Thus, schools located in affluent suburban areas would not spend three times the amount per student than their counterparts in rural or inner-city areas. All children would have equal access to the same textbooks, library materials, and computer technology.

In addition, standards would be the same throughout the nation for all students at the same grade level. Standards for teachers and school administrators would also be uniform. At any one time, a school district would know how its students are performing in comparison with those in the rest of the country.

Counterpoint: Schools should be locally controlled, not centrally controlled from Washington, D.C.

Each school district and its population is unique. Local control allows a community to influence what is taught and what values are shared. For instance, a vocational agriculture program with a curriculum that includes studying the nutritional content of vegetables is important in the Imperial Valley of California, whereas a similar curriculum in Idaho might emphasize learning the nutritional content of potatoes and in Ohio, that of corn and soybeans. In the areas of history and economics, each state would emphasize its own historical and economical importance to the nation.

Centralized control of schools as directed from Washington, D.C. would result in an education system in which every student must be on the same page on the same day. This does not provide for individual differences among either students or teachers.

Lastly, giving the power to the federal government to dictate how schools are administered would create one more huge bureaucracy that yields inefficiency and waste. Improved student achievement would not be guaranteed under such centralized management.

Other Factors Influencing the Control of American Education

In addition to the many influences on the administration and governance of schools in the United States already discussed, it is worthy to mention other factors, including professional organizations and business. Politics at the local, state, and national levels impact education.

Professional Organizations

Teachers' unions such as the American Federation of Teachers (AFT) and the National Education Association (NEA) are national organizations with state and local affiliates. Groups such as these can be powerful. For instance, both the AFT and the NEA were instrumental in establishing the U.S. Department of Education, whose

One of the great aspects of schooling is the sharing of ideas by educators. School administrators often talk on the phone, engage in discussion at meetings, or chat on the Internet about their successes and their problems. The American Association of School Administrators is one of the largest professional education organizations in the United States. Its annual conference is so large that only a handful of cities have sufficient convention center size and hotel space to host it.

Increased demands are being placed on schools administrators. New instructional standards are being developed, businesses are insisting on better-educated workers, and parents are more vocal with their concerns. Neighboring school districts are becoming more competitive. What used to be friendly athletic rivalries have now become academic challenges. Some districts even have recruiting efforts for "stealing" outstanding teachers from neighboring school districts. If vouchers become commonplace, school districts will devise ways to lure students, particularly top students, to their schools.

For the new teacher, all of this means you must give some thought to which teaching position you choose to accept. Schools that pressure principals to get high standardized test scores from their students may put undo pressure on teachers and students. One principal informed an experienced fourth-grade teacher that since her students had scored at the ninety-first percentile last year on the reading test, her students were expected to score at the ninety-fourth percentile for the coming year. The teacher found a teaching position elsewhere at less pay. The stress wasn't worth the extra income.

secretary serves at the same level of authority and influence as the secretaries of defense and labor.

Business

During the past fifteen years, many of the cries for educational reform have come from business leaders. They believe that schools can be better managed and more efficiently operated. In addition, they demand that students be more proficient and knowledgeable upon graduation than are current graduates.

In numerous school districts, business leaders are working with school administrators, teachers, and parents to improve the quality of education for students. A good example is the Omaha 2000 project, in which members of the Omaha Chamber of Commerce contribute their time and expertise to assist the Omaha public schools and parent groups in improving the learning conditions for students by getting members of the local community involved in education (Hunt 1993).

Community Interest Groups

Every community has interest groups, either formal or informal. These include ministerial associations, parent coalitions that impact curriculum and library acquisition decisions, PTA/PTO, chambers of commerce, Kiwanis clubs, Lions clubs, and Rotary clubs. In many communities, the League of Women Voters sponsors a forum for school board candidates prior to school board elections.

■ Summary

Schools are decentralized and governed locally. Boards of education set policies to ensure that the educational needs and welfare of students are considered. The superintendent of schools follows the laws and guidelines set forth by the board of education, the state legislature, Congress, and the rulings of state and federal courts.

Today, largely due to school reform efforts, school administration differs greatly from that of a decade ago. Principals devote the majority of their time to working with instructional programs. Teachers have a greater voice in curriculum matters and school governance in general. Large school districts may even have local school councils to provide input from the school's immediate neighborhood.

The federal and state government influences local education through legislation and program funding. Court decisions at both the state and federal levels have changed education; however, only federal court rulings affect all schools.

■ Reflections

Serving as a member of a board of education can be a thankless task. Only in a few states do school board members even receive compensation for their efforts, and in those cases the sum is negligible. Undoubtedly, decisions by a board of education can be very unpopular with citizens in a school district.

Consider three reasons why a person should serve as member of a school board. Why would a person be willing to go through an election for a position for which he or she will not receive any monetary reward?

In what constructive ways could you, as a school board member, improve education for children in your area? Would you be willing to be openly criticized in public by citizens and perhaps even in the newspaper and on local television?

■ Discussion Questions

1. Compare and contrast the responsibilities of the superintendent of schools and principals.
2. What recent court decisions have affected schools?
3. Why do states need a state board of education?
4. How has the U.S. Department of Education changed schooling?

■ For Further Reading

Aronstein, L. W., M. Marlow, and B. Desilets, 1990. Detours on the road to site-based management. *Educational Leadership* 47 (7):61–63.

Goldman, E. 1998. The significance of leadership style. *Educational Leadership* 55(7):20–22.

Michener, O. H., K. E. Underwood, and J.C. Fortune, 1993. Incision decisions. *The American School Board Journal* 180 (1):28–33.

Natale, J. A. 1993. Kooks, crooks, and kids. *The American School Board Journal* 180 (1):18–23.

Odden, E. R., and P. Wohlstetter. 1995. Making school-based management work. *Educational Leadership* 52 (5):32–36.

Shen, J. 1998. Do teachers feel empowered? *Educational Leadership* 55(7):35–36.

■ Surfing the 'Net

American Association of School Administrators
http://www.aasa.org
American Educational Research Association
http://www.tikkun.as.asu.edu.aera/home/html

Council of Chief State School Officers
http://www.ccsso.org
National School Boards Association
http://www.nsba.org

10

School Funding

Primary Points

- Schools receive local, state, and federal funding.

- The primary source of revenue for schools is local property taxes.

- Each school district has a budget that consists of three parts: capital outlay, debt service, and current expense.

- States provide financial support to school districts in an attempt to provide equal educational opportunities for all students.

- State funding usually comes from income and sales taxes, although increasingly states are using lottery funds to finance education.

- There are three types of state aid to school districts: general, categorical, and incentive.

- Federal funding to school districts is in the form of categorical aid.

Chapter Inquiries

- How are property taxes determined?

- Why do school districts with equal property tax rates have different levels of total property tax funds?

- How does a school district create a budget?

- How do states fund education?

- What are progressive and regressive taxes?

- In what ways does the federal government assist in the funding of school programs?

© James Shaffer

A veteran teacher, Bob Abramson is like many teachers, feeling underpaid and not respected. "I wonder about the future of school funding. Property taxes can't continue to rise. Certainly it is extremely difficult to pass a referendum to build a new school, yet our facilities are deplorable. And teaching salaries aren't the greatest. I read last week where new employees at Cisco Systems earn $70,000 a year plus another $125,000 in stock options. A new teacher won't make that kind of money in any one year of teaching.

"The state legislature talks about a new funding model. My friends in other states say that their legislatures are discussing school funding like we are. There doesn't seem to be a solution that politicians and educators agree upon. Nor one that the public will go along with."

School funding raises important issues. Inadequate funding results in poorly educated students. Without equitable funding for all schools, educational opportunities are denied to students, particularly those in impoverished communities. The goal of public education is to provide an appropriate and quality education for all students. This education is paid for by taxation at the local, state, and federal levels. However, the amount spent to educate each child varies widely from state to state. In 1993–94, Alaska spent $8,882 per student, with New York and New Jersey close behind. On the low end of expenditures was Utah, which spent $3,439 per student, with Idaho, Mississippi, and Alabama following (U.S. Department of Education 1996).

In 1970, the United States spent an average of $970 per student on education. By 1995–96, that figure had increased to $5,738 (U.S. Department of Education 1996). However, the difference is attributed to the high costs associated with special education. The expenditures for "regular" students have remained virtually constant in recent years.

In 1996, the United States spent more money to educate each elementary and secondary student of any nation, $5,738 per pupil (U.S. Department of Education 1996). Still, there exists a question of fair taxation of citizens and equitable education for all students. Figure 1 shows the amount of monies expended by schools throughout the United States between 1960 and 1996.

> *There is no magical, painless way to fund our schools more adequately. . . . We must do more to equalize school revenues by raising funds at the state level and then distributing them at the local level according to educational need.*
>
> **Terrell H. Bell**
> *Parting Words of the 13th Man*

Local Funding

While most states provide the majority of school funding, **property tax** is a substantial source of revenue at the local level for the support of local schools. Property tax is considered to be a proportionate tax in that the taxes reflect the ability to pay. Thus, if an individual owns a home with a market value of $150,000, while a friend's home in the same community is valued at $65,000, the first individual must pay higher property taxes. **Regressive taxes** such as sales tax and use tax are considered to penalize low-income groups more than middle- and high-income groups. However, sales taxes in many states are excluded from essential items such as unprepared food purchased at grocery stores and prescription drugs. Taxes on cigarettes and alcohol are considered to be use tax, since no one has an essential need to consume these items.

Figure 1 Monies expended by schools throughout the United States, 1960–95.

Source: U.S. Department of Education, National Center for Education Statistics, *Statistics of State School Systems; Statistics of Public Elementary and Secondary School Systems: Revenues and Expenditures for Public Elementary and Secondary Education;* and Common Core of Data Surveys.

FUNKY WINKERBEAN

Reprinted with special permission of North America Syndicate.

Real estate—homes, apartment buildings, businesses, industries, and farms—and personal property—cars, motorcycles, trucks, furniture, machinery, livestock, and stocks and bonds—are taxed based on the value of the property. In some states, the school district establishes a tax rate to which real estate and personal property are levied. If a school board decides the district needs increased funds, for instance to build a new elementary school or high school, then the district must increase its tax levy rate. If the increased rate is higher than that allowed by law in that state, the new tax levy must be voted on in a referendum during a regularly held public election with registered voters living within the school district. Since the majority of voters are adults who do not have children in school, it is very difficult to convince them to raise their taxes to support education.

The money a school district receives from tax revenues is spent on teacher salaries, building maintenance, teaching materials, and other educational costs. Money left over from one year can be carried over to another year. If a school district doesn't have sufficient funds, it may go into debt and borrow money to pay its expenses. Although this practice is discouraged, many school districts are forced either to take out loans or to reduce costs, including cutting the number of teachers in the district.

Throughout the U.S. and Canada, school districts are struggling with overcrowding in sometimes very old and outdated facilities. The costs of building a new school run into the millions. In 1997, the Naperville, Illinois, School District opened a new high school designed for three thousand students at a total cost of $62 million dollars. The building contains nine specialized computer labs, eight home economic kitchens, five soundproof music studios, two gyms, and a weight room. All classrooms contain computers that are linked to the Internet. According to Principal Kathryn Birkett, "Some things here may look to be above and beyond what's necessary, but this is where the technology is. The kids need to have access to computers—that's where they're doing their work and their research" (Associated Press 25 August 1997).

The 438,700 square foot, red brick building initially registered nine hundred students for the first year. However, due to rapid growth in the community, within five years the school is expected to be at or near capacity. For the past four years, at least one new elementary school, and usually two, has been built in the Naperville area.

Property Tax as Primary Source of Revenue

Property tax requires that the value of the property be established, or assessed. In many areas, the county employs local citizens to evaluate the value of property. In some cases, these assessors are temporary employees with no training in estimating the value of property. Thus, there can be discrepancies between the true value of a piece of property and its assessed value, which may be substantially higher or lower.

When an assessor appraises property, neighboring property is used as a guideline to determine value. The size of the home, number of rooms, type of structure (frame, brick, or stone), type of foundation (basement, crawl space, or concrete slab), garage (one-, two-, or three-car), and even the landscaping are all considered in an appraisement. Extras such as a swimming pool, tennis court, or greenhouse all increase the value of a property.

Industries and farms are likewise assessed. The size and number of buildings all contribute to the assessed value of a property. Typically, reassessment of all properties occurs every four years. Reassessment is done to keep current with the actual value of the property. In recent years, property on the East and West Coasts has depreciated in value. Reassessment of a house valued at $200,000 in 1989 to only $150,000 today can result in a sizable reduction in the owner's property tax bill. Likewise, in many rural areas that adjoin suburbs, old farmhouses that were assessed at $75,000 in 1990 but have been renovated and relandscaped and are now part of a new housing area may be worth $150,000 to $200,000.

Most states tax farmland at much lower rates than other commercially owned property. Because of this, some rural school districts receive far less tax monies than neighboring districts with an industry, such as a factory or an electrical generating power plant. Some property is exempt from property tax. This includes municipal, state, and federally owned government property. Churches are also exempt from property tax.

There are major drawbacks to the system of determining property tax. Whenever a homeowner makes improvements to a home, such as vinyl siding, a room addition, or a new garage, the tax on the property increases. However, if a homeowner allows a house to deteriorate, the property tax generally does not increase and may be reduced. Also, high property taxes can discourage new businesses and industries from locating in a particular area.

According to Bell (1988, 407),
An overreliance on property taxes has been a major obstacle to increasing school funding in the United States for several reasons. Growing numbers of older Americans, single adults, and childless couples make local-option tax levies difficult to pass. Real property is not a good measure of the ability to pay taxes; most taxpayers meet their tax bills from income. Farmers and others who operate capital-intensive businesses bear an unfair share of the cost of schooling. Moreover, the tax base is often largely determined by the assessed valuation of property located in property-rich school systems that serve comparably few students.

Property is not assessed at its actual market value but rather a percentage of its actual dollar value. The percentage varies from county to county, and state to state, but generally it runs about one-third to two-thirds of the true value of the property.

A school's total assessed valuation is the total value of the property within its boundaries. The assessed valuation per student in a school district is determined by dividing the total assessed valuation by the average number of students attending school in the district during the school year. If a school district has 2,500 students who attend school, and the total *assessed* valuation is $100 million, then that school district has an assessed valuation per pupil of $50,000. If the property tax rate for the school district was $5 per $100 of assessed valuation, the school district would receive $5 million for its budget from local sources. This would enable the district to spend $2,000 per student.

If a neighboring school district also had 2,500 students and the same tax rate of $5 per $100 of assessed valuation, but the total assessed valuation was $150 million, that district would receive $7.5 million in property taxes. This would be $3,000 per student, or $1,000 per student more than the neighboring school district.

Obviously, there can be tremendous differences among school districts' assessed valuations. Those school districts with industrial and office complexes, a shopping mall, or expensive homes have much more financial resources than do those districts that rely primarily on property taxes from small businesses and modestly valued homes. When considering that the latter school district is more likely to have a greater student population, the differences become even more extreme.

Court Rulings Regarding Property Tax and School Funding

In 1971, the lawsuit *Serrano v. Priest*, 487 P.2d 1241, was filed with the California Supreme Court and raised the issue of funding schools based on property taxes. The Baldwin Park school district was spending about half the amount per student as its

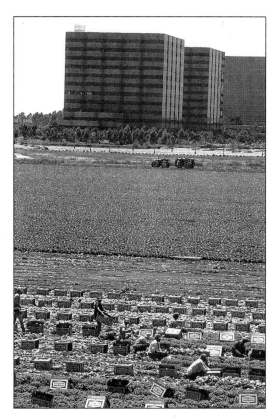

Farmland is taxed at a lower property tax rate than are commercial buildings. (© Mark Richards/PhotoEdit)

Lack of sufficient funding for schools can lead to overcrowded classrooms or lack of facilities. Here students are crowded together to view a videotape. (© Robert Daemmrich/PhotoEdit)

neighboring school district, Beverly Hills. However, property owners in the Baldwin Park school district were taxed at a rate double that of those property owners in Beverly Hills. This was because Baldwin Park was an area of low property values, while Beverly Hills had extremely high property values—fourteen times that of Baldwin Park. The California Supreme Court ruled that California's system of financing schools was unconstitutional because taxpayers were not treated equitably and students were not provided equal educational opportunities.

By 1972, other state supreme courts—Arizona, Minnesota, New Jersey, Texas, and Wyoming—made similar rulings regarding the financing of schools within their respective states. In 1973, a Texas case reached the U.S. Supreme Court. *San Antonio Independent School District v. Rodriguez* had aspects similar to *Serrano v. Priest.* One Texas school district had a far greater assessed valuation and lower tax rate than did the other. In a five-to-four decision, the Supreme Court held that local property tax was a justifiable basis for financing schools and was not in violation of the U.S. Constitution. The Court noted that a correlation between the quality of education and the amount of monies spent on education had not been proven. In addition, the poorest students were not all located in the most poorly funded school districts. The Supreme Court also stated that states should initiate taxation reform; however, little reform has occurred. In 1989, the Texas Supreme Court ruled that its state's procedures for financing its schools were unconstitutional. Several other states have made similar rulings or have cases pending.

In 1990, Oregon passed Ballot Measure 5, which reduced property taxes for schools and replaced them with state funds. The result was increased funding from the state at the expense of loss of funding to state colleges and universities.

For instance, elementary and secondary teacher education programs were dropped at both the University of Oregon and Oregon State University. By 1993–94, state funding for K–12 education began to decline. According to Smith (1995, 461), "Our unwillingness to provide for the educational needs of children will lead to massive problems of law, order, peace, and justice—and we will pay more to correct them."

In 1993, the Texas legislature passed a bill that forced the 109 property-rich school districts in the state to share their financial resources with poorer districts. Students with mental and physical disabilities receive extra allotments due to the increased costs of educating them, and all other students are treated equally under this system. Each wealthy school district has a number of choices: they can merge tax bases with one or more poorer school districts; they can send money to the state to be reallocated to poorer districts; they can contract to educate students in other districts; they can consolidate with one or more poorer districts; or they can redefine school district boundaries to move taxable property into a poorer school district and thereby increase its tax base.

In 1993, the Michigan legislature passed a bill eliminating property taxes as a source of funding for schools, but it did not pass a bill to indicate how schools would be funded. In 1994, the people of Michigan voted to increase state sales taxes to pay for financing schools. But the issue of how schools are to be financed still remains to be determined for most states.

In yet another court decision, in 1994, the U.S. Supreme Court ruled that New Jersey's funding of schools through property taxation was unconstitutional and ordered the state to eliminate disparities between rich and poor school districts by 1997 (N.J. school funding unconstitutional 1994). Obviously, school funding sources will change as states try to better equalize educational opportunities. But as Kowalski (1995, 488) points out, "State funding formulas for public education are highly political matters. Elected officials at the state level have been extremely reluctant to shift the financial burden of improving school facilities to their governmental agencies, knowing that this move would be both costly and politically precarious."

Local School Budget

Each state has specific guidelines for creating a school district's budget. The local school district determines its financial needs by anticipating both income—largely from property taxes and state and federal funding—and expenses—faculty and staff salaries, utilities, paper products, chalk, library books, gym equipment, etc.

Typically the school superintendent and his or her assistants develop the budget. They consider the number of teachers and staff members to be employed; the salary increases they will receive; the expense of health insurance for employees; the cost of new textbooks; the cost of utilities; the funding of new equipment such as computers, fax machines, and CD-ROMS; building maintenance expenses such as painting the classrooms or replacing the roof on a school or paving tennis courts; transportation costs such as a new bus with a wheelchair lift; and many other expenses. In most states, before a school district can adopt a budget, a formal public hearing, announced in the local newspaper, must be held.

The budget is divided into three areas: capital outlay, debt service, and current expenses. Capital outlay, also referred to as the building fund, is just that—major expenditures for buildings, including schools and administrative centers, land, and equipment. Debt service is the repayment of borrowed money and interest. This may be for a new school, gym, or building addition. Current expenses is often called the general or education fund. This fund, the largest of the three, meets the daily needs

California and Proposition 13

In 1978, the voters of California passed Proposition 13, which reduced and capped property taxes. In effect, the law made it almost impossible to raise property taxes in the state. Only if a piece of property is sold to a new owner can property taxes be raised.

In 1993, California spent $4,600 per pupil in grades K–12 (Reeves 1994) compared with a national average of $5,555 (U.S. Department of Education 1993). Prior to Proposition 13, California was consistently among the top five states in spending per pupil. After Proposition 13, it fell to the bottom ten, spending half as much as such states as New York and New Jersey. Before Proposition 13, 55 percent of elementary and secondary school funding in California was raised locally, primarily through property taxes. Since then less than one-third of the school funding comes from local sources, with over 60 percent coming from the state government and another 7 percent from federal funds (Reeves 1994).

Budget cuts that took effect as a result of Proposition 13 have impacted the schools in several ways. Specialized teacher positions in areas such as art, music, and physical education have been cut at many elementary schools, thereby necessitating that elementary teachers who are not as knowledgeable in these areas teach these special subjects. Field trips by bus are a rarity, as are art supplies and photocopying paper. Half of the school libraries have been closed because the school districts cannot afford to pay librarians. Many of the school libraries that were kept open are staffed by volunteers from the community. In many communities, students cannot go to public libraries because Proposition 13 cut funding for those as well.

Probably the biggest impact of Proposition 13 was class size. The typical classroom in California increased to twenty-nine students, the second largest class size in the United States (Reeves 1994). Interestingly enough, the salaries of teachers have not been greatly impacted, and California's teachers remain among the highest paid in the country. The reasons for this are that the California Teachers Association is one of the most powerful political groups in the state and that several teachers ran and were elected to school board positions. The state then led the way in reducing class size, especially for primary grades.

of the school district, including the salaries and fringe benefits of teachers, school administrators, and other employees such as secretaries and maintenance personnel. The general fund is usually 75 percent or more of a school district's budget.

Once the budget is determined and the total amount to be funded tallied, the tax rate is set. Each state sets a minimum tax rate to cover the expenses of the school districts within it. To increase the tax rate above the minimum rate, most states require that a referendum be placed on the ballot of a general election so that voters can approve it.

Unfortunately, a school district may have a tax rate at the highest possible level but still not have the same funds available for its students as another district that taxes at a much lower level. This is because the first district has low property values while the latter has high property values. It is discrepancies such as these that make many educators call for a restructuring of school funding.

State Funding

States provide financial support to school districts largely in an attempt to provide equal educational opportunities for all students. This funding comes from tax revenue from four primary sources: sales and gross receipts taxes, income taxes, licenses, and other sources. With the exception of Minnesota, which doesn't charge sales tax on clothing, sales taxes are collected on the purchase of cars, trucks, clothing, hardware, toys, jewelry, etc. Gross receipt taxes are collected on gasoline, diesel fuel, alcoholic beverages, insurance, and amusements, such as video arcade games. Income taxes are of two forms, individual and corporate. License fees include those for driver's licenses, car and truck license plates, corporations, certain occupations, such as teacher certification renewal and those in the dental, legal, and medical professions as well as barbers and hair stylists, and hunting and fishing licenses. Other tax sources include inheritance taxes and gift taxes. Each state typically has some usual tax in this area. For instance, states with large coal deposits, such as Kentucky, Illinois, Indiana, Montana, and West Virginia, have fees for mining coal. In Illinois, a portion of each traffic violation citation issued by state troopers is given to school districts to support the state-mandated driver's education program. For every speeding ticket, $10 is turned over to fund driver's education in the state.

In Illinois and Florida, all state lottery funds are devoted to their respective state education funds. However, the amounts are not in addition to the already established funds for education. The lottery funds are subtracted from the education fund, and that amount is then placed in the respective state's general revenue fund.

For those forty-six states that have sales taxes, they are collected everyday throughout the year on everything from candy bars and disposable diapers to furniture and cars. Businesses are required to collect the taxes and turn them over to the state. As we saw earlier, sales taxes are *regressive* because lower-income people must pay disproportionally. For instance, the Newton family income is $25,000 and the Warren family income is $50,000 a year. Both families need a new refrigerator, which costs $500. They live in a state that charges 5 percent sales tax, so both families will have to pay $25 in sales tax. Since the Warren family makes substantially more money each year, the $25 isn't a major concern. However, for the Newton family, earning only $25,000 a year, $25 is a substantial sum.

State income taxes are withheld from employees' paychecks by employers and turned over to the state. Between January 1 and April 15 of each year, taxpayers must report their actual income for the previous year to the state and federal internal revenue departments. If not enough money was withheld during the previous year, and there aren't enough deductions to make up the difference, the taxpayer then owes the state and federal governments income taxes. If there was too much money withheld for income taxes, then the taxpayer gets a refund.

Income taxes are *progressive* taxes. That is, the amount of tax owed increases with the ability of the taxpayer to pay. For instance, the Newtons and the Warrens live in the same state, which has a 4 percent income tax rate. The state allows a deduction for each family member of $2,500. There are four members of the Newton family. Likewise, the Warrens have four people in their family. Thus, both families are allowed to deduct $10,000 from their total income. The Newtons' would pay $600 in state income taxes ([$25,000–$10,000] × .04) while the Warrens would pay $1,600 ([$50,000–$10,000] × .04), or $1,000 more.

State Aid to Local School Districts

The tax revenue collected by the state from sales and gross receipts taxes, income taxes, license fees, and other taxes is distributed to the school districts throughout the state. However, the amount per student that is allocated to the school districts varies. One consideration for the allocation is the assessed property valuation of the

You can pay some now...

or a lot later...

(SCRAWLS reprinted by permission of NEA, Inc.)

school district. Those school districts that have large student populations but low assessed valuations are given more money in order to make the educational opportunities as equal as possible for all the students in the state.

There are three types of state aid: general, categorical, and incentive. General state aid can be spent by the school district for any area it deems appropriate. Categorical state aid must be spent solely for specific purposes as outlined by the state. Incentive aid is targeted for the creation of a new program within a school district, after which the school district itself picks up the funding for it.

The idea behind general state aid is that the state, not the federal government, is responsible for providing an education for its students. Educational opportunity should be equal for all students within the state; however, in reality this is impossible to achieve. States have developed a foundation program designed to allocate funds to school districts in order to provide students with a basic education. A foundation program is based on what funding each school district is expected, on the average, to provide for the education of its students. Every school district must provide some minimal funding for its budget. The foundation program adjusts the amount of tax funds to be returned to the school district. Impoverished school districts with low assessed valuations and that have lower-paid workers living within their boundaries receive a larger proportion of general state aid than do affluent school districts with high assessed valuation and that have taxpayers who earn six-figure salaries. An average school district might receive $3 or $4 for every $1 that an affluent school district might receive. Thus, a sliding scale inversely returns money to a school district based on the number of students and the assessed valuation of the school district.

Categorical aid is usually targeted to encourage or improve specific education programs such as programs for students with mental and physical disabilities; disadvantaged preschoolers; transportation, including the purchase of buses; vocational education, including agriculture and building trades programs; driver education; and others. Many states require school districts to match categorical aid funds. Thus, a **categorical grant** of $100,000 must be matched by $100,000 set aside for the program by the school district. In many instances, the categorical aid is provided to help establish an innovative educational program within a school district. After the first year or two, the state may then phase out the categorical aid.

A teacher ponders a question during an inservice workshop. (© Robert Kalman/Image Works)

Incentive aid is a way for state education agencies to encourage school districts to establish certain programs. The aid is designed to assist in setting up a program within a district but not to maintain the program during the following years. That responsibility falls on the school district, which must allocate funds to maintain the program.

State Grants to School Districts

In addition to general, categorical, and incentive aid, many states have grant programs to encourage the development of new educational programs. Typical programs in recent years have included assessment, math, science, and technology grants. Other programs include support for the humanities, artists, and authors-in-residence and for drug education. Funding for inservice programs designed to keep teachers up-to-date on current trends and methods in education are also provided to school districts.

State funding is often provided for specified goals. (In 1996), the California legislative passed the K–3 Class Size Reduction which called for a student-to-teacher ratio of 20 to 1. This measure included a "flood of state funding" to implement and maintain this measure (Turley and Nakai 1998, 40). In 1997, Illinois passed a law that provided a substantial amount of funding for new schools and additional classrooms because of severe overcrowding in many of its schools as well as to replace dilapidated facilities.

Federal Funding

The U.S. Constitution does not state that the federal government has the responsibility of providing education for children. Rather, this responsibility falls to the states

Steve Cooper teaches sixth grade in southern California. His class has forty-four gifted students—there's barely enough room for them to move around the classroom. The students come from a wide variety of cultures. The majority of the class is Asian American, particularly of Korean and Thai descent, as well as whites, African Americans, and a few Hispanic students.

Steve's school district is on a year-round calendar because the district lacks enough classrooms for students to attend only nine months of the year. Thus, students are rotated through the year with each attending three-quarters of the school year. There are three weeks between quarters.

Like the students, Steve gets off one quarter. However, he typically uses that time to go back to graduate school to take more coursework in education methods.

Since California has a new mandated technology program, Steve is required to take inservice training through his district and coursework at a local college to meet state certification requirements. The state is moving toward the elimination of basal readers in favor of literature-based instruction. That is, students will be taught reading through the use of children's literature books rather than the commercially published basal reader programs. In addition, portfolios, collections of work by students, are being adopted by the state to assess the progress and achievement of students in reading, writing, math, social studies, and science. Steve has had a great deal of inservice to make these transitions in his teaching, but he still feels inadequate. He recently enrolled in a reading methods course at a nearby college that meets from 5 P.M. to 10 P.M., two nights a week.

and local control. However, the federal government provides billions of dollars each year for education. This funding is usually in the form of categorical aid, not general aid. That is, all funds are targeted for specific educational purposes and must be spent by school districts solely for those purposes.

The initial federal education funding program began over two hundred years ago with the passage by Congress of the Ordinance of 1785. Sometimes called the Northwest Ordinance, the act provided for each township in the "Western" territories to have a portion of land set aside for a public school site. If you travel through the states of Ohio, Indiana, Illinois, Michigan, and Wisconsin, you may see old one- and two-room schools that were later built on those original Northwest Ordinance sites.

Opponents of federal aid for education believe that schools should be under local and state control, not federal control. They point out that whenever the federal government gets involved in any program, a large bureaucracy is created at taxpayer expense. Supporters point out that the states differ widely in terms of wealth and that federal funding helps to provide a more equitable education for all students. Figure 2 demonstrates the decline in fiscal support of local schools by both local governments and the federal government. Figure 3 shows that, in real dollars, financial support per pupil has leveled off.

Federal Programs

Ever since the GI Bill of 1944, which provided financial assistance for veterans of World War II, there has been increased federal involvement in our nation's educational programs. The GI Bill of 1944 and later versions have allowed over ten million

Figure 2
Sources of revenue for public elementary and secondary schools: 1970–71 to 1993–94

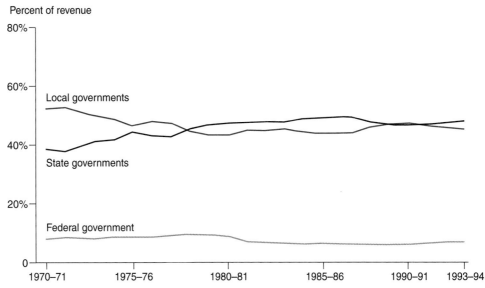

Percent of revenue

Local governments

State governments

Federal government

Source: U.S. Department of Education, National Center for Education Statistics, *Statistics of State School Systems; Revenues and Expenditures for Public Elementary and Secondary Education;* and Common Core of Data surveys.

Figure 3
Current expenditure per pupil in average daily attendance in public elementary and secondary schools: 1970–71 to 1995–96

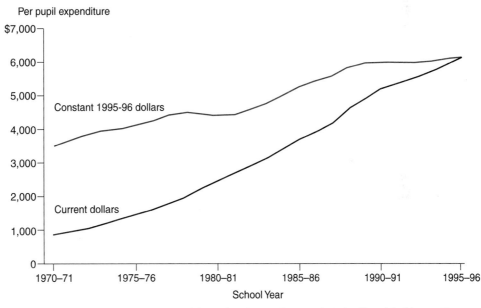

Per pupil expenditure

Constant 1995-96 dollars

Current dollars

School Year

Source: U.S. Department of Education, National Center for Education Statistics, *Statistics of State School Systems; Revenues and Expenditures for Public Elementary and Secondary Education;* and Common Core of Data surveys.

veterans to receive college or vocational education. Many teachers completed their college educations with assistance from the GI Bill. Many students today continue to benefit from an updated version of the GI Bill.

During the 1950s, the cold war led the federal government to sponsor programs to enhance the science training of teachers and students. In 1950, the National Science Foundation was created. By 1954, a program was created to encourage universities and colleges as well as state education agencies to engage in scientific research. In the late 1950s and 1960s, the National Science Foundation funded numerous summer education courses to train elementary and secondary teachers.

Point: States should allocate funding to school districts for all public schools.

Each state can best determine the needs of its students. If states fail to become involved in providing equal educational opportunities through school funding, then the likelihood of the courts or the federal government interceding greatly increases.

The states have large numbers of school districts with equally different assessed valuation levels. Some school districts with small numbers of students have substantial levels of assessed valuation, while some school districts with thousands of students have relatively little assessed valuation. Thus, there is no equity in funding for students under the current property tax system of providing revenue for the schools. The end result is that some school districts have little funds for educational materials and must pay their teachers low salaries, while their rich counterparts have more money to spend and can pay their teachers high salaries.

States could collect property taxes and redistribute them to all school districts. Or a better plan would be to increase income taxes or sales taxes, using the increased proceeds to fund all of the schools in a more equitable way.

Counterpoint: States should limit their involvement in school funding.

No procedure has been developed to fairly fund our nation's schools. And intervention at the state level will not make the educational opportunities for every student within the state equal.

Schools are governed locally. Each community within a state is unique, and that uniqueness is reflected to a great degree in its schools. If a community strongly desires good schools, the voters of that community support property tax increases through tax referendums. Likewise, if a community has little support for its schools, the voters fail to support property tax hikes.

Communities are to a large degree responsible for the businesses they attract. Thus, if a community opposes business expansion, it is indicating that it does not want the increased tax revenue that business would bring in support of the local public schools.

The launching of *Sputnik* in 1957 caused intense concern that the Russians would win the space race. The space program in the United States was fraught with problems and had suffered numerous failures. The nation's citizens became alarmed when critics and the media pointed out that American students lagged behind in math and science compared to students in other countries. In 1958, Congress enacted the **National Defense Education Act (NDEA).** Funds were provided for audiovisual equipment for classrooms, including overhead transparency and film projectors, math and science curricula materials, and inservice programs for teachers. In addition, foreign language offerings were increased. Monies from the act were set aside for college tuition for students who planned to become teachers at either the elementary or secondary level. These areas were thought to be crucial to the defense of the United States.

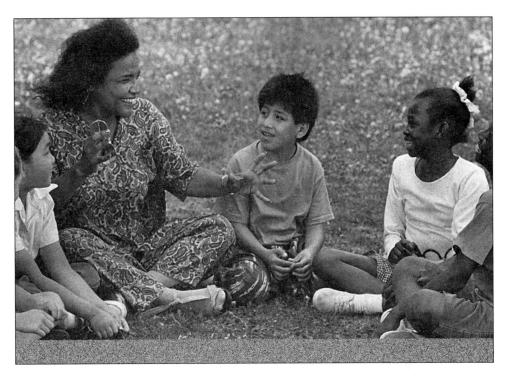

Increasingly school districts seek out bilingual and minority teachers. Some districts pay bilingual teachers higher salaries than regular classroom teachers. (© James Shaffer)

In 1965, as part of then President Lyndon B. Johnson's Great Society program, Congress passed the **Elementary and Secondary Education Act (ESEA).** Unlike the NDEA, which focused on math and science education, ESEA was passed in part to improve the educational conditions for students who were disadvantaged socially and economically. Head Start, a program for three- to five-year-olds, was created as a result of ESEA. Title I, which initially included not only remedial reading and math but also speech therapy and nursing services to school districts with a large number of disadvantaged students, was part of the ESEA of 1965.

In 1972, Congress passed Title IX of the 1972 Education Amendments to the Civil Rights Act. Later in 1974, the Women's Educational Equity Act was passed. While these bills did not provide funding for school districts, they did provide for the elimination of federal funding for any school district that did not follow federal guidelines prohibiting discrimination against females.

In 1979, the Department of Education was established as a division of the federal government with its head serving at a cabinet level position. This department oversees all federal education funding and has an annual budget of about $30 billion.

In 1981, the Educational Improvement and Consolidation Act streamlined federal funding to school districts by combining twenty-eight separately funded federal education programs into one program. This was known as a **block grant.** The first part of the block grant was a categorical grant, ESEA Title I, which provides funds to assist educationally disadvantaged students in reading and math. The second part of the program combined the twenty-eight federal programs into one. According to Broder (1994, 4B), this program is "the single biggest impact the federal government has on public education." Over $6 billion a year is given to 93 percent of all school

When school district funding becomes tight or the number of students drops significantly due to a change in demographics, school districts resort to a variety of cost-saving measures. For instance, some school districts offer financial incentives to older, experienced teachers to retire early. This enables the school district to either not fill those teaching positions or fill them with less-experienced teachers at lower salaries.

A rural midwestern school district had several students at the junior high school level with emotional problems, in addition to a major increase in child abuse by parents, a new problem encountered by the district. The school administration and school board decided to hire a school psychologist to work at the junior high level. Students who disrupted classes were sent directly to the school psychologist for immediate counseling. The result was a significant reduction in behavior problems. Unfortunately, to pay for the school psychologist, a first-grade teaching position was not filled. Thus, the average first-grade class size increased from twenty-one students to twenty-nine students.

Nationally, school districts have often cut arts education when budgets get tight. At the elementary school level, this has meant that art, music, and even physical education teaching positions are eliminated as part of a reduction in force (RIF) of teaching staff. Thus, elementary teachers have had to teach art, music, and physical education—subjects in which they have usually had minimal preparation. This also eliminates free periods for the elementary teachers to plan and prepare lessons. Media specialists are often eliminated at both the elementary and secondary levels during financial crises. At the secondary level, elective courses with small enrollments may be dropped. If the teacher of such a course is not certified to teach another subject, that individual may be a RIF victim.

districts in the United States, resulting in over five million disadvantaged students, primarily at the elementary level, receiving assistance in reading and math. Forty-three percent of the funds from Title I go to the bottom 25 percent of school districts in terms of achievement.

In 1995, the National Science Foundation awarded $105 million to seven urban school districts for five-year programs designed to improve the science, mathematics, and technological skills of minority students. The school districts that received the grants were located in Cleveland and Columbus, Ohio; Fresno and Los Angeles, California; Memphis, Tennessee; New Orleans, Louisiana; and Philadelphia, Pennsylvania (Washington Update 1995).

Many federal programs, however, remain as categorical grants. These include education for the mentally and physically disabled, bilingual education, vocational education, impact aid, ESEA Title IV civil rights programs, and the Women's Educational Equity program.

Some federal funding comes from sources other than the U.S. Department of Education. The U.S. Department of Agriculture (USDA) finances lunch programs, which provide free or reduced cost lunches for those students whose families live at or below the poverty level. Figure 4 is a pie-graph showing the proportion of education funds by federal government agency.

Figure 4
Federal funds for education, by agency: Fiscal Year 1996

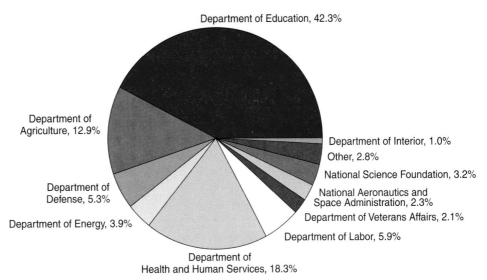

Department of Education, 42.3%

Department of Agriculture, 12.9%

Department of Interior, 1.0%

Other, 2.8%

National Science Foundation, 3.2%

National Aeronautics and Space Administration, 2.3%

Department of Veterans Affairs, 2.1%

Department of Defense, 5.3%

Department of Energy, 3.9%

Department of Labor, 5.9%

Department of Health and Human Services, 18.3%

Source: U.S. Office of Management and Budget, *Budget of the U.S. Government, Fiscal Year 1997;* and National Science Foundation, *Federal Funds for Research and Development, Fiscal Years 1994, 1995, and 1996.*

Trends in School Funding

Accountability is a term bandied about whenever school funding is discussed. The public voices its concern that teachers, school administrators, school board members, and students be held accountable. Parents are concerned that their children receive a good education, an important requirement in a technological society. Taxpayers are concerned that tax money be spent wisely and not wasted. They resist paying new taxes for education funding. Indeed only about one out of eight building referendums passes successfully.

To counter the public's cry for accountability, many states have mandated standardized tests to determine competency rates of students at the various grade levels. In addition, new types of assessment and evaluation, including portfolio assessment, are required.

Impact Fees

Many suburban and rural school districts are encountering rapid growth. Because the schools don't have enough classrooms for the increased student population, some school districts level impact fees on new housing developments. These fees, roughly $1,500 to $5,000 per house, go into the school fund to help pay for new schools and additional teachers. Housing developers fight these fees because they increase the cost of the homes they build. However, in a housing development of four hundred homes, half will have an average of two students in the local schools, or four hundred students. At twenty-five students per classroom, that means sixteen classrooms, sixteen teachers, a principal and two or three support teachers, a media specialist, school bus drivers, cafeteria workers, and maintenance personnel are needed. This is a simple breakdown. In reality, the breakdown is far more complex when children with special needs and those at the secondary level are considered.

Vouchers

Vouchers have been discussed for over three decades as a way to make schools more efficient, largely through competition. Supported by Ronald Reagan and George

Bush during their presidencies, vouchers were often discussed as part of educational reform. In theory, every student is given a voucher that allows him or her to attend a school chosen by the child's parents, regardless of where the school is located or whether the school is public or private. Previously, such choice was only available to an elite few students born to affluent parents or to talented athletes, who were given full scholarships to attend private junior high and high schools.

One argument in favor of vouchers is that public schools would improve due to competition for students from other public schools as well as from private schools. This argument suggests that expectations for students would increase, thereby creating more accountability in public schools. Indeed, with a voucher system, public schools could compete for students with other public schools within the same school district. Some proponents of vouchers believe that more public school students would elect to attend private schools, thereby reducing the need to build more public schools (Stier and Cunningham 1992).

In reality, vouchers have several problems. Many private schools represent sectarian interests, such as Catholic, Lutheran, or fundamentalist Christian. In particular, the Catholic church has come out in support of a voucher system. Vouchers would reopen many such schools, as well as schools affiliated with other religions, including fundamentalist Christian schools, through public rather than private funding. Addressing the fundamentalist schools and vouchers issue, Doerr and Menendez (1992, 167) write, "While the fundamentalist schools . . . might claim to be open to children of all faiths, few if any parents are likely to enroll their children in a school that systematically denigrates all faiths and world views other than Protestant fundamentalism. Nor would teachers of nonfundamentalist persuasions be likely to be hired by or feel comfortable teaching in such schools."

In addition, a problem with private schools is that they choose students. Any student who becomes a discipline problem, for example, can be permanently expelled. That student is thus returned to the public school, which must take the student regardless of his or her behavior problems. Likewise, private schools may elect not to educate students with emotional, mental, and/or physical disabilities, who must then attend the public schools.

While middle- and upper-class families might be able to use vouchers, the cost of transportation of lower-class students from their homes in one school district to a school in another district, even using public transportation such as buses and trains, can be prohibitive. For suburban and rural areas, public transportation may not exist. The distance to and from school becomes a factor.

In California, a voucher plan was placed on the ballot in 1993. No guidelines were established for private schools. Indeed, there was much publicity regarding a school for witchcraft, which would have been eligible to receive students under the voucher plan. Voters rejected the voucher proposition.

Critics of vouchers charge that school choice doesn't work. They point out that an open enrollment plan in Iowa led to massive white flight from urban areas in only a three-year period. Critics also cite a recent Carnegie Foundation for the Advancement of Teaching report that indicated that school choice benefited children of better-educated parents, does not necessarily improve student performance, and may widen the gap between rich and poor school districts (Cunningham, Kaull, and Burkhard 1992).

Milwaukee, Wisconsin, and the state of Vermont are both experimenting with vouchers. In both instances, parochial schools with religious ties have been excluded from participating in the programs. It is believed that the courts would strike down any voucher plan for elementary and secondary students that is associated with religious training, since this training is a violation of the First Amendment. In Milwaukee, 1,000 children from low-income families attend private schools as part of an experiment with vouchers. Currently, Bill Clinton wants increased funding for public schools while many in Congress stress school vouchers in terms of an income tax deduction for parents. There were no significant increases in achievement scores as the advocates of the voucher program had contended (Cunningham, Kaull, and Burkhard 1992).

Private Corporations

As the amount of funding per student has increased, so has interest from private sources in managing school districts or opening private schools. The Minneapolis public schools are managed by a private corporation that specializes in running school districts. In the case of the Chelsea school district in Massachusetts, Boston University, a private university, is taking over the management of the entire school district. By the mid-1990s, however, most school boards believed that a private company could not provide innovations in education and increase student achievement within the budget of the school district. Critics argue that American children should not attend schools operated by businesses that exist in "a culture where the bottom-line is everything" (Carter 1994, 2). Carter goes on to say that "rather than turning to private companies, school leaders need to create a culture in schools that is positive, rewarding, and fulfilling."

There are some companies that have made major inroads into managing public schools. Education Alternatives, Inc. (EAI), a management company that once vowed to have over two hundred school district clients by 1994, had only eleven by the end of the spring semester of 1993, and no additional school districts were added during the remainder of 1993. By 1994, twelve other school districts were negotiating with EAI. EAI has run an elementary school in inner-city Miami Beach since 1991 and runs twelve schools in Baltimore. When EAI begins working with a school district, it signs a performance contract with the school board. If the school board is dissatisfied with EAI's performance, then the contract can be terminated. One appeal of EAI in inner-city schools has been the initial money that EAI brings to improve each school—building repairs, technology improvements, and increased security. This can be up to $1 million per school (Willis 1994).

The possibility of vouchers has led several entrepreneurs and companies to open their own private schools. Even Burger King, well known as a fast-food entity, has opened accredited high schools in fourteen cities.

In the early 1990s, Whittle Communications, the creator and producer of the educational television network **Channel One,** created a division within its company to operate its own private schools. The company, headed by Chris Whittle, makes over $100 million a year from its television network, which is viewed in thousands of schools everyday. Its programs are sponsored by commercials targeted at students and their buying power. The president of Yale University stepped down from that important position and joined Whittle Communications, which had planned to open one thousand new private schools by the year 2000. Lamar Alexander, a former member of the board of directors of Whittle Communications, strongly supported vouchers during his tenure as U.S. Secretary of Education under President George Bush (Cunningham, Kaull, and Burkhard 1992). However, the Clinton administration has shifted support away from vouchers and toward increasing support of public schools. As a result, Whittle Communications changed its focus from concentrating on opening its own private schools to managing schools, beginning in 1995 (Willis 1994). However, by 1997, the company had encountered several financial setbacks and was losing money as many school districts canceled their contracts.

Charter Schools

During his presidency, George Bush proposed the creation of charter schools, a new type of American school. Great Britain has had a similar program since 1988. Charter schools are funded publicly, not privately, with funds coming from the local school district and the state department of education.

In 1991, Minnesota enacted the first law to establish charter schools based on the Bush plan. St. Paul opened the first such charter school in the fall of 1992 (Wohlstetter and Anderson 1994). Since then other states—Alaska, Arizona, California, Colorado, Connecticut, Florida, Georgia, Massachusetts, Missouri, New Jersey, New Mexico, North Carolina, Oregon, Pennsylvania, Tennessee, Washington, and Wisconsin—have passed similar legislation (Sautter 1993). Some states, such as Illinois, already had measures allowing for the creation of such schools prior to the Bush proposal.

In essence, a charter school can be established by a group of individuals—community members, teachers, parents—or by businesses. Charters to operate such schools may be granted by a local school district, the state, or the national government. Charter schools have complete autonomy.

The focus of charter schools may differ widely. For instance, charter schools may emphasize programs for high school dropouts, such as the City Academy in New York. These schools replace failing schools that have been placed on probation by their respective states and provide innovative curricula or other trailblazing approaches (Sautter 1993).

Supporters argue that charter schools offer choice for parents and students. According to Ted Kolderie, "The charter school idea offers a way to broaden quality within public education. It offers a middle way between traditional public education and the 'choice' proposals that use vouchers for private education" (Sautter 1993, 3).

Proposals to use federal funds for charter schools have been introduced in Congress. However, such proposals have yet to be passed. Kolderie insists that "the object of charter schools is not just to create a few good new schools. The object is to improve all schools. Districts do not want to lose kids and the money that comes with them. They will make improvements themselves to attract kids from charter schools, or they may make improvements before a charter even appears" (Sautter 1993, 5).

Those who oppose charter schools argue that the new schools will take the brightest students from the public schools, leaving the public schools to teach only those students with behavior problems, without the funds they need to do so.

■ Summary

The primary source of school funding is property taxes on real estate and personal property. Property tax is a progressive tax, that is, taxes reflect the individual's ability to pay. Sales tax is a regressive tax, which overly penalizes those at lower income levels.

The total assessed valuation of a school district is determined by the total amount of property assessed within the boundaries of the school district. Each school district has a property tax rate. Rich school districts with a high total assessed valuation and small numbers of students may have lower property tax rates than neighboring school districts with low total assessed valuations but large numbers of students to educate.

Each state provides funding to school districts in an attempt to provide equal educational opportunities for all students within its boundaries. This funding comes from four primary tax revenue sources: sales and gross receipts taxes; income taxes; licenses; and other sources, such as gift and inheritance taxes. Income taxes are considered progressive taxes, that is, they reflect the individual's ability to pay.

State funding may be one of three types: general, categorical, and incentive. General, or education, aid can be spent on anything that the school district deems appropriate. Salaries of teachers, school administrators, and other staff as well as educational materials may be paid from general aid. Categorical aid from the state is targeted for specific educational purposes. Incentive aid is designed to fund and initiate a new program in a school district. The district later takes over the funding costs of the program.

The federal government provides billions of dollars each year in categorical aid to school districts. These funds support such programs as Chapter I, a compensatory program designed to assist at-risk students.

■ Reflections

Think back to your high school days. Was your high school able to offer sufficient course offerings for you to attend college? Were there any classes that you would have liked to take but that weren't offered? Was the building well maintained or did the roof leak? How well was your high school equipped? Was the computer lab up-to-date? Were there sufficient library holdings for researching reports for your classes? Was there a wide choice of extracurricular activities?

Did you ever lose a good teacher or coach to another school district that paid higher salaries? Did your teachers ever strike for higher wages or additional benefits, such as health insurance coverage?

■ Discussion Questions

1. Should there be a greater emphasis on income and sales taxes to fund schools rather than property taxes?

2. Should more states use lottery or taxes on gambling to fund schools? Or does such funding set a poor moral example for impressionable students?

3. Should local school districts be subject to voters' wishes regarding school funding referendums, or should the state establish a tax levy rate for all the school districts?

4. Working in a group of four students, come up with two potential incentive programs that would be new and unique to most school districts.

■ For Further Reading

Augenblick, J. 1991. *School finance: A primer.* Denver: Education Commission of the States.

Doerr, E., and A. J. Menendez. 1992. Should tax dollars subsidize bigotry? *Phi Delta Kappan* 74 (2):165–67.

Huelskamp, R. M. 1993. Perspectives on education in America. *Phi Delta Kappan* 75 (4):718–22.

Kowalski, T. 1995. Chasing the wolves from the schoolhouse door. *Phi Delta Kappan* 76 (6):486–89.

Olson, L. 1992. "Supply side" reform or voucher? Charter school concept takes hold. *Education Week* 11, no. 17 (15 January):22.

Smith, G. A. 1995. Living with Oregon's Measure 5: The costs of property tax relief in two suburban elementary schools. *Phi Delta Kappan* 76 (6):452–57.

Swanson, A. D., and R. A. King. 1991. *School finance: Its economics and politics.* New York: Longman.

11

Teachers in the Schools

Primary Points

- A teacher's workday includes preparing for teaching, teaching, and assessing students' work.

- Like most professions, teaching can be stressful.

- The primary reason for entering the teaching profession is the desire to help children and adolescents learn.

- A teacher's attitude toward teaching and students should be positive.

- Every teacher should set goals for teaching.

- A teacher must have good classroom management skills.

Chapter Inquiries

- What is a typical workday like for a teacher?

- How can teachers reduce stress in their jobs?

- Why do so many people choose a career in teaching?

- How does your attitude as a teacher affect student learning?

- Why is goal setting important for teachers?

A Teacher's View

David Frazier Photo CD

For over twenty-five years, Margaret Metzger has taught English at Brookline High School in Brookline, Massachusetts. In her teaching, she emphasizes *how* to learn instead of *what* to learn. Margaret acknowledges that teaching can be overwhelming for the veteran teacher, let alone the beginner. According to her, teachers can control their workload and increase learning at the same time by making students more responsible for their learning.

Margaret is a strong believer in teachers taking care of themselves. Here are her four bits of advice to make one's teaching and personal life happier.

1. Purchase season tickets to events. If you don't, you'll probably feel too tired to attend or just never get around to it. Try to have lunch or dinner with a colleague or friend at least once a week. If this is no more than lunch with another teacher, so be it. Whether or not you talk shop during lunch isn't important; it's the social connection that's needed.

2. Find your own space at school. For elementary teachers and many secondary teachers, this is your own classroom. For specialty teachers or high school teachers who are forced to travel throughout the building during the day, try to find a desk or even a closet that you can call your own.

3. Even though it is sometimes difficult, stay out of petty school politics. There are power struggles within schools, and undoubtedly after getting burned a few times, you'll discover the art of self-preservation by remaining neutral.

4. Find a colleague who has a sense of humor. Teaching is a high-pressure job, and a bit of comic relief is essential for maintaining one's sanity.

"You will work very hard as you learn the craft [of teaching]. As always, your primary goal is teaching well—but a secondary goal is controlling the workload. You deserve a life of your own. . . .

"You cannot be a good teacher unless you are reading books, going to the movies, spending time alone, and maintaining a life. In order to give to others, you must take care of yourself. Teachers who generously support other people's growth also need to nurture themselves. Take care of yourself" (1996, 351).

On the outside, teaching appears to be a great profession. Teachers assist students in their learning by providing creative and motivating lessons. What a terrific career! Generally, teachers spend fewer than eight hours a day at their workplace for nine months of the year, plus they get vacations and holidays. This work schedule makes many people envious of teachers, and some believe that anyone can teach. In reality, teachers spend several hours each day before and after school developing lesson plans, assessing student work, meeting with students, creating bulletin boards, working on computers, attending curriculum meetings, and conducting parent-teacher conferences.

The truth is that not everyone can teach. Some people enter the teaching profession because they think it will be easy—they can work with kids, have the summers off, and get home before rush hour traffic. Most of these individuals fail to last out a school year. In fact, more

Teaching is this country's most honorable profession and those of us who have made the choice to teach must never forget the awesomeness and the responsibility of our choice.

Marcella L. Kysilka
Message from the
President, in Nathalie J.
Gehrke's *On Being a Teacher*

A Closer Look

Jaime Escalante

Jaime Escalante, an immigrant from Bolivia, has been recognized for his accomplishments as a high school mathematics teacher in inner-city high schools in California. He believes that every child should have an opportunity to learn and that learning can be enjoyable. Through his prodding, encouraging, and determined teaching, Escalante helps to develop his students' self-concept as well as hone their mathematical skills. Words like "ganas" (desire) and phrases like "you're the best" fill his daily interchanges with his students.

Escalante arrives early at his high school to tutor students who need it. He stays after school to do the same. His students, who are from low socioeconomic families, perform extremely well in the mathematics portion of standardized college admission examinations. Indeed, when he taught in Los Angeles, his students were accused of cheating. However, when they retook the same mathematics test using a different form, they proved they were indeed quite proficient in mathematics and had not cheated at all. They had a tremendous understanding of mathematical concepts and were equally adept at applying that understanding—all thanks to the teaching talents and encouragement of their teacher, Jaime Escalante.

In the 1980s, Escalante's teaching tactics and ability were touted in a popular film entitled *Stand and Deliver*. Escalante is deeply concerned about the lack of qualified, dedicated teachers. He says there are too many teachers who fit into the category "trabajan por la plato" (they only work for the money"). Fewer teachers bother to work before or after school these days. Incompetent and unqualified teachers are more opt to be in heavily minority schools.

In 1998, Escalante was criticized for supporting California's anti-bilingual initiative. Escalante believes that bilingual education stunts the academic growth of students (Rodriguez and Gonzales 1997, 5A). Today, Escalante continues to teach high school mathematics in Sacramento, California. He travels throughout the United States as well as foreign countries giving motivational speeches to teachers and teacher education majors.

people drop out of the teaching profession after their first year of teaching than at any other time. Some may have eventually developed into good teachers, but the stress of the first year was too much for them. For others who enter the teaching profession with idealistic visions, their dreams may be shattered by teaching in schools with discipline problems or with overdemanding parents with high expectations of their own children as well as of teachers.

Most teachers love their work. They like the challenge of motivating their students. They seek out innovative ways to present lessons. They haunt bookstores and computer software vendors, where they purchase supplies with their own monies. They attend professional conferences so they can return to their classrooms with new ideas and rekindled enthusiasm. Some teachers even admit to loving the fresh smells in a school at the beginning of a new school year—newly waxed floors, chalk dust, and new textbooks.

Most teachers stay in the profession because they enjoy working with their students and helping them learn. Ask a teacher to tell a story about his or her students and you will likely get a barrage of stories, some funny, some sad. But watch the teacher's eyes and you will probably see a sparkle of excitement. Yes, teaching is a powerful high for an individual. After teaching a lesson in which

Figure 1

Number of teachers and pupil/teacher ratios in public schools: 1960–61 to 1995–96

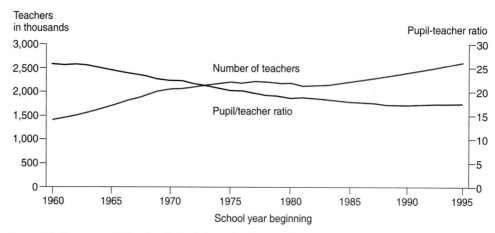

Source: U.S. Department of Education, National Center for Education Statistics, 1997. *Statistics of State School Systems; Statistics of Public Elementary and Secondary School Systems;* and *Revenues and Expenditures for Public Elementary and Secondary Education,* Washington, D.C.

students are actively involved and their curiosity is aroused to the point that electricity fills the air, you will leave the classroom so hyped up that it will take you over an hour to come down. It is a tremendous feeling unlike any other profession.

A Teacher's Workday

A typical workweek for a teacher is a required thirty-six hours, with actual classroom teaching time even less than that. A teacher's workweek is seemingly less than that of the average American worker. Coupled with the summer months off, teachers appear to have an enviable, if not somewhat cushy, job. The facts, however, tell a much different tale. While the average teacher is required to be at school thirty-six hours, a study by the National Education Association (NEA) (1993) found that the average elementary teacher worked forty-four hours and the average secondary teacher put in fifty hours. The average was forty-seven hours per week for all teachers.

Teachers devote over eight hours a week to preparing lessons, evaluating student work, and other instructional activities (National Education Association 1993). Teachers do some of these tasks during their preparation time or even during their lunch period, but most preparation takes place before or after school.

Nine out of ten teachers participate in school-related activities such as bus duty, lunchroom duty, or club advising. In some cases, the school district pays a stipend to teachers for after-school noninstructional activities such as working as a sports coach, play or concert director, marching or jazz band director, club advisor, pom-pom dance coordinator, or cheerleading coach. In all, a teacher may spend sixty to seventy hours a week in school-related work and duties (National Education Association 1993).

The pupil/teacher ratio has declined over the years, however, this statistic is somewhat misleading as more special teachers have been added in recent years. So class size hasn't decreased over the years except in states like California and Indiana which have decreased class size in the lower grades (see Figure 1).

Many teachers, such as this one, coach an after-school athletics program. (© James Shaffer)

Because of a constant influx of new theories and research findings, it is important that teachers stay current in their fields. Although every school district attempts to provide inservice staff development for their teachers, most teachers return to college to continue to learn about their teaching specialties. Most teachers enroll in master's degree programs, and some go on to complete education specialist and doctoral degrees in education. A three-credit graduate-level course during the evening, after teaching all day, can be wearisome for teachers, particularly when you consider class preparation time and the drive to the campus or extension setting. However, most teachers enjoy the camaraderie of other teachers from other school districts and the chance to discuss their successes and resolve shared problems. For some, finding solutions to difficult problems and situations, or gaining insights into a new teaching approach, spurs them on in their own classrooms. Thus, they feel rejuvenated by the challenge of advanced coursework.

Stress and Teaching

The 1980s and 1990s have been referred to as the "age of stress" (McConaghy 1992). There have been numerous books written about physical and mental wellness as well as how to cope with stress in the workplace. Teachers, like other workers in other professions, are apt to encounter stressful situations every day.

Jevne and Zingle (1992) conducted a study of the effects of stress on teachers, entitled *Striving for Health: Living with Broken Dreams*. They discovered that over six hundred of the twenty thousand teachers surveyed were on long-term medical disability leave from their teaching positions. While some of the cases were not due to stress (e.g., cancer), most were stress-related (e.g., heart conditions, mental illness).

Jevne and Zingle (1992) found that the typical teachers on long-term disability leave were slightly older than the average age of healthy teachers and were equally males and females. As compared to the group of teachers who were healthy and performing their classroom duties, the teachers on long-term disability had about the same level of educational training, years of teaching experience, sense of adequacy, and self-reported levels of personal (self and family) and job-related stress. The study indicated that mental health of teachers is as important as physical health. In addition, teachers who deny that they are under stress tend to intensify the problem, making the situation worse. The building principal plays a key role in the experiences of teachers. Principals who provide little support and encouragement are more likely to have a greater number of teachers who have difficulty coping with stress.

According to Wes Penner (McConaghy 1992, 349–50), a psychologist working with the schools in Alberta, Canada, teachers on long-term medical disability due to stress fit a profile.

> [They are] likely to be extremely sensitive; they are easily hurt and recoil or fight when criticized. However, their sensitivity has a more positive component: characteristics like intuition, creativity, flexibility, the ability to be experimental, and spontaneity. Their interpersonal relationships, including those with colleagues and students, are characterized by love, warmth, and empathy. These teachers are also subject to perfectionism. This need to perform at a higher level, without a clear concept of how much higher, can result in increased efforts and in an increasing sense of failure and inadequacy.

Obviously, teachers who possess such positive characteristics as those listed are valued by educators and the communities in which they teach. Losing such sensitive, empathic teachers to long-term disability is not only financially expensive to a school but is incalculably expensive in terms of loss of teaching talent.

Stress in teaching comes from several sources. Large classes and workloads, pressures from the community, low salaries, student misbehavior, parental demands, and lack of support and recognition from school administrators and peers can all make teaching a stressful job. Expectations by society and political pressures, both outside and inside school, will continue to intensify unless there is greater cooperation, understanding, and support from the community, political leaders, school administrators, and teachers themselves.

Most educators agree that the first year of teaching is probably the most stressful. One beginning fourth-grade teacher in a highly affluent suburban elementary school set high standards for her own teaching performance. She was sensitive to her students' needs and worked hard to meet them. She was the first to arrive each morning and usually the last to leave the school each day. She spent her lunch breaks in her classroom, working on bulletin boards and creating imaginative lesson plans that would entice her students' learning. The beginning teacher devoted weekends to schoolwork—rarely taking a break to go shopping or play tennis with friends, although she loved to do both. The parents, the majority of whom were professionals such as attorneys, doctors, or dentists, were extremely demanding of all teachers in the school. They often called or even appeared at school, insisting on knowing what and how their children were taught. By the middle of the year, the beginning teacher collapsed in her classroom and was taken by ambulance to a nearby hospital. She never returned to teaching, although everyone agreed she showed much promise and talent as a teacher.

The best way to deal with stress is to understand how to manage it. One of the most frequently mentioned ways to deal with stress is to take a break and walk outside. Obviously, we cannot leave our students and take a stroll in the neighborhood. Here are some practical suggestions for easing stress.

1. **Be organized.** Always plan ahead and make certain you have all the materials ready before you begin teaching a lesson. Don't keep rehandling the same paperwork. Collect papers, grade them, and return them to students as soon as possible—the next day preferably. Set out your wardrobe for the next day the night before. Don't plan to make an extra stop on the way to school when you can do it on the way home (e.g., getting gas, dropping off laundry or cleaning, or other personal errands).

2. **Be alert to anticipate potential problems.** Always have extra materials just in case you get a new student, for instance. If you know two students who always manage to disrupt the class, think of ways to diffuse them. Don't start a lesson unless you will have time to finish it or stop at a reasonable point.

3. **Overplan.** If the students finish the work early, always have additional related activities ready, not just busywork.

4. **Structure your class time.** Students want structure. While they can and should be given freedom to work on individual and group projects, students need to have a purpose for learning and to understand the rules and time restraints for each learning activity and assignment.

5. **Get to school early.** Be there at least thirty minutes before you are required, which is usually fifteen minutes before the students. This gives you time to review your plans for the day and say a brief hello to your fellow teachers as you get a cup of coffee from the faculty lounge.

6. **Get to know your students and colleagues as soon as possible.** Not knowing a student's name will make it harder to handle a difficult situation in class.

7. **Keep a reflective journal about your teaching.** At the end of each school day, jot down what worked successfully and what did not. If you have any suggestions for the future, note those ideas. Keep your journal in your briefcase, not at school.

8. **Keep in mind that you are a professional teacher.** Carry your briefcase back and forth to school with you each day, even if you don't open it each night. Dress comfortably but not overly casual, which might cause students to think you are one of them and weaken your authority.

9. **Provide options for students.** If you have an instructional goal that can be achieved by students through two or three different avenues, let them choose the one that best fits. Don't, however, have so many options that you cannot keep track of students.

10. **Relax.** During the day, try to take an opportunity to relax. During lunch or a free period, take a deep breath, close your eyes, and envision a pleasant setting—a beach, the mountains, etc. Relax your muscles and breathe slowly. Do this for a couple of minutes.

11. **Exercise regularly and watch your diet.** Exercise is a great way to relieve stress. Regularly exercise three times a week for at least twenty minutes each time. Diet can be a problem for beginning teachers, who often eat lots of junk food but few balanced meals. Remember, even fast-food restaurants have salads on the menu. Do try to limit fat and fried foods, and also avoid caffeine after 7:00 P.M. each evening.

12. **Learn to say no.** Serve on one or two committees, but don't overstretch yourself. Limit your commitments, and do those well.

13. **Seek advice from competent teachers.** Obviously you don't want to appear to be naive or incompetent, but as a beginning teacher you simply cannot know everything. No experienced teacher does. If you have a mentor teacher in the building in whom you can confide, do so. Or perhaps a friend who recently began teaching at another school could offer some suggestions. Usually the building principal is understanding of the many problems a beginning teacher must deal with during the first year of full-time teaching and can offer some encouragement and good advice.

The information age can be, in itself overwhelming. The morning greets you with the newspaper. At school, memos, professional journals, newsletters, and mail fill your mailbox. Your E-mail and voicemail takes another five to ten minutes to read and listen to. And then there's the parent who likes to send you a fax every now and then. The Web itself contains over a million sites, with more added every day, and you might want to explore some of them each day.

Staying afloat in the information age means managing what Reid Goldsborough (1997, 7) refers to as "infoglut." Here are four suggestions he has developed to help your survive.

1. **Do a ranking.** Evaluate your current information consumption. Which sources involve the most efficient use of your time? Which could you dispose of?

2. **Be a prospector.** Prospect for the best information source. Although there are some exceptions, often the more costly an information source, the more time efficient.

3. **Filter, filter, filter.** Filter out the junk. Don't feel compelled to read everything that crosses your desktop. Computers can be a help here—or a hindrance. By connecting to the Internet, you can quickly tap into a gold mine of authoritative information relevant to your needs. Or you can waste hours scanning the Websites of hucksters and hobbyists and reading E-mail, mailing lists, and Usenet messages written by rumormongers and idle babblers.

4. **Keep it short and sweet.** Save what's worth saving and toss the rest. Avoid letting useful information sink into pile purgatory. After you've finished scanning or reading, file information into clearly identifiable folders in a file cabinet or on your computer's hard disk.

By using Goldsborough's suggestions, you'll avoid getting cognitive overload. And you'll readily have the information you need right at your fingertips.

Chiang (1993) found that certain areas cause beginning teachers a great deal of stress—discipline and classroom management, curriculum design and lesson planning, parent conferencing, and accommodation of individual differences in students. Thus, while you are in a teacher education program, try to focus on developing skills in these particular areas.

All teachers and school administrators should be alert to signs of stress. These include physical symptoms such as headaches, indigestion, sleeping problems, and fatigue as well as emotional symptoms such as irritability or crying, feelings of anxiety, nervousness, dreading the next day, anger, being easily upset, an overwhelming sense of pressure, forgetfulness, and lack of creativity. Sometimes stress accentuates habits—excessive smoking, becoming overly critical of your own work performance, overeating or excessive drinking, or procrastination (Benson 1992). Perhaps one teacher said it best: her mark of too much stress is when she fails to

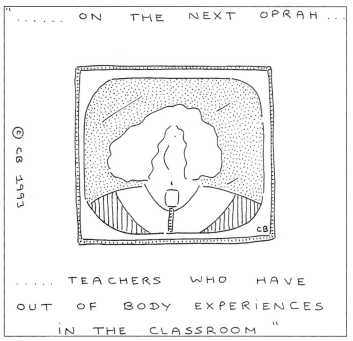

"...... ON THE NEXT OPRAH ...

..... TEACHERS WHO HAVE OUT OF BODY EXPERIENCES IN THE CLASSROOM"

(Copyright © Christopher Burke.)

laugh or when she seems to have lost her sense of humor. As Zehm and Kottler (1993, 14) wrote, "In discussing the personal dimensions of teaching, humor is the most human of all." When we fail to see and appreciate the humor in things, stress has overcome us.

The Use of Technology to Reduce Stress

Stress can generally be reduced by being more productive with your time. Many of the complex tasks of teaching can be reduced by incorporating technology. Here are a few types of computer software that can assist your teaching.

- Electronic Gradebook. This type of program combines a spreadsheet (for doing computations) with a database (for storing names of students, their addresses, phone numbers, parent's names, etc.). The spreadsheet calculates the statistical information for assignments and tests and can give the student's performance over a period of time, say a nine-week grading period.

- Portfolio Assessment Data Tools. Since many school districts require portfolios and the use of authentic assessment, this type of software is extremely helpful. Relying on a database that enables you to incorporate all of your students, you may then type in anecdotal records. It is particularly useful if you have a laptop computer that you can carry with you to (or even around in) the classroom. Some more sophisticated programs permit you to scan in examples of student work.

- Test Banks and Test Generators. These programs often accompany textbooks as ancillary materials or can be purchased independently so you can create your own tests. The program consists of a database of questions that you can either select from or have the software program randomly select. Typically the tests are true/false and multiple choice, although some have short answer or longer essay questions. If you'd prefer to have two or three versions of the same test with the test items appearing in a different order for each version, a test generator can provide multiple versions. When the program prints out a test, an accompanying answer sheet for the objective items is also printed.

- Lesson Plans. Software is available so that teachers can organize their instruction. Such programs are especially nice for the beginning teacher who can print out a professional-looking lesson for the principal's evaluation of his or her teaching.

- Time Management Tools. Some teachers carry around electronic planners, a high-tech version of the annual calendar. You can input meetings, such as faculty meetings for the year, content area meetings, curriculum committee meetings, football games, parent/teacher conferences, appointments with students, etc., and then download the information into your computer. Some schools even have a computerized master schedule of all the meetings scheduled for all of the teachers. Whenever a teacher or administrator calls a meeting, the information is sent via the school's computer network to those individuals who are to participate.

- Presentation Tools. These are software programs such as *ClarisWorks, Persuasion,* and *PowerPoint.* Typically teachers who use such programs swear by them. Rather than spending hours designing a poster and laminating it, then finding a location to safely store it for next year's class, the presentation material can be stored on a 3½-inch floppy disk. These programs let you select from a variety of fonts and sizes, colors, and background. In a realitively short period of time, you can design a class presentation that looks very professional and impressive. And you can reorganize or simplify the presentation and still save your original presentation.

- Desktop Publishing. Both ClarisWorks and Microsoft Word can be used for classroom or schoolwide newspapers.

- Poster, Banner, and Certificate Tools. These tools are essential for teachers and are available in almost every school. Customized printed materials look terrific in your classroom and take only a few minutes to create.

- Grant Writing Software. If you want to find sources of funding outside your school and school district, grant writing software can be helpful. Some programs help you find sources from a CD-ROM or by searching the Internet. Most of these programs are helpful in organizing the information into the format specified by the grant provider.

Working with Difficult People

Difficult people exist everywhere—at work, at school, at church. Adults, children, and teenagers can all fit into this category. Learning how to deal with difficult people can be very helpful to the beginning teacher. Here we will concentrate on how to work with difficult parents, administrators, and colleagues.

Before we can work effectively with difficult people, we need to be able to identify them by their actions. Friedman (1991) suggests developing a "people network" in which you identify those people you come into contact with each day. Begin by drawing a circle in the center of a piece of paper and labeling it "me." Next draw circles around your circle to represent those individuals you come into contact with every day. Write the names of those individuals in the circles, with one name per circle.

Teachers take a substantial amount of work home with them. (© Michael Siluk)

Then draw a straight line to those individuals' circles with whom you communicate and relate well. Draw a wavy line to those individuals' circles with whom you are currently having problems or generally have difficulty communicating with on an interpersonal basis.

Now think about each individual you connected to your circle with a wavy line. For each of these, write out the answers to the following questions: (1) What does this person do that causes me difficulty? and (2) I would like for this person to _____.

The next stage is to identify different behavior types in order to classify those difficult individuals and learn how to cope with them. Here are some examples as classified by Bramson (1986) and Solomon (1991).

The Complainer. *A complainer tends to be a powerless and quite frustrated individual who gripes constantly but never does anything to resolve what he or she is complaining about.*

The best way to cope with a complainer is to listen attentively to the complaint and acknowledge the complaint. However, never agree with a complainer. Limit your responses and avoid making defensive comments or accusations. Try to question the complainer and move toward having that individual identify the concerns and then move toward suggesting that he or she formulate some possible solutions to those concerns.

The Sniper. *A sniper typically attacks another individual in a group of people. The sniper may use the guise of humor to make a jabbing remark that is nothing more than a putdown.*

By letting the sniper know that you will not tolerate his or her comments, you can better cope with this type of behavior. For instance, when a sniper makes a cutting remark about you in front of others, ask the members of the group to verify the comment. It can be helpful to meet with the sniper privately, and in a professional manner inform the individual that his or her comments are not appreciated.

The Sherman Tank. *A Sherman tank tries to run over everyone, much like a bulldozer. The Sherman tank individual is always venting anger and frequently relies on abusive language and bullying tactics.*

While it is unpleasant, the best way to cope with Sherman tanks is to let them vent their anger. Make some mental or written notes as he or she is exploding. When the person begins to run out of momentum, stand up for yourself. Address the person directly by name and present your point of view ("Mrs. Johnson, you need to see my side of the situation. Your son . . ."). Avoid a direct confrontation if possible by ending the encounter by agreeing that you both disagree.

Know-It-All-Experts. *A know-it-all-expert usually knows everything about education, teaching, and children and lets you know it in a pompous, condescending way. The know-it-all-expert may be a fellow teacher or an administrator but is often a parent who has never taught or been trained to teach.*

The best approach to deal with a know-it-all-expert is to listen, thereby acknowledging what the individual has to say. Then question for facts without being confrontational. Don't try to show how much you know about a particular area or subject because this type of person will try to outdo you.

The Perfectionist. *A perfectionist has unrealistic expectations. When a parent is a perfectionist, it is extremely difficult for his or her children.*

As a teacher, you need to point out to the perfectionist how to deal with reality. The individual and his or her child need to be aware that not every assignment needs to be completed perfectly and not every test has to result in a perfect score.

A Moment in Time . . . A Decision for a Lifetime

Jim Rowan was a construction worker who decided to give up his high-paying job to enter the teaching profession. Here is his story.

"Little did I ever dream the impact that night would have on the rest of my life. Seated around a quiet flickering campfire with people I had only met earlier that day, I made my decision to be a teacher. It had taken just over twenty-one years for me to reach that decision, and now twenty years later, I have no regrets.

"The day had begun relatively normal. It was a warm, sunny, July Saturday. The night before I and several friends had got off work at a Glen Ellyn construction site, rushed home, cleaned up, packed my van with camping equipment, and had headed to the Warren Dunes in Sawyer, Michigan. These weekend journeys had been repeated nearly every summer weekend. It's a time in my life I often reflect back to, time I mark as a landmark in becoming who I am today. For it was a part of a three-year period since high school that was filled with failed college attempts; curious searches on journeys to Colorado, California, Canada, South Carolina, Mexico, Florida, Louisiana, and Iowa to name a few; hopes and dreams that always seemed to be over the next horizon; goals often set but rarely met; alcohol and drug abuse; internal and external change; questioning questions; value formation; self-structuring; the past, present, and future colliding yet fitting together; and most important it was a time filled with people. From the Pacific to the Atlantic and from Mexico to Canada, my life had been touched by people. Countless encounters with numerous shapings and reshapings had brought me to that campfire, with that group of people, on that July night. Imagine the odds!

"Earlier that day a small yellow bus had pulled into the campground. I watched approximately fifteen young children who bounded off along with five or six adults. For some reason I thought the kids were handicapped.

For another reason I went over and introduced myself and offered my assistance in setting up camp. It didn't take me long to realize that the children were not handicapped. Quite the contrary. I was impressed with their communication skills, cooperative attitudes, and ambitious work ethic. Throughout the day we crossed paths. At the beach, climbing the dunes, and at the water pump, I became more acquainted with them. It turned out that they were from a special school for gifted students located in Chicago, Illinois. They came from all over the United States and ranged in age from six to eleven. For them elementary school was like a mini adventure in college.

"By evening I was quite attached to this new group of friends. Instead of attending the normal campfire scene equipped with beer, loud music, and sexuality, I found myself instead listening to the singing of children's voices, their creativity expressed with spontaneous poetry, and their joy mixed in with laughter. I remember their smiles and eyes so full of life. I remember how fulfilled I felt. I remember the words of one of their teachers that changed my life.

"You really work well with children, Jim. You should consider becoming a teacher. Several students echoed her thoughts, and thus my life took a drastic change of course.

"I enrolled in classes that September at a community college. Attending part time and working full time, I received my Associate Degree and that fall I entered Eastern Illinois University as a full-time student in the elementary education program. I graduated two and a half years later, a certified teacher in the state of Illinois.

"As I walked up to receive my diploma, I wondered where I would have been if not for that campfire talk four years earlier. What would I have become? What occupation would I have pursued? I'm sincerely glad I will never know."

Reprinted by permission of Jim Rowan, Elementary Educator, Naperville School District 203.

Like Jim Rowan, Margaret "Meg" Hatz had no intention of becoming a teacher. Eventually Meg decided to become a special-education teacher. Here are her thoughts about her teaching career.

"How did I get 'here'? It's a long story, but I'll try to be brief. You might be surprised to learn that I did not originally intend to enter the teaching profession. No, I wanted to be a . . . marine biologist! There was only one problem (which my mother pointed out to me). We lived nowhere near an ocean and an out of state university was not an option. It was pointed out to me (again by my mother) that I was really good with the younger children in the neighborhood. Why didn't I consider teaching?

"Upon arriving at a state university, I changed my major from biology to special education with an emphasis in hearing impaired. I student taught with a regional special education cooperative, and after graduation, was offered a choice between two jobs. Well, I consulted a map and made my decision. Channahon was closer, so that's where I went.

"For eight years I taught speech and language impaired students. All was well until it was announced that the regional special-education cooperative would dissolve and I would be placed somewhere in the region. I felt as if I were a pawn in a chess game. I had no say as to a preference of schools. I must go where I was told or quit.

"I was placed in Joliet in an intermediate class for hearing impaired students. In all honesty, it was a year of unique learning experiences. I brushed up on my language signing skills, participated in a due process hearing for a student, and supervised both a practicum student and a student teacher. Finally, I arrived 'here.' I accepted an LD/BD Resource teaching position in Elmhurst.

"Well, I've had a variety of experiences. I've taught many different levels, adapted curriculum to meet the needs of a variety of learners, and been in different buildings in different districts. How has all this affected me? Over the years my teaching has evolved, and quite honestly, THANK GOD!

"I can remember my first day as a teacher. Later, my colleagues told me how cute I was because I was so cool and calm. That serenity was borne of ignorance! I had no idea what lay before me. I reflect on those early years, and think, 'Oh my goodness, I did that?!' So, I am thrilled with the changes I have made. I am still plagued by self-doubt. I ask myself, 'Are the kids learning?' I think of Mary. She is deaf, her parents speak halting English, and no one in her home signs. During an introductory lesson to *Sarah, Plain and Tall,* Mary thought of a question to guide her reading. She signed to me, 'Anna Caleb want new mother?' Yes, they are learning.

"I ask myself, 'Are the kids motivated?' I think of Bobby. He was the kind of student that would take you off on wild tangents, and think of every plausible exception (and some not plausible by any stretch of the imagination) to a generalization or rule, and always asks to alter given assignments. After reading *Angel Child, Dragon Child,* he saw story maps ready to be completed. His response was, 'Oh cool! We get to retell the story to each other after we do the story maps. I love that!' They are motivated.

"Am I doing it right? I tell my students about 'good mistakes.' Those are the kind from which we learn. If they can make them, so can I because I am a student, too.

"I hate to sound like a country song, but I have lived through some bad times. I've had quite a commute each year. My car has 112,000 miles on it! My pay has been relatively low, especially compared to my friends in other professions. I've had classrooms filled with difficult to teach students. I've taught with few available resources. But along the way, I've received support from my mother, my sister, parents of students, students, and, most recently, my husband.

(continued)

(concluded)

"I once contemplated leaving teaching. As you can imagine it had been a terrible day. I was in tears complaining about not having enough money to move out of my parents' house, trying to teach students who did not come to school and whose parents did not take an interest in their schooling, the long commute, and a feeling of utter failure. My sister responded to me by saying, 'But these kids *need* someone like you.'

"My husband nominates me for Teacher of the Year (to an imaginary audience) and, of course, I win. My mother tells me I'm the best teacher around. How she knows this I have no idea. Parents of students have written letters telling me how much their child has improved during the year. Most of all, I feel a tremendous boost when I hear a child say, 'I got it!'

"Things are a real challenge here in the trenches of teaching. But I'm teaching and, as Maxwell Smart used to say, 'And loving it!'"

Reprinted by permission of Margaret Hatz.

A Closer Look   *Oh Boy, You Have Terry!*

Dana House comes from a family of teachers. Still, pondering her first year of teaching made her full of self-doubt. She had taken a fifth-grade teaching position in a small, rural school district. Here, Dana, now an experienced third-year teacher, reflects on that first year and a problem student she had in her class.

"It was my first year of teaching. The school year had not yet begun, and I was excitedly looking over the names of the fifth graders who would comprise my very first class. Images of what their personalities might be or faces might look like formed in my mind as my eyes moved down the list name by name. I couldn't wait for the chance to meet them and make their eleven-year-old lives wonderfully enriched with all the encouragement and guidance I intended to give them. My day dream was interrupted when a long arm extended over my shoulder. A finger was pointing to one of the names on the list. A voice behind me said, 'Oh boy! You have Terry this year!'

"I wanted so badly to *like* all my students and for them to like me back. I wanted to be their source of learning, role model, friend, everything that might be missing in their homes. I wanted to be . . . SUPER

TEACHER!!! These delusions of immortality were quickly destroyed after spending approximately fifteen minutes in the same room with Terry.

"Terry was a twelve-year-old only child. His parents were in their late forties. He was on medication for hyperactivity. Terry spent most of his day with the special education teacher. His Individual Education Program (IEP) allowed him to be mainstreamed into one class — social studies. Although he was classified as a special education student, the special education teacher assured me that Terry was quite capable of fifth grade work, and his placement in special education was due almost completely to behavior. 'How strange!' I thought, 'That doesn't seem right.' Our school has no behavior disorders program and apparently the child was in special education because he could not function in a classroom of peers.

"When I inquired about Terry during lunchtime, every teacher who had him was full of stories to share. 'Terry threw a chair at me' — 'Terry put his fist through my wall' — 'Terry called me a [*-!!*-!!]' — 'Terry steals' — 'Terry lies' — 'Terry is so violent' — etc., etc. Unfortunately their

(continued)

reports of his behavior were accurate. By the end of the year (yes, I survived!) I had added, 'Terry stabbed me with a pencil' and 'Terry broke a student's finger' and many more incidents that I care to forget.

"Although I must admit I didn't much like this student, and all the methods I tried seemed to have failed, the momentary glimpses of civil behavior I caught made me refuse to give up on him.

"It was with this in mind that I agreed to have Terry in my class full-time the following year (I team teach fifth and sixth grade). The special education teacher would be in the classroom with me, but only as an observer. The other fifth and sixth grade teacher refused to deal with him on a full-time basis. 'It would be too disruptive for the rest of the class,' he said. I was very apprehensive about my decision. How could I voluntarily condemn myself to three hours with this student when last year I dreaded the forty-five minutes I had to contend with him?

"All my doubts about the decision went out the door when on the first day of class the following year, Terry came up to me and said, 'Miss House, thanks for lettin' me stay with the class. I hope I can stay all year.' With that, he bounded out the door for recess. I know it sounds like such a small simple thing on which to base a decision, but the tone of his voice and the look on his face were so sincere I wanted to hug him (definitely a new urge where Terry was concerned) and I was determined that Terry would indeed stay in our class the whole year.

"I'm not going to say that there weren't times when I felt like strangling him, but being a part of the group and not being singled out made such an incredible difference in his social and classroom behavior that the other fifth and sixth grade teacher (with a little prodding from the special education teacher and myself) let Terry in his classes the second semester. Terry's grades dropped, but they were still passing, and he was where he wanted to be . . . in the regular classroom. One might argue that his lower grades supported the notion that he was better off just being mainstreamed rather than completely included. But I think it was the best thing that ever happened to him because he likes school now. And I would never say to the seventh grade teachers, 'Oh, boy! You have Terry!'"

Reprinted by permission of Dana House.

The Nitpicker. *A nitpicker finds fault with everything. A nitpicker parent can torment a teacher with notes and phone calls on a daily basis. A nitpicker loves to find fault in others and expects perfection when perfection is not necessary.*

The best way to work with a nitpicker is to divert his or her attention to meaningful tasks or to the primary focus of an issue or project. For instance, have the nitpicker parent assist with a class activity.

Entering the Teaching Profession

There are a variety of reasons for entering the teaching profession, however, the primary reason is wanting to help children and young adults learn. The accompanying Closer Look sections were written by teachers and describe their reasons for entering the teaching profession.

Attitudes in Teaching

A teacher's **attitude** toward teaching and students is extremely important. If you don't like to teach dance and you must teach it as a physical education teacher, somehow you must hide your dislike and motivate yourself. Likewise, if your least favorite subject as a math teacher is geometry, you must still present it to your students in an interesting way. Being a band or choral director may be a terrific job except that you must work with beginning band or choral students.

Linda Mason loves Chicago, her hometown. As a teacher in the city "with big shoulders," as Frank Sinatra sings in the popular song, for almost thirty years, Linda finds that teaching has become increasingly more difficult over the years. She doesn't know if her students will all be alive tomorrow or if one will be a victim of a drive-by shooting, stabbed in a gang-related incident, or a casualty of a drug overdose. Her school has metal detectors to screen out weapons that might be hidden in their clothes or bookbags. The doors to the school and her classroom are kept locked between classes.

The curriculum has changed numerous times over the years, and Linda has attempted to keep up. Some years there aren't enough algebra and geometry textbooks to go around, and Linda has to make do with what she has.

The bureaucracy of teaching in one of the largest school systems in the nation is unbelievable. Sometimes changes are made but they don't take effect until several months or even years later. In the mid-1980s, the state of Illinois ordered reforms for the Chicago public schools. One reform was a local school council with parents and community leaders as members for every school. Linda believes that the local school councils have helped. Unfortunately, more people are interested in serving on elementary rather than high school councils.

Despite the problems, Linda believes that she has made a difference for many of her students. Linda takes pride when she goes to the grocery store where one of her former students now serves as an assistant manager or shops at Marshall Field's department store and runs into another former student, a recent graduate who now works full time as a sales clerk. There's no question that Linda believes that becoming a high school math teacher was her best choice as a profession.

Nancy Law, a fifth-grade teacher, didn't like to teach social studies but loved teaching math and science. Since her school was departmentalized and she taught math and science all day, Nancy was thrilled! She was in her element, conjuring up new ways to entice her students to love math and science. She held a math and science fair for her students. She invited guests from local labs to do demonstrations in math and science. Nancy was quite happy, and her students benefited from her enthusiasm. Alas, after a few years her school reorganized and she had to teach math and science along with social studies. Nancy disliked social studies but decided if she projected her own contempt for social studies she would never convince her students that social studies was an enjoyable subject.

Not being shy, Nancy headed straight to the teachers in her district who had reputations for loving to teach social studies. She questioned them about their teaching tactics, children's literature in social studies, and what professional journals they read. Then she enrolled in a graduate class and asked questions of the professor and her peers. Nancy became excited about teaching social studies and discovered that much of how she taught science lent itself to teaching social studies—ecology, scientific breakthroughs in history, new technology and its impact upon society. Nancy's own fervor for learning about social studies spread throughout her class, and they, too, developed a passion for social studies.

Some teachers love their subject areas but dislike some of their students. As one teacher said, "Teaching would be great if it weren't for the kids." Certainly the students of today are very different from the students of a decade ago. Teachers need to recognize and appreciate each student in their classes. A teacher cannot expect every student to like him or her, but it is important that the teacher respect every student as a learner.

Attitudes of Students

The attitudes of your students will certainly have an effect on your teaching. Some students will eagerly respond to your teaching and dive into a lesson. Other students seem to have an invisible brick wall around them to thwart your attempts to teach them. Teaching these students can be difficult indeed. Still other students may have already given up and decided they cannot learn. These may be high school students or even kindergartners. Before these students can be taught, they must develop a positive self-concept and a positive attitude toward learning. That is your responsibility—and not easily achieved.

Attitudes of Colleagues

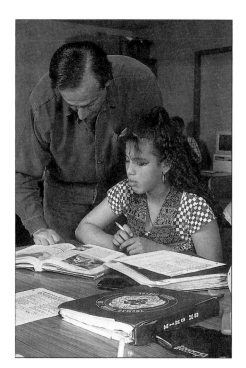

A teacher's enthusiasm for a subject can entice students to become motivated about learning a subject. (© Michael Neuman/PhotoEdit)

Teachers who share their zest for teaching are delightful co-workers. Their eyes sparkle as they share a story about a lesson that went particularly well. They suffer when a well-prepared lesson flops with the students. They work hard and put a great amount of energy and effort into their teaching. They return papers promptly so students can learn what they did right as well as how to correct their mistakes. It pains these teachers when their students don't perform well. Likewise, they beam when their students succeed. Frequently, these individuals are students' favorite teachers. They are generally popular with their colleagues and parents as well.

When teachers share both practical and emotional support with their colleagues, especially with beginning teachers, there is a professionalism that tends to bind all involved in the school together. New teachers discover that someone understands and is on their side (Stedman and Stroot 1998).

On the other hand, some teachers who have taught for several years may be tired of or disenchanted with teaching. In fact, they may be burned out. They no longer possess the spark and drive that they had when they first entered the profession. Unfortunately, some teachers in this category are eager to bemoan their plight with you and other teachers. Their world is full of despair and woe. No one has more difficult students to teach with more behavior problems. Their classes are too large and the facilities are inadequate. Parents of their students demonstrate no attributes of parenting whatsoever. As a beginning teacher, such negativism is disheartening. However, don't overlook these teachers. They probably have some good suggestions and you can benefit from their teaching experience. But try not to become intoxicated with their woebegone stories about teaching or you will likely go home depressed, wishing that you had entered another profession.

Consider this story told by June, a beginning teacher.

My first week of school flew by. Mrs. Maston came into my room to question me. She said I was fresh out of college and had to know the latest in teaching reading and writing. She insisted that I tell her. Then she asked me about math. Science wasn't her "cup of tea" as she put it but she was willing to give hands-on science a try if I'd help her. Boy, was I ever flattered! We ended up team teaching science and math. It was great!

I also encountered another teacher in my building, Mrs. Rogers. She was a first grade teacher who had a beautifully decorated classroom and did all kinds of finger plays and songs with her students. Mrs. Rogers always wore the latest fashion. Unfortunately, many of her teaching methods approached the Dark Ages. She sat the kids in straight rows and required them to do workbook page after workbook page of phonics followed by ditto page after ditto page of phonics. Very little "real" reading took place. It was like the 1950s all over again. Ugh!

At the end of the year, we had a combination retirement/birthday party. Mrs. Maston decided that age sixty-nine was a good time to retire and Mrs. Rogers turned twenty-five on the last day of school. I had learned a lot from the two of them during the school year—some teachers are old fashioned the day they begin teaching while others still find teaching to be stimulating even in their fifth decade of teaching.

Some teachers may tell woebegone stories in their second or third year of teaching while others are still honing and refining their teaching skills in their sixties. Don't expect a young teacher to always have the latest in teaching ideas and vice versa with older teachers.

Attitudes of Parents

Parental attitudes pervade any school. When parents expect their children to do their homework, by devoting less time to television and video games and more time to reading and doing assignments, teachers have substantial support. If parents tell their children that they must go to school until they are sixteen and then can drop out if they want, teachers have a struggle to make students see that schooling is valuable.

According to Ayers (1993, 39), "Parents are too often made to feel unwelcome in schools, and we too often dismiss their insights as subjective and overly involved. In fact, the insights of parents—urgent, invested, passionate, immediate—are exactly what we need."

Parents of your students will vary dramatically. Some students in your classroom may not have seen or talked with one of their parents for several years. Other students' parents will attend any school function with their child. Grandparents or aunts and uncles may serve as the parental figure for some of your students.

The attitudes of parents toward school and schooling have a major impact on your students. It is important for you to develop a good rapport with the parents of your students so that they will trust you in teaching their child. Mary Louise Ginejko teaches in an inner-city junior high school. She and her husband and their two sons visit with her students' families in their homes on a regular basis. Whenever there is a wedding or funeral in one of her students' families, Mary Louise is usually invited and attends. She tries to emphasize that her school and classroom is a community of learners—she teaches the students and they teach her and their peers as well.

Teaching Goals

As a teacher, you need to establish your teaching **goals**—that is, what you want to accomplish each year. These will differ from your curricular goals for your students. When you set your own yearly goals, you emphasize areas in which you want to improve as a teacher. Your goal may be to improve in the area of assessment or classroom management or to develop greater knowledge in a content area, for example.

Try to list three or four goals that you want to attain by the year's end, along with suggestions for reaching those goals. Early in the school year, you will sit down with your building principal or a teaching supervisor to review your goals and make sure they are appropriate and attainable. Later, you will meet to discuss your progress toward those goals and then meet again at the end of the school year. This is part of the annual review of your teaching. This process helps both you and the school district because it helps you focus on becoming a better teacher.

The Teacher as Manager

Managing the myriad duties and activities required of a teacher takes some juggling. Time and task management are essential. Some of the basic suggestions for beginning teachers in this section include learning to use time efficiently, ways to get to know your students, and how to organize your classroom and your teaching. Be sure to consider what your students already know about a topic when you plan your lessons or units of study. This way you can present a far more effective lesson (Flakes et al. 1995).

Managing Time and Paper

Here are some suggestions that can make teaching less cumbersome:

1. Make a list of what you need to accomplish each day of the week. Cross off an item when it is completed.
2. Overplan so that you have extra lessons ready if the students finish a lesson or project early or if the art teacher becomes ill and a substitute teacher cannot be found.
3. Make it a practice to touch every paper or memo only once. Otherwise you waste time handling the same papers more than once.
4. Keep your desk clear so that handling papers is easier.
5. Go through your file cabinets every few months and discard any papers no longer used or needed.
6. Evaluate papers promptly and return them to your students. This is not only a good practice for you but also a model of a good work ethic for your students.
7. Arrive at school early so you are not rushed to get set up for your first lesson.
8. Anticipate what might go wrong in a lesson and how it can be resolved.
9. Always be aware of your short-term and long-term goals and direct your teaching toward achieving those goals.

Learning Your Students' Names

Your teaching will go much more smoothly if you learn your students' names as quickly as possible. Here are some suggestions to help you:

1. On the first day of class when you take roll, say the name of the student.
2. Note any distinguishing characteristics about the student that may help you remember his or her name. For instance, John Jackson is the tallest boy in the class (an easy one to remember). Lisa Downey and Kelly McDonald look unbelievably alike but Kelly sits on the left side of the room and Lisa on the right. There are four girls named Michelle, but only two of them spell their name as Michelle, one is Michele, and one Mishelle.
3. Briefly interview the student by asking some general questions. What sports do you like? Who's your favorite author? Do you have a pet? Avoid being overly personal on the first day. With older students you may ask them to tell you

something about themselves using their initials. Write down what they say as this will help you remember them. For instance, Alan Simpson might tell you he "Always Sleeps" (you would quickly remember his name anyway if he does so in your class), while Lisa Cott might say that she "Likes Cats" and Eric Tracy might tell you that he is "Even Tempered."

4. After the student is interviewed, write down his or her name, noting any specific characteristics that stand out.

5. After school is out, write a brief note to each of your students telling them something about themselves that they shared with you as well as informing them that you are glad they are in your class. By handwriting the notes, you will make them more personable. However, by using a computer, you will have a copy to review to assist you in learning their names.

Organizing Your Classroom

Besides organizing your time and learning your students' names, you will need to organize your classroom or laboratory. Consider how much space you need, the types of activities students will be engaged in, as well as where those activities should be located within the classroom. Supplies should be readily available so either you or your students don't waste time retrieving them. You may want to set up work stations in various parts of the room where the students can work in small groups or with a partner. Windows or a lack of electrical outlets may make certain floor plans ineffective. Quiet activity areas must be located away from heavily trafficked areas.

Perhaps your most significant decision will be where to put your desk. Do you want it in the center and front of the classroom or angled in front at one side of the classroom? Will you teach sitting down (few teachers do)? Would a lectern, overhead projector, or even computer with a projection screen be better placed directly in front of students?

Other management decisions that you must make as a teacher include the amount of freedom you want to allow your students. How much flexibility are you willing to give them, and how much structure do they need? These are questions that each teacher must answer individually.

Developing a Teaching Portfolio

Increasingly, teachers are organizing **portfolios** of their teaching. These portfolios, or reflective collections, may include journals with entries that describe lessons plans or projects. By dating each entry and attaching a note with comments regarding ways to improve it or other suggestions, future lessons can be refined. Photocopies of student work or even actual pictures of projects are helpful. Even teaching artifacts (e.g., a handmade puppet or a "lung" made from a rubber glove and suspended in a gallon pickle jar) can be stored in boxes as part of a teaching portfolio.

Meg Bozzone (1994) suggests that when setting up your teaching portfolio you place any artifacts or papers in a cardboard box to be filed periodically. When filing items in your teaching portfolio, classify the contents by different categories. Make certain everything in the portfolio is dated and has a note explaining why you selected it. Create a table of contents. And lastly, set aside time to file new additions and to review your teaching portfolio.

Diane Bradley is a terrific teacher and a very funny person. She teaches in a diverse community setting. If a student has a problem, he or she will probably end up in Diane's third-grade classroom. And Diane will do everything possible to help the student get through the troubled times. Her quick wit and humor make her a very popular teacher and a good friend.

Diane says, "The best advice I can give to beginning teachers is to find a mentor who is open to new ideas and trustworthy and to find a friend who has a good sense of humor. And avoid those doom and gloomers who lurk in teachers' lounges. For if you lose your sense of humor, your teaching and personal life will suffer immensely."

"So don't be afraid of laughing with your students and with peers. Go see an absurdly hilarious movie, and laugh until you cry. Lighten up. Enjoy the pleasures of teaching and life itself."

Brian O. Kaigler, a teacher in Washington, D.C., has kept a teaching portfolio ever since his second year of teaching. Brian says that "you can't learn about how you're changing if you don't have a self-assessment tool" (Bozzone 1994, 50). Perhaps Jay Sugarman, a teacher in Brookline, Massachusetts, put it best when he wrote that "portfolios capture what we do in a day, week, and year, and during school breaks and other times when our days are less hectic we can reflect on the stories they tell. Because teachers are great collectors of stuff, our portfolios force us to pare down what we stash away and think about what we're saving and why" (Bozzone 1994, 50).

According to Hurst, Wilson, and Cramer (1998), your teaching portfolio should include: a table of contents, résumé, statement of philosophy, official documents, letters of recommendation, evaluations, photographs and visual documentation, self-goals, goals for the students of tomorrow, student and parent sentiments, thematic units, learning activities, original ideas, examples of students' work, personal data, your autobiography, reflections, and inspirational items. The portfolio should provide both support and documentaiton.

■ Summary

Teachers have the most important task of all—to teach students. As such it is important to be enthusiastic about teaching and the content area.

Teachers encounter stress as part of their lives. Recognizing the signs of stress and addressing them can help to reduce tension. Too much stress can render a teacher ineffective.

The attitudes of teachers are significant because they relate to their ability to teach. A poor attitude toward a subject area or a student can result in that attitude being shared by students in the class. Teachers also need to be aware of the attitudes of colleagues, students, and parents.

Teachers must learn to manage time and facilities. Keeping a teaching portfolio helps in both areas as teaching ideas are refined and new ones added.

■ Reflections

What type of teacher will you be? Are you very sensitive and hurt when someone criticizes you or your work? Do you cry if you read a sad story or see a sad movie? Some educators believe that sensitive people make the best teachers. Unfortunately, they often allow school events to overwhelm them. For instance, they think about a problem at school with a student or parent and can't sleep at night. In some cases, they may make themselves ill worrying about their teaching. However, students need sensitive, understanding teachers. In many instances they may not encounter such role models in their own families.

Are you the type who can stand up to anything? Does nothing anyone says offend you? Are you brusque in your manner? Or are you overly friendly and outgoing? Is it easy for you to come up with a joke?

How do you communicate with others? What kind of people give you a difficult time? How do you deal with those kinds of individuals?

How do you get along with children? with teenagers? Which do you prefer working with and why?

■ Discussion Questions

1. Consider some television actors who portray difficult people. Identify them using the categories presented in this chapter.
2. List three management characteristics that you need to improve on. Share them with a classmate. Both of you devote the next two weeks to working on your respective areas that need improving. Meet again and discuss your progress.
3. What characteristics do you want to model in your teaching?
4. List three ways you can attempt to change a parent's attitude about your teaching.

■ For Further Reading

Ayers, W. 1993. *To teach, the journey of a teacher.* New York: Teachers College Press.

Flake, C. L., T. Kuhs, A. Donnelly, and C. Ebert. 1995. Reinventing the role of teacher: Teacher as researcher. *Phi Delta Kappan* 76 (5):405–7.

Paine, B. M. 1998. Learning to teach in rural classrooms. *Phi Delta Kappan* 79(8):596-600.

Schiavone, J P. 1998. Making career transitions into classrooms. *Phi Delta Kappan* 79(8):601–602.

Turkington, C. A. 1998. *Stress management for busy people.* New York: McGraw-Hill.

Teeter, A. M. 1995. Learning about teaching. *Phi Delta Kappan* 76 (5):360–64.

Woolfolk, R. L., and P. M. Lehrer. 1984. *Principles and practices of stress management.* New York: Guilford Press.

Zehm, S.J., and J.A. Kottler. 1993. *On being a teacher: The human dimension.* Newbury Park, CA: Corwin Press.

■ Surfing the 'Net

Teachers Work Web Site
www.teachers.work.co.nz

This website has links to over one thousand sites for teachers. The sites are grouped by age of students and subject matter taught.

12

The School Curriculum

Primary Points

- A curriculum has two components: what students are to learn and how it is to be taught.

- A curriculum is developed by a committee of teachers, administrators, and sometimes parents and approved by the school board.

- Types of curricula include student-centered, integrated, core, or subject matter.

- Each subject area has its own unique aspects.

- A curriculum is influenced by such factors as technology and textbook adoption as well as new laws and societal expectations.

Chapter Inquiries

- What is the purpose of a curriculum?

- How does a curriculum change?

- How do curricula of school districts across the nation differ?

- Does the state or federal government influence a local school district's curriculum?

- How do the subject areas differ?

- How do changing standards impact a curriculum?

- How have technological advances changed curriculum development?

- How has multicultural education changed the traditional curriculum?

- How does mainstreaming differ from inclusion of special populations into regular classrooms?

Technology in the Curriculum

David Frazier Photo CD

Computer use by the general public has surged as the Internet has become a popular venue for both transmitting information and entertainment. However, only one in six teachers in the United States regularly uses computers with their students. Here are three teachers and their stories.

A high school teacher in an affluent suburban school district, Steve Grevic was born to incorporate computers in his class. "I love this stuff! I can spend hours on the computer and it seems that only a few minutes have gone by," Steve grins. His classroom is highly organized with high technological expectations of students who routinely call up Websites, even developing their own site. Steve believes that teachers must first know their subject matter and methodology and then move to folding in the appropriate media and software.

Unlike Steve, Nadine Brackemyer, a first-grade teacher in a rural school district, believes she was born to teach, not to be immersed in technology. Having taught over twenty years, she is a superb teacher with little technological background. "Computers are all the rage. They're hooking up my school to the Internet this year and I want to involve my students, but . . ." Nadine pauses and takes a deep breath before continuing, "I don't know a thing about it. I enrolled in a computer class at the university. First, I called the instructor and asked how technical it was. He asked me if I knew how to work the up and down arrows on the computer. When I said yes, he said take the class and I'll teach you from there. So I did." One evening a week after teaching twenty-four wriggly, energetic first-graders all day, Nadine drives fifty miles round trip to take her computers in the classroom course. Her teenage son answers some of her many questions when she's working at home, and her fellow teachers help when she gets stumped at school. Nadine reports, "My six-year-olds enjoy being on the computers at school. The software enhances my teaching and, surprise! I've discovered I *like* technology!"

Unlike Steve and Nadine, Theresa Rindt is a relatively new teacher in a very small rural school district with fewer than two hundred students in a K–8 building. Theresa said, "My district doesn't have much money so we've had to scrounge up funds wherever we can find them. Basically, we've applied for funds through grants from the state department of education. Also, our parent/teacher organization has purchased a computer with a thirty-one-inch monitor and cart that we can wheel between classrooms.

"When I was in college, Apple IIe's were the most popular computers. Now I'm learning about IBM compatibles, since that's what our school has. And I have no idea what kind of software to ask the school to purchase for my fifth-graders. I do know that I want to stay away from Civil War software, since our eighth-grade teacher does a fabulous job on that subject. We also have a problem in that the teacher who orders the software tends to target titles for her grade level rather than spread the titles throughout the grades and curriculum. But you know the saying, 'who has the gold, rules.' " Currently, Theresa is enrolled in a master program in elementary education which features a strong technological strand where she is discovering new software and ways of incorporating it into her teaching.

Like many teachers, Steve, Nadine, and Theresa each purchased their own computers to use at home. Steve and Theresa arranged their purchases through their respective school districts which provided programs for teachers to buy computers identical to what the school district purchased but at prices lower than an electronics store or manufacturer offered. Through a small deduction from their monthly paychecks, Steve and Theresa were able to acquire their computers and printers.

"If you teach, you just have to have a computer at home. You need the convenience it offers," Steve says. Both Nadine and Theresa agree. But, they point out, sometimes when a program doesn't perform correctly or a glitch occurs, it is very frustrating.

As Nadine sums it up, "My computer is to my teaching like my microwave is to my cooking— I can't live without it!"

"Teaching is a profession that is about change. As teachers, we are not successful if things are standing still. We work hard to nurture changes in our students' abilities. . . . In the process, we are constantly making changes in our curriculum and in ourselves" (Rowe, 1998 p. 103).

A curriculum is what students are expected to learn in the classroom as well as how it is taught. In short, a curriculum includes all educational experiences students engage in during the school day. A curriculum includes both formally prepared and hidden aspects. Formally prepared curriculum is that which has been developed and adopted by the school district. The hidden curriculum includes those positive or negative educational experiences that are beyond the scope of the written or formal curriculum, such as outstanding academic performance in math resulting in a pizza party for the class.

A good curriculum . . . addresses multiple objectives simultaneously and envisions students experiences that provoke curiosity, fire the imagination, and deepen understanding.

Ron Brandt
Overview: The Curriculum
Connection

As business and political leaders clamor that students need to learn and accomplish more, the curriculum has become a focal point. Some researchers and policy makers assert that national standards far above current learning levels are needed. Higher standards will mean that the local school curriculum must be enhanced and strengthened.

It is important that a school district adopt a common curriculum for all of its students. It is equally important that the curriculum be continuously reviewed and updated as needed so it reflects current educational trends. We will examine curricular issues in this chapter.

Purpose of the Curriculum

The curriculum of a school district reflects to a large degree the community's values and expectations. Therefore, each school district's curriculum is unique. A curriculum should be based on a philosophical stance. Typically, it is formulated by a committee comprised of teachers, school administrators, and, in many instances, parents. The committee examines a variety of materials, including but not limited to national standards established by professional organizations, state curriculum guidelines, and published textbooks. The committee makes suggestions, which are presented to the curriculum director of the district, who in turn takes the suggestions to the superintendent, who presents the final version to the board of education for adoption. The curriculum director, the superintendent, and the board of education all may offer suggestions to the committee for modification prior to acceptance by the board of education.

The curriculum must represent a balance. For instance, there should not be a greater emphasis placed on gifted education programs than on programs for students of average ability. Both should be recognized as important to the district's goals.

Figure 1
Types of
curriculum
organization

Student-centered curriculum	Integrated curriculum	Core curriculum	Subject-matter curriculum

Presently, the school district is viewed as an organization comprised of three components—the teachers, the schools, and the school board. Together, these three entities are responsible for improving instruction, that is, determining how students are taught, as well as supporting each other. This mutual support makes the school, as the workplace, a healthier environment for everyone (Joyce, Wolf, and Calhoun 1993). If a curriculum is to improve, everyone in the educational system must be involved. It must be a community effort, with everyone studying, working, and making decisions together. This process is never-ending for a school district, and as a result, teachers, administrators, and staff are engaged in continuous learning (Fullan 1993).

Fullan (1993) believes that moral purpose and change agentry, or those who have the power to make changes such as school administrators and teachers, are natural allies. He asserts that teachers and administrators must have a moral purpose—that is, to make a difference—in making improvements in the curriculum and in schools. In order to do so a change theme is essential. Fullan (1993, 12) writes, "Moral purpose keeps teachers close to the needs of children and youth; change agentry causes them to develop better strategies for accomplishing their moral goals." Like Fullan, Sirotnik (1990) believes that moral commitments to inquiry, knowledge, competence, caring, and social justice are central elements of education and public schooling without which schools will fail.

The Organization of Curriculum

Curriculum can be organized in a variety of ways. The two extremes, however, are student-centered curriculum and subject-matter curriculum. Between the student-centered curriculum and the subject-matter curriculum are the integrated and core curricula (figure 1).

Student-Centered Curriculum

A **student-centered curriculum** is usually based on a pragmatic philosophical base or a variation such as experimentalism. The activities and programs are related to the students' interests and abilities. A student-centered curriculum includes many opportunities for a child to make decisions about what is to be learned and how it will be learned. Thus, individual differences are taken into account. Typically, there is an **integration** of subjects. For instance, a lesson on the destruction of the Amazon rain forest may involve social studies, science, math, and perhaps even writing poetry. In a student-centered curriculum, the teacher serves as a facilitator or learning resource.

Subject-Matter Curriculum

A **subject-matter curriculum** emphasizes the content area as students engage in the study of disciplines. The acquisition of knowledge, with little consideration for creative and critical thinking, is stressed. In a subject-matter curriculum, students formally study algebra, geometry, botany, chemistry, geography, history, literature, physics, and zoology. Typically, a subject-matter curriculum requires that students listen intently as the teacher lectures, sharing information that has been handed down for generations. Class discussions usually follow a lecture format. At the elementary level, each subject receives a set amount of time and the instruction of subjects does not overlap. Social studies is social studies, science is science, math is math, and reading is reading. The teacher's expertise lies in the content area he or she teaches, and his or her role is that of director of **instruction.**

Integrated Curriculum

An **integrated curriculum** focuses on having students grasp basic learning principles and generalizations rather than learning facts in isolation. Thus, creative and critical thinking are emphasized.

An integrated curriculum attempts to reduce the number of separate subjects taught. For instance, reading, writing, spelling, and handwriting are taught as language arts at the elementary level. Science and social studies may be combined at the middle school level. The subjects remain the same as in the subject-matter curriculum, however, the instructional approach is holistic.

The integrated approach is more popular at the elementary and middle school levels than at the junior high and high school levels. This is because as the subject matter becomes increasingly more specific and difficult in secondary school, it is more demanding to both teach and learn. Thus, the integrated approach does not allow teachers or students the time to explore specific subjects in great depth and allows only a narrow focus within a subject.

Many elementary schools use a thematic approach for integrating the curriculum. For instance, a fifth-grade theme might be the Civil War. The students would be assigned to groups to read a novel about the Civil War. For writing, they might write letters to a main character in the novel. Using their social studies textbook, the students could use maps to locate the major battles. Math would involve considering the economic aspects of the war, such as the need for supplies for both armies as well as the number of enlisted men, officers, and casualties by both sides. Health would include a discussion of medical practices and problems, for example, Clara Barton as the first nurse in the battlefield, the lack of sanitation at the camps, the lack of food during marches, and the measles epidemic. Music would consist of a study of the songs of the period, particularly those sung by the soldiers. Art might examine the photography of Matthew Brady. Physical education might include a discussion of the soldiers' marches with full backpacks over rugged terrain and games of the period.

Some elementary schools vary the thematic approach to integrated instruction by having all grade levels identify one theme to study for a portion of the school year, usually a month. Such themes must be able to cross grade levels. For example, ecology, life in other countries, or prehistoric life could all serve as schoolwide themes, with the various grade levels sharing their knowledge with others.

Core Curriculum

The **core curriculum** has received a great deal of notoriety largely due to the success of the book *Cultural Literacy,* written by E. D. Hirsch, Jr. (1987), an English professor at the University of Virginia. Hirsch (1993, 23), founder of the Core Knowledge Foundation, advocates that to "achieve excellence and fairness in education," students need to be taught a "body of shared knowledge." For example, elementary students learn about

Teachers can greatly influence the curriculum. They are the experts in their content areas. In addition, no one knows students and their capabilities better than classroom teachers. Many teachers willingly serve on curriculum committees in order to provide input.

Bonnie Kuhrt, a teacher at Carl Sandburg Junior High School in Rolling Meadows, Illinois, has served on numerous curriculum committees during her teaching career. This means attending lots of committee meetings both before and after school begins, with a substantial amount of preparation between meetings. Bonnie serves on these committees because she cares about the students. She believes they deserve nothing but the best, and she devotes much of her energy working toward that goal.

Bonnie pours over professional journals and books, maintains contact with her former university instructors, and attends inservice programs to discover what are the latest and most effective teaching and evaluation techniques. In addition, she is not afraid to try new ideas. Her classroom often serves as a pilot program for innovative concepts and ideas in the school district. Bonnie willingly shares her ideas with colleagues as well as her enthusiasm. She is one of the first to congratulate colleagues when they enjoy success in the classroom. For Bonnie, all of the work is worthwhile if the students benefit. That is the ultimate compliment for her.

ancient Egypt, Greece, and Rome as well as the Renaissance, the Industrial Revolution, and women's suffrage.

The reason that Hirsch believes that shared knowledge is a more effective means of instruction is that completely individualized instruction is impossible. Hirsch (1993, 25) also states that "the most significant diversity faced by our schools is *not* cultural diversity but rather, diversity of academic preparation."

Largely as a result of Hirsch's influence, Virginia has adopted a core curriculum for the state. Maine has also adopted a similar core curriculum for its students.

Today, 66 percent of the course offerings at the high school level are academic in nature (Mirel and Angus 1995). This is due in part to pressure from parent groups that support individuals such as Hirsch as well as state mandates in the 1980s that established higher academic standards for high school graduation requirements. In addition, colleges and universities in the 1980s increased their entrance requirements.

As a response to the need for school reform in the 1980s and such critics as Hirsch, **outcome-based education (OBE)** became popular. According to O'Neil (1994, 6), "Outcome-based education is the simple principle that decisions about curriculum and instruction should be driven by the outcomes we'd like children to display at the end of their educational experiences." William Spady (1994, 18), a leading advocate of OBE, asserts that "outcomes are high-quality, culminating demonstrations of significant learning in context."

Outcome-based education has become quite popular in over forty-two states (Varnon and King 1993). Its widespread attraction was because "outcome-based education (OBE) has an intuitive appeal that hooks people. Simply set the outcomes you expect students to achieve, then teach and reteach in as many different ways and for as long as it takes until everyone meets them. In its simplest form, the OBE process virtually guarantees every student an education" (Evans and King 1994, 12).

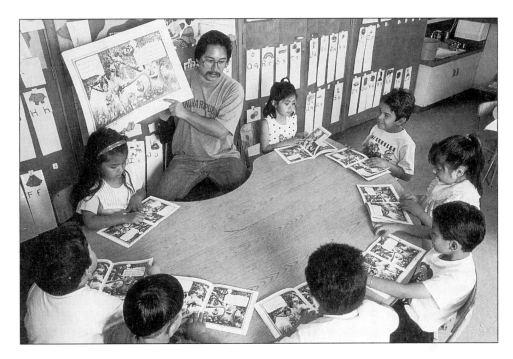

Big books allow early childhood students to see both the illustrations and the words as the teacher reads aloud the story. (© Michael Neuman/PhotoEdit)

Critics of OBE include parents of students who fail to demonstrate that they have acquired the necessary level of understanding. Littleton High School in Colorado first adopted OBE in 1991 but dropped it in 1994 after numerous complaints, including threats of lawsuits by parents of children who did not meet the graduation criteria (Davis and Felknor 1994).

In addition, Christian fundamentalists who protest that schools don't have the right to select what every child should learn, particularly in the areas of ethics and values education, have generally strongly opposed the adoption of an OBE curriculum in their schools. The state of Iowa adopted an OBE curriculum for all of its elementary and secondary schools but later dropped the curriculum as a result of lobbying by Christian fundamentalist groups.

Curriculum Content

Curriculum content includes the focus of each specific subject area. Subject areas include language arts, which is sometimes referred to as reading, literature, or English instruction, mathematics, science, social studies, the arts, physical education, foreign languages, and vocational education.

Language Arts, Reading, and English

Language arts consists of listening, speaking, reading, and writing. As infants, children first learn to listen as they become familiar with their mothers' voices. Through playing with sounds by babbling and hearing sounds made by others around them, children learn to speak. By taking frequent trips to fast-food restaurants and grocery stores, by playing store with empty cereal boxes and other food containers, or by seeing advertisements in the newspaper and on television, children learn to read environmental print, that is, printed words that appear in places where children can see them. By telling stories to children and asking them to retell them, children develop their speaking skills. By experimenting with paper and pencil, young children learn to write the most important word in their world—their own first names.

The language arts are interrelated, because as a child's skills in listening improve so do speaking, reading, and writing skills. Children who enter kindergarten with poor oral language skills typically have difficulty learning to read and write. On the other hand, children who have been read to at home, who have been encouraged to scribble marks on paper, and who have been taken to places that stimulate learning and curiosity, such as museums and zoos, are more apt to read and write easily and quickly.

Reading used to receive the primary instructional focus at the elementary level. Now educators recognize that the interrelationship between reading and listening, speaking, and writing necessitate that all be taught together. Ken Goodman (1986) not only believes that listening, speaking, reading, and writing must be taught in an integrated fashion, but he also asserts that teaching and learning must be relevant. The student must be able to make choices about what and how he or she will learn. Goodman advocates the **whole language approach,** in which students choose selections from children's literature as their primary reading source. In this approach, the teacher follows the student's lead as to what is taught.

While the whole language approach relies on children's literature, the **basal reader approach** provides reading material and corresponding questions for students, as well as more structure for the teacher. In a basal reader series, the reading material is included along with suggested questions for the teacher to ask students and suggested activities, including follow-up and extension activities. Such questions and activities must be generated by the teacher in the whole language approach. The basal reader approach is an old one, dating back to the McGuffey readers of the 1800s, but it is still the most popular approach to teaching reading in the elementary school, with roughly 75 percent of all elementary schools using it.

Basal readers are prevalent in part because of their convenience to the teacher. They are also popular because a variety of stories from various authors and illustrators are included, thus students are exposed to not only quality fiction stories but quality nonfiction pieces as well. In addition, a basal program is organized and sequenced in its presentation of skills, something classroom teachers must do themselves in a whole language program.

In recent years, the number of publishers that produce basal reader series has declined. This is a result of takeovers of one publisher by another and of the high costs of producing new basal reader series, which has driven some publishers out of business. Some of the prominent publishers in this area are Harcourt Brace, Houghton Mifflin, and Macmillan. As Strickland (1995, 295) points out, "Textbooks are no longer the dominant materials for literacy or learning in the content areas."

At the middle school and junior high school levels, listening, speaking, reading, and writing continue to be taught in an integrated approach. For instance, the class may have a literature study in which two novels are compared. Students read the novels, write journal entries indicating their own reactions to the plot, characters, and theme of each novel, and then bring the information to class, where it is discussed in small groups.

A Closer Look

Reading the Right Way: Phonics vs. Whole Language

Teaching children to read is the key to subsequent educational success and should be the most important priority of elementary school.

Yet in many inner-city, suburban and rural schools, large and growing numbers of children are reaching upper elementary levels unable to read and understand grade-appropriate material—as many as 70 to 80 percent in some inner-city schools and 30 percent in some suburban schools. The magnitude of this problem causes not only innumerable personal tragedies but also significantly drives instruction down and jeopardizes the future of our public schools.

What is most frustrating is that much of this reading failure could be prevented if schools just applied what is known about beginning reading instruction. While the field of reading seems mired in contentious debate—principally pitting phonics against whole language as the best instructional approach—a powerful and persuasive consensus has developed among educational, cognitive and medical researchers, as well as our best teachers, about the causes and cures of reading failure.

Ripe for Improvement

These ideas have been successfully implemented in thousands of classrooms in diverse settings with spectacular results. They draw from the whole language movement but also include organized skill development components such as phonemic awareness, phonics and decoding. As such, effective reading programs use elements from both traditions that have proven successful while discarding those that have proven ineffective.

Although this comprehensive approach is not driving reading instruction in most classrooms, teachers are hungry for information about specifics and willing to apply them in their classrooms and schools. Reading instruction is ripe for improvement because teachers daily face children who are not learning to read, and

they realize a gap in instruction exists. In such situations, administrative leadership is crucial.

Before change can occur, administrators need a detailed knowledge of the reading process so they don't get taken in by specious advice.

Although for most children the reading battle is lost in kindergarten and first grade, the best place to begin the search for remedies is to observe students who have difficulty reading in upper grades. In the course of working with school districts nationwide to improve reading performance, I have asked more than ten-thousand teachers to describe such students. They uniformly state (consistent with the research) that reading-deficient children in the upper primary grades exhibit:

- poor decoding skills (students struggle with too many individual words and don't know how to effectively tackle a new word);
- weak vocabulary;
- the inability to read strategically and actively;
- poor spelling;
- too few reading opportunities outside of school; and
- poor motivation, lack of confidence or avoidance behavior, all stemming from experience too much reading failure.

Rule of Thumb

Recent research has developed a powerful explanatory theory of why poor readers exhibit these behaviors. The theory is based on the two ways that proficient readers gain meaning from text: (1) from the *word*—the vocabulary concept underlying an individual word and (2) from the *passage*—from stringing those words together and thinking about their meaning.

This research shows that in proficient reading, word recognition is primarily an automatic, unconscious and

(continued)

(continued)

rapid process. Conversely, passage understanding is primarily an active, engaged, thinking process of weaving individual words into a meaningful whole, thinking about what the author is saying and connecting it to other ideas.

If readers take too much time and mental effort decoding individual words, they can't attend to passage meaning. The rule of thumb is this: A student should recognize eighteen or nineteen out of twenty words automatically or reading comprehension suffers, a construct referred to as automaticity. Additionally, by sixth grade if students are reading below 100 to 120 words a minute, they probably cannot attend to meaning properly. The 1992 National Assessment of Educational Progress showed that more than 40 percent of American fourth-graders read too slowly to understand what they were reading.

A balanced reading program should include strategies to develop both automatic word recognition *and* passage comprehension. Many reading programs used in schools fall short of this balanced approach. They de-emphasize the word side and the tools by which students become automatic with a growing number of words and over-rely on the passage side. These inadequate programs are based on the theory that the arduous instructional task of developing word recognition skills for many children can be avoided or minimized because the passage can supply word meaning. Vast amounts of research and experience now dispute this view.

One strand of studies, focusing on computer eye research, has disposed of the claims that proficient readers skip a large number of words. Actually, studies suggest, they read virtually every word and see all the letters in each word. (Try skipping a *not* in expository text.)

Other studies show that using context can help decode words only about 10 to 25 percent of the time and this rate is too slow for fluency. It is the poorer readers who rely on context-based decoding strategies. Finally, studies have demonstrated that using indirect methods first (such as context) and waiting to directly instruct those who fail to intuit the alphabetic system significantly decreases the odds that those struggling students will learn to read properly.

In first grade, recognizing individual words contributes about 80 percent of meaning. (The words and concepts of the story are simple, and if the words are recognized the meaning of the story is apparent.) In later grades, other factors increase in importance such as strategic reading ability or the ability to discuss what has been read, but recognizing individual words still remains crucial to reading for understanding.

Decoding Skills

Becoming automatic with a growing number of words depends on knowing how to use the alphabetic system to decode words. (Decoding is the ability to read through a word from left to right, generate the sounds that are connected to all the letters or letter patterns in that word and manipulate those sounds until they connect to a word in the student's speaking vocabulary). This finding is one of the most validated in reading research, and equipping each child with the ability to decode simple words should be a major goal of kindergarten and early first-grade reading instruction.

First-grade decoding ability predicts 80 to 90 percent of reading comprehension in second and third grade and still accounts for nearly 40 percent of reading comprehension by ninth grade!

Why should the ability to sound out a pseudo-word like *mot* in mid-first grade and *lote* or *blar* by late first be so predictive of later reading ability? (A pseudo-word assures that the child has not seen and memorized the word and so is a true test of decoding ability.) The reason has to do with storing words efficiently in memory for subsequent rapid retrieval.

Thoroughly decoding a word the first few times it is read forces a reader to connect information about the unique pattern of each of the letter/sound combinations to the meaning of the word. When a word is read, the letters of the word are stored in one part of the brain, the sounds in another and the meaning of the word in another so it is necessary to establish neural connections among these parts. Subsequent successful readings strengthen these mental connections and quicken the retrieval process until it occurs automatically. Additionally, early readers who want to read for meaning independently

(continued)

(continued)

need a strategy for figuring out words that they have not yet seen in print.

Theories that questioned the importance of alphabetic decoding of individual words have not withstood scientific and empirical scrutiny. Furthermore, the children's inability to figure out the sounds of printed words is implicated in most cases of reading deficiency. Compared to full alphabetic screening of a word, no other method produces fast enough retrieval for the huge numbers of words in English—there are too many words to memorize without using the generative nature of the alphabetic system. Contextual cues are essential for increasing vocabulary, resolving ambiguity in decoded words or confirming a decoded word ("Does it make sense or does it sound right?"). But context-driven decoding even aided by partial alphabetic clues is too slow and unreliable to serve as a fluent decoding tool.

For example, a recent large-scale study in New Zealand found that first-graders who use sounding-out strategies for new words as opposed to context-based strategies (skipping the word, reading to the end of the sentence, etc.) read significantly better in second and third grades than do poorer and second-language learners. These more vulnerable children tended to use the less-effective context-based method.

Extensive research and practical experience has demonstrated that learning to read does not come as naturally to most children as learning to speak does. It needs to be taught. As many as 50 percent of children will intuit the alphabetic system from the instructional strategies now in vogue—exposure to print and print activities and mini-lessons in the context of reading a story. However, many students need an organized program that teaches phonemic awareness, letter sound correspondences and decoding skills to learn to read. This need is especially true of the dyslexic, low socioeconomic and second-language children who fail under our present emphasis on indirect strategies.

Moreover, many first-grade students may seem to be progressing because they are memorizing words. Yet many remain unable to decode words and will subsequently suffer reading problems. Thus, every student needs to be evaluated to determine if he or she understands and can use the alphabetic system. Finally, almost all students' learning will be accelerated or consolidated by helping them understand the alphabetic system.

Decoding ability, vocabulary level and spelling are extremely highly correlated with reading comprehension. Pedagogically, they are connected. The best method for building vocabulary is to read extensively, and children cannot read extensively, especially when text becomes conceptually and structurally more difficult in third and fourth grade, unless they have become automatic with a large number of words and proficient at decoding and learning new words. Similarly, learning spelling patterns helps accelerate decoding and developing automaticity with written words.

A vast amount of research also has shown that learning decoding and independent reading of simple non-predictive text in first grade is developmentally appropriate. (Approximately 95 percent of children are mature enough to learn basic phonemic awareness and letter recognition in kindergarten and phonics and decoding in first grade.) These studies also found that if students are not taught these skills early, most will never recover. Only one out of eight children reading below grade level by the end of first grade will ever read grade-appropriate materials, though expensive and well-designed intervention can beat these odds.

Decoding gives students a sense of success, confidence and independence in figuring out and remembering a new word. This independence leads to real, not pretend, reading: Students know they can look at a previously unread simple text and read it. Non-decoders seldom experience this success and continually experience frustration in attempting to read.

Researchers estimate that nearly half of special education students would not need that expensive program if they were taught initially to read properly. Unfortunately, few schools make the ability to decode a primary objective in first grade, check to see which children can do it and then help the ones who can't.

Instructional Implications

To acquire the ability to decode a simple word by mid-first grade, students must have reached basic levels of phonemic awareness (the ability to hear and manipulate

(continued)

(continued)

the sounds in spoken words), recognize letters and have acquired basic concepts in print, preferably by the end of kindergarten. Then, by mid-first grade, they learn about half of the basic letter/sound correspondences (at least the consonants and short vowels and a smattering of blends, long vowels and more complex vowels) and the patterns of words using these sounds. They also master a core of high-frequency words and phonograms, how to map sounds to letter/letter patterns in sequence in written words (blending or sounding out) and how to apply this knowledge in figuring out a word that has not been read before but is in the student's speaking vocabulary.

Many students figure out how to sound out or blend after a few attempts; many others find this skill difficult and need several months to master this skill. In late first and second grades, students need to extend their letter-sound knowledge to the more complex patterns and learn to use larger orthographic patterns when they sound out a word.

Four major deficiencies in reading instruction prevent students from learning how to decode:

- Nearly 20 percent of our students do not develop threshold levels of phonemic awareness in kindergarten. (This means they cannot distinguish the discrete sounds in words and manipulate and sequence them, which is necessary to connect sounds and letters in words.) And, these children were not diagnosed and given assistance.
- Students were not taught enough about the main letter/sound correspondences and thus did not learn the alphabetic system.
- About a third of our students have difficulty in learning how to read through a word or how to sound it out and have not been taught how to do it.
- Students have not had the opportunity to practice reading a large number of words based on the beginning letter/sound patterns in text. As a result, they have not become automatic at recognizing those words.

Phonemic Awareness

One critical breakthrough in the reading field in the past decades is how important being able to hear and ma-

nipulate the discrete sound parts of words—phonemic awareness—is to learning to read. Most phonemic awareness is learned in the process of learning how print maps to sound in phonics instruction. However, threshold levels are necessary to learn phonics. If a child cannot tell what the last sound in *cat* is, that child is going to find it impossible to connect that sound with the written symbol *t* or to read through a word while keeping the letters and sounds in proper sequence.

Most children acquire basic phonemic awareness in kindergarten by such activities as rhyming and sound-word games. Unfortunately, about a sixth of our children have phonological wiring problems. Without assistance of about 12–14 hours (about 20 minutes a day) during the latter third of the kindergarten year, they will not acquire basic phonemic awareness. Many of these children end up in special education or Title I programs because they never were taught properly at the outset, and many others flounder with their reading problems remaining undetected. The implications are obvious—kindergarten programs must identify and assist those children who, without intervention, will have an extremely difficult time learning to read.

One reason for the growth of the whole language movement was the reality that many children never seemed able to learn phonics and decoding. Educators naturally were inclined to find other ways for them to learn to read. As mentioned earlier, these other ways (predictions using context and first-letter cues) are too slow and inaccurate to replace phonological decoding, and teaching children to rely on them produced large numbers of poor readers. Now we know that one key reason why many of these students didn't learn to decode was that they could not hear and abstract the sounds. The obvious solution is to ensure that children are properly prepared to learn phonics and decoding.

Phonics Instruction

Most children need an organized program that directly teaches the basic consonant/vowel combinations and that follows principles of linguistic sequencing. Such a program introduces words based on short vowel patterns and simple consonants in early first grade and then follows with the more complicated vowel marker

(continued)

(concluded)

patterns (e controlled, r controlled and vowel combinations and consonant blends and digraphs, such as ch). Those basic high-frequency words that cannot be sounded out also need to be taught in some sequence.

The sound/symbol correspondences (and high-frequency words) must be practiced and reinforced extensively in connected or decodable text. These materials contain good stories but are designed to contain large numbers of words easy enough for children to read because they represent the patterns previously taught. For example, changing the gingerbread man with its difficult "g" sound to the pancake man, which reinforces short and long "a" sounds. The problem is this: many materials in use for teaching reading in first grade are highly predictable in their vocabulary with too few decodable words. Thus, the materials are not effective for developing independent decoding skills. The opposite problem is no better; literature books that contain too many difficult words are too hard for many children beginning to read.

Finally, activities that allow students to spell and manipulate words by sorting, and changing them (change sit to set to sat) are an essential part of the curriculum for beginning readers. Just allowing students to play with the structure of words will help many students to understand the alphabetic principle.

Studies have shown that programs incorporating these elements (as well as reading to children, discussions and language-rich activities) are about twice as effective as the more indirect or unfocused methods now in wide use.

Massive Reading

The other major reasons for the growth of whole language approaches that deemphasized decoding were the sterile, unproductive nature of much phonics instruction (worksheets and paucity of connected text), and the lack of motivational and authentic reading experiences accompanying skills instruction. The decoding instruction being advocated today is much more akin to a thinking phonics program that strives for understanding of the alphabetic principle and uses engaging activities to help students learn it.

Secondly, in the latest synthesis, decoding instruction is only part of a broader language arts curriculum that does stress reading to children, writing, shared and reading activities and discussion of literature.

None of these ideas will be simple to implement. They call for the use of the right materials, restructuring of schools around these ideas and massive retraining of teachers. (A high percentage of those who have graduated from university teacher training programs in the past ten years have minimal understanding of linguistics, spelling and teaching the alphabetic code.) Without aware and dedicated leadership, this problem will not be corrected.

Source: Bill Honig is author of *Teaching Our Children to Read: The Role of Skills in a Comprehensive Reading Program,* published by Corwin Press. He is visiting distinguished professor of education at San Francisco State University and president of the Consortium of Reading Excellence, 5500 Shellmound St., Suite 140, Emeryville, Calif. 94608. E-mail: Honig@sirius.com. Bill Honig, The School Administrator, No. 8, Vol. 54

At the high school level, there is a greater tendency to break each subject into separate areas of study. For instance, students may study U.S. literature one semester and then grammar and writing the following semester.

Mathematics

Technological advancements have changed how mathematics is taught. According to Battista (1994, 463), "The last ten years have brought technological advances that have all but eliminated the need for paper-and-pencil computational skill." Mathematics emphasizes problem solving, logical structuring of mathematical ideas, functional application of mathematics content to real-world applications, integration of mathematical topics, and the use of both manipulatives and technology according to the new standards established by the National Council of Teachers of Mathematics (NCTM) (1989). The NCTM advocates collaboration among students and the need

Science is now taught in integrated themes at the elementary and secondary levels. (© James Shaffer)

for students to engage in mathematics communication. In short, the "NCTM asserts that *knowing* mathematics is *doing* mathematics and *what* students learn depends to a great degree on *how* they learn it" (Smith, Smith, and Romberg 1993, 4).

There has been much concern in recent years about math anxiety among female students. In elementary school, girls score at about the same level boys do in mathematics skill. However, by high school boys as a group outperform girls on national math achievement tests. Also, a higher percentage of boys than girls elects to take advanced math courses at the secondary level. This pattern may change as increasingly more girls enroll in such math classes as advanced geometry and calculus.

Science

Science emphasizes both *content,* that is, facts, concepts, generalizations, and theories, and *process,* that is, classification, comparison, generalization, inference, measurement, observation, and theory development. The emphasis at the elementary and middle school levels is on problem-solving skills and developing a positive attitude toward science. The emphasis at the high school level is on inquiry, problem-solving skills, and theory development.

Typically at the elementary and middle school levels, the natural sciences are emphasized—living things, the earth and the universe, and matter and energy. "Living things" includes subjects such as animals, ecology, food chains, fossils, health, the human body, life cycles, natural resources, and plants. "The earth and universe" includes subjects such as air, earthquakes, erosion, rocks and minerals, volcanoes, water, and weather. "Matter and energy" covers atoms and molecules, chemical and physical properties, light, machines, sound, magnetism, solar power, and temperature. Physical sciences are stressed at the high school level, where biology, botany, chemistry, and physics along with earth science are typical science offerings. As students move from sixth to twelfth grade, the teaching of science changes from being largely descriptive to being empirical and quantitative to the theoretical and abstract (National Science Teachers Association 1992). Most states require science to be taught in grades K–8. At the high school level, all students are usually required to study biology.

In 1997, the National Assessment Governing Board of the U.S. Department of Education administered a new science test to 123,000 fourth-, eighth-, and twelfth-graders. No set standards were established to identify basic, proficient, or advanced knowledge levels. Boys in the upper grades slightly outperformed girls. There was no difference in the lower grades. Whites outperformed African Americans and Hispanics (Associated Press, May 3, 1997).

One of the science subtests required that students perform hands-on experiments. For instance, when fourth-graders were given the task of determining whether beetles prefer light or shade, only 12 percent could successfully perform the experiment. It should be noted that few elementary schools have students conduct experiments. At the twelfth-grade level, only 26 percent of the students could completely describe how to separate an assortment of copper pellets, iron filings, sand, salt, and steel pellets using a sieve, magnet, filter paper, and water. The addition of an experiment to the testing process will add millions of dollars of expense but will prove whether students truly are able to apply their knowledge when given an unfamiliar situation.

The American Association for the Advancement of Science (AAAS) created Project 2061, which promotes the use of integrative themes in the teaching of science (Lemlech 1994). Project 2061 is designed to serve as the overriding structure of the science curricula. The suggested themes are energy, evolution, patterns of change, scale and structure, stability, and systems and interactions.

The development of a scientific attitude by students is actually the development of critical thinking. There are four areas of scientific literacy: curiosity, inventiveness, critical thinking, and persistence.

Traditionally, male students have been more interested in science than female students, particularly at the high school level. However, the number of female high school students electing to take advanced science courses such as chemistry and physics has increased in recent years.

Social Studies

The purpose of a social studies curriculum is to help students acquire citizenship skills so they can successfully participate in the economic, political, and social aspects of our nation. According to Farris and Whealon (1994, 6), "Social studies is more than a collection of facts for children to memorize; it is an understanding of how people, places, and events came about and how people can relate and respond to each other's needs and desires as well as how to develop respect for different viewpoints and cultural beliefs. In short, social studies is the study of cultural, economic, geographic, and political aspects of past, current, and future societies."

Social studies consists of the social sciences—economics, geography, history, political science (or civics), psychology, and sociology. At the elementary and middle school levels, these are integrated. Indeed, some school districts integrate the six social sciences, for example, social studies with language arts; students may read historical fiction and informational books and write reports or responses to what they read. At the high school level, the social sciences are taught separately so that teachers can go into greater depth and breadth for each social science.

The arts help motivate students and provide an outlet for their creativity in addition to developing self-esteem.
(Top left: © Myrleen Ferguson/PhotoEdit; top right: © Michael Neuman/PhotoEdit; bottom left: © Myrleen Ferguson/PhotoEdit; bottom right: © Janet Century/PhotoEdit)

Most states require elementary and middle school curricula to devote time to the study of their respective states, particularly focusing on the economic, historical, and political aspects. Likewise, most states require that high school students enroll in U.S. history, economics, and political science classes to meet graduation requirements.

Visual and Performing Arts

The visual and performing arts include art, dance, drama, and music. Aesthetic, perceptual, creative, and intellectual components are all part of each of the arts.

Elliot Eisner (Brandt 1988), a noted authority on the arts, believes that the arts should be integrated with other subjects in the curriculum. He suggests that four operations of the arts should be studied: art/music production; art/music criticism; art/music history; and aesthetics. In other words, making art or music, appreciating and enjoying it, understanding it, and making judgments about it are the areas to be studied.

Should the Arts be a Part of the School Curriculum or Taught Outside the School By Parents?

Point: The arts have no place in the school curriculum.

The arts provide little information for students to use in a job setting. Thus, schools should concentrate on the basics—reading, writing, and math—and not waste time on treating the arts as equal subjects to those that are essential life skills.

Money paid to art and music teachers should be spent on books for the library or computers. Or it could be used to hire more classroom teachers so class sizes would be smaller. Such changes would improve the test scores of students.

The arts cannot be measured as good or bad, thus, freedom of expression can be taken too far by students.

Counterpoint: Students must be exposed to quality instruction in the arts in order to develop their own artistic qualities.

The arts are needed to provide balance in our lives. The arts provide the aesthetic in our hectic lifestyle that helps us cope with the pressures of our workplaces.

Without guidance from trained teachers, students will only listen to rap or hard rock music and think that soft drink cans and clothing ads are the best art forms. Teachers can point out structure and form in both art and music so that students can truly appreciate them. By looking at examples of fine artwork by Picasso and Rembrandt on video laser disks or listening to a fugue or symphony by Bach or Mozart on a compact disk, students are exposed to some of the finest artistic creations in the world right in their own schools.

Society would be affected if students did not receive arts instruction. Newly designed buildings and houses would tend to be bland. There would be no diversion from work without the arts. There would be no music on the radio or movies and plays in the theaters. Thus, there would be no escape from the pressures of society.

The arts have traditionally received less emphasis than language arts, math, science, and social studies. "Less than .1 percent of the Department of Education's $30 billion budget is devoted to arts education" (Oddleifson 1994, 450). Indeed, when budget cuts occur, art and music are often targeted for reduction. Some school districts routinely cut art and music teachers during economic crises and then rehire them once school finances can allow for them. Eisner (1992, 592) points out that "in American schools, the arts receive about two hours of instructional time per week at the elementary level and are generally not a required subject of study at the secondary level." Eisner argues that because time is not provided for instruction in the arts, they are not considered significant in the curriculum and thus children do not develop fully.

According to Hanna (1992), the arts are an important part of a school's curriculum for a variety of reasons. Arts education has been found to have a positive effect on students' motivation, academic performance, and personal development. Eisner (1994) agrees, pointing out that the visual arts offer students an alternative to the single right answer approach of most subject areas, such as math, as well as allow for

Chapter 12   *The School Curriculum*

individuality. A strong visual arts program enables students "to view the world around them with new understanding and insight" (Eisner 1994, 2).

Physical Education, Recreation, and Leisure Time

Physical education includes physical fitness and wellness, skill and knowledge development, and psychological and social development. Forty-six states mandate that physical education be taught, although not all forty-six require it at all grade levels.

Physical education activities and experiences are developmental in nature to accommodate students' growth and coordination. Kindergarteners may learn to skip and gallop, while fifth-graders are taught how to climb ropes. Middle school students learn the techniques of volleyball, and high-schoolers are taught formal social dances.

Over the years physical education has changed from predominately skill-oriented, competitive physical activities to preparing students for lifelong physical activities that contribute to their physical and mental fitness and wellness. No longer do most schools chart the number of sit-ups or push-ups a student can perform, with the name of the most proficient student placed on a large chart in the gym. Now lifelong individual sports such as golf, swimming, and tennis are featured. Competitive lifelong sports also receive attention, for instance basketball, soccer, softball, and volleyball over dodgeball and baseball. Secondary schools may offer classes in modern dance, tai chi or yoga, and even self-defense.

Schools now provide more opportunities for females as the emphasis in physical education has changed. After-school sports now include basketball, soccer, softball, and volleyball for girls, which were available only in large schools as recently as thirty years ago.

California has six physical education goals as part of its *California Physical Education Framework* (California State Department of Education 1986). These basic goals all contribute to a student's development of physical fitness and mental wellness.

1. *Physical Activity.* To create a lifelong interest and proficiency in physical activity, students should participate in a variety of different physical activities.
2. *Physical Fitness and Wellness.* Students need to develop and maintain a high level of physical fitness and mental wellness to meet the demands of schoolwork, play, and other work.
3. *Movement Skills and Movement Knowledge.* By practicing and analyzing purposeful movement, students develop effective motor skills and understand the fundamentals of movement.
4. *Social Development and Interaction.* For students to develop appropriate social behaviors, students need to work independently and with others in regularly planned physical activities.
5. *Self-Image and Self-Realization.* To develop a positive self-image, as well as to maintain it and to achieve self-realization, students need to engage in planned physical activities.
6. *Individual Excellence.* For students to achieve the highest level of physical performance they must set realistic, attainable personal goals.

Ideally, physical education is taught five days a week; however, most schools offer it two or three days a week. In those states that require physical education through only the tenth grade, physical fitness levels of eleventh- and twelfth-grade students drop dramatically.

Today's workweek for the average American worker is longer than any time since World War II. This means there is less leisure time available for family as well as physical activities. Mental stress from demands at home and in the workplace seems to be on the increase. More and more workers complain of the burdens placed on them. Physical education at the elementary and secondary levels thus plays an even more important role in developing the motivation and desire you will need to maintain a high level of physical fitness and mental wellness throughout life.

Foreign Languages

Traditionally, foreign language offerings included only Latin. Latin was taught so that students planning to enter law or medical school could understand the terms in their respective professions. Now many high schools offer Spanish, German, and French, with large suburban districts often offering Japanese and Russian as well. Foreign language classes now emphasize the language as part of personal communication, stressing oral communication in particular. This global village approach has been adopted because so many people travel throughout the world for business and pleasure. This is a substantial change from fifty years ago. Some elementary schools, and even preschools, offer foreign languages, usually Spanish or French.

More and more students enter school with a native language other than English. In addition, immigration to the United States by people with native languages other than English has increased the number of elementary through high school students who speak little or no English upon entering school here. As a result, **bilingual education** has become a part of almost every school district in the nation.

Most universities require two years of a foreign language before students can be admitted. This has increased the demand for not only basic but upper-level foreign language courses as well.

Websites Regarding Bilingual Education

The National Clearinghouse for Bilingual Education has information on federal and state legislation, court decisions, and bilingual education.

http://www.ncbe.gwu.edu/

The Southwest Educational Development Laboratory (SEDL) has an online newsletter, *SEDLetter,* that contains online articles pertaining to minority languages. The newsletter focuses on issues important to educators who teach immigrant children.

http://www.sedl.org/culture/welcome.html

The Thomas site within the U.S. Congress on the Internet site contains the Illegal Immigration Reform and Immigrant Responsibility Act of 1996.

http://thomas.loc.gov/

Vocational Courses

Most high schools offer vocational courses designed to meet career expectations and requirements of students. Such courses include industrial education, business education, home economics, distributive education, and agriculture.

Vocational teachers complain that students are not given the opportunity to elect vocational courses because states have increased graduation requirements. These new requirements necessitate that students enroll in more academic courses in order to graduate—three years of English, two years of math, etc.

The building principal was once considered to be foremost an administrator and organizer. It was not unusual for former basketball or football coaches to be promoted to a principalship because of their organizational skills. Today, however, a principal is expected to be the instructional leader of the building.

Roland H. Andrews and Leslie L. Roberts are both principals who are indeed instructional leaders of their buildings. Both are principals of elementary schools, with Andrews at Rankin Elementary School in Greensboro, North Carolina, and Roberts at Capshaw Elementary School in Cookeville, Tennessee (Andrews 1994; Cudd and Roberts 1994).

Roland Andrews first became a principal in 1981. The school had numerous problems: the faculty did not work together well, parents were not pleased with the school, and the students were not achieving up to expectations and tended to devote a large portion of their time fighting and bickering with each other. At that point, according to Andrews, "I questioned my sanity for wanting to be a principal" (Andrews 1994, 19).

During his first three years as a principal, Andrews devoted more time to disciplining students and talking with upset parents than being an instructional leader. During the summer of 1984 he attended a summer workshop for principals, where he sat through a session on learning styles. Andrews went back to his school and worked with his teachers to implement this new curriculum. He gave each teacher the option of adopting the new approach or continuing with his or her current teaching strategy. For the teachers, the new approach meant allowing the students to work with their preferred learning style.

The teachers responded positively to the new curriculum, not only working with Andrews but by attending several workshops to train themselves in using the new techniques. Andrews decided to move slowly, and it took four years of effort for the new program to be fully implemented. The result was far fewer discipline problems, a reduction from 147 to 8 students sent to the principal's office during the school year, and improved achievement scores. Andrews was so successful as an instructional leader that his school district moved him to another school to implement the same program (Andrews 1994).

Like Andrews, Leslie Roberts is also concerned with the learning climate. Roberts observed that children who were seldom read to at home or who rarely read books themselves are at a major disadvantage in learning to write. She noted that poor readers, and even some average and good readers, in grades 1-3 tended to have problems with writing. Their vocabulary and sentence structure was limited or awkward (Cudd and Roberts 1994).

To assist students in improving their writing, Roberts went into the classroom and developed procedures for using sentence expansion with primary grade students. She created sentence stems, the beginning three or four words of a sentence, using words from the students' content area textbooks or trade books they were reading. Two to five of the sentence stems were then written on the board for the students to respond to and discuss. Students repeated the sentences orally to provide oral reinforcement. The students then individually wrote paragraphs incorporating the sentence stems. By the end of the year, their writing reflected much improvement over their initial efforts (Cudd and Roberts 1994).

Roberts recognizes that to be an effective principal, it is essential to keep up with curricular trends. Thus, she is an active member of professional organizations, including the International Reading Association. Roberts not only shares information with teachers within the building but also has published articles in *The Reading Teacher,* a publication to assist teachers and administrators in the teaching of reading and writing (Cudd and Roberts 1994).

A common complaint about vocational education is that students are not instructed in the latest technology used in the workplace. Schools often cannot afford to purchase the latest equipment. Many vocational programs are using machinery purchased in the 1970s and 1980s, or even earlier—outdated by today's standards.

In addition, the idea of a vocational education curriculum itself is often thought of as outdated. Some argue that businesses want workers who can read, write, perform math, and reason and that they are willing to train workers to perform the specified tasks that their business requires. Others argue that students have unrealistic expectations of the job market as a result of vocational training—they question how many body shop workers and cake designers are needed in a community. Yet another argument is that of gender tracking by the students themselves. Few female students enroll in welding or woodshop and few male students take floral arranging or interior design. Also, critics question if vocational education improves the likelihood of disadvantaged students obtaining a better-paying job than their parents.

Vocational educators assert that vocational education has changed. Home economics used to be taught to female students who intended to be homemakers for the rest of their lives. Now, home economics classes teach female and male students how to prepare nutritious meals quickly and basic child-care techniques, as well as how to hem a pair of pants. Both female and male students learn how to tune an engine and change a car's oil or a flat tire in auto mechanics classes.

Elective Courses

High schools typically offer courses that are not required for graduation but are offered to meet the interests and needs of students. Consumer education and driver's education are two such courses.

Consumer education is designed to assist students in discovering how to buy quality products at reasonable prices. Topics covered in this class may range from understanding the nutritional ingredients in a box of cereal, to purchasing homeowner's insurance, to evaluating the terms of a lease on an apartment, to figuring interest rates on a car loan—important skills for all of us. This course also helps students develop real-world skills; they learn how to negotiate when buying a car, how to resolve problems with purchases, and whom to contact if a product is misrepresented.

Driver's education interests most students because most apply for a driver's license during their junior or senior year of high school. In addition, many insurance companies offer auto insurance discounts for those students who have successfully completed a driver's education course. Some states, such as Illinois, require driver's education at the high school level in order for young drivers to receive a driver's license at age sixteen. Participation in driver's education is believed to reduce the number of traffic violations and accidents by teenagers.

Years ago, local car dealerships would provide new vehicles to schools for driver's education, free of charge. This changed in the late 1970s and early 1980s because of the high costs of cars. Because most school districts are now required to buy or lease cars for driver's education courses, school districts in some states charge a substantial fee, sometimes up to $300 or more, for students who enroll in these classes.

Values Education

Values and moral education continues to receive a vast amount of attention. Opponents believe that it is inappropriate to teach values and morals in the schools.

(Steve Breen)

Proponents argue that students need to have the knowledge, skills, and competencies to assist them in becoming successful citizens in our society, and that includes values and morals (Jackson 1993). Still others assert that it is impossible for teachers to distance themselves from values and moral education. By requiring students to attend class and turn assignments in on time, teachers are involved in values education.

Maryland was the first state to require high school students to engage in community service as a part of its high school graduation requirements. Over two hundred high schools throughout the nation have adopted a similar requirement. Beginning in the fall of 1993, all Maryland students were required to perform seventy-five hours of voluntary community service between eighth grade and high school graduation (Pipho 1992). The volunteer work may be in soup kitchens dishing out food for the homeless, working in day-care centers, painting and cleaning houses for impoverished elderly citizens, assisting in nursing homes, etc. These plans are largely based on the suggestion of Ernest Boyer, who asserted that by volunteering and helping others, high school students would gain self-worth and in the process realize that they can contribute to the good of society. "During high school young people should be given opportunities to reach beyond themselves and feel more responsively engaged. They should be encouraged to participate in the communities of which they are a part" (Boyer 1983, 209).

Certainly the increased level of violence in our society has led some to make the argument that if schools don't teach values and morals, then they probably won't get taught to students. When students fail to recognize and appreciate others, human life itself is not valued.

Standards and the Curriculum

Currently, establishing national standards is the trend worldwide as many countries have set learning criteria for students. This trend has affected educational practice in the United States. In an attempt to improve education, almost every state is creating its own standards. Many states take into consideration core academic standards set by professional subject-matter groups such as the National Council of Teachers of Mathematics and the combined efforts of the International Reading Association and National Council of Teachers of English. The standards developed by the various professional organizations for a specific subject area can be found by starting at the U.S. Department of Education's homepage, which lists information to direct you to the standards. The Website can be accessed at http://www.ed.gov.

Standards fall into two basic categories. First are content standards that clearly define what students should know and be able to do in various subject areas as well as for the different grade levels. Second are performance standards that provide concrete examples and definitions of how well students must learn the material in the content standards (Education Commission of the States 1996). To be most effective, there must be challenging subject matter combined with assessments to determine whether students have met the standards. In addition, there must be communication to students, parents, and the community at large to inform everyone how well the schools are doing.

Most states as well as their school districts have either recently adopted or are working to develop new curriculum standards. While most states have student assessments, only a few have tough measures to penalize those students who fail to achieve the standards.

Delaware has developed statewide standards in four core area subjects: mathematics, science, social studies, and English. The focus has been on standardizing performance measures, assessments, benchmarks, and expectations while decentralizing curriculum, instructions, and teaching practices. The 1997–98 school year was the first year that the statewide standards and assessment measures along with an accountability system went into effect. Georgia adopted a "Quality Core Curriculum" that covers not only the core subjects but also the arts and foreign languages. The core curriculum is very specific, with tests of students in grades three, five, eight, and eleven (American Federation of Teachers 1995).

One of the most highly publicized states to adopt a performance-based system is Kentucky. Major changes in school structure and teacher development took place as part of Kentucky's reform movement. After the performance-based education system was implemented, test results indicated that 78 percent of the state's schools showed gains in student achievement between 1992 and 1994. Most dramatic were the scores of fourth-graders, an increase of 22 percent, and those of eighth-graders, an increase of 13 percent. High school seniors' scores increased 12 percent (Education Commission of the States 1996).

Yet another state to demonstrate dramatic improvement after the adoption of student standards was Maryland, where results have been quite impressive. In 1993, only 113 elementary schools approached or met the standards set for third-grade mathematics. By 1995, nearly three-hundred schools fell into that category (Education Commission of the States 1996). Illinois adopted new standards in 1997.

For teacher and school administrators doing curriculum development, standards are influenced by many different factors. The national standards offered by the professional organizations need to be considered as well as those adopted by the state. In addition, the local school district must consider its clientele. The same is true for every school. If students are to be able to compete in a global society, then they must be able to perform well according to a number of standards.

Challenging Courses and Curriculum

During the education reform movement of the 1980s, most states increased the requirements for English, mathematics, science, and social studies. Between 1982 and 1994, there was a 62 percent increase in high school graduates who took three years of mathematics (National Assessment of Educational Progress 1996). However, math scores on college entrance exams have not increased appreciatively during the same period of time. This suggests that while students are taking more math courses, the curriculum has been watered down.

More challenging courses are encouraged.

All students benefit from taking challenging courses in core subject areas. When students are not exposed to demanding courses, their opportunities to learn a subject in-depth, to pursue higher education, and to succeed in a high-skill job market are diminished (Education Commission of the States 1996, 3).

Or as John Murphy (Associated Press 1996, 1), the former superintendent of the Charlotte-Mecklenburg Schools, in North Carolina, said, "We have found out that the reason most students haven't been learning much was because we weren't teaching them very much."

The Southern Regional Education Board (1996) supports the inclusion of more challenging courses in the curriculum. The board found that students who take more challenging courses know more about the subject. Students who complete a college preparatory curriculum score better on college admissions and college placement tests. Likewise, students who complete a more challenging vocational curriculum score higher on national assessments than those students who complete a more traditional vocational program.

Studies by the College Board (1996) show that minority students who mastered algebra and geometry in high school succeeded in college at almost the same rate as white students. Generally, those students whose secondary teachers emphasize algebra and geometry over basic mathematics score higher on the National Assessment of Educational Progress (NAEP) tests (Education Commission of the States 1996). In addition to the above, a study by Grouws found that

by comparison with conventional practices, instruction that emphasizes meaning and understanding is more effective at teaching advanced skills, is at least as effective at teaching basic skills, and engages children more extensively in academic learning. [The study also found that] low-income students can learn 'the basics' in a broader, more meaningful context if they are taught advanced skills at the same time (1992, 6–7).

Studies have demonstrated that for both mathematics and writing instruction, when teachers assigned challenging assignments their students performed better on tests. Teachers whose students performed in the top one-third of the writing test group assigned longer papers (three pages or more) and stressed analysis and interpretation over report and summary writing.

Research in the area of challenging courses and curriculum has found that the following actions can increase student performance:

- Setting explicit, high standards and expectations for all students;

- Eliminating or reducing low-level courses and replacing them with courses that offer challenging content;

Chapter 12 *The School Curriculum*

- Providing high-quality professional development that helps educators effectively teach all students advanced skills;
- Preparing students in elementary and middle school to take more advanced high school courses; and,
- Securing support and commitment for these policies from district officials, school board members, parents, and the community (Education Commission of the States 1996, 4–5).

Certainly the above findings should be considered in a school district's curriculum development. By increasing the challenge of coursework, pupil performance can be increased.

Block Scheduling

In the 1980s, **block scheduling** became popular in many middle, junior high, and high schools. Rather than have students move from one class to another after a 45- or 50-minute period, block scheduling enables classes to meet for extended periods of time, usually 90- to 100-minute periods, every other day of the week. The advantages to block scheduling are numerous. For instance, the longer duration of class periods enables increased discussion time for the social sciences while permitting the hard sciences additional time for teachers to demonstrate and then allow students to conduct experiments. A drawback occurs whenever a student is absent for a day—it is like missing two class sessions instead of one.

Block scheduling has been beneficial to many small school districts who share teachers, particularly those certified to teach physics, chemistry, calculus, or foreign languages. Some school districts hire retired teachers from other districts to teach a course for one semester instead of having the course extend for an entire academic year.

Teachers applaud block scheduling because it is a more efficient use of class time. Students do not need breaks every 45 to 50 minutes. Block scheduling permits greater coverage of material and increased learning. Class discussion is more apt to flow when it is not restricted by the time constraints of short periods.

For students, block scheduling translates into a need to be better prepared and organized. Students who tend to procrastinate sometimes completely forget to finish an assignment for a class. Also, with fewer breaks between classes, less socialization occurs. In short, with block scheduling, students are expected to be more responsible for their learning and more on task during the school day.

Curriculum for Diverse Populations

The 1954 *Brown v. Board of Education of Topeka,* 347 U.S. 483, decision found that African American students had the right to an education equal to that of their white counterparts. This landmark decision by the U.S. Supreme Court changed the direction of schooling for many Americans. Until that time, African American students in southern states as well as in several large metropolitan cities in northern states were segregated from white students. They were forced to attend schools only with other African American students in what were supposedly "separate but equal" educational facilities. *Brown v. Board of Education of Topeka* stated that separate educational facilities are not equal. This decision resulted in the integration of African American students into previously all-white schools. Since that time, schools have continued to struggle with the issue of diversity, including its impact on the curriculum.

Diverse populations include students from different cultures, females, gay students, and students who are physically and mentally disabled. Presenting information about these groups in the classroom raises new challenges for teachers. Some people have even questioned, though more on university campuses than in elementary and secondary schools, whether a white male teacher can effectively present material written by a white female or an Asian American author.

Educators have asked themselves to what degree science should include discussions of women scientists and pioneers and social studies include the biographies of African Americans and Asians. How should such material be presented? Certainly, teachers are becoming more familiar with cultural issues. School districts offer inservice training to assist them in incorporating new information and concepts into the curricula.

Multicultural Education

In the 1980s and 1990s, there has been a tremendous interest in **multicultural education.** One of the primary goals of multicultural education is to assist students of all cultures in developing positive attitudes toward different cultural, racial, and ethnic groups (Banks and Banks 1989). According to Sunal and Haas (1993, 346), "Being an active participant in American society requires the ability to interact with people from diverse backgrounds."

If present demographic trends continue, by the year 2000, one out of every three students will be nonwhite (Banks and Banks 1989). By the year 2020, that figure is expected to reach one out of every two students (Pallas, Natriello, and McDill 1989).

In developing a curriculum that focuses on multicultural education, teachers and administrators include not only content about other cultures but they also try to encourage students to develop empathy for others. Thus, materials and activities often have a strong affective component. For example, studying literature at the high school level would include works written by African American, Asian American, and Hispanic American authors.

According to Sleeter and Grant (1988), there are five primary approaches to teaching students about various cultures and people who are physically and mentally disabled.

1. Teaching about the exceptional and culturally different. This approach focuses on using teaching strategies to remediate deficiencies.
2. Teaching about human relations in an attempt to develop the self-confidence of all students.
3. Teaching about other cultures and groups through single-group studies in which one group is studied in depth (e.g., African Americans might be studied during February, which is Black History Month, and women might be studied in March, which is Women's Month.
4. Teaching through multicultural education to promote the strength and value of cultural diversity as well as to promote human rights and respect for those who are different from oneself. Such teaching promotes social justice and equal opportunity for all.
5. Teaching with a multicultural and social reconstructionist approach. Of all five approaches, this one deals most directly with oppression and social inequity. Teachers are encouraged to engage students in discussions around current issues, including life experiences of the students themselves.

Banks (1989) believes there are four curricular models for incorporating ethnic/multicultural content into the curricula. The levels are described below.

First Level: Contributions Approach. The focus is the highlights, heroes, and holidays of a particular culture. A lesson may depict a particular cultural trait. In the study of the Jewish culture, students might read *Mr. Blue Jeans, A Story About Levi Strauss* (Weidt, 1990), who left the Bavarian Alps to live in America where he invented the ever-popular blue jeans. In addition to reading about famous Jewish people, students would also learn about Jewish holidays such as Hanukkah and Passover.

Second Level: Additive Approach. This is similar to the contributions approach in that the basic curriculum remains the same; however, content, concepts, and themes that are reflective of other cultures are "added" to the already established curriculum. For instance, *Aunt Martha and the Golden Coin* (Rodriguez, 1993), a picture book that tells of an African-American woman who migrates north during the post-Depression era, might be added to the literature curriculum.

Third Level: Transformation Approach. Students are encouraged to view problems, themes, concerns, and concepts from the perspective of different cultural groups. For instance, a major historical event might be studied in terms of the various cultures involved, such as the completion of the transcontinental railroad as viewed by Native Americans and by Chinese and Irish railroad workers. To determine the different viewpoints, students would do research, including reading such books as Lawrence Yep's (1993) *Dragon's Gate.*

Fourth Level: Decision-Making and Social Action Approach. Students identify social problems and concerns, then make decisions and take steps to help resolve the identified problems and concerns. Typically students take action on a community level to try to improve conditions for a particular cultural/ethnic group. Students may read the local newspaper or tune in to a local radio or television station to identify a cultural or ethnic group that is being treated unfairly (Farris, 1997, p. 39).

Multicultural education has been a part of language arts and social studies curricula for quite some time. Educators are now attempting to integrate it throughout the entire curriculum.

Students with Mental and Physical Disabilities

Ever since the **Education for all Handicapped Children Act (Public Law 94-142)** was passed in 1975, students with mental and physical disabilities have been mainstreamed into regular classrooms, or least restrictive educational environments, for part of the school day (e.g. for art, physical education, or math). Now the inclusion of these students occurs throughout the entire school day, bringing additional curricular and instructional demands.

As a result of Public Law 94-142, students with mental and physical disabilities receive free and appropriate special education and related services as deemed necessary by the nature of their disabilities. Each student is to have an **individualized education plan (IEP)** outlining their individual needs. The IEP must specify the following:

1. The student's current achievement level.
2. Short-range and year-long educational goals for the student.
3. Any special services needed to implement or achieve the goals.
4. The extent to which the student can be placed in a regular classroom.
5. An annual review of the instructional goals, progress, and newly developed implementation plans.

A Special Education Teacher's View of Teaching in a Collaborative Teaching Model

Marilyn A. Scala is a learning disabilities teacher at Munsey Park Elementary School in Manhassett, New York. She wrote the following reflections about her own teaching as well as about teaching collaboratively with regular elementary classroom teachers in assisting students with learning disabilities in their classrooms. Scala (1993, 222, 228–29) writes initially about how the groups of teachers began the collaborative project.

"Heterogeneous grouping is an important aspect of . . . classrooms. [I]t seemed time to try fully heterogeneous grouping and include children with learning disabilities in the mainstream groups. I approached each teacher with whom I would be working, and the journey began. This was not a journey on bold primary roads, mapped out straight and obvious. It was more like a trip full of unexpected detours, delays, and pleasures, . . . we traveled together responding to the needs of our students. . . .

"Each year is different. Next year I will be teaching two grade levels and working with seven teachers. The teachers and I realize these (collaborative) programs do not work without an immense amount of joint planning. We cannot stuff all of our work in our briefcases and shopping bags at the end of the day and work alone in the evening. Now we are planning, discussing, and evaluating together, so our biggest need is regularly scheduled time! We must

look ahead. For next year, we are asking for common preparation periods and faculty meeting time. I also need to work with teachers on class placements for the fall. I go into rooms for specific activities depending on the needs of my students on their IEPs. Is there a way to create balanced groups and also facilitate my schedule?

"This year was successful for other reasons. Preparation. Teachers were able to balance professional growth and family responsibilities. Commitment. With the principal's support for whole language, there has been an emphasis on providing materials such as new tradebooks and multiple copies. The media specialist and teachers work and plan continually to build the resources to make our teaching and learning possible. Time. Teachers have put in the extra time and thought to make this transition work; we will continue to explore ways to facilitate our meeting and planning together. Success. A child's success at a book talk or with a finished paper is supported by the regular classroom teacher, special educator, or teacher assistant during the process, in and out of the mainstream.

Postscript, last day of school

"Mr. G. asks if we can collaborate again next year; he'll even take more children with learning disabilities. Mrs. S. is already planning poetry possibilities with me. Mrs. W. is changing grade levels. 'I feel like we're getting divorced,' she says."

The student's parent or guardian must sign the IEP to indicate that he or she took part in the planning conference and agreed to the proposed educational program for the child.

Mainstreaming has traditionally meant that a student who is mentally or physically disabled would be assigned to a special education classroom for all or part of the day, with the remaining time spent in a regular classroom. In 1986, a new term, total **inclusion,** or the regular education initiative (REI), was proposed by the U.S. Department of Education. Total inclusion means that students with mental and physical disabilities are to be educated in a regular classroom, including receiving support services within that classroom.

The total inclusion movement, or REI, has progressed rapidly in some states. Proponents suggest that it enables students with mental and physical disabilities to be with their friends. Supporters of total inclusion believe that these students can receive an appropriate education if adequate supplemental aids are provided to assist them (Sailor 1989). Another factor has been the reduction of costs because fewer special education teachers are needed and there is less need to transport students to other schools for special education classes. Some proponents believe the issue is one of civil rights for students with mental and physical disabilities. Research studies "demonstrate a small to moderate beneficial effect of inclusive education on the academic and social outcomes of special needs children" (Baker, Wang, and Walberg 1994/1995, 33).

Opponents of total inclusion point out that regular classroom teachers are not appropriately trained to work with students with mental and physical disabilities. These students' instructional and curricular needs do not coincide with those of the class at large. They argue that the curricular needs of these students cannot be provided in a typical classroom setting (Braaten et al. 1988). Some opponents point out that the needs of certain students are best met in special education settings, where adequate physical and teaching resources are available, but instead students are forced by their parents to be in a traditional classroom setting, which thereby makes the parents feel that their child is "normal."

Curricular needs of students with mental and physical disabilities are being addressed in school districts as part of the curricular process. Support teachers in areas such as speech and hearing, learning disabilities, and behavior disorders all contribute to curricular decisions.

Influences on the School's Curriculum

The curriculum of a school district is influenced by many outside factors. As we have seen, national professional organizations, such as the National Council of Teachers of Mathematics (NCTM), establish certain guidelines for teachers and school administrators, which are then adopted by the various states within particular subject areas of the curriculum. In reality, it is the classroom teacher who makes the greatest difference, because it is the teacher who decides what is taught and how it is presented.

Here we examine some of the outside factors that influence curriculum. These include technological advances and textbook adoption.

Technological Advances

New software programs for education are introduced on an almost daily basis. Whether it is a program that simulates a chick hatching out of an egg or the molecular makeup of a drop of water or a desktop publishing program for the school newspaper, software programs combined with computers have changed the curriculum. "Technological tools can foster students' abilities, revolutionize the way they work and think, and give them access to the new world" (Peck and Dorricott 1994, 11).

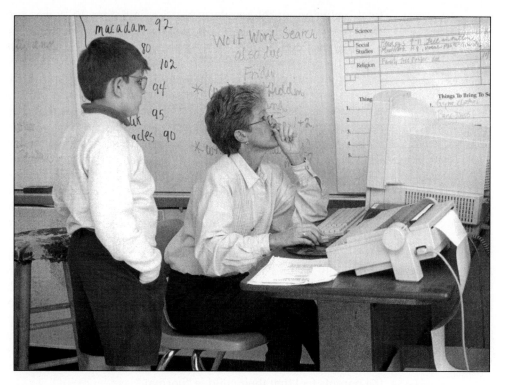

Teachers find themselves spending lots of time developing lessons with technology components. Unfortunately, most teachers learn about computers on their own with little inservice training from their school districts. This is reflected in the fact that there is a higher percentage of first graders who are computer literate than first grade teachers.
(© James Shaffer)

The expense of such programs can be prohibitive for school districts with limited funds, so students in those districts may have limited exposure to technology as part of the curriculum. The information superhighway promises to deliver information inexpensively to schools. However, each school must have the necessary technological equipment, including fiber optic cables to connect classrooms to the outside world. This will require millions of dollars to provide accessibility at a time when funding of schools from all levels—local, state, and federal—is very tight.

Computers and the School Curriculum

Computer use in schools has increased tremendously during the past decade. In classrooms, school libraries, and computer labs where once the state-of-the-art-technology was Apple IIe computers now sit faster and better-linked computers, many of which are online to the Internet. Market Research Data Retrieval (1997) surveyed the nation's eighty-five thousand public schools and discovered that 6.3 million computers were available to students in 1996–97, a 186 percent increase over the 2.2 million computers available in 1991–92. In 1996–97, Apple computers were used in 53 percent of the schools, with IBM compatibles used in 47 percent, increasing in usage by over 3 percent year.

Ten years ago the ratio of students per computer was 36.5 students per computer. By 1996–97 that ratio had been reduced to 7.3 students per computer, a significant improvement made as a result of parents clamoring for more technology in their schools. Wyoming had the lowest ratio of students per computer, four to one, while Louisiana had the highest, ten to one.

Most computer advocates believe that four computers in a classroom is the minimum number that is acceptable. Unfortunately, many schools still make computers accessible to students via carts that are rolled back and forth between classrooms as needed. Students of teachers who are timid or lack an interest in utilizing computers may get little or no computer experience.

Students in suburban schools were most likely to have computers available for their use. In wealthy professional neighborhoods, 78 percent of the schools had Internet access, many of which had access direct from classrooms. In rural schools, 66 percent of the schools had Internet access. Minority and low-income students were found to have the least accessibility to technology.

Over two-thirds of U.S. public schools have access to the Internet. This is a somewhat deceptive figure in that access is generally limited. For instance, many schools have online access available for school administrators or in libraries but not in computer labs or classrooms. A few computers in a school's library that have Internet access cannot possibly meet the needs of all students. Vermont schools ranked the highest nationally in Internet access with 92 percent of its schools linked to the Net. The lowest access was Mississippi with 44 percent of its schools having access. Kansas had the lowest ratio of students per multimedia computer, that is, those equipped with CD-ROM and newer software, with 10.7 students for every such souped-up computer in its school.

The survey by Market Research Data Retrieval also found that a half million teachers used computers, or approximately one in six teachers nationally. This figure has remained the same for many years as some teachers refuse to gain the knowledge needed to incorporate new technology into the curriculum. Preservice teacher education programs in colleges and universities train new teachers in multimedia computer use. As increasing numbers of these individuals take the place of retiring teachers and influence curricular decisions, computer usage will gain an even greater instructional focus. Another survey, the 1997 Tenth Planet Teachers and Technology Survey (Carey and Worthington 1997), found that nine out of ten teachers use computers with their students. Two or more computers were in the classroom of 52 percent of the participants. Teachers reported an average of 3.8 hours of instruction each week to teach concepts in core areas such as math, science, and social studies via the computer, while drill and practice software comprised 3.4 hours per week and educational games totaled 2.9 hours per week.

Finding appropriate, high-quality software is a challenge to teachers. Incorporating it into the curriculum is time-consuming. Even having students use the software takes up a substantial amount of time. Typically, most schools can't afford a computer specialist for their computer lab, so classroom teachers have to not only locate appropriate software but load it as well. Fortunately, with their natural curiosity, students eagerly learn aspects about software as fast, if not faster, than their teachers. Julie Foss, a first-grade teacher, was using a CD-ROM with her class. Despite having devoted a weekend to learning the nuances of the new software, she found one of her first-graders knew the ins and outs of the software far better than she because he had the CD-ROM at home. Sharing the story with other teachers, Julie laughed and said, "So I let Michael demonstrate certain portions of the software to the class until I caught up with him!"

Gopher sites

AskEric *askeric@ericir.syr.edu*

Educational journals *gopher://info.asu.edu:70/11/asc-cwis/education/journals*

K–12 Internet Resources *informns.k12.mn.us*

Kidsphere (discussion group) *kidsphere@vms.cis.pitt.edu*

National Aeronautics and Space Administration *spacelink.msfc.nasa.gov*

National School Network Testbed *copernicus.bbn.com*

University of Massachusetts K–12 Internet Resources *k12.ucs.umass.edu*

WELL (Whole Earth 'Lectronic Link) *gopher.well.sf.ca.us*

World Wide Web sites

Classroom Connect *http://www.classroom.net*

Cisco Ed Archive *http://sunsite.unc.edu/cisco/edu-arch.html*

Cyberkids (magazine) *http://www.mtlake.com/cyberkids*

Department of Instructional Technologies at San Francisco State University WWW Server *http://130.212.25.153/dit_home_page.html*

EdWeb *http://k12.cnidr.org:90*

Eisenhower National Clearinghouse on Math and Science *http://www.enc.org*

Global Network Academy (GNA) and Usenet University *http://uu-gna.mit.edu:8001/*

Gifted and Talented Homepage *http://www.eskimo.com/~user/kids.html*

Guides/Tutorials/Lists *http://library.tufts.edu/www/internet_guides.html*

Institute for Learning Sciences *http://www.ils.nwu.edu/e_for_e/index.html*

Internet in the Classroom *http://www.schnet.edu.au*

Jasper Woodbury Math series *http://peabody.vanderbilt.edu/ltc/general/ltcproj.html*

K12 Cyberspace Outpost *http://k12.cnidr.org/janice_k12/k12menu.html*

Kids Created Resources *http://sln.fi.edu/tfi/hotlists/kids.html*

Kids Internet Delight *http://www.clark.net/pub/journalism/kid.html*

Learning in Motion *http://www.learn.motion.com*

NASA's Network Applications and Information Center (NAIC) *http://naic.nasa.gov/naic/guide/*

National Reading Conference *http://www.iusb.edu/webacts/edud/EleEd/nrc/nrcindex.html*

National Reading Conference Yearbook *http://syllabus.syr.edu./EED/DJLEU/EED625/*

Roadmap for the Information Superhighway Interactive Internet Training Workshop *http://www.ll.mit.edu/Roadmap/*

Scholastic *http://scholasic.com:2005/b*

Spacelink *http://spacelink.msfc.nasa.gov*

Uncle Bob's Kids' Page *http://miso.wwa.com/~boba/kids.html*

U.S. Department of Education (ED)/Office of Educational Research and Improvement (OERI) *http://www.ed.gov/*

U.S. Department of Education/Partnership for Family Involvement in Education *http://www.ed.gov/Family/agbts.*

Web66 *http://web66.coled.umn.edu*

Increasingly, computer software and other media is becoming a part of textbook instructional packages. Science and math were areas that textbook publishers quickly targeted for computer software and videodisks. Software such as Microsoft's Magic School Bus series helps elementary teachers teach science concepts associated with astronomy, geology, the human body, and oceanology. Dorling-Kindersley Multimedia offers math, science, and social studies software for students in kindergarten through grade twelve. Topics of the CD-ROMs range from simple math to cartography, world history, space and the universe, the human body, and a 3D human skeleton. Now books with music CD-ROMs are being produced for music and band instruction.

Videodisks enable teachers to target a specific slide or a series of slides without wasting time trying to find the specific locations as would happen with a videotape. Unlike videotapes, videodisks are quite durable, being similar in construction to CD-ROMs. Unfortunately, videodisks can only hold about an hour's worth of material. National Geographic and even the Weather Channel and several other publishers and media producers offer CD-ROMs and videodisks that greatly enrich the curriculum, making the teacher's job easier.

Textbook Adoption

Since the United States does not have a national curriculum, and since each state is charged with the responsibility of educating its children, what is taught in schools varies from state to state. Each state has guidelines for school districts to follow for what will be taught at each grade level and in each subject area. For instance, in Arkansas, schools are not required to teach U.S. history to elementary students, but they must teach economics. In Illinois, all students must take driver's education before they graduate from high school.

Despite differences among the states in what is taught, there seems to be a common curriculum that pervades instruction in all states due to the textbooks used. Textbook companies provide student textbooks and workbooks, teacher's guides, and accompanying extras such as unit tests, worksheets, overhead transparencies, and learning activities. Even today, most students are taught through the use of textbooks and related materials, although the related materials today may include CD-ROMs and videodisks as well as videotapes.

To some degree, textbooks have always influenced the curriculum of a school district because each textbook has its own learning objectives and goals for students. However, there used to be more choices of textbooks than there are currently. Two decades ago, there were numerous commercial textbook companies that published graded materials for teachers and students. As profits became squeezed in the 1970s through the early 1990s, many companies were sold or merged with other companies, while others simply shut their doors. Companies such as Allyn and Bacon,

Ginn, Harcourt Brace and Jovanovich, Macmillan, Silver Burdett, and Scott Foresman, among others, were sold, many to multimedia companies such as General Cinema and Paramount. This resulted in fewer textbook choices for teachers.

Some states, such as Alabama and Indiana, have statewide textbook adoptions. Typically, every five years such states have a call for an adoption for a particular content area, such as math or social studies. The content areas are rotated each year so that a school district is not forced to adopt new textbooks in more than one content area. Teachers from different grade levels throughout an adoption state serve on committees to examine the textbooks, teacher's guides, and accompanying materials. Their input is given to the state department of education, and a decision is made about which textbooks are to be used by schools in the state. Typically, more than one series of books is adopted, with sometimes as many as five or six different companies' textbooks selected.

Developing a new textbook is an expensive business. Each basal reading series, for example, can cost from $50 to $150 million or more to design, field test, produce, and market. Two states with large student populations are California and Texas. Both have statewide adoption. Obviously, being on the state adoption lists for both California and Texas translates into large profit margins for textbook publishers. Hence in recent years, to modify an old saying, "Will it play in California and Texas?" has become the cry of textbook editors and publishers.

Both California and Texas allow the public to examine the textbooks under consideration and to discuss them in open hearings. Thus, members of influential groups, and even small but vocal groups, sometimes determine whether a particular textbook series is adopted and placed on the state's list of acceptable textbooks. For example, fundamental religious groups insist that textbooks reflect the traditional family of a father, mother, and children as well as the values of honesty and hard work. These groups resist the adoption of textbooks with stories about single-parent families or that suggest alternative lifestyles. Members of fundamentalist religions filed lawsuits in Alabama and Tennessee to eliminate certain textbooks in the schools. They lost the suit. Another group of fundamentalist parents sued a school district, claiming that the basal reading series advanced a "satanic religion." The federal judge acknowledged that the series had stories about witches and goblins but dismissed the case by saying that the series was "a far cry from fostering some pagan cult" (Zirkel 1994, 19).

Evaluation and Assessment

In previous centuries it was thought that a student's work should be evaluated based on the final product. In the 1970s, the idea of concentrating on the learning process became popular. Rather than examining the final product, such as a research paper or answers to mathematics equations, the learning process received attention. For instance, when evaluating a child's performance on a test of long division, a teacher who considered only the product would check only the final answers to problems. If you considered the learning process, you would note that the child followed the correct process but made a subtraction error that resulted in the wrong answer.

Evaluation can be *formative*, which is ongoing, day-by-day evaluation, or it can be *summative*, which looks at achievement or performance over a period of time, such as the nine-week grading period, a semester, or a year.

"In California schools, more and more teachers are relying on portfolios to put authentic student work at the center of education.

"When I started teaching seventeen years ago, I would look at student work only to give it a grade and check it off. I relied on publishers to test my students and to tell me what to teach. I would start at Chapter 1 and hope to finish the text before the end of June. In those days, my focus was on me—my plans, my lessons, my teaching. It embarrasses me now to confess this. I would like to call all of my early students and apologize for my selfishness.

"Since that time, a revolution has taken place in my classroom and in classrooms like mine across the state. In California, we have moved beyond a skill-based curriculum, which has to do with teaching, to a meaning-centered curriculum, which has to do with learning. Because of this shift, student work has become the center of education. Teachers no longer follow the guidelines of publishers but, instead, look at their students to determine what must happen next.

The Power of Portfolios

"A portfolio is one strategy teachers can use to focus on student work. In Poway, we've been using Language Arts portfolios for almost three years now. That might seem like a long time in education, but we are just beginning to reach new understandings.

"At first, we coped with the physical problems of portfolios. Who should keep them? Where to keep them? How often should we look at them? What should go inside? Since our new report card stated that 'grades' were based on a collection of work, portfolios appeared in some form in almost every elementary classroom.

"That first year, portfolios were much like the work folders that teachers had traditionally kept for students. Teachers, rather than students, made most of the selections. The portfolios were organized storage bins, where work went in but never came out. Then at the end of the year, the portfolios were sent home—much like a scrapbook for the year.

"In a few places, however, some exciting things were done with portfolios. At Los Penasquitos Elementary School, the third grade team met in a tiny storage room—portfolios in hand—to look more closely at the third grade language arts program. All the portfolios were shuffled and dealt out like a deck of cards. We then spent about forty-five minutes, silently reading and making notes. The first surprise was how accurately the portfolios portrayed our students. I remember reading through one folder and saying, 'Mary, Sarah appears to be struggling with writing. All of her pieces are short and done just to complete the assignment. Her reading list shows that she enjoys reading grade-level books.'

"'That's right,' Mary replied, surprised that I knew so much about a student I had never met. This interchange was repeated time and time again. It gave us great confidence that portfolios could provide an undistorted image of student effort and achievement.

"When we looked at the collection of portfolios as a whole, we made some important discoveries, too. Worksheets and formula writings were much less informative than student-generated topics. Our third grade team decided to spend less time on formula writing assignments that asked students to fill in the gaps—and more time teaching young writers to focus on one topic. So, although we were really looking at *student* learning, we learned a tremendous amount about our students and our third grade program.

Developing Models and Rubrics

"The power of looking directly at student work as a *team* cannot be overstated. Real student work gives teachers a starting point for conversations that get to the essence

(continued)

(concluded)

of what happens in classrooms. Samples of student work are concrete demonstrations of what is known and what is not known. They also provide teachers with signposts that mark how far we've come and point us in the direction we must follow.

"At Los Penasquitos, the principal provided released time for the grade level teams to get together. However, in schools where there is staff interest, teachers can still meet. Bernardo Heights Middle School is a perfect example. Last fall teachers on the seventh- and eighth-grade teams decided to establish schoolwide standards in writing. Using a prompt from the California Assessment Program (CAP) handbook, we asked every seventh- and eighth-grader to write about a school-related experience. Students completed these essays during a forty-five minute class period—all were first draft pieces.

"That afternoon we met to select examples of student writing to serve as models for our six-point rubric. Papers were shuffled about from stack to stack. We placed pieces that showed promise in the *high* pile, papers that looked like typical responses in the *middle* pile, and papers that raised concerns into the *lower* pile.

"In the high pile, we hoped to find 'outstanding' examples that would rate a six and 'good' ones that would rate a five. On the chalkboard, we listed characteristics that put a paper into the top category: selecting a dramatic topic, using precise vocabulary, and creating sentence variety, to name a few.

" 'I think this might be a five,' said Kathy. She read it to our tiny group and then argued for it: 'It has more sophisticated sentence structure than we normally see. The vocabulary is strong, and the details paint a clear picture. I know it's not a 'wow,' but it's clearly a 5.' "

"Our dialogue continued until we had models for each point and had annotated each piece with information for future reference. Each teacher in the group received copies of the models and annotations, and we've shared them with students and parents. We wanted everyone to have a clear understanding of how we look at student writing.

Spotlight on Students' Work

"To our surprise, the models were just one benefit of this entire process. More important, we felt, were the discussion and negotiation that occurred that afternoon. In addition to learning about student writing, we valued the opportunity to talk to one another about the work we do. That sense of being a community of learners continued for the entire year.

"Our 'community of learners' has since expanded to students and their parents. We use our models and rubrics to train young writers to examine their own work and that of their peers:

- Can you find examples of precise vocabulary?
- Can you play a videotape in your head and see the action?
- Here is a paper written last year. You said it was a three. Can you work with your group to make it a four?

"Questions like these help us to zero in on the elements that make writing come alive for the reader.

"Parents have shown their support by attending evening workshops so that they, too, can learn to look at student work through a new lens. 'This is not easy,' one mom wrote after a training session on rubrics. 'However, I think that I can help my daughter better now.'

"Teachers, students, parents—we are all focusing on real work to give us insights about learning. Sometimes, though, these insights make us uncomfortable. 'I'm going to have to re-do mine,' Tom confided to me, 'I just didn't know what *good* looked like!'

"The portfolios that fill our crates and cabinets, and sometimes cover my dining room table, are no longer scrapbooks of completed assignments. Instead they are showcases for the best work a student can do. They allow young people, like Tom, a chance to reflect, revise, and re-start, if necessary, in order to paint a portrait of themselves as learners.

"Portfolios also give me, the teacher, the same opportunity to reflect, revise, and re-start. I no longer look to publishers to tell me what to do next. My students show me the way."

From Christine Sobray Evans, "When Teachers Look at Student Work" in *Educational Leadership,* 50, 5:71–72. Reprinted with permission of the Association for Supervision and Curriculum Development. Copyright ©1993 by ASCD. All rights reserved.

In formative evaluation, the teacher may write down anecdotal records based on observations of the student. Checklists for how the student is doing, for instance, the student knows the multiplication tables for 1s, 2s, 3s, 4s, 5s, etc., may be used.

In summative evaluation, the teacher may compare dated samples of a student's writing to note strengths and weaknesses as well as growth over a set period of time. Standardized achievement tests, which are commercially prepared timed tests, may be given on an annual basis to see how well a school district's student body performs as compared to students on a national basis. This, too, is summative evaluation.

■ Summary

The curriculum is what students are to learn in the classroom and how they are to be taught. The curriculum is designed by a committee of teachers, school administrators, and often parents. The committee makes its recommendations to the school superintendent, who may make recommendations or reject the proposed curriculum. The final approval of the curriculum is by the school board.

There are four primary curriculum structures. The student-centered curriculum is based on the needs and interests of the individual student. The integrated curriculum weaves together two or more content areas, such as science and social studies, to be presented to students at one time. The core curriculum presents information that all students from all backgrounds should know. Lastly, the subject-matter curriculum presents information about each content area in depth with the teacher serving as an expert in his or her specialty.

Each content area has its own unique aspects. What is taught and how it is taught is influenced by the national professional teaching affiliation for each content area as well as state recommendations and local community expectations.

The curriculum is influenced by a variety of other factors including technological advances, textbook adoption, and laws that affect education. Recently multicultural education, values education, and the mainstreaming and inclusion of students with mental and physical disabilities into the regular classroom have impacted the curriculum.

■ Reflections

Compare the curricula of your elementary school, middle school, and high school. What were the curricula of each (student-centered, integrated, core, or subject-matter)? Recall your favorite teacher(s). Which curricular approach did he or she follow? What makes you think so?

Now consider how you will teach. Which curricular approach appeals most to you? Can you give three reasons why you feel that approach is better than the other three?

A Closer Look *Raising Academic Standards*

In order to raise academic standards for American students, voluntary standards are being developed in various subject areas. Encouraged by the success of the national Council of Teachers of Mathematics' (NCTM) *Curriculum and Evaluations Standards for School Mathematics* in 1989, other discipline-based organizations are developing standards. Thousands of teachers, scholars, administrators, parents, and other members of the public have participated in shaping academic standards of what students should know and be able to do.

While states establish their own standards voluntarily and without direction from outside agencies, they often check their standards against those developed, or being developed, by national discipline-based organizations. As of September 1995, the voluntary standards listed below have been completed and might be useful as a resource to communities seeking to establish their own standards for students. In addition, communities might want to check with state departments of education and discipline-based organizations to find out the status of other standards not yet released.

How to Obtain Copies of National Standards Documents

Arts—*Released March 1994*
Music Educators National Conference
Publications Sales
1806 Robert Fulton Drive
Reston, Virginia 22091
800-828-0229

National Standards for Arts Education; item #1605; cost $15.00

Civics and Government—*Released November 1994*
National Standards for Civics and Government
Center for Civic Education
5146 Douglas Fir Road
Calabasas, CA 91302-1467
800-350-4223

National Standards for Civics and Government; ISBN 0-89818-155-0; cost $12.00 plus s/h, discount for bulk orders (sales tax charged in CA)

English Language Arts—*Released April 1996*
National Council of Teachers of English,
Book Order Dept.,
1111 W. Kenyon Road, Urbana IL 61801-1096
ISBN 0-8141-4676-7; Member Price $13.00, Nonmember Price: $18.00; 20 copies or more: $11.00 each

Foreign Language Education—*Released November 1995*
National Standards in Foreign Language Education
American Council on the Teaching of Foreign Languages
6 Executive Boulevard
Yonkers, New York 10701-6801
914-963-8830
cost $20.00 for individual copies, ten or more copies $15.000 each.

Geography—*Released October 1994*
National Geography Standards
National Geographic Society
P.O. Box 1640
Washington, DC 20013-1640
800-368-2728
Geography for Life: National Geography Standards 1994; item #01775; ISBN 0-7922-2775-1; cost $9.00, discount for bulk orders (sales tax charged CA, DC, MD, MI, CANADA)

Science—*Released November 1995*
National Research Council
National Science Education Standards Project
2101 Constitution Ave NW HA486
Washington DC 20418
202-334-1399 or 800-624-6242
ISBN 0-309-05326-9; cost $19.95 single copy, 2–9 copies & 16.50 each, 10 or more copies $13.95 each.

(continued)

 Chapter 12 *The School Curriculum*

(concluded)

History—*Released October/November 1994*
National Center for History in the Schools
University of California, Los Angeles
10880 Wilshire Boulevard, Suite 761
Los Angeles, CA 90024-4108
310-825-4702
Three volumes available:
1. *National Standards for History* (grades K-4); cost $7.95 plus s/h for educators, $12.95 plus s/h for Institutions (sales tax charged in CA);
2. *National Standards for United States History* (grades 5–12); cost $18.95 plus s/h for educators, cost $24.95 plus s/h for institutions (sales tax charged in CA);
3. *National Standards for World History* grades 5-12), cost $18.95 plus s/h for educators, $24.95 plus s/h for institutions (sales tax charged in CA).

Mathematics—*Released 1989*
National Council of Teachers of Mathematics
Order Processing
1906 Association Drive
Reston, Virginia 22091
800-235-7566

Curriculum and Evaluation Standards for School Mathematics; Item #398E1; ISBN 0-87353-273-2; cost $25.00, discount for bulk orders

■ Discussion Questions

1. How is a curriculum designed?
2. Should parents have an equal vote on a curriculum committee?
3. Should a first-year teacher serve on a curriculum committee that interests him or her?
4. Should a teacher be dismissed for not following the school district's curriculum?
5. Should textbooks prepared by professional educators dominate a curriculum?

■ For Further Reading

Baker, E. T., M. C. Wang, and H. J. Walberg. 1994/1995. The effects of inclusion on learning. *Educational Leadership* 52 (4):33–35.

Banks, J. A., and C. A. M. Banks. 1989. *Multicultural education: Issues and perspectives.* Needham Heights, MA: Allyn & Bacon.

Barry, A. L. 1995. Easing into inclusion classrooms. *Educational Leadership* 52 (4):4–6.

Dede, C. (Ed.). 1998. *Learning with technology: 1998 ASCD yearbook.* Alexandria, VA: Association for Curriculum and Development.

Fullan, M. 1993. *Change forces: Probing the depths of educational reform.* London: Falmer Press.

Glatthorn, A. A. 1994. *Developing a quality curriculum,* Alexandria, VA: Association for Supervision and Curriculum Development.

Jacobs, H. H. 1997. *Mapping the big picture: Integrating curriculum and assessment K–12.* Alexandria, VA: Association for Supervision and Curriculum Development.

Oddleifson, E. 1994. What do we want our schools to do? *Phi Delta Kappan* 75 (6):446–52.

Scala, M. A. 1993. What whole language means for children with learning disabilities. *The Reading Teacher* 47 3:222–29.

Spady, W. G. 1994. Choosing outcomes of significance. *Educational Leadership* 51 (6):18–23.

Strickland, D. 1995. Reinventing our literacy programs: Books, basics, balance. *Reading Teacher* 48 (4):294–302.

Zirkel, P. A. 1994. The religious right and the public schools. *Catalyst for Change* 23 (2):18–20.

■ Surfing the 'Net

Curriculum Development
http://www.aads.net.1081/education/

This Website features lesson plans, curriculum guides, and projects.

13

Effective Instructional Strategies

Primary Points

- Teacher effectiveness has been examined in terms of a process-product paradigm.

- Learning theories influence how one teaches.

- Nine educational productivity factors have been identified that help students to be productive learners.

- Direct instruction relies on teacher-student awareness of the goal to be achieved and appropriate teacher modeling and explanation.

- Integrated instruction requires students to be active learners and risk takers.

- The Foxfire approach requires that students take the initiative in their own learning as well as to expand learning out into the community.

- Reflective teaching necessitates that the teacher continuously examine and reexamine his or her teaching practices.

- Cooperative and collaborative learning are based on the concept that when

working together toward a common goal, all students must contribute and as a result each learns more than he or she would individually.

- Technological advancements have made computers and electronic equipment less expensive and a valid means of instruction for students.

Chapter Inquiries

- What are the nine educational productivity factors that contribute to a student's learning?

- What are the differences in the three major learning theories?

- What makes an effective teacher?

- How does integrated instruction differ from direct instruction?

- In what ways are integrated instruction and the Foxfire approach similar?

- How can a teacher use reflective teaching to become a better teacher?

- How has technology impacted teaching?

"For me, effective teaching means having the kids with me. I learn something new about teaching every day. Often the kids clue me into how I can be more effective. Like I used to fill the chalkboard and then erase it. Then I discovered that the old stuff on the board distracted my students from the immediate stuff I wanted them to know." Jim Corrish is a young high school teacher full of ideas and energy to match.

"I learned by making mistakes, too. I used to read my so-called appropriate answer, the one I was looking for, as we went over essay test items. Then I discovered that when I had the students who had the best essay answers read their responses, the other students learned from that experience. They had never paid much attention to me. Ka ching! Bong! Now it makes sense so I do it. Maybe that's what teaching is all about. You teach the kids and the kids teach you. Everyone in the classroom learns."

Teacher preparation programs have two main goals: to help preserve teachers acquire the content they will need to teach students various subjects and to help them develop the pedagogical skills they will need to be in the classroom. Typically this is accomplished by combining coursework and participation in actual classroom settings. According to Grossman (1991, 205), "If teachers are to guide students in their journey into unfamiliar territory, they need to know the terrain as well. Both knowledge of the content and knowledge of the best ways to teach that content to students help teachers construct meaningful representations for students, representations that reflect both the nature of the subject matter and the realities of students' prior knowledge and skill."

Every teacher has a special way of doing things and a special way of thinking—a manner or style that helps characterize who he or she is. Teaching style is a composite of personality and philosophy, evidenced by behavior and attitude, what the teacher emphasizes, how he or she reacts to different situations.

Alan Orstein
Teacher Effectiveness Research: Theoretical Considerations

A major challenge of teacher preparation programs is to create situations, both in the classroom and in other settings, that both interest preservice and/or inservice teachers and help them solve either existing or created problems. By taking action to solve problems, the individual gains both knowledge and skill (Bullough 1989).

Certainly teacher education programs seek to produce teachers who are sensitive, empathetic, and responsive to the needs of their students. These programs also try to stress the need for compassion and warmth as well as enthusiasm for both teaching and subject matter.

Current trends in training teachers evolved from teacher effectiveness research, which largely developed a set of teaching practices and descriptions. These practices and descriptions were strongly suggested to be appropriate for teaching any subject at any grade level.

Teacher Effectiveness

In the early 1980s, several noted researchers, including David Berliner, Jere Brophy, Barak Rosenshine, and Lee Shulman, focused their research on what successful teachers did in the classroom. The primary theoretical framework of teacher effectiveness research is the process-product paradigm developed by Lee Shulman (1987). A collection of teaching practices soon evolved that described the effective delivery of instruction in the classroom. Since 1970, over one thousand studies have been conducted and published regarding effective teacher behavior. Nussbaum (1992, 167) defined effective teacher behaviors as being "those in-class behaviors of the teacher that are related directly either to positive student outcomes or positive evaluations of teaching." Here are some of the findings of teacher effectiveness research:

- Students should be made aware of learning goals.
- Homework needs to have feedback to be worthwhile.
- Wait time is needed (three to five seconds after a question is asked before a student is called on) to produce more thoughtful responses.
- Lessons should be taught at a lively pace.
- Initial questions in a discussion should be low-level knowledge questions, with subsequent questions being of high-level caliber to allow students to adapt to the learning setting (Farris 1993).
- Higher-order questioning, which requires more in-depth and divergent thinking, increases students' thinking ability and achievement.
- Class time should be used efficiently, for instance devoted to learning tasks rather than in moving students and/or materials from one classroom to another.
- Parental involvement is important.

These and other findings have been adopted by many teachers. School districts across the nation use them to evaluate their classroom teachers and school administrators.

Nine Educational Productivity Factors

In 1988, Herbert J. Walberg cited nine educational productivity factors that contribute to student productivity. These are divided into three categories: student aptitude, instruction, and psychological elements.

Student Aptitude
1. *Ability,* or preferably *prior achievement,* as measured by the usual achievement tests
2. *Development,* as indexed by chronological age or stage of maturation
3. *Motivation,* or *self-concept,* as indicated by personality tests or the student's willingness to persevere intensively on learning tasks

Instruction
4. The *amount of time* students engage in learning
5. The *quality of the instructional experience,* including method (psychological) and curricular (content) aspects

Psychological Elements
6. The *curriculum of the home*
7. The *morale* of the classroom social group
8. The *peer group* outside school
9. *Minimum leisure-time television viewing* (Walberg 1988, 77)

Walberg's nine educational productivity factors actually provide a bridge in the research, which changed from emphasizing effective teaching through instructional practices to emphasizing the social aspects of learning. Today, the emphasis is the interaction between the learner and the teacher. Learning and teaching are viewed as social phenomena. The following describes different views of learning and teaching.

Learning Theories

Teaching strategies require an understanding of the various learning theories. Three major views of learning exist: environmental, hereditary, and synthesized. The **environmental** theory holds that intelligence is heavily influenced by one's surroundings, even more so than by one's hereditary traits. Environmentalists such as Benjamin Bloom, Martin Deutsch, and B. F. Skinner advocate the need for supportive programs for students such as the federally funded Head Start and Title I, which provide social and academic readiness and skill development programs for reading and math for low-ability students from low-income communities.

Supporters of the environmental theory are often critical of traditional intelligence testing. They assert that such tests are biased against certain groups such as African Americans and females because of differences in social class, family environment, and gender inequity.

Several studies of the effects of one's environment upon intelligence have been conducted. Scarr and Weinberg (1976) compared African American children who were reared by their biological families with those who were adopted by nonrelatives. Those raised in the adopted families had higher intelligence scores, leading the researchers to conclude that environment had a more significant influence than heredity in determining intelligence. Husen and Tujinman (1991) reviewed numerous studies on intelligence and concluded that meaningful gains in IQ scores can occur from one generation to the next when there are improvements in the economic and social conditions, including accessibility to schooling. Such studies support compensatory intervention programs.

At the opposite end of the spectrum is the **hereditarian** view. In 1969, Arthur Jensen published the results of a study in which he claimed that Asians were superior in intelligence to Caucasians. African Americans averaged fifteen IQ test points lower than Caucasians. In his controversial findings, Jensen concluded that the disparity in intelligence scores was due to genetic differences in learning abilities and learning patterns. Opposition to Jensen's findings quickly arose as some researchers pointed out that impoverished African American women are more apt than are white women to receive inadequate or no prenatal care. Likewise, white children generally receive better medical health care than do African American children. Another factor in the IQ score difference is the biased nature of the intelligence tests.

In 1994, Richard Herrnstein, a Harvard University professor, and Charles Murray, a political analyst, published a highly controversial book, *The Bell Curve.* The authors of this book assumed that genes account for 40 to 80 percent of intelligence. The authors of *The Bell Curve* say that their findings suggest that the intermarriage of highly intelligent and well-educated people and the opposite, the intermarriage of poorly educated people of lower intelligence, will lead to a two-tiered American society, one rich and smart and the other impoverished and dumb.

Taking both environmental and hereditary factors into consideration is the **synthesizer** view, which says that both factors play an important role in intelligence. Two noted researchers in this area are Christopher Jencks and Robert Nichols. Jencks (1987) believes that heredity contributes up to .45 variance of intelligence scores while up to .35 is attributed to environmental factors. The remaining variance, about .20, is due to interaction between heredity and environment. The interaction is a result that some abilities are nurtured while others languish in specific environments. For instance, a child with an interest in music might thrive in an environment with opportunities for music lessons and concert attendance. On the other hand, a child with an interest in science who is unable to visit museums or who attends a school with a very limited science curriculum is less likely to develop advanced scientific skills.

Nichols (1978), another proponent of the synthesized learning theory, disagrees with Jencks on the portion of intelligence that can be attributed to environment and/or heredity. Nichols asserts that the proportions are not important; rather, it is the interaction between environment and heredity that is the crucial point in determining intelligence. In Nichols' opinion, parents and educators must focus on providing an enriching environment in order to nurture children and stimulate their intellect.

In 1997, researchers at the University of Pittsburgh concluded that the womb should be considered an environment that significantly affects intelligence. While there have been over two hundred studies of identical twins, who have identical genes, demonstrating similarities of IQ, this study compared fraternal twins, who have different genetic makeup, and found that they have more similar IQs than do siblings. These researchers found that 48 percent of intelligence is attributed to genes (Begley 1997). Increased research into prenatal life and its contributions may result in new findings and theories regarding genetical and environmental factors in determining IQ.

Psychological Theories

Three major psychological theories have developed. These are the behaviorist theory, which emphasizes the need for rewarding appropriate behavior, constructivism, which stresses the need for activities to stimulate intellectual growth, and Howard Gardner's multiple intelligences theory, which describes how every human being possesses eight different intelligences.

The **behaviorist** theory of psychology is grounded in the environmental view of learning. Pavlov's dogs salivated whenever a bell rang, having associated the ringing bell with food. From this early study, behaviorism grew, becoming particularly popular in the 1960s under the leadership of B. F. Skinner. Skinner said that if you gave him a newborn infant, he could train it through environmental intervention to be anything you wanted, be it a nuclear scientist or an artist. Behaviorism advocates positive reinforcement as being central to teaching children to learn new skills. By saying positive, buoyant comments to students as they succeed in completing learning tasks, they will be encouraged to continue. Giving students concrete rewards such as a movie and a popcorn party if they all score above a certain level on the six weeks review spelling test would be a classroom technique that a behaviorist would support.

While positive reinforcement is encouraged, negative reinforcement, or punishment, is considered by behaviorists to be largely ineffective in changing behavior. Hence, most behavior modification techniques emphasize the development of positive self-esteem.

Behaviorism, while not as prevalent as a psychological view today, still is widely used in schools, particularly with mentally challenged or behavior-disordered students. Those students who excel academically are given the positive reinforcement of having their names listed on the school's honor roll, which is generally published in the local paper for the community to see. Certainly the success of casinos and lotteries depends upon positive reinforcement. Some frequent riverboat gamblers claim that slot machines yield greater winnings the last few minutes of the trip. If true, the owners of the riverboats would be relying upon behaviorism, wanting their customers to leave the premises as winners feeling good so they will be eager to return, perhaps bringing even more money to gamble.

Like behaviorism, **constructivism** stresses the importance of the environment in learning. In effect, the child uses previously gained knowledge along with newly acquired knowledge to "construct" new knowledge. Constructivism has its roots in the modern-day work of Jean Piaget, a Swiss biologist. Piaget observed the behavior of his own three children and claimed that children's cognitive development occurs in stages. These stages are outlined below.

The Sensorimotor Stage

The sensorimotor stage is the shortest in duration, but it is a stage in which children make significant advances. The sensorimotor stage is from birth to about age two. During this time children learn to grasp items, sit up, eat, crawl, walk, and run. Language development is rapid during this stage, and by age ten to twelve months, children begin speaking, using nouns such as "Dada," "Mama," and "doggie." From nouns, children move on to acquire verbs, the negative (and often defiant) "NO!", and then adjectives. Pronouns are acquired late, with "me" and "mine" being among the first learned. By the time children leave the sensorimotor stage, they are using short phrases and simple sentences to convey needs, wants, and desires.

During the preoperational stage, children begin to use **assimilation** as new data is incorporated into their conceptual banks of information. Upon the child's seeing a horse for the first time, a child's parent may point out that it is a "horsey." The child will later see another horse and say "horsey." **Accommodation** occurs whenever the established conceptual framework is changed or modified upon the discovery of new information. For instance, when the child sees a mule, it is similar to a horse with its four legs and tail, but the ears have a different shape and the sound it makes is far different. Later the child will use accommodation to differentiate between kinds of horses, such as pinto, buckskin, bay, sorrel, and palomino.

The Preoperational Stage

From about age two until age seven, children are in the preoperational stage. As in the sensorimotor stage, language development gains are tremendous as they pick up the meaning of literally thousands of words. This is the period of time that parents have to "watch what they say," as all new words are appealing, especially those used by parents As one mother slowed her car for an intersection, the light turned red, prompting her three-year-old son to shout out, "Damn it!" When she inquired why he said what he did, the boy's immediate response was, "That's what Daddy always says"

The preoperational stage finds children engaging in egocentric behavior. Young children may seemingly be carrying on conversations with other children but upon listening, the observer discovers that while each child takes his or her turn in a "conversation," each individual is talking about something entirely different. Each child carries on a solitary conversation with himself or herself. Talking out loud in a monologue is commonplace. Kurtis, aged 30 months, enjoyed singing in the tub. Upon conclusion of each invented song, a combination of various sounds, Kurtis would throw back his head and yell "Yee-ooo!" Then, he would bow graciously to his audience of tub toys and say, "Thank you, duck. Thank you, frog"—as if his yellow rubber duck and green plastic frog had given him a standing ovation.

Children in this stage are much more observant of their surrounding environment, desiring to fit in. Marks on paper have meaning, so they want to write, even if it is scribbling with a crayon on the wall. Older siblings bemoan the desire of the young preoperational to always "tag along."

Superheroes, wrestling idols, Barbies, and Beanie Babies are all part of this stage. In particular, superheroes are viewed as the know-all, be-all characters who right wrongs. This is important, for at this stage of cognitive development, everything is classified by children as being good or evil, with no in-between behavior accepted by members of this age group.

The Concrete Operational Stage

From age seven through eleven or twelve, most children fall into the concrete operational stage. During this stage, active involvement with the environment is still critical. For instance, through manipulating objects, the child discovers similarities and differences, important concepts in classification. When given two different-shaped containers that hold the same quantity of liquid, the child will say that the two containers are the same size in terms of the amount that can be put in them. If two identical-sized pencils are placed next to each other and then moved apart, the concrete operational child will say that they are still the same size. This is the ability to **conserve.** Preoperational children will be unable to perform these seemingly simple tasks.

The Formal Operations Stage

At age eleven or twelve, most, but not all, children enter the formal operations stage, or the stage of abstract thinking. Some children don't enter this stage until they are teenagers; some never enter it at all. Unlike in the previous three stages which relied heavily upon firsthand experiences, such experiences are not as essential in this stage, because children in the formal operations stage can form images in their minds. Interests become more adultlike, so, for example, children in this stage may prefer to see PG-13- and R-rated movies, read adult action and mystery novels or science fiction, or engage in challenging levels of computer games.

Piaget's Four Stages of Cognitive Development	
Sensorimotor Stage	birth to age two
Preoperational Stage	age two to age seven
Concrete Operations	age seven to age twelve or thirteen
Abstract Thinking Stage	age twelve or thirteen on

Early childhood teachers observe students' behavior patterns noting how they differ in the various stages of development. By middle school level, those students who have entered the abstract thinking stage vary greatly in their academic abilities and approaches to learning new content from those who are still in the content operations stage.

Teachers who use the constructivist model plan activities during which there is interaction between the child and the environment, which requires much planning by the teacher. At the early childhood and elementary levels, the activities involve hands-on experiences. At the middle/junior high school and high school levels, the activities rely upon the ability to use abstract thinking. Typically the activities require children to solve problems. A criticism of constructivism is that such activities require large amounts of time for the students to complete. Constructivists argue that the time is put to good use because once the students go through the learning process, they retain the knowledge and concepts.

In contrast to behaviorism and constructivism, Harvard professor Howard Gardner developed the theory of **multiple intelligences,** which attributes to each learner a group of eight intelligences, each having a unique neurological pattern and course of development. Previously, it was thought by any theorists that intelligence was comprised of verbal and reasoning abilities. Gardner defines intelligence as follows:

An intelligence entails the ability to solve problems or fashion products that are of consequence in a particular setting. The problem-solving skill allows one to approach a situation in which a goal is to be obtained and to locate the appropriate route to that goal. The creation of a cultural product is crucial to capturing and transmitting knowledge or expressing one's views or feelings. The problems to be solved range from creating an end to a story to anticipating a mating move in chess to repairing a quilt. Products range from scientific theories to musical composition to successful political campaigns (Gardner 1993, 7–8).

The eight intelligences included in Gardner's theory are listed below.

1. **Linguistic Intelligence**
   This intelligence involves sensitivity to the meaning of words, their order and syntax, the sounds, rhythms, and inflections of language, and the uses of language.

2. **Musical Intelligence**
   This intelligence consists of sensitivity to rhythm, pitch, and timbre. It also has an emotional component. Gardner relates musicians' descriptions of their abilities that emphasize an individual's natural feel for music and not the reasoning or linguistic components of musical ability.

3. **Logical-Mathematical Intelligence**
   This intelligence involves interaction with objects and is often called "scientific thinking." Deductive thinking and reasoning, making computations using numbers, and recognizing abstract patterns are included.

4. **Spatial Intelligence**
   This intelligence is the capacity to perceive the physical world accurately, to perform transformations and modifications on these perceptions, and to produce or recreate forms.

5. **Body and Kinesthetic Intelligence**
   This intelligence involves the ability to use the body in highly specific and skilled ways, both for expressive and goal-directed purposes.

6. **Intrapersonal Intelligence**
   This intelligence involves the ability to access one's own feelings and to label, discriminate, and symbolize one's range of emotions in order to understand one's own behavior.

7. **Interpersonnel Intelligence**
   This intelligence involves the ability to notice and make distinctions about other people's moods, temperaments, motivations, and intentions.

8. **Naturalist Intelligence**

   This intelligence, the last to be identified by Gardner, involves the ability to classify nature such as flora and fauna, or plants and rocks.

In Gardner's opinion, the school day is designed to favor those students who perform well in reading and writing, thus emphasizing linguistic intelligence. It does not address the spatial skills of a student who can operate a film projector after seeing the teacher set it up once—the same student who may be considered a poor student because of limited reading and writing abilities. Because schools fail to nurture all eight intelligences, Gardner believes that educators have taken too narrow a view with regard to who is intelligent. Gardner asserts that educators must broaden their definition of intelligence to include all eight intelligences. In planning learning experiences for their students, teachers should include activities for each of the eight intelligences whenever possible.

The fundamental goal of education, according to Gardner, should be "genuine understanding—going beyond repetitive learning and short answers" (1993, 27). He proposes that education systems should increase the amount of learning activities they offer that involve both individual and group projects, apprenticeships, and hands-on experiences. Gardner says, "People probably learn more from the few projects they do in school than from hundreds and hundreds of hours of lectures and homework assignments" (Gursky 1992, 28). Also, Gardner asserts that schools should help students discover subject area that interest them instead of just focusing on the learning of basic skills. If schools do this, Gardner believes that children's senses of adventure, flexibility, creativity, and natural enthusiasm for learning will be enhanced rather than suppressed. This then would facilitate the attaining of a genuine understanding of whatever children would be learning and, therefore, would facilitate the transferring of this understanding to situations in everyday life.

Systematic Direct Instruction

One educator describes systematic **direct instruction** in this way: "In direct instruction, students and teacher are focused on a goal or objective, on what is to be learned; students are aware of why it is important to learn the task at hand; and students are explicitly taught how to do a particular process through teacher modeling and explanation" (Spiegel 1992, 41). Research suggests that direct teaching and memorization can be more efficient time-wise than lessons that are less directed or have no specific direction. This is especially true if the educational goals and purposes are made clear to students (Walberg 1988).

The teacher first sets specific learning goals and objectives and then incorporates instructional activities that fulfill these educational goals. A systematic curriculum must be established and maintained to prevent "learning and teaching chaos." According to Yatvin (1991, 1), without a schoolwide curriculum "that ensures a rational and orderly distribution of content and materials over the grades," rebellion will occur as every teacher creates a curriculum to meet the needs of his or her students.

Much of the research on direct instruction has been conducted by Barak Rosenshine (Rosenshine and Stevens 1986). Research findings suggest that nine teaching behaviors play an integral role in direct instruction.

1. Begin a lesson with a short review of previous, prerequisite learning.
2. Begin a lesson with a short statement of goals.
3. Present new material in small steps, with student practice after each step.

4. Give clear and detailed instructions and explanations.
5. Provide a high level of active practice for all students.
6. Ask a large number of questions, check for student understanding, and obtain responses from all students.
7. Guide students during initial practice.
8. Provide systematic feedback and corrections.
9. Provide explicit instruction and practice for seatwork exercises and, where necessary, monitor students during work (Rosenshine and Stevens 1986, 377).

Through demonstration or modeling lessons, students learn new concepts and information. However, unless the lessons are long enough, students may fail to learn enough to transfer the learning to another situation (Durkin 1990).

Standardized achievement tests are typically used to measure achievement for direct instructional purposes. The test items are typically objective in nature.

Integrated Instruction

Integrated instruction is promoted largely by supporters of the whole language movement, which emphasizes the importance of students using meaningful, relevant materials in their learning, much like the proponents of progressive education stress. The emphasis is placed on "whole to part" learning—the broader picture is viewed initially before breaking it down into smaller sections (Goodman 1986). Students acquire learning strategies that they can apply to a variety of learning situations.

In whole language instruction, students are given choices in their learning. The term *empowerment* is frequently used for both the teacher and students. The teacher and students work as a team to choose what will be learned as well as how the learning will occur. Passive learners are encouraged to take control of their learning just as their actively involved peers do. Teachers have more input into curricular decisions with this approach.

The teacher encourages risk taking as students choose how and what they will learn. Thus, students try out new ideas and theories. The whole language movement, in the strictest sense, encourages that students themselves determine what they will learn. Or as Dorothy Watson (1989, 133) wrote, "Nothing is set into classroom motion until it is validated by learners' interest and motivated by their needs." Opponents argue that students cannot be expected to know what they need to know purely from an intuitive perspective, just as an ill person cannot accurately determine what medicine or treatment is needed for a cure.

With the focus more on the learning *process* than the final *product,* the classroom becomes a community of learners, with the teacher learning from the students just as the students learn from the teacher and each other (Farris 1993). Everyone in the classroom seeks to work together to meet genuine needs and concerns (Allen et al. 1991).

One of the drawbacks to whole language and wholistic instruction is that some students, particularly those of low ability, cannot discover and use learning strategies (Rosenshine and Stevens 1984). In addition, it is argued that minority students may not benefit as much from wholistic instruction because they need more direct instruction. According to Spiegel (1992, 43), "Children from upper and middle classes come to school already knowing the codes and rules for participating in power; that is, they know how to operate within the culture of power." In contrast, many minority children, particularly those from low socioeconomic families, discover that learning is much easier if the rules are explicitly taught, as in

There are twelve primary differences between traditional skills-based instruction, commonly referred to as *direct instruction,* and nontraditional, strategy-based instruction, commonly referred to as *integrated instruction.*

Direct Instruction (Skills)	Integrated Instruction (Whole Language)
1. Children are expected to be passive participants pants in the learning process.	1. Children are expected to be active participants in the learning process.
2. The product is the msot important part of learning.	2. The process is the most important part of learning.
3. Part to whole is stressed (phonics).	3. Whole to part is stressed, as is part to whole (phonics).
4. Learning is based on a sequence of skills.	4. Learning is based on relevant, real experiences.
5. Motivtion to learn is extrinsic (material rewards such as stickers are given out).	5. Motivation to learn is intrinsic (child learns be cause of self desire to learn).
6. Children are placed in groups according to ability (low, average, high).	6. Children are grouped by interests and re grouped as topics change.
7. Competition is encouraged.	7. Cooperation is encouraged.
8. The teacher makes the decisions as to what will be taught and how it will be presented to students.	8. Students make choices as to what and how they will learn.
9. The teacher directly guides instruction, serving as a leader.	9. The teacher indirectly guides instruction, serving as facilitator.
10. Textbooks serve as the materials for teaching.	10. Children's literature and children's own writing serve as the materials for teaching.
11. Multiple choice, true–false, and essay tests are used for evaluation.	11. Samples of the children's own work are used for evaluation.
12. The classroom is book centered (the child must fit the book).	12. The classroom is child centered (the book must fit the child).

Adapted from P. J. Farris. (1993). *Language Arts: A Process Approach.* Dubuque, IA: Brown & Benchmark, p. 26. Used by permission.

direct instruction, as well as if they are told specifically why they need to learn that information (Delpit 1991). According to Delpit (1988, 287), the whole language approach, with its process-oriented instruction, "creates situations in which students ultimately find themselves held accountable for knowing a set of rules about which no one has ever directly informed them. . . . Teachers do students no service to suggest, even implicitly, that 'product' is not important. In this country students *will* be judged on their product, regardless of the process they utilized to achieve it."

Wholistic instruction stresses authentic assessment, that is, looking at what the student has done both from a process *and* a product standpoint. This includes higher-order thinking skills, depth of knowledge, and degree of connectedness to the world (Newmann and Wehlage 1993). Portfolios, a collection of the student's work such as initial and final drafts of pieces of writing, research reports, science observation notes, math problems, and lists of books read, are often used to determine student growth and achievement.

The current trend is to use whole language ideas in an integrated curriculum. Thus two or more subject areas are taught at the same time. For instance, phonics is taught as part of reading for content in the early grades. For high school in a biology class, students may study the effects of pollution at the same time as they are discussing in economics class the pros and cons of industrial pollution.

The Foxfire Approach

In the late 1960s, a young high school English teacher named Eliot Wigginton became known for his successful teaching approach called *Foxfire.* As a first-year teacher in Rabun Gap, Georgia, Wigginton struggled with teaching English to high school juniors and seniors. The textbooks were not relevant to his impoverished students from Appalachia; extrinsic motivation was insufficient. Wigginton suggested that the students help define the English curriculum by finding stories in the local community and writing about them in a class newspaper. The result was Foxfire.

Students from Wigginton's classes interviewed members of the community, in effect conducting an oral history project. Interview topics ranged from folk cures for a variety of illnesses and injuries to how to shoe a horse or make lye soap. Several collections of student essays have been published over the years, all under the Foxfire name.

Today, a network of teachers throughout the United States uses the Foxfire approach to teaching. This teaching is characterized by a respect for the learner, a commitment to achieving goals and objectives, the need for learning to go beyond the classroom and into the community, and the need to appreciate the aesthetic in learning (Wigginton 1985). The teacher's role is that of a collaborator in the learning process, focusing on developing each student's positive self-concept (Foxfire Fund 1990).

With the Foxfire approach, students make choices and decisions throughout the learning process. A final product is produced. Students typically collaborate on projects, with each doing what he or she does best (e.g., photography, interviewing, writing columns).

Reflective Thinking and Teaching

In the 1980s and early 1990s, one of the most discussed developments in educational circles was the concept of reflective thinking. Other fields, such as medicine and health care, have become aware of the value of reflective thinking in developing better doctors, nurses, and health technicians. **Reflective teaching** contrasts sharply with the simplistic, almost technical view of teaching present in the 1980s (Sparks-Langer and Colton 1991), which included the very effective teaching approach of direct instruction (Berliner and Rosenshine 1977; Rosenshine and Berliner 1978). As educators have realized that teaching is a complex, situation-specific activity, however, an increasing number have become proponents of reflective thinking and teaching.

Reflective thinking was defined by Boyd and Fales (1983) as the process of creating and clarifying the meaning of an experience, either past or present, in terms of "self." The outcome, or benefit, of the process is a change or modification in your conceptual perspective.

The concept of shifting, or changing, from one perspective to another is not a recent one. Historians point to Plato and his followers, who used reflection to challenge or change an individual's perspective. At the beginning of the twentieth century, John Dewey advocated behavior that involved active, persistent, and careful consideration of a belief or practice and its consequences (Canning 1991). Thus, Dewey was a supporter of reflective thinking and action.

Reflective thinking is a natural and spontaneous process. According to research, naming a process, that is, bringing to consciousness what we do naturally and routinely, is a significant way of supporting its use (Boyd and Fales 1983). In other words, most of us already use some form of reflection as a pathway to modify our actions or perspectives, but we are largely unaware that we do so. Thus, as we become more aware of our spontaneous reflective activity and of its importance and worth to us, our interest in discovering whether we can control our own process of reflective thinking increases. Boyd and Fales found that once people become aware of their own reflective activity, most try to harness and manipulate their own reflective processes.

Reflective thinking is a rich source for both professional and personal growth (Killion and Todnem 1991). *The Reflective Practitioner,* by Donald Schon, was first published in 1983. The book was not specifically directed toward educators, but since that time many teachers and administrators have embraced Schon's ideas on reflective thinking and how it can be used effectively in teaching. A second book by Schon, *Educating the Reflective Practitioner* (1987), elaborates on the idea of reflective thinking. In these two books, Schon describes two types of reflective thinking, reflection-on-action and reflection-in-action. Reflection-on-action involves thinking about our actions and thoughts *after* an action is completed. This is a type of hindsight thinking. Reflection-in-action occurs during the action itself. A third type of reflection, reflection-for-action, was proposed by Killion and Todnem (1991). They suggest that reflection-for-action occurs whenever reflective thinking is used to guide future actions. We examine our past and present experiences and knowledge to help us decide what to do in the future. In reflection-for-action, teachers use information gathered from both reflection-on-action and reflection-in-action, analyze it, and draw conclusions that help in future decision making.

Reflective practice is found in our everyday activities, as we redesign and reconstruct our existing thoughts (Wellington 1991). Generally speaking, reflection applied in the area of education is defined as "a way of thinking about educational matters that involves the ability to make rational choices and to assume the responsibility for those choices" (Ross 1989, 22).

Different versions of reflective practice have been suggested to create a preliminary framework of reflective thinking. Smythe (1989) provides a model of reflective thinking with four stages that are both sequential, that is, they follow one another, and cyclical, that is, they are both repetitive and expansive. Each stage actively involves the person and necessitates that a deeper level of reflection be used.

The first stage of reflective thinking, according to Smythe, is called the *describing* stage. At this stage the teacher describes the various aspects of the event under reflection. The second stage is *informing*. It is at this stage that the teacher views how a theory was applied to the event. The third stage, *confronting,* forces the teacher to reflect on how the situation was impacted by the larger social-culture milieu. Thus, the teacher must take into consideration how outside political and social forces impact on the practices employed within the classroom. This could vary from state and federal funding for educational programs to neighborhood gangs. The last stage is *reconstructing,* the primary goal of reflective thinking. This stage helps the teacher to

Marilyn Fergus, a fifth-grade teacher, keeps a journal to record her thoughts about the school day. Initially, she assigned her students the task of devoting five minutes each school day to journal writing while she, also, wrote in a journal. But she has continued the practice herself for many years.

The daily journal entries became reflections on the school day. Marilyn wrote about lesson plans that went well or activities that needed modification. She wrote about problems with the curriculum or with students and parents. Every two weeks or so, Marilyn reread portions of her journal and then wrote her reactions to her first written impressions in another area of the journal. She found herself questioning and probing her teaching methods. She also found herself seeking advice from other teachers and her principal about specific teaching approaches or discipline problems. Often, she would venture to a nearby college to peruse articles on topics that she had written about in her journal.

Marilyn believes that her reflective journal has made her a better teacher: "I ponder more, and act hastily less. While I write, I mull over the problems of my students as well as find time to celebrate each little triumph they may have. I, too, write about problems with teaching—lack of resources, textbook adoption, discipline, and so on. But I try to find one thing each time I write an entry to include that celebrates a victory, no matter how small. We all need to value what we do in teaching. My journal helps me to value and respect myself as a teacher."

see what actions might be taken in future situations. This stage enables the teacher to change direction if the course of action so warrants it. Together, these four stages of reflective thinking should improve a teacher's observations and judgments and improve the delivery of education in the classroom.

The initial steps in developing a reflective approach have been outlined by Ross (1989, 22). These include the following:

- Recognizing an educational dilemma;
- Responding to a dilemma by recognizing both the similarities to other situations and the unique qualities of the situation;
- Framing and reframing the dilemma;
- Experimenting with the dilemma to discover the consequences and implications of various situations; and
- Examining the intended and unintended consequences of an implemented solution and evaluating the solution by determining whether the consequences are desirable or not.

Increasingly, teacher education programs across the country are adopting some form of reflective thinking as part of their preservice and inservice requirements. Teacher education programs such as the Collaboration for the Improvement of Teacher Education (CITE) at Eastern Michigan University have found that technical and practical reflection are relatively easy for future teachers to learn and acquire. However, it is more difficult to achieve critical reflection (Sparks-Langer and Colton 1991).

Reflection is becoming a part of teacher education programs in the hope that these practices will carry over into individual teaching styles. Many view reflective thinking as a way teachers can improve their teaching methods. Reflective thinking permits student teachers and classroom teachers to analyze, question, probe, and reflect upon their experiences in the field.

One of the most widely used reflective thinking activities is that of journal writing. This activity is appropriate for the student teacher, as well as the novice teacher and seasoned veteran. Through journal writing, the teacher can question, make linkages between theory and practice, develop a deeper understanding of content material, and allow for experimentation with new ideas. Journal writing also requires personal involvement in addition to an occasional transformation of perspective.

Reflective thinking raises the level of consciousness, challenges complacency, and encourages a higher order of professional practice. It requires initial training in reflective techniques, but in essence it makes teachers and administrators alike aware of a practice that most of us already engage in effectively but only for short amounts of time.

Cooperative/Collaborative Learning

Competitive and individual goals are a major part of classroom instruction; however, **cooperative/collaborative learning** is being encouraged by more and more school districts. Rather than competitive learning, in which students are pitted against each other, cooperative/collaborative learning stresses the need to work together as a team to produce a final product. As such, each team member plays a crucial role; thus, if one member of the team fails, so does the entire team. According to Slavin (1988), when a group of children collaborate to accomplish a common goal, the finished product is superior to what would be produced if each student worked alone.

Serving as a social model, cooperative/collaborative learning necessitates that heterogeneous groups be created to investigate a topic or to develop a particular end product. Cooperative/collaborative learning encourages the members of the group to share any previously gained knowledge. In addition, divergent thinking is valued by the group.

To be most effective, cooperative/collaborative learning must have two elements present: (1) the students must work toward achievement of a common goal, and (2) the achievement of the goal must be dependent on the individual learning of each member of the group (Slavin 1988).

Research findings indicate that cooperative/collaborative learning can benefit all students—low ability, infused, or gifted (Augustine, Gruber, and Hanson 1989 and 1990; Watson and Rangel 1989). Because groups are formed heterogeneously, respect for different cultures is another benefit.

Johnson and Johnson (1991, 283) assert that "no matter how intellectually capable or skilled individuals are, if they do not exert considerable effort and seek to achieve challenging goals, their productivity will be low." In their review of 375 research studies, Johnson and Johnson (1989) conclude that working cooperatively to meet a shared goal yields greater effort, increased achievement, and increased productivity than when individuals work alone.

The Cooperative Learning Center, at the University of Minnesota, directed by David W. Johnson and Roger T. Johnson, has a Website (http://www.clcrc.com/) that offers lots of information.

Figure 1

Unit around subject area topic

From Bess Altwerger and Barbara M. Flores, "Theme Cycles: Creating Communities of Learners" in *Primary Voices, K–6,* January 1994. Copyright © 1994 by the National Council of Teachers of English. Reprinted with permission.

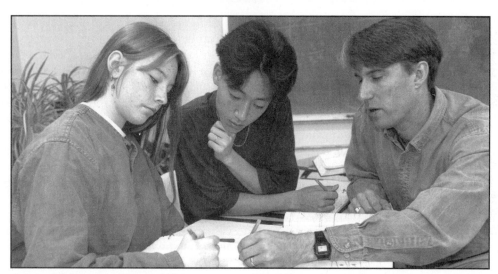

The combination of a knowledgeable, caring teacher who is willing to help his students learn makes for an effective learning environment. (© John Eastcott/Yva Momatiuk/The Image Works, Inc.)

Theme Cycles

The use of theme cycles is an integrated curriculum approach used at the elementary school level. Unlike theme units, in which one particular subject area might focus on a topic unrelated to other areas (e.g., the study of the westward movement during the 1800s in social studies, while studying fractions in math and fusion in science), theme cycles focus on one area of study for the entire curriculum (e.g., weather—reading the weather report in the newspaper and writing about how the weather affects one's outdoor activities as part of composition, graphing the daily high and low changes in the temperature outdoors as part of math, reading about historical events that were affected by the weather as part of social studies, and studying cloud formations and barometric influences in science) (figure 1).

Figure 2 The learning process using theme cycles.

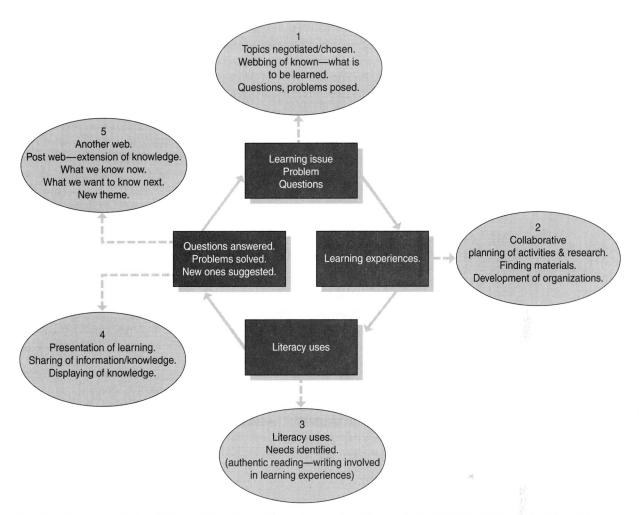

From Bess Altwerger and Barbara M. Flores, "Theme Cycles: Creating Communities of Learners" in *Primary Voices, K–6,* January 1994. Copyright © 1994 by the National Council of Teachers of English. Reprinted with permission.

Theme cycles naturally evolve into new topics because "new and related questions and problems are posed" (Altwerger and Flores 1994, 4). Five steps exist in the theme cycle, each generating another (figure 2).

1. Collectively tapped knowledge of the negotiated topic leads to collaboratively posed questions and problems by the students.
2. The questions and problems lead to the selection of learning experiences.
3. The learning experiences suggest teaching methods and materials.
4. Creative presentation of learning that is also meaningful to students leads to new areas of investigation (Altwerger and Flores 1994).

5. Extension activity that demonstrates learning occurs. This may also lead into a new theme.

The teacher, along with students, is challenged by creating new knowledge in a group process. Students are encouraged to become decision makers and to make choices. Thus, the theme cycle approach emphasizes the contributions of all students as well as the teacher, and the classroom becomes a community of learners.

Because all of the class becomes involved in the learning process in a wholistic manner, theme cycles have become popular with bilingual students. The approach seems to help maintain higher levels of student motivation.

Theme cycles at the elementary and middle school levels allow for the integration of all of the content areas. In addition, students are helped to see how one thing is connected to something else. One major drawback is the tremendous amount of preparation time on the part of the classroom teacher (Andrews-Sullivan and Negrete 1994). However, good planning on the teacher's part aids student learning.

Technology and Teacher Effectiveness

The information superhighway has reached into our schools, connecting them with information links throughout the country and even the world. Of all of our states, Iowa has developed the most comprehensive fiber optics linkage between its schools in an attempt to provide the best education possible for its students. Students can access data and communicate with other students throughout the state and beyond.

Distance Education

Distance education gained popularity in the 1980s largely because of the accessibility of satellite dishes. Rural school districts throughout the United States and Canada quickly found that distance education was a means to efficiently provide for the educational needs of students, particularly at the high school level. While it may appear to be an expensive undertaking, after the initial purchase of equipment for each classroom (video camera, television set, phone, and phone lines), the cost is relatively inexpensive. Through the use of interactive video teleconferencing, carried by satellite aboveground or fiber optic lines belowground, a handful of students in a remote Nebraska farming community, for example, can take courses such as physics, calculus, and Latin—courses that would be too expensive for their school district to provide but that are affordable through these technological advances.

In distance education, it is possible for students to view a teacher and class in another part of the state, usually a neighboring school district. The teacher can see both the students in his or her classroom as well as the students in the classroom miles away, who are projected on a television screen, thus enabling both groups of students to participate in the class discussion and to ask questions. In some instances, as many as five or six classrooms may be connected at one time as part of the interactive video connection.

Distance education can be used for a variety of educational activities. For instance, after talking about earthquakes as part of their elementary science unit, a group of sixth-graders in Ohio can use the interactive technology to have a discussion about earthquakes with sixth-graders from Los Angeles who experienced the 1994 earthquake.

"Frank & Ernest reprinted by permission of Newspaper Enterprise Association, Inc."

Computers

As the cost of computers and other technological equipment decreases, students more often have access to technology that can enhance their learning. Now students have access to the entire works of Shakespeare, the complete holdings of the Smithsonian Institute, the speeches of famous American political and civil rights leaders, archaeological findings in ancient Egypt, or an entire encyclopedia on CD-ROM disks by computer in their classroom or computer lab.

As computer chips become increasingly smaller and cheaper and able to hold more and more information, computers have become an essential classroom teaching component. Today they are as common in most classrooms as chalkboards. The ratio of students to computers in schools is about thirteen to one and dropping every year. Even kindergartners work at computer stations to develop simple math skills such as counting and the concepts of less than and more than, to learn the letters of the alphabet, or to see how mixing two basic colors creates a secondary color.

In the early 1980s, computer programs were largely "drill and kill" programs, so-called because of their similarity to boring workbook drills. There have been many advancements in software since then, however. Students engage in continual and direct two-way communication with a computer, sometimes referred to as "interactivity." Students respond to questions and receive both positive and negative feedback (Lockard, Abrams, and Many 1990).

The term **hypermedia** refers to the use of a variety of media at one time. Today's technology permits students to write a research paper using the word processing program on a computer and also to select a portion of a video laser disk to incorporate into the report. For instance, a science report on tornadoes can be made more effective by adding a video of an actual tornado. The video adds emphasis and helps the teacher to know whether the student understands the concepts presented.

School districts with limited fiscal resources are often unable to provide any computers for students. Other schools with greater financial resources not only provide computers but also regularly upgrade to newer models to keep students abreast of the latest developments. Other schools use outdated machines that lack the memory to run more sophisticated education software programs, thereby limiting what the teacher can offer to students. On the other hand, schools with better financial resources can provide networking between schools within the district. More and more schools have computer modems that enable students to communicate with others throughout the world.

Point /Counterpoint

To What Degree Should Students Have Access To Technology?

Point: The age of the information superhighway is here and should be shared with our elementary and secondary students.

We live in a highly technological world. The typical elementary or secondary student encounters myriad technological advancements every day, whether it be warming a frozen muffin in a microwave, playing a computer game with a friend, or fastening a coat with Velcro. To deprive students of technological advancements in the classroom is to ignore the real world.

Unfortunately, even when technology is included as part of the curriculum, many students have better technological access to the information superhighway than their school provides. They may have access to an on-line service at home but be working on outdated computers in their classrooms.

By learning to use technology, students are able to practice skills they will need in the workplace. In addition, technological advancements allow students to experiment with problem solving on a new, higher level. Divergent thinking can be enhanced and encouraged as new ideas are challenged.

Without the advantages of technology, students' learning is stifled and limited; this is punishing the community and society as a whole.

Counterpoint: Students should be provided with a basic education in reading, writing, and math and not in technology.

Technology is very expensive, especially since it becomes obsolete so quickly. As soon as a computer is purchased and taken out of a store, it is already outdated. Thus, schools with limited fiscal resources are not able to keep up with their well-to-do counterparts. The use of online information services is prohibitive in many underfunded districts that can barely afford to buy computers and software in the first place.

Because technology changes continuously, it is apparent that teachers have to constantly update their own technological skills. Far too often this is done on the teacher's own time, working alone with a machine.

Students must know and understand basic concepts prior to relying on technology. First-graders need to learn place value from manipulatives, not computers. Isn't it better to begin with concrete objects that a six-year-old can freely manipulate to learn place value? We're expecting technology to solve the problems of why students don't learn; in reality, it can create even more problems when students fail to understand simple concepts and are unable to apply them.

Many students have their own computers at home, enabling them to draft research reports, check spelling and grammar, and print on either a letter-quality or laser printer complete with graphs. If the students have a CD-ROM player, they may have access to atlases of the world, famous works of art, or historical information. These students have a significant advantage over students who lack such sophisticated electronic equipment and must write their papers by hand and then reread them to check for spelling and grammatical errors.

Teacher Professional Development

According to the Education Commission of the States, professional "teacher development activities are sorely inadequate, irrelevant, poorly designed, and viewed (by

As a beginning teacher, you want to have lessons that work—those the students get into and enjoy. By learning a variety of teaching strategies and collecting more along the way, you can adjust to students' needs and interests.

As a beginning teacher, I accumulated numerous ideas, many of which I revised and still find useful today. Others have been discarded or just haven't been used. I still am open to new instructional practices and find new technological developments exciting to use. Multimedia presentations get the students' attention and make it fun to teach new concepts. But hands-on materials can be just as effective. The important thing about effective instructional strategies is that they work for you as the teacher. Use what works best with your students.

school districts) as a low priority. Yet, teachers are expected to deepen their subject knowledge, broaden their array of teaching practices to meet students' diverse needs, adapt to the latest technology, and keep pace with numerous reform initiatives" (1996, 21). Professional development continues to be a problem for educators. Effective opportunities need to be expanded while useless ones are cast aside if we are to improve teaching and learning in our schools. Ann Bradley (1996, 1) said, "schools are only as good as their teachers, regardless of how high their standards, how up to date their technology or how innovative their programs. If teachers aren't given adequate opportunities to learn, they have little chance of meeting the ever increasing demands placed upon them."

The typical professional development program for teachers consists of a couple of days of inservice or less during a school year. Educators view this as being very inadequate if teachers are to improve their teaching. Some states have developed grant programs that fund school district programs that are designed to develop student and teacher standards as well as school practices and performance. Some examples include Iowa's School Improvement Program, Ohio's Venture Capital Fund, and Maine's Innovative Educational Grant. Other programs to help teachers enhance their teaching skills include the National Writing Project, designed to assist K–12 teachers in the teaching of writing, and the Urban Math Collaborative, which brings together high school mathematics teachers, university faculty, and business professionals to strengthen math instruction (Education Commission of the States 1996).

Some states have developed their own unique professional development plans. California's Subject-Matter Projects provides ongoing support for teachers in all discipline areas. Vermont's Portfolio Networks is a teacher network that helps teachers learn how to use portfolios in math and writing. The 1990 Kentucky Education Reform Act funded professional development for teachers at a rate of $23 per student. Slightly over half of that amount can be allocated for professional development by each school's decision-making council. Missouri devotes 1 percent of its state aid funds for education to professional development. Michigan is a leader in professional development, seeking long-term, sustained professional development in the improvement of teaching, learning the academic core curriculum, collaborative decision making, instructional leadership, and use of assessments to improve teaching and learning.

Summary

A wide variety of instructional approaches are available to teachers. How they are used depends on the teaching setting, the students, and the teacher.

Numerous teaching strategies have been proposed by researchers. These include traditional, direct instructional practices and nontraditional, whole language practices. Other effective teaching strategies include the Foxfire approach, cooperative/collaborative learning, and theme cycles.

As researchers moved from considering learning *products* to the learning *process,* they began considering whole language and cooperative/collaborative learning. These approaches require that the classroom become a community of learners with the teacher as the facilitator of learning. Direct instruction necessitates that the teacher serves as the conductor of learning, directing the students through the learning activities.

Advancements in technology have also changed instructional practices in the classroom. Computers are more powerful and educational software more challenging and enticing to students. Fiber optics and satellite communications now enable a student in one part of the country to communicate with another student in another part of the country.

Reflections

Marilyn Fergus stressed the need to respect and value yourself as a teacher. How do you feel about this? Do you value your accomplishments, even the small ones? Do you respect yourself as a learner? Have you ever taught someone how to do something? How did you feel afterwards? Have you ever tried to learn something but failed? What was your reaction to that event?

Keep a reflective journal for the next three weeks. Set aside some time to write in it every day. A good time is just before you go to bed. This enables you to think about all of the day's events. Reread your journal entries once a week. Write your reactions to your entries in the back of your journal. Be sure to point out positive and negative achievements.

Discussion Questions

1. Do most American businesses foster cooperative learning?
2. Increasingly there is less loyalty demonstrated in our country. For instance, players change baseball and football teams through free agency. No longer do fans support their local teams. Businesses and industry no longer guarantee lifelong employment. Discuss the advantages and disadvantages of competitive and cooperative learning.
3. Consider the nine productivity factors. In a small group, select the three productivity factors you believe are the most significant. Share with the other groups in your class.
4. What are the advantages and disadvantages of reflective teaching?

For Further Reading

Blythe, M. C., and P. M. Bradbury. 1993. Classroom by committee. *Educational Leadership* 50 (1):56–59.

Danielson, C., and L. Abrutyn. 1997. *An introduction to using portfolios in the classroom.* Alexandria, VA: Association for Supervision and Curriculum Development.

Darling-Hammond, L. 1997. *The right to learn.* San Francisco: Jossey-Bass.

Perrone, V. 1991. *A letter to teachers: Reflections on schooling and the art of teaching.* San Francisco: Jossey-Bass.

Shapiro, B. C. 1995. The NBPTS sets standards for accomplished teaching. *Educational Leadership* 52 (6):55–57.

Swaim, J. 1998. In search of an honest response. *Language Arts* 75 (2):118–125.

Wellington, B. 1991. The promise of reflective practice. *Educational Leadership* 48 (6):4–5.

■ Surfing the 'Net

Allyn and Bacon Website
http://www.abacon.com

This website contains information about education resources.

K–12 Internet Projects
http://www.hptn.orgi80/cyber.serv/aonepl

This website describes and illustrates K–12 Internet projects.

Electronic Library
http://www.elibrary.com

This website is for K–12 students and is described as an electronic library for research.

Classroom Connect
http://www.classroom.net

A variety of resources for teachers and students are included here.

http://www.gsh.org

This site contains information and resources about getting a classroom Web page online and accessing the latest Internet software.

SuperKids Educational Software Review
http://www.superkids.com

This site offers critiques of educational software for kids. It can be used by both teachers and students.

The Web as a Learning Tool
http://www.cs.uidaho.edu/

This site has information listed by area of interest.

14

Managing the Classroom Environment

Primary Points

- Classroom management involves how the teacher orchestrates student activities, materials, time, and space.

- The more classroom time devoted to learning, the more students learn.

- Students need to be actively involved in learning.

- Teachers need to give students genuine, sincere praise.

- A few simple classroom rules are best.

- From the first day of school, classroom rules must be established and followed.

- Conflict resolution and assertive discipline are two techniques to resolve inappropriate student behavior.

- Creating democratic classrooms requires students to act as responsible citizens.

Chapter Inquiries

- How does a teacher manage the classroom?

- What is the difference between time allocated to teach a subject and engagement time?

- Why is assertive discipline controversial?

- In what way is conflict resolution a "win-win" situation for both sides?

- Why should a teacher create a democratic classroom community?

© Photo Edit

Photo Disc/Families and
Lifestyles

"Be fair to all students and don't smile until Christmas." That advice summed up the extent of the classroom management instruction I received in my teacher education preparation. I felt very competent in teaching all of the core subject matters of elementary education—reading, writing, mathematics, science, and social studies, and a tad bit knowledgeable in the teaching of art, music, and physical education, which were required methods courses back in those days. Classroom management was the elusive aspect that no methods course covered, the taboo of methods courses just as sex education was, and still is, for public school teachers. My friends and I learned appropriate classroom management on the line, teaching in the trenches.

Armed with my "be fair and no smiling" advice, I headed off to my first year of teaching. My classroom was right next to the special-education wing, since the principal thought I could be the buffer between the "regular" classes and the special-education classes, an archaic view even for 1975. However, my classroom's location proved to be an asset for which I'm still grateful.

Next door was Dot Elmore, who had taught special education for years, even before it was labeled special education. When I first met her, I mistook her for a member of the school board. She had perfectly coiffured hair and more high heels and an expensive dress with matching lavish, valuable jewelry. This was my view of a bank officer or businesswoman, certainly not of a classroom teacher. And weren't teachers of primary-aged children supposed to wear pantsuits (yo, in 1975, polyester ruled!)? My second shock came when this very attractive woman entered my room with cotton swabs and Vaseline and said, "Hi, I'm Dot Elmore. Give me your glue bottles." My jaw dropped as I realized that this beautiful, elegant, graceful woman had been doomed to possess the deep, gravelly voice of Ma Kettle.

Sitting down at my work table, she removed the orange caps from the glue bottles and swabbed the inside of each bottle with a dab of Vaseline before replacing the caps. "There," she announced. "Now they won't clog up when your kids use them." My former art professor didn't have a clue about such practical matters.

Mrs. Elmore had Dorothy Hamilton in her class that year. In fact, she had all eleven Hamilton children before she retired. But Dorothy, she was the greatest challenge. Barely weighing forty-five pounds, with a scrawny, willowy body, at age seven Dorothy was commonly described by teachers in the faculty lounge as being "hell on wheels." I scoffed at their comments. No little kid could be that bad. Upon hearing her cuss out a bigger kid on the playground using words even ancient mariners didn't know, I retreated and reconsidered my opinion.

Dorothy would enter the classroom, drop to her knees, and crawl. Screams that echoed down the tiled hallway were generally emitted from her mouth. And fights!!! Dorothy could start a fight in an empty elevator.

They talk about abolishing prayer in school. That would be the wrong thing to do. First-year teachers pray more during that year than they ever do any other time in their lives. Whenever Dorothy would get into a scuffle or start a ruckus, I sent up a silent prayer of gratitude: "Thank you God for not giving me Dorothy." Frankly, I still believe if I had had Dorothy, I would have folded my tent and left teaching and you'd be stuck reading someone else's textbook. Not that I didn't have some major discipline problems of my own, but Dorothy was able to get into trouble on the hour, every hour, day after day.

After the first two weeks of school, Mrs. Elmore had Dorothy *walking* into the classroom and occupying herself by drawing or coloring until school began. I was flabbergasted. No one in college taught you how to manage such a remarkable change in a student's behavior. Naturally, Dorothy still had her occasional relapses, but the improvement was nothing short of incredible.

It was about the beginning of November when I heard a shout down the hallway followed by crying and a flurry of profanity. Upon reaching the doorway of her classroom, Dorothy dropped to her knees. crawled to the center of the room, and promptly began giving the all-time, Guiness Book of World Records temper tantrum. Mrs. Elmore had been collecting lunch money at the time. Being the good teacher, she looked down and noticed what was taking place. She picked Dorothy up and carried her to her desk. Mrs. Elmore said in a soft, but firm voice, "Now sit here, Dorothy. I don't now what happened to you on the way to school but as soon as I finish taking lunch money, we'll talk about it."

Dorothy sat at her desk, sniffling, arms crossed, livid with her teacher for taking her off center stage. Suddenly, Dorothy bolted to the writing table and returned with paper and pencil. Dorothy could barely spell her own name correctly and still didn't know the letters of the alphabet, but she was determined on that day to write. After she had filled the page with scribbles, Dorothy picked up the paper, turned it over, and loudly slapped it down on her desk as she began to fill the second page with more scribbles. By now, Mrs. Elmore had finished her fiscal duties. Dorothy slammed her pencil onto the desk, raced to Mrs. Elmore's desk, handed the paper to her teacher and said, "There. Read it." Then, turning her back defiantly toward her teacher, Dorothy crossed her arms and pointed her nose triumphantly toward the ceiling.

"Of course I'll read it, Dorothy," Mrs. Elmore calmly said. "It says, 'Dear Mrs. Elmore. I love you. Your friend, Dorothy.'"

A shocked look came over Dorothy's face as her tense body relaxed. Dorothy's rage was transformed into affection for her teacher. And Dorothy said softly, "You guessed it." Then Mrs. Elmore hugged Dorothy and they talked.

Mrs. Elmore intuitively knew that Dorothy, like all children, wanted to be accepted and loved. That isn't part of any methods class. Good teachers just know it and they do it.

In short, from the opening bell to the end of the day, the better classroom managers are thinking ahead. While maintaining a pleasant classroom atmosphere, these teachers keep planning how to organize, manage, and control activities to facilitate instruction.

David Berliner

What Do We Know About Well-Managed Classrooms? Putting Research to Work

Classroom management in the 1700s was summed up in the words of a song: "Readin', and 'ritin', and 'rithmetic. Taught to the tune of a hickory stick." Teachers have long recognized that students cannot learn in a threatening environment. Today, educators have moved away from trying to control student behavior and instead focus on the teaching process to "create, implement, and maintain a classroom environment that supports learning" (Evertson and Harris 1992, 74).

According to Lewis, Schaps, and Watson (1995, 548), to accomplish this "schools must attend simultaneously to children's intellectual, social, and ethical development." Classroom management in reality focuses on how you, the teacher, orchestrate the classroom. This includes time, structure of lessons and activities, and actual room design. If you are well organized and can present the subject-matter content in an interesting manner, then you will probably be a good classroom manager with few discipline problems.

The placement of student desks and workstations is your decision as classroom teacher and is part of classroom management. For example, if your desk is placed next to an open door, students may be distracted unnecessarily. According to Sadker and Sadker (1991, 75), "Effective teachers must be more than good classroom managers . . . they must also be good organizers of academic content and instruction." Classroom management research has concentrated on the areas of time management, student involvement, student engagement, classroom communication, teachers' managerial decisions, and the handling of misbehavior. These areas have received a substantial amount of attention during the 1980s and 1990s. This chapter examines effective classroom management and discipline techniques as well as the effective use of student and teacher time.

Classroom Management

Classroom management includes time management, student involvement, student engagement, and classroom communication. In addition, the teacher must make sound managerial decisions.

Time Management

In the 1800s, some educators believed that if students were kept working, misbehavior would be at a minimum. Thus, many teachers assigned "busy work"—tasks that filled the time but did little to teach students. Students busily wrote spelling words ten times each, completed workbook pages, wrote out incorrect sentences from English grammar books and corrected the errors, and calculated twenty-five math problems to demonstrate that they knew a single math concept, even if they got the first problem correct.

Today, teachers use class time more wisely and efficiently. The amount of class time for learning has been found to be a consistent indicator in research studies regarding achievement. The more time devoted to learning, the more learning that occurs (Walberg 1988). As a result, many educators advocate increasing the length of a school day by fifteen to thirty minutes. Other educators and some state legislators throughout the nation argue that the school year should be increased by two weeks to a month or even longer.

Research by Karweit (1988) found that the amount of time that students devote to learning varies from school to school. This is true even within the same school district. A study of beginning teachers found great differences in the amount of time devoted to subjects. For instance, when first-year elementary teachers in the Los Angeles school system were surveyed, one elementary teacher devoted 68 minutes per day to reading instruction while another spent 137 minutes; one elementary teacher spent only 16 minutes teaching mathematics while another devoted over an hour to the subject (Fisher et al. 1978).

Karweit (1988) also discovered that even in the best schools, half or less of the school day is used for instruction. This is because elementary and middle school students must take time to move from their classrooms to the art room, the library, the gym for physical education, and the music room for music. Lunch takes time, as does collecting the money to pay for it and taking the daily lunch count. Taking attendance requires more time. In addition, middle, junior high, and high school students must move from classroom to classroom throughout the day for *all* subjects within the curriculum. One student teacher was astonished to discover the amount

Students need to be motivated and involved in the learning process. (© Nita Winter/ Image Works)

of time needed to simply hand out a single sheet of paper to each of the students in her first-grade classroom—time when learning wasn't taking place among her students.

Certainly teachers cannot afford to waste valuable classroom time. It is important that the day be organized in the morning before school begins. If students need a copy of a handout for a lesson, there must be enough copies for everyone in the class. If a science lesson requires students to conduct an experiment, there must be enough materials available for all the student groups to do the experiment. If the art lesson requires that students make clay sculptures, there must be a sufficient amount of clay for all. No matter what the class, as a teacher you must plan ahead and organize the necessary materials.

Classroom time must be productive learning time for students. You can accomplish this by early in the school year establishing and instituting classroom procedures and setting academic expectations. Thus, students know from their first day in the classroom what they can and cannot do and what is and is not expected of them. Throughout the school year, you can get the most out of the time you have with students by planning lessons and activities that fit within any time constraints as well as the available learning materials. You should also sequence, pace, monitor, and assess student work as well as provide feedback to each student (Evertson and Emmer 1982).

Student Involvement

If students are given choices about what and how they are to learn, they will be actively involved in the learning process. Thus, lessons become more relevant for them and their motivation to learn increases. By capitalizing on this, you can help reduce distractions and discipline problems. Giving students choices, however, does not mean that you let them run the classroom. If as a high school algebra teacher you ask students to figure the circumference of objects described in the textbook and one student wants to apply that knowledge by calculating the circumference of the oversized tires on his car, why not let him? If he then wants to figure out how fast he is actually going at sixty-five miles per hour when the speedometer is designed for smaller tires, why not have him calculate the difference in speeds? The more relationships students see between what they are learning and their own lives, the more willing and motivated they are to learn.

When students are motivated and involved, they can devote long periods of time to one activity. Just check out the video arcade at the mall and observe children and teenagers as they concentrate on video games for an hour or more—or as long as the quarters hold out. The same is true of learning activities. Some students can sit down during the first week of school and read a book for thirty minutes without stopping. Most, however, become restless after ten or fifteen minutes. The former students probably read on a regular basis over the summer, while those less able to concentrate may not have picked up a book during the entire vacation.

Students differ in their degree of concentration and in the amount of time they remain engaged by a particular subject. Jason loves math and could devote the entire school day to learning about algorithms, but he has trouble keeping his mind on verbs in his Spanish class. Shanatt wants to be a writer and can't get enough of English literature, but he finds it difficult to concentrate on social studies. Like adults, children each have likes and dislikes. As a teacher, it will be up to you to determine these likes and dislikes and to convince your students to like the unlikable subject or topic.

Student Engagement

The time allocated to teach a subject is the amount of time you set aside each day for particular subject matter. Allocated time differs from student engagement time, which is the actual time the student is "engaged" in the learning activity. Student engagement time can vary from classroom to classroom and may range from 50 percent to over 90 percent of class time (Sadker and Sadker 1991). Also, student engagement time differs among individuals. In short, student engagement time is when the student is thinking about nothing else but the academic learning task at hand. This may be a class or group discussion, writing a report or composition, listening to your lecture or a speech by a classmate, solving chemistry or math problems, or watching a video or laser disc on art history or music composition. To foster student engagement, you must set up the lesson effectively and efficiently so that time is not wasted on trivial matters or so that the class or a group of students within the class does not get off track.

Planning and preparation can increase student engagement time. A well-designed lesson with all the necessary materials readily at hand is very important. A variety of activities can help keep students from becoming bored by the same lessons day after day. Field trips, discussions, brainstorming groups, simulations, computer software, laser discs, videos, plays, small-group work, cooperative and collaborative learning activities, guest speakers, debates, panel discussions, writing activities, independent work, and work with a partner can all enliven a lesson or curriculum unit and increase student engagement time.

Variety increases the curiosity of students. With their curiosity piqued, students want to come to class to find out what is happening and be included in the learning activity.

A substantial amount of research has been conducted on the need to give students feedback on their work. Jere Brophy (1985) found that teacher praise, while important for all students, was especially critical to low-achieving students and those from low socioeconomic backgrounds. Brophy's research indicated that a positive comment by the teacher was most effective when the praise

1. was contingent on student performance;
2. was specific, clearly indicating what the student had done well or had improved;
3. was genuine and sincere;
4. let the student know about his or her competence;
5. let the student know about the importance of his or her accomplishment;
6. ties the student's success to his or her ability or effort;
7. relies on using the student's past performance as a context for describing the quality of the present performance.

Brophy also observed the reactions of students when teachers criticized their work. He found that how the teacher worded his or her suggestions for student improvement made a difference. According to Brophy, a teacher's comments help a student in an area in which he or she is weak when they meet certain conditions:

1. The comment should be specific and contingent on student performance.
2. The comment should focus solely on student performance and not be of a personal nature.
3. The comment should provide a clear blueprint for improvement.
4. The teacher establishes a classroom environment where the student knows that making mistakes is acceptable.
5. The comment should relate eventual success to effort.
6. The comment should recognize when the student has made progress.

Classroom Communication

As a teacher, you must make certain that all of your students are involved and engaged. This involves moving through the lesson with as few interruptions and distractions as possible. Teachers must establish basic classroom communication signals. For instance, many teachers begin a lesson by looking over the class and giving an introductory statement such as, "Today, we're going to follow the trail of Lewis and Clark in their quest to find the Pacific Ocean." Other teachers look at their students until the class becomes quiet, while still others stand up and begin a class discussion or lecture no matter how students are behaving. Use of a daily seating chart with checks after student names helps to keep track of student participation.

Avoid getting in a rut by repeating phrases or becoming overly predictable. A response of "uh-huh" or "okay" isn't very encouraging to students. Such responses convey that you aren't very interested in what students have to share. An enthusiastic, sincere word of praise is much more desirable. "That's right, Ricardo!" or "good answer, Tasha" or "great point, Kurtis" are far more effective with elementary and secondary students. By calling the student by name, you are indicating that he or she is important to you as a teacher. It is very significant to a student to be recognized by name by his or her teacher. Most of all, it shows you really care.

Teachers' Managerial Decisions

Teachers are decision makers as they manage the daily routines of their classrooms. Some teachers squeeze out every minute of learning possible. They are highly organized and well prepared and they constantly think and plan ahead. This doesn't mean that they create a cold classroom atmosphere where students feel unwelcome. Rather, they are warm and enthusiastic teachers who are simply well organized and equally well versed in their craft of teaching.

As a teacher, you must decide how to arrange your classroom and how each lesson is taught. Curriculum decisions are made by the district, but you will teach designated subjects in your own way. Most teachers spend a portion of their vacations and breaks from school designing new units of study and lesson plans for their students. The managerial decisions of a teacher include choosing new activities or books to incorporate.

Strategies for Handling Misbehavior

A teacher establishes classroom rules either with his or her students or before the school year begins. There is no research that clearly indicates that one approach is better than the other. Rules are best if they are few in number, simple and easy to understand, and fair. Also, rules should be posted in the classroom for all to see, and the teacher should go over the rules on the first day of school.

Students have a tendency to rebel against unfair rules, just as adults do. Likewise, if the teacher unfairly applies the rules to one student but not another, students will become upset. Even young students have a strong sense of morality. If the teacher fails to fairly enforce the rules, chaos can result.

There are several different strategies for handling student misbehavior. Typically, a school or even a school district has adopted and implemented one approach. Regardless of the approach for handling misbehavior, it is important that as a teacher you implement and follow it from the first day of class, whether your students are at the preschool, elementary, or secondary level. It is not so much what you do to stop student misbehavior that characterizes good classroom control but rather how you avoid or prevent such misbehavior from occurring initially (Kounin 1970).

Some of the strategies for handling misbehavior include Dreikurs' four goals: shared culture, assertive discipline, conflict resolution, and group process.

Dreikurs's Four Goals of Misbehavior

Rudolf Dreikurs (Dreikurs, Grunwald, and Pepper 1971) studied children and adolescents who misbehaved. Dreikurs and his colleagues believe that for a small percentage of students it is difficult to receive recognition and approval through appropriate behavior at school. Thus, these students often misbehave to receive attention, gain control, get revenge, or withdraw from the group. Dreikurs suggests that these students actually have one or more of these goals.

According to Dreikurs's theory, as a teacher you can observe the behavior of a student to determine the student's goal. A student who seeks attention often misbehaves to get your recognition, even if that recognition is negative. Such a student may use profanity in the classroom, throw objects at other students, talk out of turn, or simply insist he or she cannot do the work and request additional help with assignments. When dealing with students who like to receive attention, you should praise these students when they are behaving appropriately as well as find ways to

"Could I see you in my office, MR. KING?"

Reprinted by permission.

give them recognition, such as assigning responsibilities and duties in the classroom. By trying to anticipate the needs of attention-demanding students in a lesson, you can defuse the situation. For example, you can ask the student a question about the lesson's main topic at the beginning of the lesson. If a student is seeking attention by misbehaving in a mild way, focus on praising his or her peers for their appropriate behavior.

A student who is trying to gain control tends to defy your authority as classroom teacher. This can lead to what Dreikurs calls a "battle of the wills." A control-seeking student tries to make you feel threatened and angry. Forcing such a student to do something against his or her will can result in a most unpleasant confrontation. If you are faced with a control-seeking student, never argue with the student. It is better to walk away from the encounter than to have an open confrontation. Whenever possible, allow students to make choices. This helps the control-oriented student. For instance, the student may select one of three books to read, the topic of a report, where in the room to work, what student to be his or her partner, etc. Giving the control-seeking student responsibility helps to defuse the situation as the student becomes a responsible student citizen of the classroom community. It is important to set up established limitations and consequences for the control-seeking student as well as for all other students. In every case, you must handle the situation in a calm, poised manner.

A student who seeks revenge inflicts emotional or physical pain on others using such tactics as critical comments, name calling, or destruction or defacing of property. The revenge-seeking student may try to embarrass you and make you feel hurt. If you respond by using the same tactics as the student, that serves only to reinforce

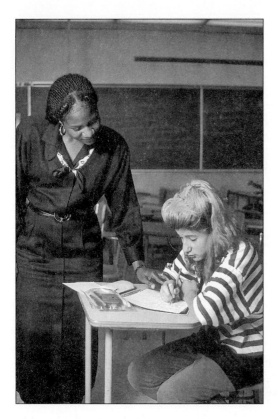

A teacher must be consistent in applying classroom management techniques. (© Mary Kate Denny/PhotoEdit)

such behavior as acceptable when in reality it is not. Try to understand that the student who seeks revenge has a basic mistrust and anger toward others. He or she believes that by using criticism and sarcasm, others can be hurt. As with the attention-seeking student, you should praise the revenge-seeking student whenever appropriate and acceptable behavior is demonstrated. Since the revenge-seeking student tends to have low self-esteem, point out to the student his or her positive attributes and abilities. The revenge-seeking student prefers to distance himself or herself from others; this student is wary of too much praise from others, especially from teachers.

The final type of student misbehavior is that of withdrawal or assumed disability. This student has given up on a specific subject or even on school completely. This student insists and actually believes that he or she cannot learn and conveys this to you by being passive in class, resisting involvement in a learning activity. A student who withdraws needs to be reassured that he or she *can* learn. Small measures of progress and achievement need to be rewarded to build the student's self-esteem. Focus on building on the student's strengths so he or she can demonstrate to peers what he or she can do. This increases the student's motivation to learn. Slowly but continuously, you should increase the amount of involvement in learning activities by this type of student. Cooperative and collaborative learning activities are useful, and you can assign students who will be supportive of the student to the group.

As teachers, we must avoid being manipulated by the students described here. We must examine our own feelings and reactions to these students. Dreikurs suggests that teachers should be alert and not fall into a pattern that reinforces student misbehavior. He suggests that teachers not constantly respond to the misbehavior of the student who seeks attention; that they avoid engaging in confrontations and battles of the will with the student who seeks control; that they not respond with sarcasm or punitiveness to the student who seeks revenge; and that they not give up on the student who has withdrawn from learning activities.

Shared Culture

Culture impacts classroom management and discipline. In 1994, an American high school student in Singapore received a jail term and four swats with a cane as part of his sentencing for spray painting cars. Singapore is a very safe country with very rigid laws. Many Americans were outraged at the harsh penalty. Other Americans embraced the idea of caning, and laws were introduced in several state legislatures, such as California, to institute **corporal punishment** for juveniles who break certain laws, such as spraying graffiti on buildings. Others called for corporal punishment to be part of school discipline policies.

Some educators believe that by establishing a common school or classroom culture, students are less apt to misbehave. Some schools create student committees to establish a school code for behavior. When a student violates the code, he or she

A Shared Ethical Culture

The James P.B. Duffy School in Rochester, New York, had severe discipline problems that affected academic performance of students. According to Wager (1993, 36) "Violence . . . punctuated the school day. Older children occasionally terrorized younger ones, sometimes extorting money from them. There were daily outbreaks of fist-fighting. Students conspired . . . to bring bicycles to school . . . so that they could run down supervising adults. Ethnic and racial groups locked horns at every opportunity. Emotionally handicapped students were in constant anarchy: they threw food, overturned furniture, and ran wildly through the building."

The principal of the building developed a list of Ten Commandments:

1. No weapons—real or toy (first offense to committee).
2. No pushing, tripping, hitting, or fighting.
3. No swearing.
4. No threatening.
5. No insulting others.
6. Stay where adults are in charge.
7. No class disruption or refusal to follow adult direction.
8. Respect things that belong to others (no stealing, extorting, destroying).
9. Do not touch fire alarms; do not bring matches.
10. No alcoholic beverages, drugs, or cigarettes (Wager 1993, 36–37).

The school has a committee of teachers and parents who volunteer to hear conflicts. On the initial offense except for bringing either a real or toy weapon to school, the teacher counsels the student who broke the rule. On the second offense, the student must appear before the committee within twenty-four hours. The student's parents and teacher must also attend. After instituting this program, discipline problems waned and academic achievement by students in the school improved dramatically.

must appear before a committee of student peers. The committee decides the consequences for the student's action.

Assertive Discipline

Assertive discipline was developed by Lee and Marlene Canter as a means to help teachers take charge of their classrooms in a firm, yet positive manner (Canter 1976). Canter believes that the focal point of his approach is to teach students responsibility by giving them choices. Teachers and school administrators seem to agree with Canter's philosophy. Over 750,000 teachers have been trained to use assertive discipline with their students (Hill 1990). Several research studies have been conducted on assertive discipline, and the results indicate that discipline problems are reduced when it is adopted and maintained (Ferre and Ferre 1992; King 1987; McCormack 1987; Parkhurst 1987). In particular, a study by Barnett and Curtis (1986) found that student teachers who had been trained to use the assertive discipline techniques were considered to be better prepared and given higher ratings than those who were not.

Typically, teachers who utilize assertive discipline adopt a limited number of classroom rules, usually four to six. Rewards for compliance as well as consequences for breaking the rules, or noncompliance, are clearly indicated. Both the classroom rules and the rewards and consequences are usually posted on a chart in the classroom. The classroom rules, consequences, and rewards for one classroom are as follows:

FoxTrot   by Bill Amend

Classroom Rules

1. Be respectful of others and their property.
2. Work quietly.
3. Raise your hand before talking in class.

Consequences

1. First infraction   = Warning
2. Second infraction   = Name on chalkboard
3. Third infraction   = Checkmark next to name on chalkboard; stay after school twenty minutes
4. Fourth infraction   = Checkmark next to name on chalkboard and immediate phone call to parent. May result in removal from class for rest of school day.

Rewards

When everyone is doing their work and following the rules, a popcorn kernel will be dropped into a jar. When the class earns one hundred popcorn kernels, we will have a pizza party or see a movie.

Assertive discipline requires that the teacher be consistent, businesslike, and firm. Infractions cannot be debated or negotiated. The teacher warns the student and then writes his or her name on the board for the second infraction.

The key to assertive discipline is that consequences are delivered to students on an individual basis but rewards are earned by the class as a whole. Thus, assertive discipline relies on peer pressure to have all class members conform to the rules and regulations.

Some educators argue that assertive discipline forces students to comply with the rules but does little to help students develop self-control or problem-solving skills (Curwin and Mendler 1988, 1989). Linda Darling-Hammond, a prominent teacher educator, believes that assertive discipline is "especially harmful to children in the early grades, when they are still developing self-regulatory behavior and social skills" (Hill 1990, 75).

Should Assertive Discipline Be Used to Handle Student Misbehavior?

Point: The use of assertive discipline in the schools helps students learn the value of obeying the law.

Assertive discipline provides structure similar to that of the reward system of our society. Adults who work hard are rewarded with a raise or a bonus in their paychecks. If students follow the rules, they should be rewarded.

Assertive discipline helps the teacher maintain classroom order. Every student and teacher knows the rules and the penalties for breaking them. Assertive discipline helps increase class learning time by decreasing the amount of time needed to deal with disruptive behavior by students.

Counterpoint: Students need to learn how to work out their difficulties with others, and assertive discipline doesn't allow them opportunities to do so.

Assertive discipline is unrealistic in that it requires students to blindly follow rules without thinking about them. Thus, students often don't understand why a rule is important.

Students need to be able to engage in small-group discussions or work with partners. Such communicative abilities are important life skills for both students and adults. Assertive discipline emphasizes a quiet classroom; however, learning often requires that students talk or do hands-on activities that make noise. Students must learn to deal with situations in which there are no set rules or teacher to penalize those individuals who misbehave.

The assertive discipline approach insists that students be quiet and that rewards be given when the entire class behaves, and these have been two areas of controversy. Certainly the whole language movement encourages students to converse amongst themselves, which conflicts with the insistence in assertive discipline that students be quiet unless they are called on. Research shows that the use of rewards decreases intrinsic motivation among students (Hill 1990).

Beyond Discipline: Creating Democratic Classrooms

Rather than emphasizing discipline, Alfie Kohn (1996) believes that the classroom should be a democratic community where students behave well because that is acceptable behavior. Teachers really cannot "manage" children, in Kohn's view. Instead we must let students know exactly how we expect them to behave and then offer positive reinforcement when they do obey. Positive reinforcement includes praise but does not include material rewards such as those offered as part of assertive discipline.

According to Kohn (1996, 120),

No degree of skill or care on the part of an educator can cause all problems in the classroom to vanish. A teacher can do only so much when her students come from homes where power is valued more than reason or love—or when the culture as a whole reflects similar priorities. Besides, when two or three dozen people spend the day together, there are bound to be conflicting needs and clashes of will that occasionally get out of hand.

Creating a classroom community requires that the teacher think in terms of problem solving. Here are ten suggestions Kohn makes to help teachers solve problems with their students.

1. Develop a relationship with all of your students. Unless you have a relationship already established, you will find it difficult if not impossible to solve a problem. "As a general rule, it's important for students to trust their teacher, to know she respects them, and to feel safe in speaking their minds with her" (1996, 122).

2. Besides having a caring relationship with their students, teachers need to develop a certain set of skills. "The teacher may need to help students learn to listen carefully, calm themselves, generate suggestions, imagine someone else's point of view, and so on. Ideally, children should have the chance to work on these skills from the time they are very young. Like us, they need guidance and practice to get better" (p. 123).

3. The teacher's role in dealing with an immediate problem or unpleasant situation is to diagnose what has happened and why. It is the underlying reasons for a given behavior that must be sought out. Punishing and rewarding students tends, in part, to be unproductive unless the underlying reasons are understood.

4. "To figure out what is really going on, we must be willing to look beyond the concrete situation in front of us. . . . [As teachers,] it is even more difficult to consider causes and contexts when that process raises questions about our own practices" (p. 124).

5. The role students play in making decisions should be expanded. When this is the case, fewer problems are likely to occur. According to Martin Hoffman (Kohn 1996, 1), "The evidence increasingly points to an innate disposition [in children] to be responsive to the plight of other people. . . . Creating people who are socially responsive does not totally depend on parents and teachers. Such socializing agents have an ally within the child."

6. "Asking students to come up with solutions will not get us very far if they feel obliged to cough up explanations, suggestions, or apologies on demand. The questions we ask them must be open-ended, with students encouraged to explore possibilities, reflect on their own motives, disagree, and, in general, to construct an authentic solution" (Kohn 1996, 126).

7. "When a student has done something cruel, our first priority is to help her understand that what she did is wrong and *why* it is wrong, so that it will not happen again. . . . We don't need to ignore what the student has done. Instead, she can be assisted in thinking about ways to make restitution or reparations. A reasonable follow-up to a destructive action may be to try to restore, replace, repair, clean up, or apologize, as the situation may dictate" (p. 127).

8. The teacher should "check back later to see how a plan worked, whether the problem got solved, whether additional or entirely new strategies may now be needed. Alternatively, another conversation may be useful just to allow the child to feel proud of himself for the resolution. Such discussions also encourage reflection on the process and consideration of whether it seemed fair and constructive. It is especially important for students to check back later when they have met as a class to solve a problem" (p. 127).

9. "Problem solving requires flexibility about logistics as well as about substance. Sometimes you will need to put off a conversation with a student even though it would have been better to talk right away. Sometimes you will have difficulty getting a student to talk openly about what is bothering him and it will make more sense to drop him a note and invite a written response. Sometimes you will notice a pattern of problems and decide to bring this up at a class meeting rather than holding private discussions with individual students. . . . Sometimes you will reach the end of your rope and have to ask a colleague, a spouse, or a student for ideas. In short, 'doing to' responses can be scripted, but 'working with' responses often have to be improvised" (p. 128).

10. "There may be times when no alternative to a 'doing to' intervention comes to mind, when one feels compelled to rely on control. If a student persists in disrupting a class meeting, even after repeated reminders that he isn't being fair to everyone else, the teacher may decide to ask him to leave (go to the vice principal's office, for instance) until he is ready to stop acting that way. Everything possible should be done to minimize the punitive impact of such a move; the teacher's tone should be warm and regretful, and she should express confidence that the two of them can eventually solve the problem together" (p. 128).

By following these suggestions, Kohn believes that we can create in our classrooms democratic communities where students are responsible citizens. In this view, "we can move beyond discipline" (Kohn 1996, 137).

Conflict Resolution

Like assertive discipline, conflict resolution or mediation programs were adopted by school districts in the 1970s and 1980s. The basis for such programs is that through communication, cooperative problem solving will result in a "win-win" resolution. This field was largely developed and applied to business management problems in the 1970s and 1980s. In 1972, the Quakers introduced the Children's Creative Response to Conflict Program in inner-city New York schools. The program used puppets, music, games, and discussion to help children learn cooperation and conflict resolution skills (Roderick 1988).

In schools, students are trained to mediate minor conflicts and problems that arise among their peers. Usually, two students serve as mediators for a problem. Students who serve as mediators do the following:

1. serve as models for their peers;
2. are alert to potential problems between students;
3. make certain that procedures are followed in conflict resolution:
   a. only one person can talk at a time;
   b. listen to both sides;
   c. ask each student what the other student is doing that he or she wants stopped;
   d. ask the other student if he or she can stop doing those things that bother the other student;
   e. ask both students to apologize and shake hands;
   f. ask both students if the problem has been resolved or if it should be turned over to a teacher;
   g. take any unresolved problems to a teacher.

One School's Conflict Resolution Program

Conflict resolution programs, which rely on students mediating problems between other students, have been instituted in many schools throughout the country. Eastwood Hills Elementary School in Raytown, Missouri, has adopted such a program.

After the teachers in the elementary school were trained in the aspects of conflict resolution, they selected students who demonstrated leadership potential, either positive or negative, respect of fellow students, good verbal skills, initiative, and the ability to commit to a year-long program. The students were selected to reflect the population of the elementary school. These students were trained to be conflict managers and help other students resolve conflicts (Holder and Martin 1993).

Several skills are emphasized when training students to be good conflict managers. First of all, a conflict manager must be a good listener. Secondly, a conflict manager must believe that conflicts can be resolved peacefully. Students work in pairs as conflict managers with two students who have a problem. One day a week, the conflict managers wear brightly colored T-shirts with "Conflict Manager" in bold print across the front so that students who have a problem can easily seek them out (Holder and Martin 1993).

In conflict resolution, certain ground rules are established. Both disputants must agree to four rules:

1. Do not interrupt the other person or the conflict manager.
2. Do not call names or use put-downs to insult the other person.
3. Be honest.
4. Agree to solve the problem.

Once both individuals agree to follow the rules, they take turns defining the problem, with both stating their feelings and why they feel that way. The last portion of conflict resolution involves finding solutions to the problem. At this point, the conflict managers ask the first student what he or she can do to resolve the part of the problem for which he or she is responsible. The second student must also agree to this. Then the conflict managers ask the second student what he or she can do to resolve the remainder of the problem for which he or she is responsible. The first student must also agree. The conflict managers then ask each student what he or she would do differently should the problem resurface. Finally, the conflict managers ask both of the students if the problem is resolved. If they believe that it has been, the conflict managers congratulate the students and tell them to inform their friends that the conflict has been resolved. The conflict managers then complete a conflict manager report form (Holder and Martin 1993; The Community Board Program 1986).

4. don't pass judgment;
5. don't attempt to police the playground, hallways, or classroom.

According to Peggy Cahoon, principal of William E. Ferron Elementary School in Las Vegas, Nevada, even students with minimal academic skills can serve as mediators. In her school, several second-graders were involved in an incident at recess time. The mediator, a second-grader with low language skills, asked, "Can you all get along, or do we need to act like those magnets we used in class today; you know, when the north and the north are put together, they repel?" Another mediator then said, "Yeah, like a skunk." The group decided they could get along without repelling each other (Cahoon 1988, 94).

In Chicago, conflict resolution is part of the high school social studies curriculum. Students study negotiation, mediation, and arbitration as they attempt to resolve problems that are presented to them. The problems range from interpersonal (e.g., you want to borrow the car and your father says no) to international (e.g., two countries disagree over fishing rights). In San Francisco, elementary and high school students are selected and trained to be conflict managers, or mediators. "The mediator does not play the role of police officer, judge, or counselor, but facilitates communication so that the disputants themselves can find a solution" (Roderick 1988, 90).

Conflict resolution and mediation programs enable students to recognize that they have choices. They learn that they do not have to stand and take abuse in a passive way or resort to violence. Through communication and action by both individuals involved in the conflict, a resolution that is acceptable to both individuals can be found.

At the elementary, middle, and junior high school levels, conflict resolution has been effective in those schools that fully utilize it. However, because of the potentially violent nature of incidents between teenagers at high schools, it has been more difficult to implement and maintain student mediation programs successfully.

Group Process

William Glasser, like Lee Canter and the proponents of conflict resolution, believes that problem behavior diminishes if students are made to feel responsible. By involving students in problem solving, Glasser argues, they better grasp a sense of responsibility to others and to themselves.

In Glasser's (1969, 1985) technique, there are five steps that the teacher needs to follow.

1. Meet with the student, one to one, and discuss the misbehavior. Be supportive, not judgmental, of the student.

2. Ask the student to tell what he or she did and how his or her behavior affected another student or the class.

3. Help the student to develop a plan of constructive behaviors that the student will enact when a similar situation arises.

4. Develop with the student a precise set of rewards for enacting the plan and consequences for failing to carry through with the plan.

5. Review the plan regularly. When necessary, along with the student, revise the plan.

By teaching problem-solving techniques to the entire class, Glasser (1969) asserts that students acquire the skills needed to solve commonplace problems that occur on a daily basis. Once students identify a problem and understand it, then they make suggestions for a solution. Glasser believes that taking class time to work through problems results in students learning how to solve their own interpersonal problems and how to gain self-control.

Straight Talk About Gangs

Does a baseball cap with a Chicago Bulls logo with one black horn have any significance? What about the number 3/22/12? It means March 22, 1912, doesn't it? Or does it? Mary Jensen, a professor at Western Illinois University, and Phillip Yerington, a police officer in a gang division, have written a book entitled *Gangs: Straight Talk, Straight Up* (1997). Gangs were once common-place only in poor, inner-city neighborhoods. While they are still concentrated in cities, they have spread to the suburbs and rural small towns. The primary reason for the extension of their territory is less

The worst part of teaching is classroom management. Some teacher education programs dismiss it completely, and that's wrong. How do you combine teaching with discipline? Contrary to what some educators say, just teaching interesting lessons isn't sufficient. You have to have a classroom structure, a classroom community, for classroom management to work.

The bottom line is that students will be disruptive from time to time. It is your job to keep things in perspective and get students back on task in a relatively short amount of time. It's not an easy job to do, but then no one ever said teaching was easy.

competition for drug sales. It is believed that between 5 and 20 percent of the students in the United States are active in gangs. New members as young as seven- or eight-year-olds are actively recruited to deliver drugs or pick up money as couriers.

Shirley Brice Heath (1997), a noted researcher, believes that a desire for high self-esteem and a need to be part of a group has led children and young adults to seek out groups in which to belong. These groups include music organizations, such as a band or choral group, martial arts clubs, athletic groups, such as soccer teams, or gangs. Formerly, this need to belong was filled by the family. The weekend tasks of gardening or cleaning the attic no longer involve the entire family. This void of togetherness and belonging must be filled for children and young adults. "Soccer moms" and "softball dads" are helping their children meet this need.

Jensen and Yerington (1997) emphasize that gang members can be extremely hostile and aggressive. They believe that those kids who are lost to street gangs cannot be salvaged by teachers. However, teachers can work with those students still in school. Schools need to establish a zero tolerance policy regarding gangs and gang behavior. Additional after-school activities to keep children involved are critical. Counseling programs are important. Punishment other than suspensions from school must be instituted. Being aware of what children are wearing, particularly colors of local gangs, or what they scribble in their notebooks can alert teachers to gang activity or gang "wannabes." Wannabes are more apt to exhibit behavior that schools can change. After a student has become a gang member, the gang generally takes control and it is extremely difficult to regain the confidence needed to sway the student away from gang activity.

As for the Chicago Bulls logo mentioned earlier, with the left horn painted black, it is a symbol of being a member of the Vice Lords. And "3/22/12" represents the third, twenty-second, and twelfth letters of the alphabet—CVL—which stands for the Conservative Vice Lords. A drawing of a crown or a gold crown worn around the neck is a symbol of the Latin Kings.

For more information about gangs, you may want to check out the following Website: http://www.courses.edu/gang_resources.html

The site has two online courses offered by the University of the Pacific: "Online Guide to Gang Signs and Graffiti" and "Gangs: Prevention, Remediation, and Parent Conferencing."

■ Summary

Effective classroom management includes being knowledgeable about the subject and developing well-prepared lessons and learning activities. A good teacher establishes a pleasant classroom atmosphere but is always thinking ahead. When a teacher is well organized and a good planner, classroom management problems are reduced.

The classroom teacher needs to consider the use of classroom time, student involvement in learning, student engagement, classroom communication, and the type of managerial decisions he or she must make. Each of these is very important to a student's learning.

Certainly student behavior plays an important role in classroom management. One of the strategies for handling student misbehavior is Dreikurs's four goals of misbehavior, which describe the actions of students who misbehave and give suggestions for dealing with these students. The four types of students are attention seekers, control seekers, revenge seekers, and those who withdraw.

Other approaches to handling misbehavior include developing a common school culture, assertive discipline, conflict resolution, and group process. Each of these are used in elementary and secondary schools throughout the United States and Canada.

■ Reflections

Recall when you were in elementary school. Do you remember having a set of classroom rules on a chart at the front of the classroom? Do you remember how punishment was doled out by the teacher?

Think back to your junior high or high school years. Who was your best teacher? Did that person have good classroom management skills? Think about your worst classroom teacher. What kind of classroom management skills did that person possess? Draw a line down the middle of a sheet of paper. List the classroom management strategies used by the good high school teacher on the left side of the page. On the right, list the corresponding classroom management strategies of the inadequate high school teacher. On another sheet, list the qualities that you want to have in managing your own classroom.

■ Discussion Questions

1. In what ways can a teacher save time in teaching lessons?
2. Select the strategy that you prefer to adopt in dealing with inappropriate behavior. Give three reasons why you prefer it.
3. Why is engagement time so important?
4. Can a strategy for dealing with misbehavior work with students in our society?
5. Why would having a common school culture work as an effective strategy for handling misbehavior?

■ For Further Reading

Canter, L. 1976. *Assertive discipline.* Los Angeles: Lee Canter Associates.

Evertson, C. M., and A. H. Harris. 1992. What we know about managing classrooms. *Educational Leadership* 49 (7):74–77.

Johnson, D. W., R. T. Johnson, L. Stevatin, and P. Hodne. 1997. The Three C's of Safe Schools. *Educational Leadership* 55 (2) 8–13.

Kauffman, J. M., J. W. Lloyd, J. Baker, and T. M. Riedel. 1995. Inclusion of all students with emotional or behavioral disorders? Let's think again. *Phi Delta Kappan* 76 (7):542–46.

Kohn, A. 1996. *Beyond discipline: From compliance to community.* Alexandria, VA: Association for Supervision and Curriculum Development.

Lewis, C. C., E. Schaps, and M. Watson. 1995. Beyond the pendulum: Creating challenging and caring schools. *Phi Delta Kappan* 76 (7):547–49.

Wong, H. K., and R. T. Wong. 1997. *The first days of school: How to be an effective teacher.* Alexandria, VA: Association for Supervision and Curriculum Development.

15

Schools and Their Environment

Primary Points

- Schools differ in the ages of students who attend and their purpose.

- Schools differ by their location—urban, suburban, and rural.

- Teachers face different challenges at different levels of schools.

Chapter Inquiries

- What are the different types of schools and how do they differ?

- How are urban, suburban, and rural schools alike, and in what ways do they differ?

- What are some of the problems teachers face at the elementary and secondary levels?

© *Photo Disc/Education*

"If you walk down the hallway, you know. How, I don't know, but you just know if it's a good school or not." Barbara Janisch is an education consultant who is in and out of schools several times each month. "I get a feeling of the staff's pride in the school. The floor is swept and clean. Elementary schools have bright, bold bulletin boards and lots of children's work on the walls. Secondary schools buzz with excitement as students shift between classes.

"The Beach Boys even had a song about it— 'Be True to Your School.' That's the feeling you get when you go through a good school. The building may be old and even the teachers as well. That's not the point. The staff cares, and the students there are getting a good education."

Schools are divided into four levels—preschools, elementary schools, middle schools or junior high schools, and high schools—with public schools generally including the last three of these levels. In the United States in 1995, there were twenty-five million students enrolled in grades K–6, nearly seven million in grades 7–8, and twelve and a half million in grades 9–12 (U.S. Department of Education 1997).

The entry level for private schools is the preschool. However, the federal government has Head Start, a free program for economically disadvantaged three- through five-year-olds. Some public school systems also provide preschools for three- to five-year-olds. Preschools are typically privately funded, usually by tuition paid by the parents.

For most children only two places exist where they can gain a successful identity and learn to follow the essential pathways. These places are the home and the school. . . . if the home is successful, the child may succeed despite the school, but that is too big an if to rely upon. We must ensure that the child's major experience in growing up, the most constant and important factor in his life, school, provides within it the two necessary pathways: a chance to give and receive love and a chance to become educated and therefore worthwhile.

William Glasser
Schools Without Failure

Preschools typically enroll children between the ages of three and five years old, although some take younger children. Preschools differ from day-care centers, which focus only on taking care of children in a safe environment. Preschools have a set curriculum of language, movement, art, and music activities. Preschoolers learn how to print their names, draw pictures, cut and glue paper, sing songs such as "The Wheels on the Bus" and "Old MacDonald Had a Farm," recite simple rhymes such as the "Itsy Bitsy Spider" and "Five Little Ducks Went Out to Play," and skip and gallop. Day-care centers may teach some of the same things, but they are primarily interested in keeping children active, feeding them snacks and lunch, and supervising their naps. They are geared toward more social interaction, while preschools are geared toward both social interaction and academic performance.

Elementary school is the first level of school that children are mandated to attend. Most states require that children begin school no later than age seven. However, traditionally children begin kindergarten at age five and enter first grade at age six. Elementary schools usually provide the first seven years of children's education before they go on to middle school or junior high.

Middle schools typically include grades 6–8, while junior high schools usually include grades 7–8 and sometimes grade 9. Middle schools generally have a more elementary focus, while junior high schools are more like high schools. In middle schools, teachers often work together in teams, something that occurs with less frequency in junior high schools. Both middle schools and junior high schools allow students to become involved in school activities, clubs, and after-school sports programs.

High schools are the culminating required public school experience for students. High schools allow students more freedom to select courses. Each state, however, has minimum guidelines of specific courses that all students must take and successfully pass to graduate. Many school activities, clubs, and after-school sports are available for student participation.

In this chapter we discuss elementary schools, middle and junior high schools, and high schools. Since schools largely reflect the values and expectations of their communities, urban, suburban, and rural settings of schools are described first.

Current Trends

Schools, particularly elementary and middle schools are changing. Many school districts now have divided into K–3, 4–5, 6–8, and 9–12 buildings. The belief is that children learn best if they are around other children of similar ages. Thus, we find early childhood buildings comprised of kindergarten through third grades, upper elementary buildings with fourth and fifth grades, middle schools with sixth through eighth grades, and high schools with ninth through twelfth grades. Some high schools only have grades ten through twelve. Schools in large cities such as Chicago and New York are more apt to have K–8 and 9–12 schools. This is largely for efficiency purposes in organization. However, the majority of U.S. school districts still have K–6, 7–8 and 9–12 buildings. Research shows that whenever a child changes schools, regardless of the reason, the child's achievement level declines. For this reason, some school districts are reluctant to restructure the age groupings of students by buildings.

Recent trends include a resurgence of multi-age grouping. Popularized in the non-graded school movement of the late 1960s and 70s, multi-age grouping was used primarily with younger children. A typical multi-age class consisted of an equal number of first, second, and third graders. At the end of the year, the third graders moved on to the fourth, fifth, and sixth grade class. New first graders took their place. Multi-age grouping has been successful in that the older students serve as role models for the younger ones.

Looping is a variation of multi-age grouping. In looping, the teacher advances along with her students. Looping is also called multiyear teaching or multiyear placement. The teacher may stay with the same group of students for two or three years. Classroom routines started in the first year, continue on day one of the second school year. Thus, students are familiar with the classroom structures and routines and are more comfortable with expectations. Looping is said to better meet the developmental needs of children. Jan Jubert, a first and second grade teacher from Lac du Flambeau, Wisconsin, says that "by staying with a teacher who really knows them and whom they trust, students are given time and high-quality instruction to succeed" (Rasmussen 1998, p. 4). Jubert goes on to say that she finds she can cover more material, do more hands-on activities, and designs more multiple intelligence activities. She has found that attendance has increased as children, particularly high risk students, find the classroom setting a secure, trusting place to be. Test scores and increased self-esteem have also improved.

Looping is done in grades K–8 but some high schools are considering it. Small high schools have been doing a variation of looping for years as the biology I teacher also teaches biology II, etc.

Block scheduling is the current trend in high schools. Longer class periods enable teachers to plan more elaborate and engaging class activities. So instead of changing classes every 50 minutes or so, students remain in the same class for 100 minutes.

Figure 1 The structure of education in the United States

NOTE—Adult education programs, while not separately delineated above, may provide instruction at the elementary, secondary, or higher education level. Chart reflects typical patterns of progression rather than all possible variations. SOURCE: U.S. Department of Education, National Center for Education Statistics.

The class meets every other day rather than every day. Such scheduling permits teachers in rural areas to rotate between schools. Thus Latin, physics or calculus teachers may teach students at two or three different high schools during one academic year. Without block scheduling, the subjects might not be offered at all.

Distance education using computers and television technology is being increasingly incorporated into high schools and, more recently, elementary and middle schools. Schools serve as sites where classes are transmitted into via fiber optic telephone lines or through satellite signals. Students can see the teacher and the teacher

Urban schools spend more money per student than do suburban and rural schools. (© Amy Etra/PhotoEdit)

can see the students by using television and video cameras. Therefore, a teacher may teach a class live in a "studio" classroom and two or three or more classes at remote sites throughout the area or even country. Such technology has much promise.

School Settings

The three school settings are urban, suburban, and rural. Urban schools are those in large cities. Suburban schools are those in smaller communities but still of substantial size. Rural schools are those in less-populated outlying areas.

Urban School Districts

Urban schools have a diverse population of students, with high percentages of African American, Hispanic, and Asian students. For instance, the Oakland Unified school district in Oakland, California; Hartford public schools in Hartford, Connecticut; Orleans Parish schools in New Orleans, Louisiana; Detroit public schools, in Detroit, Michigan; and the San Antonio school district in San Antonio, Texas, all have minority student populations of over 90 percent of their total student body. However, some urban school districts have much lower percentages of minority students. In the New York City public schools, the largest school district in the nation, about 69 percent of the students are members of minorities (U.S. Department of Education 1992).

We are a highly mobile society. This mobility causes problems in all schools but especially in urban districts. In large cities, students may move frequently within the same school district during a single school year. Because urban schools have a larger

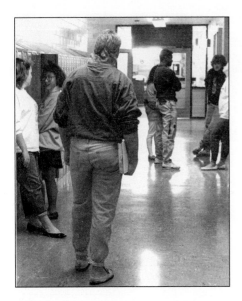

Suburban school districts may have higher expectations of teachers and students due to community values.
(© Cleo Freelance Photos)

concentration of disadvantaged students (Hill, Wise, and Shapiro 1989), this movement interferes with students' learning, particularly for those students with learning difficulties.

In urban school districts, in particular, students come from a variety of different family compositions. Some students may live with extended families, and it is not unusual for grandparents or aunts and uncles to serve as guardians of students. This disruption in the family can also interfere with students' academic achievement.

The level of violence is higher in urban schools than in either suburban or rural schools. Gangs are a major problem for high school educators. Some schools have adopted school uniforms, even at the elementary level, in an attempt to prevent students from identifying with a specific gang by the color of the clothes they wear. Drug and alcohol abuse extend from upper elementary grades through the high school grades. Urban schools also have a higher dropout rate as well as incidence of teenage pregnancies than suburban or rural schools (U.S. Department of Education 1997).

A greater number of students with special needs attend urban schools than either suburban or rural schools (Englert 1993). In addition, urban schools have a high concentration of at-risk students. According to Kagan (1990, 105–6), "At-risk students have low educational aspirations, low self-esteem, an external locus of control, and negative attitudes toward school along with a history of academic failure, truancy, and misconduct, with no indication that they lack requisite aptitudes." In Levin's (1989, 47) view, at-risk students "are concentrated among minority groups, immigrants, non–English speaking families, families headed by single mothers, and economically disadvantaged groups."

Typically, urban school districts have among the highest expenditures of money per student in the nation. On the average, teachers in urban school districts are paid higher salaries than the average teacher in their state because of the higher cost of living associated with a large urban area and strong teacher union support. Because of the needs of large numbers of at-risk students, more federal education funds are appropriated to urban districts per student than to other districts.

Suburban School Districts

Suburban school districts are among the most affluent in the nation. They have more financial resources per student than do rural school districts and even more than some urban school districts. The typical suburban school district has among the latest in technological advancements, including computers with CD-ROM players and video disk machines. Some even have video telephones so that one student can both talk with and see another student in a classroom across the country.

Like urban and rural school districts, suburban school districts have their own unique problems. Many suburban students are latchkey children—they often leave home after their parents leave for work and arrive home before their parents. This has resulted in many suburban school districts offering before- and after-school care for elementary students.

Suburban students are highly mobile. Parents are often transferred by companies from one location to another or gain employment with another company in another city or state. This means that the faces within a student's classroom may change frequently.

Like urban students, many suburban students come from single-parent families. However, most suburban students come from two-parent families in which both parents work outside of the home. This has created a problem in that many suburban students have ample amounts of money and time to spend at shopping malls but receive little attention or time from their stressed-out parents.

Rural School Districts

There are numerous rural school districts throughout the United States and Canada. Small rural districts are in nearly every state. In both New York and Oregon, a third of their respective school districts serve fewer than one thousand students. Nationally, 51 percent of all school districts are both small and rural (Schmuck and Schmuck 1992).

Rural America itself is changing as family farms get bigger in size and fewer individuals farm. Small-town merchants who a decade ago were the owners of the family-run drugstore, department store, hardware store, or restaurant are also fewer in number. Today, nationally based retailers and fast-food restaurants supply the needs of the rural community.

Schmuck and Schmuck (1992, 56–57) studied twenty-five rural school districts in twenty-one states. They write:

> Because of depressing economic times during the 1980s, schools in small districts all over America were undergoing a continuous drain on their resources, both physical and human. Their decaying buildings were barely adequate, new books and educational materials were not being purchased, new teachers with fresh ideas were not being hired, and experienced teachers were overloaded with teaching, counseling, committee work, and extracurricular activities. On top of that, many families were caving in because of unemployment or underemployment, and the stress of poverty was bringing on drinking, spouse beating, child abuse, and divorce.

Since schools are typically funded by property taxes, rural school districts are at a disadvantage for two reasons. First, there are few commercial businesses and factories located in rural areas. These businesses and factories tend to locate in communities with a larger pool of workers and that are near major transportation lines, such as railroads, airports, and interstate highways. A second problem is that while farms consist of many acres of land, usually over three hundred acres per farm, farmland is taxed at a rate lower than businesses, factories, and homes. Thus, teacher salaries in rural school districts are lower than in suburban and urban districts. Rural school districts typically have less money to spend per student.

With fewer families remaining on their farms, many farm houses have been sold or rented to other families. Some of these families stay and become a part of the rural community while others are more transient, staying a year or two at the most. Most noticeable is the increased number of at-risk students in rural schools, many of whom move in and out during a school year.

Child abuse, something rarely heard of in rural areas twenty years ago, is on the increase in rural communities as it is in suburban and urban areas. Incidents of both physical and sexual abuse have been reported in rural areas in record numbers during the past few years. Some researchers believe it is due to the economic decline in rural areas. Teachers in rural areas are often poorly trained to deal with such abuse of their students.

There are fewer discipline problems in rural schools. In addition, there seems to be more parental support. For example, many rural teachers find that the majority of parents of their students attend parent-teacher conferences in the fall and spring. It is not unusual for every student in a class to have had at least one parent attend the parent-teacher conferences.

There is less violence in rural schools than in urban and suburban schools. Typically, the community itself focuses on the schools. Friday night football or basketball games are often the highlight of the community's events for the week.

The Preschool Environment

Preschools offer children a chance to interact with other children of their own age. In addition, a structured academic program is provided. Preschool teachers read to students and talk with them in order to develop their language skills. Students learn to take turns and share as well as to be responsible. They are expected to dress themselves with little or no assistance. By the end of preschool, students know how to write their first names and the letters of the alphabet, to read some words, and to count to fifteen.

Lynn Kagan, a child psychologist from Yale University, contends that early childhood education is vitally important if children are to succeed. She believes that preschools should have a developmental curriculum based on presenting material to children when they are physically and mentally ready for it. In addition, Kagan is an advocate of strong parental involvement and coordinated services for children and families. She asserts that these three aspects should follow children from preschool to kindergarten and beyond (Lewis 1993).

Head Start is a federally funded program initially begun in the mid-1960s as part of then President Lyndon B. Johnson's Great Society programs. Designed to give an academic boost to three- to five-year-old children from low-income families, Head Start has been both praised and condemned by educators. Head Start provides stimulating experiences for preschoolers, often helping them in language and concept development. In addition, the program provides nutritious snacks for children who often do not have enough to eat or who lack proper nutrition. In some areas of the country, Head Start programs have not been successful. Some Head Start critics point out that early gains fade away by third grade. In 1998, the cost of Head Start in the U.S. will be just over four billion dollars (U.S. Department of Education, 1997).

Privately owned urban and suburban preschools are typically very academically oriented. Three- to five-year-olds are taught not only the letters of the alphabet but how to read simple books. Likewise, adding and subtracting numbers are stressed. Paper and pencil worksheets are commonplace. Preschools are less likely to be found in rural areas.

The Elementary School Environment

Elementary school is where most of us began our formal education. Your kindergarten teacher's name as well as the activities you did at that level probably come readily to mind. While we may remember good as well as bad experiences from this time, many years have passed and elementary schools have changed, so we really don't have a good image of what elementary schools are actually like today.

Structure and routine are two of the primary ingredients of an elementary school. Young children depend on constancy because it makes them feel secure when they can predict what will happen. Even minor incidents can cause young children to become upset. If the school serves white milk Monday through Thursday and chocolate milk

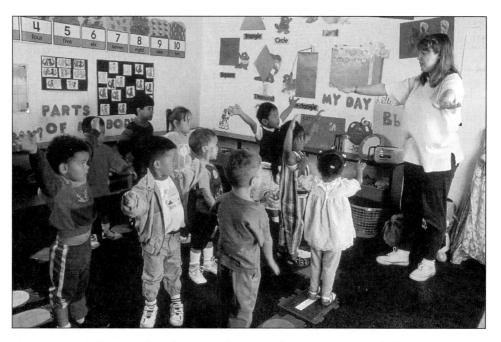

These young children are learning a simple song and its accompanying body movements.
(© Michael Neuman/PhotoEdit)

only on Fridays, and a mistake in the order causes white milk to be served on a Friday, children become disconcerted.

When elementary students enter kindergarten, they are eager to please their teacher. Enthusiasm and curiosity exudes from their small, wiggling, squirming bodies. They believe whatever the teacher says is the "word of the land," or the classroom in this case. Kindergartners treat their teacher with a kind of reverence in their respectful mannerisms. They line up when told, raise their hands to answer or ask questions, and willingly work with other students. The room is filled with cheerful, smiling faces.

As children get older their enthusiasm and often their curiosity fades. For many, instructional strategies fail to make them excited and interested in what they are learning. Some leave the elementary grades disliking school. While some take pleasant memories with them, others recall only frustration. The kinds and number of positive experiences each student has during the elementary school years are largely dependent on the elementary teacher. It is the classroom teacher that makes the difference.

Elementary Teachers

Elementary teachers are responsible for establishing the academic climate as well as the social climate in their schools. Unlike middle school and high school teachers, elementary teachers have complete responsibility for a student's learning in every content area—art, music, and physical education are usually exceptions. Thus, if an elementary teacher loves math but hates social studies, that may be conveyed to the students. It is up to the teacher to display a positive attitude toward all subjects—math, reading, science, social studies, and writing—if the students are to be interested and motivated. Teachers must also keep up to date by following current trends in all aspects of the elementary curriculum.

Gary Varrel

Elementary teachers establish a classroom routine. This includes when students can sharpen their pencils or go to the library to check out a book, how they line up to go to lunch or physical education, when they can work with other students and with how many, and numerous other daily aspects of classroom life.

As teachers, we know that it is best to keep classroom rules to a minimum—three or four at the most. "Respect for others" translates into "keep your hands off other students and their property." "Talk with permission" becomes "you can talk at certain times but not at other times." "Take turns" means "don't push and shove to be first in line." Having a set of ten or fifteen rules at the elementary level or any level is absurd because students aren't able to remember them all, let alone follow them.

The physical climate of the classroom impacts student attitudes toward learning. A warm, bright classroom with samples of students' work, several children's literature books readily available for the students to read, and an engaging bulletin board made by the students or the teacher are preferable to a classroom with no displays of children's work, few or no children's books, and a dull or even empty bulletin board. A classroom that is "too busy"—that is, has several colorful displays on the walls and windows as well as things hanging from the ceiling, and bright, commercially prepared posters or bulletin boards—can be too stimulating for some children. It is best to rotate displays of students' work. Student- or teacher-made bulletin boards are of more interest to the students and offer less distraction to the learning environment.

Structure of the Elementary School

Elementary schools are typically organized by grade levels K–6; however, there are variations. Some urban school districts include kindergarten through grade 8 at the elementary setting, with grades 9–12 as high school. Some school districts have kindergarten through grade 3 in one elementary building and grades 4–6 in another, or some similar combination.

Elementary schools can vary greatly in size, from fewer than twenty students in one- and two-room schools in remote areas of western states, to over twelve hundred students in suburban and urban areas. The average elementary school in the United States has 476 students (U.S. Department of Education 1997).

Within the elementary school itself can be different types of structural organization. While traditionally students are placed in grade levels from kindergarten through sixth, some schools offer developmental or transitional first-grade programs. These programs assist at-risk students in their move from the more socially focused kindergarten to the more academically focused first-grade classroom. In recent years, there has been a trend to group children developmentally rather than by grade level.

Some school districts mix the age levels of students within a classroom so that a primary-level class may consist of an equal number of first-, second-, and third-grade students, each of whom spends three years in the class with the same students and teacher. Thus, a community of learners is established with only a third of the class leaving each year. The older students serve as mentors to the younger students. Because the teacher knows the students so well, and the students know their teacher, the learning environment is comfortable for both. Because students feel secure and their teacher knows what to expect of them, many educators believe this is an ideal learning situation for both students and the teacher. If a student has difficulty working with a teacher, or vice versa, due to a lack of rapport or other reasons, the student may be moved to another teacher's classroom at the beginning of a new year.

Urban Elementary Schools

Urban elementary schools are often located in economically depressed areas of cities. However, some are located in relative close proximity to affluent high-rise apartment buildings, where many students live.

Urban elementary schools generally have a high percentage of minority students. Many large school districts have eight minority students for every two white students in the classroom. Also there is a higher percentage of minority teachers in urban schools than either in suburban or rural schools. However, white teachers make up the predominant group in the urban teaching force.

As a teacher in a typical urban elementary school, you can expect the majority of students to come from single-parent homes at or below the poverty level. Many parents will be illiterate. A majority of the students in kindergarten through grade 3 generally have language development problems, both with vocabulary and sentence structure as well as with articulation. They lack the stimulation of a variety of experiences, such as going to the zoo or a museum and visiting a public library on a regular basis. Those who spend time at the library often do so after school. Their parents use the facility as a safe place for their children to stay until they can pick them up after work.

Also at the early childhood level, the only things most students have ever purchased by themselves are cans of soda pop or candy from a vending machine or a round on a video game at a video arcade. Thus, identification of currency and making change are both taught. At the upper elementary level, students are searching for their own identity. Clothes are increasingly important, so schools require uniforms. Some students frequently hang around noted gang members, even running errands for them, as they attempt to move into the world of adolescence.

Most urban elementary schools lock their outside doors after students arrive in the morning and return from recess and lunch. In neighborhoods where gangs or

Are All Suburban Elementary Schools Alike?

Suburban school districts vary drastically. Steve Layne, a fifth-grade teacher who has taught in two different suburban districts outside of a large city, can attest to this. In one lower-class suburb, Steve says many of his students were latchkey children—they went home to empty houses and took care of themselves. The neighborhood was dangerous, and drugs were a problem in the community. Occasionally there were shootings. Steve had trouble arranging parent-teacher conferences because parents worked unusual hours at local factories.

Steve then moved to an upscale suburban school district. There he found that many of his students were also latchkey children, like those in the blue-collar district from which he had come. In the more affluent district, both parents worked and some parents were both professionals—businessmen and businesswomen, doctors, and lawyers. He still had difficulty arranging parent-teacher conferences because of parent work schedules. But in general, Steve believed that the students in both communities had the same needs from him as a teacher—to be accepted, loved, and taught.

drive-by shootings are prevalent, students and teachers routinely go through drills to learn to protect themselves from gunfire by dropping to the floor under their desks or tables.

Suburban Elementary Schools

While suburban elementary schools are predominately white, most are becoming more culturally diverse. Indeed, in some suburban communities, numerous cultures are represented. By having students or members of the community share the unique aspects of their cultures, all students can better appreciate and understand other cultures.

Traditionally, the suburban elementary school educated children of two-parent families, in which the father worked and the mother stayed home in the role of homemaker. Today, that has changed. In many families both parents head out the door to work each day. Even though some suburban students' parents are divorced, the overwhelming majority live with both parents.

A decade ago, suburban elementary schools had all of the parent volunteers they could use. Now, they have more students who need individual tutoring but far fewer volunteers to provide it. Instead of serving as room mothers and tutors, many mothers are now in the workplace to provide a second income for the family.

Rural Elementary Schools

Rural elementary schools are usually located in small communities. Some rural elementary school buildings were formerly high schools that were converted due to consolidation of schools into one larger district.

Because of the lack of jobs in rural communities, more parental involvement in the elementary school is sometimes seen—parents serve as volunteers or work as teacher aides. On the other hand, since most rural workers receive low salaries, many rural elementary students live at or just above the poverty level. They may lack proper clothing, food, and health care.

Rural students are often bused several miles to and from school each day. For some students, this may be a ride of up to an hour each morning and afternoon. School districts in the plains and western states often have more school bus routes with smaller buses in an attempt to lessen the riding time of their students.

Because a rural school district's boundaries may cover several miles, some districts have had to make changes in their schedules to adjust. For instance, Amboy, Illinois, is a rural district with a large territory of several square miles but few students. The district adopted an all-day, alternate-day kindergarten program in which students in the northern part of the school district attended kindergarten on Mondays, Wednesdays, and Fridays one week and Tuesdays and Thursdays the next week. Kindergartners from the southern part of the district attended the alternate days.

The Middle School and Junior High School Environment

Middle schools usually have students in grades 6–8 and **junior high schools** cover grades 7–8 or 7–9. There are over five thousand middle and junior high schools in the United States (U.S. Department of Education 1997).

There is more of a student-centered focus in middle schools than in their junior high counterparts. Middle schools are designed to be an extension of elementary school. Thus, most middle schools teach reading and language arts whereas junior high schools, considered to be preparatory schools for high school, teach English grammar and literature.

Typically, the majority of children go through puberty at this level of schooling. Girls start their pubertal growth spurt earlier than do boys, some as young as third grade, while boys begin later, usually in seventh grade.

Middle School and Junior High Teachers

Middle school teachers are usually highly student oriented. The middle school curriculum is aimed at having teaching materials fit the student rather than the student fit the teaching materials. As such, teachers are sensitive to student interests and needs. Junior high teachers, on the other hand, tend to be more focused on the subject area they teach. They are more subject-matter oriented than student oriented.

These differences are due in part to state certification requirements. Teachers who obtain teaching certification in grades K–8, or a middle school certification, typically have a student-oriented background since that is the curriculum focus of most elementary and middle school teacher education programs at colleges and universities. Teachers who obtain teaching certification in grades 7–12 are generally subject-matter oriented since they majored in a content area in the liberal arts (e.g., English, history, mathematics, earth or life sciences) in their teacher education programs in college.

Urban Middle Schools and Junior High Schools

In most large urban school districts such as Chicago, Detroit, Los Angeles, and New York City, there are no middle schools. These grades are included in the elementary schools. This means that thirteen- and fourteen-year-olds are in the same building as five- and six-year-olds. Since there is a vast difference in the physical, psychological, and sociological development of these age groups, many educators question whether they should be taught within the same school building, where they come into contact with each other on a daily basis. The primary reason for such grouping is economics. Fewer school buildings are needed when a larger school structure can accommodate grades K–8.

Suburban Middle Schools and Junior High Schools

Suburban school districts were among the first in the nation to embrace the idea of junior high schools and, later, middle schools. Junior high schools were designed to be preparatory schools for high schools. As such they still are very highly subject-matter oriented but also offer vocational courses such as home economics and basic woodshop.

Middle schools likewise offer vocational courses. However, the basic curriculum is an extension of that of the elementary school, with the focus on the students' needs and interests.

Rural Middle Schools and Junior High Schools

Many rural school districts have a middle school or junior high school. Most often the school is a junior high school, a miniature version of the local high school. In smaller rural districts, however, grades 7–12 are often housed together in the high school. This enables a junior high school teacher to teach high school classes as well. Thus, a student may have the same subject-area teacher in junior high as in high school.

The High School Environment

High school is entirely an American invention. In 1821, the first high school was established in Boston. High school allows students to select the courses in which they enroll. More freedom and independence is given to high school students than to elementary and middle or junior high students. However, hall passes are still required as well as dress codes maintained. Smoking and drinking on school grounds are prohibited.

High schools are often called *comprehensive* because of their wide variety of course selections. They offer academic programs for students who plan to attend college, a vocational program for students who plan to take jobs in the workplace upon graduation, and a general studies program for those students who haven't decided what to do after high school. Magnet high schools are specialized high schools that concentrate on one particular area of study, for example, the arts, business, or science.

High schools range in size from as few as fifty students in rural areas to as many as five thousand students in urban and suburban areas. Small high schools have very limited course offerings, while large high schools may offer more courses than a student could take in an eight-year period of study, let alone a four-year program.

About 10 percent of the nation's high schools are located in urban areas and over 50 percent are in rural areas, with many of these being combination junior high/high schools. Suburban school districts include roughly a third of the high schools in the United States.

Talented athletes are often given a higher status at the high school level than are academically talented students. This is true regardless of the community in which the high school is located—urban, suburban, or rural. Students who are not engaged in extracurricular sports or other activities, and who are not academically talented, can seemingly get lost in any high school.

High schools in large cities have come under attack in recent years. According to Boyer (1983, 16), "Troubled high schools frequently are in inner cities where problems of population dislocation, poverty, unemployment, and crime take priority over education. They also may be found in decaying suburbs or in rural communities racked by poverty and neglect." Unfortunately, today we find troubled high schools in many suburban districts as well.

Students may legally drop out of high school at age sixteen, and as a result, some high schools have high dropout rates. In 1996, for all races, the dropout rate was 11.1 percent with 7.3 percent white students and 13.0 percent African American students. The dropout rate among Hispanics is the highest for any group, at 29.4 percent (U.S. Department of Education 1997).

High school students have many more social pressures than their elementary and middle school counterparts. High school students often hold down jobs outside of school, they typically apply for a driver's license while in school, and they apply for admission to college or full-time employment upon graduation. They are learning to be adults when they have had no prior experience in the adult world. The high school years are a time when students experiment with adulthood. They may drive a car for the first time, stay out late without their parents' permission, have sex for the first time, or try alcohol or drugs.

Peer pressure is very strong for high school students. If a peer group discourages getting good grades, adolescents often weaken and conform to the group's desire. Likewise, if smoking and drinking are accepted by the peer group, students generally follow suit. Unfortunately, many male peer groups today approve of carrying guns, and many high schools across the country are encountering this phenomenon.

High School Teachers

High school teachers have completed a combination of liberal arts and education methods courses as part of their college study. Each teacher has majored in a particular content area of study, usually forty hours of coursework at the collegiate level. Most have areas of concentration or minors in another field of study, which range from eighteen to twenty-four hours of coursework.

According to Boyer (1983), to be a successful teacher at the high school level, or any level, you must

- carefully plan for each lesson;
- have educational goals for each school day;
- carefully pace and time the presentation of lessons;
- love the subject matter you teach;
- respect your students;
- have clear, specific procedures for students to follow;
- carry through with expectations of students and established goals;
- carefully measure accomplishments of students.

High school teachers may have five or six different classes for which to prepare, each with twenty-five to thirty-five students in a class period from forty-five to fifty-five minutes long. One period each day is set aside for teachers to prepare for their classes and grade papers. Inclusion requires teachers to have to work with students with a wide range of abilities. Obviously, teaching at the high school level can be very demanding.

Urban High Schools

Urban high schools were designed to hold large numbers of students, sometimes as many as five thousand students. Thus, they are often viewed as being cold and impersonal. In schools such as these, it is possible for a student to go through four years of high school and never really know a teacher or even have any friends.

Urban, or inner-city, high schools tend to offer a variety of courses, emphasizing academic and especially vocational education. Students have a more limited selection of sports and extracurricular activities than do their suburban counterparts. This is due to lack of funding for such activities. The activities are usually restricted to some degree for safety reasons. For example, most urban high schools do not allow student clubs to meet after school or hold football games on Friday nights because of security reasons.

A study by the American Institute of Stress found that the most stressful job was being a teacher in an inner-city high school (Butterfield 1994). Many urban high schools have major problems with violence and gang-related assaults. Doors are kept locked, and some schools use monitoring devices such as metal detectors and closed-circuit cameras as deterrents. It is not unusual for police squad cars to arrive and take students out of school and directly to the local police station.

Suburban High Schools

Large student bodies, usually between one thousand and two thousand students, are representative of the typical suburban high school. Suburban high schools offer more variety in their course selections than either urban or rural high schools. Typically the teaching and administrative staff are better educated than those found in urban and rural high school classrooms—the majority have master's degrees and many have earned doctoral degrees in education.

Most suburban high schools have a rigorous academic program to prepare students to attend college. At New Trier High School in a suburb of Chicago, 99 percent of the students go on to college immediately following high school graduation. Over 75 percent of the teachers at New Trier High School have doctoral degrees.

Suburban high schools typically emphasize academic extracurricular activities and clubs as well as sports. Chess club, art club, jazz band, swing choir, computer club, Spanish club, German club, math club, science club, National Honor Society are all available to students. With sports, like course selections, there are more opportunities for students. Swimming and diving, cross country, track, golf, tennis, volleyball, wrestling, football, basketball, badminton, softball, soccer, and baseball are typical offerings.

Rural High Schools

Teachers in rural high school settings may prefer to concentrate on one subject area, but generally they must teach in more than one area. For instance, a high school English teacher may also teach Spanish, while the high school advanced math teacher may also teach physics and chemistry. This also means that students have a limited number of course offerings from which to select. In some cases, a course may be offered one year but not the next because the teacher must teach another subject or the advanced class of the same subject. Students who plan to attend college may find that they lack some requirements for certain majors, particularly upper-level foreign language, mathematics, or laboratory science courses.

Classes in rural high schools are generally average to small in size, depending on the course. Higher-level courses tend to be smaller than those at the freshman and sophomore levels. The smaller student body and class sizes mean that the school is a microcosm of the community in that most students know each other. Likewise the principal and most teachers recognize the students and know their first names.

A Beginning Teacher in an Inner-City School

After high school, LouAnne Johnson joined the Navy to help finance her college education. After working her way through college, she took a commission in the Marines. When she completed her tour of duty, LouAnne took a teaching position in an inner-city high school in California. After teaching for four years, she wrote a book, *My Posse Don't Do Homework,* in which she shared her teaching experiences. LouAnne believes that teaching is the best thing she has ever done in her life. She has made a difference in the lives of many of her students. This is an excerpt from *My Posse Don't Do Homework.*

"I decided to write notes to the parents of every student in both of my classes. I wrote the notes in three batches: The first students to receive them were the 'bad' kids because I thought they needed the most encouragement. It was difficult, at times, to find something positive to say, but I didn't lie. I didn't tell parents that their kids were rocket scientists, but I did include a statement in each note to the effect that I was happy to have the child in my class, or pleased to have the chance to be his or her teacher for some reason—the student's wit, charming personality, delightful sense of humor, courteous behavior, impeccable dress, ability to get along with other kids, quick grasp of subject matter, and so on. In most cases, the notes didn't address the subject of academic achievement; most of them simply praised the student as a person.

"When I handed the notes, unsealed, to the kids and asked them to give them to their parents or guardians, I invariably got the same response from the students: What did I do now? I told the kids they were free to read the notes, but they had to take them home. A few of the kids crumpled up the notes and threw them on the floor on their way out of the room, which hurt my feelings a little bit and annoyed me quite a lot because it was taking much longer

than I had anticipated to write fifty-six notes by hand. But the results were worth the effort. I was amazed. Of course, a few kids still held out, but most of them changed their perceptions of themselves. Jason was no longer a mouthy brat; he was a 'quick-witted young man whose comments added a welcome touch of humor to class discussions.' Sherri, a straight D student, held her head high, proud to be 'a young lady whose tasteful clothes and gracious manner set a good example for other students.' Danny, my hyperactive desk thumper, had never thought of himself before as a 'bright and charming young man with boundless energy.'

"When the students with good study habits and high grades realized that their academically less successful counterparts had received complimentary notes to take home, several of them privately requested similar notes. I assured them that every student in class would receive a note as soon as I could turn them out. The model student notes were easy to write. I complimented them on their neat handwriting, their high-quality work, their excellent attendance, their high test scores, and the like. But I tried to remember to include a personal compliment in each note, since the kids valued those more highly than the academic kudos.

"As I approached the third batch of notes—for the 'middle' students who were neither especially good nor noticeably bad—I was appalled to realize that I couldn't picture some of those kids in my mind, although I thought I knew them all so well. Sometimes a trivial detail such as hair color escaped me; other times it was the entire body that disappeared, leaving me with a mental image of a young face floating above a school desk. I realized then why so many good kids are so easily lost in our school system—they have softer voices, better

(continued)

manners, less extreme personalities. They don't cause problems or constantly seek attention or assistance in class. They go along with the program and fade into the background, often by choice, but sometimes simply because they are overshadowed by the others. I took extra care and spent a lot of time on that final batch of notes and when I distributed them to the students, I looked into each one's face until I was satisfied that I saw the boy or girl looking back at me.

"After writing all the individual notes, I actually felt the bonding between the students and me that I'd read about but hadn't experienced before. It was a wonderful feeling and it completely changed the dynamics of the classroom. When the students truly believed that I liked them just as they were, it was no longer Teacher versus Students. It became Teacher and Students versus Curriculum. Together, we hated vocabulary exercises, grammar exams, reading proficiency tests, and spelling quizzes, but we had to do them. Teaching was the best thing I had ever done in my life. Before I knew it, June raced around the corner and crashed into the classroom, spinning all my students out into the summer sun."

From LouAnne Johnson, *My Posse Don't Do Homework.* © 1992 by LouAnne Johnson. Reprinted by permission of St. Martin's Press, Inc., New York, NY.

Suburban, urban, and rural schools usually offer activities such as basketball to students. (© James Shaffer)

Extracurricular activities in a rural high school are limited. Typical offerings are a foreign language club, usually Spanish, math or science club, computer club, pep band, choir, art club, and National Honor Society. Sports tend to include cross country, track, softball for girls and baseball for boys, basketball, volleyball, wrestling, and football. Very small high schools may not have football but offer soccer instead,

Chapter 15 *Schools and Their Environment*

Talking It Over

Go back to your old high school and you'll see changes. In fact, all schools change. And changes are occurring more dramatically and rapidly than ever before. The walls may be the same, but what's taking place inside those walls is a transition from the old to the new.

Charles Darwin wrote, "It is not the strongest of the species that survive, nor the most intelligent, but the one most responsive to change" (Pritchett 1996, 60). You'll be changing your own teaching as you continually incorporate new ideas and methodology.

although in Kansas and Nebraska, small high schools play seven- or eight-person football rather than the required eleven players.

Often students from small rural high schools may be penalized when applying for college admission and scholarships because they haven't taken as rigorous a course load, been involved in as many extracurricular activities, or had a large student body with which to compare themselves. Most college admission programs attempt to take these factors into consideration, but still it is difficult to determine whether a student who ranks third in a class of forty-one students is a better candidate than a suburban high school student who ranks twenty-first out of 487 students.

■ Summary

Preschools, elementary schools, middle schools or junior high schools, and high schools are the different levels of schooling in the United States. Students are required to attend only elementary through high school. However, students may drop out of school at age sixteen.

School settings differ as do the levels. Schools are located in rural, suburban, and urban settings. Because each school in every community is unique, teachers need to become familiar with community expectations and desires as well as other aspects of the community, such as the cultures represented, the economic base, and community values.

■ Reflections

Recall the high school you attended. Was it urban, suburban, or rural? How big was your graduating class? What were the class sizes for the various subjects?

Make a list of the course selections you had. Which ones did you take? Which ones would you have liked to take but could not? Were the teachers well prepared to teach their particular subject areas?

What extracurricular activities were available? Which did you join? Was there a sense of school spirit?

Write a two-page paper expressing how you would improve your former high school if money was not a problem.

■ Discussion Questions

1. How do preschools differ from day-care centers for three- to five-year-olds?
2. Describe a typical elementary school. If you had the opportunity to create a perfect elementary school, what would you do?
3. How do middle schools differ from junior high schools?
4. In what ways does peer pressure affect students?
5. How can high schools be improved?

■ For Further Reading

Boyer, E. 1983. *High school: A report on secondary education in America.* New York: The Carnegie Foundation for the Advancement of Teaching.

Johnson, L. A. 1992. *My posse don't do homework.* New York: St. Martin's Press.

Jorgensen, C. M. 1998. *Restructuring high school for all students.* Baltimore: Paul H. Brookes.

Lewis, A. C. 1993. The payoff from a quality preschool. *Phi Delta Kappan* 74 (10):748–49.

Schmuck, R. A., and P. A. Schmuck. 1992. *Small districts big problems: Making school everybody's house.* Newbury Park, CA: Corwin Press.

Sheppo, K. G., S. J. Hartsfield, S. Ruff, C. A. Jones, and M. Holinga. 1995. How an urban school promotes inclusion. *Educational Leadership* 52 (4):82–84.

Sizer, T. R. 1984. *Horace's compromise: The dilemma of the American high school.* Boston: Houghton Mifflin.

16

Education in Other Countries

Primary Points

- Most industrialized countries have national standards for their students.

- Nations in the European Community share educational ideas while still respecting each nation's individuality and culture.

- British teachers emphasize individual attention for their students.

- Asian students tend to be quieter in class and more respectful of their teachers than students in other countries.

- Japanese students have a longer school year than do American students.

Chapter Inquiries

- How are the British grant schools like charter schools in the United States?

- How are Germany and Japan alike in their educational systems?

- What are some of the primary criticisms of Japanese schools?

- Why do the United States and the Catholic Church play an important role in the future of Polish schools?

- How has education changed in South Africa?

"I student taught in Australia and consider myself a better teacher for the experience," says Joyce Westbrook, who has taught for fifteen years. "Through that experience I learned that kids have more similarities than differences. I also learned to prepare my own lessons from my own materials rather than relying upon commercially prepared textbooks. That required a lot of my time and thought. I knew exactly what I wanted the activity to teach, and I had to orchestrate it completely."

Photo Disc/Education

Education is of primary concern to world leaders. The economic summits held by industrialized nations, along with the overall concern about developments in less advanced nations, are evidence of this. There are over 950 million illiterate people in the world, and two-thirds of them are women. In addition, over 100 million school-age children, primarily in impoverished developing nations, do not have access to school (Glazer 1994). Obviously, there is a great need for education to be improved as well as made available to children throughout the world.

The educational systems of industrialized nations are often compared (figure 1).

We must foster and pursue international cooperation and understanding if we are to resolve the pressing problems confronting the nations of the world. And education, as it has in the past, will play a primary role in that crucial effort.

Jerry Kopp
A World at Risk

Many industrialized countries have national standards for their students. For instance France, Germany, and Japan have long had national standards. Great Britain has had local standards but now is moving toward implementing national standards with performance-based testing of student growth in different subject areas (Maeroff 1992). With the passage of Goals 2000, the United States is now developing national standards for its students. In February, 1998, a report was released that indicated U.S. students performed worse than students in fourteen other nations in math and physics. Those U.S. students who performed best in math received five hours of instruction per week (Holland, 1998). Studies such as these are used to gauge how U.S. compares with the rest of the world.

Education differs not only in curriculum but in how it is used and applied. For instance, high school students in the United States spend only 1,460 hours in academic core classes while students in other industrialized nations devote much more time studying the academic areas—3,528 hours for German students, 3,280 hours for French students, and 3,170 hours for Japanese students (National Education Commission on Time and Learning 1994). It should be noted, however, that high school students in the United States attend comprehensive high schools whereas there are different types of high schools in Germany, France, and Japan. Thus, a student in the United States is being compared with those foreign students who attend high schools with an academic focus, not a technical or business focus.

Many of the problems faced by the United States are those encountered by other nations. According to Kopp (1992, 347), "The roots of the world's educational problems are amazingly similar, despite the diverse histories, cultures, and social forces that have shaped the various nations. Yet the reasons these problems have surfaced today are quite different and have led to some very different attempts at resolution."

This chapter provides an overview of the educational systems of several nations throughout the world.

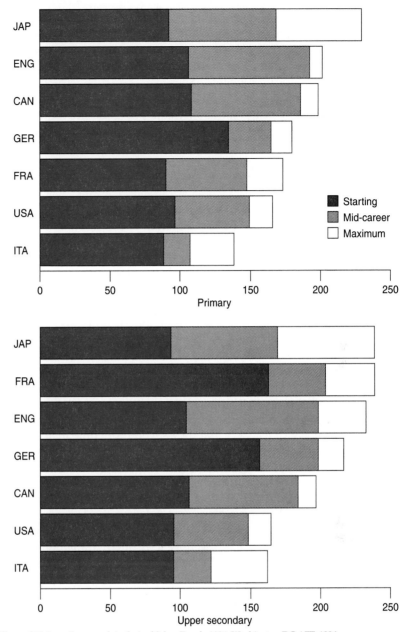

Figure 1
Teacher salaries as a percentage of 1996 GDP in the seven major industrialized nations

From F. Howard Nelson, *Survey and Analysis of Salary Trends*, 1996. Washington DC:AFT, 1996.

North American Countries

Canada and Mexico differ greatly in their educational systems. Because the United States is the leading free nation in the world as well as located between the two, its educational programs and advancements are observed by both countries. All three countries, however, have very different educational systems.

Canada

Education in Canada has been influenced by educational programs in Great Britain and the United States as well as those in New Zealand and Australia. Students in

Canada attend school for 190 days rather than 180 days as in the United States. The individual provinces control the educational system within their respective boundaries, and the federal government has little influence on the schools.

Kindergarten is provided to five-year-olds, but, as in the United States, compulsory education begins at age six. The school structure generally consists of elementary schools (grades K–5), middle schools (grades 6–8), and high schools (grades 9–12). Rural schools in the western provinces are more apt to include grades K–8.

Schools are provided with curriculum guides that are developed at the province level, similar to state curricular guidelines in the United States. Students are taught from a developmental approach; that is, the teacher begins where the student is and has the student engage in learning activities that he or she can manage. Some Canadian elementary schools are nongraded and operate on a continuous progress approach. This places greater emphasis on the individual learner. In addition, there is a great emphasis on the integration of subjects and on small-group projects.

There are both public and private schools in Canada. The public schools are coeducational. Forty percent of Canadian students attend private religious schools that are partially or fully funded by public taxes. Over 90 percent of the private religious schools are Catholic, and most are in the province of Quebec (McAdams 1993). In the 1900's, at the high school level in particular, many boys attended private schools called "colleges" while girls attended "academies." Today boys and girls attend coeducational high schools.

Canadian law gives applicants who are Canadian citizens the first opportunity for all teaching positions before considering those from other nations.

Canada is similar to the United States in that each province, like each state, has jurisdiction over the education of students and teacher certification within its boundaries. For example, in 1994, the province of Ontario approved the requirement of all preservice teachers that they spend more time in actual classroom settings as part of their teacher education programs. In Quebec, where most residents speak French, French-speaking students are taught English for an hour each day, while English-speaking students are taught French an hour each day.

The curricula of schools in Canada tend to be a mixture of those found in Great Britain, Australia, New Zealand, and the United States. For example, whole language is quite popular in Canadian elementary schools, as it is in these countries. Other subject areas also have a distinctly Canadian curricula. For instance, teachers rely on children's and young adult books authored by Canadians in their elementary and secondary classrooms. At the secondary level, teachers in social studies may have their students read *Canada and the World,* a magazine designed solely for Canadian students.

Mexico

As compared to the United States and Canada, Mexico has a less sophisticated public education system, with fewer requirements of both teachers and students. There are both public and private schools in Mexico, with the majority of the private schools run by the Catholic Church.

Affluent Mexicans send their children to private schools, which generally have rigorous academic standards. The majority of Mexican parents send their children to local public schools, where the standards are far lower, as are fiscal resources. Classes are large, and the teachers possess minimal training. Professional development for teachers is virtually unheard of because of the poor funding.

Access to universities in Mexico is quite limited. Thus, the lower class tends to have little hope of improving their social status through education. Many students obtain only a minimal education before they seek jobs that are nearly always low-paying manual labor positions.

European Countries

The European Community agreement has affected educational programs in member countries. The Maastricht Treaty encourages the sharing of information regarding education. The treaty's education points include "the development of quality education by encouraging cooperation between the Member States" and while respecting each country's rights and responsibility for educating its students, sharing the "content of teaching and the organizations of educational systems and their cultural and linguistic diversity" (Peck 1994, 421). Youth and teacher exchange programs have been created due to the agreement. Distance education, which relies on teleconferencing technology, for example, connecting a classroom in France with one in Belgium, is also promoted.

For those countries that do not belong to the European Community, primarily former communist nations, education lags behind as democratic and free economic principles are instituted. There is a grave lack of qualified teachers. Fiscal problems along with a lack of materials and lab and computer equipment are encountered by students.

Czechoslovakia

Czechoslovakia is not a member of the European Community. Unlike other former communist block countries, education has been left to professional educators rather than politicians.

The primary question in Czechoslovakia is the structure of the schools. Currently there is an eight-year common school and a four-year secondary school. Others propose a four-year primary school with an eight-year elite school for those who choose to attend. Technical schools would be available for those students who do not desire to attend the elite schools (Rust 1992).

Private schools have been established to cater to children of the wealthy. In addition, they provide experimentation with the traditional, state-governed curricula of the schools.

Denmark

One of the leading early child-care programs is in Denmark, a socialist nation, which requires by law that day-care facilities must be available for all children. The Danish child-care system has long been recognized internationally. Day care is available, easily accessible, and widely supported by the general population (Corsini 1991).

The government subsidizes high-quality, comprehensive child care for infants as young as six months old through seven-year-olds. In addition, after-school care is provided for those children of school age (Polakow 1997).

The Danes, like the citizens of other Scandinavian countries, place a strong emphasis on the family. By Danish law, mothers must be paid for maternity leave, four weeks prior to the birth of the child and for fourteen weeks afterwards. This is a paid parental leave, for one or both parents. When the infant reaches six months of age, another leave may be requested, this time twenty-six weeks is available with the parent(s) receiving 80 percent of his and/or her pay. If the employer agrees, the leave can be extended for fifty-two more weeks, or until the child is two years old. The ratio of caregivers to infants and toddlers is 1:2 (Polakow 1997).

Education in Denmark is marked by student attendance at a *folkeskole,* a school for children between the ages of seven and sixteen. Government regulations keep folkeskoler small, usually around three hundred students, with no more than twenty-eight students per class. The average class size is eighteen. Children enter school at age seven, a year older than in most nations of the world.

Students attend school in the mornings and go home in the early afternoon. No lunch is served, but a midmorning snack time is provided. The school year is two hundred days; however, breaks are often provided during the school year for students to attend school camps and overnight field trips, which are all supervised by teachers.

After attending a folkeskole for nine years, about 40 percent of the students go on to an upper secondary school that is a preparatory school for college. Ten percent of students tend to drop out, while the remaining 50 percent go on to commercial schools or vocational schools or take apprenticeships in the workforce (McAdams 1993).

The curriculum consists of instruction in Danish, and older children receive instruction in English as well. Biology, mathematics, and physical education and sport are required studies, as are Christian studies. Since Denmark is heavily Lutheran, this religion is studied in the schools as well as other religions. Students aren't formally evaluated until they are in the fifth grade.

Danish teachers have always been politically active, using their influence to apply innovative ideas in the schools and to urge legislators to pass laws to support education and children's rights. Teachers take this responsibility seriously as they continually update their skills by participating in professional inservice and taking additional graduate-level coursework. Teachers heavily influence curricular decisions in schools in terms of content taught, textbook selection, and methods utilized (Birkvad 1997).

In 1994, Denmark passed the Act on the Folkeskole so that a national curriculum for schools could be suggested. As a result of this legislation, the minister of education changed the guidelines for teaching in individual subject areas and has "identified key areas of knowledge and skills" (Birkvad 1997, 612).

Teachers work together with their students. Teamwork among teachers is encouraged, with teachers working with one or two classes. Both teachers and students give input as to the lesson planning, and project-oriented teaching is supported.

Assessment of academic, personal, and social behavior is done regularly, with the teacher maintaining close contact with both pupils and their parents. Individual goals are set based upon teacher-pupil discussions.

Danish teachers are paid according to the level of their students. Elementary teachers are paid less than those at the upper secondary schools. Most teachers live comfortably as middle-class citizens, since their salaries are almost 50 percent more than those who work in factories (Nelson 1991). Principals are paid substantially more than teachers. Teachers are not formally evaluated.

France

In France, education is run by the central government. Thus, on any given day in any school in France, all students at the same grade level will be precisely on the same textbook page. Between the ages of six and sixteen, children are required to attend school. Preschool is available for youngsters between the ages of two and six, with 35 percent of two-year-olds and 97 percent of three-year-olds attending. For children ages four through six, nearly 100 percent attend (American Federation of Teachers and National Center for Improving Science Education 1994).

Primary school, called *ecole primaire*, begins at age six and lasts for five years. Students then enter secondary school, called college, which is four years. From primary through secondary school, students are taught from a national core curriculum. Upon completing college, students then enter the *lycee*, which offers a two-year technical/vocational program and a three-year academic program, called the *baccalaureat*, for those who plan to attend a university. In 1992, over half of the students earned the baccalaureat.

French students are given examinations to determine whether they are competent in the subject areas they study. The exams are national and developed by the Ministry of Education, but they are graded by teachers selected from their respective regions who are supervised by central government inspectors.

Students who live near their school may walk home for lunch. Those who bring their lunch to school will probably have bread, cheese, and red wine in their lunch bag.

Germany

Children in Germany attend school in their neighborhood, often walking to school. They attend a four-year primary school called the *Grundschule* from ages six to ten. This school groups children by age but not ability. The school day is four hours long with a six-day school week. According to McAdams (1993, 99), "The German reputation for neatness, order, and thoroughness is evident in the exercise books, handicraft projects, and homework assignments of elementary school students. . . . In day-to-day projects the teacher demands that the student produce the *whole job*."

After completion of primary school, fifth- and sixth-grade students attend a two-year *Orientierungsstufe* school, which focuses on orienting and preparing students to attend secondary school. Secondary schools consist of three types: lower, middle, and upper. In effect, at what is comparable to the junior high level in the United States, German students are divided into three groups according to their career options. The best academic students enroll in the *Gymnasium*, those who might have technical or managerial abilities enroll in the *Realschule*, and the *Hauptschule*, or main school, is attended by the remainder of students. In recent years, German parents have encouraged far more of their children to attend the Gymnasium and enrollment has increased greatly.

The German education system is undergoing changes due to the unification of East Germany into the Federal Republic of Germany, "a society of sixty million people virtually taking over another—bankrupt—society of sixteen million people" (Durr 1992, 391). The West German education system is noted for its high academic standards and the East German for its turning out of socialists.

Currently, German educators are redesigning curricula and retraining teachers from East Germany, where there is a shortage of qualified teachers. Many of the East German teachers taught only Marxism and Leninism and need to be retrained to teach democracy and free enterprise, along with foreign languages. Dismissing these teachers rather than retraining them would only lead to more unemployment in an area of already high unemployment.

Teachers are paid on a national scale with adjustments made according to the cost of living in the area in which they live. Primary school teachers are paid less than secondary teachers. The average German teacher's salary is higher than that of American teachers, by roughly 10 percent (Nelson 1991).

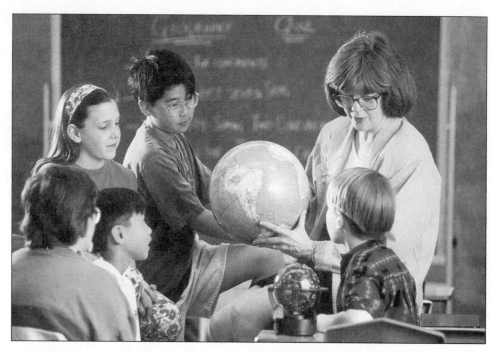

Many schools in Great Britain have diverse student populations. (© Bob Christ/PhotoEdit)

Societal and family structures in Germany and the United States are often compared. The United States has a higher infant mortality rate than in Germany. The poverty rate for U.S. children is nearly double that of German children (17 percent as compared with 8 percent). In addition, German families tend to be more stable, with a divorce rate one-third that of the United States. Students tend to have more financial support from the family in Germany, thereby allowing them more time to concentrate on their education. For instance, German high school students are less likely to be employed outside the home than are American students (Jaeger 1992).

Great Britain

Great Britain has long been a nation of social class consciousness. This has influenced its schools. Of all the major industrial nations to provide free secondary education for all students, Great Britain was the last to adopt this policy (McAdams 1993).

Like schools in the United States, British schools are also undergoing reform. In 1988, the Education Reform Act was passed by Parliament. It allows schools to have local governance, with budgetary and staffing decisions made by the local board. In addition, schools may elect to be grant schools funded directly by the national government. These schools are encouraged to experiment with different educational theories; however, they are still subject to the same review as other schools in the country (Maeroff 1992).

Children enter primary school at age five and continue there until they are eleven. The first three years of primary schooling are called infant school, with the final three referred to as junior school. The school year is 190 days in length, with several short vacations, or holidays, during the school year and a six-week summer vacation. This is a common European school calendar.

In most British schools, students are required to wear uniforms.
(© Topham/Image Works)

British schools focus on developmentally appropriate learning activities. Study begins where each student is intellectually and proceeds from there. There is no retention of students. Each student works at his or her own pace, no matter how fast or how leisurely it may be.

In the primary schools, students receive individual attention and rarely work with a partner or in small groups. The pace of learning is slow, and no pressure is placed on the students to learn. At lunchtime, children are seated at tables and food is passed around in bowls and on platters, similar to a home setting rather than that of a school.

Very few British schools require students to complete workbook drill pages as in other industrialized nations. Instead, each student writes in a journal, filling several each school year. Thus, the link between reading and writing is much closer than in some countries, including the United States.

Students are required to "sit for exams"—a series of examinations that determine whether or not the student can go on to the next level of schooling or be moved to a vocational track.

At age sixteen, students are no longer required to attend school and thus compulsory education ends. Unlike the United States, British high school students do not receive diplomas to signify that they have completed high school. When they leave school, sixteen-year-olds either try to find work, a difficult task with Britain's high unemployment rate, or enter a vocational school or university.

Members of the predominantly white lower class in Britain largely believe that they cannot escape their class. This is unlike the United States, where education is the primary means for lower-class citizens to rise in the social structure. In addition, British universities do not have open enrollment as do those in the United States. Students must have high grades from quality prep schools and recommendations to enter a university. The United States offers financial aid to those who cannot afford the tuition and fees, something unavailable to students in Great Britain.

Sweden

In Sweden, until recently a socialistic nation, there is a strong emphasis on children and the family. Sweden has generous family leave policies for parents with newborns. In addition, the government provides child care. The emphasis on the family and the importance of meeting the needs of young children is very strong in the Swedish culture. Thus, children in Sweden have opportunities and advantages that children in other nations do not. Students who desire to attend a university receive support from the state. During the summer holiday when the schools are closed, librarians from the public libraries actually roam the streets to entice elementary and secondary students to go to the library and enroll in reading programs.

Swedish children enter school at age seven, the oldest enrollment age of any nation except Denmark. It should be noted, however, that Sweden has a lower incidence of reading problems than that reported by other nations in the world.

Poland

Poland is not a member of the European Community. Historically, Polish schools were run by the Catholic Church, and teachers were expected to promote the values and interests of the Church. After World War II, the communist regime used the school system in the same way for its own purpose (Rust 1992).

The structure of the Polish school system includes an eight-year common school followed by three options for students: the four-year *lycee,* or academic school, which leads to study at a university; a four- or five-year technical school; or a three-year vocational training school. Each school has its own local school board. Teachers can make curriculum changes fairly readily.

It remains to be seen what changes will be made in Polish schools. However, the Catholic Church still wields substantial power in Poland. Also, the United States, with its common school and trade ties to Poland, has much influence.

Republic of Ireland

Ireland has always held education in high regard. During the Middle Ages, for instance, Ireland was known as "the island of saints and scholars."

During the late twentieth century, economic decline let to major education reform in Ireland. In 1995, the government issued a document entitled "Charting Our Education Future." Regional school boards were added to oversee local schools as well as to report to the state education board. Each school has a board of management on which teachers may serve. In 1996, the government budget for education doubled that of thirty years ago (Lennon and White 1997).

The skill levels of Irish students have increased in recent years, helping Ireland's economy improve as many international businesses, particularly technology firms, have built facilities there.

Asian Countries

Culture plays a major role in education in Asian nations. Most of the teachers in Asian countries, particularly at the secondary and college levels, are males (figure 2), and there is a greater emphasis for boys to be educated than girls.

Classes are often much larger in Asian schools than those in industrialized nations. However, since the teacher is treated with great respect and students are required to remain quiet unless they are called on, classroom discipline problems are

Figure 2 Teacher gender percentages in various countries

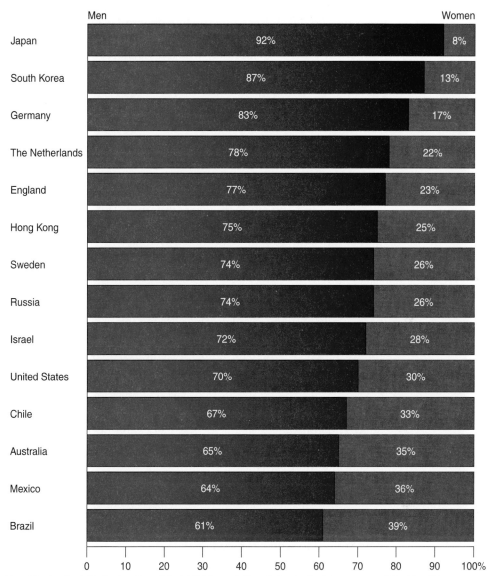

From The Academic Profession. Copyright © 1994 Carnegie Foundation for the Advancement of Teaching, Princeton, New Jersey. Reprinted by permission.

quite minimal. Tardiness is considered to be an insult to the teacher. Students who misbehave in class, disrupting the learning of their peers, are severely punished.

In addition to these aspects, each Asian country has its own distinct educational attributes.

China

The largest student population in the world belongs to China, although the Chinese government restricts the number of children a family may have. Thus, it is quite evident that "each child receives the best parents can give in terms of education and attention" (Fuhler 1994). The Chinese value boys over girls because boys carry on the family name. Indeed, there are instances in China of female infants being murdered. It isn't surprising then that the educational system is focused on boys.

It is quite rare for a Chinese student to live in a single-parent family. Chinese parents are much more critical than are American parents of the education their children receive. Likewise, Chinese students are far less likely to believe that they are performing above average in a subject as compared to American students, even if they really are doing extremely well (Stevenson et al. 1990).

Attendance in school is compulsory in China. However, Chinese children are older when they first begin school. Chinese students are usually a half year older when they enter school than are American students. Classrooms are highly structured and very quiet, with little opportunity for social interaction with peers (Fuhler 1994).

South Korea

In South Korea, school is very structured and students are expected to study hard and display self-discipline. The teacher is authoritarian and fully in control of the classroom, and the students wear uniforms. The curriculum is quite demanding, with lecture being the primary form of instructional delivery. National exams are part of the South Korean educational system.

Classes are quite large; often forty to fifty students crowd into cold, poorly heated classrooms. Despite that, Korean thirteen-year-old students were found to score the highest on mathematics of fourteen nations that supplied test data (Jaeger 1992).

"Education mania" has been the label given to the frenzy that Korean parents, particularly mothers, display. The Korean mother sees that homework is completed, makes sure extra tutoring is provided, and even schedules the after-school time of middle and high schoolers so that the children are engaged in special enrichment or tutoring programs. The Korean mother maintains a close link with her children's school, typically visiting four or five times a year. When corporal punishment is doled out, most of the time it is done by mothers (Ellinger and Beckham 1997).

Preschoolers and kindergarten students are tutored in music and art while elementary students are given private instruction in English, writing in Korean, and music. While the focus with young children is on enjoyment of music, serious study begins in middle school.

Education in South Korea is compulsory for students through the sixth grade; however, most students attend high school with the tuition being paid by their parents. High school students attend school from 8 A.M. until 4 P.M., Monday through Friday, and until noon on Saturdays. From 6 P.M. until 10 P.M. each weekday, students return to school for study hall.

Japan

The Japanese society differs greatly from that of the United States and other nations. Less than 6 percent of Japanese children live in single-parent homes compared with 25 percent of American children. The divorce rate in Japan is four times less than that in the United States. The Japanese infant mortality rate is half that of the United States (Jaeger 1992).

Japanese public schools are run by the Japanese Ministry of Education, Science, and Culture, or Monbusho (Stevenson 1991). There is no retention of students, not even at the kindergarten and first-grade levels. Compulsory education ends after completion of the ninth grade, which is why the Japanese have such a low dropout rate at the high school level. Only those students who want to go to high school and can pass the necessary entrance exams attend (Boylan 1993). Japan has two types of high schools, academic and vocational (Stevenson, 1998).

Japanese students are very respectful of their teacher. These fifth-graders are giving their teacher their full attention. (© Andy Sacks/Tony Stone)

In the United States and other nations, teachers are primarily responsible for students' cognitive growth and academic achievement. This is not true in Japan, where teachers encourage memorization of information by students (Boylan 1992). One educator observed that "one of the most important aspects of Japanese science education is to find ways to inculcate the ideals of beauty and orderliness in nature, love of nature, adjustment to nature, and not to conquer nature" (Takemura 1991, 8).

Students at all levels are given time for extracurricular activities. At the elementary level, almost all of the cleaning of the school facilities is done by the students, who are supervised by their teachers. There are no cafeterias, rather food is delivered to the classroom and the students take turns serving it. Thus student interaction through clubs, activities, cleaning activities, and discussions at lunch is very important in developing social skills (Stevenson 1991).

The Japanese school curriculum is targeted at high-achieving students. Even the textbooks are written at grade levels above the actual grade in which they are used. Thus, most of the students may not understand what the teacher is discussing. For instance, a passing score to enter calculus is only 35 percent, however, most students in a calculus class have not passed the initial prerequisite exam (Goya 1993). Textbooks, which are published by private publishing companies that follow the national curriculum, have very similar content. Each local school board adopts the textbooks to be used in its schools (Stevenson 1991).

In Japan, there is a six-day school week, Monday through Saturday, with Saturday afternoons off. The school year begins in April (Goya 1993) and consists of 240 days compared with 180 in the United States (Boylan 1993). The school year consists of three terms separated by three vacations: summer (July 21 to August 25), winter (December 25 to January 10), and spring (March 25 to April 7) (Stevenson 1991).

Students are taught early that their academic performance in school is a reflection on their family. Thus, a good grade on a test brings pride to a student's family, a poor grade dishonor. Perhaps because of this pressure, there is a higher percentage of suicide among Japanese teenagers than in any other country.

The Japanese education system requires that children be given examinations at different age levels throughout their school career. The first exam is given to all children at age three to determine which nursery/preschool they will attend, which in turn influences the elementary and secondary school and even college opportunities available. Japanese students are tracked into different schools, whereas in the United States students are tracked into different programs within a school. It is not surprising to find parents crying upon receipt of their child's test scores—tears of relief or tears of anxiety. Thus, children are strongly encouraged to study for tests.

To enter high school, students must pass an entrance examination, which costs a minimum of $200. Students who fail the test must retake it and pay the fee again (Boylan 1993). Failure to pass the high school entrance examination is "truly a catastrophe for Japanese students" (Goya 1993, 126). High school entrance exams in Japan are not based on a student scoring above a certain percentile or answering a specified number of questions correctly. Rather, the tests are related to the number of openings. If a high school has four hundred openings and 410 students taking the entrance test, the lowest ten students are eliminated (Goya 1993). Thus, the passing cutoff score actually fluctuates depending on how other students in the test group perform.

The requirement for graduating from high school is that the student must retake the same entrance test he or she took to enter high school. The student must score as well or higher than he or she did the first time. Thus, Japan has incredibly high graduation rates for its high school students (Boylan 1993).

Once students pass university entrance exams in a particular area of study, they may enter a university. However, if students decide after completing a semester or more at the university to change their area of study, they must drop out and take university entrance exams in the new area to be pursued (Goya 1993).

In the United States, high schools are comprehensive and free (table 1). In Japan, all high schools charge tuition. Japanese students who decide not to go on to high school go to business or technical schools, which are not considered as prestigious as high school (Reischauer 1977). Students at the business high schools are primarily female and are expected to graduate, work for a few years in an office, and then marry and permanently leave the workforce. They learn how to serve tea, how to be polite to customers, and basic bookkeeping and business machine skills (Goya 1993). The current Japanese school system, including its examination program and tracking of students, serves important social functions but not necessarily academic functions (Kiefer 1970).

Parents seek outside help for their children from jukus, or tutoring schools, which are a major service industry in Japan. Jukus are both expensive and indispensable. One of every three primary grade students in Japan receives supplementary help from a juku, or tutor (Goya 1993). Students work with jukus after school and on Saturday afternoons. Those students in secondary school who plan to study at a college or university work with jukus one or two days a week. According to James Fallows (1992), jukus are essential to the Japanese because the schools are so poor. The typical university student has spent from one to four years enrolled in a juku program before passing the university's entrance exams.

To become a teacher in Japan, you must have an undergraduate degree with a major in education, pass a written examination in your area of specialty, and then student teach for two weeks. Most student teachers are required to teach at least one

Table 1 School Governance and Finance

	Canada	Denmark	England	Germany	Japan	USA
Political control of education	Small federal role, strong provincial role, and moderate local control.	Strong national direction and control with regional control at county and municipal levels.	Dramatic move toward strong national control and smaller role for local education agencies under 1988 education law.	Significant federal coordination, with real power with German states.	Strong national control of all important aspects of education.	Small national role, states have potential for strong role but tradition of local control is still the norm.
Role of local school boards	Similar to U.S.A. model, although with fewer powers over taxation and curriculum authority.	Boards of local schools composed of parents, teachers, and students. Major financial and curriculum decisions are made by regional or national governments.	Boards of local schools composed of parents and teachers. These boards have some control over operating processes of schools, although major power is at national level.	Local parent councils have little power. Teachers not involved in governance. Most major decisions are made at regional level of state education system.	Local boards of parents operate in a manner similar to U.S. PTO groups. Power is reserved at the national and prefectural levels.	Local boards consist of community members and some parents. Major decisions on budgets, salaries, curriculum, and tax levels are made by local boards.
Financing of the schools	While financial support varies among the provinces, on average, 9 percent of funds are raised at the federal level, 66 percent by the provinces, 18 percent by local school districts, and 7 percent by private funding.	All major costs such as salaries are paid by the national government. Local funds support items such as texts and supplies.	Eighty percent of school costs are paid from national funds while 20 percent of expenses are met by local taxes.	The German states bear the major costs of education, including monies for teacher salaries. Small amounts are contributed by the federal and local government.	The national government pays 50 percent of educational costs in Japan, 25 percent is paid by the prefecture level, and 25 percent by local taxes.	Fifty percent of funding is provided by state government, 44 percent by local taxes, and 6 percent by federal sources. Heavy reliance on local property taxes.
Educational equity	Funding system provides for equity within a province. There is significant disparity of resources among the provinces. Provincial curriculum guides promote equity within each province.	National financing within this small nation provides for an equitable distribution of school funding. National curriculum promotes equal education.	Majority funding from national level provides a good degree of equity, although residential patterns affect socioeconomic level of school population. New common curriculum will promote equal education.	Major funding at state level provides equity within a German state, but there is disparity in educational resources among the sixteen states. Coordinated educational goals among the states also promote equality.	National and prefectural funding provide for equitable financing of public schools in Japan. Common curriculum also promotes equal education.	Great disparity among states regarding ability to raise funds for education. High dependence on local funding also creates great disparities within states, and even within counties.
Use of public funds for private and denominational schools	Assuming they follow provincial curriculum and other regulations, private and denominational schools are funded on same basis as public schools in most provinces.	Denmark pays 85 percent of the costs to operate nonpublic schools. Even so, only 10 percent of parents choose private schools. Religious instruction is given in the public schools.	English maintained and voluntary schools receive public funds for private and denominational schools. Religious act of worship is required by law in all English schools.	Support for private education varies among German states, although most states generously support nonpublic schools. Religion is taught in public schools.	Ninety-seven percent of Japanese students attend public schools for the first nine grades. Private high schools, attended by 25 percent of the students, receive some state support. Moral instruction is provided in the public schools.	Public support for private schools in the U.S.A. is generally limited to areas such as busing, health services, or textbooks. Religion is carefully excluded from public schools, and there is a continuing argument over funding for private schools.

From *Lessons From Abroad*. Copyright © 1993 by Technomic Publishing Company, Inc., Lancaster PA. Reprinted by permission.

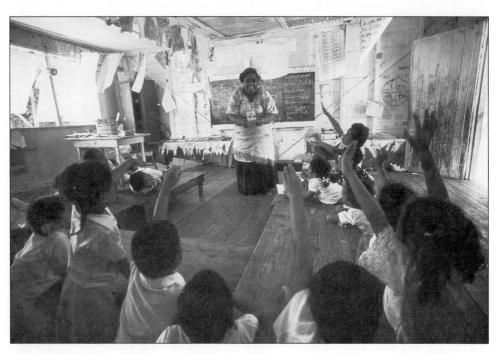

These Tonga students are taking a language class in Vaváu. (© David Hiser/Tony Stone)

but not more than two classes (Boylan 1992). Teachers are rotated every few years so that they don't teach in one school for several years. Likewise, school administrators are also moved from one school to another (Stevenson, 1991).

Japanese teachers are extremely dedicated. They spend a large amount of their free time outside of school preparing lessons and developing curricula for their students. According to McAdams (1993, 207), "A professional can be defined as one who possesses a specialized body of knowledge and skill by the larger society, has automony in performing his or her work, and is subject to peer review and sanctions. The teacher in Japan possesses all of these attributes, while the American teacher fares poorly when measured against the same criteria."

While most U.S. teachers devote little time out of school to professional development, Japanese teachers spend many hours working on lesson plans and engaging in a variety of professional development activities outside of the school day (Sato and McLaughlin 1992). Each school has a head teacher who coordinates cooperative efforts among its teachers. For instance, teachers work together in developing lessons and teaching materials (Stevenson 1991).

Interestingly enough, while many Americans look to the efficiency of the Japanese schools, the Japanese government looks to American schools for its educational innovations. One concern by Japanese businesspeople is that the Japanese school system doesn't train students to think creatively, as does the American school system. This is cited when the two nations are compared in terms of the number of Nobel Prize winners, of which the United States clearly predominates.

Thailand

Thai students are expected to learn academics as well as culture in school. For instance, they are forbidden to cross their legs and point their feet at the teacher since the feet are considered to be the most unholy part of the body. Likewise, it is inappropriate for the teacher to pat a child on the head, the most holy part of the body.

Thailand's teachers are predominately male. They are treated with respect by their students. Class sizes are larger than in European or North American schools.

In 1994, Thailand began subsidizing the school lunch program to offer free or reduced price milk to elementary and secondary students. Additional support for food products is under consideration.

Australia

The Australian curriculum consists of four study areas rather than individual subject areas. Reading and writing are taught together in the elementary schools. The other major content areas are math, social studies/science, and physical/social education.

The Australian government supports both public and private schools. This came about in the 1980s, when many private schools began to fail because of lack of funds. To prevent the collapse of private schools, which would have resulted in overcrowding in its public schools, the Australian parliament voted to assist in the funding of both types of schools.

The requirements for becoming a teacher in Australia changed in the 1980s. Formerly, students could attend a technical college and obtain a teaching degree in two or three years or attend a university and complete an additional semester of work in addition to a four-year academic program. Half of Australia's teachers have less than four years of college. In the future, prospective teachers will need to complete a four-year teacher preparation program at a university. There are no additional requirements for becoming a building principal.

Teachers begin teaching in rural areas. After three years they may apply to teach in a suburban or urban school. Beginning teachers make $18,000 (US) with $30,000 (US) being the highest teaching salary. Income tax is 48½% with books taxed at 22½%, so materials can be scarce.

New Zealand

New Zealand, a seemingly small country, has been a major leader, particularly at the elementary level, in curricular developments. The whole language movement and Reading Recovery, a program to assist at-risk six-year-olds in learning to read and write, began in New Zealand. New Zealand secondary schools, called colleges, offer several curricular choices to students. In addition to the core subjects, students may enroll in such diverse classes as forestry and Japanese (Belsky 1994).

Teachers in New Zealand devote much of their time to educating the whole child. Thus, elementary students in the lower grades learn to swim, play the flute, run in races, and create artwork, as well as concentrate on academics such as math, reading, writing, and spelling (Jarchow 1992).

The school building itself consists of a main building with several portable classrooms. Whenever one school's enrollment decreases and another's nearby increases, the buildings are simply moved to the other school site.

Students in intermediate and secondary schools are required to wear uniforms to school each day. This is to give a sense of belonging to a school, thereby building school spirit. In addition, no one can tell the difference between the rich and the poor students.

Relaxation and conversation are considered to be important for both students and teachers. Everyone in a New Zealand school takes a tea break promptly at 10 A.M. each morning. While the students have snacks and play, the teachers and principal drink their tea or coffee, eat biscuits (cookies), and engage in an informal discussion. In addition, common courtesy is expected. Any teacher or parent who cannot attend a meeting sends a note of apology.

At the high school level, single-sex schools are available. Many female students elect to attend an all-girl high school because they believe that it is in their academic best interest. Those who select coeducational high schools believe that such schools offer a better social atmosphere for them.

Susan Rogers, a parent who moved with her family to New Zealand, believes that New Zealand has higher education standards and offers a better quality of schooling. In Novato, California, her son had to share a science book with a classmate because of his middle school's financial problems. Now he is able to select from several courses and is assigned his own textbook. According to Rogers, "In the United States, we open too many prisons and close too many schools" (Belsky 1994, 62).

Middle Eastern Countries

In most Middle Eastern countries, teachers are viewed with respect. Indeed they are almost revered. There is a shortage of teachers in the Middle East.

Egypt

Girls are more likely to receive an education, including a university education, in Egypt than in any other Middle Eastern country except Israel. Likewise, there is a higher percentage of female teachers than in other Middle Eastern countries. However, almost all secondary teachers are males. As the influence of conservative Muslims increases in Egypt, the rights of women decrease, which will affect educational opportunities for females.

The British influence still lingers in Egyptian schools. Students must sit for exams, for example. Students are encouraged to pursue advanced education at universities in other countries.

Turkey

In Turkey, teaching is considered by the public to be a holy profession. Parents bring their children to school on the first day of classes to entrust them to their teachers. In fact, teachers have a great deal of influence over a child both legally and socially.

According to Sezai Kaya (Ryan and Cooper 1992), teachers in Turkey receive a salary that is one of the highest among public servants. Teaching salaries are based on several factors, including education, years of service, and the geographical location in which the individual teaches. Unlike most countries, teachers in rural areas and less developed areas receive higher salaries than their counterparts in the cities. Teachers also receive fringe benefits of lower-cost goods and services through government-supported teacher markets. In addition, there is a shortage of teachers and school buildings because of Turkey's high birth rate. Most schools have double or triple shifts of students each day. The typical teacher then has either the morning or afternoon free. A major fringe benefit is Turkey's two-month paid summer vacation for teachers.

Schools in Africa often lack sufficient materials. Here are elementary students in Dakar, Senegal, Africa. (© Superstock)

African Countries

One of the first universities in the world was the university at Timbuktu. Today, education in African nations tends to vary from country to country. Those nations that were colonialized have tended to retain similarities to their colonial European countries. Thus, Belgium, France, Great Britain, and the Netherlands have greatly impacted the educational system of the different African nations.

Kenya

One of the most modern African nations is Kenya. Students in its schools are taught English, which is the language of international business. The schools are structured much like the British schools and are academically oriented. However, most high school students are male, as are the teachers. Students must pass exams to progress to the next level of schooling.

Nigeria

Teachers are given much respect in Nigeria, where most are male. The educational system of Great Britain has influenced the schools in Nigeria. Students sit for exams, and English is taught.

Because of its economic development, Nigeria, like Kenya, has an advanced educational system compared to other African nations.

South Africa

From 1652 until 1991, when Parliament ruled that South Africans could no longer be classified by race from birth, South Africa had white rule. In 1994, the first free elections were held.

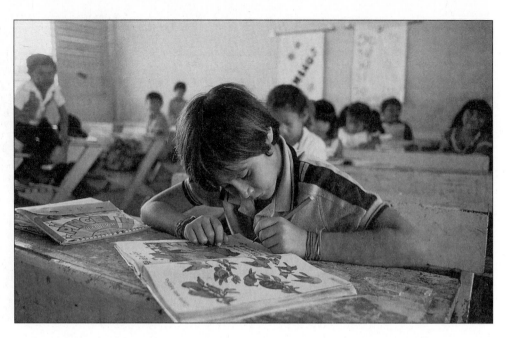

These students attend a primary school in Yucatan, Mexico. (© Bob Daemmrich/Tony Stone)

Schools in South Africa today still suffer from the years of neglect and misman-agement. As recently as 1991, the per capita expenditures for white students were four times greater than those for black students. Teachers in white schools were paid more so that good teachers often left black schools. Basic materials such as pencils, paper, and chalk are still in short supply for some schools. Class sizes are often unbe-lievably large—for example, 110 in a twelfth-grade language class (Murphy 1992).

The curriculum is based on the South African national examinations. Rigorous tests administered by outside school officials are given to high school students as a graduation requirement. The questions require that the students be bilingual and fa-miliar with European rather than South African history and literature. Rote learning is promoted.

Teachers are authoritarian and generally have minimal training. In 1991, only half the elementary teachers had high school diplomas. Only 20 percent of the secondary teachers had graduated from college.

The curriculum itself was affected by the apartheid regime. Since censorship was widespread for many years, there are few quality pieces of literature available for students to read. Social studies textbooks were heavily biased and contained no pho-tos or illustrations of blacks doing leisure-time activities, although there were exam-ples of blacks working. Until the downfall of apartheid, there were no photos of a smiling black person published in white newspapers as part of the censorship rules (Rochman 1994).

In South Africa, eight languages are commonplace. This makes it difficult for teachers to acquire textbooks and literature because publishers find it to be finan-cially to their disadvantage to publish only a few copies of any one work.

Teachers are viewed by students with respect. Like many African nations, most teachers, particularly at the secondary level, are male.

Due to the growth of the Internet, you can E-mail messages to people in over 150 countries. Thus, it makes sense for us to consider how students in other nations are educated. What are they doing that's successful? What doesn't work with their students?

Two elementary teachers read about teachers in Japan rotating schools in order to keep on top of their teaching practices. They asked their principal to rotate teachers in their building. A fifth-grade teacher who had been at that level for twenty-two years wasn't amused. During the year, she struggled with her third-grade class but then discovered she liked teaching third grade, despite having to retool for a new grade level. Other teachers found themselves regaining the old spark for teaching they thought they had lost.

As a beginning teacher, you'll compare your own teaching style with that of your colleagues in the building and in your district. Don't stop there. Education knows no boundaries. What are they doing to educate workers in corporations? What can you take back to your class that will make you a better teacher? Keep your door open to new ideas. Then teaching will always be an exhilarating experience.

International Education Organizations

The World Confederation of Organizations of the Teaching Profession (WCOTP) is a group of over one hundred teaching organizations, including the AFT and NEA, that support international goodwill and understanding and defend the rights and moral interests of teachers throughout the world. A primary focus of WCOTP is to encourage a closer relationship between teachers from different nations.

There are several professional organizations that have members of various nationalities. The International Reading Association (IRA) has long encouraged teachers and school administrators from all nations to become members and attend one of its many conferences and congresses throughout the world. Other organizations include Kappa Delta Pi and Phi Delta Kappa, education honoraries with chapters throughout the world.

Teaching in Another Country

The International Schools Services (ISS) holds an annual recruitment in which teaching candidates can interview for positions in over one hundred overseas schools. Typically, these events are held in February in three different U.S. locations. Preference is given to those individuals who have taught at least two years in the United States. In addition, those who have expertise in two or more teaching areas, have advanced degrees, are interested in multicultural education, and/or have talent in an extracurricular area have a greater chance of being selected. Information can be obtained from ISS, Educational Staffing, P.O. Box 5910, Princeton, NJ 08543 or by calling (609)452–0990. In the United States, the University of Northern Iowa, Cedar Falls, Iowa 50614, and in Canada, the Queens University in Kingston, Ontario K7L 3N6, Canada, hold annual international recruitment fairs for teachers (Rabbitt 1992).

■ Summary

Students in Canada attend a longer school year than do their U.S. counterparts. The Canadian educational system is heavily influenced by that of Great Britain. Students are taught individually from a developmental perspective.

Education varies greatly in Mexico, where the best schools are private and operated by the Catholic Church. The public schools have much lower academic standards and less-qualified teachers.

Asian students tend to be well behaved and hold their teachers in high regard. Exams are given to students before they can progress to higher levels of education. Chinese and Japanese students are taught to appreciate art, music, and dance at an early age.

The formation of the European Community and the fall of communism have radically affected education in Europe. Great Britain, which until 1988 had local standards for students, now has national standards as do France and Germany.

Former communist nations that are not members of the European Community are experiencing economic problems that affect their respective educational systems and the quality of education. There is a shortage of qualified teachers because many teachers were trained to teach only Marxist-Leninist indoctrination to their students.

■ Reflections

Interview a student at your college or university who is a native of another country. If you don't know such a student, contact your college's international student office and they will put you in touch with one.

Ask the student what his or her elementary school years were like. How was the school designed? What were the teachers like? What kind of learning activities were there? Do the same for high school. Discuss the differences between how you were both educated in the schools you attended.

■ Discussion Questions

1. In what ways does the culture of a nation influence its educational system?
2. How does education in Great Britain compare with that in the United States?
3. How does the professional commitment of teachers in Japan compare with that of American teachers?
4. How do the requirements for becoming a teacher differ among various countries?

■ For Further Reading

Jaeger, R. M. 1992. World class standards, choice, and privatization: Weak measurement serving presumptive policy. *Phi Delta Kappan* 74 (2):118–28.

McAdams, R. 1993. *Lessons from abroad: How other countries educate their children.* Lancaster, PA: Technomic Publishing.

Miller, R. 1995. Mexico's role in U.S. education—a well-kept secret. *Phi Delta Kappan* 76 (6):470–74.

Murphy, J. T. 1992. Apartheid's legacy to black children. *Phi Delta Kappan* 73 (5):367–74.

Salom, A. K. and R. Truax. 1998. In Equador: Developing child-centered learning. *Educational Leadership,* 55 (5): 66–69

Stevenson, H. W. 1998. A study of three cultures: Germany, Japan, and the United States—An overview of the TIMSS Case Study Project. *Phi Delta Kappan,* 79 (7): 524–529.

Epilogue

Eleven Ways to Be a Great Teacher

by Donald C. Wesley, Principal
Orchard Park High School, Orchard Park, New York

Recently, I was asked to speak to a class of undergraduate college students who were preparing to be teachers about my expectations for those entering the profession. I came up with "Don Wesley's Top 11 Non-Traditional Expectations for Teachers." Here they are:

1. *Empathize.* If you are not and never have been a student having trouble, a parent, an administrator, or the teacher next door, can you imagine what it must be like? Can you see yourself as the other? This is the beginning of understanding.

   I recall telling one of my students that she would make a great teacher. Even as a student in high school, she had a strong capacity to empathize. She wanted to be an engineer then. Today she is an outstanding science teacher and activities advisor. Popular and trusted, she has nurtured this ability to imagine life in the shoes of others.

2. *Create partnerships with families, administrators, and other teachers.* It won't be easy. Partnerships of this kind meet resistance. They must be forged. Somebody has to keep trying. Decide that it will be you.

   Sarah provides consultant teacher services to disabled students. In a meeting to review a student's program, a parent unfairly criticized her. With an amazing display of composure, Sarah listened to the harsh words and kept her focus on the problem. Months later, the parent was working with us as a partner, the anger gone. It all started with Sarah's focus.

3. *Account to others.* Organize. Don't wing it. Be able to explain. Keep careful records. Know when things happened or didn't happen. Let the record show that you did your part; you tried. Don't get caught not knowing facts, dates, times, and numbers. Be convincing and thorough.

   A well-meaning father was convinced that his son was just being a normal kid until Linda, the boy's classroom teacher, calmly took this parent through situation after situation of documented attempts to give the student the benefit of the doubt and work on changing his behavior. The evidence was compelling. The father came over to the teacher's side, convinced that his son did indeed have behavior problems, and that he needed to help the teacher.

4. *Embrace adversity.* (This is also known as *Face the beast.*) Conflict, contention, failure, and fears are the experiences that teach us. To deal with adversity in others while maintaining respect and concern for them is an accomplishment.

   In addition to handling issues with students, teachers have strong disagreements with colleagues. When I brought Jack and Wendy together to resolve their differences over the way each was handling lunch duty supervision, we had a few moments of frank, somewhat heated, conversation. To their credit, they moved past the anger and frustration and built an effective team, each better understanding the viewpoint of the other. Even in their intense disagreement, they maintained a mutual respect that provided a basis to rebuild after the dispute.

5. *Practice the long view.* Consider the strategic consequences of tactical decisions. Your students will become adults. What will they say of you then? Were you real, honest, fair, and right? What students are today is not what they might become. Are you willing to treat them as if they can become something better, as if they are already on their way?

   Here's a tale of two teachers. Teacher A labels her students just days after they start class. It's as if A shelves them according to categories: bright, lazy, careless, and mature. A's opinion doesn't change over time. There is no reconsideration. A's alumni, for the most part, don't come back to visit; they don't write letters.

   Teacher B encourages students from day one to be the best they can be. B's conversations, even when involving discipline, never belittle. B is always reminding them that soon they will be out there making a contribution. B's alumni think often and gratefully of B. They send notes, they call, they stop by. They become friends.

6. *Demonstrate competency and interest* not only in your subject specialty but in others as well. And help students become competent and interested.

   Steve is a fine artist and art teacher. He also coaches track and is a gifted trumpet player. Yvette teaches math and directs plays and musicals. Karen is a media specialist who helps students daily in their search for information. The message in their actions is clear. There is joy in cultivating competency in everything we do.

7. *Never quit. Go the distance.* Keep believing in your students even when they are failing, disruptive, suspended, or thrown out. Believe in them when they do not believe in themselves. Draw the line, and do what you must, but be ready when your lesson finally takes hold—and *they* begin to believe.

   Administrators are teachers too. I see students for discipline problems every day. I want them to know that discipline is not personal; it's business. I can respect them and care for them while I am being the disciplinarian. Often, they come back wiser and willing to take responsibility. In the classroom or the principal's office, it's great to be there when the light finally comes on.

8. *Accept responsibility* for doing the job to the best of your ability every day. Teach responsibility by being responsible.

   Regardless of which students appear in her classes or which duties she has, Carol is one of those teachers who leaves things better than she found them. She is a self-starter who familiarizes herself with the expectations of the task and then pushes beyond them. Papers are returned promptly, and averages are always available. It seems to rub off. Her students seldom turn things in late, and they catch her enthusiasm.

9. *Reflect and contribute to reflection.* Read, think, write. Communicate your questions and ideas. Share with colleagues. Publish. Teaching is largely a thinking life—forward to a plan, backward to an evaluation. It is constant reflection.

   Dave is always processing and reprocessing. He takes mental and written notes on everything. Without any major effort beyond his involvement in committees, activities, and conversations, he makes contributions to positive change and growth. His rhetoric is replete with questions, but he does not worry the answers into being. They will come, he always says, in the process. It works.

10. *Admit mistakes and fix them* as soon as possible. Don't wait until tomorrow. Make fixing a top priority. It solidifies credibility. It keeps you humble. It teaches by example.

    I once assigned a group of student interns to supervision duties without consulting their cooperating teachers. When two of these teachers advised me that I had interfered with their own plans for working with these future teachers, I was stunned. It took a few minutes to get past my strong urge to defend my actions as important and within my authority. I canceled the assignments and apologized to each cooperating teacher privately. We worked out other arrangements for the supervision.

11. *Wait patiently, expectantly, and intensely* for your work to have an effect, for your students to succeed, for your reputation to grow, for your skills to sharpen, and for your alumni to choose to visit you and to let you know how you did.

    I became a high school English teacher by necessity at a time when a liberal arts graduate could be hired in the absence of certified candidates. I tried to leave the profession repeatedly in my first three years. Then a strange thing happened. Alumni came back to see me. They taught me that the joy in teaching is often a matter of waiting. It's like planting and nurturing a seed you hope will grow into something full and mature and useful. Everything teachers do is related to planting, pruning, nurturing, and strengthening. But we become impatient. We think we have failed with some. We forget that each individual is unique. In the rush to meet standards and to perform well, it is sometimes furthest from our thoughts to wait with confidence, remembering that it is the nature of the seed to grow.

    I have listed each expectation beginning with a verb. The first letters of each, when combined in reverse order, create an acrostic which describes how I think of teaching. It is "War and Peace," an epic undertaking full of battles, losses, and victories punctuated with periods of alternating despair and euphoria. It is not for the timid, the faint of heart, the aloof, the distant, or the uncommitted. It is down and dirty, five live shows a day. There is no more honorable or ennobling way to make a living. I recommend it highly.

Student Resource Guide

Contents

Goals 2000: Educate America Act

The Goals 2000 Act Supporting Community Efforts to Reach Challenging Goals and High Standards

Since 1983, when the report "A Nation at Risk" sent alarming signals across America that our nation's public schools were not preparing our youth for the changing times, many state and local leaders have been engaged in school reform. What we have all learned from their experiences has shaped the principles underlying the Goals 2000: Educate America Act—the need for high expectations for students, full participation by parents, educators and communities in education, safe and disciplined learning environments, quality teaching and professional development, the effective use of technology in learning, long-term systemwide improvement efforts, and communities and states custom-making school improvement efforts to meet their needs.

Goals 2000 has drawn broad support from both major political parties, parents, and representatives of the business community, governors, teachers, labor, school administrators, state legislators, school boards, and state school superintendents.

The Act recognizes that there is no simple or cookie cutter approach to improving education. It supports a wide array of state and local approaches to raise academic achievement, and to provide a safe, disciplined learning environment for all children. The Goals 2000 Act "reaffirms that the responsibility for control of education is reserved to the states and local school systems."

Major Directions of Goals 2000

Improving Student Achievement—High Expectations for All

What we've learned: We've learned that children often meet expectations set for them. U.S. Education Secretary—and former South Carolina Governor—Richard Riley cites the urgent need for "ending the tyranny of low expectations" that is blocking the progress of many of our students.

What Goals 2000 helps states and communities to do: States and communities are being asked to make their own high expectations concrete by establishing standards for what children should learn and know how to do. These standards would be in core academic subjects, such as math, science and English. Voluntary national standards could be used as models for academic excellence to help set challenging learning standards.

Source: United States Department of Education.

Increasing Parent and Community Involvement in Education

What we've learned: While schools have been given an important responsibility for helping communities and parents to educate children, we have learned that schools cannot do it alone. Students simply achieve more when there is meaningful parental and community involvement in their children's education. Parents and families are often our "secret weapon" to improve student learning. The American family is the rock on which a solid education can and must be built.

What Goals 2000 helps states and communities to do: The Goals 2000 Act encourages the building of strong family-school partnerships for learning. Schools need to open their doors for parental and community involvement in the design and implementation of school improvement efforts. At the state and local level, broad-based panels will develop and oversee the implementation of improvement efforts, including strengthening parental involvement in learning.

Finally, Goals 2000 authorizes the creation of parent resource centers to support strong and effective parental involvement.

Making Schools Safe, Drug-Free, and Disciplined

What we've learned: Students learn better when they are in orderly environments in which they feel safe. Such environments also make it possible for teachers to focus on teaching and provide students with real opportunities for learning.

What Goals 2000 helps states and communities to do: States and communities can address ways to make schools safe, drug-free, and more disciplined as part of their improvement efforts. In addition, Title VII of Goals 2000, entitled the Safe Schools Act, authorizes the Secretary of Education to award competitive grants to school districts to help them reduce violence. Grants of up to $3 million each may be made for periods up to two years. These funds can support activities ranging from the installation of metal detectors to comprehensive violence prevention efforts, which might include mentoring programs and the training of school personnel in conflict resolution.

Related activities could also be supported by the crime prevention authority in the crime bill that recently passed Congress. This bill provides substantial new funds for community and school efforts to prevent and reduce violence.

Upgrading Teacher Training and Professional Development

What we've learned: Improving student achievement depends on the ability of teachers to teach challenging subject matter to all students, and to manage effectively an orderly learning environment. Prospective and current teachers need sustained and meaningful opportunities to learn how to do these things well.

What Goals 2000 helps states and communities to do: Participating states will develop competitive grant processes to award at least 60 percent of Goals 2000 funds in the first year—and at least 90 percent in subsequent years—to school districts for the development of reform plans, *and* for improving professional development opportunities for prospective and current teachers. Subgrants for professional development will be awarded by the state to school districts working with institutions of higher education and other non-profit organizations.

Bringing Technology into the Schools

What we've learned: The use of educational technologies—including computers in the classroom—can improve student achievement, support professional development, and increase the learning resources available to our students. In this information age, students must be prepared to use computers and other technology in school and beyond.

What Goals 2000 helps states and communities to do: Goals 2000 funds can be used by states to integrate technology into their school improvement efforts. It also creates an Office of Educational Technology within the Department of Education, charged with supporting state and local efforts to bring technology into the classrooms.

Supporting Long-Term and Systemwide Efforts

What we've learned: Improving schools involves intensive and long-term effort. Moreover, success depends on ensuring that all parts of an educational system are working together to help all children reach challenging academic standards. Reforms are less likely to lead to gains in student achievement when focus is placed on only one piece of an educational system, rather than on all pieces and how they fit together. A piecemeal approach, for example, might focus on professional development or educational technology without looking at challenging standards for what communities want their children to learn, or rigorous assessments of learning.

What Goals 2000 helps states and communities to do: At the heart of Goals 2000 is the grant program for the development and implementation of long-term comprehensive school improvements. Participating states and communities are being supported in their efforts to set high academic standards and goals, and improve all aspects of education to reinforce the achievement of these standards and goals—including parent involvement, the use of better assessments, professional development, technology, and how related education and training initiatives can work together to improve student achievement.

Communities, States Tailoring Improvements to Their Needs

What we've learned: Improvements in education are most likely to take place when schools, districts, and states have the flexibility and support needed to custom-make their own strategies to improve student achievement. This approach is particularly effective when new flexibility is exchanged for accountability based on results.

This lesson highlights the need for a new role of government at all levels—one that focuses on removing unnecessary barriers to improvement, and supporting those closest to the classroom and community as they work to improve their schools.

What Goals 2000 helps states and communities to do: Under Goals 2000, the focus of government shifts from rules and compliance, and toward flexibility and support for high student achievement and accountability for results. Moreover, Goals 2000 provides support for communities and state to custom-make their own improvement efforts to meet their own needs. The two-page Goals 2000 application and the absence of any regulations associated with the Goals 2000 plans are important—and unprecedented—manifestations of this new partnership.

The Goals 2000 Act provides new waiver authority to the Secretary of Education to cut through federal red tape in education. Once a state reform plan is approved, the state may ask the Secretary to waive requirements of certain federal education programs that the state has determined impede the implementation of state or local plans. State educational agencies may also submit waiver requests on behalf of local educational agencies and schools.

In addition, six states will be selected for participation in an education flexibility demonstration program. This provision authorizes the Secretary to *delegate* his waiver authority to state educational agencies.

Helping to Reach the National Education Goals

The Goals 2000 Act formalizes in law eight national education goals. These goals constitute a lighthouse that can guide the efforts of communities and states to improve education. The Goals are: By the year 2000 . . .

School readiness. All children in America will start school ready to learn.

Increased graduation rate. The high school graduation rate will increase to at least 90 percent.

Improved student achievement. All students in America will be competent in the core academic subjects.

Adult literacy and lifelong learning. Every adult American will be literate and possess the skills necessary to compete in the economy of the twenty-first century.

Teacher education and professional development. All teachers will have the opportunity to acquire the knowledge and skills needed to prepare U.S. students for the next century.

Best in math and science. U.S. students will be first in the world in math and science.

Safe, disciplined, and drug-free schools. Every school in America will be safe, disciplined, and drug-free.

Parental involvement. Every school will promote parental involvement in their children's education.

Conclusion

Together, these school improvement efforts—supported by Goals 2000—can help create a new ethic of learning in this country and play a critical role in helping children reach challenging goals and standards. These efforts can help create better education and training opportunities—geared to the needs of states and local communities—to best support children's success in school, in the workplace, and as responsible citizens in our nation's democracy.

Goals 2000: Educate America Act Supporting Communities and States to Improve Student Achievement

Overview

- The Goals 2000 Act provides resources to states and communities to develop and implement comprehensive education reforms aimed at helping students reach challenging academic and occupational skill standards.

Legislative Review

- On March 23, 1994, the House of Representatives approved the final Goals 2000 bill by a bipartisan vote of 306–121. On March 26, the Senate approved Goals 2000 by a bipartisan vote of 63–22.
- The President signed the bill into law March 31, 1994.

Timetable and Funding

- Congress appropriated $105 million for Goals 2000 for fiscal year 1994. First-year funds became available to the states on July 1, 1994. The President asked Congress for a substantial increase for fiscal year 1995. A House-Senate conference committee determines the final appropriation for Goals 2000 for each fiscal year through the year 2000.
- For first-year funding, states were asked to submit an application describing how a broad-based citizen panel would develop an action plan to improve their schools. The application also described how subgrants will be made for local education improvement and better teacher preservice and professional development programs.
- During the first year, states used at least 60 percent of their allotted funds to award subgrants to local school districts for the development or implementation of local and individual school improvement efforts, and for better teacher education programs and professional development activities.

- In succeeding years, at least 90 percent of each state's funds will be used to make subgrants for the implementation of the state, local, and individual school improvement plans and to support teacher education and professional development.
- During the first year, local districts used at least 75 percent of the funds they received to support individual school improvement initiatives. After the first year, districts passed through at least 85 percent of the funds to schools.

Components of the "Goals 2000: Educate America Act"

Title I: Setting High Expectations for Our Nation: the National Education Goals

Formalizes in law the original six National Education Goals. These goals concern: readiness for school; increased school graduation rates; student academic achievement and citizenship; mathematics and science performance; adult literacy; and safe, disciplined, and drug-free schools. The Act adds two new goals that encourage parental participation and better professional development for teachers and principals.

Title II: Public Accountability for Progress Toward the Goals and Development of Challenging, Voluntary, Academic Standards

Establishes in law the bipartisan National Education Goals Panel, which will: report on the nation's progress toward meeting the goals; build public support for taking actions to meet the goals; and review the voluntarily-submitted national standards and the criteria for certification of these standards developed by the National Education Standards and Improvement Council.

- Creates the National Education Standards and Improvement Council, made up of a bipartisan, broad base of citizens and educators, to examine and certify voluntary national and state standards submitted on a voluntary basis by states and by organizations working on particular academic subjects.
- Authorizes grants to support the development of voluntary assessment systems aligned to state standards, and for the development of *model* opportunity-to-learn standards.

Title III: Supporting Community and State Efforts to Improve Education

- The central purpose of the Goals 2000 Act is to support, accelerate, and sustain state and local improvement efforts aimed at helping students reach challenging academic and occupational standards.

Broad-Based Citizen Involvement in State Improvement Efforts

- The Governor and the Chief State School Officer will each appoint half the members of a broad-based panel. This panel will be comprised of teachers, principals, administrators, parents, representatives of business, labor, and higher education, and members of the public, as well as the chair of the state board of education and the chairs of the appropriate authorizing committees of the state legislature.
- States that already have a broad-based panel in place that has made substantial progress in developing a reform plan may request that the Secretary of Education recognize the existing panel.

Comprehensive Improvement Plan Geared to High Standards of Achievement

- The State Planning Panel is responsible for developing a comprehensive reform plan.
- States with reform plans already in place that meet the Act's requirements will not have to develop new plans for Goals 2000. The U.S. Secretary of Education may approve plans, or portions of plans, already adopted by the state.

- In order to receive Goals 2000 funds after the first year, a state has to have an approved plan or have made substantial progress in developing it.
- A peer review process will be used to review the state plans and offer guidance to the State Planning Panel. The U.S. Department of Education also will offer other technical assistance and support by drawing on the expertise of successful educators and leaders from around the nation.

In general, the plans are to address:

- Strategies for the development or adoption of content standards, student performance standards, student assessments, and plans for improving teacher training.
- Strategies to involve parents and the community in helping all students meet challenging state standards and to promote grass-roots, bottom-up involvement in reform.
- Strategies for ensuring that all local educational agencies and schools in the state are involved in developing and implementing needed improvements.
- Strategies for improved management and governance, and for promoting accountability for results, flexibility, site-based management, and other principles of high-performance management.
- Strategies for providing all students an opportunity to learn at higher academic levels.
- Strategies for assisting local educational agencies and schools to meet the needs of school-age students who have dropped out of school.
- Strategies for bringing technology into the classroom to increase learning.

Funds are also available to states to support the development of a state technology plan, to be integrated with the overall reform plan.

Broad-Based Involvement in Local Education Improvement Efforts

- Each local school district that applies for Goals 2000 funds will be asked to develop a broad consensus regarding a local improvement plan.
- Local districts will encourage and assist schools in developing and implementing reforms that best meet the particular needs of the schools. The local plan would include strategies for ensuring that students meet higher academic standards.

Waivers and Flexibility

- State educational agencies may apply to the U.S. Secretary of Education for waivers of certain requirements of Department of Education programs that impede the implementation of the state or local plans. States may also submit waiver requests on behalf of local school districts and schools.
- The Secretary may select up to six states for participation in an education flexibility demonstration program, which allows the Secretary to delegate his waiver authority to State education agencies.
- The Act specifies certain statutory and regulatory programmatic requirements that may not be waived, including parental involvement and civil rights laws.

Title IV. Support for Increased Parental Involvement

- This title creates parental information and resource centers to increase parents' knowledge and confidence in child-rearing activities and to strengthen partnerships between parents and professionals in meeting the educational needs of children. Parent resource centers will be funded by the U.S. Department of Education beginning in fiscal year 1995.

Title V. National Skill Standards Board

- This title creates a National Skill Standards Board to stimulate the development and adoption of a voluntary national system of occupational skill standards and certification. This Board will serve as a cornerstone of the national strategy to enhance workforce skills. The Board will be responsible for identifying broad clusters of major occupations in the U.S. and facilitating the establishment of voluntary partnerships to develop skill standards for each cluster. The Board will endorse those skill standards submitted by the partnerships that meet certain statutorily prescribed criteria.

Relationship of Goals 2000 to Other Federal Education Programs

- State participation in all aspects of the Goals 2000 Act is voluntary and is not a precondition for participation in other federal programs.

- The Goals 2000 Act is a step toward making the federal government a better partner—a supportive partner—in local and state comprehensive improvement efforts aimed at helping all children reach higher standards. The proliferation of many sets of rules and regulations for different federal education programs has often interfered with local school, community, or state efforts to improve schools. The Goals 2000 Act is designed to be flexible and supportive of community-based improvements in education.

- Other new and existing education and training programs will fit within the Goals 2000 framework of challenging academic and occupational standards, comprehensive reform, and flexibility at the state and local levels. The aim is to give schools, communities, and states the option of coordinating, promoting, and building greater coherence among federal programs and between federal programs and state and local education reforms.

- For example, the School-to-Work Opportunities Act will support state and local efforts to build a school-to-work transition system that will help youth acquire the knowledge, skills, abilities, and labor-market information they need to make a smooth transition from school to career-oriented work and to further education and training. Students in these programs could be expected to meet the same academic standards established in states under Goals 2000 and will earn portable, industry-recognized skill certificates that are benchmarked to high-quality standards.

- Similarly, the Clinton Administration's proposed reauthorization of the Elementary and Secondary Education Act (ESEA) allows states that have developed their own standards and assessments under Goals 2000 to use them for students participating in ESEA programs, thereby providing one set of standards and assessments for states and schools to use for their own reform needs and, at the same time, to meet federal requirements.

Federal Programs for Education and Related Activities

The following is a summary of federally funded education programs and federal laws that apply to schooling.

1787 *Northwest Ordinance* authorized land grants for the establishment of educational institutions.

1802 *An Act Fixing the Military Peace Establishment of the United States* established the U.S. Military Academy. (The U.S. Naval Academy was established in 1845 by the Secretary of the Navy.)

1862 *First Morrill Act* authorized public land grants to the states for the establishment and maintenance of agricultural and mechanical colleges.

1867 *Department of Education Act* authorized the establishment of the Department of Education.*

1876 *Appropriation Act,* Department of the Treasury established the U.S. Coast Guard Academy.

1890 *Second Morrill Act* provided for money grants for support of instruction in the agricultural and mechanical colleges.

1917 *Smith-Hughes Act* provided for grants to states for support of vocational education.

1918 *Vocational Rehabilitation Act* provided for grants for rehabilitation through training of World War I veterans.

1919 *An Act to Provide for Further Educational Facilities* authorized the sale by the federal government of surplus machine tools to educational institutions at 15 percent of acquisition cost.

1920 *Smith-Bankhead Act* authorized grants to states for vocational rehabilitation programs.

1935 *Bankhead-Jones Act* (Public Law 74–182) authorized grants to states for agricultural experiment stations.

*The Department of Education as established in 1867 was later known as the Office of Education. In 1980, under P.L. 96-88, it became a cabinet-level department. Therefore, for purposes of consistency, it is referred to as the "Department of Education" even in those tables covering years when it was officially the Office of Education. 1911 State Marine School Act authorized federal funds to be used for the benefit of any nautical school in any of eleven specified state seaport cities.

Source: National Center for Education Statistics, *Digest of Education Statistics 1996,* U.S. Department of Education, National Center for Educational Statistics.

Agricultural Adjustment Act (Public Law 74–320) authorized 30 percent of the annual customs receipts to be used to encourage the exportation and domestic consumption of agricultural commodities. Commodities purchased under this authorization began to be used in school lunch programs in 1936. The National School Lunch Act of 1946 continued and expanded this assistance.

1936   *An Act to Further the Development and Maintenance of an Adequate and Well-balanced American Merchant Marine* (Public Law 84–415) established the U.S. Merchant Marine Academy.

1937   *National Cancer Institute Act* established the Public Health Service fellowship program.

1941   *Amendment to Lanham Act of 1940* authorized federal aid for construction, maintenance, and operation of schools in federally impacted areas. Such assistance was continued under Public Law 815 and Public Law 874, 81st Congress, in 1950.

1943   *Vocational Rehabilitation Act* (Public Law 78–16) provided assistance to disabled veterans.

School Lunch Indemnity Plan (Public Law 78–129) provided funds for local lunch food purchases.

1944   *Servicemen's Readjustment Act* (Public Law 78–346) known as the GI Bill, provided assistance for the education of veterans.

Surplus Property Act (Public Law 78–457) authorized transfer of surplus property to educational institutions.

1946   *National School Lunch Act* (Public Law 79–396) authorized assistance through grants-in-aid and other means to states to assist in providing adequate foods and facilities for the establishment, maintenance, operation, and expansion of nonprofit school lunch programs.

George-Barden Act (Public Law 80–402) expanded federal support of vocational education.

1948   *United States Information and Educational Exchange Act* (Public Law 80–402) provided for the interchange of persons, knowledge, and skills between the United States and other countries.

1949   *Federal Property and Administrative Services Act* (Public Law 81–152) provided for donation of surplus property to educational institutions and for other public purposes.

1950   *Financial Assistance for Local Educational Agencies Affected by Federal Activities* (Public Law 81–815 and P.L. 81–874) provided assistance for construction (Public Law 815) and operation (Public Law 874) of schools in federally affected areas.

Housing Act (Public Law 81–475) authorized loans for construction of college housing facilities.

1954   *An Act for the Establishment of the United States Air Force Academy and Other Purposes* (Public Law 83–325) established the U.S. Air Force Academy.

Cooperative Research Act (Public Law 83–531) authorized cooperative arrangements with universities, colleges, and state educational agencies for educational research.

National Advisory Committee on Education Act (Public Law 83–532) established a National Advisory Committee on Education to recommend needed studies of national concern in the field of education and to propose appropriate action indicated by such studies.

School Milk Program Act (Public Law 83–597) provided funds for purchase of milk for school lunch programs.

1956   *Library Services Act* (Public Law 84–911) provided grants to states for extension and improvement of rural public library services.

1957   *Practical Nurse Training Act* (Public Law 84–911) provided grants to states for practical nurse training.

1958   *National Defense Education Act* (Public Law 85–865) provided assistance to state and local school systems for strengthening instruction in science, mathematics, modern foreign languages, and other critical subjects; improvement of state statistical services; guidance, counseling, and testing services and training institutes; higher education student loans and fellowships; foreign language study and training provided by colleges and universities; experimentation and dissemination of information on more effective utilization of television, motion pictures, and related media for educational purposes; and vocational education for technical occupations necessary to the national defense.

Education of Mentally Retarded Children Act (Public Law 85–926) authorized federal assistance for training teachers of the handicapped.

Captioned Films for the Deaf Act (Public Law 85–905) authorized a loan service of captioned films for the deaf.

1961   *Area Redevelopment Act* (Public Law 87–27) included provisions for training or retraining of persons in redevelopment areas.

1962   *Manpower Development and Training Act* (Public Law 87–415) provided training in new and improved skills for the unemployed and underemployed.

Communications Act of 1934, Amendment (Public Law 87–447) provided grants for the construction of educational television broadcasting facilities.

Migration and Refugee Assistance Act of 1962 (Public Law 87–510) authorized loans, advances, and grants for education and training of refugees.

1963   *Health Professions Educational Assistance Act* (Public Law 88–129) provided funds to expand teaching facilities and for loans to students in the health professions.

Vocational Education Act of 1963 (Public Law 88–210) increased federal support of vocational education schools; vocational work-study programs; and research, training, and demonstrations in vocational education.

Higher Education Facilities Act of 1963 (Public Law 88–204) authorized grants and loans for classrooms, libraries, and laboratories in public community colleges and technical institutes, as well as undergraduate and graduate facilities in other institutions of higher education.

1964   *Civil Rights Act of 1964* (Public Law 88–352) authorized the Commissioner of Education to arrange for support for institutions of higher education and school districts to provide inservice programs for assisting instructional staff in dealing with problems caused by desegregation.

Economic Opportunity Act of 1964 (Public Law 88–452) authorized grants for college work-study programs for students from low-income families; established a Job Corps program and authorized support for work-training programs to provide education and vocational training and work experience opportunities in welfare programs; authorized support of education and training activities and of community action programs, including Head Start, Follow Through, and Upward Bound; and authorized the establishment of Volunteers in Service to America (VISTA) .

1965   *Elementary and Secondary Education Act* (Public Law 89–10) authorized grants for elementary and secondary school programs for children of low-income families; school library resources, textbooks, and other instructional materials for school children; supplementary educational centers and services; strengthening state education agencies; and educational research and research training.

Health Professions Educational Assistance Amendments (Public Law 89–290) authorized scholarships to aid needy students in the health professions.

Higher Education Act of 1965 (Public Law 89–329) provided grants for university community service programs, college library assistance, library training and research, strengthening developing institutions, teacher training programs, and undergraduate instructional equipment. Authorized insured student loans, established a National Teacher Corps, and provided for graduate teacher training fellowships.

Medical Library Assistance Act (Public Law 89–291) provided assistance for construction and improvement of health sciences libraries.

National Foundation on the Arts and the Humanities Act (Public Law 89–209) authorized grants and loans for projects in the creative and performing arts, and for research, training, and scholarly publications in the humanities.

National Technical Institute for the Deaf Act (Public Law 89–36) provided for the establishment, construction, equipping, and operation of a residential school for postsecondary education and technical training of the deaf.

National Vocational Student Loan Insurance Act (Public Law 89–287) encouraged state and nonprofit private institutions and organizations to establish adequate loan insurance programs to assist students to attend postsecondary business, trade, technical, and other vocational schools.

Disaster Relief Act (Public Law 89–313) provided for assistance to local education agencies to help meet exceptional costs resulting from a major disaster.

1966 *International Education Act* (Public Law 89–698) provided grants to institutions of higher education for the establishment, strengthening, and operation of centers for research and training in international studies and the international aspects of other fields of study.

National Sea Grant College and Program Act (Public Law 89–688) authorized the establishment and operation of Sea Grant Colleges and programs by initiating and supporting programs of education and research in the various fields relating to the development of marine resources.

Adult Education Act (Public Law 89–750) authorized grants to states for the encouragement and expansion of educational programs for adults, including training of teachers of adults and demonstrations in adult education (previously part of Economic Opportunity Act of 1964) .

Model Secondary School for the Deaf Act (Public Law 89–694) authorized the establishment and operation, by Gallaudet College, of a model secondary school for the deaf.

Elementary and Secondary Education Amendments of 1966 (Public Law 89–750) in addition to modifying existing programs, authorized grants to assist states in the initiation, expansion, and improvement of programs and projects for the education of handicapped children.

1967 *Education Professions Development Act* (Public Law 90–35) amended the Higher Education Act of 1965 for the purpose of improving the quality of teaching and to help meet critical shortages of adequately trained educational personnel.

Public Broadcasting Act of 1967 (Public Law 90–129) established a corporation for Public Broadcasting to assume major responsibility in channeling federal funds to noncommercial radio and television stations, program production groups, and ETV networks; conduct research, demonstration, or training in matters related to noncommercial broadcasting; and award grants for construction of educational radio and television facilities.

1968 *Elementary and Secondary Education Amendments of 1967* (Public Law 90–247) modified existing programs, authorized support of regional centers for education of handicapped children, model centers and services for deaf-blind children, recruitment of personnel and dissemination of information on education of the handicapped; technical assistance in education to rural areas; support of dropout prevention projects; and support of bilingual education programs.

Handicapped Children's Early Education Assistance Act (Public Law 90–538) authorized preschool and early education programs for handicapped children.

Vocational Education Amendments of 1968 (Public Law 90–576) modified existing programs and provided for a National Advisory Council on Vocational Education, and collection and dissemination of information for programs administered by the Commissioner of Education.

Higher Education Amendments of 1968 (Public Law 90–575) authorized new programs to assist disadvantaged college students through special counseling and summer tutorial programs, and programs to assist colleges to combine resources of cooperative programs and to expand programs that provide clinical experiences to law students.

1970 *Elementary and Secondary Education Assistance Programs, Extension* (Public Law 91–230) authorized comprehensive planning and evaluation grants to state and local education agencies; provided for the establishment of a National Commission on School Finance.

National Commission on Libraries and Information Services Act (Public Law 91–345) established a National Commission on Libraries and Information Science to effectively utilize the nation's educational resources.

Office of Education Appropriation Act (Public Law 91–380) provided emergency school assistance to desegregating local education agencies.

Environmental Education Act (Public Law 91–516) established an Office of Environmental Education to develop curriculum and initiate and maintain environmental education programs at the elementary-secondary levels; disseminate information; provide training programs for teachers and other educational, public, community, labor, and industrial leaders and employees; provide community education programs; and distribute material dealing with environment and ecology.

Drug Abuse Education Act of 1970 (Public Law 527) provided for development, demonstration, and evaluation of curriculums on the problems of drug abuse.

1971 *Comprehensive Health Manpower Training Act of 1971* (Public Law 92–257) amended Title VII of the Public Health Service Act, increasing and expanding provisions for health worker training and training facilities.

Nurse Training Act of 1971 (Public Law 92–158) amended Title VIII, Nurse Training, of the Public Health Service Act, increasing and expanding provisions for nurse training facilities.

1972 *Drug Abuse Office and Treatment Act of 1972* (Public Law 92–255) established a Special Action Office for Drug Abuse Prevention to provide overall planning and policy for all federal drug-abuse prevention functions; a National Advisory Council for Drug Abuse Prevention; community assistance grants for community mental health center for treatment and rehabilitation of persons with drug-abuse problems, and, in December 1974, a National Institute on Drug Abuse.

Education Amendments of 1972 (Public Law 92–318) established the Education Division in the U.S. Department of Health, Education, and Welfare and the National Institute of Education; general aid for institutions of higher education; federal matching grants for state student incentive grants; a national commission on financing postsecondary education; state advisory councils on community colleges; a Bureau of Occupational and Adult Education and state grants for the design, establishment, and conduct of postsecondary occupational education; and a bureau-level Office of Indian Education. Amended current Office of Education programs to increase their effectiveness and better meet special needs. Prohibited sex bias in admission to vocational, professional, and graduate schools, and public institutions of undergraduate higher education.

1973 *Older Americans Comprehensive Services Amendment of 1973* (Public Law 93–29) made available to older citizens comprehensive programs of health, education, and social services.

Comprehensive Employment and Training Act of 1973 (Public Law 93–203) provided for opportunities for employment and training to unemployed and underemployed persons. Extended and expanded provisions in the Manpower Development and Training Act of 1962, Title I of the Economic Opportunity Act of 1962, Title I of the Economic Opportunity Act of 1964, and the Emergency Employment Act of 1971 as in effect prior to June 30, 1973.

1974 *Educational Amendments of 1974* (Public Law 93–380) provided for the consolidation of certain programs; and established a National Center for Education Statistics.

Juvenile Justice and Delinquency Prevention Act of 1974 (Public Law 93–415) provided for technical assistance, staff training, centralized research, and resources to develop and implement programs to keep students in elementary and secondary schools; and established, in the Department of Justice, a National Institute for Juvenile Justice and Delinquency Prevention.

1975   *Indian Self-Determination and Education Assistance Act* (Public Law 93–638) provided for increased participation of Indians in the establishment and conduct of their education programs and services.

Harry S Truman Memorial Scholarship Act (Public Law 93–642) established the Harry S Truman Scholarship Foundation and created a perpetual education scholarship fund for young Americans to prepare and pursue careers in public service.

Indochina Migration and Refugee Assistance Act of 1975 (Public Law 94–23) authorized funds to be used for education and training of aliens who have fled from Cambodia or Vietnam.

Education of the Handicapped Act (Public Law 994–142) provided that all handicapped children have available to them a free appropriate education designed to meet their unique needs.

1976   *Educational Broadcasting Facilities and Telecommunications Demonstration Act of 1976* (Public Law 94–309) established a telecommunications demonstration program to promote the development of nonbroadcast telecommunications facilities and services for the transmission, distribution, and delivery of health, education, and public or social service information.

Education Amendments of 1976 (Public Law 94–482) extended and revised federal programs for education assistance for higher education, vocational education, and a variety of other programs.

1977   *Youth Employment and Demonstration Projects Act of 1977* (Public Law 95–93) established a youth employment training program that includes, among other activities, promoting education-to-work transition, literacy training and bilingual training, and attainment of certificates of high school equivalency.

1978   *Career Education Incentive Act* (Public Law 95–207) authorized the establishment of a career education program for elementary and secondary schools.

Tribally Controlled Community College Assistance Act (Public Law 95–471) provided federal funds for the operation and improvement of tribally controlled community colleges for Indian students.

Education Amendments of 1978 (Public Law 95–561) established a comprehensive basic skills program aimed at improving pupil achievement (replaced the existing National Reading Improvement program) ; and established a community schools program to provide for the use of public buildings.

Middle Income Student Assistance Act (Public Law 95–566) modified the provisions for student financial assistance programs to allow middle-income as well as low-income students attending college or other postsecondary institutions to qualify for federal education assistance.

1979   *Department of Education Organization Act* (Public Law 96–88) established a Department of Education containing functions from the Education Division of the Department of Health, Education, and Welfare along with other selected education programs from HEW, the Department of Justice, Department of Labor, and the National Science Foundation.

1980   *Asbestos School Hazard Protection and Control Act of 1980* (Public Law 96–270) established a program for inspection of schools for detection of hazardous asbestos materials and provided loans to assist educational agencies to contain or remove and replace such materials.

1981   *Education Consolidation and Improvement Act of 1981* (Public Law 97–35) consolidated 42 programs into 7 programs to be funded under the elementary and secondary block grant authority.

1983   *Student Loan Consolidation and Technical Amendments Act of 1983* (Public Law 98–79) established 8 percent interest rate for Guaranteed Student Loans and extended Family Contribution Schedule.

Challenge Grant Amendments of 1983 (Public Law 98–95) amended Title III, Higher Education Act, and added authorization of the Challenge Grant program. The Challenge Grant program provides funds to eligible institutions on a matching basis as incentive to seek alternative sources of funding.

Education of Handicapped Act Amendments (Public Law 98–199) added Architectural Barrier amendment and clarified participation of handicapped children in private schools.

1984 *Education for Economic Security Act* (Public Law 98–377) added new science and mathematics programs for elementary, secondary, and postsecondary education. The new programs include magnet schools, excellence in education, and equal access.

Carl D. Perkins Vocational Education Act (Public Law 98–524) continues federal assistance for vocational education through fiscal year 1989. The act replaces the Vocational Education Act of 1963. It provides aid to the states to make vocational education programs accessible to all persons, including handicapped and disadvantaged, single parents and homemakers, and the incarcerated.

Human Services Reauthorization Act (Public Law 98–558) reauthorized the Head Start and Follow Through programs through fiscal year 1986. It also created a Carl D. Perkins scholarship program, a National Talented Teachers Fellowship program, a Federal Merit Scholarships program, and a Leadership in Educational Administration program.

1985 *Montgomery GI Bill—Active Duty* (Public Law 98–525) , brought about a new GI Bill for individuals who initially entered active military duty on or after July 1, 1985.

Montgomery GI Bill—Selected Reserve (Public Law 98–525) , is an education program for members of the Selected Reserve (which includes the National Guard) who enlist, reenlist, or extend an enlistment after June 30, 1985, for a six-year period.

1986 *Handicapped Children's Protection Act* (Public Law 99–372) allows parents of handicapped children to collect attorney's fees in cases brought under the Education of the Handicapped Act and provides that the Education of the Handicapped Act does not preempt other laws, such as Section 504 of the Rehabilitation Act.

The Drug-Free Schools and Communities Act of 1986 (Public Law 99–570) , part of the Anti-Drug Abuse Act of 1986, authorizes funding for fiscal years 1987–89. Establishes programs for drug abuse education and prevention, coordinated with related community efforts and resources, through the use of federal financial assistance.

1987 *Higher Education Act Amendments of 1987* (Public Law 100–50) makes technical corrections, clarifications, or conforming amendments related to the enactment of the Higher Education Amendments of 1986.

1988 *The Augustus F. Hawkins-Robert T. Stafford Elementary and Secondary School Improvement Amendments of 1988* (Public Law 100–297) reauthorizes through 1993 major elementary and secondary education programs including: Chapter 1, Chapter 2, Bilingual Education, Math-Science Education, Magnet Schools, Impact Aid, Indian Education, Adult Education, and other smaller education programs.

Technology-Related Assistance for Individuals with Disabilities Act of 1988 (Public Law 100–407) provides financial assistance to states to develop and implement consumer-responsive statewide programs of technology-related assistance for persons of all ages with disabilities.

The Omnibus Trade and Competitiveness Act of 1988 (Public Law 100–418) authorizes new and expanded education programs. Title VI of the Act, Education and Training for American Competitiveness, authorizes new programs in literacy, math-science, foreign language, vocational training, international education, technology training, and technology transfer. The Omnibus Drug Abuse Prevention Act of 1988 (Public Law 100–690) authorizes a new teacher training program under the Drug-Free Schools and Communities Act, an early childhood education program to be administered jointly by the Departments of Health and Human Services and Education, and a pilot program for the children of alcoholics.

Stewart B. McKinney Homeless Assistance Act (Public Law 100–628) extends for two additional years programs providing assistance to the homeless, including literacy training for homeless adults and education for homeless youths.

Tax Reform Technical Amendments (Public Law 100–647) authorizes an Education Savings Bond for the purpose of postsecondary educational expenses. The bill grants tax exclusion for interest earned on regular series EE savings bonds.

1989   *The Children with Disabilities Temporary Care Reauthorization Act of 1989* (Public Law 101–127) revises and extends the programs established in the Temporary Child Care for Handicapped Children and Crises Nurseries Act of 1986.

The Drug-Free Schools and Communities Act Amendments of 1989 (Public Law 101–226) amends the Drug-Free Schools and Communities Act of 1986 to revise certain requirements relating to the provision of drug abuse education and prevention programs in elementary and secondary schools.

1990   *The Childhood Education and Development Act of 1989* (Public Law 101–239) authorized the appropriations to expand Head Start programs and programs carried out under the Elementary and Secondary Education Act of 1965 to include child-care services.

The Excellence in Mathematics, Science and Engineering Education Act of 1990 (Public Law 101–589) promotes excellence in American mathematics, science, and engineering education by creating a national mathematics and science clearinghouse, establishing regional mathematics and science education consortia, establishing three new mathematics, science, and engineering scholarship programs, and creating several other mathematics, science, and engineering education programs.

The Student Right-To-Know and Campus Security Act (Public Law 101–542) requires institutions of higher education receiving federal financial assistance to provide certain information with respect to the graduation rates of student-athletes at such institutions. The act also requires the institution to certify that it has a campus security policy and will annually submit a uniform crime report to the Federal Bureau of Investigation (FBI) .

The Children's Television Act of 1990 (Public Law 101–437) requires the Federal Communications Commission to reinstate restrictions on advertising during children's television, and enforces the obligation of broadcasters to meet the educational and informational needs of the child audience.

The Americans with Disabilities Act of 1990 (Public Law 101–336) prohibits discrimination against persons with disabilities.

The McKinney Homeless Assistance Amendments Act of 1990 (Public Law 101–645) reauthorized the Stewart B. McKinney Homeless Assistance Act programs of grants to state and local education agencies for the provision of support services to homeless children and youth.

The National Assessment of Chapter 1 Act (Public Law 101–305) requires the Secretary of Education to conduct a comprehensive national assessment of programs carried out with assistance under Chapter 1 of Title I of the Elementary and Secondary Education Act of 1965.

The Augustus F. Hawkins Human Services Reauthorization Act of 1990 (Public Law 101–510) authorized appropriations for fiscal years 1991–1994 to carry out the Head Start Act, the Follow Through Act, the Community Services Block Grant Act, and the Low-Income Home Energy Assistance Act of 1981.

The National and Community Service Act of 1989 (Public Law 101–610) increased school and college-based community service opportunities and authorized the President's Points of Light Foundation.

The School Dropout Prevention and Basic Skills Improvement Act of 1990 (Public Law 101–600) improves secondary school programs for basic skills improvements and dropout reduction.

The Medical Residents Student Loan Amendments Act of 1989 (Enacted in Public Law 101–239, the Omnibus Budget Reconciliation Act of 1989) amended the Higher Education Act of 1965 to eliminate student loan deferments for medical students serving in internships or residency programs.

The Asbestos School Hazard Abatement Reauthorization Act of 1990 (Public Law 101–637) reauthorized the Asbestos School Hazard Abatement Act of 1984, which provided financial support to elementary and secondary schools to inspect for asbestos, and to develop and implement an asbestos management plan. In addition, the act provides for programs of information, technical, and scientific assistance and training.

The Eisenhower Exchange Fellowship Program (Public Law 101–454) provided a permanent endowment for the Eisenhower Exchange Fellowship Program.

The Tribally Controlled Community College Reauthorization (Public Law 101–477) reauthorized the Tribally Controlled Community College Assistance Act and the Navajo Community College Act.

The Environmental Education Act (Public Law 101–619) promotes environmental education by the establishment of an Office of Environmental Education in the Environmental Protection Agency and the creation of several environmental education programs.

The Anti-Drug Education Act of 1990 and the Drug Abuse Resistance Education (DARE) Act of 1990 (Both bills were enacted as part of Public Law 101–647, the Comprehensive Crime Control Act of 1990.) amends the Drug-Free Schools and Communities Act and raises funding levels for schools personnel training, funds the replication of successful drug education programs, helps local education agencies to cooperate with law enforcement agencies and allows funds to be used for after-school programs. The Drug Abuse Resistance Education Act establishes a program of grants to HEW for Drug Abuse Resistance Education (DARE) programs.

The Public Service Assistance Education Act (enacted as part of Department of Defense Authorization Act, Public Law 101–510) gives federal agencies authority to provide new educational benefits to employees by paying for an employee to obtain an academic degree for which there is an agency shortage of qualified personnel, and by repaying up to $6,000 per year of the student loan of a qualified employee in exchange for a three-year commitment.

The 1990 Budget Reconciliation Act (Public Law 101–508) included a set of student aid provisions that were estimated to yield a savings of $2 billion over five years. These provisions included delayed Guaranteed Student Loan disbursements, tightened ability-to-benefit eligibility, and expanded pro rata refund policy and the elimination of student aid eligibility at high default schools.

1991   *A bill to amend title 38, United States Code, with respect to veterans education and employment programs, and for other purposes* (Public Law 102–16) revises and extends eligibility for veterans' education and employment programs.

National Literacy Act of 1991 (Public Law 102–73) established the National Institute for Literacy, the National Institute Board, and the Interagency Task Force on Literacy. Amends various federal laws to establish and extend various literacy programs.

Dire Emergency Supplemental Appropriations for Consequences of Operation Desert Shield/ Desert Storm, Food Stamps, Unemployment Compensation Administration, Veterans Compensation and Pensions, and Other Urgent Needs Act of 1991 (Public Law 102–27) makes dire emergency supplemental appropriations for FY 1991 for the additional costs of Operation Desert Shield/Operation Desert Storm and other programs.

Higher Education Technical Amendments of 1991 (Public Law 102–26) amends the Higher Education Act of 1965 to resolve legal and technical issues relating to federal postsecondary student assistance programs and to prevent undue burdens on participants in Operation Desert Storm, and for other purposes.

Intelligence Authorization Act, Fiscal Year 1992 (Public Law 102–183) provides for the establishment of a National Security Education Board and a National Security Education Trust Fund within the Treasury.

National Defense Authorization Act for Fiscal Year 1992 and 1993 (Public Law 102–190) authorizes appropriations for military functions of the Department of Defense. Includes Defense Manufacturing Education program and plan for science, mathematics, and engineering education.

Rehabilitation Act Amendments of 1991 (Public Law 102–52) amends the Rehabilitation Act of 1973 to reauthorize funding for various programs, including vocational rehabilitation services, research and training, supplementary services and facilities, the National Council on Disability, the Architectural and Transportation Barriers Compliance Board, employment opportunities for individuals with handicaps, and comprehensive services for independent living. Reauthorizes funding for the Helen Keller National Center for Deaf-Blind Youths and Adults (under the Helen Keller National Center Act) and for the President's Committee on Employment of People with Disabilities.

Amend the School Dropout Demonstration Assistance Act of 1988 to extend authorization of appropriations through fiscal year 1993 and for other purposes (Public Law 102–103) revises and reauthorizes programs under: 1) the School Dropout Demonstration Assistance Act of 1988; and 2) the Star Schools Program Assistance Act. Revises the functional literacy program, and adds a life skills program, for state and local prisoners under the National Literacy Act of 1991.

A bill making appropriations for the Department of the Interior and related agencies for the fiscal year ending September 30, 1992, and for other purposes (Public Law 102–154) amends the Anti-Drug Abuse Act of 1988 to extend the authorization of appropriations for drug abuse education and prevention programs relating to youth gangs and for runaway and homeless youth. Directs the Secretary of Health and Human Services to report annually on the program of drug education and prevention relating to youth gangs.

Federal Supplemental Compensation Act of 1991 (Public Law 102–164) revises procedures for student loan debt collection.

Joint resolution to declare it to be the policy of the United States that there should be a renewed and sustained commitment by the Federal government and the American people to the importance of adult education (Public Law 102–74) declares it to be the policy of the United States that: 1) the twenty-fifth anniversary of federal aid to improve the basic and literacy skills of adults through the Adult Education Act (AEA) should be recognized and observed; and 2) there should be a continued commitment to federal aid for educating adults through AEA to increase adult literacy and assure a productive work force and a competitive United States in the twenty-first century.

National Commission on a Longer School Year Act (Public Law 102–62) establishes the National Education Commission on Time and Learning. Directs the Secretary of Education to: 1) make grants for research in the teaching of writing; and 2) carry out a program to educate students about the history and principles of the Constitution, including the Bill of Rights. Amends the Elementary and Secondary Education Act of 1965 to revise requirements for law-related education program grant and contract applications, review, and award periods. Establishes the National Council on Education Standards and Testing.

High-Performance Computing Act of 1991 (Public Law 102–194) directs the president to implement a National High-Performance Computing Program. Provides for: 1) establishment of a National Research and Education Network; 2) standards and guidelines for high-performance networks; and 3) the responsibility of certain federal departments and agencies with regard to the Network.

National and Community Service Technical Amendments Act of 1991 (Public Law 102–10) amends the National and Community Service Act to make various technical amendments.

Persian Gulf Conflict Supplemental Authorization Personnel Benefits Act of 1991 (Public Law 102–25) authorizes supplemental appropriations: 1) to the Department of Defense in connection with Operation Desert Storm; and 2) for certain national security programs. Revises various military personnel benefits provisions, especially with respect to those personnel serving on active duty in connection with Operation Desert Storm.

Veterans' Educational Assistance Amendments of 1991 (Public Law 102–127) restores certain educational benefits available to reserve and active-duty personnel under the Montgomery GI Bill to students whose course studies under such programs were interrupted by being called to active duty or given increased work in connection with the Persian Gulf War.

Individuals with Disabilities Education Act Amendments of 1991 (Public Law 102–119) amends the Individuals with Disabilities Education Act (IDEA) to extend the authorization of appropriations and revise various features of the early intervention program of services for infants and toddlers with disabilities.

National Sea Grant College Program Authorization Act of 1991 (Public Law 102–186) amends the National Sea Grant College Program Act to: 1) authorize appropriations; and 2) repeal provisions authorizing grants relating to marine affairs and resource management.

National Commission on Libraries and Information Science Act Amendments of 1991 (Public Law 102–95) amends the National Commission on Libraries and Information Science Act to revise provisions, and authorize appropriations, for the National Commission on Libraries and Information Science.

Civil Rights Act of 1991 (Public Law 102–166) amends the Civil Rights Act of 1964, the Age Discrimination in Employment Act of 1967, and the Americans with Disabilities impact, tests, mixed motives, judgment finality, foreign discrimination, seniority systems, fees, and time limits. Establishes the Technical Assistance Training Institute.

Dropout Prevention Technical Correction Amendments of 1991 (Public Law 102–159) amends federal law relating to impact aid to restore provisions for the Secretary of Education to make certain preliminary payments to local education agencies.

1992   *Higher Education Amendments of 1992* (Public Law 102–325) amends the Higher Education Act of 1965 to revise and reauthorize funding for its various programs.

Ready-To-Learn Act (Public Law 102–545) amends the General Education Provisions Act to establish Ready-To-Learn Television programs to support educational programming and support materials for preschool and elementary school children and their parents, child-care providers, and educators.

Job Training Reform Amendments of 1992 (Public Law 102–367), a bill to amend the Job Training Partnerships Act, the Carl Perkins Vocational Education Act, and the Adult Education Act.

National Commission of Time and Learning, Extension (Public Law 102–359) amends the National Education Commission on Time and Learning Act to extend the authorization of appropriations for such Commission, amends the Elementary and Secondary Education Act of 1965 to revise provisions for (1) a specified civic education program; (2) schoolwide projects for educationally disadvantaged children, and provides for additional Assistant Secretaries of Education.

1993   *Student Loan Reform Act* (Public Law 103–66) reforms the student aid process by phasing in a system of direct lending designed to provide savings for taxpayers and students. Students will be able to choose among a variety of repayment options, including income contingency.

National Service Trust Act (Public Law 103–82) amends the National and Community Service act of 1990 to establish a corporation for National Service and enhance opportunities for national service. In addition, the Act provides education grants up to $4,725 per year for 2 years to people age 17 years or older who perform community service before, during, or after postsecondary education.

Higher Education Technical Amendments Act (Public Law 103–208) amends the Higher Education Act to make technical changes and conforming amendments.

NAEP Assessment Authorization (Public Law 103–33) authorizes the use of NAEP for state-by-state comparisons.

Migrant Student Record Transfer System Extension (Public Law 103–59) extends the operation of the migrant student record transfer system.

1994 *Goals 2000: Educate America Act* (Public Law 103–227) establishes a new federal partnership through a system of grants to states and local communities to reform the nation's education system. The Act formalizes the national education goals and establishes the National Education Goals Panel. It also creates a National Education Standards and Improvement Council (NESIC) to provide voluntary national certification of state and local education standards and assessments and establishes the National Skill Standards Board to develop voluntary national skill standards.

School-To-Work Opportunities Act of 1994 (Public Law 103–239) establishes a national framework within which states and communities can develop School-To-Work Opportunities systems to prepare young people for first jobs and continuing education. The act also provides money to states and communities to develop a system of programs that include work-based learning, school-based learning, and connecting activities components. School-To-Work programs will provide students with a high school diploma (or its equivalent), a nationally recognized skill certificate, and an associate degree (if appropriate) and may lead to a first job or further education.

Safe School Act of 1994 (Part of Public Law 103–227) authorizes the award of competitive grants to local educational agencies with serious crime to implement violence prevention activities such as conflict resolution and peer mediation.

Educational Research, Development, Dissemination, and Improvement Act of 1994 (Part of Public Law 103–227) authorizes the educational research and dissemination activities of the Office of Educational Research and Improvement. The regional educational laboratories and university-based research and development centers are authorized.

Student Loan Default Exemption Extension (Public Law 103–235) amends the Higher Education Act of 1965 to extend until July 1, 1998 the effective date for cohort default rate extension for historically black colleges and universities, tribally controlled community colleges, and Navajo community colleges.

Improving America's Schools Act (Public Law 103–382) reauthorizes and revamps the Elementary and Secondary Education Act. The legislation includes Title I, the federal government's largest program providing educational assistance to disadvantaged children; professional development and technical assistance programs; a safe and drug-free schools and communities provision; and provisions promoting school equity.

1995 *Unfunded Mandate Reform Act of 1995* (Public Law 104–4) curbs the practice of imposing unfunded federal mandates on states and local governments; to strengthen the partnership between the federal government and state, local, and tribal governments, and for other purposes.

Paperwork Reduction Act of 1995 (Public Law 104–13) furthers the goals of the Paperwork Reduction Act to have federal agencies become more responsible and publicly accountable for reducing the burden of federal paperwork.

Amendment to the Elementary and Secondary Education Act of 1965 (Public Law 104–5) amends a provision of Part A of title IX of the Elementary and Secondary Education Act of 1965, relating to Indian education, to provide a technical amendment, and for other purposes.

1997 *1997 Tax Reform Law* (Public Law 105) provides $400 federal income tax deduction per child. The law establishes the Hope Scholarship that provides up to $1,500 per child tax credit for college tuition and fees per first two years of postsecondary education. A Lifetime Learning Credit was also created which enables families to claim up to 20 percent of $5,000 in tuition and fees (increasing to $10,000 in 2003). The Education IRA was established in which taxpayers may set aside up to $500 per child per year until the child reaches age 18 for funding postsecondary education.

A Bill of Rights for High School Students

Neither students nor teachers shed their constitutional rights to freedom of speech or expression at the schoolhouse gate. That has been the unmistakable holding of the Supreme Court for almost fifty years. (*Tinker* v. *Des Moines*, 1969)

The following statement of students' rights is intended as a guide to students, parents, teachers, and administrators who are interested in developing proper safeguards for student liberties. IT IS NOT A SUMMARY OF THE LAW, BUT SETS FORTH IN A GENERAL WAY WHAT THE ACLU THINKS *SHOULD* BE ADOPTED. . . .

Article I. Expression

A. Students shall be free to express themselves and disseminate their views without prior restraints through speech, essays, publications, pictures, armbands, badges, and all other media of communication. Student expression may be subject to disciplinary action only in the event that such expression creates a significant physical disruption of school activities.

B. No reporter for a student publication may be required to reveal a source of information.

C. Students shall have the right to hear speakers and presentations representing a wide range of views and subjects in classes, clubs, and assemblies. Outside speakers and presentations may be limited only by considerations of time, space, and expense.

D. Students shall be free to assemble, demonstrate, and picket peacefully, to petition and to organize on school grounds or in school buildings subject only to reasonable limitations on time, place, and manner designed to avoid significant physical obstruction of traffic or significant physical disruption of school activities.

E. Students shall be free to determine their dress and grooming as they see fit, subject only to reasonable limitations designed to protect student safety or prevent significant ongoing disruption of school activities.

F. No student shall be required to participate in any way in patriotic exercises or be penalized for refusing to participate.

Article II. Religion

A. Students shall be free to practice their own religion or no religion.

B. There shall be no school-sanctioned religious exercises or events.

C. Religious history, ideas, institutions, and literature may be studied in the same fashion as any other academic subject.

Article III. Privacy

A. Students should be free from undercover surveillance through the use of mechanical, electronic, or other secret methods, including undercover agents, without issuance of a warrant.

B. Students should be free from warrantless searches and seizures by school officials in their personal effects, lockers, or any other facilities assigned to their personal use. General housekeeping inspections of lockers and desks shall not occur without reasonable notice.

C. Student record files
   1. A student's permanent record file shall include only information about academic competence and notation of the fact of participation in school clubs, sports, and other such school extracurricular activities. This file shall not be disclosed to any person or agency outside the school, except to the student's parents or guardian, without the student's permission.
   2. Any other records (e.g., medical or psychological evaluations) shall be available only to the student, the student's parents or guardian, and the school staff. Such other records shall be governed by strict safeguards for confidentiality and shall not be available to others in or outside of the school even upon consent of the student.
   3. A record shall be kept, and shall be available to the student, of any consultation of the student's files, noting the date and purpose of the consultation and the name of the person who consulted the files.
   4. All records shall be open to challenge and correction by the student.
   5. A student's opinions shall not be disclosed to any outside person or agency.

Article IV. Equality

A. No organization that officially represents the school in any capacity and no curricular or extracurricular activity organized by school authorities may deny or segregate participation or award or withhold privileges on the basis of race, color, national origin, sex, religion, creed, or opinions.

Article V. Government

A. All students may hold office and may vote in student elections. These rights shall not be denied for any reason.

B. Student government organizations and their operation, scope, and amendment procedures shall be established in a written constitution formulated with full and effective student participation.

Article VI. Due process

A. Regulations concerning student behavior shall be formulated with full and effective student participation. Such regulations shall be published and made available to all students. Regulations shall be fully, clearly, and precisely written.

B. No student shall be held accountable by school authorities for any behavior occurring outside the organized school day or off school property (except during school-sponsored events) unless such behavior presents a clear, present, and substantial ongoing danger to persons and property in the school.

C. There shall be no cruel, unusual, demeaning, or excessive punishments. There shall be no corporal punishment.

D. No student shall be compelled by school officials to undergo psychological therapy or use medication without that student's consent. No student may be required to participate in any psychological or personality testing, research project, or experiment without that student's written, informed, and willing consent. The nature, purposes, and possible adverse consequences of the testing, project, or experiment shall be fully explained to the student.

E. A student shall have the right to due process in disciplinary and investigative proceedings. In cases that may involve serious penalties, such as suspension for more than three days, expulsion, transfer to another school, a notation on the student's record, or long-term loss of privileges:

1. A student shall be guaranteed a formal hearing before an impartial board. That student shall have the right to appeal hearing results.
2. Rules for hearings and appeals shall be written and published, and there shall be full and effective student participation in their formulation.
3. The student shall be advised in writing of any charges brought against that student.
4. The student shall have the right to present evidence and witnesses and to cross-examine adverse witnesses. The student shall have the right to have an advisor of his or her own choosing present.
5. The hearing shall be open or private as the student chooses.
6. The student shall have a reasonable time to prepare a defense.
7. A student may not be compelled to incriminate himself or herself.
8. The burden of proof, beyond a reasonable doubt, shall be upon the school.
9. A written record of all hearings and appeals shall be made available to the student, at the school's expense.
10. A student shall be free from double jeopardy.

Domains
of Learning

The levels of cognitive learning evaluate depth of learning. The levels are numbered from the most superficial to the most advanced.

1.00 Knowledge
    1.10 Knowledge of specifics
    1.20 Knowledge of ways and means of dealing with specifics
    1.30 Knowledge of the universals and abstractions in a field

2.00 Comprehension
    2.10 Translation
    2.20 Interpretation
    2.30 Extrapolation

3.00 Application

4.00 Analysis

4.10 Analysis of elements
4.20 Analysis of relationships
4.30 Analysis of organizational principles

5.00 Synthesis
    5.10 Production of a unique communication
    5.20 Production of a plan or proposed set of operations
    5.30 Derivation of a set of abstract relations

6.00 Evaluation
    6.10 Judgments in terms of internal evidence
    6.20 Judgments in terms of external criteria

Source: Benjamin S. Bloom, ed., *Taxonomy of Educational Objectives* (New York: Longmans, Green, 1956), pp. 6–8.

Different levels of affective learning are classified as follows:

1.00 Receiving (attending)
    1.10 Awareness
    1.20 Willingness to receive
    1.30 Controlled or selected attention

2.00 Responding
    2.10 Acquiescence in responding
    2.20 Willingness to respond
    2.30 Satisfaction in response

3.00 Valuing
    3.10 Acceptance of a value

3.20 Preference for a value
3.30 Commitment

4.00 Organization
    4.10 Conceptualization of a value
    4.20 Organization of a value system

5.00 Characterization by a value or value complex
    5.10 Generalized set
    5.20 Characterization

Source: David R. Krathwohl, Benjamin S. Bloom, and Bertram B. Masia, eds. *Taxonomy of Educational Objectives* (New York: McKay, 1964), pp. 176–193.

Levels of learning for the psychomotor domain are as follows:

1.00 Reflex movements
    1.10 Segmental reflexes
    1.20 Intersegmental reflexes
    1.30 Suprasegmental reflexes

2.00 Basic-fundamental movements
    2.10 Locomotor movements
    2.20 Nonlocomotor movements
    2.30 Manipulative movements

3.00 Perceptual abilities
    3.10 Kinesthetic discrimination
    3.20 Visual discrimination
    3.30 Auditory discrimination
    3.40 Tactile discrimination
    3.50 Coordinated abilities

4.00 Physical abilities
    4.10 Endurance
    4.20 Strength
    4.30 Flexibility
    4.40 Agility

5.00 Skilled movements
    5.10 Simple adaptive skills
    5.20 Compound adaptive skills
    5.30 Complex adaptive skills

6.00 Nondiscursive communication
    6.10 Expressive movement
    6.20 Interpretive movement

Source: Anita J. Harrow, *A Taxonomy of the Psychomotor Domain* (New York: McKay, 1972), pp. 1–2.

Professional Journals

American Educational Research Journal
American Educational Research Association, 1230 17th Street NW, Washington, D.C. 20036
(202) 223-9485

American Educator
American Federation of Teachers, Local 231 AFL-CIO 7451 Thira, Detroit, MI 48202
(202) 797-4400

American Middle School Education
National Middle School Institute, Box 16149, Columbus, OH 43216
(614) 369-8005

American School Board Journal
National School Boards Association, 1680 Duke Street, Alexandria, VA 22314
(703) 838-6722

Arts and Activities
Publishers Development Corporation, 591 Camino de la Reina, Suite 200, San Diego, CA 92108
(619) 297-8520

Behavioral Disorders Journal
Council for Exceptional Children, 1920 Association Drive, Reston, VA 22091
(703) 620-3660

Business Education World
McGraw-Hill, Inc., 1221 Avenue of the Americas, New York, NY 10020
(212) 512-4736

Cable in the Classroom
I D G Peterborough, 80 Elm Street, Peterborough, NH 03458
(603) 924-0100

Canadian Council of Teachers of English Newletter
Canadian Council of Teachers of English, Box 4520 Sta. C, Calgary Alta. T2T 5N3, Canada
(403) 244-4487

Canadian Journal of Education
Canadian Society for The Study of Education, 14 Henderson Avenue, Ottawa Ont. K1N 7P1, Canada
(613) 230-3532

Canadian Social Studies
Faculty of Education, 4-116 Education N., Edmonton, Alta. T6G 2G5, Canada
FAX (403) 492-0236

Canadian Vocational Journal
Canadian Vocational Association, PO Box 3435, Station D, Ottawa Ont. K1P 6L4, Canada
(613) 596-2515

Catalyst for Change
(National School Development Council) East Texas School Study

Council, East Texas State University, Commerce, TX 75428
(903) 886-5521

Challenge
Good Apple, 1204 Buchanan Street, Box 299, Carthage, IL 62321-0299
(217) 357-3981

Childhood Education
Association for Childhood Education International, 11141 Georgia Avenue, Suite 200, Wheaton, MD 20902
(301) 942-2443

Clearing House
Heldref Publications, 4000 Albemarle Street NW, Washington, D.C. 20016
(202) 362-6445

Cognition and Instruction
Lawrence Erlbaum Associates, 365 Broadway, Hillsdale, NJ 07642
(201) 666-4110

Computers & Education
Pergamon Press, Inc., Journals Division, 660 White Plains Road, Tarrytown, NY 10591-5153
(914) 524-9200

Computers in Education Journal
American Society for Engineering Education, Computers in Education Division, Box 68, Port Royal Square, Port Royal, VA 22535
(804) 742-5611

Computers in the Schools
Haworth Press, Inc., 10 Alice Street,
Binghamton, NY 13904
(800) 342-9678

The Computing Teacher
International Council for
Computers in Education, University
of Oregon, 1787 Agate Street,
Eugene, OR 97403
(503) 686-4414

Creative Classroom
Children's Television Workshop,
One Lincoln Plaza, New York, NY
10023
(212) 595-3456

Curriculum Review
Curriculum Review Company,
212 West Superior Street, Suite 200,
Chicago, IL 60610-3533
(312) 922-8245

Dialogue in Instrumental Music
Education
D I M E, Humanities Building,
School of Music, University of
Wisconsin, Madison, WI 53706-1483
(608) 263-3220

Early Years
Trentham Books Ltd, Westview
House, 734 London Road, Oakhill,
Stoke-on-Trent, Staffs. ST4 5NP,
England
0782-745567/FAX 0782-745553

Education Digest
Prakken Publications, PO Box 8623,
Ann Arbor, MI 48107
(313) 769-1211

Educational Leadership
Association for Supervision and
Curriculum Development, 225
North Washington Street,
Alexandria, VA 22314
(703) 549-9110

Educational Measurement, Issues and
Practice
National Council on Measurement
in Education, 1230 17th Street NW,
Washington, D.C. 20036
(202) 223-9318

Educational Technology
Educational Technology
Publications, 720 Palisade Avenue,
Englewood Cliffs, NJ 07632
(201) 871-4007

Electronic Learning
Scholastic Inc., 730 Broadway, New
York, NY 10003-9538
(212) 505-3000

The Elementary School Journal
University of Chicago Press, PO Box
37005, Chicago, IL 60637
(312) 962-7600

English in Education
National Association for the
Teaching of English, Birley School
Annexe, Fox Lane Site, Frecheville,
Sheffield S12 4WY, England
0742-390081

English Journal
National Council of Teachers in
English, 1111 Kenyon Road,
Urbana, IL 61801

Exceptional Children
Council for Exceptional Children,
1920 Association Drive, Reston, VA
22091
(703) 620-3660

Exceptionality Education Canada
University of Calgary Press, 2500
University Drive NW, Calgary,
Alta. T2N 1N4, Canada
(403) 220-7578

Feminist Teacher
Feminist Teacher, Ballantine 442
Indiana University, Bloomington,
IN 47405
(812) 855-3042

Focus on Exceptional Children
Love Publishing Company, 1777
South Bellaire Street, Denver, CO
80222
(303) 757-2579

Guide to Federal Funding for
Education
Education Funding Research
Council, 4301 Fairfax Drive
Number 875, Arlington, VA
22203-1627
(703) 528-1000

Harvard Educational Review
Harvard Educational Review,
6 Appian Way, Suite 349, Gutman
Library, Cambridge, MA 02138
(617) 495-3432

The High School Journal
University of North Carolina Press,
Box 2288, Chapel Hill, NC
27515-2288
(919) 966-3561

History of Education Quarterly
School of Education, Indiana
University, Bloomington, IN 47405
(812) 855-9334

Human Communication and Its
Disorders
Ablex Publishing Corporation,
355 Chestnut Street, Norwood, NJ
07648
(201) 767-8450

Instructor
Instructor, 545 Fifth Avenue,
New York, NY 10017
(212) 503-2888

The International Schools Journal
European Council of International
Schools, 21B Lavant Street, St
Petersfield Hampshire GU32 3EL,
England

Journal of American Indian Education
Arizona State University, College of
Education, Bureau of Educational
Research and Services, Tempe, AZ
85281
(602) 965-6292

Journal of Childhood Communication Disorders
Council for Exceptional Children, Division for Children with Communication Disorders, 1920 Association Drive, Reston, VA 22091-1589
(703) 620-3660

Journal of Curriculum and Supervision
Association for Supervision and Curriculum Development,
225 North Washington Street, Alexandria, VA 22314
(703) 549-9110

Journal of Early Intervention
Special Press, 474 North Lake Shore Drive, Number 3910, Chicago, IL 60611-3400
(703) 446-0500

Journal of Education
Boston University, School of Education, 605 Commonwealth Avenue, Boston, MA 02215
(617) 353-3230

Journal of Educational Measurement
National Council on Measurement in Education, 1230 17th Street NW, Washington, D.C. 20036
(202) 223-9318

Journal of Educational Psychology
American Psychological Association, 1400 North Uhle Street, Arlington, VA 22201
(703) 247-7703

Journal of Educational Research
Heldref Publications,
4000 Albemarle Street NW, Washington, DC 20016
(202) 362-6445

Journal of Learning Disabilities
Pro-Ed Inc, 8700 Shoal Creek Boulevard, Austin, TX 78757-6897
(512) 451-3246

Journal of Moral Education
Carfax Publishing Company,
PO Box 25 Abingdon, Oxfordshire OX14 3UE, England
US subscriptions: 85 Ash Street, Hopkinton, MA 01748
01-580-6784

Journal of Multicultural Counseling and Development
American Association for Counseling Development, 5999 Stevenson Avenue, Alexandria, VA 22304

Journal of Physical Education, Recreation and Dance
American Alliance for Health, Physical Education, Recreation, and Dance, 1990 Association Drive, Reston, VA 22091
(703) 476-3400

Journal of Reading
International Reading Association, 800 Barksdale Road, Newark, DE 19714-8139
(800) 336-READ

Journal of Rural and Small Schools
West Washington University, Miller Hall 359, Bellingham, WA 98225
(206) 676-3576

Journal of School Psychology
Pergamon Press Inc, Maxwell House, Fairview Park, Elmsford, NY 10523.
Canada subscriptions: 150 Consumers Road, Suite 104, Willowdale Ontario M2J 1P9, Canada
(914) 592-7700

Journal for Vocational Special Needs Education
National Association of Vocational Education Special Needs Personnel, 518 East Nebraska Hall, University of Nebraska, Lincoln, NE 68508-0515
(402) 472-2365

Journal of Vocational and Technical Education
Omicron Tau Theta, 215 Lane Hall, Blacksburg, VA 24061
(703) 231-5471

Language Arts
National Council of Teachers of English, 1111 Kenyon Road, Urbana, IL 61801
(217) 328-3870

Learning
Education Today Company, Inc., 530 University Avenue, Palo Alto, CA 94301
(215) 646-8700

Lectura y Vida
International Reading Association, Inc., 800 Barksdale Road, Box 8139, Newark, DE 19714-8139
(302) 731-1600

Mathematics in School
Longman Group UK Ltd., Westgate House, The High, Harlow, Essex CM20 1YR, England
0279-442601

Mathematics Teacher
National Council of Teachers of Mathematics, 1906 Association Drive, Reston, VA 22091
(703) 620-9840

Mathematics Teaching
Association of Teachers of Mathematics, 7 Shaftesbury Street, Derby DE3 8YB, England
0332-46599

Media and Methods
American Society of Educators, 1429 Walnut Street, Philadelphia, PA 19102
(215) 563-3501

Microcomputers in Education
John Mongillo, Editor & Publisher, 1125 Point Judith Road, Apartment E7, Narragansett, RI 02882-5541
(203) 655-3798

Middle School Journal
National Middle School
Association, 4807 Evanswood
Drive, Columbus, OH 43229-6292
(614) 848-8211

Minority Funding Report
Government Information Services,
4301 Fairfax Drive Suite 875,
Arlington, VA 22203-1627
(703) 528-1000

NASSP Bulletin
National Association of Secondary
School Principals, 1904 Association
Drive, Reston, VA 22091-1598
(703) 860-0200

NEA Today
National Education Association,
1201 16th Street NW, Washington,
D.C. 20036

Perspectives in Education and Deafness
Gallaudet University, Pre-College
Programs, KDES PAS-6, 800 Florida
Avenue NE, Washington, D.C.
20002-3695
(202) 651-5340

Philosophy of Education
Philosophy of Education Society,
Illinois State University, Normal, IL
61761
(309) 438-5422

Principal
National Association of Elementary
School Principals, 1615 Duke Street,
Alexandria, VA 22314
(703) 684-3345

PTA Communicator
Texas Congress of Parents and
Teachers, 408 West 11th Street,
Austin, TX 78701
(512) 476-6769

PTA Today
National Congress of Parents and
Teachers, 700 North Rush Street,
Chicago, IL 60611
(312) 787-0977

Reading Horizons
College of Education, Western
Michigan University, Kalamazoo,
MI 49008
(616) 387-3470

Reading Improvement
Project Innovation, 1362 Santa Cruz
Court, Chula Vista, CA 92010

Reading Psychology
Taylor & Francis, 1900 Frost Road,
Suite 101, Bristol, PA 19007-1598
(800) 821-8312

Reading Research and Instruction
College Reading Association,
Department of Curriculum &
Instruction, Pittsburg State
University, Pittsburg, KS 66762
(316) 235-4494

Reading Research Quarterly
International Reading Association,
Inc., 800 Barksdale Road, Box 8139,
Newark, DE 19714-8139
(302) 731-1600

Reading Teacher
International Reading Association,
Inc., 800 Barksdale Road, Box 8139,
Newark, DE 19714-8139
(302) 731-1600

Rural Special Education Quarterly
National Rural Project, Western
Washington University,
Bellingham, WA 98225
(206) 676-3576

School Arts
Davis Publications Inc, 50 Portland
Street, Printers Building, Worcester,
MA 01608
(508) 754-7201

The School Counselor
American Association for
Counseling Development, 5999
Stevenson Avenue, Alexandria, VA
22304
(703) 823-9800

*School Library Media Folders of Ideas
for Library Excellence*
Libraries Unlimited, Inc., Box 3988,
Englewood, CO 80155-3988

Science and Children
National Science Teachers
Association, 1742 Connecticut
Avenue NW, Washington, D.C.
20009
(202) 328-5800

Social Studies and the Young Learner
National Council for the Social
Studies, 3501 Newark Street, NW,
Washington, D.C. 20016
(202) 966-7840

Teaching Exceptional Children
Council for Exceptional Children,
1920 Association Drive, Reston, VA
22091
(703) 620-3660

Teaching Pre K–8
Early Years, Inc., 325 Post Road
West, Westport, CT 06880

Urban Education
SAGE Publications Inc, 2111 West
Hillcrest Drive, Newbury Park, CA
91320
(805) 499-0721

Free Resources

Apple Education News
Apple Computer, Inc.,
10381 Bandley Drive,
Cupertino, CA 95014
(408) 974-2552

G P N Educational Video Catalog,
Elementary-Secondary
Great Plains National Instructional
Television Library, Box 80669,
Lincoln, NE 68501
(402) 472-2007

Journal of Outdoor Education
Journal of Outdoor Education c/o
The Editor, Box 299, Oregon, IL
61061
(815) 732-2111

Educators Grade Guide to Free
Teaching Aids ($44.95)
Educators Guide to Free Films,
Filmstrips, and Slides ($32.95)
Educators Guide to Free Guidance
Materials ($28.95)
Educators Guide to Free Health,
Physical Education & Recreation
Materials ($27.95)

Educators Guide to Free Science
Materials ($27.95)
Educators Guide to Free Social
Studies Materials ($28.95)
Educators Guide to Free Videotapes
($27.95)
Educators Index of Free Materials
($46.95)
All from
Educators Progress Service Inc,
214 Center Street, Randolph, WI
53956
(414) 326-3126 (plus $3.95 per guide
for postage and handling)

Professional Organizations

American Alliance for Health, Physical Education, Recreation and Dance (AAHPERD)
1900 Association Dr., Reston, VA 22091
(703) 476-3400
http://www.aahperd.org

American Association of Physics Teachers (AAPT)
5112 Berwyn Rd., College Park, MD 20740
(301) 345-4200
http://www.aapt.org

American Association of School Administrators (AASA)
1801 N. Moore St., Arlington, VA 22209
(703) 528-0700
http://www.aasa.org

American Association of Teachers of French (AATF)
57 E. Armory Ave., Champaign, IL 61820
(217) 333-2842
http://www.aatf.org

American Association of Teachers of Spanish and Portuguese (AATSP)
PO Box 6349, Mississippi State, MS 39762
(601) 325-2041
http://www.aatsp.org

American Montessori Society (AMS)
150 5th Ave., Ste. 203, New York, NY 10011
(212) 924-3209

American Schools Association (ASA)
3069 Amwiler Rd., Ste. 4, Atlanta, GA 30360
(404) 449-7141
http://www.asa.org

American String Teachers Association (ASTA)
4020 McEwen, No. 105, Dallas, TX 75244
(214) 233-3116
http://www.asta.org

American Vocational Association (AVA)
1410 King St., Alexandria, VA 22314
(703) 683-3111
http://www.ava.org

Association for Childhood Education International (ACEI)
11501 Georgia Ave., Ste. 312 Wheaton, MD 20902
(301) 942-2443

Association for Supervision and Curriculum Development (ASCD)
1250 N. Pitt St., Alexandria, VA 22314-1403
(703) 549-9110
http://www.ascd.org/

Association for World Travel Exchange (AWTE)
38 W. 88th St., New York, NY 10024
(212) 787-7706

Business Professionals of America
5454 Cleveland Ave., Columbus, OH 43231
(614) 895-7277

College Reading and Learning Association (CRLA)
Chemekata Community College, PO Box 14007 Salem, OR 97309
(503) 399-2556
http://www.crla.org

Council for Children with Behavioral Disorders (CCBD)
c/o Council for Exceptional Children 1920 Association Dr., Reston, VA 22091-1589
(703) 620-3660
http://www.ccbd.org

Council for Exceptional Children (CEC)
1920 Association Dr., Reston, VA 22091-1589
(703) 620-3660
http://www.cec.sped.org

Cousteau Society, The (TCS)
870 Greenbriar Cir., Ste. 402, Chesapeake, VA 23320
(804) 523-9335

Distributive Education Clubs of America (DECA)
1908 Association Dr., Reston, VA 22091
(703) 860-5000

Division on Mental Retardation of the Council for Exceptional Children (CEC-MR)
245 Cedar Springs Dr., Athens, GA 30605
(706) 546-6132
http://www.cec.sped.org

Earthwatch
680 Mt. Auburn St., Box 403, Watertown, MA 02272
(617) 926-8200

Educational Theatre Association (ETA)
3368 Central Pky., Cincinnati, OH 45225-2392
(513) 559-1996

Federation Internationale des Mouvements d'Ecole Moderne (FIMEM)
Wilhelm-Leuschnerstrasse 6B, W-4350 Recklinghausen, Germany 2361-42501

Future Homemakers of America
1910 Association Dr., Reston, VA 22091
(703) 476-4900

German Teachers Association (GTA)
Nordstrasse 53, W-5300 Bonn 1, Germany
(228) 231266

International Reading Association (IRA)
800 Barksdale Rd., PO Box 8139 Newark, DE 19714-8139
(302) 731-1600
http://www.ira.org

International Thespian Society (ITS)
3368 Central Pky., Cincinnati, OH 45225-2392
(513) 559-1996

Investment Education Institute (IEI)
1515 E. 11 Mile Rd., Royal Oak, MI 48067
(313) 543-0612

Junior Achievement
1 Education Way
Colorado Springs, CO 80906
(719) 540-8000
http://www.ja.org

Music Teachers National Association (MTNA)
617 Vine St., Ste. 1432
Cincinnati, OH 45202
(513) 421-1420

National Art Education Association (NAEA)
1916 Association Dr., Reston, VA 22091-1590
(703) 860-8000

National Association for the Education of Young Children (NAEYC)
1834 Connecticut Ave. NW Washington, D.C. 20009
(202) 232-8777
http://www.naeyc.org/

National Association for Girls and Women in Sport (NAGWS)
1900 Association Dr., Reston, VA 22091
(703) 476-3450

National Association for Sport and Physical Education (NASPE)
1900 Association Dr., Reston, VA 22091
(703) 476-3410

National Association of Elementary School Principals (NAESP)
1615 Duke St., Alexandria, VA 22314
(703) 684-3345
http://www.naesp.org

National Association of Partners in Education (NAPE)
209 Madison St., Ste. 401 Alexandria, VA 22314
(703) 836-4880

National Association of Secondary School Principals (NASSP)
1904 Association Dr., Reston, VA 22091
(703) 860-0200
http://www.nassp.org

National Association of Student Activity Advisers (NASAA)
1904 Association Dr., Reston, VA 22090
(703) 860-0200

National Business Education Association (NBEA)
1914 Association Dr., Reston, VA 22091
(703) 860-8300
http://www.nbea.org

National Catholic Educational Association (NCEA)
1077 30th St. NW, Ste. 100 Washington, D.C. 20007
(202) 337-6232
http://www.ncea.org

National Council for the Social Studies (NCSS)
3501 Newark St. NW Washington, D.C. 20016
(202) 966-7840
http://www.ncss.org

National Council of Teachers of English (NCTE)
1111 Kenyon Rd., Urbana, IL 61801
(217) 328-3870
http://www.ncte.org

National Council of Teachers of Mathematics (NCTM)
1906 Association Dr., Reston, VA 22091-1593
(703) 620-9840
http://www.nctm.org

National FFA Organization (NFFAO)
National FFA Center, Box 15160, 5632 Mt. Vernon Memorial Hwy. Alexandria, VA 22309-0160
(703) 360-3600
http://www.agriculture.com/contents/FFA/index.html

National Forensic League (NFL)
PO Box 38, Ripon, WI 54971
(414) 748-6206

National Head Start Association
(NHSA)
201 N. Union St., Ste. 320
Alexandria VA 22314
(703) 739-0875
http://www.nhsa.org

National Middle School
Association (NMSA)
4807 Evanswood Dr.,
Columbus, OH 43229
(614) 848-8211
http://www.nmsa.org

National PTA — National Congress
of Parents and Teachers
700 N. Rush St., Chicago, IL 60611
(312) 787-0977
http://www.pta.org

National Science Teachers
Association (NSTA)
1742 Connecticut Ave. NW
Washington, D.C. 20009-1171
(202) 328-5800
http://www.nsta.org

National Student Nurses'
Association (NSNA)
555 W. 57th St., Ste. 1327
New York, NY 10019
(212) 581-2211
http://www.nsna.org/

National Vocational Agricultural
Teachers' Association (NVATA)
PO Box 15440,
Alexandria, VA 22309
(703) 780-1862

Plymouth Rock Foundation (PRF)
Fisk Mill, PO Box 577
Marlborough, NH 03455
(603) 876-4685

Quest International
537 Jones Rd., PO Box 566
Granville, OH 43023-0566
(614) 552-6400

Teachers of English to Speakers of
Other Languages (TESOL)
1600 Cameron St., Ste. 300
Alexandria, VA 22314-2751
(703) 836-0774
http://www.tesol.edu/.

Technology Student Association
(TSA)
1914 Association Dr.,
Reston, VA 22091
(703) 860-9000

Vocational Industrial Clubs of
America (VICA)
PO Box 3000, Leesburg, VA 22075
(703) 777-8810

Current Minimum Requirements for Earning an Initial Certificate for Teaching Public Elementary and Secondary Schools

State	College B.A. Degree	General Ed. as Specified by SEA	Pedagogical Studies as Specified by SEA	Studies of Subject Matter as Specified by SEA	Pedagogical Studies as Specified by SEA	Basic Skills in Reading	Basic Skills in Mathematics	Basic Skills in Writing	Examination of Teaching Proficiency	Examination of Subject Matter Knowledge	Other
	1	2	3	4	5	6	7	8	9	10	11
Alabama	x	x	x	x	x	x	x	x		x	(1)
Alaska	x										
Arizona	x	x	x	x	x	x	x^1	x^1	x		
Arkansas	x	x	x	x	x					x	(1)
California	x			x	x	x	x	x		x^1	
Colorado	x	x	x	x	x		x	(2)			(1)
Connecticut	x	x			x	x^1	x^1				
Delaware	x					x	x	x			(1)
Dist. of Columbia	x	x	x	x	x						
Florida	x	x		x	x	x	x	x	x		
Georgia	x	x	x	x	x	x^1	x^1			x^2	
Hawaii	x					x	x	x			
Idaho	x	x	x	x	x	x^1					
Illinois	x	x	x	x	x						
Indiana	x	x	x	x	x						
Iowa	x	x	x	x	x						
Kansas	x	x	x	x	x				x^1		
Kentucky	x	x		x	x	x	x	x	x^1	x^1	

	College B.A. Degree	General Ed. as Specified by SEA	Pedagogical Studies as Specified by SEA	Studies of Subject Matter as Specified by SEA	Pedagogical Studies as Specified by SEA	Basic Skills in Reading	Basic Skills in Mathematics	Basic Skills in Writing	Examination of Teaching Proficiency	Examination of Subject Matter Knowledge	Other
Louisiana	x	x		x						x	
Maine	x	x		x^1	x	x^2					
Maryland	x	x^1		x	x						
Massachusetts	x			x	x						
Michigan	x	x	x	x	x						
Minnesota	x	x	x	x^1	x	x^2	x^2	x^2			
Mississippi	x	x	x^1	x	x	x	x	x	x	x	(2)
Missouri	x	x	x	x	x						
Montana	x	x	x	x	x	x	x^1	x			
Nebraska	x	x	x	x	x	x	x	x		x	
Nevada	x	x	x	x	x	x	x^1	x		x^2	
New Hampshire	x	x	x	x	x	x	x	x			
New Jersey	x	x	x	x	x	x	x	x	x	x^1	
New Mexico	x					x	x	x			
New York	x			x^1	x	x^2					
N. Carolina	x	x	x	x	x	x	x	x	x	x	
N. Dakota	x	x	x	x	x						(1)
Ohio	x	x		x	x	x	x	x		x^1	(2)
Oklahoma	x	x	x	x	x	x^1	x^1	x^1		x	
Oregon	x			x	x	x	x^1	x			
Pennsylvania	x										(1)
Rhode Island	x			x^1							
S. Carolina	x	x	x	x	x	x	x	x		x	
S. Dakota	x	x	x	x	x						
Tennessee	x	x	x	x	x	x	x	x			(1)
Texas	x	x		x	x	x^1	x^1	x^1		(2)	
Utah	x	x		x	x						(1)
Vermont	x	x	x	x	x	x	x	x			
Virginia	x	x	x	x	x	x	x	x	x	x	
Washington	x	x	x	x	x	x	x	x	x^1	x^1	
W. Virginia	x	x		x	x	x	x^1				
Wisconsin	x	x	x	x	x						
Wyoming	x	x	x	x	x						

Footnotes

Alabama
1. Exam of knowledge of concepts common to all teaching areas (including mainstreaming).

Arizona
1. Elementary level only.

Arkansas
1. NTE Professional Knowledge for both Elementary and Secondary.

California
1. Exempted from exam if completed a Commission-approved subject matter program.

Colorado
1. Six semester hours of recent course work (within the past five years).
2. Basic skills in oral English and written English but no writing sample required.

Connecticut
1. Elementary level only.

Delaware
1. Vocational Ed Skills Test for Secondary Vocational Ed Program.

Georgia
1. Elementary level only.
2. On-the-job assignment for both levels.

Idaho
1. Elementary level only.

Kansas
1. Examination required beginning May 1986.

Kentucky
1. Effective 1985–86 school year and thereafter.

Maine
1. Secondary level only.
2. Elementary level only.

Minnesota
1. Secondary level only.
2. Elementary level only.

Mississippi
1. Elementary level only.
2. National Teachers' Exam.

Montana
1. Elementary level only.

Nevada
1. Elementary level only.
2. Exams are given at the I.H.E (Institute of Higher Education).

New Jersey

1. As of September 1, 1985.

New York

1. Secondary level only.
2. Elementary level only.

North Dakota

1. North Dakota Native American Studies.

Ohio

1. Secondary level only.
2. Applicants for both Elementary and Secondary Certificates must complete an approved program.

Oklahoma

1. Student must show proficiency in reading, writing, and mathematics prior to admission to an approved program. The college assesses for those skills.

Oregon

1. Elementary level only.

Pennsylvania

1. Completion of an approved program and a recommendation by a college are required. Currently Pennsylvania's teacher certification standards are being revised. More specific requirements may be established in the future.

Rhode Island

1. Secondary level only.

Tennessee

1. All three sections of the NTE Commons Exam.

Texas

1. As of May 1, 1984, Pass/Fail level on these tests is required for admission to the institution's program.
2. Certification examinations are required at all levels as of May 1, 1986.

Utah

1. Metric competencies and reading/reading in content fields.

Washington

1. These exams are not formal, uniform state examinations. Rather, an assessment in the programs.

West Virginia

1. Elementary level only.

Education Agencies and Certification Offices (by state)

Note: Be sure to address correspondence to the State Teacher Certification office.

Alabama
Department of Education
Gordon Persons Office Building
50 North Ripley Street
Montgomery, AL 36130-3901
(205) 242-9977
http://www.alsde.edu

Alaska
Department of Education
P.O. Box F
801 West 10th Street, Suite 200
Juneau, AK 99801-1894
(907) 465-2810
http://www.educ.state.ak.us

American Samoa
Department of Education
Pago Pago, AS 96799
(OS) 684-633-5237
none

Arizona
Department of Public Instruction
P.O. Box 25609
1535 West Jefferson
Phoenix, AZ 85002
(602) 542-4368
http://ade.state.az.us

Arkansas
Department of Education
4 State Capitol Mall
Little Rock, AR 72201-1071
(501) 682-4342
http://arkedu.ik12.ar.us/

California
Department of Education
721 Capitol Mall
Sacramento, CA 95814
(916) 657-5485
http://goldmine.cde.ca.gov

Commission on Teaching
Credentialing
Box 944270
Sacramento, CA 94244-7000
(916) 445-7254
http://goldmine.cde.ca.gov

Colorado
Department of Education
210 E. Colfax Avenue
Denver, CO 80203
(303) 866-6628
http://www.
cde.state.co.us

Connecticut
Department of Education
Box 2219
Hartford, CT 06145-2219
(203) 566-5201
http://www.aces.k12.ct.us/csdf

Delaware
Department of Public Instruction
P.O. Box 1402, Townsend Bldg. No.
279
Federal and Lockeman Streets
Dover, DE 19903
(302) 739-4688
http://www.dpi.state.de.us

Department of Defense
Dependents Schools
Department of Defense
Office of Dependents Schools
1225 Jefferson Davis Hall
Crystal Gateway #2, Suite 1500
Alexandria, VA 22202
(703) 746-7844
http://www.ed.gov/pubs/
AchGoal/1/dod.html

District of Columbia
Division of State Services Teacher
Education
415 12th Street, N.W., Room 1013
Washington, D.C. 20004
(202) 724-4246
http://www.K12.dc.us

Florida
Department of Education
Room PL 08, Capitol Bldg.
Tallahassee, FL 32301
(904) 487-1785
http://www.firn.edu/doe/
index.html

Bureau of Teacher Certification
Florida Education Center
325 W. Gaines, Room 201
Tallahassee, FL 32399
(904) 488-2317
http://www.firn.edu/doe/
index.html

Georgia
Department of Education
2066 Twin Towers East
Atlanta, GA 30334-5020
(404) 657-9000
http://www.doe.k12.ga.us

Guam
Department of Education
P.O. Box DE
Agana, GM 96910
(OS) 671-472-8901
none

Hawaii
Department of Education
P.O. Box 2360
Honolulu, HI 96804
(808) 586-3420
http://www.K12.hi.us

Idaho
Department of Education
L.B. Jordan Office Bldg.
650 West State Street
Boise, ID 83720-3650
(208) 334-3475
http://www.sde.state.id.us

Illinois
Board of Education
100 North First Street
Springfield, IL 62777
(217) 782-4321
http://www.isbe.state.il.us

Indiana
Teacher Licensing
251 East Ohio Street, Suite 201
Indianapolis, IN 46204-2133
(317) 232-9010
http://www.doe.state.in.us

Department of Education
Room 229, State House
Indianapolis, IN 46204-2798
(317) 232-6665
http://www.doe.state.in.us

Iowa
Department of Education
Grimes State Office Bldg.
East 14th and Grand Streets
Des Moines, IA 50319-0147
(515) 281-3245
http://www.state.ia.us/educate

Kansas
Department of Education
Kansas State Education Bldg.
120 East 10th Street
Topeka, KS 66612-1182
(913) 296-2288
http://www.ksbe.state.ks.us

Kentucky
Department of Education
18th Floor-Capital Plaza Tower
500 Mero Street
Frankfort, KY 40601
(502) 564-4606
http://www.kde.state.ky.us

Louisiana
Department of Education
P.O. Box 94064
Baton Rouge, LA 70804-9064
(504) 342-3490
http://www.doe.state.la.us

Maine
Department of Education
State House Station 23
Augusta, ME 04333
(207) 287-5944
http://www.state.me.us/
education/homepage.htm

Maryland
Department of Education
200 West Baltimore Street
Baltimore, MD 20201
(301) 333-2142
http://sailor.lib.md.us/msde

Massachusetts
Department of Education
350 Main Street
Malden, MA 02148
(617) 770-7517
http://info.doe.mass.edu

Michigan
Department of Education
P.O. Box 30008
Lansing, MI 48909
(517)373-3310
http://www.mde.state.mi.us

Minnesota
Department of Education
616 Capitol Square Bldg.
St. Paul, MN 55101

(612) 296-2046
http://www.educ.state.mn.us

Mississippi
Department of Education
Box 771
550 High Street
Jackson, MS 39205-0771
(601) 359-3483
http://mdek12.state.ms.us

Missouri
Department of Elementary and
Secondary Education
P.O. Box 480
205 Jefferson Street
Jefferson City, MO 65102
(314) 751-0051
http://services.dese.state.mo.us

Montana
Office of Public Instruction
P.O. Box 202501
106 State Capitol
Helena, MT 59620-2501
(406) 444-3150
http://161.7.114.15/OPI/OPIHTML

Nebraska
Department of Education
301 Centennial Mall South
Box 94987
Lincoln, NE 68509-4987
(800) 371-4642
http://www.NDE.State.NE.US

Nevada
Department of Education
1850 E. Sahara, Suite 200
Las Vegas, NV 89158
(702) 386-5401
fsouth@nsn.k12.unr.edu (email only
for Nevada)

New Hampshire
Department of Education
101 Pleasant Street
State Office Park South
Concord, NH 03301
(603) 271-2407
http://www.state.nh.us/doe/
education.html

New Jersey
Department of Education
CN 503

Trenton, NJ 08625-0503
(609) 292-2070
http://www.state.nj.us/education

New Mexico
Department of Education
Education Building
300 Don Gaspar
Santa Fe, NM 87501-2786
(505) 827-6587
http://sde.state.nm.us

New York
Office of Teaching
Room 5A11-CEC
State Education Department
Albany, NY 12230
(518) 474-3901
http://www.nysed.gov

North Carolina
Department of Public Instruction
301 North Wilmington Street
Raleigh, NC 27601-2825
(919) 733-4125
http://www.dpi.state.nc.us

North Dakota
Department of Public Instruction
State Capitol Building, 11th Floor
600 Boulevard Avenue East
Bismarck, ND 58505-0440
(701) 224-2264
http://www.sendit.nodak.edu/dpi

Northern Mariana Islands
Department of Education
Commonwealth of the Northern
Mariana Islands
P.O. Box 1370 CK
Saipan, MP 96950
(OS) 670-322-6451
none

Ohio
Department of Education
65 South Front Street, Room 1012
Columbus, OH 43266-0308
(614) 466-3593
http://www.ode.ohio.gov

Oklahoma
Professional Standards
Department of Education

Oliver Hodge Memorial Education
Building
2500 North Lincoln Boulevard,
Room 211
Oklahoma City, OK 73105-4599
(405) 521-3337
http://sde.state.ok.us

Oregon
Teacher Standards and Practices
Commission
630 Center Street, N.E., Suite 200
Salem, OR 97310
(503) 378-3586
http://www/ode.state.or.us

Department of Education
700 Pringle Parkway, S.E.
Salem, OR 97310-0290
(503) 378-3573
http://www/ode.state.or.us

Pennsylvania
Department of Education
333 Market Street, 10th Floor
Harrisburg, PA 17126-0333
(717) 787-2967
http://www/cas.psu.edu/pde.html

Puerto Rico
Department of Education
P.O. Box 759
Hato Rey, PR 00919
(809) 751-5372
none

Rhode Island
Department of Education
22 Hayes Street
Providence, RI 02908
(401) 277-2675
http://instruct.ride.ri.net/ride home
page.html

South Carolina
Department of Education
10006 Rutledge Building
1429 Senate Street
Columbia, SC 29201
(803) 734-8492
http://www.state.sc.us/sde

Office of Education Professions
Teacher Certification Section
1015 Rutledge Building

Columbia, SC 29201
(803) 774-8466
http://www.state.sc.us/sde

South Dakota
Teacher Education & Certification
Department of Education
700 Governors Drive
Pierre, SD 57501-2291
(605) 773-3553
http://www.state.sd.us/state/
executive/deca/

Tennessee
Department of Education
100 Cordell Hull Building
Nashville, TN 37243-0375
(615) 741-2731
http://www.state.tn.us/other/sde/
homepage.htm

Office of Teacher Licensing
710 James Robertson Parkway
5th Floor, Gateway Plaza
Nashville, TN 37243-0377
(615) 741-1644
http://www.state.tn.us/other/sde/
homepage.htm

Texas
Texas Education Agency
William B. Travis Building
1701 North Congress Avenue
Austin, TX 78701-1494
(512) 463-8976
http://www.tea.texas.gov

Utah
Office of Education
250 East 500 South Street
Salt Lake City, UT 84111
(801) 538-7740
http://www.usoe.k12.ut.us

Vermont
Department of Education
120 State Street
Montpelier, VT 05602-2703
(802) 828-2445
http://www.state.vt.us/educ

Virgin Islands
Department of Education
44-46 Kogens Gade
Charlotte Amalie, VI 00802

(809) 774-2810
none

Virginia
Department of Education
James Monroe Building
Fourteenth and Franklin Streets
P.O. Box 6-Q
Richmond, VA 23216-2120
(804) 225-2755
http://www.pen.k12.va.us/go/
VDOE

Office of Professional Licensure
Department of Education
P.O. Box 2120
Richmond VA 23216-2120
(804) 225-2022
http://www.pen.k12.va.us/go/
VDOE

Washington
Department of Public Instruction
Old Capitol Building
P.O. Box 47200
Olympia, WA 98504-7200
(206) 753-6773
http://www.ospi.wednet.edu

West Virginia
Department of Education
Building 6, Room 337
1900 Kanawha Blvd., East
Charleston, WV 25305-0330
(800) 982-2378
http://access.k12.wv.us

Wisconsin
Teacher Education, Licensing and
Placement
Department of Public Instruction

Box 7841
125 South Webster Street
Madison, WI 53707-7841
(608) 266-1027
http://badger.state.wi.us/agencies/
dpi

Wyoming
Department of Education
2300 Capitol Avenue
Hathaway Building, 2nd Floor
Cheyenne, WY 82002
(307) 777-7291
http://www.k12.wy.us/
wdehome.html

U.S. Department of Education
www.ed.gov

Canadian Education Agencies

Employment & Immigration
Canada
Public Inquiries Centre
Public Affairs Branch
140 Promenade du Portage,
Phase IV
Hull PQ K1A OJ9
(819) 994-6313

Statistics Canada
Statistical Reference Centre (NCR)
Ottawa, ON K1A OT6
(613) 951-8116

Alta.: Alberta Education
Communications Branch
Devonian Bldg.
11160 Jasper Ave., 2nd Floor
Edmonton, AB T5K OL2
(403) 427-2285

Alberta Advanced Education &
Career Development
City Centre
10155 - 102 St., 7th Floor
Edmonton, AB T5J 4L5
(403) 422-4495

B.C.: Ministry of Education #325
620 Superior Street
Victoria, BC V8V 1X4
(604) 356-2500

Man.: Manitoba Education &
Training #221
1200 Portage Avenue
Winnipeg, MB R3G OT5
(204) 945-6176

N.B.: Department of Education
P.O. Box 6000
Fredericton, NB E3B 5H1
(506) 453-3678

Nfld.: Department of Education
Information Officer
Confederation Building
P.O. Box 8700
St. John's, NF A1B 4J6
(709) 729-5097

N.S.: Department of Education,
Publication & Communication
P.O. Box 578
Trade Mart
Halifax, NS B3J 2S9
(902) 424-5570

Ont.: Ministry of Education &
Training,
Communications & Marketing
Branch
Mowat Block
900 Bay Street, 14th Floor
Toronto, ON M7A 1L2
(416) 325-2929

Toll Free: 1-800-387-5514
TDD: 1-800-263-2892

P.E.I.: Department of Education &
Human Resources
P.O. Box 2000
Charlottetown, PE C1A 7N8
(902) 368-4600

Que.: Ministere del'Education,
Direction
des communications, 11e etage
1035 De La Chevrotiere
Quebec, PQ G1R 5A5
(418) 643-7095

Sask.: Saskatchewan Education,
Training & Employment, Inquiries
2220 College Avenue
Regina, SK S4P 3V7
(306) 787-6030

N.W.T.: Department of Education
Culture & Employment
P.O. Box 1320
Yellowknife, NT X1A 2L9
(403) 873-7529

Yukon: Yukon Education
P.O. Box 2703
Whitehorse, YT Y1A 2C6
(403) 667-5141

Directory of Chief State School Offices

Alabama
Superintendent of Education
State Department of Education
Gordon Persons Office Building
50 North Ripley St
Montgomery, AL 36130-3901
(205) 242-9700
Term of office: Appointed by the state board of education for a four-year term.

Alaska
Commissioner of Education
State Department of Education
Alaska State Office Building
Pouch F
Juneau, AK 99811
(907) 465-2800
Term of office: Appointed by the state board of education with the concurrence of the governor and serving at the will of the board.

Arizona
Superintendent of Public Instruction
State Department of Education
1535 W. Jefferson St.
Phoenix, AZ 85007
(602) 542-4361
Term of office: Elected by popular vote for a four-year term.

Arkansas
Director, General Education Division

State Department of Education
Four State Capitol Mall, Room 304A
Little Rock, AR 72201-1071
(501) 682-4204
Term of office: Appointed by the state board of education and serving at the will of the governor.

California
Superintendent of Public Instruction
State Department of Education
721 Capitol Mall
Sacramento, CA 95814
(916) 657-5485

Colorado
Commissioner of Education
State Department of Education
201 East Colfax Ave.
Denver, CO 80203-1706
(303) 866-8805
Term of office: Appointed by the state board of education and serving at the will of the board.

Connecticut
Commissioner of Education
State Department of Education
165 Capitol Ave.
Room 305, State Office Building
Hartford, CT 06106
(203) 566-5061
Term of office: Appointed by the state board of education and confirmed by the governor.

Delaware
Superintendent of Public Instruction
State Department of Public Instruction
P.O. Box 1402 Townsend Building, #279
Federal and Locherman Sts.
Dover, DE 19903
(302) 739-4601
Term of office: Appointed by the state board of education and serving at the will of the board.

District of Columbia
Superintendent of Public Schools
District of Columbia Public Schools
415 12th St., NW
Washington, D.C. 20004
(202) 724-4222
Term of office: Appointed by the school board for a three-year term.

Florida
Commissioner of Education
State Department of Education
Capitol Building, Room PL 08
Tallahassee, FL 32301
(904) 487-1785
Term of office: Elected by popular vote for a four-year term.

Georgia
Superintendent of Schools
State Department of Education
2066 Twin Towers East

Reprinted with permission from *Education Week*, Vol. 12, No. 23, March 3, 1993.

205 Butler St.
Atlanta, GA 30334
(404) 656-2800
Term of office: Elected by popular
vote for a four-year term.

Hawaii
Superintendent of Education
Department of Education
1390 Miller St., #307
Honolulu, HI 96804
(808) 586-3230
Term of office: Appointed by the
state board of education and
serving at the will of the board.

Idaho
Superintendent of Public
Instruction
State Department of Education
Len B. Jordan Office Building
650 West State St.
Boise, ID 83720
(208) 334-3300
Term of office: Elected by popular
vote for a four-year term.

Illinois
Superintendent of Education
State Department of Education
100 North First St.
Springfield, IL 62777
(217) 782-2221
Term of office: Appointed by the
state board of education and
serving at the will of the board.

Indiana
Superintendent of Public
Instruction
State Department of Education
State House, Room 229
Indianapolis, IN 46204-2798
(317) 232-6665
Term of office: Elected by popular
vote for a four-year-term.

Iowa
Director of Education
State Department of Education
Grimes State Office Building
East 14th and Grand Sts.
Des Moines, IA 50319-0146
(515) 281-5294

Term of office: Appointed by the
governor and serving at the will of
the governor.

Kansas
Commissioner of Education
State Department of Education
120 South East 10th St.
Topeka, KS 66612
(913) 296-3202
Term of office: Appointed by the
state board of education and
serving at the will of the board.

Kentucky
Commissioner of Education
State Department of Education
Capitol Plaza Tower
500 Metro St.
Frankfort, KY 40601
(502) 564-3141
Term of office: Serving under a
contract with the state board of
education.

Louisiana
Superintendent of Education
State Department of Education
626 North Fourth St.
P.O. Box 94064
Baton Rouge, LA 70804-9064
(504) 342-3602
Term of office: Appointed by the
state board of secondary and
elementary education.

Maine
Commissioner of Education
Maine Department of Education
State House Station 23
Augusta, ME 04333
(207) 287-5114
Term of office: Appointed by the
governor for a four-year term, and
serving a term concurrent with that
of the governor.

Maryland
Superintendent of Schools
State Department of Education
200 West Baltimore St.
Baltimore, MD 21201
(410) 333-2200

Term of office: Appointed by the
state board of education for a four-
year term.

Massachusetts
Commissioner of Education
State Department of Education
Quincy Center Plaza
1385 Hancock St.
Quincy, MA 02169
(617) 770-7321
Term of office: Appointed by the
state board and serving at the will
of the board.

Michigan
Superintendent of Public
Instruction
State Department of Education
P.O. Box 30008
608 West Allegan St.
Lansing, MI 48909
(517) 373-3354
Term of office: Appointed by the
state board of education for a three-
year term.

Minnesota
Commissioner of Education
State Department of Education
712 Capitol Square Building
550 Cedar St.
St. Paul, MN 55101
(612) 296-2358
Term of office: Appointed by the
governor for a four-year term
concurrent with that of the
governor.

Mississippi
Superintendent of Education
State Department of Education
P.O. Box 771
550 High St., Room 501
Jackson, MS 39205-0771
(601) 359-3513
Term of office: Appointed to the
position by the board of education.

Missouri
Commissioner of Education
Department of Elementary and
Secondary Education
P.O. Box 480
205 Jefferson St., 6th Floor

Jefferson City, MO 66102
(314) 751-4446
Term of office: Appointed by the state board of education and serving at the will of the board.

Montana
Superintendent of Public Instruction
State Office of Public Instruction
106 State Capitol
Helena, MT 59620
(406) 444-3680
Term of office: Elected by popular vote for a four-year term.

Nebraska
Commissioner of Education
State Department of Education
P.O. Box 94967
301 Centennial Mall, South
Lincoln, NE 68509
(402) 471-5020
Term of office: Appointed by the state board of education with a three-year contract.

Nevada
Superintendent of Public Instruction
State Department of Education
400 West King St.
Capitol Complex
Carson City, NV 89710
(702) 687-3100
Term of office: Appointed by the state board of education and serving at the discretion of the board.

New Hampshire
Commissioner of Education
State Department of Education
101 Pleasant St.
State Office Park South
Concord, NH 03301
(603) 271-3144
Term of office: Appointed by the state board of education and serving at the discretion of the board.

New Jersey
Commissioner of Education
State Department of Education

225 West State St. CN 500
Trenton, NJ 08625-0500
(609) 292-4450
Term of office: Appointed by the governor with state Senate approval.

New Mexico
Superintendent of Public Instruction
State Department of Education Building
300 Don Gasper
Santa Fe, NM 87501-2786
(505) 827-8516
Term of office: Appointed by the state board of education and serving at the discretion of the board.

New York
Commissioner of Education
State Education Department
111 Education Building
Washington Ave.
Albany, NY 12234
(518) 474-5844
Term of office: Appointed by the board of regents and serving at the discretion of the board.

North Carolina
Superintendent of Public Instruction
State Department of Public Instruction
Education Building, Room 194
116 West Edenton St.
Raleigh, NC 27603-1712
(919) 733-3813
Term of office: Elected by popular vote for a four-year term.

North Dakota
Superintendent of Public Instruction
State Department of Public Instruction
State Capitol Building 11th Floor
600 Boulevard Ave. East
Bismarck, ND 58505-0440
(701) 224-2261
Term of office: Elected by popular vote for a four-year term.

Ohio
Superintendent of Public Instruction
State Department of Education
65 South Front St., Room 808
Columbus, OH 43266-0308
(614) 466-3304
Term of office: Appointed by the state board of education and serving at the discretion of the board.

Oklahoma
Superintendent of Public Instruction
Secretary of Education
State Department of Education
Oliver Hodge Memorial Education Building
2500 North Lincoln Blvd.
Oklahoma City, OK 73105-4599
(405) 521-3301
Term of office: Elected by popular vote for a four-year term.

Oregon
Superintendent of Public Instruction
State Department of Education
700 Pringle Parkway, S.E.
Salem, OR 97310
(503) 378-3573
Term of office: Elected by popular vote for a four-year term.

Pennsylvania
Secretary of Education
State Department of Education
333 Market St., 10th Floor
Harrisburg, PA 17126-0333
(717) 787-5820
Term of office: Appointed by the governor and serving at the discretion of the governor.

Rhode Island
Commissioner of Education
State Department of Education
22 Hayes St.
Providence, RI 02908
(401) 277-2031
Term of office: Appointed by the state board of education and serving at the discretion of the board.

South Carolina
Superintendent of Education
State Department of Education
1006 Rutledge Building
1429 Senate St.
Columbia, SC 29201
(803) 734-8492
Term of office: Elected by popular vote for a four-year term.

South Dakota
Secretary of Education
Department of Education and Cultural Affairs
700 Governors Dr.
Pierre, SD 57501
(605) 773-3134
Term of office: Appointed by the state board of education and serving at the discretion of the governor.

Tennessee
Commissioner of Education
State Department of Education
100 Cordell Hull Building
Nashville, TN 37219
(615) 741-2731
Term of office: Appointed by the governor and serving concurrently with the governor's term.

Texas
Commissioner of Education
Texas Education Agency
William B. Travis Building
1701 North Congress Ave.
Austin, TX 78701-1494
(512) 463-8985
Term of office: Appointed by the state board of education for a four-year term.

Utah
Superintendent of Public Instruction
State Office of Education
250 East 500 South
Salt Lake City, UT 84111
(801) 538-7510
Term of office: Appointed by the state board of education with approval of the governor and serving at the board's discretion.

Vermont
Commissioner of Education
State Department of Education
120 State St.
Montpelier, VT 05602-2703
(802) 828-3135
Term of office: Appointed by the state board of education, with approval of the governor, and serving at the board's discretion.

Virginia
Superintendent of Public Instruction
State Department of Education
James Monroe Building
14th and Franklin Streets
Richmond, VA 23216-2060
(804) 225-2023
Term of office: Appointed by the governor and confirmed by the General Assembly for four years concurrent with the governor's term.

Washington
Superintendent of Public Instruction
State Department of Public Instruction

Old Capitol Building, Washington & Legion
P.O. Box 47200
Olympia, WA 98504
(208) 506-6904
Term of office: Elected by popular vote for a four-year term.

West Virginia
Superintendent of Schools
State Department of Education
1900 Kanawha Blvd., East
Building 6 Room B-358
Charleston, WV 25305
(304) 558-2081
Term of office: Appointed by the state board of education and serving at the discretion of the board.

Wisconsin
Superintendent of Public Instruction
State Department of Public Instruction
125 South Webster St.
Post Office Box 7841
Madison, WI 53707
(608) 266-1771
Term of office: Elected by popular vote for a four-year term.

Wyoming
Superintendent of Public Instruction
State Department of Education
2300 Capitol Avenue, 2nd Floor
Hathaway Building
Cheyenne, WY 82002-0060
(302) 777-7675
Term of office: Elected by popular vote for a four-year term.

Source: Council of Chief State School Officers.

Methods of Selecting Chief State School Officers

	Appointed by State Board of Education	Appointed by Governor	Elected by People
Alabama	X		
Alaska	X		
Arizona			X
Arkansas	X		
California			X
Colorado	X		
Connecticut	X		
Delaware	X		
Florida			X
Georgia			X
Hawaii	X		
Idaho			X
Illinois	X		
Indiana			X
Iowa		X	
Kansas	X		
Kentucky	X		
Louisiana	X		
Maine		X	
Maryland	X		
Massachusetts	X		

Source: National Association of State Boards of Education.

	Appointed by State Board of Education	Appointed by Governor	Elected by People
Michigan	X		
Minnesota		X	
Mississippi	X		
Missouri	X		
Montana			X
Nebraska	X		
Nevada	X		
New Hampshire	X		
New Jersey		X	
New Mexico	X		
New York	X		
North Carolina			X
North Dakota			X
Ohio	X		
Oklahoma			X
Oregon			X
Pennsylvania		X	
Rhode Island	X		
South Carolina			X
South Dakota	X		
Tennessee		X	
Texas		X	
Utah	X		
Vermont	X		
Virginia		X	
Washington			X
West Virginia	X		
Wisconsin			X
Wyoming			X
District of Columbia	X		

Methods of Selecting State School Board Members

	Elected by People or Representatives	Appointed by Governor	Other
Alabama	X		
Alaska		X	
Arizona	X		
Arkansas		X	
California		X	
Colorado	X		
Connecticut		X	
Delaware		X	
Florida	X		
Georgia		X	
Hawaii	X		
Idaho		X	
Illinois		X	
Indiana		X	
Iowa		X	
Kansas	X		
Kentucky		X	
Louisiana			X
Maine		X	
Maryland		X	
Massachusetts		X	

Source: National Association of State Boards of Education.

(continued on next page)

Source: National Association of State Boards of Education.

	Elected by People or Representatives	Appointed by Governor	Other
Michigan	X		
Minnesota		X	
Mississippi			X
Missouri		X	
Montana		X	
Nebraska	X		
Nevada	X		
New Hampshire		X	
New Jersey		X	
New Mexico			X
New York	X		
North Carolina		X	
North Dakota		X	
Ohio	X		
Oklahoma		X	
Oregon		X	
Pennsylvania		X	
Rhode Island		X	
South Carolina	X		
South Dakota		X	
Tennessee		X	
Texas	X		
Utah	X		
Vermont		X	
Virginia		X	
Washington	X		
West Virginia		X	
Wisconsin	(NO BOARD)		
Wyoming		X	
District of Columbia	X		

Computer Companies

Apple Computer, Inc.
20525 Mariani Avenue
Cupertino, CA 95014
(408) 996-1010

AST Computer
16215 Alton Parkway
Irvine, CA 92619-7005
(714) 727-4141

AT&T Co. Communications Group
295 N. Maple Ave.
Basking Ridge, NJ 07920
(201) 221-8851

Compaq Computer Corporation
P.O. Box 692000
Houston, TX 77269-2000
(713) 370-0670

Dell Computer Corporation
9505 Arboretum Blvd.
Austin, TX 78759-7299
(512) 728-8797

Digital Equipment Corp.
146 Main St.

Maynard, MA 01754
(617) 897-1111

Gateway 2000 Computers
610 Gateway Drive
N. Sioux City, SD 57049-2000
(605) 232-2222

Hewlett-Packard
3000 Hanover St.
Palo Alto, CA 94304
(415) 857-1501

IBM Corporation
Old Orchard Road
Armonk, NY 10504
(914) 765-1900

Leading Edge
117 Flanders Road
West Borough, MA 01581
(508) 836-4800

NEC Technologies
1414 Massachusetts Ave.
Boxboro, MA 01719
(508) 264-8000

Packard Bell
31717 La Tienda Drive
West Lake Village, CA 91362
(818) 865-1555

Panasonic Computer Products
Two Panasonic Way 76-0
Secaucus, NJ 07094
(201) 392-4500

Tandy Corporation/Radio Shack
Dept. 88-A-530
300 One Tandy Center
Fort Worth, TX 76102
(817) 390-3011

Texas Instruments, Inc.
Data Systems Group
P.O. Box 809063, DSG-163
Dallas, TX 75380
(800) 527-3500

Zenith Data Systems Corporation
2150 E. Lake Cook Rd.
Buffalo Grove, IL 60089
(708) 808-5000

Source: John H. Johansen, et al., *American Education: An Introduction to Teaching,* 7th ed. 1993. Dubuque, Iowa: Times Mirror Higher Education Group, Inc.

Educational Software Companies from A-to-Z

The following list of companies is but a small sample of the over 1,000 educational software companies listed by the PEP Registry on the World Wide Web.

Academic Software, Inc.
331 W. 2nd St.
Lexington, KY 40507
10800-842-2357
www.acsw.com

Advantage Learning Systems, Inc.
P.O. Box 8036
Wisconsin Rapids, WI 54495
1-800-338-4204
www.advlearn.com

Afrolink Software
P.O. Box 36708
Los Angeles CA 90036-0708
(213) 731-5465
www.trip.com/~griotech/
blistmac.htm

Barnum Software
3450 Lack Shore Ave, Suite 200A
Oakland, Ca 94610
1-800-553-9155
www.thequartermile.com

Broderbund Software
PO Box 6125
Novato, CA 94948-6125
800-548-1798
Educational Support Line
800-474-8840
www.broderbund.com/

Cognitive Technologies
Corporation
5009 Cloister Dr.
Rockville, MD 20852
1-800-335-0781
www.cogtech.com

COMPAQ
P.O. Box 692000
Houston, TX 77269-2000
281-370-0670
www.compaq.com

DiscoverWare Inc.
fifth floor, 926 5th ave. sw
calgary, alberta
canada T2P 0N7
403.237.0426
1.800.465.3641
www.discoverware.com

Educational Software Products
Kate Lockner & Sales Inquiries—
ESP
299 Tanager Court
Deerfield, IL 60015
1-888-377-3776
www.expexpert.com

Expert Software, Inc.
800 Douglas Road
Executive Tower
Coral Gables, Florida 33134-3160

(305) 567-9990 Phone
www.expertsoftware.com

Falcon Software, Inc.
One Hollis Street
Wellesley, MA 02181 USA
Phone (781) 235-1767
www.falconsoftware.com

Gryphon Software Corporation
7220 Trade Street
San Diego, CA 92121 USA
(619) 536-8815
Product Orders: (888) 8GRYPHON
World Wide Web:
http://www.gryphonsw.com/

Girl Tech., Inc.
Public Relations
PO Box 4062
San Rafael, CA
93913-4062
(415) 256-1510
www.girltech.com

Harcourt Brace & Company
Order Fulfillment Department
6277 Sea Harbor Drive
Orlando, FL 32887
Toll Free: 1-800-225-5425
www.hbschool.com

Source: PEP Registry of Educational Software Publishers PEP: Resources for Parents, Educators & Publishers http://www.microweb.com/pepsite/
Software/publishers.html

Houghton Mifflin
1900 S. Batavia Avenue
Geneva, IL 60134-3399
(800) 733-2828
www.eduplace.com

Info Math
1-888-math-456
www.infomath.com

IBM K-12 Education
1-800-IBM-4EDU
www.solutions.ibm.com/K12

Jon Noonan Educational Software
Box 427
Mira Loma, CA
USA 91752-0427
909-360-5944
www.pe.net/~jnes

Jostens Learning Corporation
9920 Pacific Heights Blvd.
San Diego, Ca 92121
800-521-8538
www.jlc.com

K12 Micromedia Publishing
16 Mckee Dr.
Mahwah, NJ 07430
800-292-1997
www.k12mmp.com

KnowWonder, Inc
1-888-KNOWNDR (566-9637)
www.knowwonder.com

Knowledge Revolution
66 Bovet Road, Suite 200
San Mateo, CA 94402
800-766-6615
www.krev.com

The Learning Box
4508 Valleycrest Dr.
Arlington, TX 76013
800-743-9450
www.learningbox.com

The Learning Company, Inc.
One Athenaeum Street
Cambridge, MA 02477
617.494.1200
www.learningco.com

MathMedia Educational Software,
Inc.
3100 Dundee Road, Suite 703
Northbrook Illinois 60062
1-888-FOR-MATH
www.mathmedia.com

McGraw-Hill School Division
Corporate Headquarters
1221 Avenue of the Americas
New York, NY 10020
(212) 512-2000
www.mmhschool.com

Microsoft
10700 Northrup Way
Box 97200
Bellevue, WA 98009
(206) 828-8080
www.microsoft.com

NECTAR Foundation
10 Bowhill Ave.
Nepean, Ontario
Canada K2E6S7
613-224-3031
http://spdcs.crcssb.edu.on.ca/
nectar

Nordic Software
(800)- 306-6502
www.nordiscsoftware.com

OnScreen Science, Inc.
46 Wallace St., Suite 20
Somerville, MA 02144
(800) 617-6416
www.onscreen-sci.com

Oryx Press
P.O. Box 33889
Phoenix, Arizona 85067-3889
800-279-6799
www.oryxpress.com

Paper Trail Software
P.O. Box 36262
Las Vegas, NV 89133
Voice Mail or Fax: 702-656-1950
http://www.tcd.net/~papertrl/

Point Software
P.O. Box 710
St. Petersburg, Florida 33731
(813) 896-7711
www.netizard.com

Queue, Inc.
338 Commerce Drive
Fairfield, CT 06432
203-335-0906
800-232-2224
www.queueinc.com

RJ Cooper & Associates
24843 Del Prado #283
DanaPoint, CA 92629
800-RJCooper
www.rjcooper.com

Scholastic Order Processing
2931 East McCarty Street
Jefferson City, MO 65101
800-223-4011
www.scholastic.com

Science Education Softward Inc.
(SESI)
PO Box 60790
Palo Alto, CA 94306
415-367-6457 (voice) 415-366-2744
(fax)
www.hungryfrog.com

Tom Snyder Productions
80 Coolidge Hill Road
Watertown, MA 02172
1-800-342-0236
www.techtsp.com

TeacherSoft, Inc.
903 East 18th Street, 2nd Floor
Plano, TX 75074
U.S.A.
Voice: 972-424-7882
www.teachersoft.com

Texas Learning Technology Group
Attn: Cathy Austin
P.O. Box 2947
Austin, Texas 78768-2947
1-800-580-8584, ext. 6101
www.tasb.org

Universal Learning Technology
39 Cross Street
Peabody, MA 01960
(508) 538-0036
www.cast.org

Ventura Educational Systems
P.O. Box 425
910 Ramona Avenue–Suite E

Grover Beach, Ca 93433
800-336-1022
www.venturaaes.com

Visions Technology in Education
710 N.E. Cleveland Ave.
Gresham, OR 97030 Suite 130
800-877-0858
www.visteched.com

Weaver Instructional Systems, Inc.
6161 28th Street SE
Grand Rapids, MI 49546
800-634-8916
www.wisesoft.com

WorldSoft Technical Services

775 N 1570 W
Pleasant Grove, UT 84062
(801) 796-3822 voice
www.worldsoft.com

Xavier Educational Software Ltd.
Department of Psychology
University of Wales Bangor
Gwynedd. UK. LL57 2DG.
Tel: +44 (0) 1248 382616
www.psych.bangor.ac.uk/
deptpsych/xavier/xavier.html

Xlsoft International
12K Mauchly
Irvine, CA 92618
Tel: 714-453-2781

www.xisoft.com

Yale University Press
Order Department
PO Box 209040
New Haven, CT 06520
800-987-7323
www.yale.edu

Zimgraphics, Lts.
26 Scollard Street
Toronto, Ontario, Canada M5R 1E9
(416) 929-8155, Sales—
(800) 929-8155
http://www.netusa.com/pcsoft/
library/p_1028.htm

Resources and Hotlines

AIDS Action Council & Foundation......................................(202) 986-1300
AIDS Clinical Trials Information Service...............................(800) 874-2572
AIDS Helpline (Health Professionals) ....(800) 548-4659
Al-Anon & Alateen ....(800) 356-9996
Alcoholics Anonymous ....(800) 452-7990
American Foundation for AIDS Research (AmFar)........................(212) 682-7440
American Red Cross (AIDS Education)..................................(703) 206-7180
American Suicide Foundation...(800) 531-4477
Ask A Nurse...(800) 535-1111
Boys Town ....(800) 448-3000
Bureau of Indian Affairs, Child Abuse Hotline ....(800) 633-5155
Child Find of America ....(800) 426-5678
Child Help USA National Child Abuse Hotline..........................(800) 422-4453
Child Quest International Sighting Line ....(800) 248-8020
Children's Rights of America ....(800) 442-4673
Crisis Nursery & Respite Referral....................................(800) 473-1727
Families Anonymous ....(800) 736-9805
Literacy Hotline/Department of Education ....(800) 228-8813
Names Project ....(415) 882-5500
National AIDS Hotline..(800) 342-2437
National AIDS Hotline (Hearing Impaired) ....(800) 243-7889
National AIDS Information Clearinghouse..............................(800) 458-5231
National AIDS Program Office ....(202) 690-5471
National Center for Missing & Exploited Children ....(800) 843-5678
National Clearinghouse for Alcohol & Drug Info ....(800) 729-6686
National Coalition Against Domestic Violence ....(303) 839-1852
National Cocaine Hotline...(800) 262-2463
National Council on Alcoholism and Chemical Dependency Hope Line ....(800) 622-2255
National Criminal Justice Reference Service...........................(301) 251-5500
National Family Planning & Reproductive Health Organization ....(202) 563-7742
National Foundation for Cancer Research ....(800) 321-2873
National Health Information Center ....(800) 336-4797
National Institute on Drug Abuse Hotline ....(800) 662-4357
National Mental Health Association ....(800) 433-5959
Office of Minority Health Resource Center............................(800) 444-6472
National Pediatric HIV Resource Center...............................(800) 362-0071
National Referral Network for Kids in Crisis ....(800) 543-7283
National Runaway Hotline ....(800) 621-4000

National Service Organizations

Action for Child Protection
4724C Park Rd.
Charlotte, NC 28209
(704) 529-1080
(704) 529-1132 FAX

AIDS Clinical Trials Information
Service (ACTIS)
P.O. Box 6421
Rockville, MD 20849-6421
(800) 874-2572
(800) 243-7012 Deaf Access (TTY)
(301) 217-0023 International Line
(301) 738-6616 FAX

American Academy of Child &
Adolescent Psychiatry
3615 Wisconsin Ave., N.W.
Washington, D.C. 20016
(800) 333-7636
(202) 966-2891 FAX

American Association for Marriage
& Family Therapy
1100 17th Street, N.W., 10th Floor
Washington, D.C. 20036
(202) 452-0109
(202) 223-2329 FAX

American Association on Mental
Retardation
444 North Capitol St., N.W., Suite
846
Washington, D.C. 20001-1512
(800) 424-3688
(202) 387-2193 FAX

American Association of School
Administrators
1801 North Moore Street
Arlington, VA 22209-9988
(703) 528-0700
(703) 841-1543 FAX

American Bar Association
750 North Lake Shore Dr.
Chicago, IL 60611
(800) 621-6159
Family Law Section
(312) 988-5613
(312) 988-6281 FAX

American Bar Association Center
on Children & the Law
1800 M. Street, N.W., Suite S-200
Washington, D.C. 20036
(212) 331-2250

American College of Nurse-
Midwives
818 Connecticut Ave., N.W., Suite
900
Washington, D.C. 20006
(202) 728-9860
(202) 728-9897 FAX

American Foundation for AIDS
Research (AmFAR)
733 Third Ave., 12th Floor
New York, NY 10017
(212) 682-7440
(212) 682-9812 FAX

American Foundation for the Blind
(AFB)
11 Penn Plaza, Suite 300
New York, NY 10001
(800) 232-5463
(212) 620-2158 TDD
(212) 727-7418 FAX

American Home Economics
Association
1555 King Street
Alexandria, VA 22314
(703) 706-4600
(703)706-4663 FAX

American Humane Association -
Children's Division
63 Inverness Drive East
Englewood, CO 80112-5117
(800) 227-4645
(303) 792-5333 FAX

American National Red Cross
430 17th Street, N.W.
Washington, D.C. 20006
(202) 737-8300
(202) 639-3000 FAX

American Nurses Association
600 Maryland Ave., S.W., Suite 100
West
Washington, D.C. 20024-4444
(202) 554-4444
(202) 554-2262 FAX

American Occupational Therapy
Association (AOTA)
4720 Montgomery Lane -
P.O. Box 31220
Bethesda, MD 20284-1220
(301) 652-2682
(800) 377-8555 TDD
(301) 948-5512 FAX

American Professional Society on
the Abuse of Children
407 S. Dearborn, Suite 1300
Chicago, IL 60605
(312) 554-0166
(312) 554-0919 FAX

American Psychological
Association
750 1st Street, N.E.
Washington, D.C. 20002
(800) 374-2721
(202) 336-6069 FAX

American Public Health Association
1015 15th Street, N.W., Suite 300
Washington, D.C. 20005
(202) 789-5600
(202) 789-5661 FAX

American Public Welfare
Association
810 1st Street, N.E., Suite 500
Washington, D.C. 20002-4267
(202) 682-0100
(202) 289-6555 FAX

American Social Health Association
P.O. Box 13827
Research Triangle Park, NC 27709
(919) 361-8400
(919) 361-8425 FAX

American Society for Adolescent
Psychiatry
4330 East West Highway, Suite 1117
Bethesda, MD 20814-4408
(301) 718-6502
(301) 656-0989 FAX

American Speech-Language-
Hearing Association (ASHA)
10801 Rockville Pike
Rockville, MD 20852
(800) 638-8255
(301) 571-0457 FAX

American Youth Work Center
1200 17th St., N.W. 4th Floor
Washington, D.C. 20036
(202) 785-0764
(202) 728-0657 FAX

Armed Services YMCA of the USA
6225 Brandon Ave., Suite 215
Springfield, VA 22150-2510
(703) 866-1260
(703) 866-9215 FAX

Association for the Advancement of
Rehabilitation Technology (RESNA)
1700 N. Moore St., Suite 1540
Arlington, VA 22200
(703) 524-6686
(703) 524-6630 FAX

Association on American Indian
Affairs, Inc.
245 5th Ave., Suite 1801
New York, NY 10016
(800) 895-2242
(212) 685-4692 FAX

Association for the Care of
Children's Health
7910 Woodmont Ave., Suite 300
Bethesda, MD 20814-3015
(301) 654-6549
(301) 986-4553 FAX

Association for Childhood
Education International
11501 Georgia Ave., Suite 315
Wheaton, MD 20902
(800) 423-3563

Association on Mental Retardation
(ARC)
P.O. Box 1047
Arlington, TX 76004
(817) 261-6003
(817) 277-0553 TDD

Association for Persons with Severe
Handicaps
(206) 361-8870

Autism Society of America
7910 Woodmont Ave., Suite 650
Bethesda, MD 20814
(800) 328-8476

Big Brothers/Big Sisters of America
230 North 13th Street
Philadelphia, PA 19107
(215) 567-7000
(215) 567-0394 FAX

Boys & Girls Clubs of America
1230 W. Peachtree Street
Atlanta, GA 30309
(404) 815-5700

Boy Scouts of America
P.O. Box 152079
1325 Walnut Hill Lane
Irving, TX 75015-2079
(214) 580-2000
(214) 580-2502 FAX

Boys Town National Research
Hospital
555 North 30th Street
Omaha, NE 68131
(402) 498-6511
(402) 498-6638 FAX

The Bureau of At Risk Youth
645 New York Ave.
Huntington, NY 11743
(800) 999-6884
(516) 673-4544 FAX

Business Responds to AIDS
Resource Services (BRTA)
P.O. Box 6003
Rockville, MD 20849
(800) 458-5231
(800) 243-7012 Deaf Access Line
(TDD)

Camp Fire Boys & Girls
4601 Madison Ave.
Kansas, City, MO 64112
(800) 669-6884
(816) 756-0258 FAX

The Annie E. Casey Foundation
701 St. Paul Street
Baltimore, MD 21202
(401) 547-6600

Catholic Charities USA
1731 King Street, Suite 200
Alexandria, VA 22314
(703) 549-1390
(703) 549-1656 FAX

Center for the Study of Social Policy
1250 Eye Street, N.W., Suite 503
Washington, D.C. 20005
(202) 371-1565
(202) 371-1472 FAX

Center for the Study of Youth Policy
University of PA
School of Social Work
4200 Pine Street, 2nd Floor
Philadelphia, PA 19104-4090
(215) 898-2229
(215) 573-2791 FAX

Child Find of America, Inc.
P.O. Box 277
New Paltz, NY 12561
(800) 426-5678
(914) 255-5706 FAX

CHILDHELP USA
6463 Independence Ave.
Woodland Hills, CA 91367
(818) 347-7280
(800) 422-4453 HOTLINE
(818) 593-3257 FAX

Child Quest International
1440 Koll Circle, Suite 103
San Jose, CA 95112
(408) 453-9601
(800) 248-8020 Sighting Line
(408) 453-1927 FAX

Children of Alcoholics Foundation
P.O. Box 4185
Grand Central Station
New York, NY 10163-4185
(800) 359-2623
(212) 754-0664 FAX

Children's Defense Fund
25 E. Street, N.W.
Washington, D.C. 20001
(800) 233-1200
(202) 662-3510 FAX

The Children's Foundation
725 15th Street, N.W., Suite 505
Washington, D.C. 20005
(202) 347-3300
(202) 347-3382 FAX

The Children's Health Fund
317 East 64th Street
New York, NY 10021
(212) 535-9400
(212) 535-7488 FAX

Children's Research Center
6409 Odana Road
Madison, WI 53719
(608) 274-8882
(608) 274-3151 FAX

Child Welfare Institute
1349 W. Peachtree Street, N.E.
Atlanta, GA 30309
(404) 876-1934
(404) 876-7949 FAX

Child Welfare League of America
(CWLA)
440 First Street, N.W., Suite 310
Washington, D.C. 20001-2085
(202) 638-2952
(202) 638-4004 FAX

Cities in Schools, Inc.
1199 N. Fairfax St., Suite 300
Alexandria, VA 22314
(703) 519-8999
(703) 519-7213 FAX

Council on Adoptable Children, Inc.
666 Broadway, Suite 820
New York, NY 10012
(212) 475-0222
(212) 475-1972 FAX

Council for Exceptional Children
1920 Association Drive
Reston, VA 22091
(800) 328-0272
(703) 264-9494 FAX

Council of Jewish Federations
730 Broadway
New York, NY 10003
(212) 475-5000
(212) 529-5842 FAX

Covenant House
346 West 17th Street
New York, NY 10011-5002
(212) 727-4000
(800) 999-9999 HOTLINE
(212) 989-9098 FAX

Devereux National Headquarters
Box 400
19 So. Waterloo Rd.
Devon, PA 19333
(610) 964-3000

Education Commission of the States
707 17th Street, Suite 2700
Denver, CO 80202-3427
(303) 299-3600
(303) 296-8332 FAX

Family Resource Coalition
200 South Michigan Avenue., 16th
Floor
Chicago, IL 60604
(312) 341-0900
(312) 341-9361 FAX

Family Service America, Inc.
11700 West Lake Park Drive
Milwaukee, WI 53224
(800) 221-2681
(414) 359-1074 FAX

Family Violence & Sexual Assault
Institute
1310 Clinic Drive
Tyler, TX 75701
(903) 595-6600
(903) 595-6799 FAX

Foundation for Hospice &
Homecare
519 C Street, N.E.
Washington, D.C. 20002
(202) 547-6586
(202) 546-8968 FAX

Giarretto Institute
232 East Gish Road
San Jose, CA 95112
(408) 453-7616
(408) 453-9064 FAX

Girls Incorporated
30 East 33rd St.
New York, NY 10016
(212) 689-3700
(212) 683-1253 FAX

Girl Scouts of the USA
420 5th Avenue
New York, NY 10018
(800) 223-0624
(212) 852-6514 FAX

Incest Survivors Resource Network
International
P.O. Box 7375
Las Cruces, NM 88006-7375
(505) 521-4260

Institute for Urban & Minority
Education
P.O. Box 40
Teachers College, Columbia
University
New York, NY 10027
(212) 678-3433

International Child Resource
Institute (ICRI)
1810 Hopkins
Berkeley, CA 94707
(510) 644-1000
(510) 525-4106 FAX

Joint Action in Community
Services, Inc. (JACS)
5225 Wisconsin Ave., N.W., Suite
404
Washington, D.C. 20015
(202) 537-0996

Robert F. Kennedy Memorial
1206 30th Street, N.W.
Washington, D.C. 20007
(202) 333-1880
(202) 333-4903 FAX

KidsPeace National Centers
5300 KidsPeace Drive
Orefield, PA 18069-9101
(800) 845-3123
(212) 799-8001 FAX

Learning Disabilities Association of
America
4156 Library Road
Pittsburgh, PA 15234
(412) 341-1515
(412) 344-0224 FAX

Mental Health Association
National Headquarters
1021 Prince Street
Alexandria, VA 22314-2971
(800) 969-6642
(703) 684-5968 FAX

Military Family Resource Center
4015 Wilson Blvd., Suite 903,
Tower 3
Arlington, VA 22203-5190
(703) 696-5806
(703) 696-6344 FAX

National Adoption Center
1500 Walnut Street, Suite 701
Philadelphia, PA 19102
(800) 862-3678
(215) 735-9410 FAX

National Alliance for the Mentally
Ill
200 N. Glebe Rd., Suite 1015
Arlington, VA 22203-3754
(800) 950-6264
(703) 524-9094 FAX

National Association of Anorexia
Nervosa & Associated Disorders
(ANAD)
Box 7
Highland Park, IL 60035
(708) 831-3438
(708) 433-4632 FAX

National Association for Childcare
Resource & Referral Agencies
2116 Campus Drive, S.E.
Rochester, MN 55904
(800) 462-1660
(507) 287-2411 FAX

National Association for the
Education of Young Children
1509 16th Street, N.W.
Washington, D.C. 20036-1426
(800) 424-2460
(202) 328-1846 FAX

National Association of Former
Foster Children, Inc.
P.O. Box 874
New York, NY 10268-0874
(212) 332-0078

National Association of Homes and
Services for Children
1701 K. Street, N.W., Suite 200
Washington, D.C. 20006-1503
(800) 220-1016
(202) 331-7476 FAX

National Association of Services
and Conservation Corps
666 11th Street, N.W., Suite 500
Washington, D.C. 20001
(202) 737-6272
(202) 737-6277

National Black Child Development
Institute, Inc.
1023 15th Street, N.W., Suite 600
Washington, D.C. 20005
(800) 556-2234
(202) 234-1738 FAX

National Center on Child Abuse
and Neglect
P.O. Box 1182
Washington, D.C. 20013
(800) 394-3366
(202) 205-8221 FAX

National Center on Institutions &
Alternatives
635 Slaters Lane, Suite G-100
Alexandria, VA 22314
(703) 684-0373
(703) 549-4077 FAX

National Center for Missing and
Exploited Children
2101 Wilson Blvd., Suite 550
Arlington, VA 22201
(703) 235-3900
(800) 843-5678 Report Information
Line
(703) 235-4067 FAX

National Center for Youth Law
114 Sansome Street, Suite 900
San Francisco, CA 94104
(415) 543-3307
(415) 956-9024 FAX

National Child Labor Committee
1501 Broadway, Room 1111
New York, NY 10036
(212) 840-1801
(212) 768-0963 FAX

National Child Safety Council
P.O. Box 1368
Jackson, MI 49204
(517) 764-6070
(517) 764-3068 FAX

National Coalition Against
Domestic Violence
P.O. Box 18749
Denver, CO 80218-0749
(303) 839-1852
(303) 831-9251 FAX

National Coalition for Hispanic
Health & Human Services
(COSSMHO)
1501 16th Street
Washington, D.C. 20036
(202) 387-5000
(202) 797-4353 FAX

National Committee to Prevent
Child Abuse (NCPCA)
332 South Michigan Ave., Suite 1600
Chicago, IL 60604
(800) 244-5373
(312) 939-8962 FAX

National Council for Adoption
1930 17th Street, N.W.
Washington, D.C. 20009
(202) 328-1200
(202) 332-0935 FAX

National Council on Child Abuse
and Family Violence
1155 Connecticut Ave., N.W.,
Suite 400
Washington, D.C. 20036
(800) 222-2000
(202) 467-4924 FAX

National Council on Crime &
Delinquency
685 Market Street, Suite 620
San Francisco, CA 94105
(415) 896-6223
(415) 896-5109 FAX

National Council on Family
Relations
3989 Central Ave., N.E., Suite 550
Columbia Heights, MN 55421
(612) 781-9331
(612) 781-9348 FAX

National Council of Jewish Women
53 West 23rd Street
New York, NY 10010
(212) 645-4048
(212) 645-7466 FAX

National Council of Negro Women
1001 G Street, N.W., Suite 800
Washington, D.C. 20001
(202) 628-0015
(202) 628-0233 FAX

National Court Appointed Special
Advocate Association (CASA)
2722 Eastlake Ave., East, Suite 220
Seattle, WA 98102
(800) 628-3233
(206) 323-8137 FAX

National Crime Prevention Council
1700 K Street, N.W., 2nd Floor
Washington, D.C. 20006-3817
(202) 466-6272
(202) 296-1356 FAX

National Criminal Justice Reference
Service (NCJRS)
1600 Research Boulevard
Rockville, MD 20850
(800) 851-3420

Justice Statistics Clearinghouse
(800) 732-3277

National Victims Resource Center
(800) 627-6872

Justice Assistance Clearinghouse
(800) 688-4252

National Diabetes Information
Clearinghouse
Box NDIC—One Information Way
Bethesda, MD 20892-3560
(301) 654-3327
(301) 907-8906 FAX

The National Directory of Children,
Youth & Families Services
P.O. Box 1837
Longmont, CO 80502-1837
(800) 343-6681
(303) 776-5831 FAX

National Down Syndrome Society
666 Broadway, Suite 800
New York, NY 10012-2317
(800) 221-4602
(212) 979-2873 FAX

National Easter Seal Society
230 W. Monroe St., Suite 1800
Chicago, IL 60606
(800) 221-6827
(312) 726-4258 TDD

National Education Association
1201 16th Street, N.W.
Washington, D.C. 20036
(202) 833-4000
(202) 822-7974 FAX

National Exchange Club
Foundation for the Prevention of
Child Abuse
3050 Central Ave.
Toledo, OH 43606
(419) 535-3232
(419) 535-1989 FAX

National Fathers' Network
16120 N.E. Eighth Street
Bellevue, WA 98008
(206) 747-4004 or (206) 284-2859

National Foster Parent Association
226 Kilts Drive
Houston, TX 77024-6214
(713) 467-1850
(713) 827-0919 FAX

National 4-H Council
7100 Connecticut Ave.
Chevy Chase, MD 20815
(301) 961-2800
(301) 961-2894 FAX

National Head Start Association
201 N. Union St., Suite 320
Alexandria, VA 22314
(703) 739-0875
(703) 739-0878 FAX

National Health Information Center
P.O. Box 1133
Washington, D.C. 20013-1133
(800) 336-4797
(301) 468-7394 FAX

National Hospital for Kids in Crisis
5300 KidsPeace Drive
Orefield, PA 18069
(800) 446-9543
(215) 799-8801 FAX

National Information Center for Children & Youth with Disabilities
P.O. Box 1492
Washington, D.C. 20013
(800) 695-0285
(202) 884-8441 FAX

National Information Center for Deafness (NICD)
800 Florida Ave., N.E.
Washington, D.C. 20002
(202) 651-5051
(202) 651-5052 TDD
(202) 651-5054 FAX

National Institute for Citizen Education in Law
711 G St., S.E.
Washington, D.C. 20003
(202) 546-6644
(202) 546-6649 FAX

National Job Corps Alumni Association
607 14th St., N.W., Suite 610
Washington, D.C. 20005
(800) 424-2866
(800) 733-5627 HOTLINE
(202) 638-3807 FAX

National Kidney & Urologic Diseases Information Clearinghouse
3 Information Way
Bethesda, MD 20892-3580
(301) 654-4415

National Lekotek Center
2100 Ridge Ave.
Evanston, IL 60201-2796
(800) 366-7529
(708) 328-5514 FAX

National Organization for Victim Assistance
1757 Park Rd., N.W.
Washington, D.C. 20010
(800) 879-6682
(202) 462-2255 FAX

National PTA Headquarters
330 N. Wabash Ave., Suite 2100
Chicago, IL 60611-2511
(312) 670-6782
(312) 670-6783 FAX

National Pediatric HIV Resource Center
15 South Ninth Street
Newark, NJ 07107
(800) 362-0071
(201) 485-2752 FAX

National Rehabilitation Information Center
8455 Colesville Rd., Suite 935
Silver Springs, MD 20910-3319
(800) 346-2742 TDD & Voice
(301) 587-1967 FAX

National Resource Center for Family Centered Practice
112 North Hall
Iowa City, IA 52242
(319) 335-2200
(319) 335-2204 FAX

National School Boards Association
1680 Duke Street
Alexandria, VA 22314
(703) 838-6722

National Urban League
500 East 62nd Street
New York, NY 10021
(212) 310-9000
(212) 593-8250 FAX

National Victim Center
309 West 7th St., Suite 705
Ft. Worth, TX 76102
(800) 394-2255
(817) 877-3396 FAX

National Youth Employment Coalition
1001 Connecticut Ave., N.W., Suite 719
Washington, D.C. 20036
(202) 659-1064
(202) 775-9733 FAX

Obsessive Compulsive Disorder Foundation
P.O. Box 70
Milford, CT 06460
(203) 878-5669

Orphan Foundation of America
1500 Massachusetts Ave., N.W., Suite 448
Washington, D.C. 20005
(800) 950-4673
(202) 223-9079 FAX

Pacific Institute for Research & Evaluation
7315 Wisconsin Ave., Suite 1300 West
Bethesda, MD 20814
(301) 951-4233
(301) 907-8637 FAX

Parents Helping Parents, Inc.
3041 Olcott Street
Santa Clara, CA 95054
(408) 727-5775

Pretrial Services Resource Center
1325 G St., N.W., Suite 1020
Washington, D.C. 20005
(202) 638-3080
(202) 347-0493 FAX

Resources for Children with Special Needs, Inc.
200 Park Ave., South, Suite 816
New York, NY 10003
(212) 677-4650
(212) 254-4070 FAX

The Salvation Army National Headquarters
P.O. Box 269
615 Slaters Lane
Alexandria, VA 22313-0269
(703) 684-5500
(703) 684-3478 FAX

Save the Children International & National Office
54 Wilton Road
Westport, CT 06880
(203) 221-4000
(203) 454-3914 FAX

Survivors of Incest Anonymous, Inc.
World Service Office
P.O. Box 21817
Baltimore, MD 21222
(410) 282-3400

ToughLove International
P.O. Box 1069
100 Mechanic Street
Doylestown, PA 18901
(800) 333-1069
(215) 348-9874 FAX

United Cerebral Palsy Association
1160 L St., N.W., Suite 700
Washington, D.C. 20036

United Jewish Appeal-Federation of
Jewish Philanthropies of NY
130 East 59th Street
New York, NY 10022
(212) 980-1000
(212) 888-7538 FAX

U.S. Catholic Conference
3211 4th Street, N.E.
Washington, D.C. 20017-1194
(202) 541-3000
(202) 541-3322 FAX

U.S. Center for Disease Control &
Prevention National AIDS
Clearinghouse
P.O. Box 6003
Rockville, MD 20849-6003
(800) 458-5231
(800) 243-7012 Deaf Access Line
(TTY/TDD)
(301) 217-0023 International Line
(301) 738-6616 FAX

Volunteers of America National
Headquarters Office
3939 North Causeway Blvd., Suite
400
Metairie, LA 70002-1784
(800) 899-0089
(504) 837-4200 FAX

Women in Community Service
(WICS)
1900 N. Beauregard St., Suite 103
Alexandria, VA 22311
(800) 442-9427
(703) 671-4489 FAX

World Association for Infant Mental
Health
Kellogg Building #27
Michigan State University
E. Lansing, MI 48824-1022
(517) 432-3793

YWCA of The U.S.A. National
Board
726 Broadway
New York, NY 10003
(212) 614-2700
(212) 677-9716 FAX

Youth Policy Institute
1221 Massachusetts Ave., N.W.,
Suite B
Washington, D.C. 20005
(202) 638-2144
(202) 638-2325 FAX

Youth Service America
1101 15th St., N.W., Suite 200
Washington, D.C 20005
(202) 296-2992
(202) 296-4030 FAX

Canadian Federal Agencies

Canada provides health care programs to its citizens through the Department of National Health in conjunction with the provinces and municipalities. The Department of Human Resources Development provides income maintenance and social service programs. Programs are supported by a combination of federal-provincial-municipal funding.

Related federal agencies have responsibility for Indian affairs and development of the territories, work force resources, employment services, immigration, unemployment compensation, and veterans affairs.

Department of National Health

The department is composed of five branches. The program branches are described in the following paragraphs.

Policy and Consultation Branch

The objective of the Policy and Consultation Branch is to provide advice to the Minister, Deputy Minister, and program branches on social and health trends and issues, policy requirements, strategic planning, and information needs relative to departmental objectives, priorities, and programs. The branch undertakes policy research and analysis and coordinates many major policy initiatives within the department.

The Communications Directorate provides strategic communications advice, media and public relations, and publishing and distribution services and organizes conferences and special events.

The newly created Women's Health Bureau plays an advocacy, liaison, and education role with other government and nongovernmental organizations to ensure that Canada's health care system responds to issues affecting women's health.

The branch is also responsible not only for Canada's participation in matters involving international and federal/provincial liaison in the areas of health and social affairs, but also for developing Canada's position on international health issues, advising on bilateral relations with foreign governments, and monitoring international health matters. Finally, the branch administers the Access to Information Act and the Privacy Act, coordinates Canada's drug strategy, and coordinates, monitors, and advises on departmental policies and programs as they relate to women and their families.

Health Protection Branch

This branch is concerned with protecting the health of Canadians. Its role is "to protect and improve the well-being of the Canadian public by defining, advising on, and managing risks to health."

The branch identifies, assesses, and manages risks to health associated with food, drugs (including immunizing agents and biologics), radiation-emitting and medical devices, consumer products, and environmental contaminants. It also investigates the occurrence and cause of communicable and noncommunicable diseases, and injury. These activities require extensive cooperation with provincial health agencies and authorities, with provincially authorized professional licensing bodies, service institutions, universities, and international agencies.

The responsibility for protecting Canadians from certain types of health hazards, such as environmental contaminants, is shared with other federal departments, and often entails interagency cooperation across the two levels of government.

The branch supports health care services provided by the provinces by ensuring the safety and effectiveness of the drugs and devices on which medicine depends, and by providing national laboratory facilities for diagnostic reference services and the evaluation of diagnostic reagents and methods. The branch also provides specialized analytical services and expert testimony for national, provincial, and local law enforcement agencies that control drug abuse and trafficking.

Medical Services Branch

The branch provides health services, health promotion, and assessment services to a wide clientele through the following programs:

Indian and Northern Health Services. Assists status Indians, Inuit, and residents of the Yukon Territory to attain a level of health comparable to that of other Canadians.

Noninsured Health Benefits. Provides health benefits to Inuit and status Indians beyond those paid by provincial governments.

Program Transfer, Policy, and Planning. Works with native communities to help them take control over the administration and the delivery of health care within their own communities.

Occupational and Environmental Health. Provides an occupational health and safety program for the Public Service and provides environmental health services to native communities.

Health Advisory Services. Provides medical assessments of immigrants and civil aviation personnel. In addition it ensures the provision of health and social services under national emergency conditions.

Health Programs and Services Branch

The primary responsibility of this branch is to develop, promote, and support measures designed to preserve and improve the health and social well-being of Canadian residents. The branch also has a major role in providing leadership and coordination in assisting the provinces and territories to bring their health services to, and maintain them at, national standards.

Children's Bureau

The main role of the Children's Bureau is to encourage effective policies and programs relating to the health, welfare, and development of children and families. The bureau promotes coordination within the federal government and consults with other levels of government and nongovernmental organizations on federal initiatives relating to children. The bureau is responsible for the coordination of Canada's implementation of the United Nations Convention on the Rights of the Child, ratified on December 11, 1991, and is currently preparing Canada's progress report to the United Nations.

In addition, the bureau has developed Canada's Action Plan for Children, which is Canada's response to the World Summit for Children. It provides a framework for addressing the long-term needs of Canadian children and has served as a basis for the development of Brighter Futures, a comprehensive five-year federal strategy announced in May 1992, to improve the lives of Canadian children.

The bureau is also responsible for the implementation and coordination of the Brighter Futures initiative, a group of long-term programs designed to address conditions of risk during the earliest years in a child's life.

In addition, Canada has a long-standing commitment to working with other countries to address global issues, and Canada has worked for the welfare of the world's children by participating with multilateral organizations and by maintaining bilateral relations.

The Partners for Children Fund, administered by the Children's Bureau, represents the federal government's response to the Declaration on the Survival, Protection, and Development of Children and the Plan of Action. The purpose of the fund is to support projects that demonstrate Canada's continuing commitment to action as a result of the World Summit recommendations through appropriate nongovernmental and nonprofit organizations working internationally to improve the lives of children.

Seniors Secretariat

A Seniors Secretariat provides information and support to the Minister of State for Seniors. This secretariat is responsible for the following functions: (1) meeting with federal government departments and agencies to coordinate and encourage programs and policies for seniors; (2) consulting with provincial governments on matters related to seniors; (3) consulting with organizations for seniors, professional groups, voluntary associations, and individual seniors to learn more about seniors' needs; (4) developing a communications program to inform seniors of the services and benefits available to them and to keep decision makers aware of the real needs of Canada's seniors; and providing, at the federal level, an information and referral service. Seniors community programs such as New Horizons, Seniors Independence programs, and Ventures in Independence are contribution programs for older Canadians. Seniors and other stakeholders can work together on issues that promote the independence and quality of life of Canada's aging population.

New Horizons

The New Horizons Program encourages older, retired Canadians to share their skills, talents, and experience through activities that are of benefit to themselves and to their community. The program provides financial help to assist seniors to join with others of their age in group projects that they themselves initiate, organize, develop, and control.

Seniors Independence Program

This program provides financial assistance to eligible groups for health, education, and social well-being projects designed to enhance the quality of life and independence of seniors. Seniors must be actively involved in project design and delivery. Priority is given to community-based projects that direct attention to the needs of women seniors, seniors living in rural and remote areas, and seniors who are less advantaged due to life circumstances.

Ventures in Independence

This program offers business, labor, and other levels of government increased coinvestment opportunities with seniors.

Family Violence Prevention Division

Established in December 1986 to coordinate federal involvement and leadership in the area of family violence, the division, in consultation with the provinces, territories, professional associations, and nongovernmental organizations, promotes the development and implementation of policies, programs, and community-based services relating to the prevention and reduction of family violence. It has been responsible for coordinating funding mechanisms and processes within the federal government under the Family Violence and Child Sexual Abuse Initiatives. A new four-year (1991–1995) federal Family Violence Initiative ensures continuity of funding to increase public awareness of the problem, encourage effective prevention efforts, improve the skills and knowledge of workers, enhance information exchange, and improve treatment and support for victims, their families, and offenders.

The division includes the National Clearinghouse on Family Violence, which provides resource materials and a referral service to professionals and the public on all aspects of family violence.

Human Resources Development Canada

Income Security Programs Branch

This branch is responsible for the administration of the Canada Pension Plan, the Old Age Security Program, and the Children's Special Allowances program.

Canada Pension Plan

The Canada Pension Plan is a contributory social insurance program designed to provide a basic level of income protection against the contingencies of retirement, disability, and death. The plan operates in all parts of Canada, except in the province of Québec where a similar program, the Québec Pension Plan (QPP) is in force. The plan provides three main types of benefits: retirement pensions, disability pensions for contributors and benefits for their dependent children, and survivors benefits consisting of a lump-sum death benefit payable to the deceased contributor's estate, a monthly pension for the surviving spouse, and monthly benefits for dependent children.

Old Age Security

Under the Old Age Security (OAS) Act, pensions are paid on a universal, noncontributory basis to those aged sixty-five and over who meet certain residence requirements. A Guaranteed Income Supplement (GIS) may be added to the basic pension in the case of pensioners who have little or no income outside of their basic OAS pension. Likewise, a Spouse's Allowance (SPA) may be paid on an income-tested basis to the spouse of an OAS/GIS pensioner if the spouse is sixty to sixty-four years of age and meets the residence requirements. A similar benefit is available to sixty to sixty-four-year-old widow(er)s.

Children's Special Allowances

The Children's Special Allowances are amounts paid to assist in the support of children under the care of provincial departments, agencies, and institutions, including children in foster care. The monthly amount is equivalent to the basic amount of the Child Tax Benefit.

Social Service Programs Branch

This branch administers three major federal-provincial cost-sharing programs and five grants and contributions programs. It has responsibility for developing and implementing the federal approach on child care, family violence, and seniors. It also has responsibility for coordinating departmental activities related to the National Strategy for the Integration of Persons with Disabilities. It provides consultation and advice to provincial officials, voluntary organizations, and consumer groups on family and children's services, community development, voluntary actions, and rehabilitation. The Seniors Secretariat supports the Minister of State for Seniors by enhancing the quality of life for Canada's seniors.

Cost-Shared Programs Directorate

This directorate administers all department programs that are based on cost-sharing agreements with the provinces.

Canada Assistance Plan

Under agreements signed with all provinces and territories, the federal government, through the Canada Assistance Plan (CAP), shares eligible costs that these jurisdictions and their municipalities incur in the provision of a wide range of social assistance and welfare service programs to needy persons.

CAP shares in the cost of the following programs that are administered by the province.

Financial Assistance—Provinces and territories receive cost sharing for assistance they and their municipalities provide to persons in need. Assistance must be provided on the basis of a test of need which takes into account an individual's budgetary requirements and any income and resources available to meet these requirements. Assistance includes aid to persons in need for basic requirements (i.e., food, shelter, clothing, fuel, utilities, household supplies, and personal requirements) and may also include aid for travel and transportation, for certain health services (such as drugs and dental care) and for special needs as determined by each province or territory such as civil legal aid, wheelchairs, prostheses, and essential repairs to homes.

Institutional Care—Federal sharing is available to the provinces and territories of costs they and their municipalities incur in the provision of residential care to persons in need of facilities that qualify as homes for special care under CAP (i.e., homes for the aged, nursing homes, child-care facilities, hostels for transients, and shelters for battered women).

Since April 1, 1977, cost sharing of residential care for adult persons in need has been limited under CAP due to the introduction of new funding arrangements pursuant to the Extended Health Care Services Program of the Federal-Provincial Fiscal Arrangements and Federal Post-Secondary Education and Health Contributions Act, which subsumed the major responsibility for federal financial support to the provinces and territories for long-term adult residential care.

Certain facilities providing short-term residential care to adults are not included in this new financing arrangement and, consequently, CAP continues to share in the full cost to the provinces and territories of maintaining adult persons in need in these facilities (i.e., hostels for transients, homes for unmarried mothers, and crisis intervention centers such as shelters for battered women).

There has been no change to the capacity of CAP to share in the cost to the provinces and territories of providing residential care to children who qualify as persons in need within the scope of the plan. Cost sharing in residential care for children under CAP was not affected by the funding arrangement pursuant to the Federal-Provincial Fiscal Arrangements and Federal Post-Secondary Education and Health Contributions Act.

Welfare Services—The federal government shares in certain costs to the provinces and territories that they and their municipalities incur in providing welfare services to persons in need and persons likely to become in need. Welfare services are defined as services having as their objective the lessening, removal, or prevention of the causes and effects of poverty, child neglect, or dependence on public assistance and include day-care services, homemaker services, counseling services, adoption services, rehabilitation services, information and referral services on a wide range of child welfare services, as well as the administration of public assistance programs.

Work Activity Projects—Under CAP the federal government shares in costs that provinces and territories incur in operating work activity projects. These projects provide a comprehensive approach to social rehabilitation in that they are aimed at resolving the personal, family, or environmental problems of persons who have difficulty in securing or maintaining employment or in undertaking training. Projects are designed to help improve the motivation and work capacity of participants and prepare them for entry or return to employment or further vocational training.

Vocational Rehabilitation of Disabled Persons

Under agreements signed with all the provinces and territories, the federal government, through the Vocational Rehabilitation of Disabled Persons Act (VRDP), contributes 50 percent of the costs incurred by the provinces toward a comprehensive vocational rehabilitation program for physically and mentally disabled persons. As of April 1, 1990, a new three-year agreement with all provinces and territories took effect.

Services to individuals under a comprehensive vocational rehabilitation program include assessment; counseling; restorative services; provision of prostheses, wheelchairs, technical aids, and other devices; vocational training and employment placement; provision of tools, books, and equipment necessary for employment; maintenance allowances as required by each individual; follow-up goods and services; and goods and services to prevent the loss of employment of disabled persons facing a vocational crisis. Recent initiatives include establishing appeal procedures for disabled persons who are refused service because they are deemed ineligible.

There is also provision within the VRDP to fund vocational rehabilitation research projects undertaken by individual researchers and organizations. This fund is administered by the National Welfare Grants Division of the Social Services Program Branch.

Alcohol and Drug Treatment and Rehabilitation

This new federal-provincial cost-sharing agreement, which took effect April 1, 1988, is a component of Canada's Drug Strategy announced in 1987. It enables the federal government to extend financial support to provinces in order to increase the availability of alcohol and drug programming in Canada. Youths are the prime target group; however, other groups at risk, such as women and the elderly, are also being served. This agreement complements the VRDP, which supports provincial programming for alcohol and drug treatment and rehabilitation in the context of vocational rehabilitation. The initial two-year agreement, developed jointly with the provinces, has been signed by eight provinces. A new three-year agreement took effect as of April 1, 1990. Negotiations continue with the remaining provinces and territories to conclude the new (1990–1993) agreement. Services covered in the agreement include assessment, early intervention, special access services, detoxification, counseling, aftercare, information on the availability and accessibility of services, and work initiatives.

Social Development Directorate

This directorate provides contributions to community groups, social service organizations, schools of social work, individuals, and other levels of government for research and demonstration activities. It also provides sustaining grants to national voluntary social service organizations. The directorate is responsible for the National Welfare Grants, National Adoption Desk, Disabled Persons Unit, Family Violence Prevention Division, child-care programs, New Horizons program, and the Seniors Independence program.

National Welfare Grants

This is a national and social research and development program that provides consultation and financial support to stimulate knowledge development, identify social policy and service needs and gaps, and recommend action in critical areas of social welfare.

National Adoption Desk

The National Adoption Desk represents provincial and territorial (except Québec) adoption authorities in dealings with foreign authorities on intercountry adoption matters, provides consultative and liaison services to the provinces/territories in the area of international adoption, negotiates intercountry adoption agreements and programs, and coordinates adoption cases between provincial/territorial and foreign authorities.

Child-Care Programs Division

This division has three principal components: the Child Care Initiatives Fund (CCIF), the Child Care Regional Consultants, and the National Child Care Information Centre (NCCIC). The CCIF, announced in 1987, supports research, development, and demonstration projects relating to child care over a seven-year period. The Child Care Regional Consultants are liaison officers between the provincial/territorial government and the federal government who provide advice and consultation to groups and organizations regarding child-care issues as well as the CCIF. The NCCIC is a national focal point for information and promotion of quality child-care services in Canada. Current literature is available, free of charge, on a wide range of child-care matters. The NCCIC has a resource center with a diverse selection of information and research data on child-care issues, and a distribution center that disseminates publications, articles, fact sheets, posters, and information kits on relevant child-care issues.

Disabled Persons Unit

The mandate of this unit is to promote and support the development of programs and initiatives that enhance opportunities for disabled persons to live and work within the community. Working extensively with nongovernment and private sector groups and individuals, the unit provides a consultation and brokerage function whereby resources of government and nongovernment sectors are effectively linked to initiatives of merit in the area of services to disabled persons.

Under the National Strategy for the Integration of Persons with Disabilities, the Disabled Persons Unit also administers the Ability Program, which provides funding in support of initiatives that advance the community and economic integration of persons with disabilities and social integration of children and youths with disabilities.

Where to Write

Inquiries regarding **federal health programs** should be addressed to:
Communications Branch
Department of National Health
Jeanne Mance Bldg., 19th Fl.
Ottawa, ON K1A 0K9

Inquiries regarding **federal income security and social service programs** should be addressed to:
Communications Branch
Human Resources Development Canada
140 Promenade du Portage
Hull, PQ K1A 0J9

Inquiries regarding **welfare, social services, and health care programs administered by the provinces and territories** should be addressed to the appropriate provincial or territorial agency (see the **Where to Write** sections for each province and territory).

Department of National Health

Office of the Minister
Jeanne Mance Bldg.
Ottawa, ON K1A 0K9
Tel: (613) 957-0200
Diane Marleau, M.P., Min.,
(613) 957-0200

Office of the Deputy Minister
Michele S. Jean, Dep. Min.,
(613) 957-0213
Susan Fletcher, Exec. Dir., National
Advisory Council on Aging,
(613) 957-1971

Corporate Services Branch
Robert Lafleur, Asst. Dep. Min.,
(613) 952-3984
O. Marquardt, Dir. Gen., Financial
Administration, (613) 957-7762
J. Butler, Dir., Departmental
Administration, (613) 952-0947
M. Williams, Dir. Gen., Facilities
Mgmt. Srvs., (613) 957-3375
H. Valin, Act. Dir., Departmental
Srvs., (613) 957-9247
B. Smith, Dir., Parliamentary
Relations, (613) 952-0665
S. Harisson, Dir., CMB, Exec.
Secretariat, (613) 952-4104
F. Bull, Dir. Gen., Informatics,
(613) 954-8713

Human Resources Directorate
Robert Joubert, Dir. Gen.,
(613) 957-3236

Communications Directorate
Joel Weiner, Dir. Gen.,
(613) 957-2979
Sandra Lavigne, Dir., Operations
and Planning Div., (613) 957-2981
Carole Peacock, Dir., Media and
Pub. Relations Div., (613) 957-2987;
FAX: (613) 952-7266

Policy and Consultation Branch
André Juneau, Asst. Dep. Min.,
(613) 957-3059

Judith Ferguson, Dir. Gen., Health
Policy, (613) 957-3066
Health Policy Division
Guy Bujold, Dir., (613) 957-3081
Strategic Planning Division
Lyle Makosky, Dir., (613) 957-3026
Canada Drug Strategy Secretariat
I. Malyalewsky, Exec. Dir.,
(613) 957-3507
Women's Health Bureau
Abby Hoffman, Dir., (613) 957-1940

International Affairs Directorate
E.M. Aiston, Act. Dir. Gen.
Health Affairs Directorate
E.M. Aiston, Dir., (613) 957-7298
International Information and
Planning Directorate
Patricia Dunn Erickson, Chf.,
(613) 957-7288
Social Development Directorate
D. Ogston, Dir. Gen., (613) 957-8672

Medical Services Branch
Jeanne Mance Bldg.
de l'Eglantine St.
Ottawa, ON K1A 0L3
Marie Fortier, Act. Asst. Dep. Min.,
(613) 957-7701
Public Service Health
G.I. Lynch, Dir. Gen., (613) 957-7669
Indian and Northern Health
Services
M. McNaughton, Dir. Gen.,
(613) 952-9616
Health Advisory Services
L. Davies, Act. Dir. Gen.,
(613) 957-7665
Program Transfer and Policy
Planning
P. Blais, Act. Dir. Gen.,
(613) 957-3402

Health Protection Branch
Kent Foster, Asst. Dep. Min.,
(613) 957-1804
Drugs Directorate
D. Michols, Dir. Gen., (613) 957-0369

Food Directorate
S.W. Gunner, Dir. Gen.,
(613) 957-1821
Field Operations
J.R. Elliott, Dir., (613) 957-1794
Environmental Health Directorate
R. Hickman, Dir. Gen.,
(613) 954-0291
Laboratory Centre for Disease
Control
J. Losos, Dir. Gen., (613) 957-0315
Finance and Administration
Directorate
M.T. McElrone, Dir., (613) 957-1014

**Health Programs and Services
Branch**
Jeanne Mance Bldg.
de l'Eglantine St.
Ottawa, ON K1A 1B4
Kay Stanley, Asst. Dep. Min.,
(613) 954-8524
Health Insurance
Bruce Davis, Dir. Gen.,
(613) 954-8674
Health Services
Diane Kirkpatrick, Dir. Gen.,
(613) 954-8629
Extramural Research Programs
Mary Ellen Jeans, Dir. Gen.,
(613) 954-8538
Health Promotion
Catherine Lane, Dir. Gen.,
(613) 957-7792
Policy and Planning
Judy Lockette, Dir., (613) 954-8532
Office of the Principal Nursing
Officer
M.J. Flaherty, (613) 957-1975
Seniors Secretariat
S. Hansen, Exec. Dir., (613) 954-8536
New Horizons Program
E. Kwavnick, Dir., (613) 957-2881
Family Violence Programs
E. Scott, Dir., (613) 957-0622
Seniors Independence Program
D. O'Flaherty, Dir., (613) 952-9529

Reprinted with permission of Department of Health Canada.

Human Resources Development Canada

140 Promenade du Portage
Hull, PQ K1A 0J9
Lloyd Axworthy, Min.,
(819) 994-2482

Jean-Jacques Noreau, Dep. Min.,
(819) 994-4514
François Pouliot, Assoc. Dep. Min.,
(819) 994-4520

Strategic Policy
Harvey Lazar, Sr. Asst. Dep. Min.,
(819) 994-4272
Kathy O'Hara, Asst. Dep. Min.,
(819) 997-1094

Employment
Kristina Liljefors, Exec. Dir.,
(819) 953-7362

Human Resource Services
Jean Claude Bouchard, Asst. Dep.
Min., (613) 994-1791

Insurance
Hy Braiter, Exec. Dir.,
(819) 994-1600

Systems
David McNaughton, Exec. Mgr.,
(819) 994-1592

Financial and Administrative
Services
W.E.R. (Bob) Little, Asst. Dep. Min.,
(819) 994-2521

Income Security Programs
Monique Plante, Asst. Dep. Min.,
(819) 957-3111

Labour
Michael McDermott, Sr. Asst. Dep.
Min., (819) 997-1493

Social Development and Education
Ian C. Green, Asst. Dep. Min.,
(819) 957-2953

Related Federal Agencies

Department of Indian Affairs and Northern Devleopment
Les Terrasses de la Chaudière
10 Wellington St., North Tower
Hull, PQ K1A 0H4
Tel: (819) 997-0002
Ronald A. Irwin, Min.,
(819) 997-0002
Dan Goodleaf, Dep. Min.,
(819) 997-0133
Richard Van Loon, Assoc. Dep.
Min., (819) 997-0854
Claims and Indian Government
John Sinclair, Asst. Dep. Min.,
(819) 953-3180
Policy and Strategic Direction
Jack Stagg, Asst. Dep. Min.,
(819) 994-7555
Lands and Trust Services
Wendy F. Porteous, Asst. Dep. Min.,
(819) 953-5577
Northern Affairs
John Rayner, Asst. Dep. Min.,
(819) 953-3760
Corporate Services
Alan Williams, Asst. Dep. Min.,
(819) 997-0020
Regional Directors General
Gerry Kerr, Atlantic, (902) 661-6262

Guy McKenzie, Québec,
(418) 648-3270
Audrey Doerr, Ontario,
(416) 973-6201
Brenda D. Kustra, Manitoba,
(204) 983-2475
Myler Savill, Saskatchewan,
(306) 780-5950
Ken Kirby, Alberta, (403) 495-2835
John Watson, British Columbia,
(604) 666-5201
Mike Ivanski, Yukon, (403) 667-3300
Warren Johnson, Northwest
Territories, (403) 920-8111

Ministry of the Solicitor General
Sir Wilfrid Laurier Bldg.
340 Laurier Ave., West
Ottawa, ON K1A 0P8
Tel: (613) 995-7548
Herb Gray, Sol. Gen., (613) 991-2924
Correctional Service of Canada
John Edwards, Comm.,
(613) 995-5481
National Parole Board
Michel Dagenais, Chair,
(613) 954-1150
Royal Canadian Mounted Police
N.D. Inkster, Comm., (613) 993-0400

Canadian Security Intelligence
Service
Raymond Protti, Dir., (613) 993-9620

Department of Veteran Affairs
Daniel J. MacDonald Bldg.
P.O. Box 7700
Charlottetown, PE C1A 8M9
Tel: (902) 566-8330
66 Slater St.
Ottawa, ON K1A 0P4
David Collenette, Min., National
Defence and Veterans Affairs,
(613) 996-3100
David Nicholson, Dep. Min.,
(613) 996-6881
Veterans Services
(Vacant), Asst. Dep. Min.,
(902) 566-8100
Administration
S. Rainville, Asst. Dep. Min.,
(902) 566-8047
Veterans Appeal Board
T. Whalen, Chair, (902) 566-8636
Canadian Pension Commission
M. Chartier, Chair, (902) 566-8800
Bureau of Pensions Advocates
Keith Bell, Chf. Pensions Advocate,
(902) 566-8640

Department of Health Canada

Office of the Minister
Brooke Claxton Building
Ottawa, ON K1A 0K9
Tel: (613) 957-0200
The Honorable Allan Rock
(613) 957-0200

Office of the Deputy Minister
Michèle S. Jean, Deputy Minister
(613) 957-0213
Alan Nymark, Associate Deputy
Minister (613) 954-5904
Sylvie Dufresne, Director General,
Departmental Secretariat
(613) 941-2000
Hélène Valin, Director,
Departmental Service (613) 957-9247
Bob Houston, Director,
Parliamentary Relations
(613) 952-0665

Corporate Services Branch
Robert S. Lafleur, Senior Associate
Deputy Minister (613) 952-3984
Gordon Peters, Director, Internal
Audit (613) 957-4362
Orvel Marquardt, Director General,
Departmental Planning and
Financial Administration
Directorate (613) 957-7762
Robert Joubert, Director General,
Human Resources Directorate
(613) 957-3236
Marie Williams, Director General,
Assets Management Directorate
(613) 957-3375
Fruji Bull, Director General,
Information Management Services
Directorate (613) 954-8713

Policy and Consultation Branch
André Juneau, Assistant Deputy
Minister (613) 957-3059
Abby Hoffman, Director General,
Women's Health Bureau
(613) 957-1940
Malcolm Brown, Director General,
Intergovernmental Affairs
Directorate (613) 957-3081
Sange de Silva, Director General,
Strategic Planning and Review

Directorate (613) 954-8072
Director General, Health Policy and
Information Directorate
(613) 957-3066
Ed Aiston, Director General,
International Affairs Directorate
(613) 957-7298
Patricia Dunn Erickson, Director,
International Information Division
(613) 957-7288
Andrew Simon, Director General,
Office of Health and the
Information Highway
(613) 954-7532
Carla Gilders, Director General,
Communications and Consultation
Directorate (613) 957-2979
Director, Communications Services
(613) 957-2987

Health Promotion and Programs Branch
Jeanne Mance Building
Ottawa, On K1A 0K9
Ian Potter, Assistant Deputy
Minister (613) 954-8525
Judy Lockett, A/Director General,
Management Planning and
Operations Directorate
(613) 954-8532
Catherine Lane, Director General,
Population Health Directorate
(613) 957-7792
Nancy Garrard, Director, Division
of Aging and Seniors (613) 957-1967
Jim Mintz, Director, Partnerships
and Marketing Division
(613) 954-2402
Diane C. Kirkpatrick, Director
General, Strategies and Systems for
Health Directorate (613) 954-8629
Janet Davies, Director, Health Issues
(613) 941-1977
David Allan, Family Violence
(613) 957-2866

Health Protection Branch
Health Protection Building
Ottawa, On K1A 0K9
Dr. Joseph Z. Losos, Assistant
Deputy Minister (613) 957-1804

Ian Shugart, Visiting Assistant
Deputy Minister (613) 941-4332
Joel Weiner, Executive Director,
Office of Scientific and Regulatory
Affairs (613) 952-3665
Executive Director, Office of
Laboratory Rationalization
(613) 957-7894
Dann M. Michols, Director General,
Therapeutic Products Directorate
(613) 957-0369
Dr. George Paterson, Director
General, Food Directorate
(613) 957-1821
Rod Raphael, A/Director General,
Environmental Health Directorate
(613) 954-0291
Dr. Michael Shannon, Director
General, Laboratory Centre for
Disease Control (613) 957-0316
Radiation Protection Bureau
(613) 954-6647

Medical Services Branch
Jeanne Mance Building
Ottawa, ON K1A 0K9
Paul F. Cochrane, Assistant Deputy
Minister (613) 957-7701
Dr. Gillian I. Lynch, Director
General, Occupational and
Environmental Health Services
Directorate (613) 957-7669
Paul Glover, Director General, First
Nations and Inuit Health Programs
(613) 952-9616
Dr. Jay A. Wortman, Director
General, Non-Insured Health
Benefits Directorate (613) 954-8825
Ross Leeder, A/Director General,
Program Policy, Transfer Secretariat
and Planning (613) 957-3402

Pest Management Regulatory Agency
2250 Riverside Drive
Ottawa, ON K1A 0K9
Dr. Claire Franklin, Executive
Director (613) 736-3708

Parent-Teacher Conferences

Communicating with each student's parents is one of the most important tasks you will do as a teacher. A link between the student's family and the classroom is critical in helping the student develop his or her skills to the fullest. Each elementary and secondary school arranges parent-teacher conferences for all students. During these conferences, you share the student's academic and social strengths and weaknesses with the parent(s), who, in turn, provide insights into the student's development and background. As teachers, we need to carefully plan for these formally arranged parent-teacher conferences. Here are some suggestions.

1. Try to make the parents feel comfortable. Remember that coming to school to talk to a teacher is not a daily habit for parents. Some may have had unpleasant school experiences themselves. It is your responsibility to put the parent at ease. Suggest that your school provide coffee or juice and cookies for those parents who arrive early, or offer it yourself.

2. Begin *and* end the conference on a positive note. Beginning on a positive note will help the parent(s) feel more relaxed and less defensive about their child. Ending on a positive note makes them feel good about their child, themselves, and you as their child's teacher.

3. Share with parents positive attributes that you have observed in their child. For a few students, it may be difficult to readily point out a positive quality, but if you try, you will find one. The trait may or may not be academic, such as knowing all the multiplication tables up to eight or being able to write a biography. It could pertain to work habits, such as always handing in homework on time (even if the homework is done wrong most of the time, the student does do it!), arriving on time for class, or being honest in saying he or she doesn't understand something. Whatever it is, point it out at the beginning of the conference.

4. Maintain a professional composure and manner, including confidentiality. Don't talk about other students. If parents want to talk about another student, change the direction of discussion and bring it back to their child.

    Don't second guess other teachers, school administrators, or the school board in front of parents. You may not fully agree with your colleagues, but you should never demonstrate unprofessional behavior by questioning their views or decisions with parents.

    Make certain that other parents cannot overhear your discussion with another set of parents about another student.

5. Remember that the parent should dominate the discussion. After all, these meetings are "parent-teacher" conferences, not "teacher-parent" conferences. You need to open the discussion, present evidence of the student's work, and, most important, be a good listener. Answer the parents' questions directly. Avoid educational jargon, and use language that parents can readily understand.

6. Above all, be honest. Don't paint a picture of an outstanding student when the child isn't. Don't be overly critical either. Being a parent is a very difficult job.

Keeping these suggestions in mind, review the following examples of ways to think about parent-teacher conferences in three different situations—early childhood, middle school, and special education. Some of these can be adopted for secondary parent-teacher conferences as well.

Early Childhood Conference Model

The following model was designed to assist teachers in the process of interacting with parents, particularly in scheduled meetings. Although all conferences are different and there are no set answers, the model provides ideas to help teachers communicate effectively and establish partnerships with parents.

When meeting with parents, time is limited and in some cases both teacher and parent may be nervous and/or uncomfortable. The following guidelines may enable teachers to better prepare and work through problems in conferencing. To date, there are no models from which teachers can learn conferencing skills. This model is based on the literature concerning conferencing techniques and research on effective conferencing. Lawler's previous teaching experience has also contributed significantly to the design.

The Lawler Model*

L—*LOCATE* records, materials, etc., necessary for effectively interacting with parents.

A—*ARRANGE* the environment for a relaxed, pleasant atmosphere.

W—*WORK* toward "partnerships" with parents. (Do *not* dominate the conference!)

L—*LISTEN* more than 50 percent of the planned conference time.

E—*EVALUATE* the conference as it proceeds.

R—*RESPOND* to the parents in terms of follow-up.

L—*Locate* records, materials, etc., necessary for effectively interacting with parents.

1. Plan an agenda, selecting two to four priority goals for each child (5).
2. Send the agenda to parents with a note requesting time preferences for the conference.
3. Ask the parents if they have concerns to discuss (5).

A—*Arrange* the environment for a relaxed, pleasant atmosphere.

4. Arrange the environment so that parents will feel comfortable. The room should be neat and orderly. Examples of children's work should be displayed attractively. Show the parents where their child sits, works, etc. (*Note:* Providing a small table and chair outside the classroom also supports the idea of comfort for parents who have to wait.)
5. Have adult-sized chairs in which the parents and you may sit.
6. Greet each parent at the door using *your* first name. Clarify parents' names with your records. Many children are from divorced, blended, and stepparent families today. All family members are not addressed by the same last name.
7. Sit beside or at an angle from the parent. *Never* sit behind your desk or at a table across from the parent. It is intimidating.

---

*The Lawler Model, published in Lawler, 1991, *Parent-Teacher Conferencing in Early Childhood Education.* Washington DC: NEA. Reprinted by permission of the author.

W—*Work* toward partnerships with parents (do not dominate the conference).

8. Begin on a positive note. Think of something good to say about each child. (If you cannot think of anything positive to say about a particular child, ask colleagues for help. Be sure to begin on a positive note.)

9. Keep a notepad nearby and take notes. You cannot remember the suggestions/ recommendations of all parents. Parents should also see that their input is important enough for you to record and utilize. (*Note:* If parents object to your writing comments, assure them it is for your benefit only, that conference discussions are confidential.)

10. Discuss educational plans and concerns.

11. Be clear and concise. Do not use jargon. (Even the names of tests—for example, MAT-6 [Metropolitan Achievement Test, Version 6]—should be explained.)

12. Do not talk down to parents. If you practice in front of a mirror and your eyebrows are never in a relaxed position, but are always raised, this is a sure sign that you are, indeed, talking in a condescending manner.

13. Base judgments on available *facts* from actual situations. Never repeat comments of other teachers or students to parents. Document behavior when discussing incidents. No one can be expected to relate detailed information concerning all students to all parents. Keep records.

14. Be constructive in all suggestions to parents (26). We know that parents consider their children extensions of themselves. When a teacher is criticizing the child, parents also feel criticized. Parents may often feel intimidated by teachers, regarding knowledge of parenting skills (or lack thereof). Teachers are the experts in the eyes of parents (generally). Be careful.

15. Offer more than one solution to a problem. Treat parents as adults by providing alternatives so that they may have specific input and feel that they contribute.

L—*Listen* more than 50 percent of the planned conference time. The information gained *from* the parent is equally as important as the information you have to share.

16. Talk less than 50 percent of the scheduled time. You are a facilitator, not a director or dictator.

17. Listen carefully and paraphrase for clarification. If parents are intimidated and/or nervous, they may not express themselves well. While hearing back the message you received, they may realize that it was not the one they meant to send. Give them support and assistance in this interactive process through paraphrasing.

E—*Evaluate* the conference as it proceeds.

18. Make necessary adjustments in the agenda while conferencing.

19. Mentally ask yourself how the conference is proceeding.

20. Ask for and accept suggestions from parents. Some teachers are often afraid of what they might hear. Be open-minded and willing to listen and respond to parental suggestions. Remember, the parent has known the child much longer than you have known the child.

R—*Respond* to the parent in terms of follow-up.

21. Make *educational plans* for future accomplishment of goals and objectives. If parents are to become partners, they must be included in some way by making follow-up arrangements. When a conference ends and the parent is "dismissed" by the teacher, the parent often feels as if he/she is no longer needed and has no further part to play in the educational process. Parents come to school from many walks of life and, as in working with children, teachers must work with them on their levels. A single conference during the school year is not enough to develop a partnership with the parent.

22. Allow for parental input in *all* aspects of the child's education. Always make educational plans with the parents to *respond* to their needs and those of the child.

23. Summarize the key points of the conference.

24. Plan for follow-up communication. (This item is often omitted, but it is most important.) Never end a conference without planning what type of future interaction will occur between you and the parent. Follow-up may consist of a note sent home, a note from the parent, a phone call, or (ideally) a face-to-face conference.

The Parent-Teacher Conference in the Middle School*

Parent interest in schools has never been greater than at present. Parents expect full information about school programs and particularly information about the progress of their children. They are entitled to it. The parent-teacher conference is an important vehicle for communication. It provides for a two-way exchange of information about the student. It may be used as a supplement to the report card, but, because it can do much more than a report card alone, it is increasingly being used. However, to make the best use of this technique requires careful planning on the part of middle school staff. In some schools, the student also participates in the conference, making it a three-way exchange of information.

What Parents Want to Know

1. What subjects the students will study—the curriculum for the year.
2. An explanation of the grading system and how it works.
3. How much emphasis is placed on the basics and on other studies.
4. Pertinent school policies, school rules, and procedures, including discipline.
5. How parents can help students learn.
6. Homework policies.
7. What you, the teacher, expect of the student.
8. How well students get along with others (i.e., are they well liked)?

What Teachers Can Learn from the Conference

1. Information about how the student is treated at home.
2. How the student feels about school, teacher, and other students as reported by parents.
3. Strengths or interests the student has that may not have shown up in school.
4. Any problems regarding homework or study habits that show up at home.

Tips for Better Parent-Teacher Conferences

1. Prepare for the conference! Make an outline covering major points you want to discuss. You might want to send a copy of this brief outline of topics home to parents after they have confirmed the parent-teacher conference date and time. Stick to the outline!
2. Be courteous and cheerful.
3. Give the parents a chance to talk first and to share their views and their problems.
4. Be a good listener.
5. Be truthful but tactful. Don't forget that a child is a most precious possession!

*From Louis G. Romano and Nicholas P. Georgiady, *Building an Effective Middle School*. Copyright © 1994 Wm. C. Brown Communications, Inc., Dubuque, Iowa. Reprinted by permission of Times Mirror Higher Education Group, Inc., Dubuque, Iowa. All Rights Reserved.

6. Try to avoid prescribing solutions. Offer suggestions and alternatives. Give parents a part in deciding any action to be taken.

7. Begin and end on a positive note.

The value the parent-teacher conference can have is quite apparent when one examines the lists of expectations held by parents and teachers. Both parents and teachers learn more about each student. Teachers learn how the child is treated at home and what bearing, if any, this may have on behavior in school. Parents can learn about the year's work for students, what is expected of students, how the teacher and the school function, and most importantly, that teacher and school are there to help in every way possible. Besides direct benefits for learning by students, the parent-teacher conference has great public relations potential that cannot be overlooked.

Parent-Teacher Conferences for Exceptional Children*

Be aware of some basic do's and don'ts of parent-educator relationship building. Although lists seldom provide a comprehensive statement of desired outcomes, they can serve to remind individuals of certain basic elements that need to be considered. This also applies to the creation of trust between parents and educators.

Do's

1. Maintain a sense of humor.
2. Be accepting of yourself and the parents and family members with whom you work.
3. Demonstrate warmth and sensitivity.
4. Be positive.
5. Demonstrate respect for the parents and families with whom you work.
6. Be sincere.
7. Listen.
8. Use language that parents and family members can understand.
9. Attend to the emotions and body language of parents and family members.
10. Reinforce parents when it is appropriate.

Don'ts

1. Don't attempt to be a sage who has all the answers.
2. Don't make premature judgments.
3. Don't be overly critical.
4. Don't threaten, ridicule, or blame parents and families.
5. Avoid arguing with parents and family members.
6. Avoid strong expressions of surprise and concern.
7. Avoid making promises and agreements that you may not be able to keep.
8. Don't patronize parents and family members.
9. Avoid making moralistic judgments.
10. Don't minimize what parents and family members have to say about their child.

*Simpson, R. L., *Conferencing Parents of Exceptional Children*, 2d ed. Copyright © 1990 Austin, Texas: Pro-Ed: 146–7; 266–7.

Preconference Planning

The success of the parent-educator progress report conference will be highly correlated with preconference planning efforts (Barsch 1969; Ehly, Conoley, and Rosenthal 1985). These planning efforts should involve attention to the following:

- The child's records, including the IEP [individualized education program] and previous parent-educator conference notes, should be reviewed carefully.
- An outline of those items to be discussed should be prepared.
- The conferencer should review standardized test data that may need to be reinterpreted to the parents and family members.
- A careful selection of papers and work samples should be made in preparation for the conference. These samples should be representative and illustrative of particular concepts and should be dated and sequentially arranged for comparative purposes.
- Parents should be provided a folder of their child's work to take with them after the conference. This work sample should be representative of their child's performance and consistent with feedback provided by the conferencer. Evaluative comments should be provided on the papers to aid parents and family members in understanding the concepts being illustrated.
- Educators should plan for an acceptable environment for the session. This should include a professional and confidential setting. In addition, the conferencer should make arrangements for adult-size furniture for all participants and pad and pencil for note taking.
- Parents and family members should be prepared to participate in the conference.
- The educator should prepare each child for the conference. This will basically consist of apprising the child of the purpose and nature of the session to be conducted with the parents and the materials to be reviewed. The pupil should be offered an opportunity for input into the agenda. Finally, it is recommended that participation of the pupil in the session be considered. In instances in which such participation is appropriate, the pupil should be provided training (e.g., information, discussion opportunities, and role playing) in participating in the conference. These preliminary efforts can aid in reducing the anxiety of both the pupil and the parents.

Off the Shelf

The following list includes books from the self-help section of many libraries and bookstores. These books address areas that you or your students may need help with. This is not an exhaustive list but will give you an idea of what is available. The books are listed alphabetically by title. Check the author's credentials when looking for resources, and remember that self-help books cannot replace mental (or physical) health professionals.

Body Traps by Judith Rodin. William Morrow.

The Boys & Girls Book About Divorce by Richard Gardner. Jason Aronson.

Conversationally Speaking by Alan Garner. Lowell House Extension Press.

Coping with Difficult People by Robert Bramson. Dell Publishing.

Coping Skills Interventions for Children and Adolescents by Susan G. Forman. Jossey-Bass Publishers.

Drama of the Gifted Child by Alice Miller. Harper Collins.

Frames of Mind: The Theory of Multiple Intelligences by Howard Gardner. Harper Collins.

How to Get Control of Your Time and Your Life by Alan Lakein. Signet.

How to Save the Children by Amy Hatkoff and Karen Kelly Klopp. Simon & Schuster.

The Ideal Problem Solver by Bransford Stein. W.H. Freeman and Company.

Magic of Conflict by T. Crum. Simon & Schuster.

The New York Times Parents' Guide to the Best Books for Children by Eden Lipson. Random House.

Organize Yourself by Ronni Eisenberg. Macmillan.

Organizing for the Creative Person by Dorothy Lehmkohl and Dolores Cotter Lamping. Crown Publishers.

People Skills by Robert Bolton. Touchstone.

The Relaxation and Stress Reduction Workbook by Martha Davis, Elizabeth Eshelman, and Matthew McKay. New Harbinger.

The Seven Habits of Highly Effective People by Stephen R. Covey. Simon & Schuster.

Shyness by Philip G. Zimbaro. Addison Wesley.

Speaking Your Mind in 101 Difficult Situations by Don Gabor. Simon & Schuster.

Stress Management by Edward A. Charlesworth and Ronald G. Nathan. Ballantine.

The Stress Solution by Lyle Miller and Alma Dell Smith. Pocket Books.

To Listen to a Child by T. Berry Brazelton. Addison Wesley.

Understanding Culture's Influence on Behavior by Richard Brislin. Harcourt Brace Jovanovich.

What to Say When You Talk to Yourself by Shad Helmstetter. Pocket Books.

The Job Search Process

Begin Your Preparation Early

The fall market can begin the previous November for college/university and in March for public school jobs. *Be flexible* regarding location, levels you will teach, school size, etc.; know what you want, but be willing to adjust to the reality of the market. ***Keep a record* of all your job-search activities,** so you will know what has been done and what you still need to do.

1. *Assess yourself and your goals.* What do you want to teach and where? Do you have personal preferences or limitations, and what alternatives have you or will you consider? What are your strengths and weaknesses?

2. *Locate job information sources,* and evaluate the market in your field(s). Use the placement office, your department faculty, friends, colleagues in the field, and professional associations and/or journals and other publications. Stay up-to-date on job search techniques.

3. *Prepare/collect the necessary materials* for your job search, and make sure everything is current and will be available when needed:

   - EMPLOYMENT CREDENTIAL, including references, to be sent by your placement office.
   - RÉSUMÉ, to copy and send with letters and to take to interviews.
   - LETTERS—of application; of inquiry to a specific school or location; of follow-up to indicate continued interest; of thank-you for interviews—do samples to follow later.
   - PERSONAL FILE—copies of résumé; transcripts; lesson plans and special programs developed; personal references and other evaluations not in your credential; photos; tapes; slides; performance programs; exhibit lists; publications lists; personal statement; etc.—to send when requested and to take to interviews.

4. *Apply for jobs,* when you hear of an opening, by sending an application letter and your résumé. Write inquiry letters and send a résumé to specific areas in which you are interested. If and when the employer so requests, also send materials from your personal file, ask your placement office to send credentials, and have the transcript office send a copy of your transcript. Late in the year, or when there are close deadlines, you may want to phone the employer to find out what you can do to speed up the process and to encourage an interview.

Source: Educational Placement & Career Services, University of Wisconsin–Madison, Madison, Wisconsin. Reprinted by permission.

5. ***Prepare for interviews;*** plan what questions you will ask, and find out what employers are looking for and what questions can typically be expected from them. Use libraries, chambers of commerce, colleagues, and the placement office to research schools and communities.

6. ***Follow up*** on applications periodically; do not wait to be contacted. Send thank-you letters for interviews, and follow up if you are not contacted by an agreed-upon date. Remain *active* in your job search—be assertive! REMEMBER that you are responsible for finding your job.

Typical Interview Questions (K–12)

For the Teacher Candidate

In preparing yourself for the employment interview, consider kinds of questions that the interviewer may ask you. Most interviewers ask questions that fall into four major categories: (1) personal qualifications and background, (2) interpersonal relationships, (3) the teaching-learning process, and (4) professional qualifications and experience. The following questions are representative of those that might be posed in each of the four categories:

A. *Personal Qualifications and Background*

1. Why do you want to teach?
2. What gives you the most satisfaction as a teacher?
3. What can you contribute to our school?
4. Tell me about your personal background.
5. What are your hobbies and interests?
6. What would you like to be doing professionally five years from now?
7. Why do you think you will be a successful teacher?
8. Why should I hire you instead of other applicants?
9. What extra-duty activities would you be willing to assist with?
10. What are your strongest traits? Your weakest trait(s)?

B. *Interpersonal Relationships*

1. What quality in other people is most important to you?
2. Would you enjoy team-teaching?
3. What do you believe your role and obligations to be toward other faculty members?
4. What techniques do you use in developing rapport with students?
5. How do your students react to your teaching?
6. What are the qualities of some of the best teachers you have studied under or worked with?
7. How do you feel you relate with minority students in the classroom?
8. What do you see your relationship to be with the parents of the students in your classroom?

Source: Educational Placement & Career Services, University of Wisconsin–Madison, Madison, Wisconsin. Reprinted by permission.

9. How would you work with students in your classroom who are handicapped or disadvantaged in some way?

10. What procedures work best for you in maintaining discipline?

C. *The Teaching-Learning Process*

1. How do you handle curricular content in classes with many levels of ability?

2. How would you individualize instruction in your classroom?

3. What do you consider to be the most worthwhile innovations in your particular field(s)?

4. Describe the role of the teacher in the learning process.

5. What do you consider to be an ideal learning environment?

6. How would you organize and what would you include in a unit lesson plan?

7. What "pet" ideas or innovations do you plan to use in your teaching?

8. How do you expect to motivate students?

9. What do you think of the letter grade system?

10. What would you do or how would you treat a student who refused to do the work assigned?

D. *Professional Qualifications and Experience*

1. Why did you choose your particular area of preparation?

2. What have you learned from your student teaching experience?

3. What grade level do you feel most competent teaching? Why?

4. What out-of-school experiences have you had working with children?

5. What kinds of work experience have you had other than teaching?

6. What courses do you feel competent to teach?

7. How effective has your university been in preparing you for teaching?

8. What is the purpose or place of your subject on the school curriculum?

9. How do you define education?

10. What would you do if . . . ? (hypothetical situations regarding curriculum, methods, texts, student relationships, professionalism, and discipline)

For the Employer

You will want to be prepared to obtain information as well as give it, so if the employer does not cover everything you want to know, do not hesitate to ask about the following and anything else you may have questions on:

A. *The Teaching Assignment*

1. Specific information concerning classload and subjects to be taught

2. Extra-class assignments

3. Physical facilities

4. Available equipment/teaching aids

5. Texts

6. Other responsibilities

B. *Information About the School*

1. Educational philosophy, programs, future plans

2. The school curriculum

3. Availability of study guides and special supervisory help

4. Length of school periods, school day, and school year
5. Number of teachers in system
6. Personnel data concerning staff, that is, average age, number of years of experience, etc.
7. Student data, teacher-pupil ratio
8. Nature and condition of physical plant
9. Special classes/mainstreaming
10. Record and grading system
11. Enrollment trends

C. *Information About the Community*
1. Location and population of community
2. Transportation facilities
3. Educational and cultural background of community
4. Tax base or financial ability of community to support schools
5. Recreational opportunities
6. Churches available
7. Nature of vocational groups
8. Civic activities and vigor of community

D. *Personal Information*
1. Availability and cost of housing
2. General cost of living
3. Salary details and nature of "fringe" benefits

Letters
of Inquiry

The purpose of the letter of inquiry is to introduce yourself to an employer and to inquire if a vacancy exists or is anticipated in the fields for which you are qualified. You write a letter of inquiry when you are interested in a specific school or location and want to know about the availability of jobs there. It is not an application for a specific position, but rather an inquiry about possible openings, whether full-time, part-time or substitute. Whenever possible, address the letter to a particular individual (e.g., personnel officer, district administrator, principal, department chairperson). Names of appropriate individuals can be found in directories available in your placement office or in the reference room of some libraries.

The *opening paragraph* of a letter of inquiry should state why you are writing to the employer and the type of position you are seeking. You may also want to include a sentence or two on why you want to live or teach in the employer's area.

The *middle paragraph(s)* should include information on your qualifications in your field, based on your education and past experiences. Mention where and when you received your latest college degree, as well as your major and minor teaching fields. It may be helpful to include extracurricular interests like coaching to enhance your background. Since you will be enclosing a *résumé* with your letter of inquiry, don't repeat everything from it in your letter; rather, limit your comments to highlights of your résumé, emphasizing special skills or experiences.

The *concluding paragraph* should indicate the name and address of the placement office where your employment credential is on file, and information on how you can be contacted. In closing, you will also want to request application forms and/or information about the school district. One page should be ample for the inquiry letter.

It is time consuming to write letters of inquiry, but the time spent will hopefully result in your obtaining a teaching position. A typed (or even handwritten) letter is preferable to letters that have been copied by machine. This letter provides a first impression of you, and first impressions are important, whether in a letter of inquiry or the first few minutes of a job interview.

Responses to letters of inquiry vary. Some schools, especially those with a small clerical staff, may ignore your letter unless a legitimate vacancy exists. Enclosing a stamped, self-addressed envelope may encourage a response. Other districts may send you a postcard indicating they have no openings in your field, but that they will keep your résumé on file in case an opening does occur. Some schools will automatically send you an application form and perhaps some information on their district. This does not necessarily mean that they have a vacancy, but you will need to complete the application form to be considered for a position if one does open.

Source: Eucational Placement & Career Services, University of Wisconsin–Madison, Madison, Wisconsin. Reprinted by permission.

Consider the best time to send letters of inquiry. Elementary and secondary schools generally begin their search for teachers in the spring. Letters sent too early might be ignored, while those sent in March, April, and May will probably get the most response. You may need to send letters in the spring, *and* again in late June or July, to maintain contact with those districts that have at least acknowledged your first letter. By showing continued interest in a school district, you will enhance your chances of being considered as a prospective candidate when vacancies arise. Keep a record of the schools to which you have written, as well as the responses they have made to your letters of inquiry, so you will know which schools need to be contacted again.

The Letter
of Application

A letter of application is written to a prospective employer when you know an opening for which you are qualified actually exists. The letter will provide the employer with a first impression of you, including your ability to communicate, so it is important to construct the letter carefully and type it neatly on good-quality stationery. Check for spelling, punctuation, and grammatical errors. Address your letter to the individual whose name is given in the vacancy listing, and include a copy of your résumé with the letter of application.

Since you have some information about the position (e.g., tenth-grade English and advisor to the school yearbook), the letter of application can and should be more specifically written than a letter of inquiry. You will want to highlight information from your résumé that relates to the position (e.g., that you student taught at the tenth-grade level, that you have several credits in journalism, or that you were the editor of your high school annual).

The *opening paragraph* typically states why you are writing to the employer and how you learned of the job vacancy.

Middle paragraphs deal with your qualifications for the position based on your educational background and experiences. You might want to include certification information, particularly if you will be licensed in more than one field. Personal data should be included when it is relevant; an example would be your interest in supervising extracurricular activities. The body of the letter should not be too stiff or formal—let some of your personality come through. A letter that looks like a standard application letter that could have been written by any of a hundred different people will not enhance your employment chances. Another way to personalize the letter would be to gather information about the school so that you can identify ways in which you would be an asset to their program. Although it is not always possible to obtain much information, it can be useful when it is available. Library reference rooms contain copies of college catalogs, and college placement offices often have booklets on school districts which you can review before writing your letter. How much time you have to apply will often affect how much research you can do prior to writing your letter.

In the *final paragraph* you will want to list the address of the placement office where your employment credential is on file and indicate how the employer may contact you. Express an interest in obtaining an interview, and give some indication of when you would be available for an interview.

Upon receiving your application letter and a copy of your résumé, the employer will review them and typically respond in one of the following ways: by merely acknowledging receipt of your materials, asking for more material, sending you an application form, or arranging for an interview. Unfortunately, some employers do not respond at all. This may occur if a large number of individuals apply for a position. If this happens to you, you may want to write a follow-up letter or even phone the employer to see if your letter and résumé arrived and to find out when you can expect to hear from him or her. Keep a record of where you have applied, when you applied, and the response to your application.

Source: Eucational Placement & Career Services, University of Wisconsin–Madison, Madison, Wisconsin. Reprinted by permission.

The
Résumé

The résumé is a brief account of your educational, personal, and experienctial qualifications for a position. It is used as a general introduction to accompany the letters of application or inquiry you send to potential employers, to promote a job interview. *The completed résumé should be one to two pages long for positions in education.*

As you begin your résumé, review your qualifications for the type of position you are seeking. What is unique about your preparation and background in terms of both your formal and informal experiences and the skills you have acquired? You'll want to emphasize those facets of your experience and preparation that qualify you for the type of position you are seeking. This could mean that you'll need *more than one* résumé, for different types of jobs.

Résumés are structured in different ways. Ideas for format can be found in library reference books and at your placement office, where sample résumé may be available for review. The résumé should be concisely written, orderly in format, and neatly typed. Do a rough draft first to plan the layout and provide for revisions. You may use either short phrases or complete sentences, but try to be consistent in style throughout the résumé. Summarize your experiences, but not so briefly that you omit important information that may distinguish your résumé from the others being reviewed. It may help to ask these questions regarding the information: Does it contribute to my expertise as an educator? And, is it something the employer wants and needs to know?

Listed below are some kinds of information you should include in your résumé, depending on your background. Use the categories and titles that best fit your background. Remember to anticipate your qualifications, that is, include any degree, experience, etc. that you will have by the time you are employed.

1. *Identification*—Your name, present address, and phone number, including zip code and area code, should be listed at the top of the résumé. It is often advisable to list another address and phone number, either permanent or work, where you can be contacted if you can't be reached at your current address. This is particularly important for students, whose addresses often change during the summer when employers will be trying to contact them.

2. *Employment Objective*—This is a statement of the type of job you are pursuing and can serve as a focal point from which the rest of the résumé emanates. It may include your areas of teaching interests and competencies as well as information on the extracurricular activities you are qualified to supervise, research interests, etc. An employment objective tells the employer what you can do for him or her. If you have several possible objectives, you may need different résumés, or you may use your letter of application, instead of your résumé, to indicate your objective.

Source: Eucational Placement & Career Services, University of Wisconsin–Madison, Madison, Wisconsin. Reprinted by permission.

3. *Educational Background*—Include information on the schools and colleges you have attended, dates of attendance, and degrees earned, or, if no degree, credits taken. List in order of *most recent first.* Those seeking specialist positions in the public schools will want to include information on their graduate work, both completed and in progress, including area of specialization.

4. *Certificates or Teaching Licenses*—All public school candidates must include information on the fields in which they are licensed to teach or will be eligible to teach by the date of employment. Include the state in which you are licensed, fields, grade levels, and, in Wisconsin, the certification code number(s) for the field(s).

5. *Work Experience*—Employers want to know about your previous work experiences and the *skills* and *responsibilities* those jobs required. Simply listing employment experience is not enough for the résumé. First, prioritize your experiences, with those most relevant to your objective listed first. Indicate the position you held (e.g., English teacher), the employer and location, and the dates. Then *briefly* describe the important aspects (skills, responsibilities) of the experience. If you have a long list of jobs, divide them into separate categories, such as "Teaching Experience," "Volunteer Experience," etc. for clarity. Non-teaching experiences can be included in this section. Be sure to indicate how these experiences have enhanced your teaching abilities.

   For those seeking *teaching* positions, you might include the kinds of courses taught, age level of students, type of school (e.g., open classroom), administrative responsibilities, a unit you developed, a technique you implemented to teach a unit already in place, a description of the learning center you constructed, curriculum development you participated in, and so forth. Stress the contributions you made over and above the expected duties. Student teaching experience, teaching internships, assistantships, and practica should be included and so identified. You may also have non-school work experience, such as summer employment and volunteer experience related to the type of position you are seeking, for example, a camp counselor or tutor experience.

   Those seeking *specialist or administrative* positions may want to include teaching, administrative experiences, special courses taught or developed, etc. Non-school experience may also be listed, especially if it covers a six-month period or longer.

6. *Professional Activities*—A *brief* indication of your activities, such as memberships, research, publications, exhibits, performances, repertoire, presentations, speeches/addresses, workshops, etc., should also be included in the résumé. Memberships might include community and service groups, also, if they are important to the picture you want to present. Each activity can have its own category or be listed with a similar activity if you have only a few entries for each. *If you have a long list of activities in any of these categories, indicate that it is available upon request and put only the most recent/significant entries on your résumé. Keep the list in your personal file to send with the résumé and/or to take to interviews. Remember that the résumé itself should be brief.*

7. *Special Abilities/Interests*—You should emphasize your experience and education in areas that employers find especially valuable, such as coaching, reading education, multi-ethnic education, urban education, etc. Even if you are not aware of a specific need or are unsure of what commitment you want to make to extracurriculars, list your experience on the résumé. A résumé is a tool used to get an interview. A list of extracurriculars may give you the edge in getting the interview. Some individuals may want to create a separate section on the résumé for their coaching experiences and other extracurricular activities.

8. *Honors, Scholarships, and Awards*—Include in this category any college, professional, or community recognitions that are significant to your background. You may need to be specific about the award. Not all employers know, for example, that Phi Eta Sigma is a national freshman honorary fraternity.

9. *References*—It is important to list references who can be specific about your professional competencies or previous employment experiences. Provide a title (e.g., Professor, Cooperating Teacher) and complete address for each reference. Also, list telephone

numbers, since many employers want to speak directly to those listed as references. Remember to obtain permission from those persons you've listed to use their names and telephone numbers.

Remember that employers who read your résumé usually know nothing about you. Have you provided them with enough information to present a clear picture of who you are and what your background has been, yet not so much as to overwhelm them? Have you geared the résumé to the kind of job you want? Does your résumé tell them what makes you different, in terms of interests, skills, preparation, and experience, from the others who will be applying for the same job? Since you are applying for a professional job, did you first present your qualifications and then let the employer see you as a person? A well-done résumé often determines who gets selected for an interview, so it is worth the time spent in careful preparation.

Before you type the final copy, consider having others, such as your placement consultant or someone who has had experience in hiring, read your résumé. They may have helpful suggestions. During the layout of the document, utilize underlining, capital letters, bold print, and white space to highlight key ideas and categories. Be prepared to revise your résumé as your experiences and job interests change. And keep your résumé current and applicable to the kinds of positions you are applying for.

You will need several copies of your résumé, to send to prospective employers. A reputable copy center will reproduce your résumé on higher quality paper so it is clear and readable. Check the phone directory for locations of copy centers. If you wish to have your résumé copied on colored paper or have the layout done by a printer, expect to pay more. Some printers will type and do layout as well as make the copies for you. Remember that although unusual layout, printing, or colored paper may be pluses in producing a high-quality résumé, it is the *content* that matters most.

Job Search
Timetable Checklist

This checklist is designed to help graduating students who are seeking teaching positions make the best use of their time as they conduct job searches. We encourage you to use this checklist in conjunction with the services and resources available from your college or university career planning and placement office.

August/September *(12 months prior to employment)*	_____ Attend any applicable orientations/ workshops offered by your college placement office.
	_____ Register with your college placement office and inquire about career services.
	_____ Begin to define career goals by determining the types, sizes and geographic locations of school systems in which you have an interest.
October *(11 months prior to employment)*	_____ Begin to identify references and ask them to prepare letters of recommendation for your credential or placement files.
	_____ See a counselor at your college placement office to discuss your job-search plan.
November *(10 months prior to employment)*	_____ Check to see that you are properly registered at your college placement office.
	_____ Begin developing a résumé and a basic cover letter.
	_____ Begin networking by contacting friends, faculty members, etc., to inform them of your career plans. If possible, give them a copy of your résumé.
December/January *(8–9 months prior to employment)*	_____ Finalize your résumé and make arrangements for it to be reproduced. You may want to get some tips on résumé reproduction from your college placement office.
	_____ Attend any career planning and placement workshops designed for education majors.
	_____ Use the directories available at your college placement office to develop a list of school systems in which you have an interest.
	_____ Contact school systems to request application materials.
	_____ If applying to out-of-state school systems, contact the appropriate State Departments of Education to determine testing requirements.
February *(7 months prior to employment)*	_____ Check the status of your credential or placement file at your college placement office.
	(continued on next page)

From *1995 ASCUS Annual.* Copyright © 1995 Association for School, College and University Staffing, Evanston, Illinois. Reprinted by permission.

	_____ Send completed applications to school systems, with a résumé and cover letter.
	_____ Inquire about school systems which will be recruiting at your college placement office, and about the procedures for interviewing with them.
March/April *(5–6 months prior to employment)*	_____ Research school systems with which you will be interviewing.
	_____ Interview on campus and follow up with thank you letters.
	_____ Continue to follow up by phone with school systems of interest.
	_____ Begin monitoring the job vacancy listings available at your college placement office.
May/August *(1–4 months prior to employment)*	_____ Just before graduation, check to be sure you are completely registered with your college placement office, and that your credential or placement file is in good order.
	_____ Maintain communication with your network of contacts.
	_____ Subscribe to your college placement office's job vacancy bulletin.
	_____ Revise your résumé and cover letter if necessary.
	_____ Interview off campus and follow up with thank you letters.
	_____ If relocating away from campus, contact a college placement office in the area to which you are moving and inquire about available services.
	_____ Continue to monitor job vacancy listings and apply when qualified and interested.
	_____ Begin considering job offers. Ask for more time to consider offers, if necessary.
	_____ Accept the best job offer. Inform those associated with your search of your acceptance.

Glossary of
Important Terms

academic engaged time   The time a student spends on academically related activities or materials while actual learning is taking place.

academic freedom   The freedom of teachers to teach about a topic or issue or to use teaching materials without fear of penalty, reprisal, or harassment so long as the instruction meets the curriculum guidelines of the school district.

academic learning skills   Competencies in subject matter areas such as English, math, science, and social studies.

academy   A kind of private or semiprivate secondary school during the early to middle 1800s. In its later years, the academy was similar to a college.

accommodation   When newly gained knowledge causes one to redefine and/or interpret previous knowledge. For instance, a child may know that all dogs bark until encountering an African basenji, which only whines.

accountability   Holding teachers and/or school administrators responsible for student achievement and learning.

aesthetics   A branch of philosophy that examines the questions of beauty and art.

alternative certification   Teacher certification obtained through a state without completing a state-approved teacher education program through a college or university.

alternative school   A school, public or private, that provides learning opportunities different from local public schools; for example, a school that emphasizes the arts or math and science.

American Federation of Teachers (AFT)   Founded in 1916, it is the second largest teachers association or union in the United States.

Americans with Disabilities Act (ADA)   Federal legislation passed in 1990 that ensures that individuals with disabilities cannot be discriminated against.

assertive discipline   Classroom management approach that establishes clear expectations and limits of student behavior as well as appropriate consequences if rules are broken.

assimilation   The process of acquiring new information and knowledge.

at-risk students   Students who are considered to be more likely than an average student of being a low achiever or of dropping out of school.

attitude   An individual's predisposition to act in either a positive or negative manner toward others, ideas, or events.

authentic assessment   The attempt to measure student performance on actual academic tasks rather than through testing.

axiology   The area of philosophy that examines value issues, particularly ethics and aesthetics.

back-to-basics   Placing the emphasis on reading, writing, and math (the three Rs) at the elementary level and on academic subjects such as English, math, science, and social studies at the secondary level.

basal reader approach   A method of teaching children in grades K–8 to read that uses textbooks including stories, informational pieces, and poetry, along with supportive reading and writing activities. In addition, the textbooks have detailed teacher's manuals with suggested questions and student activities.

bilingual education   Instruction provided in students' native language for those students whose first (birth) language is not English.

block grants Education grants from the federal government to the states for specific purposes. Each state, in turn, selects specific programs to fund, based on the federal guidelines that describe how the monies are to be spent.

block scheduling When large chunks of time are arranged for classes at the middle, junior high or high school level. For instance, a class may meet twice a week for 120 minutes per class session.

board of education (local) A group of citizens, usually elected but sometimes appointed, given authority by the state to operate the public schools of a school district.

Brown v. Board of Education of Topeka A 1954 U.S. Supreme Court decision that held that it was unconstitutional to have segregated schools because the students in such schools were not educated equally.

categorical grant Federal grant designated for specific purposes.

CD-ROM (compact disc-read only memory) A disc that can store several hundred megabytes of data.

certification State government review and approval that a teaching candidate has met certain specific standards.

Channel One A free commercial cable television program shown in classrooms that provides brief news programs accompanied by commercials to public schools.

Chapter I A federal program under the Educational Consolidation and Improvement Act that provides funds to improve the education of economically disadvantaged students, particularly in reading, writing, and math.

character The sum of an individual's lifelong habits that in turn greatly determine how that person will react to challenges and events.

charter schools Public schools that have been given special permission by the school district and the state to deliver an alternative educational program that better meets the needs of the community's students.

child-centered curriculum A curriculum that focuses on the developmental needs and interests of students in combination with meeting academic goals. Such a curriculum is based on the theories of Rousseau, Pestalozzi, and Froebel.

choice Allowing parents to decide which school within a school district their child will attend.

classroom management The procedures and criteria established by the teacher with the students to ensure that instruction will occur efficiently without undue interruptions.

collective bargaining A system for reaching agreements and resolution of differences between employers and employees (teachers and the school board).

common school A publicly supported and locally controlled school that is free to all children. Horace Mann was the champion of this type of school.

compensatory education Federal or state funding to provide a more equal educational opportunity for disadvantaged children (e.g., Chapter I and Head Start).

comprehensive school A public high school that offers a variety of curricular choices, from academic to vocational, to meet the needs of all of its students.

conserve The ability to recognize that things retain their size. For instance, a pencil is the same size regardless of where it is placed on a table or that a child doesn't disappear just because he is under a blanket.

consolidation The combining of two or more smaller school districts into one larger school district.

constructivism Rooted in cognitive psychology, a theory that people learn by building or constructing their own knowledge through active learning (i.e., hands-on, firsthand experiences) rather than through direct instruction (being told specific information).

contract A legal agreement between two or more parties in which one party agrees to do something (such as teach) in exchange for something else (salary and fringe benefits).

cooperative/collaborative learning An instructional method in which children work together in small groups to accomplish a common learning goal. Each student must do his or her work for the group to meet its goal.

core curriculum A common course of study for all students that stresses language arts, math, science, and social studies at the elementary level and English, math, science, social studies, and a foreign language at the high school level.

corporal punishment Punishment administered for disciplinary reasons that relies on physical punishment (e.g., paddling).

culture A set of beliefs, values, and mores of a group of people.

curriculum The planned instructional organization and experiences of a school to meet its educational goals and objectives for its students.

dame school A school in early colonial days operated by a woman in her own home.

defacto **segregation** School segregation resulting from housing patterns in neighborhoods.

de jure **segregation** School segregation resulting from laws or government action.

direct instruction   An organized, systematic instructional approach in which the teacher presents the material or knowledge in small segments to the students.

distance education   Use of technology to link teachers and students in two or more different locations or schools.

drug-free schools   One of the goals of Goals 2000, a federal education act passed by Congress in 1994.

due process   A formalized legal procedure that protects an individual's constitutional rights.

education   The lifelong process of acquiring knowledge, skills, and values through either formal means, such as schooling, or informal means, such as firsthand experiences or vicarious experiences gained through reading books or discussions with others.

Education for All Handicapped Children Act Amendment   Federal legislation that extended Public Law 94-142 to provide early intervention for young children between the ages of birth and age two.

Education for All Handicapped Children Act (Public Law 94-142)   Federal legislation passed in 1975 providing for the education of students with disabilities, including students with hearing and/or vision impairments, mental retardation, emotional disturbance, and learning disabilities.

Elementary and Secondary Education Act (ESEA)   A federal law passed by Congress in 1965 to improve educational conditions for students who are disadvantaged socially or emotionally. The Head Start and Title I programs began under ESEA.

elementary school   An educational institution for children in kindergarten through grade 6 or 8.

epistemology   An area of philosophy that examines knowing and theories of knowledge.

essentialism   An educational philosophy that emphasizes basic skills such as reading, writing, and math at the elementary level and English, geography, history, mathematics, and science at the secondary level.

ethics   An area of philosophy that questions right and wrong and good and bad.

existentialism   The philosophy that examines the way in which individuals create their own meaning and purpose in life.

experimentalism   The philosophical stance that believes learning takes place when an individual attempts to try something new.

expulsion   The dismissal of a student, usually as a consequence of misbehavior at school, for a long period of time, from one semester to permanent dismissal.

fair use   A federal law that allows teachers to make copies of materials for use with students for educational purposes under certain limited conditions.

gender equity   Treating students of both sexes fairly by providing equal educational and extracurricular opportunities.

goals   Educational purposes of a school or school district.

Goals 2000   Federal legislation passed in 1994 that sets the following as national education goals: every adult will be literate; schools free of drugs, alcohol, and firearms; a 90 percent graduation rate; competencies in English, math, science, foreign languages, civics and government, economics, arts, history, and geography; professional development of teachers; and every school will promote partnerships with parents of students.

Head Start   A federally funded program that provides educational opportunities for economically disadvantaged preschoolers.

heterogeneous grouping   Grouping of students with varying abilities and achievement levels.

high school   A school for upper-level students, commonly referred to as secondary school, usually including grades 9–12.

homogeneous grouping   Grouping of students by ability or achievement levels.

hornbook   A flat, wooden board with a parchment made from a cow's horn that usually contained the alphabet, numerals, and the Lord's Prayer. This was used to teach students during the colonial period.

hypermedia   Computer technology that links a video laser disc, graphics, sound, and text together.

idealism   The philosophy that asserts that reality is spiritual in nature. Individuals must attempt to attain ideals or models of perfection.

inclusion   Educating a student with a mental, physical, or emotional disability in a regular classroom.

individualized education program (IEP)   A written educational program as required by Public Law 94-142 that outlines the current level of performance and short- and long-term educational goals for students with mental, physical, or emotional disabilities.

in loco parentis   A legal term meaning "in the place of a parent." A teacher or school administrator assumes the responsibility and rights of a parent while the student is in school.

instruction   The methods and materials used by the teacher as part of the curriculum to develop students' skills.

integrated curriculum   This curriculum approach emphasizes having students grasp basic learning principles and generalizations rather than learning isolated facts. Creative and critical thinking are stressed.

integration   The combining of people or things. For instance, having students of different cultures work together or teaching different subjects together (e.g., science and social studies).

Internet   A computer network that enables over 20 million people throughout the world to communicate with one another or retrieve information.

junior high school   An educational institution that usually has students who are young adolescents in grades 7 and 8 and sometimes 9.

kindergarten   A division of school for children between the ages of four and six, with the majority being five years old. First started in Germany in the 1900s by Froebel, who referred to it as "a children's garden."

land-grant college   A state college or university offering agricultural or mechanical curricula that was originally established and funded by Congress by the Morrill Act of 1862.

Latin grammar school   A college preparatory school during the colonial period that stressed Latin and Greek.

learner outcomes   Statements of what students should know and be able to do after having been taught a specific lesson or unit.

least restrictive environment   A requirement of Public Law 94-142 that students with disabilities be included in regular education programs to the greatest extent possible.

logic   An area of philosophy that includes the study of reasoning. Logic is the study of deductive inference.

magnet school   A type of alternative school in which instruction is focused around a particular curricular area such as math and science or the fine arts. Students may elect to attend the magnet school instead of their neighborhood school. Magnet schools have been used to encourage students of all racial backgrounds to attend, thereby promoting voluntary desegregation.

metaphysics   An area of philosophy that focuses on the nature of existence.

middle school   An educational institution that is an extension of the elementary school and usually has students in grades 6–8.

multicultural education   Teaching approaches that foster the understanding and appreciation of the various cultures in society.

multiple intelligences   Howard Gardner's theory that identifies seven dimensions of intellectual capacities of individuals used in problem solving and the creation of ideas.

National Board for Professional Teaching Standards   A new professional agency that sets standards for teachers. At this time, such an endorsement of teachers is voluntary.

National Defense Education Act (NDEA)   A federal law passed by Congress in 1958 in response to the former Soviet Union's launch of *Sputnik.* The law provided funds to improve the teaching of math and science and provide technological equipment for classroom use. In addition, loans were made available to college students to encourage them to enroll in teacher education programs.

National Education Association (NEA)   Founded in 1857, it is the largest teachers' association in the United States. Sponsors National Education Week in November each year.

National Teacher Examinations (NTE) Standardized tests designed and administered by the Educational Testing Service (ETS) to measure teachers' general knowledge, professional knowledge, and communication skills. In addition, there are specific subject area tests. Some states use the NTE test scores to screen for new teacher candidates.

normal school   A teacher preparatory college begun in the 1800s that required students to attend for two or four years. Pedagogy, or teaching methods, were emphasized. Horace Mann and Henry Barnard were strong advocates of normal schools.

objectives   The basic goal or goals of a lesson plan.

on-task behavior   Student engagement in learning activities as part of the lesson's objectives and goals.

outcome-based education (OBE)   A reform approach by William Spady that emphasizes general learning outcomes rather than specific content to be covered. Every student is expected to meet a school's learning outcomes. If a student successfully completes the assessment measure for the learning outcome, enrichment activities are then assigned to him or her until the other students in the class pass the assessment measure. In addition, students are expected to understand and respect others. OBE is very controversial and is especially criticized by conservative religious groups.

pedagogy   Methods used to teach students.

perennialism   An area of philosophy that views human nature as constant, with little change occurring over time. In education, the purpose of schools is considered to be the development of intellect.

philosophy   The search for the meaning of life. In Western culture, five aspects of philosophy are considered: metaphysics, ethics, aesthetics, epistemology, and logic.

Plessy v. Ferguson   In 1896, the U.S. Supreme Court ruled that separate but equal accommodations for African Americans was constitutional. In education, this was interpreted to mean that African Americans and white students could attend separate schools. This was overturned with the *Brown v. Board of Education of Topeka* U.S. Supreme Court ruling in 1954.

portfolios   An authentic assessment measure that uses the student's actual work to demonstrate what has been achieved as well as what needs to be learned.

pragmatism   The belief that truth is tested by its practical results. Thus, truth is relative depending on the various circumstances in which it is tested.

Praxis   Three standardized tests that were developed by the Educational Testing Service to measure competencies of beginning teachers.

preschool   A school for infants through five-year-olds that has a structured curriculum.

principal   The administrator responsible for both building and curricular operations of a school.

progressivism   A type of educational philosophy that views nature as everchanging, thus requiring learners to be problem solvers.

property tax   A local tax on land and buildings such as a person's home or a business office complex. Property tax is considered to be a proportionate tax in that the taxes reflect a person's or company's ability to pay.

realism   An area of philosophy that states that ideas or universals have an absolute existence. A view that decisions should be based on facts and reality, disregarding emotions or imagination.

reflective teaching   A teacher's practice of reviewing and thinking about what he or she has taught and how it could be improved.

regressive tax   A tax on items that is paid at the time of purchase, such as sales, tobacco, and gasoline taxes.

reminiscence   A term coined by Plato. It is a process that individuals recall the truths or ideas present at their birth. These truths and ideas are brought forth through learning.

scholasticism   Was a method of inquiry, scholarship, and teaching developed by educators during the Middle Ages. St. Thomas Aquinas was the best known of the Scholastics.

school district   A governmental unit created under state statutes to administer the local school system. Its purpose is to educate.

schooling   Formal instruction based on standardized practices in an institution.

self-fulfilling prophecy   Students' behavior that reflects teachers' expectations. If a teacher expects a student to achieve, the student will perform well. Likewise, if the student is expected to perform poorly, the student will perform poorly.

site-based management   Administrative decisions made by a team of school administrators and teachers at the school level rather than handed down from a school district's central administration.

socialization   The process of social learning in which the child discovers what is and is not acceptable behavior in society.

social reconstructionism   The educational theory that it is up to the schools and teachers to make reforms that will cure societal problems.

special education   The educational programming for students with emotional, mental, and/or physical disabilities.

staff development or inservice training   Organized efforts by a school or school district to enhance the professional skills of teachers and school administrators.

state board of education   The primary education policy-setting committee for a state. Members are usually appointed by the governor and serve staggered terms.

state department of education   The state office of education under the direction of the state board of education and the state superintendent of instruction. The office distributes state and federal funds to school districts, certifies teachers and school administrators, collects and analyzes data pertaining to the schools, and establishes criteria and approves college and university teacher education programs.

student-centered curriculum   This curriculum approach is based on pragmatism and experimentalism, in which activities and programs are designed based on student interests and abilities.

subject-matter curriculum   This curriculum approach emphasizes the content areas with little consideration for creative and critical thinking.

superintendent of schools   A school administrator who is employed by the local school board as its chief executive in overseeing the operation of the district's schools and educational programs. Requires a special school administrative certificate by the state beyond that of being a school principal.

suspension   The exclusion of a student from attending classes for a short period of time due to the student's misbehavior.

teacher empowerment   When the school district asks teachers to provide increased input into the educational process (i.e., make curricular decisions as to what will be taught and how).

teaching portfolio   Collection of lesson plans, teaching units, samples of students' work, and videotapes of actual lessons taught that demonstrate the quality of teaching.

tenure   A legal term meaning that after a specified time of employment as a teacher in a district (usually two or three years, depending on the state), the teacher cannot be dismissed without sufficient cause.

time on task   The amount of time students are actively engaged in academic work during a lesson, or class period, or in a school day.

Title IX   Part of the 1972 federal Education Amendment Act that requires that schools provide equal access for female students. School districts that discriminate against females by not allowing them access to an educational program or activity cannot receive federal funds.

tort liability   The responsibility for damages due to improper behavior or conduct of an individual. This is a civil, not a criminal, wrongdoing.

tracking   The homogeneous grouping of students by ability or achievement levels for learning, usually at the secondary school levels (junior high and high school). Such grouping is discriminatory and unconstitutional.

U.S. Department of Education   A department of the federal government headed by the U.S. secretary of education to oversee federal educational programs.

U.S. secretary of education   This individual heads the U.S. Department of Education and serves on the president of the United States' Cabinet.

values   The attitude of an individual as to what in life is and is not important.

voucher   In return for a written statement (or voucher), parents may elect that their child attend a school they believe best meets his or her educational needs.

whole language approach   An approach that advocates teaching reading, writing, listening, and speaking together through relevant, meaningful experiences in which both the teacher and the student are given choices. It stresses the classroom as a community of learners, the teacher included.

Text and
Art References

A look at parental involvement in schools. 1993. *Reading TODAY* (October/November):17.

Aardema, V. 1977. *Who's in rabbit's house?* Illustrated by D. Dillon and L. Dillon. New York: Dial Press.

Adkinson, J. A. 1980–81. Strategies to promote women's careers in school administration. *Administrator's Notebook* 29:155–88.

Adler, A. J. 1990. *Healing the hurt through self help and professional support.* New York: PIA Press.

Adler, M. J. 1988. *Reforming education: The opening of the American mind.* New York: Macmillan.

Adler, M. J. 1984. Introduction. In M . J. Adler, ed. *The paideia proposal: An educational syllabus.* New York: Macmillan, 1–14.

Alexander, L. 1964. *The book of three.* New York: Holt, Rinehart & Winston.

Allen, J., B. Michalove, B. Shockley, and M. West. 1991. "I'm really worried about Joseph. " Reducing the risks of literacy learning. *Reading Teacher* 44 (6): 458–72.

Altwerger, B., and B. Flores. 1994. Theme cycles: Creating a community of learners. *Primary Voices, K–6* 2 (1):2–6.

American Association of University Women. 1993. *Hostile hallways: The AAUW Survey on sexual harassment in America's schools.* Washington, D.C.: The American Association of University Women.

American Federation of Teachers. 1996. *A bill of rights and responsibilities for learning: Standards of conduct, standards for achievement.* Washington, D.C.: American Federation of Teachers.

American Federation of Teachers. 1995. *Making standards matter.* Washington, D.C.: American Federation of Teachers.

American Federation of Teachers and National Center for Improving Science Education. 1994. *What college-bound students abroad are expected to know about biology: Exams from England and Wales, France, Germany, and Japan.* Washington, D.C.: American Federation of Teachers.

American Psychological Association. 1993. *Violence and youth: Psychology's response,* vol. 1. Washington, D.C.: American Psychological Association.

Anderson, J. 1994. Alternative approaches to organizing the school day and year: A national commission examines new structures for improving student learning. *The School Administrator* 3 (51): 8–15.

Andrews, R. H. 1994. Recreating an environment for learning. *The School Administrator* 51 (1):19, 22.

Andrews-Sullivan, M., and E. O. Negrete. 1994. Our struggles with theme cycle. *Primary Voices, K–6* 2 (1):15–18.

Armstrong, D. G., K. T. Henson, and T. V. Savage. 1993. *Education: An introduction.* New York: Macmillan.

Aronstein, L. W., M. Marlow, and B. Desilets. 1990. Detours on the road to site-based management. *Educational Leadership* 47 (7):61–63.

ASCD Panel on Moral Education. 1988. Moral education in the life of the school. *Educational Leadership* 45 (8):7–8.

Associated Press. 1997. 'Exciting' $62M high school opens today in Naperville. *Rockford Register Star,* 25 August.

Associated Press. 1997. One man's vision turned into a national reality. *Rockford Register Star,* 27 April.

Associated Press. 1997. U.S. Kids weak in science analysis. *Rockford Register Star,* 3 May.

Associated Press. 1996. On test day, educational fervor grips South Korea. *Rockford Register Star,* 17 November.

Associated Press. 1994. Students working—and learning—at mall. *Bloomington (MN) Daily Herald,* 13 May.

Associated Press. 1993. Survey: Schools not safe. *Rockford Register Star,* 17 December: 3A.

Association of American Publishers. 1991. How to request copyright permissions. *The Chronicle of Higher Education* (4 September):A23.

Augustine, D. K., K. D. Gruber, and L. R. Hanson. 1989 and 1990. Cooperation works! *Educational Leadership* 47 (4):4–7.

Ayers, W. 1993. *To teach, the journey of a teacher.* New York: Teachers College Press.

Bagley, W. 1934. An essentialist's platform for the advancement of American education. *Educational Administration and Supervision* 24:241–56.

Baker, E. T., M. C. Wang, and H. J. Walberg. 1994/1995. The effects of inclusion on learning. *Educational Leadership* 52 (4):33–35.

Banks, J. A. 1994. Transforming the mainstream curriculum. *Educational Leadership* 51 (8):10–13.

Banks, J. A., and C. A. M. Banks. 1989. *Multicultural education: Issues and perspectives.* Needham Heights, MA: Allyn & Bacon.

Barnett, E., and F. Curtis. 1986. *The effect of assertive discipline training on student teachers.* Phoenix, AZ: CIJE Document Reproduction Service No. EJ 3561648.

Barrington, B. L., and B. Hendricks. 1989. Differentiating characteristics of high school graduates, dropouts, and nongraduates. *Journal of Educational Research* 82 (July/August):309–19.

Bartlett, J., and J. Kaplan. 1992. *Bartlett's familiar quotations.* 16th ed. New York: Little, Brown.

Batesky, J. 1987. Inservice education: Increasing teacher effectiveness using the Hunter lesson design. *Journal of Physical Education, Recreation, and Dance* (September): 88–93.

Battista, M. T. 1994. Teacher beliefs and the reform movement in mathematics education. *Phi Delta Kappan* 75 (6):462–70.

Bear, T., S. Schenk, and L. Buckner. 1993. Supporting victims of child abuse. *Educational Leadership* 50 (4):42–47.

Beck, R. H. 1986. The Iliad: Principles and lessons, *Educational Theory* (3):179–95.

Begley, S. 1997. Wombs with a view. *Newsweek,* 11 August.

Bell, T. H. 1988. Parting words of the 13th man. *Phi Delta Kappan* 69 (6):400–407.

Belsky, G. 1994. Escape from America. *Money* 23 (7): 60–70.

Benson, H. 1992. *The wellness book.* New York: Fireside.

Berliner, D. 1985. What do we know about well-managed classrooms? Putting research to work. *Instructor* 94 (6):15.

Berliner, D.C. 1983. The executive functions of teaching. *Instructor* 93 (2):28–33, 36, 38, 40.

Berliner, D.C., and B. A. Rosenshine. 1977. The acquisition of knowledge in the classroom. In R. C. Anderson, R. J. Spiro, and W. E. Montague, eds. *Schooling and the acquisition of knowledge.* Hillsdale, NJ: Erlbaum.

Berreth, D., and S. Berman. 1997. The moral dimensions of schools. *Educational Leadership* 54 (8):24–27.

Bestor, A. 1956. *The restoration of learning: A program for redeeming the unfulfilled promise of American education.* New York: Alfred A. Knopf.

Bestor, A. 1953. *Educational wastelands: Retreat from learning in our public schools.* Urbana, IL: University of Illinois Press.

Birkvad, B. 1997. Teacher professional development in Denmark. *Kappan* 78 (8):611–14.

Blankenhorn, D. 1995. *Fatherless America: Confronting our most urgent problem.* New York: Institute for American Values.

Blum, D. E. 1991. Copyright ruling on anthologies may spur vigilance. *The Chronicle of Higher Education* (10 April):A14.

Bonuso, C., and C. Shakeshaft. 1983. The gender of secondary school principals. *Integrated Education* 21:143–46.

Boyd, E. M., and A. W. Fales. 1983. Reflective learning: Key to learning from experience. *Journal of Humanistic Psychology* 23 (2):99–117.

Boyer, E. 1983. *High school.* New York: Harper and Row.

Boyer, E. 1983. *High school: A report on secondary education in America.* New York: Harper and Row.

Boyko, C., and K. Colen. 1996. *Hold fast to your dreams.* New York: Scholastic.

Boylan, P. W. 1993. A letter from Japan. *Phi Delta Kappan* 74 (7):581–82.

Bozzone, M. 1994. The professional portfolio: Why you should start one now. *Instructor* 103 (9):48–50.

Braaten, S., J. M. Kauffmann, B. Braaten, L. Polsgrove, and C. M. Nelson. 1988. The regular education initiative: Patent medicine for behavior disorders. *Exceptional Children* 55 (1):21–28.

Bradley, A. 1996. The missing link. *Education Week,* 17 April, 1.

Bradley, A., and J. Ponessa. 1997. Education community mourns 'the loss of a visionary.' *Education Week,* 5 March, 30–31.

Brameld, T. 1956. *Toward a reconstructed philosophy of education.* New York: Holt, Rinehart & Winston.

Bramson, R. 1986. *Coping with difficult people.* New York: Simon & Schuster.

Brandt, R. 1994. On educating for diversity: A conversation with James A. Banks. *Educational Leadership* 51 (8):3–8.

Brandt, R. 1988. On discipline-based art education: A conversation with Elliot Eisner. *Educational Leadership* 45 (4):6–9.

Broder, D. 1994. School can't go it alone. *Rockford Register Star,* 20 February, 4B.

Brophy, J. 1981. Teacher praise: A functional analysis. *Review of Educational Research* 51 (1):5–32.

Brown, L. M., and C. Gilligan. 1990. *The psychology of women and the development of girls.* Paper presented at the meeting of the Society for Research on Adolescence, March, Atlanta, GA.

Bucci, J. A., and A. F. Reitzammer. 1992. Teachers make the critical difference in dropout prevention. *The Educational Forum* 57 (1):63–70.

Buck, P. S. 1948. *The big wave.* New York: John Day.

Bullough, R. V., Jr. 1989. Teacher education and teacher reflectivity. *Journal of Teacher Education* 40 (2):15–21.

Burgess, D. M., and A. P. Streissguth. 1992. Fetal alcohol syndrome and fetal alcohol effects: Principles for educators. *Phi Delta Kappan* 74 (1): 24–26, 28, 30.

Butterfield, J. 1994. Unload stress for 1994. *USA Weekend,* 2 January, 4–5.

Butts, R. F., and L. A. Cremin. 1953. *A history of education in American culture.* New York: Holt, Rinehart & Winston.

Cahoon, P. 1988. Mediator magic. *Educational Leadership* 45 (4):92–93.

California State Department of Education. 1986. *California Physical Education Framework.* Sacramento, CA: California Department of Education.

Campbell, J. K. 1967. *Col. Francis W. Parker.* New York: Columbia Teachers College Press.

Canning, E. 1991. What teachers say about reflection. *Educational Leadership* 48 (6):18–21.

Canter, L. 1976. *Assertive discipline.* Los Angeles: Lee Canter Associates.

Capkova, D. 1970. The recommendations of Comenius regarding the education of young children. In C. H. Dobinson, ed. *Comenius and contemporary education: An international symposium.* Hamburg, Germany: UNESCO Institute for Education, 17–33.

Carey, A. R., and K. Worthington. 1997. Elementary computing. *USA Today,* November 6: 1A.

Carmony, M. 1994. Personal communication, 21 February.

Carson, R. 1962. *Silent spring.* Boston: Houghton Mifflin.

Carter, G. R. 1994. Is privatization the answer? *ASCD Update* 36 (3):2.

Chiang, L. H. 1993. The voices of beginning teachers: Positive impacts from the Indiana beginning teacher internship program. In P. J. Farris and J. Summers, eds. *Perspectives and possibilities in teacher education.* Terre Haute, IN: Indiana and Illinois Associations of Teacher Educators, 63–65.

Children at risk: A photo essay. 1992. *Phi Delta Kappan* 74 (1):15–17.

Children of Alcoholics Foundation. 1992. *Children of alcoholics at work: We need to know more.* New York: Children of Alcoholics Foundation.

Children's Defense Fund. 1991. *The state of America's children.* Washington, D.C.: Children's Defense Fund.

Civil Rights Project. 1997. *Deepening segregation in American Schools.* Cambridge, MA: Harvard University.

CNN Plus: CNN Interactive Custom Newsline. 1997. U.S. violent crime rate takes sharp drop. June 1 (http://www.cnn.com).

Colorado Department of Education. 1988. *The school's role in the prevention/intervention of child abuse and neglect.* Denver: Colorado Department of Education.

Commager, H. S. 1962. McGuffey and his readers. *Saturday Review* 44 (16 June):50–61, 69–70.

Commission on the Reorganization of Secondary Education. 1918. *Cardinal principles of secondary education,* bulletin no. 35. Washington, D.C.: U.S. Government Printing Office.

Community Update. 1997. U.S. mayors support President Clinton's call to action for American education. Washington, D.C.: Office of Intergovernmental and Interagency Affairs, U.S. Department of Education. July/August.

Conant, J. 1959. *The American high school today.* New York: McGraw-Hill.

Connell, C. 1993. Kids' gun wounds costly. Associated Press, *Rockford Register Star,* 26 November, 1A–2A.

Cordasco, F. 1976. *A brief history of education.* Totowa, NJ: Littlefield, Adams, & Company.

Corkill, P. J., and J. R. Hendricks. 1997. Learning the law and loving the school attorney less. *The School Administrator* 54 (10):6–9.

Corsini, D. A. 1991. Family day care in Denmark: A model for the United States? *Young Children* 56 (7):10–15.

Counts, G. S. 1932. *Dare the school build a new social order?* New York: John Day.

Cowan, D., and T. Puck. 1984. Science. In M. J. Adler, ed. *The paideia proposal: An educational syllabus.* New York: Macmillan.

Cox, M., and R. Alm. 1995. *By our own bootstraps: Economic opportunity and the dynamics of income distribution.* Dallas: Federal Reserve Bank of Dallas.

Cremin, L. A. 1957. *The republic and the school: Horace Mann on the education.* New York: Columbia University Press.

Crunden, R. M. 1984. *Ministers of reform: The Progressives' achievement in American education, 1889–1920.* Urbana, IL: University of Illinois Press.

Csikszentmihalyi, M., and J. McCormick. 1986. The influence of teachers. *Phi Delta Kappan* 67(6):415–19.

Cudd, E. T., and L. L. Roberts. 1994. A scaffolding technique to develop sentence sense and vocabulary. *The Reading Teacher* 47 (4):346–48.

Cunningham, P., M. Kaull, and B. Burkhard. 1992. School vouchers, pro/con: A recipe for disaster. *Rockford Register Star,* 29 November, 5B.

Curio, J. L., and P. F. First. 1993. *Violence in the schools: How to proactively prevent and defuse it.* Newbery Park, CA: Corwin Press.

Curwin, R., and A. Mendler. 1989. We repeat, let the buyer beware: Response to Canter. *Educational Leadership* 46 (6):83.

Curwin, R., and A. Mendler. 1988. Packaged discipline programs: Let the buyer beware. *Educational Leadership* 46 (2):68–71.

Darling-Hammond, L. 1997. *The right to learn: A blueprint for creating schools that work.* San Francisco: Jossey-Bass.

Davis, A., and C. Felknor. 1994. The demise of performance-based graduation in Littleton. *Educational Leadership* 51 (6):8–11.

De Guimps, R. 1896. *Pestalozzi: His life and work.* New York: D. Appleton and Company.

Defoe, D. 1966. *Robinson Crusoe.* Ann Arbor: University Microfilms.

Delpit, L. D. 1991. A conversation with Lisa Delpit. *Language Arts* 68: 541–47.

Delpit, L. D. 1988. The silenced dialogue: Power and pedagogy in educating other people's children. *Harvard Educational Review* 58 (3):280–98.

Deutschman, A., and R. Tetzeli. 1994. Your desktop in the year 1996. *Fortune,* 11 July, 86–98.

Dewey, E. 1916. *New schools for old.* New York: Dutton.

Dewey, J. 1909. *Moral principles in education.* Boston: Houghton Mifflin.

Dewey, J. 1899. *School and society.* Chicago: University of Chicago Press.

Dewey, J. 1916. *Democracy and education: An introduction to the philosophy of education.* New York: Macmillan.

Dickens, C. 1840. *Oliver Twist.* New York: Wm. H. Colyer.

Doerr, E., and A. J. Menendez. 1992. Should tax dollars subsidize bigotry? *Phi Delta Kappan* 74 (2):165–67.

Dreikurs, R., B. Grunwald, and F. Pepper. 1971. *Maintaining sanity in the classroom: Illustrated teaching techniques.* New York: Harper and Row.

Duncan, L. 1992. *Who killed my daughter?* New York: Delacorte Press.

Durkin, D. 1990. Dolores Durkin speaks on instruction. *The Reading Teacher* 43 (6):472–76.

Durr, K. 1992. East German education: A system in transition. *Phi Delta Kappan* 73 (5):390–93.

Edelman, M. W. 1992. Commencement address, Washington University, St. Louis, Missouri, 15 May.

Education Commission of the States. 1996. *The ABCs of investing in student performance.* Denver, CO: Education Commission of the States.

Eisner, E. W. 1994. Rethinking visual arts programs for all students. *ASCD Curriculum Update.* Reston, VA: Association for Supervision and Curriculum Development.

Eisner, E. W. 1992. The misunderstood role of the arts in human development. *Phi Delta Kappan* 73 (8): 591–95.

Elam, S. M., L. C. Rose, and A. M. Gallup. 1994. The 26th annual Phi Delta Kappa/Gallup poll of the public's attitudes toward the public schools. *Phi Delta Kappan* 76(1):41–56.

Elam, S. M., L. C. Rose, and A. M. Gallup. 1993. The 25th annual Phi Delta Kappa/Gallup Poll of the public's attitudes toward the public schools. *Phi Delta Kappan* 75 (2):137–52, 157.

Eliot, G. 1861. *Silas Marner.* Edinbourgh: W. Blackwood and Sons.

Ellinger, T. R., and G. M. Beckham. 1997. South Korea: Placing education on top of the family agenda. *Kappan* 78 (8):624–25.

Ely, V. 1947. *I quote.* New York: George W. Stewart Publisher.

Epstein, J. L. 1995. School/family/community partnerships: Caring for the children we share. *Kappan* 76 (9):699–701.

Evans, K. M., and J. A. King. 1994. Research on OBE: What we know and don't know. *Educational Leadership* 51 (6):12–17.

Evertson, C. M., and A. H. Harris. 1992. What we know about managing classrooms. *Educational Leadership* 49 (7):74–77.

Evertson, C. M., and E. T. Emmer. 1982. Effective management at the beginning of the school year in junior high classes. *Journal of Educational Psychology* 74 (4):485–98.

Fallows, J. 1991. Strengths, weaknesses, and lessons of Japanese education. *Education Digest* 49 (1):55–59.

Farris, P. J. 1997. *Language arts: Process, product, and assessment.* Dubuque, IA: Times Higher Education Group.

Farris, P. J. 1993. *Language arts: A process approach.* Dubuque, IA: Brown & Benchmark.

Farris, P. J. 1992. *Achieving adult literacy.* Bloomington, IN: Phi Delta Kappa.

Farris, P. J. 1986. Author's personal conversation with Ralph Tyler, DeKalb, IL, 5 March.

Farris, P. J. 1980. *A study of the effects on attitude from listening to McGuffey readers and Dr. Seuss books.* Unpublished doctoral dissertation, Indiana State University, Terre Haute, IN.

Farris, P. J., and B. J. Smith. 1993. Alternative certification: Much ado about nothing? *Contemporary Education* 65(1):34–36.

Farris, P. J., and T. Whealon. 1994. Bringing together social studies and whole language: A look at social studies. In P. J. Farris and S. M. Cooper, eds. *Elementary social studies: A whole language approach.* Dubuque, IA: Brown & Benchmark, 1–23.

Fege, A. F. 1997. Parental rights: Yes! Parental rights legislation: No! *Educational Leadership* 55 (3):76–79.

Feldman, C. 1993. Top students display casual attitude toward honesty. *The Northern Star* 21 October, 1.

Ferre, V., and L. Ferre. 1992. Effectiveness of assertive discipline in a rural setting. *Rural Educator* 14 (2):6–8.

Film scene to be cut. 1993. *Rockford Register Star,* 21 October, 1A.

First, P. F., and G. R. Cooper. 1992. Access to education by homeless children. In P. F. First, ed. *Educational policy for school administrators.* Needham Heights, MA: Allyn & Bacon, 104–13.

Fisher, N. F., E. Marleave, L. Cahen, M. Dishaw, M. Moore, and D. Berliner. 1978. *Teaching behaviors, academic learning time, and student achievement: Final report of beginning teacher evaluation study.* San Francisco, CA: Far West Regional Education Laboratory.

Flakes, C. L., T. Kuhs, A. Donnelly, and C. Ebert. 1995. Reinventing the role of the teacher: Teacher as researcher. *Phi Delta Kappan* 76 (5):405–7.

Foxfire Fund. 1990. *The foxfire approach: Perspectives and core practices.* Rabun Gap, GA: Foxfire Fund.

Friedman, P. 1991. *How to deal with difficult people.* New York: Skillpath Communications.

Frymier, J. 1984. *One hundred good schools.* West Lafayette, IN: Kappa Delta Pi.

Fuhler, C. J. 1994. Personal communication with author, 13 November.

Fullan, M. 1993. *Change forces: Probing the depths of educational reform.* London: Falmer Press.

Galotti, K. M., S. F. Kozberg, and M. C. Farmer. 1990. *Gender and developmental differences in adolescents' conceptions of moral reasoning.* Paper presented at the meeting of the Society for Research on Adolescence, March, Atlanta, GA.

Gannett News Service. 1997. High School enrollment to swell 13% in 10 years. 22 August.

Gannett News Service. 1997. NEA votes peer review of teachers. 7 July.

Gardner, H. 1993. *Multiple intelligences.* New York: Basic Books.

Gehrke, N. J. 1987. *On being a teacher.* West Lafayette, IN: Kappa Delta Pi Honor Society.

Gilligan, C. 1990. Teaching Shakespeare's sister. In C. Gilligan, N. Lyons, and T. Hanmer, eds. *Making connections: The relational worlds of adolescent girls at Emma Willard School.* Cambridge, MA: Harvard University Press.

Gilligan, C. 1982. *In a different voice.* Cambridge, MA: Harvard University Press.

Gilligan, C., M. L. Brown, and A. G. Rogers. 1990. Psyche embedded: A place for body, relationships, and culture in personality theory. In A. I. Rabin, R. A. Zucker, R. Emmons, and S. Frank, eds. *Studying lives and persons.* New York: Springer.

Glasser, W. 1992. *The quality school.* New York: Harper and Row.

Glasser, W. 1985. *Control theory: A new explanation of how we control our lives.* New York: Harper and Row.

Glasser, W. 1969. *Schools without failure.* New York: Harper and Row.

Glazer, S. M. 1994. Glazer testifies before U.S. Congress. *Reading Today* 11 (6):6.

Glazer, S. M. 1994. Teachers and education: Are we somehow tied to a class system? *Reading Today* 11 (6):3.

Goldberg, M. 1998. Bringing the voices of the people to the people. *Phi Delta Kappan, 79*(8), 613–615.

Goldberg, M. F. 1990. Portrait of Madeline Hunter. *Educational Leadership* 47 (5):141–43.

Goldman, E. 1998. The significance of leadership style. *Educational Leadership* 55 (7):20–22.

Goldsborough, R. 1997. Staying afloat in a rising ride of data. *Reading Today* (October/November): 7.

Goodlad, J. 1984. *A place called school.* New York: McGraw-Hill.

Goodman, K. 1986. *What's whole in whole language?* Portsmouth, NH: Heinemann.

Gooler, D. D. 1991. *Professorial vitality: A critical issue in higher education.* DeKalb, IL: LEPS Press.

Gordon, R. 1998. Balancing real-world problems with real-world results. *Phi Delta Kappan,* 79 (5):390–393.

Gough, P. B. 1992. Another bad rap. *Phi Delta Kappan* 74 (1):3.

Goya, S. 1993. The secret of Japanese education. *Phi Delta Kappan* 75 (2):126–29.

Green, M., ed. 1967. *Existential encounters for teachers.* New York: Random House.

Griffith, D. R. 1992. Prenatal exposure to cocaine and other drugs: Developmental and educational prognoses. *Phi Delta Kappan* 74 (1):30–34.

Grossman, P. 1991. Mapping the terrain: Knowledge growth in teaching. In H. C. Waxman and H. J. Walberg, eds. *Effective teaching: Current research.* Berkeley, CA: McCutchan Publishing, 203–16.

Grouws, D. A. 1992. Mathematics. *Handbook of research on improving student achievement.* Arlington, VA: Education Research Service.

Gursky, D. 1992. The unschooled mind. *The Education Digest* 58:27–29.

Gursky, D. 1992. Spare the child? *Teacher Magazine* 3 (5):16–19.

Gutek, G. L. 1991. *Cultural foundations of education: A biographical introduction.* New York: Macmillan.

Gutek, G. L. 1988. *Philosophical and ideological perspectives on education.* Needham Heights, MA: Allyn & Bacon.

Hamm, R. L. 1974. *Philosophy and education: Alternatives in theory and practice.* Danville, IL: Interstate.

Hanna, J. L. 1992. Connections: Arts, academics, and productive citizens. *Phi Delta Kappan* 73 (8):601–7.

Hanson, R. A., and R. L. Mullis. 1985. Age and gender differences in empathy and moral reasoning among adolescents. *Child Study Journal* 15:181–88.

Harmin, M. 1988. Value clarity, high morality: Let's go for both. *Educational Leadership* 45 (8):24–30.

Harran, M. J. ed. 1985. *Luther and learning: The Wittenburg University Luther Symposium.* Cranbury, NJ: Associated University Presses.

Heath, S. B. 1997. Trackville revisited. Speech presented at National Council of Teachers of English, Charlotte, NC, April 11.

Helburn, S., ed. 1995. *Cost, quality, and child outcomes in child care centers.* ERIC Document Reproduction Service, No. ED 386-297.

Hemingway, E. 1940. *For whom the bell tolls.* Philadelphia: Blakiston.

Henry, T. 1994. Violence in schools grows more severe. *USA Today,* 4 January, 1A.

Herrnstein, R., and C. Murray. 1994. *The Bell Curve.* New York: Random House.

Hersh, R. 1994. The culture of neglect. *Newsweek,* 26 September, 12–13.

Hewitt, P. B. 1993. Effects of non-institutional variables on attrition rates of beginning teachers. ERIC Document Reproduction Service, No. ED 372–072.

Hiatt, D. B. 1994. No limit to the possibilities: An interview with Ralph Tyler. *Phi Delta Kappan* 75(10):786–87.

Hill, D. 1994. The doctor is in. *Teacher Magazine* (February):18–25.

Hill, D. 1990. Order in the classroom. *Teacher* 1 (7): 70–77.

Hill, P. T., A. E. Wise, and L. Shapiro. 1989. *Educational progress: Cities mobilize to improve their schools.* Santa Monica, CA: Center for the Study of the Teaching Profession.

Hirsch, E. D., Jr. 1993. The core knowledge curriculum—What's behind its success? *Educational Leadership* 50 (8):23–25.

Hirsch, E. D., Jr., 1987. *Cultural literacy.* Boston: Houghton Mifflin.

Hodgkinson, H. 1992. *A democratic look at tomorrow.* Washington, D.C.: Institute for Educational Leadership.

Holder, C. M., and B. N. Martin. 1993. Kids can work it out: Problem solvers/peacemakers. *The Delta Kappa Gamma Bulletin* 59 (2):25–28.

Holland, A. C. 1998. Report Says test scores in U.S. lag after 4th grade. *Chicago Tribune,* 25 February.

Holmes, S. A. 1990. Rights bill for the disabled sent to Bush. *New York Times,* 14 July, 7.

Horton, L. 1992. Drug and alcohol education. *The Educational Forum* 57 (1):84–89.

Howard, L., and P. Rogers. 1994. Do clothes make the delinquent? *Newsweek,* 7 March, 8.

Huelskamp, R. M. 1993. Perspectives on education in America. *Phi Delta Kappan* 74 (9):718–22.

Hunt, S. 1993. Omaha to share education ideas. *Rockford Register Star,* 10 July, 1A–2A.

Hunter, M. 1982. *Mastery teaching.* El Segundo, CA: TIP Publications.

Hunter, M., and D. Russell. 1981. Planning for effective instruction: Lesson design. In M. Hunter and D. Russell, Eds. *Increasing Your Teaching Effectiveness.* Palo Alto, CA: The Learning Institute.

Hurst, B. C. Wilson, and G. Cramer. 1998. Professional teaching portfolios: Tools for reflection, growth, and advancement. *Phi Delta Kappan,* 79(8):578–582.

Husen, T., and A. Tujinman. 1991. The contribution of formal schooling to the increase in intellectual capital. *Educational Researcher* 1:17–25.

Hutchins, R. M. 1968. *The learning society.* New York: Praeger.

Ingram, M. F. 1954. *Toward an education.* New York: Comet Press.

Ingrassia, M. 1993. Endangered family. *Newsweek,* 23 August, 16–27.

Ingrassia, M., P. Annin, N. A. Biddle, and S. Miller. 1993. Life means nothing. *Newsweek,* 19 July, 16–17.

Jackson, M. 1993. Issue. *ASCD Curriculum Update.* Reston, VA: Association for Supervision and Curriculum Development.

Jaeger, R. M. 1992. World class standards, choice, and privatization: Weak measurement serving presumptive policy. *Phi Delta Kappan* 74 (2):118–28.

Jarchow, E. 1992. Ten ideas worth stealing from New Zealand. *Phi Delta Kappan* 73 (5):394–95.

Jencks, C. 1987. Genes and crime. *New York Review of Books* (12 February):33–41.

Jensen, A. R. 1969. How much can we boost IQ and scholastic achievement? *Harvard Educational Review* 3:1–123

Jensen, M., and P. Yerington. 1997. *Gangs: Straight talk, straight up.* Davenport, IA: Sopris West.

Jevne, R., and H. Zingle. 1992. *Striving for health: Living with broken dreams.* Edmonton, Alberta, Canada: Alberta School Employee Benefit Plan.

Johnson, D. W., and R. T. Johnson. 1991. Classroom instruction and cooperative learning. In H. C. Waxman and H. J. Walberg, eds. *Effective teaching: Current Research.* Berkeley, CA: McCutchan Publishing, 277–93.

Johnson, D. W., and R. T. Johnson. 1989. *Cooperation and competition: Theory and research.* Edina, MN: Interaction Book Company.

Johnson, J. A., H. W. Collins, V. L. Dupruis, and P. Musiel. 1997. *Foundations of American Education.* Needham Heights, MA: Allyn & Bacon.

Jones, J. H. 1994a. A few observations from the frontier. *The School Administrator* 3 (51):20.

Jones, J. H. 1994b. Ahead of the times in Murfreesboro: How one district overcame skepticism about the extended school day. *The School Administrator* 3 (51):16, 18–21.

Jones, K. 1994. Interview by author. Orlando, FL, 5 June.

Jorgensen, C. M. 1998. *Restructuring high school for all students.* Baltimore: Paul H. Brookes.

Joyce, B., J. Wolf, and E. Calhoun. 1993. *The self-renewing school.* Alexandria, VA: Association for Supervision and Curriculum Development.

Justin, N. 1993. Spring Creek gun incident: Parents have their say. *Rockford Register Star,* 21 October, 1A–2A.

Kagan, D. M. 1990. How schools alienate students at risk: A model for examining proximal classroom variables. *Educational Psychologist* 25 (2):105–25.

Kansas Department of Education. 1991. *And now they fly: GED success stories.* Topeka, KS: Kansas Department of Education.

Kantrowitz, B. 1988. A tale of abuse. *Newsweek,* 3 December, 56–59.

Kantrowitz, B., and D. Rosenberg. 1994. In a class of their own. *Newsweek,* 10 January, 58.

Karweit, N. 1988. Time-on-Task: The second time around. *NASSP Bulletin* 72 (5):31–39.

Kenny, D. J., and T. S. Watson. 1993. Improving school safety by empowering students. *The Educational Forum* 57 (1):50–62.

Kiefer, C. W. 1970. The psychological interdependence of family, school, and bureaucracy in Japan. *American Anthropologist* 70 (2):66–75.

Killion, J. P., and G. R. Todnem. 1991. A process for personal theory building. *Educational Leadership* 48 (6):14–16.

King, D. 1987. *Using assertive discipline.* Bloomington, IN: RIE Document Reproduction Service No. ED 283803.

Kirst, M. W. 1993. Strengths and weaknesses of American education. *Phi Delta Kappan* 74 (8):613–18.

Knowles, J. G., S. E. Marlow, and J. A. Muchmore. 1992. From pedagogy to ideology: Origins and phases of home education in the United States, 1970–1990. *American Journal of Education* 100:195–235.

Knox, G. A. 1994. Seven rules to year-round schooling: Research and dialogue make implementation possible. *The School Administrator* 3 (51):22–25.

Kohlberg, L. 1986. A current statement on some theoretical issues. In S. Modgil and C. Modgil, eds. *Lawrence Kohlberg.* Philadelphia: Falmer.

Kohlberg, L. 1969. Stage and sequence: The cognitive-developmental approach to socialization. In D. A. Goslin, ed. *Handbook of socialization theory and research.* Chicago: Rand McNally.

Kohlberg, L. 1958. *The development of modes of moral thinking and choice in the years 10 to 16.* Unpublished doctoral dissertation. University of Chicago.

Kohn, A. 1998. Only for *My* kid: How privileged parents undermine school reform. Phi Delta Kappan, 79(8):568–577.

Kohn, A. 1996. *Beyond discipline: From compliance to community.* Alexandria, VA: Association for Supervision and Curriculum Development.

Kopp, J. 1992. A world at risk. *Phi Delta Kappan* 73 (5):347.

Kounin, J. S. 1970. *Discipline and group management in classrooms.* New York: Holt, Rinehart & Winston.

Kowalski, T. 1995. Chasing the wolves from the schoolhouse door. *Phi Delta Kappan* 76 (6):486–89.

Kozol, J. 1988. *Rachel and her children: Homeless families in America.* New York: Crown.

Labaree, D. F. 1989. Career ladders and the early public high school teacher: A study of inequality and opportunity. In D. Warren, ed. *American teachers: Histories of a profession at work.* New York: Macmillan.

Lackey, G. H., and M. D. Rowls. 1989. *Wisdom in education.* Columbia, SC: University of South Carolina.

Lacy, M. 1997. Clinton unveils reading program. *Rockford Register Star,* 27 April.

Lapp, D., and J. Flood. 1992. *Teaching reading to every child.* 3d ed. New York: Macmillan.

Lascarides, V. C. 1990. "J. A. Comenius: Reflections in the new world." Paper presented at the International Conference for the History of Education, Prague, Czechoslovakia, ERIC Document (ED 337249), August.

Lemlech, J. K. 1994. *Curriculum and instructional methods for the elementary and middle school.* 3d ed. New York: Macmillan.

Lemming, J. S. 1992. The influences of contemporary issues curricula on school-aged youth. *Review of Research in Education* 18:111–61.

Lennon, C., and J. White. 1997. The reform of school governance in the Republic of Ireland. *Kappan 78* (8):632–34.

Leslie, C., N. Biddle, D. Rosenberg, and J. Wayne. 1993. Girls will be girls. *Newsweek,* 2 August, 44.

Levin, H. M. 1988. Accelerating elementary education for disadvantaged students. In Council of Chief State School Officers, ed. *School success for students at risk: Analysis and recommendations of the Council of Chief State School Officers.* Orlando, FL: Harcourt, Brace, Jovanovich, 209–26.

Lewis, A. C. 1994. Goals 2000 is not more of the same. *Phi Delta Kappan* 75 (9):660–61.

Lewis, A. C. 1993. The payoff from a quality preschool. *Phi Delta Kappan* 74 (10):748–49.

Lewis, B. 1993. *Islam and the West.* New York: Oxford University.

Lewis, C. C., E. Schaps, and M. Watson. 1995. Beyond the pendulum: Creating challenging and caring schools. *Phi Delta Kappan* 76 (7):547–49.

Lindgren, A. 1950. *Pippi Longstocking.* New York: Viking.

Lockard, J., P. Abrams, and W. Many. 1990. *Microcomputers for educators.* Glenview, IL: Scott, Foresman/Little, Brown.

Losee, S. 1994. DaVinci Time & Space. *Fortune,* 11 July, 136.

Lyman, I. 1994. A mother's day of home schooling. *Wall Street Journal,* 11 July, A3.

Lyons, N. 1990. Dilemmas of knowing: Ethical and epistemological dimensions of teachers' work and development. *Harvard Educational Review* 60 (2): 159–80.

Maeroff, G. 1992. Focusing on urban education in Britain. *Phi Delta Kappan* 73 (5):352–58.

Maeroff, G. I. 1998. Altered destinies: Making life better for schoolchildren in need. *Phi Delta Kappan,* 79 (6):424–433.

Magnet, M. 1992. The American family, 1992. *Fortune,* 10 August, 42–47.

Males, M. 1993. Schools, society, and 'teen' pregnancy. *Phi Delta Kappan* 74 (7):566–68.

Mann, H. 1848. *Twelfth annual report on education.* Boston: Massachusetts Department of Education.

Market Research Data Retrieval. 1997. *Technology in education.* Shelton, CN: Dun & Bradstreet.

Markgraf, J. 1997. Conversation with Pamela J. Farris, 18 May.

Marshall, C. A. 1995. Teacher supply and demand: Where are candidates needed? *Kappa Delta Pi Record* 31(2):52–55.

Marx, K., and F. Engels. 1963. *The communist manifesto.* New York: Russell.

Mayer, F. 1960. *A history of educational thought.* Columbus, OH: Merrill.

Mayer, S. 1997. *What money can't buy.* Cambridge, MA: Harvard University Press.

Maynes, M. J. 1985. *Schooling in Western Europe: A social history.* New York: State University of New York Press.

McAdams, R. 1993. *Lessons from abroad: How other countries educate their children.* Lancaster, PA: Technomic Publishing.

McConaghy, T. 1992. Teacher wellness: An educational concern. *Phi Delta Kappan* 74 (4):349–50.

McCormack, S. 1987. *Assertive discipline: What do we really know?* Bloomington, IN: RIE Document Reproduction Service No. ED 286618.

McGuffey, W. H. 1879. *McGuffey's first eclectic reader, revised edition.* Cincinnati, OH: Van Antwerp, Bragg, and Company.

McGuffey, W. H. 1935. Lecture on the relative duties of parents and teachers. *Transactions of Fifth Western Institute and College for Professional Teachers.* Cincinnati: Executive Commission.

McLaughlin, M., and M. E. Vogt. 1996. *Portfolios in teacher education.* Newark, DE: International Reading Association.

McPartland, J., W. Jordan, N. Legters, and R. Balfanz. 1997. Finding safety in small numbers. *Education Leadership* 55 (2):14–17.

Meade, G. H. 1964. *Selected writings.* Indianapolis: Bobbs-Merrill.

Meehan, P. 1998. Beyond a chocolate crunch bar: A teacher examines her philosophy of teaching reading. *The Reading Teacher* 51 (4):314–328.

Meek, A. 1998. America's teachers: Much to celebrate. *Educational Leadership,* 55 (5):12–16.

Mellon, J. 1988. *Bullwhip days: The slaves remember.* New York: Avon.

Metropolitan Life. 1993. *Metropolitan life survey of the American teacher.* Hartford, CN: Metropolitan Life.

Metzger, M. 1996. Maintaining a life. *Kappan* 77 (5): 346–51.

Michener, O. H., K . E. Underwood, and J. C. Fortune. 1993. Incision decisions. *The American School Board Journal* 180 (1):28–33.

Minnick, H. C. 1936. *William Holmes McGuffey and his readers.* New York: American Book Company.

Mirel, J., and D. Angus. 1995. Rhetoric and reality in the American high school curriculum. In D. Ravitch and M. Vinovskis, eds. *Historical considerations on current educational reform.* Baltimore: Johns Hopkins Press, 35–48.

More dads at home, too. 1994. *Washington Post,* 20 May, 3A.

Morris, V. C. 1970. An overview: Existentialism and education. In J. Park, ed. *Selected readings in the philosophy of education.* 3d ed. New York: Macmillan, 303–15.

Morris, V. C. 1961. *Philosophy and the American school: An introduction to the philosophy of education.* Boston: Houghton Mifflin.

Morrison, G. S. 1997. *Teaching in America.* Boston: Allyn and Bacon.

Mosier, R. D. 1947. *Making the American Mind: Social and moral ideas in the McGuffey readers.* New York: King's Crown Press.

Moskowitz, F. 1991. *And the bridge is love: Life stories.* Boston: Beacon Press.

Murphy, J. T. 1992. Apartheid's legacy to black children. *Phi Delta Kappan* 73 (5):367–74.

Mydans, S. 1989. Correction: California calls evolution "a fact and a theory." *New York Times,* 14 November, 12.

N.J. school funding unconstitutional. 1994. *Washington Post,* 13 July, 3A.

National Assessment of Educational Progress. 1996. Results from the NAEP 1994 Reading Assessment—at a glance. *NAEP 1994 Reading: A first look (Revised Edition).* Washington, D.C.: National Assessment of Educational Progress.

National Association of Secondary School Principals. 1996. Breaking ranks: *Changing an American institution.* Reston, VA: Author.

National Center for Education Statistics. 1995. *Statistics in brief: Mathematics course taking and gains in mathematics achievement.* Washington, D.C.: U.S. Department of Education.

National Commission on Excellence in Education. 1983. *A nation at risk: The imperative for educational reform.* Washington, D.C.: U.S. Department of Education.

National Council of Teachers of Mathematics. 1989. *Curriculum and evaluation standards for school mathematics.* Reston, VA: Association for Supervision and Curriculum Development.

National Education Association. 1993. *The status of the American public school teacher.* Washington, D.C.: National Education Association.

National Education Association. 1992. *Estimates of school statistics.* Washington, D.C.: National Education Center.

National Education Association. 1893. *Report of the Committee on Secondary School Studies.* Washington, D.C.: U.S. Government Printing Office.

National Education Commission on Time and Learning. 1994. *Prisoners of Time.* Washington, D.C.: U.S. Government Printing Office.

National Science Teachers Association. 1992. *The content core: A guide for curriculum designers.* Washington, D.C.: National Science Teachers Association and the U.S. Department of Education.

Nelson, F. H. 1991. *International comparisons of public spending on education.* Washington, D.C.: American Federation of Teachers, 37.

Newmann, F. M., and G. C. Wehlage. 1993. Five standards of authentic instruction. *Educational Leadership* 50 (7):8–12.

Nichols, R. C. 1978. Policy implications of the IQ controversy. In L. S. Schulman, ed., *Review of Research in Education.* Itasca, IL: Peacock.

Nicklin, J. L. 1994. Annenberg shifts priorities. *The Chronicle of Higher Education* (12 January):A18.

North Carolina State Department of Public Instruction. 1986. *Report of the state superintendent of schools.* Raleigh, NC: State Department of Public Instruction.

Nussbaum, J. F. 1992. Effective teacher behaviors. *Communication Education* 41 (2):167–80.

Odden, E. R., and P. Wohlstetter. 1995. Making school-based management work. *Educational Leadership* 52 (5):32–36.

Oddleifson, E. 1994. What do we want our schools to do? *Phi Delta Kappan* 75 (6):446–52.

Ohles, J. S., ed. 1978. *Biographical dictionary of American educators.* Westport, CN: Greenwood Press.

1.6 million kids home alone. 1994. Gannett News Service, 20 May, 3A.

O'Neil, J. 1997. Building schools and communities. *Educational Leadership* 54 (8):6–10.

O'Neil, J. 1994. Aiming for new outcomes. *Educational Leadership* 51 (6):8–11.

Orstein, A. C. 1991. Teacher effectiveness research: Theoretical considerations. In H. C. Waxman and H. J. Walberg, eds. *Effective teaching: Current Research.* Berkeley, CA: McCutchan Publishing, 63–80.

Orstein, A. C., and D. U. Levine. 1989. *Foundations of Education.* 4th ed. Boston: Houghton Mifflin.

Pallas, A. M., G. Natriello, and E. L. McDill. 1989. The changing state of the disadvantaged population: Current dimensions and future trends. *Educational Researcher* 18 (5):16–22.

Parker, F. W. 1894. *Talks on pedagogics: An outline of the theory of concentration.* Chicago: E. L. Kellogg.

Parkhurst, K. 1987. *Supplementing assertive discipline with conflict resolution to develop social skills at the intermediate level.* Bloomington, IN: RIE Document Reproduction Service No. ED 296802.

Paterson, K. 1978. *The great Gilly Hopkins.* New York: HarperCollins.

Paulsen, G. 1987. *Hatchet.* New York: Bradbury.

Peck, B. T. 1994. Education and training in the European Community: The next phase. *Phi Delta Kappan* 75 (5):355–56.

Peck, K. L., and D. Dorricott. 1994. Why use technology? *Educational Leadership* 51 (7):11–14.

Pedram, M. 1963. *A critical comparison of the educational theories and practices of John Amos Comenius with John Dewey's concept of experience.* Unpublished doctoral dissertation, University of Kansas.

Pigford, A. B., and S. Tonnsen. 1993. *Women in school leadership.* Lancaster, PA: Technomic Publishing.

Pinloche, A. 1901. *Pestalozzi and the foundation of the modern elementary school.* New York: Charles Scribner's and Sons.

Pipho, C. 1992. Caught between competing visions. *Phi Delta Kappan* 74 (2):102–3.

Polakow, V. 1997. Who cares for the children? *Kappan* 78 (8):604–610.

Pollin, R. 1992. Rossonomics. *The Nation* 255:456–57.

Press, A. 1994. Tacking toward moderation. *Newsweek,* 11 July, 58.

Pritchett, P. 1996. *Mindshift.* Houston: Pritchett and Associates.

Rabbitt, M. 1992. International recruitment centers for international schools. *Phi Delta Kappan* 73 (5):409–10.

Rafferty, M. 1962. *Suffer little children.* New York; Signet.

Rase, D. 1992. War on welfare dependency. *U.S. News and World Report,* 20 April, 34–40.

Rasmussen, K. 1998. Looping—discovering the benefits of multiyear teaching. Education Update 40 (2) 1, 3–4.

Raths, L., M. Harmin, and S. Simon. 1978. *Values and teaching.* 2d ed. Columbus, OH: Merrill.

Ratner, J., ed. 1939. *Intelligence in the modern world: John Dewey's philosophy.* New York: Random House.

Ravitch, D., and J. P. Viteritti. 1997. *New schools for a new century.* New Haven, CT: Yale University Press.

Rawls, W. 1976. *Summer of the monkeys.* New York: Dell.

Rawls, W. 1961. *Where the red fern grows.* New York: Doubleday.

Reeves, R. 1994. The tax revolt that wrecked California. *Money* 23 (1):90–103.

Reischauer, E. O. 1977. *The Japanese.* Tokyo: Tuttle.

Reno, J. 1994. *CNN Headline News,* 7 July.

Reno urges crackdown on TV violene "soon." 1993. *Rockford Register Star,* 21 October, 2A.

Richman, L. S. 1992. Struggling to save our kids. *Fortune,* 10 August, 34–40.

Rippa, S. A. 1992. *Education in a Free Society: An American History.* 7th ed. White Plains, NY: Longman.

Robbins, J. 1990. *Public schools as public forums.* Bloomington, IN: Phi Delta Kappa.

Robin, B. 1997. Evaluating an education Web site. *ATE Newsletter* (May–June):6.

Robin, B., E. Keeler, and R. Miller, 1996. *Educator's guide to the Web.* Houston: MIS Press.

Rochman, H. 1994. Multiculturalism and literature. Annual International Children's Literature Lecture, Northern Illinois University, DeKalb, IL, 12 April.

Roderick, T. 1988. Johnny can learn to negotiate. *Educational Leadership* 45 (4):86–91.

Rodriguez, R., and P. Gonzales. 1997. The two tongues of Jaime Escalante. 14 December. *The Rockford Register-Star.*

Rothberg, I. C., M. H. Futrell, and J. M. Lieberman. 1998. National Board Certification: Increasing participation and assessing impacts. *Phi Delta Kappan,* 79(6):424–427.

Rosenberg, D., L. Beachy, P. Annin, S. D. Lewis, J. Gordon, P. Katel, and M. Liu. 1993. Wild in the streets. *Newsweek,* 2 August, 40–46.

Rosenshine, B., and R. Stevens. 1986. Teaching functions. In M. E. Wittrock, ed. *Handbook of Research on Teaching.* 3d ed. New York: Macmillan, 376–91.

Rosenshine, B., and R. Stevens. 1984. Classroom instruction in reading. In P. D. Pearson, ed. *Handbook of Reading Research.* New York: Longman, 745–98.

Rosenshine, B. A., and D. C. Berliner. 1978. Academic engaged time. *British Journal of Teacher Education* 4 (1):3–16.

Ross, D. D. 1989. First steps in developing a reflective approach. *Journal of Teacher Education* 40 (2):22–30.

Rousseau, J. J. 1911. *Emile.* Translated by B. Foxley. New York: Dutton.

Rowe, D. W. 1998. Examining teacher talk: Revealing hidden boundaries for curricular change. *Language Arts* 75 (2):103–107.

Rubin, L. J. 1994. Ralph W. Tyler: A remembrance. *Phi Delta Kappan* 75(10):784–85.

Rury, J. 1989. Who became teachers?: The social characteristics of teachers in American history. In D. Warren, ed. *American teachers: Histories of a profession at work.* New York: Macmillan.

Rust, V. D. 1992. Educational responses to reforms in East Germany, Czechoslovakia, and Poland. *Phi Delta Kappan* 73 (5):375–77.

Ryan, K., and J. M. Cooper. 1998. *Those who can, teach.* Boston: Houghton Mifflin.

Ryan, K., and J. M. Cooper. 1992. *Those who can, teach.* 6th ed. Boston: Houghton Mifflin.

Sadker, M. P., and D. M. Sadker. 1991. *Teachers, schools, and society.* 2d ed. New York: McGraw-Hill.

Sadler, J. E. 1970. Comenius as a man. In C. H. Dobinson, ed. *Comenius and contemporary education: An International Symposium.* Hamburg, Germany: UNESCO Institute for Education, 9–16.

Sagor, R. D. 1992. Three principals who make a difference. *Educational Leadership* 49 (5):13–18.

Sailor, W. 1989. The educational, social, and vocational integration of students with the most severe disabilities. In D. K. Lipsky and A. Gartner, eds. *Beyond separate education: Quality education for all.* Baltimore, MD: Paul H. Brookes, 54–87.

Salinger, J. D. 1951. *Catcher in the rye.* Boston: Little Brown.

Salmon, A. K. and R. Truax. 1998. In Equador: Developing child-centered learning. *Educational Leadership* 55(5):66–69.

Sappir, S. 1998. Global ethics in a high school curriculum. *Educational Leadership* 55 (6):80–82.

Sarason, S. B. 1977. *Work, aging, and social change: Professionals and the one life-one career imperative.* New York: The Free Press, Macmillan.

Sautter, R. C. 1993. *Charter schools: A new breed of public schools* (Report 2). Oak Brook, IL: North Central Regional Educational Laboratory.

Savage, D. 1994. Drawing the church-state line. *Los Angeles Times,* 31 March, 1.

Sawyer, F. 1989. "Nightline," ABC Network.

Scala, M. A. 1993. What whole language means for children with learning disabilities. *The Reading Teacher* 47 (3):222–29.

Scarr, S., and R. A. Weinberg. 1976. I.Q. test performance of black children adopted by white families. *American Psychologist* (7):726–39.

Schmuck, P. A. 1986. Networking: a new word, a different game. *Educational Leadership* 43:60–61.

Schmuck, R. A., and P. A. Schmuck. 1992. *Small districts big problems: Making school everybody's house.* Newbury Park, CA: Corwin Press.

Schon, D. A. 1987. *Educating the Reflective Practitioner.* San Francisco: Jossey Bass.

Schon, D. A. 1983. *The Reflective Practitioner.* New York: Basic Books.

Seidel, S., and C. Williams. 1997. Initiative produces better prepared teachers. *ATE Newsletter* (May–June):4.

Senator no fan of 'Buffcoat and Beaver.' (sic) 1993. *Rockford Register Star,* 21 October, 1A.

Shanker, A. 1994. Where we stand: Inclusion and ideology. *New York Times,* 6 February, E23.

Shannon, P. 1993. Developing democratic voices. *The Reading Teacher* 47 (2):86–94.

Shen, J. 1998. Do teachers feel empowered? *Educational Leadership* 55 (7):35–36.

Shen, J. 1997. The evolution of violence in schools. *Educational Leadership* 55 (2):18–20.

Shulman, L. 1987. Knowledge and teaching: Foundations and the new reform. *Harvard Educational Review* 3:1–22.

Shurtleff, N., ed. 1853. *Records of the Governor and Company of the Massachusetts Bay in New England, vol. 2.* Boston: Order of the Legislature.

Simmons, B. J. 1995. Developing and using portfolios. *Kappa Delta Pi Record* 31(2):56–59.

Sirotnik, K. A. 1990. Society, schooling, teaching, and preparing to teach. In J. I. Goodlad, R. Soder, and K. A. Sirotnik, eds. *The moral dimensions of teaching.* San Francisco: Jossey Bass.

Sizer, T. 1985. *Horace's compromise: The dilemma of the American high school.* Boston: Houghton Mifflin.

Slavin, R. 1988. Cooperative revolution catches fire. *School Administrator* 45 (1):9–13.

Slavin, R. E., N. L. Karweit, and B. A. Wasik. 1993. Preventing early school failure: What works? *Educational Leadership* 50 (4):10–18.

Sleeter, C. E., and C. Grant. 1988. *Making choices for multicultural education: Five approaches to race, class, and gender.* Columbus, OH: Merrill.

Smail, W. M. 1966. *Quintilian on education.* New York: Teacher's College Press.

Smith, G. A. 1995. Living with Oregon's Measure 5: The costs of property tax relief in two suburban elementary schools. *Phi Delta Kappan* 76 (6):452–57.

Smith, M. A., J. Kalvelage, and P. A. Schmuck. 1982. *Women getting together and getting ahead* (RO 9-30-8). Newton, MA: WEEA Publishing Center.

Smith, S. Z., M. E. Smith, and T. A. Romberg. 1993. What the NCTM standards look like in one classroom. *Educational Leadership* 50 (8):4–7.

Smythe, J. 1989. Developing and sustaining critical reflection in teacher education. *Journal of Teacher Education* 40 (2):2–9.

Solomon, M. 1991. *Working with difficult people.* Englewood Cliffs, NJ: Prentice Hall.

Sophocles. 1978. *Oedipus the king.* New York: Oxford University Press.

Sousa, D. A. 1990. The evidence is in classrooms. *Educational Leadership* 46 (4):82.

Spady, W. G. 1994. Choosing outcomes of significance. *Educational Leadership* 51 (6):18–23.

Sparks-Langer, G. M., and A. B. Colton. 1991. Synthesis of research on teachers' reflective thinking. *Educational Leadership* 48 (6):37–43.

Spiegel, D. L. 1992. Blending whole language and systematic direct instruction. *Reading Teacher* 46 (1):38–44.

Sprout, A. L. 1994. Medio Multimedia. *Fortune,* 11 July, 140–41.

Stedman, P. and S. A. Stroot. 1998. Teachers helping teachers. *Educational Leadership* 55(5):37–38.

Stecklow, L. 1997. Disney's model school. *Rockford Register Star* 21 June: 6A.

Steinbeck, J. 1978. *The grapes of wrath.* Franklin Center, PA: Franklin Library.

Stevens, L. J., and M. Price. 1992. Meeting the challenge of educating children at risk. *Phi Delta Kappan* 74 (1):18–23.

Stevenson, H. W. 1998. A study of three cultures: Germany, Japan, and the United States—An overview of the TIMSS Case Study Project. *Phi Delta Kappan* 79 (7) 524–529.

Stevenson, H. W. 1991. Japanese elementary school education. *The Elementary School Journal* 92 (1): 109–20.

Stevenson, H. W., S. Lee, C. Chen, M. Lummis, J. Stigler, L. Fan, and F. Ge. 1990. Mathematics achievement of children in China and the United States. *Child Development* 61 (4):1053–66.

Stier, M. P., and L. G. Cunningham. 1992. School vouchers, pro/con: An effective means of reform. *Rockford Register Star,* 29 November, 5B.

Stowe, H. B. 1972. *Uncle Tom's cabin.* New York: Dutton.

Stowe, H. B. 1965. *Uncle Tom's cabin.* New York: Viking.

Strauber, S. K., S. Stanley, and C. Wagenknecht. 1990. Site-based management at Central-Hower. *Educational Leadership* 47 (7):64–66.

Strickland, D. 1995. Reinventing our literacy programs: Books, basics, balance. *Reading Teacher* 48 (4): 294–302.

Sunal, C S., and M. E. Haas. 1993. *Social studies and the elementary/middle school students.* Orlando, FL: Harcourt Brace.

Swaim, J. 1998. In search of an honest response. *Language Arts* 75 (2):118–125.

Takemura, S. 1991. A study of the knowledge base for science teaching as perceived by elementary school teachers in Japan and the United States. Paper presented at the annual meeting of JUSTEC, Stanford University, July.

Taylor, M. 1976. *Roll of thunder, hear my cry.* New York: Dial Press.

Teeter, A. M. 1995. Learning about teaching. *Phi Delta Kappan* 76(5):360–64.

Texas Education Agency. 1992. *Alternative teacher certification in Texas.* Austin, TX: Texas Education Agency.

Texas to force its richer schools to share the wealth. 1993. *Chicago Tribune,* Associated Press, 30 May, 5.

The Community Board Program. 1986. *Starting a conflict manager's program.* San Francisco: The Community Board Program.

Thomas, B. R. 1990. The school as a moral learning community. In J. I. Goodlad, R. Soder, and K. A. Sirotnik, eds. *The moral dimensions of teaching.* San Francisco: Jossey Bass.

Thut, I. N. 1957. *The story of education.* New York: McGraw-Hill.

Torrey, B., ed. 1968. *The writings of Henry David Thoreau, vols. II–III.* New York: Ams Press.

Traub, J. 1997. What can public schools learn? *The New York Times,* November 9: 13

Turley, S. and K. Nakai. 1998. Coping with class size reduction in California. *Educational Leadership* 55 (5):40–43.

Twain, M. 1885. *The adventures of Huckleberry Finn.* New York: Pennyroyal Press.

U.S. Census Bureau. 1996. *Statistical abstract of the United States.* Washington, D.C.: U.S. Government Printing Office.

U.S. Department of Commerce Bureau of the Census. 1996. *1996 U.S. census report.* Washington, D.C.: U.S. Government Printing Office.

U.S. Department of Education. 1996. *1996 Official Education Census Data.* Washington, D.C.: U.S. Department of Education.

U.S. Department of Education. 1996. *Digest of Education Statistics.* Washington, D.C.: U.S. Government Printing Office.

U.S. Department of Education. 1994a. *Digest of education statistics, 1993.* Washington, D.C.: National Center for Education Statistics.

U.S. Department of Education. 1994b. *Mini-digest of education statistics 1993.* Washington, D.C.: National Center for Education Statistics.

UNESCO. 1957. *John Amos Comenius on education.* Introduction by J. Piaget. New York: Teachers College Press.

Underwood, J. K. 1997. Four implications of IDEA's reauthorization. *The School Administrator* 54 (10): 24–27.

Vacca, R. S., and H. C. Hudgins, Jr. 1982. *Liability of school officials and administrators for civil rights torts.* Charlottesville, VA: The Michie Company.

Van Doren, G. 1984. English language and literature. In M. J. Adler, ed. *The paideia program: An educational syllabus.* New York: Macmillan, 59–70.

VanWagenen, L. and K. M. Hibbard. 1998. Building teacher Portfolios. *Educational Leadership* 55 (5): 26–29.

Varnon, C . J., and R. L. King. 1993. A tidal wave of change—OBE in the USA. *Outcomes* 12 (1):16–19.

Vsdansky, M. L. 1993. Census language not foreign at home. *USA Today,* 28 April, 1A, 11A.

Wager, B. R. 1993. No more suspension: Creating a shared ethical culture. *Educational Leadership* 50 (4):34–37.

Walberg, H. J. 1988. Synthesis of research on time and learning. *Educational Leadership* 45 (6):76–85.

Walker, A. 1982. *The color purple.* New York: Harcourt Brace Jovanovich.

Walker, B. 1976. *Curriculum evolution as portrayed through old textbooks.* Terre Haute, IN: Curriculum Research and Development Center, Indiana State University.

Waller, R. J. 1992. *The bridges of Madison County.* New York: Warner.

Wallerstein, J., and S. Blakeslee. 1989. *Second chances: Men, women, and children a decade after divorce.* New York: Ticknor & Fields.

Warren, R. P. 1982. *All the king's men.* San Diego: Harcourt Brace Jovanovich.

Washington update. 1995. *Chronicle of Higher Education* (3 March):A28.

Watson, D. 1989. Defining and describing whole language. *Elementary School Journal* 90 (2):129–41.

Watson, D., and L. Rangel. 1989. Can cooperative learning be evaluated? *School Administrator* 46 (6):13–17.

Wellington, B. 1991. The promise of reflective practice. *Educational Leadership* 48 (6):4–5.

What's news. 1995. *Wall Street Journal,* 23 February, 1.

Whitman, D., and D. Friedman. 1992. The war over "family values." *U.S. News and World Report,* 8 June, 35–36.

Whitmire, R. 1997. Abused children more likely to be arrested. Associated Press, 5 August.

Whitmire, R. 1994. Report: Juveniles as victims on rise. Gannett News Service, 18 July.

Wigginton, E. 1985. *Sometimes a shining moment.* New York: Doubleday.

Willis, D. 1994. "Educating Our Children." WRTV, Indianapolis, IN., 12 July.

Willis, S. 1994. Public schools, private managers. *ASCD Update* 36 (3):1–2.

Wilson, J. Q. 1992. Point of view: Scholars must expand our understanding of criminal behavior. *Chronicle of Higher Education* (10 June):A40.

Winerip, M. 1994. All under one roof: Shopping and education. *New York Times,* 2 May.

Wohlstetter, P., and L. Anderson. 1994. What can U.S. charter schools learn from England's grant-maintained schools? *Phi Delta Kappan* 75 (6):486–91.

Woo, L. C. 1985. Women administrators: profiles of success. *Phi Delta Kappan* (December):285–88.

Yatvin, J. 1991. *Developing a whole language program.* Richmond, VA: Virginia State Reading Association.

Yulish, S. M. 1980. *The search for a civic religion.* Washington, D.C.: University Press of America.

Yussen, S. R. 1977. Characteristics of moral dilemmas written by adolescents. *Developmental Psychology* 13:162–63.

Zehm, S. J., and J. A. Kottler. 1993. *On being a teacher: The human dimension.* Newbury Park, CA: Corwin Press.

Zirkel, P. 1998. Courtside: Hostile environment. *Phi Delta Kappan* 79 (5):409–410.

Zirkel, P. A. 1994. Student dress goads. *Phi Delta Kappan* 75 (7):570–71.

Zirkel, P. A. 1994. The religious right and the public schools. *Catalyst for Change* 23 (2):18–20.

Zirkel, P. A. 1978. *A digest of Supreme Court decisions affecting education.* Bloomington, IN: Phi Delta Kappa.

Zirkel, P. A., and I. B. Gluckman. 1991. Invocations and benedictions at school events. *NASSP Bulletin* 81 (2):105–9.

Zirkel, P. A., and I. B. Gluckman. 1990. Pledge of Allegiance. *NASSP Bulletin* 74:115–17.

Name and Subject Index

547

In loco parentis principle, 181–182
Incentive aid
    from states, 270, 271
Inclusion
    disadvantages of, 62–63
    examples of, 296–297
    trend toward, 58, 333
Income taxes
    school funding from, 269
India
    ancient, 102
Individual education plans (IEPs)
    for disabled students, 163–164
Individualized education
        program (IEP), 331–332
Inductive logic, 93
Industrialized nations
    teacher salaries in, 411
Information
    managing, 290
Informing
    in reflective thinking, 357
Ingram, Margaret Fogelsong, 124
Ingrassia, M., 209, 212, 226
Inservice training
    examples of, 272
    for teachers, 287, 365
Institutio Oratoria, 109
Instruction time
    and learning, 372–373
Instructional strategies
    cooperative/collaborative
        learning, 359
    direct instruction, 353–354, 355
    Foxfire approach, 356
    integrated instruction, 354–356
    reflective teaching, 356–359
    theme cycles, 360–362
    using technology, 362–364
Integrated curriculum, 309
Integrated instruction, 354–356
Integration
    of American colleges, 153–154
Intelligence
    and environment, 348–349
    and heredity, 348–349
    interpersonal, 352
    prenatal effects on, 349
    psychological theories
        of, 349–353
Internal barriers
    for aspiring female
        administrators, 67–68
International Reading
        Association, 429
International Schools
        Services, 429
Internet
    access in schools, 335
    instructional use of, 362–364
    legal issues about, 176–178
    See also Websites; World Wide
        Web
Internships
    for women in
        administration, 67
Interviews
    for teaching jobs, 26–27
Intrapersonal intelligence, 352
Ireland
    educational system in, 418
Islam
    influence on education, 99, 100

Jackson, M., 326
Jaeger, R. M., 416, 420

Japan
    educational system in, 420–424
Jarchow, E., 425
Jefferson, T., philosophy of, 78
Jen, 102, 186
Jencks, C., 348
Jensen, A., 348
Jensen, M., 385, 386
Jevne, R., 287, 288
Joe Camel, 44
Johansen, J. H., 135, 150
Johnson, D. W., 359
Johnson, J. A., 135, 150
Johnson, L., 11–13
Johnson, LouAnn, 405
Johnson, R. T., 359
Jones, J. H., 55
Jones, K., 17
Jordan, W., 233
Journals
    to reduce stress, 289
    as reflective tools, 358, 359
Joyce, B., 308
Judicial system
    oversight of schools, 159
Jukus, 422
Junior high schools
    creation of, 136
    environment of, 401–402
Justin, N., 227

Kagan, D. M., 394
Kagan, Lynn, 396
Kalvelage, J., 66, 67
Kant, I., idealism of, 77
Kantrowitz, B., 46, 208, 219
Kaplan, J., 80
Karweit, N. L., 211, 214, 372
Katel, P., 226, 227, 228
Kauffmann, J. M., 333
Kaull, M., 278, 279
Keeler, E., 71
Kenny, D. J., 228
Kentucky Education Reform
        Act, 365
Kenya
    educational system in, 427
Kiefer, C. W., 422
Kierkegaard, S., philosophy
        of, 79–80
Killion, J. P., 357
Kilpatrick, W. H., 85
Kindergarten
    all-day, alternate-day, 401
    introduction in
        America, 134–135
    origin of, 119
King, D., 379
King, J. A., 310
King, R. L., 310
Kirst, M. W., 213
Know-it-all
    pesonality type, 293
Knowles, J. G., 57
Knox, G. A., 55, 56
Kohlberg, Lawrence
    views on moral
        development, 188–189
Kohn, A., 381, 382, 383
Kopp, J., 410
Kopp, W., 64
Kottler, J. A., 291
Kounin, J. S., 376
Kowalski, T., 267
Kozberg, F. S., 189
Kuhs, T., 301

Labaree, D. F., 124
Lacey, M., 234
Lackey, G. H., 140
Land Ordinance of 1785, 129
Land-grant colleges
    creation of, 152–153
Language
    and perennialism, 87
Language arts
    curriculum for, 311–317
Language development
    in early childhood, 350–351
Languages
    of students, 38
Lapp, D., 138
Lascarides, V. C., 117
Latchkey children, 210–211, 394,
        400
Latin grammar schools, 126
Law, Nancy, 298
Leadership
    attributes of, 68
Learning
    and instruction time, 372–373
    theories of, 348–349
    See also Intelligence
Learning disabilities
    causes of, 208–209, 214
Lee, S., 420
Legal issues
    child abuse, 176
    copyright, 178–179
    court system, 159
    discrimination, 170–171
    due process, 171–172
    freedom of
        expression, 173–176
    jurisdiction in school
        matters, 158–159
    liability, 172–173, 198
    peer review of teachers, 167
    residence requirements, 180
    right to education, 180
    school discipline, 183
    student conduct, 174–176,
        181–182
    for students with
        disabilities, 163–164
    teacher certification and
        licensing, 165–168
    teacher lifestyles, 179
    teaching contracts, 165
    and technology, 176–178
    tenure, 168–169
Legters, N., 233
Lemlech, J. K., 319
Lemming, J. S., 225
Lemon test, 160
Lemon v. Kurtzman, 160
Lennon, C., 418
Leslie, C., 226
Lesson plans
    software for, 292
    student involvement
        in, 373–374
    on World Wide Web, 29
Levin, H. M., 394
Levine, D. V., 128
Lewis, A. C., 54, 396
Lewis, C. C., 371
Lewis, S. D., 226, 227, 228
Li, 187
Liability, 172–173
Liability insurance
    for schools, 173
Licenses
    school funding from, 269

Lieberman, J. M., 52
Lindgren, A., 87
Linguistic intelligence, 352
Literacy
    worldwide, 410
Literature
    classics of, 86–87, 91
    teaching, 112
Liu, M., 226, 227, 228
Local ordinances
    affecting schools, 158
Local School Authority, 248–251
    defense of, 258
Local school councils, 249, 298
Lockard, J., 363
Locke, John
    influence on education, 115,
        121
Logic, 93
Logical-mathematical
        intelligence, 352
Long-term disability
    and stress, 287–288
Looping, 391
Losee, S., 70
Lotteries
    school funding from, 269
Lummis, M., 420
Lün Yu, 101
Luther, Martin
    influence on education, 113,
        114, 121
Lycos, 30
Lyman, I., 60
Lyons, N., 199

Maastricht Treaty, 413
Maeroff, G. I., 32, 410, 416
Magellan, 30
Magnet high schools, 402
Magnet, M., 203, 213, 214, 225
Magnet schools, 239
Mainstreaming, 62–63, 332
    See also Inclusion
Males, M., 202
Mall of America
    high school in, 59
Mankiller, Wilma P., 147
Mann, Horace
    and common school
        movement, 130–133
    philosophy of, 78
Many, W., 363
Marijuana
    use by children, 225
Markgraf, J., 232
Markgraf, John, 247
Marleave, E., 372
Marlow, M., 250
Marlow, S. E., 57
Marshall, C. A., 20
Martin, B. N., 384
Marx, K., 36
Mason, Linda, 298
Matching grants
    from states, 270
Maternity leave
    in Denmark, 413–414
    for teachers, 171
Mathematics
    curriculum for, 317–318
    curriculum standards for, 343
Mayer, F., 77, 84, 133
McAdams, R., 412, 414, 415, 416,
        424
McConaghy, T., 287, 288
McCormack, S., 379

World Confederation of
Organizations of the
Teaching Profession, 429
World Wide Web
educational website
checklist, 71
legal issues about, 176–178
Worthington, K., 335

Writing
assessment of, 339–340
development of, 99–100, 102

Yahoo, 30
Yale University
origin of, 150

Yatvin, J., 353
Year-round school calendars
examples of, 55–56
Yep, L., 331
Yerington, P., 385, 386
Yulish, S. M., 188
Yussen, S. R., 189

Zehm, S. J., 291
Zingle, H., 287, 288
Zirkel, P. A., 161, 162, 171, 180,
182, 338